ABSOLUTE C++

5TH EDITION

ABSOLUTE C++

5TH EDITION

Walter Savitch
University of California, San Diego

Contributor
Kenrick Mock
University of Alaska Anchorage

PEARSON

Boston Columbus Indianapolis New York San Francisco Upper Saddle River
Amsterdam Cape Town Dubai London Madrid Milan Munich Paris Montréal Toronto
Delhi Mexico City São Paulo Sydney Hong Kong Seoul Singapore Taipei Tokyo

Vice President and Editorial Director, ECS:
Marcia Horton
Executive Editor: Matt Goldstein
Editorial Assistants: Chelsea Kharakozova/
Emma Snider
Vice President Marketing: Patrice Jones
Marketing Manager: Yez Alayan
Marketing Coordinator: Kathryn Ferranti
Vice President and Director of Production:
Vince O'Brien
Managing Editor: Jeff Holcomb
Senior Production Project Manager: Marilyn Lloyd
Manufacturing Manager: Nick Skilitis

Operations Specialist: Lisa McDowell
Text Designer: Joyce Cosentino Wells
Cover Designer: Anthony Gemmellaro
Cover Image: © Shutterstock
Media Editor: Dan Sandin
Manager, Rights and Permissions: Michael Joyce
Text Permissions—assessment: Dana Weightman
Text Permissions—clearance: Nicole Coffineau/
Creative Compliance
Full-Service Vendor: GEX Publishing Services
Project Management: GEX Publishing Services
Printer/Binder: Edwards Brothers
Cover Printer: Lehigh-Phoenix Color

This book was composed in InDesign. Basal font is Adobe Garamond 10/12. Display font is Optima LT Std.

Credits and acknowledgments borrowed from other sources and reproduced, with permission, in this textbook appear on the appropriate page within text.

Many of the designations by manufacturers and sellers to distinguish their products are claimed as trademarks. Where those designations appear in this book, and the publisher was aware of a trademark claim, the designations have been printed in initial caps or all caps.

Library of Congress Cataloging-in-Publication Data

Savitch, Walter J.
Absolute C++ / Walter Savitch ; contributor, Kenrick Mock. -- 5th ed.
   p. cm.
Includes bibliographical references and index.
ISBN 978-0-13-283071-3 (alk. paper)
1. C++ (Computer program language) I. Mock, Kenrick. II. Title.
QA76.73.C153S279 2010
005.13'3--dc23

2012001325

1 2 3 4 5 6 7 8 9 10—EB—15 14 13 12

ISBN-10: 0-13-283071-X
ISBN-13: 978-0-13-283071-3

Preface

This book is designed to be a textbook and reference for programming in the C++ language. Although it does include programming techniques, it is organized around the features of the C++ language, rather than any particular curriculum of techniques. The main audience I had in mind is undergraduate students who had not had extensive programming experience with the C++ language. As such, this book is a suitable C++ text or reference for a wide range of users. The introductory chapters are written at a level that is accessible to beginners, while the boxed sections of those chapters serve to introduce more experienced programmers to basic C++ syntax. Later chapters are also understandable to beginners, but are written at a level suitable for students who have progressed to these more advanced topics. *Absolute C++* is also suitable for anyone learning the C++ language on their own. (For those who want a textbook with more pedagogical material and more on very basic programming technique, try my text *Problem Solving with C++*, Eighth Edition, Pearson Education.)

The C++ coverage in this book goes well beyond what a beginner needs to know. In particular, it has extensive coverage of inheritance, polymorphism, exception handling, and the Standard Template Library (STL), as well as basic coverage of patterns and the unified modeling language (UML).

CHANGES IN THIS EDITION

This fifth edition presents the same programming philosophy as the fourth edition. For instructors, you can teach the same course, presenting the same topics in the same order with no changes in the material covered or the chapters assigned. Changes include:

- Chapter 1 now includes a short introduction to the string class and Chapter 2 includes a short introduction to reading data from a text file. Together, this material allows instructors to present students with problems of larger scale and real-world applicability as early as Chapter 2.

- Chapter 12 now includes a section on using `stringstream` to convert between strings and other data types.

- Chapter 13 briefly describes tail recursion and gives an example of mutual recursion.

- Ten new self-test exercises have been added along with twenty-five new Programming Projects. By request, some of these are longer and less prescriptive projects that give the student more practice designing programming solutions.

- Several errors that were found in the fourth edition have been corrected.

- Fifteen new VideoNotes have been added to the book's website (www.pearsonhighered.com/savitch) for a total of forty-six videos. These VideoNotes walk students through the process of problem solving and coding to reinforce key programming concepts. An icon appears in the margin of the book when a video is available regarding the corresponding topic in the text.

ANSI/ISO C++ STANDARD

This edition is fully compatible with compilers that meet the latest ANSI/ISO C++ standard.

STANDARD TEMPLATE LIBRARY

The Standard Template Library (STL) is an extensive collection of preprogrammed data structure classes and algorithms. The STL is perhaps as big a topic as the core C++ language, so I have included a substantial introduction to STL. There is a full chapter on the general topic of templates and a full chapter on the particulars of STL, as well as other material on, or related to, STL at other points in the text.

OBJECT-ORIENTED PROGRAMMING

This book is organized around the structure of C++. As such, the early chapters cover aspects of C++ that are common to most high-level programming languages but are not particularly oriented toward object-oriented programming (OOP). For a reference book—and for a book for learning a second language—this makes sense. However, I consider C++ to be an OOP language. If you are programming in C++ and not C, you must be using the OOP features of C++. This text offers extensive coverage of encapsulation, inheritance, and polymorphism as realized in the C++ language. Chapter 20, on patterns and UML, gives additional coverage of OOP-related material.

FLEXIBILITY IN TOPIC ORDERING

This book allows instructors wide latitude in reordering the material. This is important if a book is to serve as a reference. This is also in keeping with my philosophy of accommodating the instructor's style, rather than tying the instructor to my own personal preference of topic ordering. Each chapter introduction explains what material must already have been covered before each section of the chapter can be covered.

ACCESSIBLE TO STUDENTS

It is not enough for a book to present the right topics in the right order. It is not even enough for it be correct and clear to an instructor. The material also needs to be presented in a way that is accessible to the novice. Like my other textbooks, which proved to be very popular with students, this book was written to be friendly and accessible to the student.

SUMMARY BOXES

Each major point is summarized in a boxed section. These boxed sections are spread throughout each chapter. They serve as summaries of the material, as a quick reference source, and as a quick way to learn the C++ syntax for a feature you know about in general but for which you do not know the C++ particulars.

SELF-TEST EXERCISES

Each chapter contains numerous self-test exercises. Complete answers for all the self-test exercises are given at the end of each chapter.

VIDEO NOTES

VideoNote

VideoNotes are step-by-step videos that guide readers through the solution to an end of chapter problem or further illuminate a concept presented in the text. Icons in the text indicate where a VideoNote enhances a topic. Fully navigable problems allow for self-paced instruction. VideoNotes are located at www.pearsonhighered.com/savitch.

OTHER FEATURES

Pitfall sections, programming technique sections, and examples of complete programs with sample input and output are given throughout each chapter. Each chapter ends with a summary and a collection of programming projects.

ONLINE PRACTICE AND ASSESSMENT WITH MyProgrammingLab

MyProgrammingLab helps students fully grasp the logic, semantics, and syntax of programming. Through practice exercises and immediate, personalized feedback, MyProgrammingLab improves the programming competence of beginning students who often struggle with the basic concepts and paradigms of popular high-level programming languages.

A self-study and homework tool, a MyProgrammingLab course consists of hundreds of small practice problems organized around the structure of this textbook. For students, the system automatically detects errors in the logic and syntax of their code submissions and offers targeted hints that enable students to figure out what went wrong—and why. For instructors, a comprehensive gradebook tracks correct and incorrect answers and stores the code inputted by students for review.

MyProgrammingLab is offered to users of this book in partnership with Turing's Craft, the makers of the CodeLab interactive programming exercise system. For a full demonstration, to see feedback from instructors and students, or to get started using MyProgrammingLab in your course, visit www.myprogramminglab.com.

SUPPORT MATERIAL

The following support materials are available to all users of this book at www.pearsonhighered.com/cssupport:

- Source code from the book

The following resources are available to qualified instructors only at www.pearsonhighered.com/irc. Please contact your local sales representative for access information.

- Instructor's Manual with Solutions
- PowerPoint® slides

ACKNOWLEDGMENTS

Numerous individuals have contributed invaluable help and support to making this book happen. Frank Ruggirello and Susan Hartman at Addison-Wesley first conceived the idea and supported the first edition, for which I owe them a debt of gratitude. A special thanks to Matt Goldstein who was the editor for the second, third, and fourth editions. His help and support were critical to making this project succeed. Chelsea Kharakozova, Marilyn Lloyd, Yez Alayan, and the other fine people at Pearson Education also provided valuable support and encouragement.

The following reviewers provided suggestions for the book. I thank them all for their hard work and helpful comments.

Richard Albright	University of Delaware
J. Boyd Trolinger	Butte College
Jerry K. Bilbrey, Jr	Francis Marion University
Albert M. K. Cheng	University of Houston
David Cherba	Michigan State University
Fredrick H. Colclough	Colorado Technical University
Drue Coles	Boston University
Stephen Corbesero	Moravian College
Christopher E. Cramer	
Ron DiNapoli	Cornell University
Qin Ding	Pennsylvania State University, Harrisburg
Martin Dulberg	North Carolina State University
H. E. Dunsmore	Purdue University
Evan Golub	University of Maryland
Terry Harvey	University of Delaware
Joanna Klukowska	Hunter College, CUNY
Lawrence S. Kroll	San Francisco State University
Stephen P. Leach	Florida State University
Alvin S. Lim	Auburn University
Tim H. Lin	Cal Poly Pomona
R. M. Lowe	Clemson University
Jeffrey L. Popyack	Drexel University
Amar Raheja	Cal Poly Pomona
Victoria Rayskin	University of Central Los Angeles
Loren Rhodes	Juniata College
Jeff Ringenberg	University of Michigan

Victor Shtern   Boston University
Aaron Striegel   University of Notre Dame
J. Boyd Trolinger   Butte College
Chrysafis Vogiatzis   University of Florida
Joel Weinstein   Northeastern University
Dick Whalen   College of Southern Maryland

A special thanks goes to Kenrick Mock (University of Alaska Anchorage) who executed the updating of this edition. He once again had the difficult job of satisfying me, the editor, and himself. I thank him for a truly excellent job.

Walter Savitch

LOCATION OF VIDEONOTES IN THE TEXT

www.pearsonhighered.com/savitch

 VideoNote

Brief Contents

Contents

xx Contents

Chapter 7 Constructors and Other Tools 275

Chapter 8 Operator Overloading, Friends, and References 321

C++ Basics 1

C++ Basics

The Analytical Engine has no pretensions whatever to originate anything. It can do whatever we know how to order it to perform. It can follow analysis; but it has no power of anticipating any analytical relations or truths. Its province is to assist us in making available what we are already acquainted with.

ADA AUGUSTA, *Countess of Lovelace*

Introduction

This chapter introduces the C++ language and gives enough detail to allow you to handle simple programs involving expressions, assignments, and console input/output (I/O). The details of assignments and expressions are similar to those of most other high-level languages. Every language has its own console I/O syntax, so if you are not familiar with C++, that may look new and different to you.

1.1   Introduction to C++

Language is the only instrument of science.

SAMUEL JOHNSON

This section gives an overview of the C++ programming language.

Origins of the C++ Language

The C++ programming language can be thought of as the C programming language with classes (and other modern features) added. The C programming language was developed by Dennis Ritchie of AT&T Bell Laboratories in the 1970s. It was first used for writing and maintaining the UNIX operating system. (Up until that time, UNIX systems programs were written either in assembly language or in a language called B, a language developed by Ken Thompson, the originator of UNIX.) C is a general-purpose language that can be used for writing any sort of program, but its success and popularity are closely tied to the UNIX operating system. If you wanted to maintain your UNIX system, you needed to use C. C and UNIX fit together so well that soon not just systems programs but almost all commercial programs that ran under UNIX were written in the C language. C became so popular that versions of the language were written for other popular operating systems; its use is thus not limited to computers that use UNIX. However, despite its popularity, C was not without its shortcomings.

The C language is peculiar because it is a high-level language with many of the features of a low-level language. C is somewhere in between the two extremes of a very high-level language and a low-level language, and therein lies both its strengths and its weaknesses. Like (low-level) assembly language, C language programs can directly manipulate the computer's memory. On the other hand, C has the features of a high-level language, which makes it easier to read and write than assembly language. This makes C an excellent choice for writing systems programs, but for other programs (and in some sense even for systems programs) C is not as easy to understand as other languages; also, it does not have as many automatic checks as some other high-level languages.

To overcome these and other shortcomings of C, Bjarne Stroustrup of AT&T Bell Laboratories developed C++ in the early 1980s. Stroustrup designed C++ to be a better C. Most of C is a subset of C++ and so most C programs are also C++ programs. (The reverse is not true; many C++ programs are definitely not C programs.) Unlike C, C++ has facilities for classes and so can be used for object-oriented programming.

C++ and Object-Oriented Programming

Object-oriented programming (OOP) is a currently popular and powerful programming technique. The main characteristics of OOP are encapsulation, inheritance, and polymorphism. Encapsulation is a form of information hiding or abstraction. Inheritance has to do with writing reusable code. Polymorphism refers to a way that a single name can have multiple meanings in the context of inheritance. Having made those statements, we must admit that they will hold little meaning for readers who have not heard of OOP before. However, we will describe all these terms in detail later in this book. C++ accommodates OOP by providing classes, a kind of data type combining both data and algorithms. C++ is not what some authorities would call a "pure OOP language." C++ tempers its OOP features with concerns for efficiency and what some might call "practicality." This combination has made C++ currently the most widely used OOP language, although not all of its usage strictly follows the OOP philosophy.

The Character of C++

C++ has classes that allow it to be used as an object-oriented language. It allows for overloading of functions and operators. (All these terms will be explained eventually, so do not be concerned if you do not fully understand some terms.) C++'s connection to the C language gives it a more traditional look than newer object-oriented languages, yet it has more powerful abstraction mechanisms than many other currently popular languages. C++ has a template facility that allows for full and direct implementation of algorithm abstraction. C++ templates allow you to code using parameters for types. The newest C++ standard, and most C++ compilers, allow multiple namespaces to accommodate more reuse of class and function names. The exception handling facilities in C++ are similar to what you would find in other programming languages. Memory management in C++ is similar to that in C. The programmer must allocate his or her own memory and handle his or her own garbage collection. Most compilers will allow you to do C-style memory management in C++ since C is essentially a subset of C++. However, C++ also has its own syntax for a C++ style of memory management, and you are advised to use the C++ style of memory management when coding in C++. This book uses only the C++ style of memory management.

C++ Terminology

functions

All procedure-like entities are called **functions** in C++. Things that are called *procedures*, *methods*, *functions*, or *subprograms* in other languages are all called *functions* in C++. As we will see in the next subsection, a C++ **program** is basically just a function called main; when you run a program, the run-time system automatically invokes the function named main. Other C++ terminology is pretty much the same as most other programming languages, and in any case, will be explained when each concept is introduced.

program

A Sample C++ Program

Display 1.1 contains a simple C++ program and two possible screen displays that might be generated when a user runs the program. A C++ program is really a function definition for a function named main. When the program is run, the function named main is invoked. The body of the function main is enclosed in braces, {}. When the program is run, the statements in the braces are executed.

The following two lines set up things so that the libraries with console input and output facilities are available to the program. The details concerning these two lines and related topics are covered in Section 1.3 and in Chapters 9, 11, and 12.

```
#include <iostream>
using namespace std;
```

VideoNote
Compiling and
Running a C++
Program

The following line says that main is a function with no parameters that returns an int (integer) value:

```
int main ( )
```

int main()

Some compilers will allow you to omit the int or replace it with void, which indicates a function that does not return a value. However, the previous form is the most universally accepted way to start the main function of a C++ program.

The program ends when the following statement is executed:

```
return 0;
```

return 0;

This statement ends the invocation of the function main and returns 0 as the function's value. According to the ANSI/ISO C++ standard, this statement is not required, but many compilers still require it. Chapter 3 covers all these details about C++ functions.

Display 1.1   A Sample C++ Program

```
1    #include <iostream>
2    using namespace std;

3    int main( )
4    {
5        int numberOfLanguages;

6        cout << "Hello reader.\n"
7             << "Welcome to C++.\n";

8        cout << "How many programming languages have you used? ";
9        cin >> numberOfLanguages;

10       if (numberOfLanguages < 1)
11           cout << "Read the preface. You may prefer\n"
12                << "a more elementary book by the same author.\n";
13       else
14           cout << "Enjoy the book.\n";

15       return 0;
16   }
```

Sample Dialogue 1

```
Hello reader.
Welcome to C++.
How many programming languages have you used? 0
Read the preface. You may prefer
a more elementary book by the same author.
```
⟶ *User types in 0 on the keyboard. User input is shown in bold.*

Sample Dialogue 2

```
Hello reader.
Welcome to C++.
How many programming languages have you used? 1
Enjoy the book
```
⟶ *User types in 1 on the keyboard. User input is shown in bold.*

Variable declarations in C++ are similar to what they are in other programming languages. The following line from Display 1.1 declares the variable numberOfLanguages:

```
int numberOfLanguages;
```

The type int is one of the C++ types for whole numbers (integers).

If you have not programmed in C++ before, then the use of cin and cout for console I/O is likely to be new to you. That topic is covered a little later in this chapter, but the general idea can be observed in this sample program. For example, consider the following two lines from Display 1.1:

```
cout << "How many programming languages have you used? ";
cin >> numberOfLanguages;
```

C-string

The first line outputs the text within the quotation marks to the screen. The text inside the quotation marks is called a **string**, or to be more precise, a **C-string**. The second line reads in a number that the user enters at the keyboard and sets the value of the variable numberOfLanguages to this number.

The lines

```
cout << "Read the preface. You may prefer\n"
     << "a more elementary book by the same author.\n";
```

string

output two strings instead of just one string. The details are explained in Section 1.3 later in this chapter, but this brief introduction will be enough to allow you to understand the simple use of cin and cout in the examples that precede Section 1.3. The symbolism \n is the newline character, which instructs the computer to start a new line of output.

Although you may not yet be certain of the exact details of how to write such statements, you can probably guess the meaning of the if-else statement. The details will be explained in the next chapter.

(By the way, if you have not had at least some experience with some programming languages, you should read the preface to see if you might prefer a more elementary book. You need not have had any experience with C++ to read this book, but some minimal programming experience is strongly suggested.)

1.2   Variables, Expressions, and Assignment Statements

Once a person has understood the way variables are used in programming, he has understood the quintessence of programming.

E. W. DIJKSTRA, *Notes on Structured Programming*

Variables, expressions, and assignments in C++ are similar to those in most other general-purpose languages.

Identifiers

identifier

The name of a variable (or other item you might define in a program) is called an **identifier**. A C++ identifier must start with either a letter or the underscore symbol, and all the rest of the characters must be letters, digits, or the underscore symbol. For example, the following are all valid identifiers:

```
x  x1  x_1  _abc  ABC123z7  sum  RATE  count  data2  bigBonus
```

All the names shown are legal and would be accepted by the compiler, but the first five are poor choices for identifiers because they are not descriptive of the identifier's use. None of the following are legal identifiers, and all would be rejected by the compiler:

```
12  3X  %change  data-1  myfirst.c  PROG.CPP
```

The first three are not allowed because they do not start with a letter or an underscore. The remaining three are not identifiers because they contain symbols other than letters, digits, and the underscore symbol.

Although it is legal to start an identifier with an underscore, you should avoid doing so, because identifiers starting with an underscore are informally reserved for system identifiers and standard libraries.

case-sensitive

C++ is a **case-sensitive** language; that is, it distinguishes between uppercase and lowercase letters in the spelling of identifiers. Hence, the following are three distinct identifiers and could be used to name three distinct variables:

```
rate  RATE  Rate
```

However, it is not a good idea to use two such variants in the same program, since that might be confusing. Although it is not required by C++, variables are usually spelled with their first letter in lowercase. The predefined identifiers, such as main, cin, cout, and so forth, must be spelled in all lowercase letters. The convention that is now becoming universal in object-oriented programming is to spell variable names with a mix of upper- and lowercase letters (and digits), to always start a variable name with a lowercase letter, and to indicate "word" boundaries with an uppercase letter, as illustrated by the following variable names:

```
topSpeed, bankRate1, bankRate2, timeOfArrival
```

This convention is not as common in C++ as in some other object-oriented languages, but is becoming more widely used and is a good convention to follow.

A C++ identifier can be of any length, although some compilers will ignore all characters after some (large) specified number of initial characters.

Identifiers

A C++ identifier must start with either a letter or the underscore symbol, and the remaining characters must all be letters, digits, or the underscore symbol. C++ identifiers are case sensitive and have no limit to their length.

keyword or reserved word

There is a special class of identifiers, called **keywords** or **reserved words**, which have a predefined meaning in C++ and cannot be used as names for variables or anything else. In the code displays of this book keywords are shown in a different color. A complete list of keywords is given in Appendix 1.

Some predefined words, such as cin and cout, are not keywords. These predefined words are not part of the core C++ language, and you are allowed to redefine them. Although these predefined words are not keywords, they are defined in libraries required by the C++ language standard. Needless to say, using a predefined identifier for anything other than its standard meaning can be confusing and dangerous and thus should be avoided. The safest and easiest practice is to treat all predefined identifiers as if they were keywords.

Variables

Every variable in a C++ program must be *declared* before it is used. When you **declare** a variable you are telling the compiler—and, ultimately, the computer—what kind of data you will be storing in the variable. For example, the following are two definitions that might occur in a C++ program:

declare

```
int numberOfBeans;
double oneWeight, totalWeight;
```

The first defines the variable numberOfBeans so that it can hold a value of type int, that is, a whole number. The name int is an abbreviation for "integer." The type int is one of the types for whole numbers. The second definition declares oneWeight and totalWeight to be variables of type double, which is one of the types for numbers with a decimal point (known as **floating-point numbers**). As illustrated here, when there is more than one variable in a definition, the variables are separated by commas. Also, note that each definition ends with a semicolon.

floating-point number

Every variable must be declared before it is used; otherwise, variables may be declared anyplace. Of course, they should always be declared in a location that makes the program easier to read. Typically, variables are declared either just before they are used or at the start of a block (indicated by an opening brace, {). Any legal identifier, other than a reserved word, may be used for a variable name.[1]

C++ has basic types for characters, integers, and floating-point numbers (numbers with a decimal point). Display 1.2 lists the basic C++ types. The commonly used type for integers is int. The type char is the type for single characters. The type char can be treated as an integer type, but we do not encourage you to do so. The commonly

---
[1] C++ makes a distinction between *declaring* and *defining* an identifier. When an identifier is declared, the name is introduced. When it is defined, storage for the named item is allocated. For the kind of variables we discuss in this chapter, and for much more of the book, what we are calling a *variable declaration* both declares the variable and defines the variable, that is, allocates storage for the variable. Many authors blur the distinction between variable definition and variable declaration. The difference between declaring and defining an identifier is more important for other kinds of identifiers, which we will encounter in later chapters.

used type for floating-point numbers is double, and so you should use double for floating-point numbers unless you have a specific reason to use one of the other floating-point types. The type bool (short for *Boolean*) has the values true and false. It is not an integer type, but to accommodate older code, you can convert back and forth between bool and any of the integer types. The programmer can also define types for arrays, classes, and pointers, all of which are discussed in later chapters of this book.

Display 1.2 Simple Types

TYPE NAME	MEMORY USED	SIZE RANGE	PRECISION
short (also called short int)	2 bytes	-32,768 to 32,767	Not applicable
int	4 bytes	-2,147,483,648 to 2,147,483,647	Not applicable
long (also called long int)	4 bytes	-2,147,483,648 to 2,147,483,647	Not applicable
float	4 bytes	approximately 10^{-38} to 10^{38}	7 digits
double	8 bytes	approximately 10^{-308} to 10^{308}	15 digits
long double	10 bytes	approximately 10^{-4932} to 10^{4932}	19 digits
char	1 byte	All ASCII characters (Can also be used as an integer type, although we do not recommend doing so.)	Not applicable
bool	1 byte	true, false	Not applicable

The values listed here are only sample values to give you a general idea of how the types differ. The values for any of these entries may be different on your system. *Precision* refers to the number of meaningful digits, including digits in front of the decimal point. The ranges for the types float, double, and long double are the ranges for positive numbers. Negative numbers have a similar range, but with a negative sign in front of each number.

Variable Declarations

All variables must be declared before they are used. The syntax for variable declarations is as follows.

SYNTAX

Type_Name Variable_Name_1, Variable_Name_2...;

EXAMPLES

```
int count, numberOfDragons, numberOfTrolls;
double distance;
```

unsigned

Each of the integer types has an **unsigned** version that includes only nonnegative values. These types are unsigned short, unsigned int, and unsigned long. Their ranges do not exactly correspond to the ranges of the positive values of the types short, int, and long, but are likely to be larger (since they use the same storage as their corresponding types short, int, or long, but need not remember a sign). You are unlikely to need these types, but may run into them in specifications for predefined functions in some of the C++ libraries, which we discuss in Chapter 3.

Assignment Statements

The most direct way to change the value of a variable is to use an **assignment statement**. In C++ the equal sign is used as the assignment operator. An assignment statement always consists of a variable on the left-hand side of the equal sign and an expression on the right-hand side. An assignment statement ends with a semicolon. The expression on the right-hand side of the equal sign may be a variable, a number, or a more complicated expression made up of variables, numbers, operators, and function invocations. An assignment statement instructs the computer to evaluate (that is, to compute the value of) the expression on the right-hand side of the equal sign and to set

assignment statement

Assignment Statements

In an assignment statement, first the expression on the right-hand side of the equal sign is evaluated and then the variable on the left-hand side of the equal sign is set equal to this value.

SYNTAX

Variable = Expression;

EXAMPLES

```
distance = rate * time;
count = count + 2;
```

the value of the variable on the left-hand side equal to the value of that expression. The following are examples of C++ assignment statements:

```
totalWeight = oneWeight * numberOfBeans;
temperature = 98.6;
count = count + 2;
```

The first assignment statement sets the value of totalWeight equal to the number in the variable oneWeight multiplied by the number in numberOfBeans. (Multiplication is expressed using the asterisk, *, in C++.) The second assignment statement sets the value of temperature to 98.6. The third assignment statement increases the value of the variable count by 2.

In C++, assignment statements can be used as expressions. When used as an expression, an assignment statement returns the value assigned to the variable. For example, consider

```
n = (m = 2);
```

The subexpression (m = 2) changes the value of m to 2 and returns the value 2. Thus, this sets both n and m equal to 2. As you will see when we discuss precedence of operators in detail in Chapter 2, you can omit the parentheses, so the assignment statement under discussion can be written as

```
n = m = 2;
```

We advise you not to use an assignment statement as an expression, but you should be aware of this behavior because it will help you understand certain kinds of coding errors. For one thing, it will explain why you will not get an error message when you mistakenly write

```
n = m = 2;
```

when you meant to write

```
n = m + 2;
```

(This is an easy mistake to make since = and + are on the same keyboard key.)

Lvalues and Rvalues

Authors often refer to *lvalue* and *rvalue* in C++ books. An **lvalue** is anything that can appear on the left-hand side of an assignment operator (=), which means any kind of variable. An **rvalue** is anything that can appear on the right-hand side of an assignment operator, which means any expression that evaluates to a value.

Introduction to the `string` class

Although C++ lacks a simple data type to directly manipulate strings (sequences of text), there is a `string` class that may be used to process strings in a manner similar to the data types we have seen thus far. The `string` class is a class and a simple data type such as an `int` is discussed in Chapter 6. The distinction between a class and a simple data type such as an `int` is discussed in Chapter 6. Further details about the `string` class are discussed in Chapter 9.

To use the `string` class we must first include the `string` library by adding the following line of code at the top of your program:

```
#include <string>
```

string

You declare variables of type `string` just as you declare variables of types `int` or `double`. For example, the following declares one variable of type string and stores the text "durian" in it:

```
string fruit;
fruit = "durian";
```

PITFALL: Uninitialized Variables

A variable has no meaningful value until a program gives it one. For example, if the variable `minimumNumber` has not been given a value either as the left-hand side of an assignment statement or by some other means (such as being given an input value with a `cin` statement), then the following is an error:

```
desiredNumber = minimumNumber + 10;
```

This is because `minimumNumber` has no meaningful value, and so the entire expression on the right-hand side of the equal sign has no meaningful value. A variable like `minimumNumber` that has not been given a value is said to be **uninitialized**. This situation is, in fact, worse than it would be if `minimumNumber` had no value at all. An uninitialized variable, like `minimumNumber`, will simply have some garbage value. The value of an uninitialized variable is determined by whatever pattern of zeros and ones was left in its memory location by the last program that used that portion of memory.

One way to avoid an uninitialized variable is to initialize variables at the same time they are declared. This can be done by adding an equal sign and a value, as follows:

uninitialized variable

```
int minimumNumber = 3;
```

This both declares `minimumNumber` to be a variable of type `int` and sets the value of the variable `minimumNumber` equal to 3. You can use a more complicated expression involving operations such as addition or multiplication when you initialize a variable inside the declaration in this way. As another example, the following declares three variables and initializes two of them:

```
double rate = 0.07, time, balance = 0.00;
```

PITFALL: (continued)

C++ allows an alternative notation for initializing variables when they are declared. This alternative notation is illustrated by the following, which is equivalent to the preceding declaration:

```
double rate(0.07), time, balance(0.00);  ■
```

Initializing Variables in Declarations

You can initialize a variable (that is, give it a value) at the time that you declare the variable.

SYNTAX

```
Type_Name Variable_Name_1 = Expression_for_Value_1,
         Variable_Name_2 = Expression_for_Value_2,...;
```

EXAMPLES

```
int count = 0, limit = 10, fudgeFactor = 2;
double distance = 999.99;
```

SYNTAX

Alternative syntax for initializing in declarations:

```
Type_Name Variable_Name_1 (Expression_for_Value_1),
         Variable_Name_2 (Expression_for_Value_2),...;
```

EXAMPLES

```
int count(0), limit(10), fudgeFactor(2);
double distance(999.99);
```

TIP: Use Meaningful Names

Variable names and other names in a program should at least hint at the meaning or use of the thing they are naming. It is much easier to understand a program if the variables have meaningful names. Contrast

```
x = y * z;
```

with the more suggestive

```
distance = speed * time;
```

The two statements accomplish the same thing, but the second is easier to understand. ■

More Assignment Statements

A shorthand notation exists that combines the assignment operator (=) and an arithmetic operator so that a given variable can have its value changed by adding, subtracting, multiplying by, or dividing by a specified value. The general form is

```
Variable Operator = Expression
```

which is equivalent to

```
Variable = Variable Operator (Expression)
```

The *Expression* can be another variable, a constant, or a more complicated arithmetic expression. The following list gives examples.

EXAMPLE	EQUIVALENT TO
`count += 2;`	`count = count + 2;`
`total -= discount;`	`total = total - discount;`
`bonus *= 2;`	`bonus = bonus * 2;`
`time /= rushFactor;`	`time = time / rushFactor;`
`change %= 100;`	`change = change % 100;`
`amount *= cnt1 + cnt2;`	`amount = amount * (cnt1 + cnt2);`

Self-Test Exercises

1. Give the declaration for two variables called `feet` and `inches`. Both variables are of type `int` and both are to be initialized to zero in the declaration. Give both initialization alternatives.

2. Give the declaration for two variables called `count` and `distance`. `count` is of type `int` and is initialized to zero. `distance` is of type `double` and is initialized to 1.5. Give both initialization alternatives.

3. Write a program that contains statements that output the values of five or six variables that have been defined, but not initialized. Compile and run the program. What is the output? Explain.

Assignment Compatibility

As a general rule, you cannot store a value of one type in a variable of another type. For example, most compilers will object to the following:

```
int intVariable;
intVariable = 2.99;
```

The problem is a type mismatch. The constant 2.99 is of type double, and the variable intVariable is of type int. Unfortunately, not all compilers will react the same way to the previous assignment statement. Some will issue an error message, some will give only a warning message, and some compilers will not object at all. Even if the compiler does allow you to use the previous assignment, it will give intVariable the int value 2, not the value 3. Since you cannot count on your compiler accepting the previous assignment, you should not assign a double value to a variable of type int.

assigning int values to double variables

Even if the compiler will allow you to mix types in an assignment statement, in most cases you should not. Doing so makes your program less portable, and it can be confusing.

There are some special cases in which it is permitted to assign a value of one type to a variable of another type. It is acceptable to assign a value of an integer type, such as int, to a variable of a floating-point type, such as type double. For example, the following is both legal and acceptable style:

```
double doubleVariable;
doubleVariable = 2;
```

The style shown will set the value of the variable named doubleVariable equal to 2.0.

mixing types

Although it is usually a bad idea to do so, you can store an int value such as 65 in a variable of type char and you can store a letter such as 'Z' in a variable of type int. For many purposes, the C language considers characters to be small integers, and perhaps unfortunately, C++ inherited this from C. The reason for allowing this is that variables of type char consume less memory than variables of type int; thus, doing arithmetic with variables of type char can save some memory. However, it is clearer to use the type int when you are dealing with integers and to use the type char when you are dealing with characters.

The general rule is that you cannot place a value of one type in a variable of another type—though it may seem that there are more exceptions to the rule than there are cases that follow the rule. Even if the compiler does not enforce this rule strictly, it is a good rule to follow. Placing data of one type in a variable of another type can cause problems because the value must be changed to a value of the appropriate type and that value may not be what you would expect.

integers and Booleans

Values of type bool can be assigned to variables of an integer type (short, int, long), and integers can be assigned to variables of type bool. However, it is poor style to do this. For completeness and to help you read other people's code, here are the details: When assigned to a variable of type bool, any nonzero integer will be stored as the value true. Zero will be stored as the value false. When assigning a bool value to an integer variable, true will be stored as 1, and false will be stored as 0.

Literals

literal constant

A **literal** is a name for one specific value. Literals are often called **constants** in contrast to variables. Literals or constants do not change value; variables can change their values. Integer constants are written in the way you are used to writing numbers. Constants of type int (or any other integer type) must not contain a decimal point. Constants of type double may be written in either of two forms. The simple form for double constants is like the everyday way of writing decimal fractions. When written in this form a double constant must contain a decimal point. No number constant (either integer or floating-point) in C++ may contain a comma.

scientific notation or floating-point notation

A more complicated notation for constants of type double is called **scientific notation** or **floating-point notation** and is particularly handy for writing very large numbers and very small fractions. For instance, 3.67×10^{17}, which is the same as

    367000000000000000.0

is best expressed in C++ by the constant 3.67e17. The number 5.89×10^{-6}, which is the same as 0.00000589, is best expressed in C++ by the constant 5.89e-6. The e stands for *exponent* and means "multiply by 10 to the power that follows." The e may be either uppercase or lowercase.

Think of the number after the e as telling you the direction and number of digits to move the decimal point. For example, to change 3.49e4 to a numeral without an e, you move the decimal point four places to the right to obtain 34900.0, which is another way of writing the same number. If the number after the e is negative, you move the decimal point the indicated number of spaces to the left, inserting extra zeros if need be. So, 3.49e-2 is the same as 0.0349.

The number before the e may contain a decimal point, although it is not required. However, the exponent after the e definitely must *not* contain a decimal point.

What Is Doubled?

Why is the type for numbers with a fractional part called double? Is there a type called "single" that is half as big? No, but something like that is true. Many programming languages traditionally used two types for numbers with a fractional part. One type used less storage and was very imprecise (that is, it did not allow very many significant digits). The second type used double the amount of storage and so was much more precise; it also allowed numbers that were larger (although programmers tend to care more about precision than about size). The kinds of numbers that used twice as much storage were called double-precision numbers; those that used less storage were called single precision. Following this tradition, the type that (more or less) corresponds to this double-precision type was named double in C++. The type that corresponds to single precision in C++ was called float. C++ also has a third type for numbers with a fractional part, which is called long double.

Constants of type char are expressed by placing the character in single quotes, as illustrated in what follows:

```
char symbol = 'Z';
```

Note that the left and right single quote symbols are the same symbol.

quotes Constants for strings of characters are given in double quotes, as illustrated by the following line taken from Display 1.1:

```
cout << "How many programming languages have you used? ";
```

Be sure to notice that string constants are placed inside double quotes, while constants of type char are placed inside single quotes. The two kinds of quotes mean different things. In particular, 'A' and "A" mean different things. 'A' is a value of type char and can be stored in a variable of type char. "A" is a string of characters. The fact that the string happens to contain only one character does *not* make "A" a value of type char. Also notice that for both strings and characters, the left and right quotes are the same.

C-string Strings in double quotes, like "Hello", are often called **C-strings**. A C-string is not the same as the string class introduced earlier although both are used to store sequences of text and we sometimes use the two interchangeably. The difference is explained in detail in Chapter 9. Experts recommend you use the string class when possible instead of a C-string for purposes of security and flexibility.

The type bool has two constants, true and false. These two constants may be assigned to a variable of type bool or used anyplace else an expression of type bool is allowed. They must be spelled with all lowercase letters.

Escape Sequences

escape sequence A backslash, \, preceding a character tells the compiler that the sequence following the backslash does not have the same meaning as the character appearing by itself. Such a sequence is called an **escape sequence**. The sequence is typed in as two characters with no space between the symbols. Several escape sequences are defined in C++

If you want to put a backslash, \, or a quote symbol, ", into a string constant, you must escape the ability of the " to terminate a string constant by using \", or the ability of the \ to escape, by using \\. The \\ tells the compiler you mean a real backslash, \, not an escape sequence; the \" tells it you mean a real quote, not the end of a string constant. A stray \, say \z, in a string constant will have different effects on different compilers. One compiler may simply give back a z; another might produce an error. The ANSI/ISO standard states that unspecified escape sequences have undefined behavior. This means a compiler can do anything its author finds convenient. The consequence is that code that uses undefined escape sequences is not portable. You should not use any escape sequences other than those provided by the C++ standard. These C++ control characters are listed in Display 1.3.

Naming Constants

Numbers in a computer program pose two problems. The first is that they carry no mnemonic value. For example, when the number 10 is encountered in a program, it gives no hint of its significance. If the program is a banking program, it might be the number of branch offices or the number of teller windows at the main office. To understand the program, you need to know the significance of each constant. The second problem is that when a program needs to have some numbers changed, the changing tends to introduce errors. Suppose that 10 occurs twelve times in a banking program—four of the times it represents the number of branch offices, and eight of the times it represents the number of teller windows at the main office. When the bank opens a new branch and the program needs to be updated, there is a good chance that some of the 10s that should be changed to 11 will not be, or some that should not be changed will be. The way to avoid these problems is to name each number and use the name instead of the number within your program. For example, a banking program might have two constants with the names BRANCH_COUNT and WINDOW_COUNT.

Display 1.3   Some Escape Sequences

SEQUENCE	MEANING
\n	New line
\r	Carriage return (Positions the cursor at the start of the current line. You are not likely to use this very much.)
\t	(Horizontal) Tab (Advances the cursor to the next tab stop.)
\a	Alert (Sounds the alert noise, typically a bell.)
\\	Backslash (Allows you to place a backslash in a quoted expression.)
\'	Single quote (Mostly used to place a single quote inside single quotes.)
\"	Double quote (Mostly used to place a double quote inside a quoted string.)

The following are not as commonly used, but we include them for completeness:

\v	Vertical tab
\b	Backspace
\f	Form feed
\?	Question mark

Both these numbers might have a value of 10, but when the bank opens a new branch, all you need do to update the program is change the definition of BRANCH_COUNT.

How do you name a number in a C++ program? One way to name a number is to initialize a variable to that number value, as in the following example:

```
int  BRANCH_COUNT = 10;
int  WINDOW_COUNT = 10;
```

There is, however, one problem with this method of naming number constants: You might inadvertently change the value of one of these variables. C++ provides a way of marking an initialized variable so that it cannot be changed. If your program tries to change one of these variables, it produces an error condition. To mark a variable declaration so that the value of the variable cannot be changed, precede the declaration with the word const (which is an abbreviation of *constant*). For example,

const

```
const int BRANCH_COUNT = 10;
const int WINDOW_COUNT = 10;
```

If the variables are of the same type, it is possible to combine the previous two lines into one declaration, as follows:

```
const int BRANCH_COUNT = 10, WINDOW_COUNT = 10;
```

However, most programmers find that placing each name definition on a separate line is clearer. The word const is often called a **modifier**, because it modifies (restricts) the variables being declared.

modifier

A variable declared using the const modifier is often called a **declared constant.** Writing declared constants in all uppercase letters is not required by the C++ language, but it is standard practice among C++ programmers.

declared constant

Once a number has been named in this way, the name can then be used anywhere the number is allowed, and it will have exactly the same meaning as the number it names. To change a named constant, you need only change the initializing value in the const variable declaration. The meaning of all occurrences of BRANCH_COUNT, for instance, can be changed from 10 to 11 simply by changing the initializing value of 10 in the declaration of BRANCH_COUNT.

Display 1.4 contains a simple program that illustrates the use of the declaration modifier const.

Arithmetic Operators and Expressions

As in most other languages, C++ allows you to form expressions using variables, constants, and the arithmetic operators: + (addition), - (subtraction), * (multiplication), / (division), and % (modulo, remainder). These expressions can be used anyplace it is legal to use a value of the type produced by the expression.

All the arithmetic operators can be used with numbers of type int, numbers of type double, and even with one number of each type. However, the type of the value produced and the exact value of the result depend on the types of the numbers being combined. If both operands (that is, both numbers) are of type int, then the result of combining them with an arithmetic operator is of type int. If one or both of the operands are of type double, then the result is of type double. For example, if the variables baseAmount and increase are of type int, then the number produced by the following expression is of type int:

mixing types

```
baseAmount + increase
```

However, if one or both of the two variables are of type double, then the result is of type double. This is also true if you replace the operator + with any of the operators -, *, or /.

More generally, you can combine any of the arithmetic types in expressions. If all the types are integer types, the result will be the integer type. If at least one of the subexpressions is of a floating-point type, the result will be a floating-point type. C++ tries its best to make the type of an expression either `int` or `double`, but if the value produced by the expression is not of one of these types because of the value's size, a suitable different integer or floating-point type will be produced.

You can specify the order of operations in an arithmetic expression by inserting parentheses. If you omit parentheses, the computer will follow rules called **precedence rules** that determine the order in which the operations, such as addition and multiplication, are performed. These precedence rules are similar to rules used in algebra and other mathematics classes. For example,

precedence rules

$$x + y * z$$

is evaluated by first doing the multiplication and then the addition. Except in some standard cases, such as a string of additions or a simple multiplication embedded inside an addition, it is usually best to include the parentheses, even if the intended

Display 1.4   Named Constant

```
1   #include <iostream>
2   using namespace std;
3
4   int main( )
5   {
6       const double RATE = 6.9;
7       double deposit
8       cout << "Enter the amount of your deposit $";
9       cin >> deposit;
10      double newBalance;
11      newBalance = deposit + deposit*(RATE/100);
12      cout << "In one year, that deposit will grow to\n"
13           << "$" << newBalance << " an amount worth waiting for.\n";
14      return 0;
15  }
```

Sample Dialogue

```
Enter the amount of your deposit $100
In one year, that deposit will grow to
$106.9 an amount worth waiting for.
```

Naming Constants with the const Modifier

When you initialize a variable inside a declaration, you can mark the variable so that the program is not allowed to change its value. To do this, place the word const in front of the declaration, as described here:

SYNTAX

const *Type_Name Variable_Name = Constant;*

EXAMPLES

```
const int MAX_TRIES = 3;
const double PI = 3.14159;
```

order of operations is the one dictated by the precedence rules. The parentheses make the expression easier to read and less prone to programmer error. A complete set of C++ precedence rules is given in Appendix 2.

Integer and Floating-Point Division

integer division
When used with one or both operands of type double, the division operator, /, behaves as you might expect. However, when used with two operands of type int, the division operator yields the integer part resulting from division. In other words, integer division discards the part after the decimal point. So, 10/3 is 3 (not 3.3333...), 5/2 is 2 (not 2.5), and 11/3 is 3 (not 3.6666...). Notice that the number *is not rounded*; the part after the decimal point is discarded no matter how large it is.

the % operator
The operator % can be used with operands of type int to recover the information lost when you use / to do division with numbers of type int. When used with values of type int, the two operators / and % yield the two numbers produced when you perform the long division algorithm you learned in grade school. For example, 17 divided by 5 yields 3 with a remainder of 2. The / operation yields the number of times one number "goes into" another. The % operation gives the remainder. For example, the statements

```
cout << "17 divided by 5 is " << (17 / 5) << "\n";
cout << "with a remainder of " << (17 % 5) << "\n";
```

yield the following output:

```
17 divided by 5 is 3
with a remainder of 2
```

negative integers in division
When used with negative values of type int, the result of the operators / and % can be different for different implementations of C++. Thus, you should use / and % with int values only when you know that both values are nonnegative.

PITFALL: Division with Whole Numbers

When you use the division operator / on two integers, the result is an integer. This can be a problem if you expect a fraction. Moreover, the problem can easily go unnoticed, resulting in a program that looks fine but is producing incorrect output without you even being aware of the problem. For example, suppose you are a landscape architect who charges $5,000 per mile to landscape a highway, and suppose you know the length of the highway you are working on in feet. The price you charge can easily be calculated by the following C++ statement:

```
totalPrice = 5000 * (feet/5280.0) ;
```

This works because there are 5,280 feet in a mile. If the stretch of highway you are landscaping is 15,000 feet long, this formula will tell you that the total price is

```
5000 * (15000/5280.0)
```

Your C++ program obtains the final value as follows: 15000/5280.0 is computed as 2.84. Then the program multiplies 5000 by 2.84 to produce the value 14200.00. With the aid of your C++ program, you know that you should charge $14,200 for the project.

Now suppose the variable feet is of type int, and you forget to put in the decimal point and the zero, so that the assignment statement in your program reads

```
totalPrice = 5000 * (feet/5280) ;
```

It still looks fine, but will cause serious problems. If you use this second form of the assignment statement, you are dividing two values of type int, so the result of the division feet/5280 is 15000/5280, which is the int value 2 (instead of the value 2.84 that you think you are getting). The value assigned to totalPrice is thus 5000*2, or 10000.00. If you forget the decimal point, you will charge $10,000. However, as we have already seen, the correct value is $14,200. A missing decimal point has cost you $4,200. Note that this will be true whether the type of totalPrice is int or double; the damage is done before the value is assigned to totalPrice. ■

Self-Test Exercises

4. Convert each of the following mathematical formulas to a C++ expression.

$$3x \qquad 3x + y \qquad \frac{x + y}{7} \qquad \frac{3x + y}{z + 2}$$

5. What is the output of the following program lines when they are embedded in a correct program that declares all variables to be of type char?

```
a = 'b';
b = 'c';
c = a;
cout << a << b << c << 'c';
```

Self-Test Exercises (continued)

6. What is the output of the following program lines when they are embedded in a correct program that declares number to be of type int?

```
number = (1/3) * 3;
cout << "(1/3) * 3 is equal to " << number;
```

7. Write a complete C++ program that reads two whole numbers into two variables of type int and then outputs both the whole number part and the remainder when the first number is divided by the second. This can be done using the operators / and %.

8. Given the following fragment that purports to convert from degrees Celsius to degrees Fahrenheit, answer the following questions:

```
double c = 20;
double f;
f = (9/5) * c + 32.0;
```

a. What value is assigned to f?

b. Explain what is actually happening, and what the programmer likely wanted.

c. Rewrite the code as the programmer intended.

Type Casting

type cast

A **type cast** is a way of changing a value of one type to a value of another type. A type cast is a kind of function that takes a value of one type and produces a value of another type that is C++'s best guess of an equivalent value. C++ has four to six different kinds of casts, depending on how you count them. There is an older form of type cast that has two notations for expressing it, and there are four new kinds of type casts introduced with the latest standard. The new kinds of type casts were designed as replacements for the older form; in this book, we will use the newer kinds. However, C++ retains the older kind(s) of cast along with the newer kinds, so we will briefly describe the older kind as well.

Let's start with the newer kinds of type casts. Consider the expression 9/2. In C++ this expression evaluates to 4 because when both operands are of an integer type, C++ performs integer division. In some situations, you might want the answer to be the double value 4.5. You can get a result of 4.5 by using the "equivalent" floating-point value 2.0 in place of the integer value 2, as in 9/2.0, which evaluates to 4.5. But what if the 9 and the 2 are the values of variables of type int named n and m? Then, n/m yields 4. If you want floating-point division in this case, you must do a type cast from int to double (or another floating-point type), such as in the following:

```
double ans = n/static_cast<double>(m);
```

The expression

```
static_cast<double>(m)
```

is a type cast. The expression `static_cast<double>` is like a function that takes an `int` argument (actually, an argument of almost any type) and returns an "equivalent" value of type `double`. So, if the value of `m` is 2, the expression `static_cast<double>(m)` returns the double value 2.0.

Note that `static_cast<double>(n)` does not change the value of the variable `n`. If `n` has the value 2 before this expression is evaluated, then `n` still has the value 2 after the expression is evaluated. (If you know what a function is in mathematics or in some programming language, you can think of `static_cast<double>` as a function that returns an "equivalent" value of type `double`.)

You may use any type name in place of `double` to obtain a type cast to another type. We said this produces an "equivalent" value of the target type. The word equivalent is in quotes because there is no clear notion of equivalent that applies to any two types. In the case of a type cast from an integer type to a floating-point type, the effect is to add a decimal point and a zero. The type cast in the other direction, from a floating-point type to an integer type, simply deletes the decimal point and all digits after the decimal point. Note that when type casting from a floating-point type to an integer type, the number is truncated, not rounded. `static_cast<int>(2.9)` is 2; it is not 3.

This `static_cast` is the most common kind of type cast and the only one we will use for some time. For completeness and reference value, we list all four kinds of type casts. Some may not make sense until you reach the relevant topics. If some or all of the remaining three kinds do not make sense to you at this point, do not worry. The four kinds of type cast are as follows:

```
static_cast<Type>(Expression)
const_cast<Type>(Expression)
dynamic_cast<Type>(Expression)
reinterpret_cast<Type>(Expression)
```

We have already discussed `static_cast`. It is a general-purpose type cast that applies in most "ordinary" situations. The `const_cast` is used to cast away constantness. The `dynamic_cast` is used for safe downcasting from one type to a descendent type in an inheritance hierarchy. The `reinterpret_cast` is an implementation-dependent cast that we will not discuss in this book and that you are unlikely to need. (These descriptions may not make sense until you cover the appropriate topics, where they will be discussed further. For now, we only use `static_cast`.)

The older form of type casting is approximately equivalent to the `static_cast` kind of type casting but uses a different notation. One of the two notations uses a type name as if it were a function name. For example, `int(9.3)` returns the int value 9; `double(42)` returns the value 42.0. The second, equivalent, notation for the older form of type casting would write `(double)42` instead of `double(42)`. Either notation can be used with variables or other more complicated expressions instead of just with constants.

Although C++ retains this older form of type casting, you are encouraged to use the newer form of type casting. (Someday, the older form may go away, although there is, as yet, no such plan for its elimination.)

As we noted earlier, you can always assign a value of an integer type to a variable of a floating-point type, as in

```
double d = 5;
```

type coercion

In such cases C++ performs an automatic type cast, converting the 5 to 5.0 and placing 5.0 in the variable d. You cannot store the 5 as the value of d without a type cast, but sometimes C++ does the type cast for you. Such an automatic conversion is sometimes called a **type coercion**.

Increment and Decrement Operators

increment operator

decrement operator

The ++ in the name of the C++ language comes from the increment operator, ++. The **increment operator** adds 1 to the value of a variable. The **decrement operator**, --, subtracts 1 from the value of a variable. They are usually used with variables of type int, but they can be used with any numeric type. If n is a variable of a numeric type, then n++ increases the value of n by 1 and n-- decreases the value of n by 1. So n++ and n-- (when followed by a semicolon) are executable statements. For example, the statements

```
int n = 1, m = 7;
n++
cout << "The value of n is changed to " << n << "\n";
m--;
cout << "The value of m is changed to " << m << "\n";
```

yield the following output:

```
The value of n is changed to 2
The value of m is changed to 6
```

An expression like n++ returns a value as well as changing the value of the variable n, so n++ can be used in an arithmetic expression such as

```
2*(n++)
```

The expression n++ first returns the value of the variable n, and *then* the value of n is increased by 1. For example, consider the following code:

```
int n = 2;
int valueProduced = 2*(n++);
cout << valueProduced << "\n";
cout << n << "\n";
```

This code will produce the output

```
4
3
```

Notice the expression 2*(n++). When C++ evaluates this expression, it uses the value that number has *before* it is incremented, not the value that it has after it is incremented. Thus, the value produced by the expression n++ is 2, even though the increment operator changes the value of n to 3. This may seem strange, but sometimes

v++ versus ++v

it is just what you want. And, as you are about to see, if you want an expression that behaves differently, you can have it.

The expression n++ evaluates to the value of the variable n, and *then* the value of the variable n is incremented by 1. If you reverse the order and place the ++ in front of the variable, the order of these two actions is reversed. The expression ++n first increments the value of the variable n and then returns this increased value of n. For example, consider the following code:

```
int n = 2;
int valueProduced = 2*(++n);
cout << valueProduced << "\n";
cout << n << "\n";
```

This code is the same as the previous piece of code except that the ++ is before the variable, so this code will produce the following output:

```
6
3
```

Notice that the two increment operators in n++ and ++n have the same effect on a variable n: They both increase the value of n by 1. But the two expressions evaluate to different values. Remember, if the ++ is *before* the variable, the incrementing is done *before* the value is returned; if the ++ is *after* the variable, the incrementing is done *after* the value is returned.

Everything we said about the increment operator applies to the decrement operator as well, except that the value of the variable is decreased by 1 rather than increased by 1. For example, consider the following code:

```
int n = 8;
int valueProduced = n--;
cout << valueProduced << "\n";
cout << n << "\n";
```

This produces the ouput

```
8
7
```

On the other hand, the code

```
int n = 8;
int valueProduced = --n;
cout << valueProduced << "\n";
cout << n << "\n";
```

produces the output

```
7
7
```

n-- returns the value of n and then decrements n; on the other hand, --n first decrements n and then returns the value of n.

You cannot apply the increment and decrement operators to anything other than a single variable. Expressions such as `(x + y)++`, `--(x + y)`, `5++`, and so forth, are all illegal in C++.

The increment and decrement operators can be dangerous when used inside more complicated expressions, as explained in the following Pitfall.

PITFALL: Order of Evaluation

For most operators, the order of evaluation of subexpressions is not guaranteed. In particular, you normally cannot assume that the order of evaluation is left to right. For example, consider the following expression:

```
n + (++n)
```

Suppose `n` has the value 2 before the expression is evaluated. Then, if the first expression is evaluated first, the result is 2 + 3. If the second expression is evaluated first, the result is 3 + 3. Since C++ does not guarantee the order of evaluation, the expression could evaluate to either 5 or 6. The moral is that you should not program in a way that depends on order of evaluation, except for the operators discussed in the next paragraph.

Some operators do guarantee that their order of evaluation of subexpressions is left to right. For the operators `&&` (and), `||` (or), and the comma operator (which is discussed in Chapter 2), C++ guarantees that the order of evaluations is left to right. Fortunately, these are the operators for which you are most likely to want a predicable order of evaluation. For example, consider

```
(n <= 2) && (++n > 2)
```

Suppose `n` has the value 2, before the expression is evaluated. In this case you know that the subexpression `(n <= 2)` is evaluated before the value of `n` is incremented.

You thus know that `(n <= 2)` will evaluate to `true` and so the entire expression will evaluate to `true`.

Do not confuse order of operations (by precedence rules) with order of evaluation. For example,

```
(n + 2) * (++n) + 5
```

always means

```
((n + 2) * (++n)) + 5
```

However, it is not clear whether the `++n` is evaluated before or after the `n + 2`. Either one could be evaluated first.

Now you know why we said that it is usually a bad idea to use the increment (`++`) and decrement (`--`) operators as subexpressions of larger expressions.

If this is too confusing, just follow the simple rule of not writing code that depends on the order of evaluation of subexpressions. ∎

1.3   Console Input/Output

Garbage in means garbage out.

Programmer's saying

Simple console input is done with the objects `cin`, `cout`, and `cerr`, all of which are defined in the library `iostream`. In order to use this library, your program should contain the following near the start of the file containing your code:

```
#include <iostream>
using namespace std;
```

Output Using `cout`

cout

The values of variables as well as strings of text may be output to the screen using `cout`. Any combination of variables and strings can be output. For example, consider the following from the program in Display 1.1:

```
cout << "Hello reader.\n"
     << "Welcome to C++.\n";
```

This statement outputs two strings, one per line. Using `cout`, you can output any number of items, each either a string, a variable, or a more complicated expression. Simply insert a `<<` before each thing to be output.

As another example, consider the following:

```
cout << numberOfGames << " games played.";
```

This statement tells the computer to output two items: the value of the variable `numberOfGames` and the quoted string `" games played."`.

Notice that you do not need a separate copy of the object `cout` for each item output. You can simply list all the items to be output, preceding each item to be output with the arrow symbols `<<`. The previous single `cout` statement is equivalent to the following two `cout` statements:

```
cout << numberOfGames;
cout << " games played.";
```

You can include arithmetic expressions in a `cout` statement, as shown by the following example, where `price` and `tax` are variables:

```
cout << "The total cost is $" << (price + tax);
```

expression in a
cout statement

Parentheses around arithmetic expressions, such as `price + tax`, are required by some compilers, so it is best to include them.

The two `<` symbols should be typed without any space between them. The arrow notation `<<` is often called the **insertion operator**. The entire `cout` statement ends with a semicolon.

spaces in output

Notice the spaces inside the quotes in our examples. The computer does not insert any extra space before or after the items output by a `cout` statement, which is why the quoted strings in the examples often start or end with a blank. The blanks keep the various strings and numbers from running together. If all you need is a space and there is no quoted string where you want to insert the space, then use a string that contains only a space, as in the following:

```
cout << firstNumber << " " << secondNumber;
```

Similarly, if you place the '+' symbol between two variables of type `string` then this operator concatenates (i.e. joins) the two strings together to create one longer string. For example, the code

```
string day1 = "Monday", day2="Tuesday";
cout << day1 + day2;
```

results in the concatenated string of

```
"MondayTuesday"
```

New Lines in Output

As noted in the subsection on escape sequences, `\n` tells the computer to start a new line of output. Unless you tell the computer to go to the next line, it will put all the output on the same line. Depending on how your screen is set up, this can produce anything from arbitrary line breaks to output that runs off the screen. Notice that the `\n` goes inside the quotes. In C++, going to the next line is considered to be a special character, and the way you spell this special character inside a quoted string is `\n`, with no space between the two symbols in `\n`. Although it is typed as two symbols, C++ considers `\n` to be a single character that is called the **newline character.**

newline character

If you wish to insert a blank line in the output, you can output the newline character `\n` by itself:

```
cout << "\n";
```

Another way to output a blank line is to use `endl`, which means essentially the same thing as `"\n"`. So you can also output a blank line as follows:

```
cout << endl;
```

Although `"\n"` and `endl` mean the same thing, they are used slightly differently; `\n` must always be inside quotes, and `endl` should not be placed in quotes.

deciding between \n and endl

A good rule for deciding whether to use `\n` or `endl` is the following: If you can include the `\n` at the end of a longer string, then use `\n`, as in the following:

```
cout << "Fuel efficiency is "
     << mpg << " miles per gallon\n";
```

On the other hand, if the `\n` would appear by itself as the short string `"\n"`, then use `endl` instead:

```
cout << "You entered " << number << endl;
```

Starting New Lines in Output

To start a new output line, you can include \n in a quoted string, as in the following example:

```
cout << "You have definitely won\n"
     << "one of the following prizes:\n";
```

Recall that \n is typed as two symbols with no space in between the two symbols. Alternatively, you can start a new line by outputting endl. An equivalent way to write the previous cout statement is as follows:

```
cout << "You have definitely won" << endl
     << "one of the following prizes:" << endl;
```

TIP: End Each Program with \n or endl

It is a good idea to output a newline instruction at the end of every program. If the last item to be output is a string, then include a \n at the end of the string; if not, output an endl as the last output action in your program. This serves two purposes. Some compilers will not output the last line of your program unless you include a newline instruction at the end. On other systems, your program may work fine without this final newline instruction, but the next program that is run will have its first line of output mixed with the last line of the previous program. Even if neither of these problems occurs on your system, putting a newline instruction at the end will make your programs more portable. ∎

Formatting for Numbers with a Decimal Point

When the computer outputs a value of type double, the format may not be what you would like. For example, the following simple cout statement can produce any of a wide range of outputs:

```
cout << "The price is $" << price << endl;
```

If price has the value 78.5, the output might be

```
The price is $78.500000
```

or it might be

```
The price is $78.5
```

or it might be output in the following notation (which was explained in the subsection entitled "Literals"):

```
The price is $7.850000e01
```

format for double values

It is extremely unlikely that the output will be the following, however, even though this is the format that makes the most sense:

```
The price is $78.50
```

To ensure that the output is in the form you want, your program should contain some sort of instructions that tell the computer how to output the numbers.

magic formula

There is a "magic formula" that you can insert in your program to cause numbers that contain a decimal point, such as numbers of type double, to be output in everyday notation with the exact number of digits after the decimal point that you specify. If you want two digits after the decimal point, use the following magic formula:

```
cout.setf(ios::fixed);
cout.setf(ios::showpoint);
cout.precision(2);
```

If you insert the preceding three statements in your program, then any cout statements that follow these statements will output values of any floating-point type in ordinary notation, with exactly two digits after the decimal point. For example, suppose the following cout statement appears somewhere after this magic formula and suppose the value of price is 78.5.

```
cout << "The price is $" << price << endl;
```

The output will then be as follows:

```
The price is $78.50
```

outputting money amounts

You may use any other nonnegative whole number in place of 2 to specify a different number of digits after the decimal point. You can even use a variable of type int in place of the 2.

We will explain this magic formula in detail in Chapter 12. For now, you should think of this magic formula as one long instruction that tells the computer how you want it to output numbers that contain a decimal point.

If you wish to change the number of digits after the decimal point so that different values in your program are output with different numbers of digits, you can repeat the magic formula with some other number in place of 2. However, when you repeat the magic formula, you only need to repeat the last line of the formula. If the magic formula has already occurred once in your program, then the following line will change the number of digits after the decimal point to five for all subsequent values of any floating-point type that are output:

```
cout.precision(5);
```

Outputting Values of Type double

If you insert the following "magic formula" in your program, then all numbers of type double (or any other type of floating-point number) will be output in ordinary notation with two digits after the decimal point:

```
cout.setf(ios::fixed);
cout.setf(ios::showpoint);
cout.precision(2);
```

You can use any other nonnegative whole number in place of the 2 to specify a different number of digits after the decimal point. You can even use a variable of type int in place of the 2.

Output with cerr

cerr

The object cerr is used in the same way as cout. The object cerr sends its output to the standard error output stream, which normally is the console screen. This gives you a way to distinguish two kinds of output: cout for regular output, and cerr for error message output. If you do nothing special to change things, then cout and cerr will both send their output to the console screen, so there is no difference between them.

On some systems you can redirect output from your program to a file. This is an operating system instruction, not a C++ instruction, but it can be useful. On systems that allow for output redirection, cout and cerr may be redirected to different files.

Input Using cin

cin

You use cin for input more or less the same way you use cout for output. The syntax is similar, except that cin is used in place of cout and the arrows point in the opposite direction. For example, in the program in Display 1.1, the variable numberOfLanguages was filled by the following cin statement:

```
cin >> numberOfLanguages;
```

You can list more than one variable in a single cin statement, as illustrated by the following:

```
cout << "Enter the number of dragons\n"
     << "followed by the number of trolls.\n";
cin >> dragons >> trolls;
```

If you prefer, the above cin statement can be written on two lines, as follows:

```
cin >> dragons
    >> trolls;
```

Notice that, as with the cout statement, there is just one semicolon for each occurrence of cin.

how cin works

When a program reaches a cin statement, it waits for input to be entered from the keyboard. It sets the first variable equal to the first value typed at the keyboard, the second variable equal to the second value typed, and so forth. However, the program does not read the input until the user presses the Return key. This allows the user to backspace and correct mistakes when entering a line of input. Display 1.5 illustrates reading an int and a string in the same program along with a simple calculation.

separate numbers with spaces

whitespace

Numbers in the input must be separated by one or more spaces or by a line break. These delimiting characters are called **whitespace**. When you use cin statements, the computer will skip over any number of blanks or line breaks until it finds the next input value. Thus, it does not matter whether input numbers are separated by one space or several spaces or even a line break. This same behavior holds when you are reading data into a string. This means that you cannot input a string that contains spaces. This may sometimes cause errors, as indicated in Display 1.5, Sample Dialogue 2. In this case, the user intends to enter "Mr. Bojangles" as the name of the pet, but the string is only read up to "Mr." since the next character is a space. The "Bojangles" string is ignored by this program but would be read next if there was another cin statement. Chapter 9 describes a technique to input a string that may include spaces.

You can read in integers, floating-point numbers, characters, or strings using cin. Later in this book we will discuss the reading in of other kinds of data using cin.

Display 1.5   Using cin and cout with a string (part 1 of 2)

```
1   //Program to demonstrate cin and cout with strings
2   #include <iostream>          Needed to access the
3   #include <string>            string class.

4   using namespace std;
5   int main( )
6   {
7       string dogName;
8       int actualAge;
9       int humanAge;

10      cout << "How many years old is your dog?" << endl;
11      cin >> actualAge;
12      humanAge = actualAge * 7;

13      cout << "What is your dog's name?" << endl;
14      cin >> dogName;

15      cout << dogName << "'s age is approximately " <<
16          "equivalent to a " << humanAge << " year old human."
17          << endl;

18      return 0;
19  }
```

(continued)

Display 1.5   Using `cin` and `cout` with a string (part 2 of 2)

Sample Dialogue 1

How many years old is your dog?

5

What is your dog's name?

Rex

Rex's age is approximately equivalent to a 35 year old human.

Sample Dialogue 2

How many years old is your dog?

10

What is your dog's name?

Mr. Bojangles ←——— *"Bojangles" is not read into*
                      dogName because cin stops
                      input at the space.

Mr.'s age is approximately equivalent to a 70 year old human.

`cin` Statements

A `cin` statement sets variables equal to values typed in at the keyboard.

SYNTAX

```
cin >> Variable_1 >> Variable_2 >> . . . ;
```

EXAMPLES

```
cin >> number >> size;
cin >> timeLeft
    >> pointsNeeded;
```

Self-Test Exercises

9. Give an output statement that will produce the following message on the screen.

```
The answer to the question of
Life, the Universe, and Everything is 42.
```

10. Give an input statement that will fill the variable theNumber (of type int) with a number typed in at the keyboard. Precede the input statement with a prompt statement asking the user to enter a whole number.

Self-Test Exercises (continued)

11. What statements should you include in your program to ensure that when a number of type double is output, it will be output in ordinary notation with three digits after the decimal point?

12. Write a complete C++ program that writes the phrase Hello world to the screen. The program does nothing else.

13. Give an output statement that produces the letter 'A', followed by the newline character, followed by the letter 'B', followed by the tab character, followed by the letter 'C'.

14. The following code intends to input a user's first name, last name, and age. However, it has an error. Fix the code.

```
string fullName;
int age;
cout << "Enter your first and last name." << endl;
cin >> fullName;
cout << "Enter your age." << endl;
cin >> age;
cout << "You are " << age << " years old, " << fullName << endl;
```

15. What will the following code output?

```
string s1 = "5";
string s2 = "3";
string s3 = s1 + s2;
cout << s3 << endl;
```

TIP: Line Breaks in I/O

It is possible to keep output and input on the same line, and sometimes it can produce a nicer interface for the user. If you simply omit a \n or endl at the end of the last prompt line, then the user's input will appear on the same line as the prompt. For example, suppose you use the following prompt and input statements:

```
cout << "Enter the cost per person: $";
cin >> costPerPerson;
```

When the cout statement is executed, the following will appear on the screen:

```
Enter the cost per person: $
```

When the user types in the input, it will appear on the same line, like this:

```
Enter the cost per person: $1.25
```

1.4   Program Style

In matters of grave importance, style, not sincerity, is the vital thing.

OSCAR WILDE, *The Importance of Being Earnest*

C++ programming style is similar to that used in other languages. The goal is to make your code easy to read and easy to modify. We will say a bit about indenting in the next chapter. We have already discussed defined constants. Choice of variable names and careful indenting should eliminate the need for very many comments, but any points that still remain unclear deserve a comment.

Comments

There are two ways to insert comments in a C++ program. In C++, two slashes, //, are used to indicate the start of a comment. All the text between the // and the end of the line is a comment. The compiler simply ignores anything that follows // on a line. If you want a comment that covers more than one line, place a // on each line of the comment. The symbols // do not have a space between them.

Another way to insert comments in a C++ program is to use the symbol pairs /* and */. Text between these symbols is considered a comment and is ignored by the compiler. Unlike the // comments, which require an additional // on each line, the /*-to-*/ comments can span several lines, like so:

```
/*This is a comment that spans

three lines. Note that there is no comment

symbol of any kind on the second line.*/
```

Comments of the /* */ type may be inserted anywhere in a program that a space or line break is allowed. However, they should not be inserted anywhere except where they are easy to read and do not distract from the layout of the program. Usually, comments are placed at the ends of lines or on separate lines by themselves.

Opinions differ regarding which kind of comment is best to use. Either variety (the // kind or the /* */ kind) can be effective if used with care. One approach is to use the // comments in final code and reserve the /**/-style comments for temporarily commenting out code while debugging.

It is difficult to say just how many comments a program should contain. The only correct answer is "just enough," which of course conveys little to the novice programmer. It will take some experience to get a feel for when it is best to include a comment. Whenever something is important and not obvious, it merits a comment. However, too many comments are as bad as too few. A program that has a comment on each line will be so buried in comments that the structure of the program is hidden in a sea of obvious observations. Comments like the following contribute nothing to understanding and should not appear in a program:

```
distance = speed * time; //Computes the distance traveled.
```

when to comment

1.5 Libraries and Namespaces

C++ comes with a number of standard libraries. These libraries place their definitions in a *namespace*, which is simply a name given to a collection of definitions. The techniques for including libraries and dealing with namespaces will be discussed in detail later in this book. This section discusses enough details to allow you to use the standard C++ libraries.

Libraries and include Directives

C++ includes a number of standard libraries. In fact, it is almost impossible to write a C++ program without using at least one of these libraries. The normal way to make a library available to your program is with an include directive. An include directive for a standard library has the form

<code>#include</code>

```
#include <Library_Name>
```

For example, the library for console I/O is iostream. So, most of our demonstration programs will begin

```
#include <iostream>
```

Compilers (preprocessors) can be very fussy about spacing in include directives. Thus, it is safest to type an include directive with no extra space: no space before the #, no space after the #, and no spaces inside the <>.

An include directive is simply an instruction to include the text found in a file at the location of the include directive. A library name is simply the name of a file that includes all the definition of items in the library. We will eventually discuss using include directives for things other than standard libraries, but for now we only need include directives for standard C++ libraries. A list of some standard C++ libraries is given in Appendix 4.

preprocessor

C++ has a **preprocessor** that handles some simple textual manipulation before the text of your program is given to the compiler. Some people will tell you that include directives are not processed by the compiler but are processed by a preprocessor. They're right, but the difference is more of a word game than anything that need concern you. On almost all compilers, the preprocessor is called automatically when you compile your program.

Technically speaking, only part of the library definition is given in the header file. However, at this stage, that is not an important distinction, since using the include directive with the header file for a library will (on almost all systems) cause C++ to automatically add the rest of the library definition.

Namespaces

namespace

A **namespace** is a collection of name definitions. One name, such as a function name, can be given different definitions in two namespaces. A program can then use one of these namespaces in one place and the other in another location. We will discuss namespaces in detail later in this book. For now, we only need to discuss the namespace std. All the standard libraries we will be using are defined in the std (standard) namespace. To use any of these definitions in your program, you must insert the following using directive:

using
namespace

```
using namespace std;
```

Thus, a simple program that uses console I/O would begin

```
#include <iostream>
using namespace std;
```

If you want to make some, but not all, names in a namespace available to your program, there is a form of the using directive that makes just one name available. For example, if you only want to make the name cin from the std namespace available to your program, you could use the following using directive:

```
using std::cin;
```

Thus, if the only names from the std namespace that your program uses are cin, cout, and endl, you might start your program with

```
#include <iostream>
using std::cin;
using std::cout;
using std::endl;
```

instead of

```
#include <iostream>
using namespace std;
```

Older C++ header files for libraries did not place their definitions in the std namespace, so if you look at older C++ code, you will probably see that the header file names are spelled slightly differently and the code does not contain any using directive. This is allowed for backward compatibility. However, you should use the newer library header files and the std namespace directive.

PITFALL: Problems with Library Names

The C++ language is constantly in transition. If you are using a compiler that has not yet been revised to meet the new standard, then you will need to use different library names.

If the following does not work

```
#include <iostream>
```

use

```
#include <iostream.h>
```

PITFALL: (continued)

Similarly, other library names are different for older compilers. Appendix 5 gives the correspondence between older and newer library names. This book always uses the new compiler names. If a library name does not work with your compiler, try the corresponding older library name. In all probability, either all the new library names will work or you will need to use all old library names. It is unlikely that only some of the library names have been made up to date on your system.

If you use the older library names (the ones that end in .h), you do *not* need the using directive

```
using namespace std;
```

Chapter Summary

• C++ is *case sensitive*. For example, count and COUNT are two different identifiers.

• Use meaningful names for variables.

• Variables must be declared before they are used. Other than following this rule, a variable declaration may appear anyplace.

• Be sure that variables are initialized before the program attempts to use their value. This can be done when the variable is declared or with an *assignment statement* before the variable is first used.

• You can assign a value of an integer type, like int, to a variable of a floating-point type, like double, but not vice versa.

• Almost all number constants in a program should be given meaningful names that can be used in place of the numbers. This can be done by using the modifier const in a variable declaration.

• Use enough parentheses in arithmetic expressions to make the order of operations clear.

• The object cout is used for console output.

• A \n in a quoted string or an endl sent to console output starts a new line of output.

• The object cerr is used for error messages. In a typical environment, cerr behaves the same as cout.

• The object cin is used for console input.

• In order to use cin, cout, or cerr, you should place the following directives near the beginning of the file with your program:

```
#include <iostream>
using namespace std;
```

- There are two forms of comments in C++: Everything following // on the same line is a comment, and anything enclosed in /* and */ is a comment.

- Do not over comment.

Answers to Self-Test Exercises

1. `int feet = 0, inches = 0;`
   `int feet(0), inches(0);`

2. `int count = 0;`
   `double distance = 1.5;`
   `int count(0);`
   `double distance(1.5);`

   `public static void main(String[] args)`

3. The actual output from a program such as this is dependent on the system and the history of the use of the system.

   ```
   #include <iostream>
   using namespace std;

   int main( )
   {
       int first, second, third, fourth, fifth;
       cout << first << " " << second << " " << third
            << " " << fourth << " " << fifth << "\n";

       return 0;
   }
   ```

4. `3*x`
   `3*x`
   `3*x`
   `(x + y)/7` Note that `x + y/7` is not correct.
   `(3*x + y)/(z + 2)`

5. `bcbc`

6. `(1/3) * 3 is equal to 0`

   Since 1 and 3 are of type int, the / operator performs integer division, which discards the remainder, so the value of 1/3 is 0, not 0.3333.... This makes the value of the entire expression 0 * 3, which of course is 0.

7. ```
   #include <iostream>
   using namespace std;

   int main( )
   {
       int number1, number2;
       cout << "Enter two whole numbers: ";
       cin >> number1 >> number2;
       cout << number1 << " divided by " << number2
            << " equals " << (number1/number2) << "\n"
   ```
   ```

```
                    << "with a remainder of " << (number1%number2)
                    << "\n";

            return 0;
      }
```

8. a. `52.0`

   b. `9/5` has int value `1`. Since the numerator and denominator are both `int`, integer division is done; the fractional part is discarded. The programmer probably wanted floating-point division, which does not discard the part after the decimal point.

   c. `f = (9.0/5) * c + 32.0;`

      or

      `f = 1.8 * c + 32.0;`

9. ```
   cout << "The answer to the question of\n"
        << "Life, the Universe, and Everything is 42.\n";
   ```

10. ```
    cout << "Enter a whole number and press Return: ";
    cin >> theNumber;
    ```

11. ```
    cout.setf(ios::fixed);
    cout.setf(ios::showpoint);
    cout.precision(3);
    ```

12. ```
    #include <iostream>
    using namespace std;

    int main( )
    {
        cout << "Hello world\n";

        return 0;
    }
    ```

13. ```
    cout << 'A' << endl << 'B' << '\t' << 'C';
    ```

    Other answers are also correct. For example, the letters could be in double quotes instead of single quotes. Another possible answer is the following:

    ```
    cout << "A\nB\tC";
    ```

14. `cin` only reads up to the next whitespace, so the first and last name cannot be read into a single string as written if there is a space between the first name and last name. For now the easiest solution is to read the first and last name into two separate variables:

    ```
    string first, last;
    int age;

    cout << "Enter your first and last name." << endl;
    cin >> first >> last;
    cout << "Enter your age." << endl;
    cin >> age;
    cout << "You are " << age << " years old, " << first <<
            " " << last << endl;
    ```

15. The `+` operator concatenates two string operands. The result is `s3 = "53"`. If `s1` and `s2` were numeric data types then the values would be added.
    ```

Programming Projects

Visit www.myprogramminglab.com to complete select exercises online and get instant feedback.

1. A metric ton is 35,273.92 ounces. Write a program that will read the weight of a package of breakfast cereal in ounces and output the weight in metric tons as well as the number of boxes needed to yield one metric ton of cereal.

2. A government research lab has concluded that an artificial sweetener commonly used in diet soda will cause death in laboratory mice. A friend of yours is desperate to lose weight but cannot give up soda. Your friend wants to know how much diet soda it is possible to drink without dying as a result. Write a program to supply the answer. The input to the program is the amount of artificial sweetener needed to kill a mouse, the weight of the mouse, and the weight of the dieter. To ensure the safety of your friend, be sure the program requests the weight at which the dieter will stop dieting, rather than the dieter's current weight. Assume that diet soda contains one-tenth of 1% artificial sweetener. Use a variable declaration with the modifier `const` to give a name to this fraction. You may want to express the percentage as the `double` value `0.001`.

3. Workers at a particular company have won a 7.6% pay increase retroactive for six months. Write a program that takes an employee's previous annual salary as input and outputs the amount of retroactive pay due the employee, the new annual salary, and the new monthly salary. Use a variable declaration with the modifier `const` to express the pay increase.

4. Negotiating a consumer loan is not always straightforward. One form of loan is the discount installment loan, which works as follows. Suppose a loan has a face value of $1,000, the interest rate is 15%, and the duration is 18 months. The interest is computed by multiplying the face value of $1,000 by 0.15, yielding $150. That figure is then multiplied by the loan period of 1.5 years to yield $225 as the total interest owed. That amount is immediately deducted from the face value, leaving the consumer with only $775. Repayment is made in equal monthly installments based on the face value. So the monthly loan payment will be $1,000 divided by 18, which is $55.56. This method of calculation may not be too bad if the consumer needs $775 dollars, but the calculation is a bit more complicated if the consumer needs $1,000. Write a program that will take three inputs: the amount the consumer needs to receive, the interest rate, and the duration of the loan in months. The program should then calculate the face value required in order for the consumer to receive the amount needed. It should also calculate the monthly payment.

5. Write a program that determines whether a meeting room is in violation of fire law regulations regarding the maximum room capacity. The program will read in the maximum room capacity and the number of people to attend the meeting. If the number of people is less than or equal to the maximum room capacity, the program announces that it is legal to hold the meeting and tells how many additional people may legally attend. If the number of people exceeds the maximum room capacity, the program announces that the meeting cannot be held as planned due to fire

regulations and tells how many people must be excluded in order to meet the fire regulations.

6. An employee is paid at a rate of $16.78 per hour for regular hours worked in a week. Any hours over that are paid at the overtime rate of one and one-half times that. From the worker's gross pay, 6% is withheld for Social Security tax, 14% is withheld for federal income tax, 5% is withheld for state income tax, and $10 per week is withheld for union dues. If the worker has three or more dependents, then an additional $35 is withheld to cover the extra cost of health insurance beyond what the employer pays. Write a program that will read in the number of hours worked in a week and the number of dependents as input and that will then output the worker's gross pay, each withholding amount, and the net take-home pay for the week.

7. One way to measure the amount of energy that is expended during exercise is to use metabolic equivalents (MET). Here are some METS for various activities:

Running 6 MPH: 10 METS

Basketball: 8 METS

Sleeping: 1 MET

The number of calories burned per minute may be estimated using the formula

Calories/Minute = 0.0175 × 1 MET × (Weight in kilograms)

Write a program that inputs a subject's weight in pounds, the number of METS for an activity, and the number of minutes spent on that activity, and then outputs an estimate for the total number of calories burned. One kilogram is equal to 2.2 pounds.

8. The Babylonian algorithm to compute the square root of a positive number **n** is as follows:

1. Make a **guess** at the answer (you can pick n/2 as your initial guess).
2. Compute **r** = **n** / **guess**.
3. Set **guess** = (**guess** + **r**) / 2.
4. Go back to step 2 for as many iterations as necessary. The more steps 2 and 3 are repeated, the closer **guess** will become to the square root of **n**.

Write a program that inputs a double for **n**, iterates through the Babylonian algorithm five times, and outputs the answer as a double to two decimal places. Your answer will be most accurate for small values of **n**.

9. The video game machines at your local arcade output coupons depending on how well you play the game. You can redeem 10 coupons for a candy bar or 3 coupons for a gumball. You prefer candy bars to gumballs. Write a program that inputs the number of coupons you win and outputs how many candy bars and gumballs you can get if you spend all of your coupons on candy bars first and any remaining coupons on gumballs.

10. Write a program that allows the user to enter a time in seconds and then outputs how far an object would drop if it is in freefall for that length of time. Assume no friction or resistance from air and a constant acceleration of 32 feet per second due to gravity. Use the equation

$$\text{Distance} = \frac{1}{2} \times \text{acceleration} \times \text{time}^2$$

VideoNote

Solution to
Programming
Project 1.11

11. Write a program that inputs an integer that represents a length of time in seconds. The program should then output the number of hours, minutes, and seconds that corresponds to that number of seconds. For example, if the user inputs 50391 total seconds then the program should output 13 hours, 59 minutes, and 51 seconds.

12. A simple rule to estimate your ideal body weight is to allow 110 pounds for the first 5 feet of height and 5 pounds for each additional inch. Write a program with a variable for the height of a person in feet and another variable for the additional inches and input values for these variables from the keyboard. Assume the person is at least 5 feet tall. For example, a person that is 6 feet and 3 inches tall would be represented with a variable that stores the number 6 and another variable that stores the number 3. Based on these values calculate and output the ideal body weight.

Flow of Control 2

2 Flow of Control

"Would you tell me, please, which way I ought to go from here?"
"That depends a good deal on where you want to get to," said the Cat.

LEWIS CARROLL, *Alice in Wonderland*

Introduction

As in most programming languages, C++ handles flow of control with branching and looping statements. C++ branching and looping statements are similar to branching and looping statements in other languages. They are the same as in the C language and very similar to what they are in the Java programming language. Exception handling is also a way to handle flow of control. Exception handling is covered in Chapter 18.

2.1 Boolean Expressions

He who would distinguish the true from the false must have an adequate idea of what is true and false.

BENEDICT SPINOZA, *Ethics*

Boolean expression

Most branching statements are controlled by Boolean expressions. A **Boolean expression** is any expression that is either true or false. The simplest form for a Boolean expression consists of two expressions, such as numbers or variables, which are compared with one of the comparison operators shown in Display 2.1. Notice that some of the operators are spelled with two symbols, for example, ==, !=, <=, or >=. Be sure to notice that you use a double equal == for the equal sign and that you use the two symbols != for not equal. Such two-symbol operators should not have any space between the two symbols.

Building Boolean Expressions

&& means "and"

You can combine two comparisons using the "and" operator, which is spelled && in C++. For example, the following Boolean expression is true provided x is greater than 2 *and* x is less than 7:

```
(2 < x) && (x < 7)
```

When two comparisons are connected using an &&, the entire expression is true, provided both of the comparisons are true; otherwise, the entire expression is false.

The "and" Operator, &&

You can form a more elaborate Boolean expression by combining two simpler Boolean expressions using the "and" operator, &&.

SYNTAX FOR A BOOLEAN EXPRESSION USING &&

```
(Boolean_Exp_1) && (Boolean_Exp_2)
```

SYNTAX (WITHIN AN if-else STATEMENT)

```
if ( (score > 0) && (score < 10))
    cout << "score is between 0 and 10.\n";
else

    cout << "score is not between 0 and 10.\n";
```

If the value of score is greater than 0 and the value of score is also less than 10, then the first cout statement will be executed; otherwise, the second cout statement will be executed. (if-else statements are covered a bit later in this chapter, but the meaning of this simple example should be intuitively clear.)

You can also combine two comparisons using the "or" operator, which is spelled || in C++. For example, the following is true provided y is less than 0 *or* y is greater than 12:

```
(y < 0) || (y < 12)
```

When two comparisons are connected using a ||, the entire expression is true provided that one or both of the comparisons are true; otherwise, the entire expression is false.

You can negate any Boolean expression using the ! operator. If you want to negate a Boolean expression, place the expression in parentheses and place the ! operator in front of it. For example, !(x < y) means "x is *not* less than y." The ! operator can usually be avoided. For example, !(x < y) is equivalent to x >= y. In some cases you can safely omit the parentheses, but the parentheses never do any harm. The exact details on omitting parentheses are given in the subsection entitled "**Precedence Rules**."

|| means "or"

PITFALL: Strings of Inequalities

Do not use a string of inequalities such as x < z < y. If you do, your program will probably compile and run, but it will undoubtedly give incorrect output. Instead, you must use two inequalities connected with an &&, as follows:

```
(x < z) && (z < y)
```

Display 2.1 Comparison Operators

MATH SYMBOL	ENGLISH	C++ NOTATION	C++ SAMPLE	MATH EQUIVALENT
=	Equal to	==	x + 7 == 2*y	x + 7 = 2y
≠	Not equal to	!=	ans != 'n'	ans ≠ 'n'
<	Less than	<	count < m + 3	count < m + 3
≤	Less than or equal to	<=	time <= limit	time ≤ limit
>	Greater than	>	time > limit	time > limit
≥	Greater than or equal to	>=	age >= 21	age ≥ 21

The "or" Operator, ||

You can form a more elaborate Boolean expression by combining two simpler Boolean expressions using the "or" operator, ||.

SYNTAX FOR A BOOLEAN EXPRESSION USING ||

(*Boolean_Exp_1*) || (*Boolean_Exp_2*)

EXAMPLE WITHIN AN if-else STATEMENT

```
if ( (x == 1) || (x == y) )
    cout << "x is 1 or x equals y.\n";
else
    cout << "x is neither 1 nor equal to y.\n";
```

If the value of x is equal to 1 or the value of x is equal to the value of y (or both), then the first cout statement will be executed; otherwise, the second cout statement will be executed. (if-else statements are covered a bit later in this chapter, but the meaning of this simple example should be intuitively clear.)

Evaluating Boolean Expressions

As you will see in the next two sections of this chapter, Boolean expressions are used to control branching and looping statements. However, a Boolean expression has an independent identity apart from any branching or looping statement you might use it in. A variable of type `bool` can store either of the values `true` or `false`. Thus, you can set a variable of type `bool` equal to a Boolean expression. For example,

```
bool result = (x < z) && (z < y);
```

A Boolean expression can be evaluated in the same way that an arithmetic expression is evaluated. The only difference is that an arithmetic expression uses operations such as +, *, and / and produces a number as the final result, whereas a Boolean expression uses relational operations such as == and < and Boolean operations such as &&, ||, and ! and produces one of the two values `true` or `false` as the final result. Note that ==, !=, <, <=, and so forth, operate on pairs of any built-in type to produce a Boolean value `true` or `false`.

First let's review evaluating an arithmetic expression. The same technique will work to evaluate Boolean expressions. Consider the following arithmetic expression:

```
(x + 1) * (x + 3)
```

Assume that the variable `x` has the value 2. To evaluate this arithmetic expression, you evaluate the two sums to obtain the numbers 3 and 5, and then you combine these two numbers 3 and 5 using the * operator to obtain 15 as the final value. Notice that in performing this evaluation, you do not multiply the expressions (x + 1) and (x + 3). Instead, you multiply the values of these expressions. You use 3; you do not use (x + 1). You use 5; you do not use (x + 3).

The computer evaluates Boolean expressions the same way. Subexpressions are evaluated to obtain values, each of which is either `true` or `false`. These individual values of `true` or `false` are then combined according to the rules in the tables shown in Display 2.2. For example, consider the Boolean expression

```
!( (y < 3) || (y > 7) )
```

which might be the controlling expression for an `if-else` statement. Suppose the value of `y` is 8. In this case (y < 3) evaluates to `false` and (y > 7) evaluates to `true`, so the previous Boolean expression is equivalent to

```
!( false || true )
```

Consulting the tables for || (which is labeled OR), the computer sees that the expression inside the parentheses evaluates to `true`. Thus, the computer sees that the entire expression is equivalent to

```
!(true)
```

Consulting the tables again, the computer sees that !(true) evaluates to `false`, and so it concludes that `false` is the value of the original Boolean expression.

truth tables

Display 2.2   Truth Tables

AND

Exp_1	Exp_2	Exp_1 && Exp_2
true	true	true
true	false	false
false	true	false
false	false	false

OR

Exp_1	Exp_2	Exp_1 || Exp_2
true	true	true
true	false	true
false	true	true
false	false	false

NOT

Exp	!(Exp)
true	false
false	true

The Boolean (bool) Values Are true and false

true and false are predefined constants of type bool. (They must be written in lowercase.) In C++, a Boolean expression evaluates to the bool value true when it is satisfied and to the bool value false when it is not satisfied.

Precedence Rules

Boolean expressions (and arithmetic expressions) need not be fully parenthesized. If you omit parentheses, the default precedence is as follows: Perform ! first, then perform relational operations such as <, then &&, and then ||. However, it is a good practice to include most parentheses to make the expression easier to understand. One place where parentheses can safely be omitted is a simple string of &&'s or ||'s (but not a mixture of the two). The following expression is acceptable in terms of both the C++ compiler and readability:

```
(temperature > 90) && (humidity > 0.90) && (poolGate == OPEN)
```

parentheses

Since the relational operations > and == are performed before the && operation, you could omit the parentheses in the previous expression and it would have the same meaning, but including some parentheses makes the expression easier to read.

When parentheses are omitted from an expression, the compiler groups items according to rules known as **precedence rules**. Most of the precedence rules for C++ are given in Display 2.3. The table includes a number of operators that are not discussed until later in this book, but they are included for completeness and for those who may already know about them.

precedence rules

Display 2.3   Precedence of Operators (part 1 of 2)

Operator	Description	
::	Scope resolution operator	*Highest precedence (done first)*
.	Dot operator	
->	Member selection	
[]	Array indexing	
( )	Function call	
++	Postfix increment operator (placed after the variable)	
--	Postfix decrement operator (placed after the variable)	
++	Prefix increment operator (placed before the variable)	
--	Prefix decrement operator (placed before the variable)	
!	Not	
-	Unary minus	
+	Unary plus	
*	Dereference	
&	Address of	
new	Create (allocate memory)	
delete	Destroy (deallocate)	
delete []	Destroy array (deallocate)	
sizeof	Size of object	
( )	Type cast	
*	Multiply	
/	Divide	
%	Remainder (modulo)	
+	Addition	
-	Subtraction	
<<	Insertion operator (console output)	*Lower precedence (done later)*
>>	Extraction operator (console input)	

(continued)

Display 2.3   Precedence of Operators (part 2 of 2)

All operators in part 2 are of lower precedence than those in part 1.

<	Less than	
>	Greater than	
<=	Less than or equal to	
>=	Greater than or equal to	
==	Equal	
!=	Not equal	
&&	And	
||	Or	
%	Modulo and assign	
/	Divide and assign	
*	Multiply and assign	
-	Subtract and assign	
+	Add and assign	
=	Assignment	
? :	Conditional operator	
throw	Throw an exception	
,	Comma operator	

higher precedence

Lowest precedence (done last) ←

lower precedence

If one operation is performed before another, the operation that is performed first is said to have **higher precedence.** All the operators in a given box in Display 2.3 have the same precedence. Operators in higher boxes have higher precedence than operators in lower boxes.

When operators have the same precedences and the order is not determined by parentheses, then unary operations are done right to left. The assignment operations are also done right to left. For example, x = y = z means x = (y = z). Other binary operations that have the same precedences are done left to right. For example, x + y + z means (x + y) + z.

Notice that the precedence rules include both arithmetic operators such as + and * as well as Boolean operators such as && and ||. This is because many expressions combine arithmetic and Boolean operations, as in the following simple example:

```
(x + 1) > 2 || (x + 1) < -3
```

If you check the precedence rules given in Display 2.3, you will see that this expression is equivalent to

```
((x + 1) > 2) || ((x + 1) < -3)
```

because > and < have higher precedence than ||. In fact, you could omit all the parentheses in the previous expression and it would have the same meaning, although it would be harder to read. Although we do not advocate omitting all the parentheses, it might be instructive to see how such an expression is interpreted using the precedence rules. Here is the expression without any parentheses:

```
x + 1 > 2 || x + 1 < -3
```

The precedences rules say first apply the unary -, then apply the +'s, then the > and the <, and finally apply the ||, which is exactly what the fully parenthesized version says to do.

The previous description of how a Boolean expression is evaluated is basically correct, but in C++, the computer actually takes an occasional shortcut when evaluating a Boolean expression. Notice that in many cases you need to evaluate only the first of two subexpressions in a Boolean expression. For example, consider the following:

```
(x >= 0) && (y > 1)
```

If x is negative, then (x >= 0) is false. As you can see in the tables in Display 2.2, when one subexpression in an && expression is false, then the whole expression is false, no matter whether the other expression is true or false. Thus, if we know that the first expression is false, there is no need to evaluate the second expression. A similar thing happens with || expressions. If the first of two expressions joined with the || operator is true, then you know the entire expression is true, no matter whether the second expression is true or false. The C++ language uses this fact to sometimes save itself the trouble of evaluating the second subexpression in a logical expression connected with an && or ||. C++ first evaluates the leftmost of the two expressions joined by an && or ||. If that gives it enough information to determine the final value of the expression (independent of the value of the second expression), then C++ does not bother to evaluate the second expression. This method of evaluation is called **short-circuit evaluation**.

Some languages other than C++ use **complete evaluation**. In complete evaluation, when two expressions are joined by an && or ||, both subexpressions are always evaluated and then the truth tables are used to obtain the value of the final expression.

short-circuit evaluation

complete evaluation

PITFALL: Integer Values Can Be Used as Boolean Values

C++ sometimes uses integers as if they were Boolean values and `bool` values as if they were integers. In particular, C++ converts the integer 1 to `true` and converts the integer 0 to `false`, and vice versa. The situation is even a bit more complicated than simply using 1 for `true` and 0 for `false`. The compiler will treat any nonzero number as if it were the value `true` and will treat 0 as if it were the value `false`. As long as you make no mistakes in writing Boolean expressions, this conversion causes no problems. However, when you are debugging, it might help to know that the compiler is happy to combine integers using the Boolean operators `&&`, `||`, and `!`.

For example, suppose you want a Boolean expression that is `true` provided that `time` has not yet run out (in some game or process). You might use the following:

```
!time > limit
```

This sounds right if you read it out loud: "not `time` greater than `limit`." The Boolean expression is wrong, however, and unfortunately, the compiler will not give you an error message. The compiler will apply the precedence rules from Display 2.3 and interpret your Boolean expression as the following:

```
(!time) > limit
```

This looks like nonsense, and intuitively it is nonsense. If the value of `time` is, for example, 36, what could possibly be the meaning of `(!time)`? After all, that is equivalent to "not 36." But in C++, any nonzero integer converts to `true` and 0 is converted to `false`. Thus, 136 is interpreted as "not `true`" and so it evaluates to `false`, which is in turn converted back to 0 because we are comparing to an `int`.

What we want as the value of this Boolean expression and what C++ gives us are not the same. If `time` has a value of 36 and `limit` has a value of 60, you want the previously displayed Boolean expression to evaluate to `true` (because it is *not* `true` that `time > limit`). Unfortunately, the Boolean expression instead evaluates as follows: `(!time)` evaluates to `false`, which is converted to 0, so the entire Boolean expression is equivalent to

```
0 > limit
```

That in turn is equivalent to `0 > 60`, because 60 is the value of `limit`, and that evaluates to `false`. Thus, the above logical expression evaluates to `false`, when you want it to evaluate to `true`.

There are two ways to correct this problem. One way is to use the `!` operator correctly. When using the `!` operator, be sure to include parentheses around the argument. The correct way to write the above Boolean expression is

```
!(time > limit)
```

integers convert to bool

PITFALL: (continued)

Another way to correct this problem is to completely avoid using the `!` operator. For example, the following is also correct and easier to read:

```
if (time <= limit)
```

You can almost always avoid using the `!` operator, and some programmers advocate avoiding it as much as possible. ■

Both short-circuit evaluation and complete evaluation give the same answer, so why should you care that C++ uses short-circuit evaluation? Most of the time you need not care. As long as both subexpressions joined by the `&&` or the `||` have a value, the two methods yield the same result. However, if the second subexpression is undefined, you might be happy to know that C++ uses short-circuit evaluation. Let's look at an example that illustrates this point. Consider the following statement:

```
if ( (kids != 0) && ((pieces/kids) >= 2) )
    cout << "Each child may have two pieces!";
```

If the value of `kids` is not zero, this statement involves no subtleties. However, suppose the value of `kids` is zero; consider how short-circuit evaluation handles this case. The expression (`kids!=0`) evaluates to `false`, so there would be no need to evaluate the second expression. Using short-circuit evaluation, C++ says that the entire expression is `false`, without bothering to evaluate the second expression. This prevents a run-time error, since evaluating the second expression would involve dividing by zero.

Self-Test Exercises

1. Determine the value, `true` or `false`, of each of the following Boolean expressions, assuming that the value of the variable `count` is 0 and the value of the variable `limit` is 10. Give your answer as one of the values `true` or `false`.

a. `(count == 0) && (limit < 20)`

b. `count == 0 && limit < 20`

c. `(limit > 20) || (count < 5)`

d. `!(count == 12)`

e. `(count == 1) && (x < y)`

f. `(count < 10) || (x < y)`

g. `! ( (count < 10) || (x < y) ) && (count >= 0) )`

h. `((limit / count) > 7) || (limit < 20)`

i. `(limit < 20) || ((limit / count) > 7)`

j. `((limit / count) > 7) && (limit < 0)`

k. `(limit < 0) && ((limit / count) > 7)`

l. `(5 && 7) + (!6)`

(continued)

Self-Test Exercises (continued)

2. You sometimes see numeric intervals given as

   2 < x < 3

   In C++ this interval does not have the meaning you may expect. Explain and give the correct C++ Boolean expression that specifies that x lies between 2 and 3.

3. Consider a quadratic expression, say

   $x^2 - x - 2$

   Describing where this quadratic is positive (that is, greater than 0) involves describing a set of numbers that are either less than the smaller root (which is −1) or greater than the larger root (which is 2). Write a C++ Boolean expression that is true when this formula has positive values.

4. Consider the quadratic expression

   $x^2 - 4x + 3$

   Describing where this quadratic is negative involves describing a set of numbers that are simultaneously greater than the smaller root (1) and less than the larger root (3). Write a C++ Boolean expression that is true when the value of this quadratic is negative.

2.2   Branching Mechanisms

When you come to a fork in the road, take it.

Attributed to YOGI BERRA

if-else Statements

if-else statement

An **if-else statement** chooses between two alternative statements based on the value of a Boolean expression. For example, suppose you want to design a program to compute a week's salary for an hourly employee. Assume the firm pays an overtime rate of one-and-one-half times the regular rate for all hours after the first 40 hours worked. When the employee works 40 or more hours, the pay is then equal to

rate * 40 + 1.5 * rate * (hours - 40)

if-else Statement

The if-else statement chooses between two alternative actions based on the value of a Boolean expression. The syntax is shown next. Be sure to note that the Boolean expression must be enclosed in parentheses.

SYNTAX: A SINGLE STATEMENT FOR EACH ALTERNATIVE

```
if (Boolean_Expression)
    Yes_Statement
else
    No_Statement
```

If the Boolean_Expression evaluates to true, then the Yes_Statement is executed. If the Boolean_Expression evaluates to false, then the No_Statement is executed.

SYNTAX: A SEQUENCE OF STATEMENTS FOR EACH ALTERNATIVE

```
if (Boolean_Expression)
{
    Yes_Statement_1
    Yes_Statement_2
        ...
    Yes_Statement_Last
}
else
{
    No_Statement_1
    No_Statement_2
        ...
    No_Statement_Last
}
```

EXAMPLE

```
if (myScore > yourScore)
{
    cout << "I win!\n";
    wager = wager + 100;
}
else
{
    cout << "I wish these were golf scores.\n";
    wager = 0;
}
```

However, if the employee works less than 40 hours, the correct pay formula is simply

```
rate * hours
```

The following `if-else` statement computes the correct pay for an employee whether the employee works less than 40 hours or works 40 or more hours,

```
if (hours > 40)
    grossPay = rate * 40 + 1.5 * rate * (hours - 40);
else
    grossPay = rate * hours;
```

The syntax for an `if-else` statement is given in the accompanying box. If the Boolean expression in parentheses (after the `if`) evaluates to `true`, then the statement before the `else` is executed. If the Boolean expression evaluates to `false`, the statement after the `else` is executed.

Notice that an `if-else` statement has smaller statements embedded in it. Most of the statement forms in C++ allow you to make larger statements out of smaller statements by combining the smaller statements in certain ways.

Remember that when you use a Boolean expression in an `if-else` statement, the Boolean expression must be enclosed in parentheses.

parentheses

Compound Statements

You will often want the branches of an `if-else` statement to execute more than one statement each. To accomplish this, enclose the statements for each branch between a pair of braces, { and }, as indicated in the second syntax template in the box entitled "`if-else` Statement." A list of statements enclosed in a pair of braces is called a **compound statement**. A compound statement is treated as a single statement by C++ and may be used anywhere that a single statement may be used. (Thus, the second syntax template in the box entitled "`if-else` Statement" is really just a special case of the first one.)

There are two commonly used ways of indenting and placing braces in `if-else` statements, which are illustrated here:

if-else with multiple statements

compound statement

```
if (myScore > yourScore)
{
    cout << "I win!\n";
    wager = wager + 100;
}
else
{
    cout << "I wish these were golf scores.\n";
    wager = 0;
}
```

and

```
if (myScore > yourScore){
    cout << "I win!\n";
    wager = wager + 100;
} else {
    cout << "I wish these were golf scores.\n";
    wager = 0;
}
```

The only differences are the placement of braces. We find the first form easier to read and therefore prefer it. The second form saves lines, so some programmers prefer the second form or some minor variant of it.

PITFALL: Using = in Place of ==

Unfortunately, you can write many things in C++ that you would think are incorrectly formed C++ statements but which turn out to have some obscure meaning. This means that if you mistakenly write something that you would expect to produce an error message, you may find that the program compiles and runs with no error messages but gives incorrect output. Since you may not realize you wrote something incorrectly, this can cause serious problems. For example, consider an if-else statement that begins as follows:

```
if (x = 12)
    Do_Something
else
    Do_Something_Else
```

Suppose you wanted to test to see if the value of x is equal to 12, so that you really meant to use == rather than =. You might think the compiler would catch your mistake. The expression

```
x = 12
```

is not something that is satisfied or not. It is an assignment statement, so surely the compiler will give an error message. Unfortunately, that is not the case. In C++ the expression x = 12 is an expression that returns a value, just like x + 12 or 2 + 3. An assignment expression's value is the value transferred to the variable on the left. For example, the value of x = 12 is 12. We saw in our discussion of Boolean value compatibility that nonzero int values are converted to true. If you use x = 12 as the Boolean expression in an if-else statement, the Boolean expression will always evaluate to true.

This error is very hard to find, because it looks right. The compiler can find the error without any special instructions if you put the 12 on the left side of the comparison: 12 == x will produce no error message, but 12 = x will generate an error message. ■

Self-Test Exercises

5. Does the following sequence produce division by zero?

```
j = -1;
if ((j > 0) && (1/(j + 1) > 10))
    cout << i << endl;
```

6. Write an if-else statement that outputs the word High if the value of the variable score is greater than 100 and Low if the value of score is at most 100. The variable score is of type int.

7. Suppose savings and expenses are variables of type double that have been given values. Write an if-else statement that outputs the word Solvent, decreases the value of savings by the value of expenses, and sets the value of expenses to zero provided that savings is at least as large as expenses. If, however, savings is less than expenses, the if-else statement simply outputs the word Bankrupt and does not change the value of any variables.

8. Write an if-else statement that outputs the word Passed provided the value of the variable exam is greater than or equal to 60 and also the value of the variable programsDone is greater than or equal to 10. Otherwise, the if-else statement outputs the word Failed. The variables exam and programsDone are both of type int.

9. Write an if-else statement that outputs the word Warning provided that either the value of the variable temperature is greater than or equal to 100, or the value of the variable pressure is greater than or equal to 200, or both. Otherwise, the if-else statement outputs the word OK. The variables temperature and pressure are both of type int.

10. What is the output of the following? Explain your answers.

a. if (0)
```
        cout << "0 is true";
    else
        cout << "0 is false";
    cout << endl;
```

b. if (1)
```
        cout << "1 is true";
    else
        cout << "1 is false";
    cout << endl;
```

c. if (-1)
```
        cout << "-1 is true";
    else
        cout << "-1 is false";
    cout << endl;
```

Note: This is an exercise only. This is *not* intended to illustrate programming style you should follow.

Omitting the else

Sometimes you want one of the two alternatives in an `if-else` statement to do nothing at all. In C++ this can be accomplished by omitting the `else` part. These sorts of statements are referred to as **if statements** to distinguish them from `if-else` statements. For example, the first of the following two statements is an `if` statement:

```
if (sales >= minimum)
    salary = salary + bonus;
cout << "salary = $" << salary;
```

If the value of `sales` is greater than or equal to the value of `minimum`, the assignment statement is executed and then the following `cout` statement is executed. On the other hand, if the value of `sales` is less than `minimum`, then the embedded assignment statement is not executed. Thus, the `if` statement causes no change (that is, no bonus is added to the base salary), and the program proceeds directly to the `cout` statement.

Nested Statements

As you have seen, `if-else` statements and `if` statements contain smaller statements within them. Thus far we have used compound statements and simple statements such as assignment statements as these smaller substatements, but there are other possibilities. In fact, any statement at all can be used as a subpart of an `if-else` statement or of other statements that have one or more statements within them.

When nesting statements, you normally indent each level of nested substatements, although there are some special situations (such as a multiway `if-else` branch) where this rule is not followed.

Multiway `if-else` Statement

The multiway `if-else` statement is not really a different kind of C++ statement. It is simply an ordinary `if-else` statement nested inside `if-else` statements, but it is thought of as a kind of statement and is indented differently from other nested statements so as to reflect this thinking.

The syntax for a multiway `if-else` statement and a simple example are given in the accompanying box. Note that the Boolean expressions are aligned with one another, and their corresponding actions are also aligned with each other. This makes it easy to see the correspondence between Boolean expressions and actions. The Boolean expressions are evaluated in order until a `true` Boolean expression is found. At that point the evaluation of Boolean expressions stops, and the action corresponding to the first `true` Boolean expression is executed. The final `else` is optional. If there is a final `else` and all the Boolean expressions are `false`, the final action is executed. If there is no final `else` and all the Boolean expressions are `false`, then no action is taken.

if statement

indenting

multiway if-else

Multiway if-else Statement

SYNTAX

```
if (Boolean_Expression_1)
    Statement_1
else if (Boolean_Expression_2)
    Statement_2
        .
        .
        .
else if (Boolean_Expression_n)
    Statement_n
else
    Statement_For_All_Other_Possibilities
```

EXAMPLE

```
if ((temperature < -10) && (day == SUNDAY))
    cout << "Stay home.";
else if (temperature < -10) // and day != SUNDAY
    cout << "Stay home, but call work.";
else if (temperature <= 0) // and temperature >= -10
    cout << "Dress warm.";
else // temperature > 0
    cout << "Work hard and play hard.";
```

The Boolean expressions are checked in order until the first true Boolean expression is encountered, and then the corresponding statement is executed. If none of the Boolean expressions is true, then the *Statement_For_All_Other_Possibilities* is executed.

The switch Statement

switch
statement

The **switch statement** is the only other kind of C++ statement that implements multiway branches. Syntax for a switch statement and a simple example are shown in the accompanying box.

When a switch statement is executed, one of a number of different branches is executed. The choice of which branch to execute is determined by a **controlling**

controlling
expression

expression given in parentheses after the keyword switch. The controlling expression for a switch statement must always return either a bool value, an enum constant (discussed later in this chapter), one of the integer types, or a character. When the switch statement is executed, this controlling expression is evaluated and the computer looks at the constant values given after the various occurrences of the case identifiers. If it finds a constant that equals the value of the controlling expression, it executes the code for that case. You cannot have two occurrences of case with the same constant value after them because that would create an ambiguous instruction.

switch Statement

SYNTAX

```
switch (Controlling_Expression)
{
    case Constant_1:
        Statement_Sequence_1
        break;
    case Constant_2:
        Statement_Sequence_2
        break;
            .
            .
            .
    case Constant_n:
        Statement_Sequence_n
        break;
    default:
        Default_Statement_Sequence
}
```

You need not place a break statement in each case. If you omit a break, that case continues until a break (or the end of the switch statement) is reached.

EXAMPLE

```
int vehicleClass;
double toll;
cout << "Enter vehicle class: ";
cin >> vehicleClass;

switch (vehicleClass)
{
    case 1:
        cout << "Passenger car.";
        toll = 0.50;
        break;
    case 2:
        cout << "Bus.";
        toll = 1.50;
        break;
    case 3:
        cout << "Truck.";
        toll = 2.00;
        break;
    default:
        cout << "Unknown vehicle class!";
}
```

If you forget this break, then passenger cars will pay $1.50.

break statement

The switch statement ends when either a break statement is encountered or the end of the switch statement is reached. A **break statement** consists of the keyword break followed by a semicolon. When the computer executes the statements after a case label, it continues until it reaches a break statement. When the computer encounters a break statement, the switch statement ends. If you omit the break statements, then after executing the code for one case, the computer will go on to execute the code for the next case.

Note that you can have two case labels for the same section of code, as in the following portion of a switch statement:

```
case 'A':
case 'a':

    cout << "Excellent. "
        << "You need not take the final.\n";

    break;
```

default

Since the first case has no break statement (in fact, no statement at all), the effect is the same as having two labels for one case, but C++ syntax requires one keyword case for each label, such as 'A' and 'a'.

If no case label has a constant that matches the value of the controlling expression, then the statements following the default label are executed. You need not have a default section. If there is no default section and no match is found for the value of the controlling expression, then nothing happens when the switch statement is executed. However, it is safest to always have a default section. If you think your case labels list all possible outcomes, then you can put an error message in the default section.

Self-Test Exercises

11. What output will be produced by the following code?

```
int x = 2;
cout << "Start\n";
if (x <= 3)
    if (x != 0)
        cout << "Hello from the second if.\n";
    else
        cout << "Hello from the else.\n";
cout << "Start again\n";
if (x > 3)
    if (x != 0)
        cout << "Hello from the second if.\n";
    else
        cout << "Hello from the else.\n";
cout << "End again\n";
cout << "End\n";
```

Self-Test Exercises (continued)

12. What output will be produced by the following code?

```
int extra = 2;
if (extra < 0)
    cout << "small";
else if (extra == 0)
    cout << "medium";
else
    cout << "large";
```

13. What would be the output in Self-Test Exercise 12 if the assignment were changed to the following?

```
int extra = -37;
```

14. What would be the output in Self-Test Exercise 12 if the assignment were changed to the following?

```
int extra = 0;
```

15. Write a multiway if-else statement that classifies the value of an int variable n into one of the following categories and writes out an appropriate message.

```
n < 0 or 0 ≤ n ≤ 100 or n > 100
```

PITFALL: Forgetting a break in a switch Statement

If you forget a break in a switch statement, the compiler will not issue an error message. You will have written a syntactically correct switch statement, but it will not do what you intended it to do. Notice the annotation in the example in the box entitled "switch Statement." ■

TIP: Use switch Statements for Menus

The multiway if-else statement is more versatile than the switch statement, and you can use a multiway if-else statement anywhere you can use a switch statement. However, sometimes the switch statement is clearer. For example, the switch statement is perfect for implementing menus. Each branch of the switch statement can be one menu choice. ■

Enumeration Types

An **enumeration type** is a type whose values are defined by a list of constants of type int. An enumeration type is very much like a list of declared constants. Enumeration types can be handy for defining a list of identifiers to use as the case labels in a switch statement.

When defining an enumeration type, you can use any int values and can define any number of constants. For example, the following enumeration type defines a constant for the length of each month:

```
enum MonthLength { JAN_LENGTH = 31, FEB_LENGTH = 28,
MAR_LENGTH = 31, APR_LENGTH = 30, MAY_LENGTH = 31,
JUN_LENGTH = 30, JUL_LENGTH = 31, AUG_LENGTH = 31,
SEP_LENGTH = 30, OCT_LENGTH = 31, NOV_LENGTH = 30,
DEC_LENGTH = 31 };
```

As this example shows, two or more named constants in an enumeration type can receive the same int value.

If you do not specify any numeric values, the identifiers in an enumeration type definition are assigned consecutive values beginning with 0. For example, the type-definition

```
enum Direction { NORTH, SOUTH, EAST, WEST };
```

is equivalent to

```
enum Direction { NORTH = 0, SOUTH = 1, EAST = 2, WEST = 3 };
```

The form that does not explicitly list the int values is normally used when you just want a list of names and do not care about what values they have.

Suppose you initialize an enumeration constant to some value, say

```
enum MyEnum { ONE = 17, TWO, THREE, FOUR = -3, FIVE };
```

then ONE takes the value 17; TWO takes the next int value, 18; THREE takes the next value, 19; FOUR takes -3; and FIVE takes the next value, -2. In short, the default for the first enumeration constant is 0. The rest increase by 1 unless you set one or more of the enumeration constants.

Although the constants in an enumeration type are given as int values and can be used as integers in many contexts, remember that an enumeration type is a separate type and treat it as a type different from the type int. Use enumeration types as labels and avoid doing arithmetic with variables of an enumeration type.

The Conditional Operator

It is possible to embed a conditional inside an expression by using a ternary operator known as the **conditional operator** (also called the *ternary operator* or *arithmetic* if). Its use is reminiscent of an older programming style, and we do not advise using it. It is included here for the sake of completeness (and in case you disagree with our programming style).

The conditional operator is a notational variant on certain forms of the `if-else` statement. This variant is illustrated as follows. Consider the statement

```
if (n1 > n2)
    max = n1;
else
    max = n2;
```

This can be expressed using the conditional operator as follows:

```
max = (n1 > n2) ? n1 : n2;
```

conditional operator expression

The expression on the right-hand side of the assignment statement is the **conditional operator expression**:

```
(n1 > n2) ? n1 : n2
```

The `?` and `:` together form a ternary operator known as the conditional operator. A conditional operator expression starts with a Boolean expression followed by a `?` and then followed by two expressions separated with a colon. If the Boolean expression is true, then the first of the two expressions is returned; otherwise, the second of the two expressions is returned.

Self-Test Exercises

16. Given the following declaration and output statement, assume that this has been embedded in a correct program and is run. What is the output?

```
enum Direction { N, S, E, W };
// ...
cout << W << " " << E << " " << S << " " << N << endl;
```

17. Given the following declaration and output statement, assume that this has been embedded in a correct program and is run. What is the output?

```
enum Direction { N = 5, S = 7, E = 1, W };
// ...
cout << W << " " << E << " " << S << " " << N << endl;
```

2.3   Loops

Few tasks are more like the torture of Sisyphus than housework, with its endless repetition: the clean becomes soiled, the soiled is made clean, over and over, day after day.

SIMONE DE BEAUVOIR

**loop body
iteration**

Looping mechanisms in C++ are similar to those in other high-level languages. The three C++ loop statements are the `while` statement, the `do-while` statement, and the `for` statement. The same terminology is used with C++ as with other languages. The code that is repeated in a loop is called the **loop body.** Each repetition of the loop body is called an **iteration** of the loop.

The `while` and `do-while` Statements

**`while` and
`do-while`
compared**

The syntax for the `while` statement and its variant, the `do-while` statement, is given in the accompanying box. In both cases, the multistatement body syntax is a special case of the syntax for a loop with a single-statement body. The multistatement body is a single compound statement. Examples of a while statement and a `do-while` statement are given in Displays 2.4 and 2.5.

Syntax for `while` and `do-while` Statements

A `while` STATEMENT WITH A SINGLE-STATEMENT BODY

```
while (Boolean_Expression)
    Statement
```

A `while` STATEMENT WITH A MULTISTATEMENT BODY

```
while (Boolean_Expression)
{
    Statement_1
    Statement_2
      .
      .
      .
    Statement_Last
}
```

A `do-while` STATEMENT WITH A SINGLE-STATEMENT BODY

```
do
    Statement
while (Boolean_Expression);
```
*Do not forget
the final
semicolon.*

A `do-while` STATEMENT WITH A MULTISTATEMENT BODY

```
do
{
    Statement_1
    Statement_2
      .
      .
      .
    Statement_Last
} while (Boolean_Expression);
```

Display 2.4   Example of a while Statement

```
1    #include <iostream>
2    using namespace std;

3    int main( )
4    {
5        int countDown;

6        cout << "How many greetings do you want? ";
7        cin >> countDown;

8        while (countDown > 0)
9        {
10           cout << "Hello ";
11           countDown = countDown - 1;
12       }

13       cout << endl;
14       cout << "That's all!\n";

15       return 0;
16   }
```

Sample Dialogue 1

```
How many greetings do you want? 3
Hello Hello Hello
That's all!
```

Sample Dialogue 2

```
How many greetings do you want? 0
That's all!
```

*The loop body is executed
zero times*

The important difference between the while and do-while loops involves *when* the controlling Boolean expression is checked. With a while statement, the Boolean expression is checked *before* the loop body is executed. If the Boolean expression evaluates to false, the body is not executed at all. With a do-while statement, the body of the loop is executed first and the Boolean expression is checked *after* the loop body is executed. Thus, the do-while statement always executes the loop body at least once. After this start-up, the while loop and the do-while loop behave the same. After each iteration of the loop body, the Boolean expression is again checked; if it is true, the loop is iterated again. If it has changed from true to false, the loop statement ends.

Display 2.5   Example of a do-while Statement

```
1   #include <iostream>
2   using namespace std;

3   int main( )
4   {
5       int countDown;

6       cout << "How many greetings do you want? ";
7       cin >> countDown;

8       do
9       {
10          cout << "Hello ";
11          countDown = countDown - 1;
12      } while (countDown > 0);

13      cout << endl;
14      cout << "That's all!\n";

15      return 0;
16  }
```

Sample Dialogue 1

```
How many greetings do you want? 3
Hello Hello Hello
That's all!
```

Sample Dialogue 2

```
How many greetings do you want? 0
Hello
That's all!
```

⟵————————— The loop body is always
executed at least once.

executing the body zero times

The first thing that happens when a while loop is executed is that the controlling Boolean expression is evaluated. If the Boolean expression evaluates to false at that point, the body of the loop is never executed. It may seem pointless to execute the body of a loop zero times, but that is sometimes the desired action. For example, a while loop is often used to sum a list of numbers, but the list could be empty. To be more specific, a checkbook balancing program might use a while loop to sum the values of all the checks you have written in a month—but you might take a month's vacation and write no checks at all. In that case, there are zero numbers to sum and so the loop is iterated zero times.

Increment and Decrement Operators Revisited

In general, we discourage the use of the increment and decrement operators in expressions. However, many programmers like to use them in the controlling Boolean expression of a `while` or `do-while` statement. If done with care, this can work out satisfactorily. An example is given in Display 2.6. Be sure to notice that in `count++` `<= numberOfItems`, the value returned by `count++` is the value of `count` before it is incremented.

Self-Test Exercises

18. What is the output of the following?

```
int count = 3;
while (count-- > 0)
    cout << count << " ";
```

19. What is the output of the following?

```
int count = 3;
while (--count > 0)
    cout << count << " ";
```

20. What is the output of the following?

```
int n = 1;
do
    cout << n << " ";
while (n++ <= 3);
```

21. What is the output of the following?

```
int n = 1;
do
    cout << n << " ";
while (++n <= 3);
```

22. What is the output produced by the following? (x is of type int.)

```
int x = 10;
while (x > 0)
{
    cout << x << endl;
    x = x - 3;
}
```

23. What output would be produced in the previous exercise if the > sign were replaced with <?

(continued)

Self-Test Exercises (continued)

24. What is the output produced by the following? (x is of type int.)

```
int x = 10;
do
{
    cout << x << endl;
    x = x - 3;
} while (x > 0);
```

25. What is the output produced by the following? (x is of type int.)

```
int x = -42;
do
{
    cout << x << endl;
    x = x - 3;
} while (x > 0);
```

26. What is the most important difference between a `while` statement and a `do-while` statement?

The Comma Operator

The **comma operator** is a way of evaluating a list of expressions and returning the value of the last expression. It is sometimes handy to use in a `for` loop, as indicated in our discussion of the `for` loop in the next subsection. We do not advise using it in other contexts, but it is legal to use it in any expression.

The comma operator is illustrated by the following assignment statement:

```
result = (first = 2, second = first + 1);
```

The comma operator is the comma shown in the center of the previous statement. The **comma expression** is the expression on the right-hand side of the assignment operator. The comma operator has two expressions as operands. In this case the two operands are

```
first = 2 and second = first + 1
```

The first expression is evaluated, and then the second expression is evaluated. As you may recall from Chapter 1, the assignment statement, when used as an expression, returns the new value of the variable on the left side of the assignment operator. So, this comma expression returns the final value of the variable `second`, which means that the variable `result` is set equal to 3.

Since only the value of the second expression is returned, the first expression is evaluated solely for its side effects. In the previous example, the side effect of the first expression is to change the value of the variable `first`.

You may have a longer list of expressions connected with commas, but you should only do so when the order of evaluation is not important. If the order of evaluation is important, you should use parentheses. For example,

```
result = ((first = 2, second = first + 1), third = second + 1);
```

comma operator

comma expression

sets the value of `result` equal to 4. However, the value that the following gives to `result` is unpredictable, because it does not guarantee that the expressions are evaluated in order:

```
result = (first = 2, second = first + 1, third = second + 1);
```

For example, `third = second + 1` might be evaluated before `second = first + 1`.[1]

Display 2.6   The Increment Operator in an Expression

```
1   #include <iostream>
2   using namespace std;

3   int main( )
4   {
5       int numberOfItems, count,
6           caloriesForItem, totalCalories;

7       cout << "How many items did you eat today? ";
8       cin >> numberOfItems;
9       totalCalories = 0;
10      count = 1;
11      cout << "Enter the number of calories in each of the\n"
12           << numberOfItems << " items eaten:\n";

13      while (count++ <= numberOfItems)
14      {
15          cin >> caloriesForItem;
16          totalCalories = totalCalories
17                          + caloriesForItem;
18      }

19      cout << "Total calories eaten today = "
20           << totalCalories << endl;
21      return 0;
22  }
```

Sample Dialogue

```
How many items did you eat today? 7
Enter the number of calories in each of the
7 items eaten:
300 60 1200 600 150 1 120
Total calories eaten today = 2431
```

[1] The C++ standard does specify that the expressions joined by commas should be evaluated left to right. However, our experience has been that not all compilers conform to the standard in this regard.

for statement

The for Statement

The third and final loop statement in C++ is the **for statement**. The for statement is most commonly used to step through some integer variable in equal increments. As we will see in Chapter 5, the for statement is often used to step through an array. The for statement is, however, a completely general looping mechanism that can do anything that a while loop can do.

For example, the following for statement sums the integers 1 through 10:

```
sum = 0;
int n;
for (n = 1; n <= 10; n++)
    sum = sum + n;
```

A for statement begins with the keyword for followed by three things in parentheses that tell the computer what to do with the controlling variable. The beginning of a for statement looks like the following:

```
for (Initialization_Action; Boolean_Expression; Update_Action)
```

The first expression tells how the variable, variables, or other things are initialized; the second gives a Boolean expression that is used to check for when the loop should end; and the last expression tells how the loop control variable is updated after each iteration of the loop body.

The three expressions at the start of a for statement are separated by two—and only two—semicolons. Do not succumb to the temptation to place a semicolon after the third expression. (The technical explanation is that these three things are expressions, not statements, and so do not require a semicolon at the end.)

A for statement often uses a single int variable to control loop iteration and loop ending. However, the three expressions at the start of a for statement may be any C++ expressions; therefore, they may involve more (or even fewer) than one variable, and the variables may be of any type.

Using the comma operator, you can add multiple actions to either the first or the last (but normally not the second) of the three items in parentheses. For example, you can move the initialization of the variable sum inside the for loop to obtain the following, which is equivalent to the for statement code we showed earlier:

```
for (sum = 0, n = 1; n <= 10; n++)
    sum = sum + n;
```

Although we do not advise doing so because it is not as easy to read, you can move the entire body of the for loop into the third item in parentheses. The previous for statement is equivalent to the following:

```
for (sum = 0, n = 1; n <= 10; sum = sum + n, n++);
```

Display 2.7 for Statement

for Statement Syntax

```
for (Initialization_Action; Boolean_Expression; Update_Action)
    Body_Statement
```

EXAMPLE

```
for (number = 100; number >= 0; number--)
    cout << number
         << " bottles of beer on the shelf.\n";
```

EQUIVALENT while LOOP SYNTAX

```
Initialization_Action;
while (Boolean_Expression)
{
    Body_Statement
    Update_Action;
}
```

EQUIVALENT EXAMPLE

```
number = 100;
while (number >= 0)
{
    cout << number
         << " bottles of beer on the shelf.\n";
    number--;
}
```

Sample Dialogue

```
100 bottles of beer on the shelf.
99 bottles of beer on the shelf.
            .
            .
            .
0 bottles of beer on the shelf.
```

Display 2.7 shows the syntax of a for statement and also describes the action of the for statement by showing how it translates into an equivalent while statement. Notice that in a for statement, as in the corresponding while statement, the stopping condition is tested before the first loop iteration. Thus, it is possible to have a for loop whose body is executed zero times.

The body of a `for` statement may be, and commonly is, a compound statement, as in the following example:

```
for (number = 100; number >= 0; number--)
{
    cout << number
         << " bottles of beer on the shelf.\n";
    if (number > 0)
        cout << "Take one down and pass it around.\n";
}
```

The first and last expressions in parentheses at the start of a `for` statement may be any C++ expression and thus may involve any number of variables and may be of any type. In a `for` statement, a variable may be declared at the same time as it is initialized. For example,

```
for (int n = 1; n < 10; n++)
    cout << n << endl;
```

Compilers may vary in how they handle such declarations within a `for` statement. This is discussed in Chapter 3 in the subsection entitled "Variables Declared in a `for` Loop." It might be wise to avoid such declarations within a `for` statement until you reach Chapter 3, but we mention it here for reference value.

`for` Statement

SYNTAX

```
for (Initialization_Action; Boolean_Expression; Update_Action)
    Body_Statement
```

EXAMPLE

```
for (sum = 0, n = 1; n <= 10; n++)
    sum = sum + n;
```

See Display 2.7 for an explanation of the action of a `for` statement.

TIP: Repeat-N-Times Loops

A `for` statement can be used to produce a loop that repeats the loop body a predetermined number of times. For example, the following is a loop body that repeats its loop body three times:

```
for (int count = 1; count <= 3; count++)
    cout << "Hip, Hip, Hurray\n";
```

The body of a `for` statement need not make any reference to a loop control variable, such as the variable `count`. ∎

PITFALL: Extra Semicolon in a for Statement

You normally do not place a semicolon after the parentheses at the beginning of a for loop. To see what can happen, consider the following for loop:

```
for (int count = 1; count <= 10; count++) ;
    cout << "Hello\n";
```

If you did not notice the extra semicolon, you might expect this for loop to write Hello to the screen ten times. If you do notice the semicolon, you might expect the compiler to issue an error message. Neither of those things happens. If you embed this for loop in a complete program, the compiler will not complain. If you run the program, only one Hello will be output instead of ten Hellos. What is happening? To answer that question, we need a little background.

One way to create a statement in C++ is to put a semicolon after something. If you put a semicolon after x++, you change the expression

```
x++
```

into the statement

```
x++;
```

empty
statement

If you place a semicolon after nothing, you still create a statement. Thus, the semicolon by itself is a statement, which is called the **empty statement** or the **null statement**. The empty statement performs no action, but it still is a statement. Therefore, the following is a complete and legitimate for loop, whose body is the empty statement:

```
for (int count = 1; count <= 10; count++);
```

This for loop is indeed iterated ten times, but since the body is the empty statement, nothing happens when the body is iterated. This loop does nothing, and it does nothing ten times!

This same sort of problem can arise with a while loop. Be careful not to place a semicolon after the closing parenthesis that encloses the Boolean expression at the start of a while loop. A do-while loop has just the opposite problem. You must remember always to end a do-while loop with a semicolon. ∎

PITFALL: Infinite Loops

A while loop, do-while loop, or for loop does not terminate as long as the controlling Boolean expression is true. This Boolean expression normally contains a variable that will be changed by the loop body, and usually the value of this variable is changed in a way that eventually makes the Boolean expression false and therefore

(continued)

PITFALL: (continued)

terminates the loop. However, if you make a mistake and write your program so that the Boolean expression is always true, then the loop will run forever. A loop that runs forever is called an **infinite loop**.

Unfortunately, examples of infinite loops are not hard to come by. First let us describe a loop that does terminate. The following C++ code will write out the positive even numbers less than 12. That is, it will output the numbers 2, 4, 6, 8, and 10, one per line, and then the loop will end.

```
x = 2;
while (x != 12)
{
    cout << x << endl;
    x = x + 2;
}
```

The value of x is increased by 2 on each loop iteration until it reaches 12. At that point, the Boolean expression after the word while is no longer true, so the loop ends.

Now suppose you want to write out the odd numbers less than 12, rather than the even numbers. You might mistakenly think that all you need do is change the initializing statement to

```
x = 1;
```

But this mistake will create an infinite loop. Because the value of x goes from 11 to 13, the value of x is never equal to 12; thus, the loop will never terminate.

This sort of problem is common when loops are terminated by checking a numeric quantity using == or !=. When dealing with numbers, it is always safer to test for passing a value. For example, the following will work fine as the first line of our while loop:

```
while (x < 12)
```

With this change, x can be initialized to any number and the loop will still terminate. A program that is in an infinite loop will run forever unless some external force stops it. Since you can now write programs that contain an infinite loop, it is a good idea to learn how to force a program to terminate. The method for forcing a program to stop varies from system to system. The keystrokes Control-C will terminate a program on many systems. (To type Control-C, hold down the Control key while pressing the C key.)

In simple programs, an infinite loop is almost always an error. However, some programs are intentionally written to run forever (in principle), such as the main outer loop in an airline reservation program, which just keeps asking for more reservations until you shut down the computer (or otherwise terminate the program in an atypical way). ■

infinite loop

Self-Test Exercises

27. What is the output of the following (when embedded in a complete program)?:

```
for (int count = 1; count < 5; count++)
    cout << (2 * count) << " ";
```

28. What is the output of the following (when embedded in a complete program)?:

```
for (int n = 10; n > 0; n = n - 2)
{
    cout << "Hello ";
    cout << n << endl;
}
```

29. What is the output of the following (when embedded in a complete program)?:

```
for (double sample = 2; sample > 0; sample = sample - 0.5)
    cout << sample << " ";
```

30. Rewrite the following loops as for loops.

   a.
```
int i = 1;
while(i <= 10)
{
    if (i < 5 && i != 2)
        cout << 'X';

    i++;
}
```

   b.
```
int i = 1;
while(i <=10)
{
    cout << 'X';
    i = i + 3;
}
```

   c.
```
long n = 100;
do
{
    cout 6 < 'X';
    n = n + 100;
} while (n < 1000);
```

31. What is the output of this loop? Identify the connection between the value of n and the value of the variable log.

```
int n = 1024;
int log = 0;
for (int i = 1; i < n; i = i * 2)
    log++;
cout << n << " " << log << endl;
```

(continued)

Self-Test Exercises (continued)

32. What is the output of this loop? Comment on the code. (This is not the same as the previous exercise.)

```
int n = 1024;
int log = 0;
for (int i = 1; i < n; i = i * 2);
    log++;
cout << n << " " << log << endl;
```

33. What is the output of this loop? Comment on the code. (This is not the same as either of the two previous exercises.)

```
int n = 1024;
int log = 0;
for (int i = 0; i < n; i = i * 2);
    log++;
cout << n << " " << log << endl;
```

34. For each of the following situations, tell which type of loop (while, do-while, or for) would work best.

a. Summing a series, such as $1/2 + 1/3 + 1/4 + 1/5 + \ldots + 1/10$.

b. Reading in the list of exam scores for one student.

c. Reading in the number of days of sick leave taken by employees in a department.

d. Testing a function to see how it performs for different values of its arguments.

35. What is the output produced by the following? (x is of type int.)

```
int x = 10;
while (x > 0)
{
    cout << x << endl;
    x = x + 3;
}
```

The break and continue Statements

In previous subsections, we have described the basic flow of control for the while, do-while, and for loops. This is how the loops should normally be used and is the way they are usually used. However, you can alter the flow of control in two ways, which in rare cases can be a useful and safe technique. The two ways of altering the flow of control are to insert a break or continue statement. The break statement ends the loop. The continue statement ends the current iteration of the loop body. The break statement can be used with any of the C++ loop statements.

We described the break statement when we discussed the switch statement. The break statement consists of the keyword break followed by a semicolon. When executed, the break statement ends the nearest enclosing switch or loop statement. Display 2.8 contains an example of a break statement that ends a loop when inappropriate input is entered.

Display 2.8   A break Statement in a Loop

```
1   #include <iostream>
2   using namespace std;

3   int main( )
4   {
5       int number, sum = 0, count = 0;
6       cout << "Enter 4 negative numbers:\n";

7       while (++count <= 4)
8       {
9           cin >> number;

10          if (number >= 0)
11          {
12              cout << "ERROR: positive number"
13                   << " or zero was entered as the\n"
14                   << count << "th number! Input ends "
15                   << "with the " << count << "th number.\n"
16                   << count << "th number was not added in.\n";
17              break;
18          }

19          sum = sum + number;
20      }

21      cout << sum << " is the sum of the first "
22           << (count - 1) << " numbers.\n";

23      return 0;
24  }
```

Sample Dialogue

```
Enter 4 negative numbers:
-1 -2 -3 4
ERROR: positive number or zero was entered as the
4th number! Input ends with the 4th number.
4th number was not added in
-6 is the sum of the first 3 numbers.
```

continue statement

The **continue statement** consists of the keyword `continue` followed by a semi-colon. When executed, the `continue` statement ends the current loop body iteration of the nearest enclosing loop statement. Display 2.9 contains an example of a loop that contains a `continue` statement.

Display 2.9 A continue Statement in a Loop

```
1   #include <iostream>
2   using namespace std;
3   int main( )
4   {
5       int number, sum = 0, count = 0;
6       cout << "Enter 4 negative numbers, ONE PER LINE:\n";
7       while (count < 4)
8       {
9           cin >> number;
10          if (number >= 0)
11          {
12              cout << "ERROR: positive number (or zero)!\n"
13                   << "Reenter that number and continue:\n";
14              continue;
15          }
16          sum = sum + number;
17          count++;
18      }
19      cout << sum << " is the sum of the "
20           << count << " numbers.\n";
21      return 0;
22  }
```

Sample Dialogue

```
Enter 4 negative numbers, ONE PER LINE:
1
ERROR: positive number (or zero)!
Reenter that number and continue:
-1
-2
3
ERROR: positive number!
Reenter that number and continue:
-3
-4
-10 is the sum of the 4 numbers.
```

One point that you should note when using the continue statement in a for loop is that the continue statement transfers control to the update expression. So, any loop control variable will be updated immediately after the continue statement is executed.

Note that a break statement completely ends the loop. In contrast, a continue statement merely ends one loop iteration; the next iteration (if any) continues the loop. You will find it instructive to compare the details of the programs in Displays 2.8 and 2.9. Pay particular attention to the change in the controlling Boolean expression.

Note that you never absolutely need a break or continue statement. The programs in Displays 2.8 and 2.9 can be rewritten so that neither uses either a break or continue statement. The continue statement can be particularly tricky and can make your code hard to read. It may be best to avoid the continue statement completely or at least use it only on rare occasions.

Nested Loops

VideoNote
Nested Loop
Example

It is perfectly legal to nest one loop statement inside another loop statement. When doing so, remember that any break or continue statement applies to the innermost loop (or switch) statement containing the break or continue statement. It is best to avoid nested loops by placing the inner loop inside a function definition and placing a function invocation inside the outer loop. We describe how to write your own functions in Chapter 3.

Self-Test Exercises

36. What does a break statement do? Where is it legal to put a break statement?

37. Predict the output of the following nested loops:

```
int n, m;
for (n = 1; n <= 10; n++)
    for (m = 10; m >= 1; m--)
        cout << n << " times " << m
             << " = " << n * m << endl;
```

2.4   Introduction to File Input

You shall see them on a beautiful quarto page, where a neat rivulet of text shall meander through a meadow of margin.

RICHARD BRINSLEY SHERIDAN, *The School for Scandal*

input stream

By now you should be familiar with using cin to read data from the keyboard. cin is an example of something called an **input stream**. We can also connect an input stream to a file on the disk. Once this is set up we can read from the file in almost exactly the same way we read from cin. Details about reading from and writing to files are not discussed until Chapter 12 and require an understanding of programming concepts we have not yet covered. However, we can provide just enough here so that your programs can read from text files. This will allow you to work on problems with real-world data that would otherwise be too much work to type into the program every time it is run.

Reading From a Text File Using ifstream

A text file is a file stored in the text format. You can create them with programs like Notepad in Windows, TextEdit on a Mac, or vi/nano/emacs on a UNIX machine. Most word processors and many other programs will also save files in the text format. To read from a text file we need to include the fstream library and create an ifstream object which is placed in the std namespace. Thus, your program would contain

```
#include <fstream>
using namespace std;
```

You can then declare an input stream just as you would declare any other variable.

```
ifstream inputStream;
```

Next you must connect the inputStream variable to a text file on the disk.

```
inputStream.open("filename.txt");
```

You can specify a pathname (a directory or folder) when giving the file name. The details of how to specify a pathname vary a little from system to system, so consult with a local guru for the details (or do a little trial-and-error programming). In our examples we will use a simple file name, which assumes that the file is in the same directory (folder) as the one in which your program is running.

Once you have declared an input stream variable and connected it to a file using the open function, your program can take input from the file using the extraction operator, >>, the same way as cin.

For example, you can use inputStream >> intVar to read an integer from the file, inputStream >> strVar to read a string (up to a whitespace character) from the file, etc. C++ begins reading from the beginning of the file and proceeds toward the end as data is read. When the program is done with the file it should be closed with inputStream.close( ) which will release any resources that have been allocated in association with the file.

A complete example is shown in Displays 2.10 and 2.11. Display 2.10 shows the contents of a text file named player.txt. This file can be created by any program that saves in the plain text format. As an example, let us say that the file contains information about the last player to play a game. The first line of the file contains the high score of the player, 100510, and the second line contains the name of the player, Gordon Freeman. The program in Display 2.11 reads in this information and displays it. The values are simply read in using the stream extraction operator, >>.

Display 2.10   Sample Text File, player.txt, to Store a Player's High Score and Name

```
100510
Gordon Freeman
```

Display 2.11   Program to Read the Text File in Display 2.10

```
1   #include <iostream>
2   #include <fstream>
3   #include <string>

4   using namespace std;
5   int main( )
6   {
7       string firstName, lastName;
8       int score;
9       fstream inputStream;

10      inputStream.open("player.txt");

11      inputStream >> score;
12      inputStream >> firstName >> lastName;

13      cout << "Name: " << firstName << " "
14                       << lastName << endl;
15      cout << "Score: " << score << endl;
16      inputStream.close();

17      return 0;
18  }
```

Sample Dialogue

```
Name: Gordon Freeman
Score: 100510
```

Often you will want to know if the program has read everything in a file. One way to do this is to note that the stream extraction operator returns true if the read was successful and false if it was not. So if we attempt to read past the end of the file then >> will return false and we can ignore the result. This may look a bit strange because on one line we are both performing a read action and checking a Boolean result. Display 2.12 uses a while loop to read every line of data from the player.txt file as a string and outputs it.

Display 2.12   Using a Loop to Read the Text File in Display 2.10 (part 1 of 2)

```
1   #include <iostream>
2   #include <fstream>
3   #include <string>

4   using namespace std;
5   int main( )
```

(continued)

Display 2.12 Using a Loop to Read the Text File in Display 2.10 (part 2 of 2)

```
 6   {
 7       string text;
 8       fstream inputStream;
 9
10       inputStream.open("player.txt");
11       while (inputStream >> text)                    Evaluates to false
12       {                                              when there is no data left
13           cout << text << endl;                      to read from the file
14       }
15       inputStream.close();
16
18       return 0;
19   }
```

Sample Dialogue

```
100510
Gordon
Freeman
```

Self-Test Exercises

38. The following code is supposed to output every word in the file and only every word in the file, but it does not quite work. What is wrong?

```
bool moreToRead = true;
while (moreToRead)
{
    string text;
    moreToRead = inputStream >> text;
    cout << text << endl;
}
```

39. Consider a file of high scores. The first line is an integer that stores the number of records in the file. The records alternate between the name of the player (first name only) and the player's score. Here is a sample file named scores.txt consisting of three entries:

```
3
Gordon
500
Mario
550
Illidan
385
```

Self-Test Exercises (continued)

Write code that reads the file and outputs the player's name and score on one line, e.g.,

```
Gordon, 500
Mario, 550
Illidan, 385
```

40. Modify your solution to Self-Test Exercise 39 to output only the name and score of the player with the highest score.

Chapter Summary

- *Boolean expressions* are evaluated similar to the way arithmetic expressions are evaluated.

- The C++ branching statements are the *if-else statement* and the *switch statement*.

- A switch statement is a multiway branching statement. You can also form multiway branching statements by nesting if-else statements to form a multiway if-else statement.

- A switch statement is a good way to implement a menu for the user of your program.

- The C++ loop statements are the *while*, *do-while*, and *for statements*.

- A do-while statement always iterates its *loop body* at least one time. Both a while statement and a for statement might iterate their loop body zero times.

- A for loop can be used to obtain the equivalent of the instruction "repeat the loop body n times."

- A loop can be ended early with a *break statement*. A single iteration of a loop body may be ended early with a continue statement. It is best to use break statements sparingly. It is best to completely avoid using continue statements, although some programmers do use them on rare occasions.

- An *input stream* can be used to read from a file in a manner similar to using cin to read from the keyboard.

Answers to Self-Test Exercises

1. a. true.
   b. true. Note that expressions a and b mean exactly the same thing. Because the operators = = and < have higher precedence than &&, you do not need to include the parentheses. The parentheses do, however, make it easier to read. Most people find the expression in a easier to read than the expression in b, even though they mean the same thing.
   c. true.

d. `true`.

e. `false`. Since the value of the first subexpression, (`count == 1`), is `false`, you know that the entire expression is `false` without bothering to evaluate the second subexpression. Thus, it does not matter what the values of `x` and `y` are. This is *short-circuit evaluation.*

f. `true`. Since the value of the first subexpression, (`count < 10`), is `true`, you know that the entire expression is `true` without bothering to evaluate the second subexpression. Thus, it does not matter what the values of `x` and `y` are. This is *short-circuit evaluation.*

g. `false`. Notice that the expression in g includes the expression in f as a subexpression. This subexpression is evaluated using short-circuit evaluation as we described for f. The entire expression in g is equivalent to

```
!( (true || (x < y)) && true )
```

which in turn is equivalent to `!( true && true )`, and that is equivalent to `!(true)`, which is equivalent to the final value of `false`.

h. This expression produces an error when it is evaluated because the first subexpression, `((limit/count) > 7)`, involves a division by zero.

i. `true`. Since the value of the first subexpression, (`limit < 20`), is `true`, you know that the entire expression is `true` without bothering to evaluate the second subexpression. Thus, the second subexpression,

```
((limit/count) > 7)
```

is never evaluated, so the fact that it involves a division by zero is never noticed by the computer. This is *short-circuit evaluation.*

j. This expression produces an error when it is evaluated because the first subexpression, `((limit/count) > 7)`, involves a division by zero.

k. `false`. Since the value of the first subexpression, (`limit < 0`), is `false`, you know that the entire expression is `false` without bothering to evaluate the second subexpression. Thus, the second subexpression,

```
((limit/count) > 7)
```

is never evaluated, so the fact that it involves a division by zero is never noticed by the computer. This is *short-circuit evaluation.*

1. If you think this expression is nonsense, you are correct. The expression has no intuitive meaning, but C++ converts the `int` values to `bool` and then evaluates the `&&` and `!` operations. Thus, C++ will evaluate this mess. Recall that in C++, any nonzero integer converts to `true` and 0 converts to `false`, so C++ will evaluate

```
(5 && 7) + (!6)
```

as follows. In the expression (`5 && 7`), the 5 and 7 convert to `true`; true && true evaluates to true, which C++ converts to 1. In the expression (`!6`) the 6 is converted to `true`, so `!(true)` evaluates to `false`, which C++ converts to 0. Thus, the entire expression evaluates to 1 + 0, which is 1. The final value is thus 1. C++ will convert the number 1 to `true`, but the answer has little intuitive meaning as `true`; it is perhaps better to just say the answer is 1. There is no need to become proficient at evaluating these nonsense expressions, but doing a few will help you to understand why the compiler does not give you an error message when you make the mistake of mixing numeric and Boolean operators in a single expression.

2. The expression `2 < x < 3` is legal. However, it does not mean

```
(2 <58.164 pt x) && (x < 3)
```

as many would wish. It means `(2 < x) < 3`. Since `(2 < x)` is a Boolean expression, its value is either `true` or `false` and is thus converted to either `0` or `1`, either of which is less than 3. So, `2 < x < 3` is always `true`. The result is `true` regardless of the value of `x`.

3. `(x < -1) || (x > 2)`

4. `(x > 1) && (x < 3)`

5. No. In the Boolean expression, `(j > 0)` is `false` (`j` was just assigned `-1`). The `&&` uses short-circuit evaluation, which does not evaluate the second expression if the truth value can be determined from the first expression. The first expression is `false`, so the second does not matter.

6.
```
if (score > 100)
    cout << "High";
else
    cout << "Low";
```

You may want to add `\n` to the end of the previously quoted strings, depending on the other details of the program.

7.
```
if (savings >= expenses)
{
    savings = savings - expenses;
    expenses = 0;
    cout << "Solvent";
}
else
{
    cout << "Bankrupt";
}
```

You may want to add `\n` to the end of the previously quoted strings, depending on the other details of the program.

8.
```
if ( (exam >= 60) && (programsDone >= 10) )
    cout << "Passed";
else
    cout << "Failed";
```

You may want to add `\n` to the end of the previously quoted strings, depending on the other details of the program.

9.
```
if ( (temperature >=100) || (pressure >= 200) )
    cout << "Warning";
else
    cout << "OK";
```

You may want to add `\n` to the end of the previously quoted strings, depending on the other details of the program.

10. All nonzero integers are converted to `true`; 0 is converted to `false`.

   a. `0 is false`

   b. `1 is true`

   c. `-1 is true`

11. `Start`

   `Hello from the second if.`

   `End`

   `Start again`

   `End again`

12. `large`

13. `small`

14. `medium`

15. Both of the following are correct:

```
if (n < 0)
    cout << n << " is less than zero.\n";
else if ((0 <= n) && (n <= 100))
    cout << n << " is between 0 and 100 (inclusive).\n";
else if (n >100)
    cout << n << " is larger than 100.\n";
```

   and

```
if (n < 0)
    cout << n << " is less than zero.\n";
else if (n <= 100)
    cout << n << " is between 0 and 100 (inclusive).\n";
else
    cout << n << " is larger than 100.\n";
```

16. `3 2 1 0`

17. `2 1 7 5`

18. `2 1 0`

19. `2 1`

20. `1 2 3 4`

21. `1 2 3`

22. `10`

   `7`

   `4`

   `1`

23. There would be no output; the loop is iterated zero times.

24. `10`

   `7`

   `4`

   `1`

25. `-42`

26. With a do-while statement, the loop body is always executed at least once. With a while statement, there can be conditions under which the loop body is not executed at all.

27. 2 4 6 8

28. Hello 10
    Hello 8
    Hello 6
    Hello 4
    Hello 2

29. 2.000000 1.500000 1.000000 0.500000

30. a. `for (int i = 1; i <= 10; i++)`
        `    if (i < 5 && i != 2)`
        `        cout << 'X';`

    b. `for (int i = 1; i <= 10; i = i + 3)`
        `    cout << 'X';`

    c. `cout << 'X'; // necessary to keep output the same. Note`
        `             // also the change in initialization of n`
        `for (long n = 200; n < 1000; n = n + 100)`
        `    cout << 'X';`

31. The output is 1024 10. The second number is the base 2 log of the first number. (If the first number is not a power of 2, then only an approximation to the base 2 log is produced.)

32. The output is 1024 1. The semicolon after the first line of the for loop is probably a pitfall error.

33. This is an infinite loop. Consider the update expression, `i = i * 2`. It cannot change i because its initial value is 0, so it leaves i at its initial value, 0. It gives no output because of the semicolon after the first line of the for loop.

34. a. A for loop
    b. and c. Both require a while loop because the input list might be empty.
    d. A do-while loop can be used because at least one test will be performed.

35. This is an infinite loop. The first few lines of output are as follows:
    10
    13
    16
    19
    21

36. A break statement is used to exit a loop (a while, do-while, or for statement) or to terminate a switch statement. A break statement is not legal anywhere else in a C++ program. Note that if the loops are nested, a break statement only terminates one level of the loop.

37. The output is too long to reproduce here. The pattern is as follows:

```
1 times 10 = 10
1 times 9 = 9
```

•
•
•

```
1 times 1 = 1
2 times 10 = 20
2 times 9 = 18
```

•
•
•

```
2 times 1 = 2
3 times 10 = 30
```

38. The variable `moreToRead` is not set to `false` until we attempt to read past the last item in the file. This means that we will output an extra newline on the last loop iteration. We can address this by outputting the value read first and then reading the next string (and possibly end of file) at the end of the loop iteration. This also handles the case where the file is empty.

```
string text;
bool moreToRead = inputStream >> text;
while (moreToRead)
{
    cout << text << endl;
    moreToRead = inputStream >> text;
}
```

39. The following code reads the first line and then loops that many times.

```
fstream inputStream;

inputStream.open("player.txt");
int numScores;
inputStream >> numScores;
for (int i = 0; i < numScores; i++)
{
    string name;
    int score;
    inputStream >> name;
    inputStream >> score;
    cout << name << ", " << score << endl;
}
inputStream.close();
```

40. This solution remembers the highest score and name seen so far and outputs it after the loop is over.

```
fstream inputStream;
inputStream.open("player.txt");
int numScores;
int highScore = -1;
string highName = "";
inputStream >> numScores;
for (int i = 0; i < numScores; i++)
{
    string name;
    int score;
    inputStream >> name;
    inputStream >> score;
    if (score > highScore)
    {
        highScore = score;
        highName = name;
    }
}
inputStream.close();
cout << highName << " has the high score of "
     << highScore << endl;
```

Programming Projects

Visit www.myprogramminglab.com to complete select exercises online and get instant feedback.

1. It is difficult to make a budget that spans several years, because prices are not stable. If your company needs 200 pencils per year, you cannot simply use this year's price as the cost of pencils two years from now. Because of inflation the cost is likely to be higher than it is today. Write a program to gauge the expected cost of an item in a specified number of years. The program asks for the cost of the item, the number of years from now that the item will be purchased, and the rate of inflation. The program then outputs the estimated cost of the item after the specified period. Have the user enter the inflation rate as a percentage, such as 5.6 (percent). Your program should then convert the percentage to a decimal fraction, such as 0.056, and should use a loop to estimate the price adjusted for inflation. (*Hint:* Use a loop.)

2. You have just purchased a stereo system that cost $1,000 on the following credit plan: no down payment, an interest rate of 18% per year (1.5% per month), and monthly payments of $50. The monthly payment of $50 is used to pay the interest, and whatever is left is used to pay part of the remaining debt. Hence, the first month you pay 1.5% of $1,000 in interest. That is $15 in interest. The remaining $35 is deducted from your debt, which leaves you with a debt of $965.00. The next month you pay interest of 1.5% of $965.00, which is $14.48. Hence, you can deduct $35.52 (which is $50 - $14.48) from the amount you owe.

Write a program that will tell you how many months it will take you to pay off the loan, as well as the total amount of interest paid over the life of the loan. Use a loop to calculate the amount of interest and the size of the debt after each month. (Your final program need not output the monthly amount of interest paid and remaining debt, but you may want to write a preliminary version of the program that does output these values.) Use a variable to count the number of loop iterations and hence the number of months until the debt is zero. You may want to use other variables as well. The last payment may be less than $50 if the debt is small, but do not forget the interest. If you owe $50, then your monthly payment of $50 will not pay off your debt, although it will come close. One month's interest on $50 is only 75 cents.

3. Suppose you can buy a chocolate bar from the vending machine for $1 each. Inside every chocolate bar is a coupon. You can redeem seven coupons for one chocolate bar from the machine. You would like to know how many chocolate bars you can eat, including those redeemed via coupon, if you have n dollars.

For example, if you have 20 dollars then you can initially buy 20 chocolate bars. This gives you 20 coupons. You can redeem 14 coupons for two additional chocolate bars. These two additional chocolate bars give you two more coupons, so you now have a total of eight coupons. This gives you enough to redeem for one final chocolate bar. As a result you now have 23 chocolate bars and two leftover coupons.

Write a program that inputs the number of dollars and outputs how many chocolate bars you can collect after spending all your money and redeeming as many coupons as possible. Also output the number of leftover coupons. The easiest way to solve this problem is to use a loop.

4. Write a program that finds and prints all of the prime numbers between 3 and 100. A prime number is a number that can only be divided by one and itself (i.e., 3, 5, 7, 11, 13, 17, ...).

One way to solve this problem is to use a doubly-nested loop. The outer loop can iterate from 3 to 100, while the inner loop checks to see whether the counter value for the outer loop is prime. One way to decide whether the number n is prime is to loop from 2 to n − 1; if any of these numbers evenly divides n, then n cannot be prime. If none of the values from 2 to n − 1 evenly divide n, then n must be prime. (Note that there are several easy ways to make this algorithm more efficient.)

5. In cryptarithmetic puzzles, mathematical equations are written using letters. Each letter can be a digit from 0 to 9, but no two letters can be the same. Here is a sample problem:

```
SEND + MORE = MONEY
```

A solution to the puzzle is $S = 9$, $R = 8$, $O = 0$, $M = 1$, $Y = 2$, $E = 5$, $N = 6$, $D = 7$

Write a program that finds solutions to the following cryptarithmetic puzzle:

```
TOO + TOO + TOO + TOO = GOOD
```

The simplest technique is to use a nested loop for each unique letter (in this case T, O, G, D). The loops would systematically assign the digits from 0–9 to each letter. For example, it might first try $T = 0$, $O = 0$, $G = 0$, $D = 0$, then $T = 0$, $O = 0$, $G = 0$, $D = 1$, then $T = 0$, $O = 0$, $G = 0$, $D = 2$, etc. up to $T = 9$, $O = 9$, $G = 9$, $D = 9$. In the loop body, test that each variable is unique and that the equation is satisfied. Output the values for the letters that satisfy the equation.

6. Buoyancy is the ability of an object to float. Archimedes' Principle states that the buoyant force is equal to the weight of the fluid that is displaced by the submerged object. The buoyant force can be computed by

$$F_b = V \times \gamma$$

where F_b is the buoyant force, V is the volume of the submerged object, and γ is the specific weight of the fluid. If F_b is greater than or equal to the weight of the object, then it will float, otherwise it will sink.

Write a program that inputs the weight (in pounds) and radius (in feet) of a sphere and outputs whether the sphere will sink or float in water. Use $\gamma = 62.4$ lb/ft^3 as the specific weight of water. The volume of a sphere is computed by $(4/3)\pi r^3$.

7. Write a program that calculates the total grade for N classroom exercises as a percentage. The user should input the value for N followed by each of the N scores and totals. Calculate the overall percentage (sum of the total points earned divided by the total points possible) and output it as a percentage. Sample input and output are shown as follows:

```
How many exercises to input? 3
Score received for exercise 1: 10
Total points possible for exercise 1: 10
Score received for exercise 2: 7
Total points possible for exercise 2: 12
Score received for exercise 3: 5
Total points possible for exercise 3: 8
Your total is 22 out of 30, or 73.33%.
```

8. Write a program that finds the temperature, as an integer, that is the same in both Celsius and Fahrenheit. The formula to convert from Celsius to Fahrenheit is as follows:

$$\text{Fahrenheit} = \frac{9}{5}\,\text{Celsius} + 32$$

Your program should create two integer variables for the temperature in Celsius and Fahrenheit. Initialize the temperature to 100 degrees Celsius. In a loop, decrement the Celsius value and compute the corresponding temperature in Fahrenheit until the two values are the same.

VideoNote
Solution to
Programming
Project 2.9

9. (This is an extension of an exercise from Chapter 1.) The Babylonian algorithm to compute the square root of a positive number **n** is as follows:

   1. Make a **guess** at the answer (you can pick n/2 as your initial guess).
   2. Compute **r = n / guess**.
   3. Set **guess= (guess + r) / 2.**
   4. Go back to step 2 for as many iterations as necessary. The more steps 2 and 3 are repeated, the closer **guess** will become to the square root of **n.**

   Write a program that inputs a double for **n,** iterates through the Babylonian algorithm until the guess is within 1% of the previous guess, and outputs the answer as a double to two decimal places. Your answer should be accurate even for large values of n.

10. Create a text file that contains the text "I hate C++ and hate programming!" Write a program that reads in the text from the file and outputs each word to the console but replaces any occurrence of "hate" with "love." Your program should work with any line of text that contains the word "hate," not just the example given in this problem.

VideoNote
Solution to
Programming
Project 2.10

11. (This is an extension of an exercise from Chapter 1.) A simple rule to estimate your ideal body weight is to allow 110 pounds for the first 5 feet of height and 5 pounds for each additional inch. Create the following text in a text file. It contains the names and heights in feet and inches of Tom Atto (6'3"), Eaton Wright (5'5"), and Cary Oki (5'11"):

    ```
    Tom Atto
    6
    3
    Eaton Wright
    5
    5
    Cary Oki
    5
    11
    ```

    Write a program that reads the data in the file and outputs the full name and ideal body weight for each person. Use a loop to read the names from the file. Your program should also handle an arbitrary number of entries in the file instead of handling only three entries.

12. This problem is based on a "Nifty Assignment" by Steve Wolfman (http://nifty.stanford.edu/2006/wolfman-pretid). Consider lists of numbers from real-life data sources, for example, a list containing the number of students enrolled in different course sections, the number of comments posted for different Facebook status updates, the number of books in different library holdings, the number of votes per precinct, etc. It might seem like the leading digit of each number in the list should be 1–9 with an equally likely probability. However, Benford's Law states that the leading digit is 1 about 30% of the time and drops with larger digits. The leading digit is 9 only about 5% of the time.

    Write a program that tests Benford's Law. Collect a list of at least one hundred numbers from some real-life data source and enter them into a text file. Your program should loop through the list of numbers and count how many times 1 is the first digit, 2 is the first digit, etc. For each digit, output the percentage it appears as the first digit.

    If you read a number into the string variable named strNum then you can access the first digit as a char by using strNum[0]. This is described in more detail in Chapter 9.

Function Basics 3

3 Function Basics

Introduction

If you have programmed in some other language, then the contents of this chapter will be familiar to you. You should still scan this chapter to see the C++ syntax and terminology for the basics of functions. Chapter 4 contains the material on functions that might be different in C++ than in other languages.

A program can be thought of as consisting of subparts such as obtaining the input data, calculating the output data, and displaying the output data. C++, like most programming languages, has facilities to name and code each of these subparts separately. In C++ these subparts are called *functions*. Most programming languages have functions or something similar to functions, although they are not always called by that name in other languages. The terms *procedure*, *subprogram*, and *method*, which you may have heard before, mean essentially the same thing as *function*. In C++ a function may return a value, but whether the subpart returns a value or not, it is still called a function in C++. This chapter presents the basic details about C++ functions. Before telling you how to write your own functions, we will first tell you how to use some predefined C++ functions.

3.1   Predefined Functions

Do not reinvent the wheel.

Common saying

C++ comes with libraries of predefined functions that you can use in your programs. There are two kinds of functions in C++: functions that return (produce) a value and functions that do not return a value. Functions that do not return a value are called **void functions**. We first discuss functions that return a value and then discuss void functions.

Predefined Functions That Return a Value

We will use the sqrt function to illustrate how you use a predefined function that returns a value. The sqrt function calculates the square root of a number. (The square root of a number is that number which, when multiplied by itself, will produce the

void function

number you started out with. For example, the square root of 9 is 3 because 3^2 is equal to 9.) The function sqrt starts with a number, such as 9.0, and computes its square root, in this case 3.0. The value the function starts out with is called its **argument**. The value it computes is called the **value returned**. Some functions may have more than one argument, but no function has more than one value returned.

argument

value returned

The syntax for using functions in your program is simple. To set a variable named theRoot equal to the square root of 9.0, you can use the following assignment statement:

```
theRoot = sqrt(9.0);
```

The expression sqrt(9.0) is known as a **function call** or **function invocation**. An argument in a function call can be a constant, such as 9.0, a variable, or a more complicated expression. A function call is an expression that can be used like any other expression. For example, the value returned by sqrt is of type double; therefore, the following is legal (although perhaps stingy):

function call or function invocation

```
bonus = sqrt(sales)/10;
```

sales and bonus are variables that would normally be of type double. The function call sqrt(sales) is a single item, just as if it were enclosed in parentheses. Thus, the previous assignment statement is equivalent to

```
bonus = (sqrt(sales))/10;
```

You can use a function call wherever it is legal to use an expression of the type specified for the value returned by the function.

Display 3.1 contains a complete program that uses the predefined function sqrt. The program computes the size of the largest square doghouse that can be built for the amount of money the user is willing to spend. The program asks the user for an amount of money and then determines how many square feet of floor space can be purchased for that amount. That calculation yields an area in square feet for the floor of the doghouse. The function sqrt yields the length of one side of the doghouse floor.

The cmath library contains the definition of the function sqrt and a number of other mathematical functions. If your program uses a predefined function from some library, then it must contain an **include directive** that names that library. For example, the program in Display 3.1 uses the sqrt function and so it contains

#include directive

```
#include <cmath>
```

This particular program has two include directives. It does not matter in what order you give these two include directives. include directives were discussed in Chapter 1. Definitions for predefined functions normally place these functions in the std namespace and so also require the following using directive, as illustrated in Display 3.1:

```
using namespace std;
```

Display 3.1   A Predefined Function That Returns a Value

```
1   //Computes the size of a doghouse that can be purchased
2   //given the user's budget.
3   #include <iostream>
4   #include <cmath>
5   using namespace std;
6
7   int main( )
8   {
9       const double COST_PER_SQ_FT = 10.50;
10      double budget, area, lengthSide;
11
12      cout << "Enter the amount budgeted for your doghouse $";
13      cin >> budget;
14
15      area = budget / COST_PER_SQ_FT;
16      lengthSide = sqrt(area);
17
18      cout.setf(ios::fixed);
19      cout.setf(ios::showpoint);
20      cout.precision(2);
21
22      cout << "For a price of $" << budget << endl
            << "I can build you a luxurious square doghouse\n"
            << "that is " << lengthSide
            << " feet on each side.\n";

        return 0;
    }
```

Sample Dialogue

```
Enter the amount budgeted for your doghouse $25.00
For a price of $25.00
I can build you a luxurious square doghouse
that is 1.54 feet on each side.
```

#include may not be enough

Usually, all you need to do to use a library is to place an include directive and a using directive for that library in the file with your program. If things work with just these directives, you need not worry about doing anything else. However, for some libraries on some systems you may need to give additional instructions to the compiler or explicitly run a linker program to link in the library. The details vary from one system to another; you will have to check your manual or ask a local expert to see exactly what is necessary.

A few predefined functions are described in Display 3.2. More predefined functions **abs and labs** are described in Appendix 4. Notice that the absolute value functions **abs** and **labs** are

Functions That Return a Value

For a function that returns a value, a function call is an expression consisting of the function name followed by arguments enclosed in parentheses. If there is more than one argument, the arguments are separated by commas. If the function call returns a value, then the function call is an expression that can be used like any other expression of the type specified for the value returned by the function.

SYNTAX

Function_Name(Argument_List)

where the *Argument_List* is a comma-separated list of arguments:

Argument_1, Argument_2,..., Argument_Last

EXAMPLES

```
side = sqrt(area);
cout << "2.5 to the power 3.0 is "
     << pow(2.5, 3.0);
```

in the library with header file `cstdlib`, so any program that uses either of these functions must contain the following directive:

```
#include <cstdlib>
```

Also notice that there are three absolute value functions. If you want to produce the absolute value of a number of type `int`, use `abs`; if you want to produce the absolute value of a number of type `long`, use `labs`; and if you want to produce the absolute value of a number of type `double`, use `fabs`. To complicate things even more, `abs` and

fabs   `labs` are in the library with header file `cstdlib`, whereas `fabs` is in the library with header file `cmath`. `fabs` is an abbreviation for *floating-point absolute value*. Recall that numbers with a fraction after the decimal point, such as numbers of type `double`, are often called *floating-point numbers*.

pow   Another example of a predefined function is `pow`, which is in the library with header file `cmath`. The function `pow` can be used to do exponentiation in C++. For example, if you want to set a variable `result` equal to x^y, you can use the following:

```
result = pow(x, y);
```

Hence, the following three lines of program code will output the number 9.0 to the screen, because $(3.0)^{2.0}$ is 9.0:

```
double result, x = 3.0, y = 2.0;
result = pow(x, y);
cout << result;
```

Display 3.2   Some Predefined Functions

All these predefined functions require using namespace std; as well as an include directive.

NAME	DESCRIPTION	TYPE OF ARGUMENTS	TYPE OF VALUE RETURNED	EXAMPLE	VALUE	LIBRARY HEADER
sqrt	Square root	double	double	sqrt(4.0)	2.0	cmath
pow	Powers	double	double	pow(2.0,3.0)	8.0	cmath
abs	Absolute value for int	int	int	abs(-7) abs(7)	7 7	cstdlib
fabs	Absolute value for double	double	double	fabs(-7.5) fabs(7.5)	7.5 7.5	cmath
labs	Absolute value for long	long	long	labs(-70000) labs(70000)	70000 70000	cstdlib
ceil	Ceiling (round up)	double	double	ceil(3.2) ceil(3.9)	4.0 4.0	cmath
floor	Floor (round down)	double	double	floor(3.2) floor(3.9)	3.0 3.0	cmath
exit	End program	int	void	exit(1);	None	cstdlib
rand	Random number	None	int	rand( )	Varies	cstdlib
srand	Set seed for rand	unsigned int	void	srand(42);	None	cstdlib

arguments have a type

Notice that the previous call to pow returns 9.0, not 9. The function pow always returns a value of type double, not of type int. Also notice that the function pow requires two arguments. A function can have any number of arguments. Moreover, every argument position has a specified type, and the argument used in a function call should be of that type. In many cases, if you use an argument of the wrong type, some automatic type conversion will be done for you by C++. However, the results may not be what you intended. When you call a function, you should use arguments of the type specified for that function. One exception to this caution is the automatic conversion of arguments from type int to type double. In many situations, including calls to the function pow, you can safely use an argument of type int (or other integer type) when an argument of type double (or other floating-point type) is specified.

void Functions

A void function performs some action, but does not return a value. For a void function, a function call is a statement consisting of the function name followed by arguments enclosed in parentheses and then terminated with a semicolon. If there is more than one argument, the arguments are separated by commas. For a void function, a function invocation (function call) is a statement that can be used like any other C++ statement.

SYNTAX

Function_Name(Argument_List);

where the *Argument_List* is a comma-separated list of arguments:

Argument_1, Argument_2, . . . , Argument_Last

EXAMPLE

```
exit(1);
```

restrictions on pow

Many implementations of pow have a restriction on what arguments can be used. In these implementations, if the first argument to pow is negative, then the second argument must be a whole number. It might be easiest and safest to use pow only when the first argument is nonnegative.

Predefined void Functions

A void function performs some action, but does not return a value. Since it performs an action, a void function invocation is a statement. The function call for a void function is written similar to a function call for a function that returns a value, except that it is terminated with a semicolon and is used as a statement rather than as an expression. Predefined void functions are handled in the same way as predefined functions that return a value. Thus, to use a predefined void function, your program must have an include directive that gives the name of the library that defines the function.

exit

For example, the function **exit** is defined in the library cstdlib, and so a program that uses that function must contain the following at (or near) the start of the file:

```
#include <cstdlib>
using namespace std;
```

The following is a sample invocation (sample call) of the function exit:

```
exit(1);
```

The exit Function

The exit function is a predefined void function that takes one argument of type int. Thus, an invocation of the exit function is a statement written as follows:

```
exit(Integer_Value);
```

When the exit function is invoked (that is, when the previous statement is executed), the program ends immediately. Any Integer_Value may be used, but by convention, 1 is used for a call to exit that is caused by an error, and 0 is used in other cases.

The exit function definition is in the library cstdlib and it places the exit function in the std namespace. Therefore, any program that uses the exit function must contain the following two directives:

```
#include <cstdlib>
using namespace std;
```

An invocation of the exit function ends the program immediately. Display 3.3 contains a toy program that demonstrates the exit function.

Note that the exit function has one argument, which is of type int. The argument is given to the operating system. As far as your C++ program is concerned, you can use any int value as the argument, but by convention, 1 is used for a call to exit that is caused by an error, and 0 is used in other cases.

Display 3.3   A Function Call for a Predefined void Function

```
1    #include <iostream>
2    #include <cstdlib>
3    using namespace std;

4    int main( )
5    {
6        cout << "Hello Out There!\n";
7        exit(1);

8        cout << "This statement is pointless,\n"
9             << "because it will never be executed.\n"
10            << "This is just a toy program to illustrate exit.\n";

11       return 0;
12   }
```

This is just a toy example. It would produce the same output if you omitted these lines.

Sample Dialogue

```
Hello Out There!
```

A `void` function can have any number of arguments. The details on arguments for `void` functions are the same as they were for functions that return a value. In particular, if you use an argument of the wrong type, then, in many cases, some automatic type conversion will be done for you by C++. However, the results may not be what you intended.

Self-Test Exercises

1. Determine the value of each of the following arithmetic expressions.

`sqrt(16.0)`	`sqrt(16)`	`pow(2.0, 3.0)`
`pow(2, 3)`	`pow(2.0, 3)`	`pow(1.1, 2)`
`abs(3)`	`abs(-3)`	`abs(0)`
`fabs(-3.0)`	`fabs(-3.5)`	`fabs(3.5)`
`ceil(5.1)`	`ceil(5.8)`	`floor(5.1)`
`floor(5.8)`	`pow(3.0, 2)/2.0`	`pow(3.0, 2)/2`
`7/abs(-2)`	`(7 + sqrt(4.0))/3.0`	`sqrt(pow(3, 2))`

2. Convert each of the following mathematical expressions to a C++ arithmetic expression.

a. $\sqrt{x + y}$ b. $x^{y + 7}$ c. $\sqrt{area + fudge}$

d. $\dfrac{\sqrt{time + tide}}{nobody}$ e. $\dfrac{-b \pm \sqrt{b^2 - 4ac}}{2a}$ f. $|\, x - y \,|$

3. Write a complete C++ program to compute and output the square roots of the whole numbers 1 to 10.

4. What is the function of the `int` argument to the `void` function `exit`?

A Random Number Generator

A random number generator is a function that returns a "randomly chosen" number. It is unlike the functions we have seen so far in that the value returned is not determined by the arguments (of which there are usually none) but rather by some global conditions. Since you can think of the value returned as being a random number, you can use a random number generator to simulate random events, such as the result of throwing dice or flipping a coin. In addition to simulating games of chance, random number generators can be used to simulate things that strictly speaking may not be random but that appear to us to be random, such as the amount of time between the arrival of cars at a toll booth.

rand

RAND
_MAX

The C++ library with header file <cstdlib> contains a random number function named rand. This function has no arguments. When your program invokes rand, the function returns an integer in the range 0 to RAND_MAX, inclusive. (The number generated might be equal to 0 or RAND_MAX.) RAND_MAX is a defined integer constant whose definition is also in the library with header file <cstdlib>. The exact value of RAND_MAX is system-dependent but will always be at least 32767 (the maximum two-byte positive integer). For example, the following outputs a list of ten "random" numbers in the range 0 to RAND_MAX:

```
int i;
for (i = 0; i < 10; i++)
    cout << rand( ) << endl;
```

scaling

You are more likely to want a random number in some smaller range, such as the range 0 to 10. To ensure that the value is in the range 0 to 10 (including the end points), you can use

```
rand( ) % 11
```

This is called **scaling**. The following outputs ten "random" integers in the range 0 to 10 (inclusive):

```
int i;
for (i = 0; i < 10; i++)
    cout << (rand( ) % 11) << endl;
```

Random number generators, such as the function rand, do not generate truly random numbers. (That's the reason for all the quotes around "random.") A sequence of calls to the function rand (or almost any random number generator) will produce a sequence of numbers (the values returned by rand) that appear to be random. However, if you could return the computer to the state it was in when the sequence of calls to rand began, you would get the same sequence of "random numbers." Numbers that appear to be random but really are not, such as a sequence of numbers generated by calls to rand, are called **pseudorandom numbers.**

pseudorandom
number

A sequence of pseudorandom numbers is usually determined by one number known as the **seed**. If you start the random number generator with the same seed, over and over, then each time it will produce the same (random-looking) sequence of numbers. You can use the function srand to set the seed for the function rand. The void function srand takes one (positive) integer argument, which is the seed. For example, the following will output two identical sequences of ten pseudorandom numbers:

seed

srand

```
int i;
srand(99);
for (i = 0; i < 10; i++)
    cout << (rand( ) % 11) << endl;
srand(99);
for (i = 0; i < 10; i++)
    cout << (rand( ) % 11) << endl;
```

There is nothing special about the number 99, other than the fact that we used the same number for both calls to srand.

Note that the sequence of pseudorandom numbers produced for a given seed might be system-dependent. If rerun on a different system with the same seed, the sequence of pseudorandom numbers might be different on that system. However, as long as you are on the same system using the same implementation of C++, the same seed will produce the same sequence of pseudorandom numbers.

Pseudorandom Numbers

The function rand takes no arguments and returns a pseudorandom integer in the range 0 to RAND_MAX (inclusive). The void function srand takes one argument, which is the seed for the random number generator rand. The argument to srand is of type unsigned int, so the argument must be nonnegative. The functions rand and srand, as well as the defined constant RAND_MAX, are defined in the library cstdlib, so programs that use them must contain the following directives:

```
#include <cstdlib>
using namespace std;
```

These pseudorandom numbers are close enough to true random numbers for most applications. In fact, they are often preferable to true random numbers. A pseudorandom number generator has one big advantage over a true random number generator: The sequence of numbers it produces is repeatable. If run twice with the same seed value, it will produce the same sequence of numbers. This can be very handy for a number of purposes. When an error is discovered and fixed, the program can be rerun with the same sequence of pseudorandom numbers as those that exposed the error. Similarly, a particularly interesting run of the program can be repeated, provided a pseudorandom number generator is used. With a true random number generator every run of the program is likely to be different.

Display 3.4 shows a program that uses the random number generator rand to "predict" the weather. In this case the prediction is random, but some people think that is about as good as weather prediction gets. (Weather prediction can actually be very accurate, but this program is just a game to illustrate pseudorandom numbers.)

Note that in Display 3.4, the seed value used for the argument of srand is the month times the day. That way if the program is rerun and the same date is entered, the same prediction will be made. (Of course, this program is still pretty simple. The prediction for the day after the 14th may or may not be the same as the 15th, but this program will do as a simple example.)

Probabilities are usually expressed as a floating-point number in the range 0.0 to 1.0. Suppose you want a random probability instead of a random integer. This can be produced by another form of scaling. The following generates a pseudorandom floating-point value between 0.0 and 1.0:

floating-point random numbers

```
(RAND_MAX - rand( ))/static_cast<double>(RAND_MAX)
```

Display 3.4   A Function Using a Random Number Generator (part 1 of 2)

```
1    #include <iostream>
2    #include <cstdlib>
3    using namespace std;
4    int main( )
5    {
6        int month, day;
7        cout << "Welcome to your friendly weather program.\n"
8             << "Enter today's date as two integers for the month "  <<
                "and the day:\n";
9        cin >> month;
10       cin >> day;
11       srand(month * day);
12       int prediction;
13       char ans;
14       cout << "Weather for today:\n";
15       do
16       {
17           prediction =  rand( ) % 3 ;
18           switch (prediction)
19           {
20               case 0:
21                   cout << "The day will be sunny!!\n";
22                   break;
23               case 1:
24                   cout << "The day will be cloudy.\n";
25                   break;
26               case 2:
27                   cout << "The day will be stormy!\n";
28                   break;
29               default:
30                   cout << "Weather program is not " <<
                            "functioning properly.\n";
31           }
32           cout << "Want the weather for the next day?(y/n) : ";
33           cin >> ans;
34       } while (ans == 'y' || ans == 'Y');
35       cout << "That's it from your 24-hour weather program.\n";
36       return 0;
37   }
```

Display 3.4   A Function Using a Random Number Generator (part 2 of 2)

Sample Dialogue

```
Welcome to your friendly weather program.
Enter today's date as two integers for the month and the day:
2 14
Weather for today:
The day will be cloudy.
Want the weather for the next day?(y/n): y
The day will be cloudy.
Want the weather for the next day?(y/n): y
The day will be stormy!
Want the weather for the next day?(y/n): y
The day will be stormy!
Want the weather for the next day?(y/n): y
The day will be sunny!!
Want the weather for the next day?(y/n): n
That's it from your 24-hour weather program.
```

The type cast is made so that we get floating-point division rather than integer division.

Self-Test Exercises

5. Give an expression to produce a pseudorandom integer number in the range 5 to 10 (inclusive).

6. Write a complete program that asks the user for a seed and then outputs a list of ten random numbers based on that seed. The numbers should be floating-point numbers in the range 0.0 to 1.0 (inclusive).

3.2   Programmer-Defined Functions

A custom-tailored suit always fits better than one off the rack.

MY UNCLE, THE TAILOR

The previous section told you how to use predefined functions. This section tells you how to define your own functions.

Defining Functions That Return a Value

You can define your own functions, either in the same file as the main part of your program or in a separate file so that the functions can be used by several different programs. The definition is the same in either case, but for now we will assume that the function definition will be in the same file as the main part of your program. This subsection discusses only functions that return a value. A later subsection tells you how to define void functions.

Display 3.5 contains a sample function definition in a complete program that demonstrates a call to the function. The function is called totalCost and takes two arguments—the price for one item and the number of items for a purchase. The function returns the total cost, including sales tax, for that many items at the specified price. The function is called in the same way a predefined function is called. The definition of the function, which the programmer must write, is a bit more complicated.

The description of the function is given in two parts. The first part is called the **function declaration** or **function prototype.** The following is the function declaration (function prototype) for the function defined in Display 3.5:

```
double totalCost(int numberParameter, double priceParameter);
```

The first word in a function declaration specifies the type of the value returned by the function. Thus, for the function totalCost, the type of the value returned is double. Next, the function declaration tells you the name of the function; in this case, totalCost. The function declaration tells you (and the compiler) everything you need to know in order to write and use a call to the function. It tells you how many arguments the function needs and what type the arguments should be; in this case, the function totalCost takes two arguments, the first one of type int and the second one of type double. The identifiers numberParameter and priceParameter are called **formal parameters,** or **parameters** for short. A formal parameter is used as a kind of blank, or placeholder, to stand in for the argument. When you write a function declaration, you do not know what the arguments will be, so you use the formal parameters in place of the arguments. Names of formal parameters can be any valid identifiers. Notice that a function declaration ends with a semicolon.

Although the function declaration tells you all you need to know to write a function call, it does not tell you what value will be returned. The value returned is determined by the function definition. In Display 3.5 the function definition is in lines 24 to 30 of the program. A function definition describes how the function computes the value it returns. A function definition consists of a *function header* followed by a *function body.* The **function header** is written similar to the function declaration, except that the header does *not* have a semicolon at the end. The value returned is determined by the statements in the *function body.*

The **function body** follows the function header and completes the function definition. The function body consists of declarations and executable statements enclosed within a pair of braces. Thus, the function body is just like the body of the main part of a program. When the function is called, the argument values are plugged in for the formal parameters, and then the statements in the body are executed.

function declaration or function prototype

type for value returned

formal parameter

function definition

function header

function body

Display 3.5   A Function Using a Random Number Generator

```
 1   #include <iostream>
 2   using namespace std;
 3   double totalCost(int numberParameter, double priceParameter);
 4   //Computes the total cost, including 5% sales tax,
 5   //on numberParameter items at a cost of priceParameter each.

 6   int main( )
 7   {
 8       double price, bill;
 9       int number;

10       cout << "Enter the number of items purchased: ";
11       cin >> number;
12       cout << "Enter the price per item $";
13       cin >> price;

14       bill = totalCost(number, price);

15       cout.setf(ios::fixed);
16       cout.setf(ios::showpoint);
17       cout.precision(2);
18       cout << number << " items at "
19            << "$" << price << " each.\n"
20            << "Final bill, including tax, is $" << bill
21            << endl;

22       return 0;
23   }

24   double totalCost(int numberParameter, double priceParameter)
25   {
26       const double TAXRATE = 0.05; //5% sales tax
27       double subtotal;

28       subtotal = priceParameter * numberParameter;
29       return (subtotal + subtotal*TAXRATE);
30   }
```

*Function declaration;
also called the function
prototype*

Function call

*Function
head*

*Function
body*

*Function
definition*

Sample Dialogue

```
Enter the number of items purchased: 2
Enter the price per item: $10.10
2 items at $10.10 each.
Final bill, including tax, is $21.21
```

**return
statement**

The value returned by the function is determined when the function executes a `return` *statement*. (The details of this "plugging in" will be discussed in Chapter 4.)

A **return statement** consists of the keyword `return` followed by an expression. The function definition in Display 3.5 contains the following `return` statement:

```
return (subtotal + subtotal * TAXRATE) ;
```

When this `return` statement is executed, the value of the following expression is returned as the value of the function call:

```
(subtotal + subtotal * TAXRATE)
```

The parentheses are not needed. The program will run the same if the parentheses are omitted. However, with longer expressions, the parentheses make the `return` statement easier to read. For consistency, some programmers advocate using these parentheses even with simple expressions. In the function definition in Display 3.5 there are no statements after the `return` statement, but if there were, they would not be executed. When a `return` statement is executed, the function call ends.

Note that the function body can contain any C++ statements and that the statements will be executed when the function is called. Thus, a function that returns a value may do any other action as well as return a value. In most cases, however, the main purpose of a function that returns a value is to return that value.

Either the complete function definition or the function declaration (function prototype) must appear in the code before the function is called. The most typical arrangement is for the function declaration and the `main` part of the program to appear in one or more files, with the function declaration before the `main` part of the program, and for the function definition to appear in another file. We have not yet discussed dividing a program across more than one file, and so we will place the function definitions after the `main` part of the program. If the full function definition is placed before the `main` part of the program, the function declaration can be omitted.

Alternate Form for Function Declarations

You are not required to list formal parameter names in a function declaration (function prototype). The following two function declarations are equivalent:

```
double totalCost(int numberParameter, double priceParameter) ;
```

and

```
double totalCost(int, double) ;
```

We will usually use the first form so that we can refer to the formal parameters in the comment that accompanies the function declaration. However, you will often see the second form in manuals.

This alternate form applies only to function declarations. *A function definition must always list the formal parameter names.*

PITFALL: Arguments in the Wrong Order

When a function is called, the computer substitutes the first argument for the first formal parameter, the second argument for the second formal parameter, and so forth. Although the computer checks the type of each argument, it does not check for reasonableness. If you confuse the order of the arguments, the program will not do what you want it to do. If there is a type violation due to an argument of the wrong type, then you will get an error message. If there is no type violation, your program will probably run normally but produce an incorrect value for the value returned by the function. ■

PITFALL: Use of the Terms *Parameter* and *Argument*

The use of the terms *formal parameter* and *argument* that we follow in this book is consistent with common usage, but people also often use the terms *parameter* and *argument* interchangeably. When you see the terms *parameter* and *argument*, you must determine their exact meaning from context. Many people use the term *parameter* for both what we call *formal parameters* and what we call *arguments*. Other people use the term *argument* both for what we call formal *parameters* and what we call *arguments*. Do not expect consistency in how people use these two terms. (In this book we sometimes use the term *parameter* to mean *formal parameter*, but this is more of an abbreviation than a true inconsistency.) ■

Functions Calling Functions

A function body may contain a call to another function. The situation for these sorts of function calls is the same as if the function call had occurred in the main part of the program; the only restriction is that the function declaration (or function definition) must appear before the function is used. If you set up your programs as we have been doing, this will happen automatically, since all function declarations come before the main part of the program and all function definitions come after the main part of the program. Although you may include a function *call* within the definition of another function, you cannot place the *definition* of one function within the body of another function definition.

EXAMPLE: A Rounding Function

The table of predefined functions (Display 3.2) does not include any function for rounding a number. The functions ceil and floor are almost, but not quite, rounding functions. The function ceil always returns the next-highest whole number (or its argument if it happens to be a whole number). So, ceil(2.1) returns 3.0, not 2.0.

(continued)

EXAMPLE: (continued)

The function `floor` always returns the nearest whole number less than (or equal to) the argument. So, `floor(2.9)` returns `2.0`, not `3.0`. Fortunately, it is easy to define a function that does true rounding. The function `round` rounds its argument to the nearest integer. For example, `round(2.3)` returns `2`, and `round(2.6)` returns `3`.

To see that `round` works correctly, let's look at some examples. Consider `round(2.4)`. The value returned is the following (converted to an `int` value),

```
floor(2.4 + 0.5)
```

which is `floor(2.9)`, or `2.0`. In fact, for any number that is greater than or equal to `2.0` and strictly less than `2.5`, that number plus `0.5` will be less than `3.0`, and so `floor` applied to that number plus `0.5` will return `2.0`. Thus, `round` applied to any number that is greater than or equal to `2.0` and strictly less than `2.5` will return `2`. (Since the function declaration for `round` specifies that the type for the value returned is `int`, we have type cast the computed value to the type `int`.)

Now consider numbers greater than or equal to `2.5`; for example, `2.6`. The value returned by the call `round(2.6)` is the following (converted to an `int` value),

```
floor(2.6 + 0.5)
```

which is `floor(3.1)`, or `3.0`. In fact, for any number that is greater than `2.5` and less than or equal to `3.0`, that number plus `0.5` will be greater than `3.0`. Thus, `round` called with any number that is greater than `2.5` and less than or equal to `3.0` will return `3`.

Thus, `round` works correctly for all arguments between `2.0` and `3.0`. Clearly, there is nothing special about arguments between `2.0` and `3.0`. A similar argument applies to all nonnegative numbers. So, `round` works correctly for all nonnegative arguments.

Display 3.6   The Function round (part 1 of 2)

```
1    #include <iostream>
2    #include <cmath>
3    using namespace std;
4    int round(double number);
5    //Assumes number >= 0.
6    //Returns number rounded to the nearest integer.
7    int main( )
8    {
9        double doubleValue;
10       char ans;
```

Testing program for the function round

Display 3.6   The Function round (part 2 of 2)

```
11      do
12      {
13          cout << "Enter a double value: ";
14          cin >> doubleValue;
15          cout << "Rounded that number is " << round(doubleValue) <<
                endl;
16          cout << "Again? (y/n): ";
17          cin >> ans;
18      } while (ans == 'y' || ans == 'Y');
19      cout << "End of testing.\n";

20      return 0;
21  }
22  //Uses cmath:
23  int round(double number)
24  {
25      return static_cast<int>(floor(number + 0.5));
26  }
```

Sample Dialogue

```
Enter a double value: 9.6
Rounded, that number is 10
Again? (y/n): y
Enter a double value: 2.49
Rounded, that number is 2
Again? (y/n): n
End of testing.
```

Self-Test Exercises

7. What is the output produced by the following program?

```
#include <iostream>
using namespace std;
char mystery(int firstParameter, int secondParameter);
int main( )
{
    cout << mystery(10, 9) << "ow\n";
    return 0;
}
```

(continued)

Self-Test Exercises (continued)

```
char mystery(int firstParameter, int secondParameter)
{
    if (firstParameter >= secondParameter)
        return 'W';
    else
        return 'H';
}
```

8. Write a function declaration (function prototype) and a function definition for a function that takes three arguments, all of type int, and that returns the sum of its three arguments.

9. Write a function declaration and a function definition for a function that takes one argument of type double. The function returns the character value 'P' if its argument is positive and returns 'N' if its argument is zero or negative.

10. Can a function definition appear inside the body of another function definition?

11. List the similarities and differences between how you invoke (call) a predefined (that is, library) function and a user-defined function.

Functions That Return a Boolean Value

The returned type for a function can be the type bool. A call to such a function returns one of the values true or false and can be used anywhere that a Boolean expression is allowed. For example, it can be used in a Boolean expression to control an if-else statement or to control a loop statement. This can often make a program easier to read. By means of a function declaration, you can associate a complex Boolean expression with a meaningful name. For example, the statement

```
if (((rate >= 10) && (rate < 20)) || (rate == 0))
{
    ...
}
```

can be made to read

```
if (appropriate(rate))
{
    ...
}
```

provided that the following function has been defined:

```
bool appropriate(int rate)
{
    return (((rate >= 10) && (rate < 20)) || (rate == 0));
}
```

Self-Test Exercises

12. Write a function definition for a function called `inOrder` that takes three arguments of type `int`. The function returns `true` if the three arguments are in ascending order; otherwise, it returns `false`. For example, `inOrder(1, 2, 3)` and `inOrder(1, 2, 2)` both return `true`, whereas `inOrder(1, 3, 2)` returns `false`.

13. Write a function definition for a function called `even` that takes one argument of type `int` and returns a `bool` value. The function returns `true` if its one argument is an even number; otherwise, it returns `false`.

14. Write a function definition for a function `isDigit` that takes one argument of type `char` and returns a `bool` value. The function returns `true` if the argument is a decimal digit; otherwise, it returns `false`.

Defining `void` Functions

In C++ a `void` function is defined in a way similar to that of functions that return a value. For example, the following is a `void` function that outputs the result of a calculation that converts a temperature expressed in degrees Fahrenheit to a temperature expressed in degrees Celsius. The actual calculation would be done elsewhere in the program. This `void` function implements only the subtask for outputting the results of the calculation.

```
void showResults(double fDegrees, double cDegrees)
{
    cout.setf(ios::fixed);
    cout.setf(ios::showpoint);
    cout.precision(1);
    cout << fDegrees
         << " degrees Fahrenheit is equivalent to\n"
         << cDegrees << " degrees Celsius.\n";
}
```

void function definition

As the previous function definition illustrates, there are only two differences between a function definition for a `void` function and for a function that returns a value. One difference is that we use the keyword `void` where we would normally specify the type of the value to be returned. This tells the compiler that this function will not return any value. The name `void` is used as a way of saying "no value is returned by this function." The second difference is that a `void` function definition does not require a `return` statement. The function execution ends when the last statement in the function body is executed.

A `void` function call is an executable statement. For example, the previous function `showResults` might be called as follows:

void function call

```
showResults(32.5, 0.3);
```

If the previous statement were executed in a program, it would cause the following to appear on the screen:

```
32.5 degrees Fahrenheit is equivalent to
0.3 degrees Celsius.
```

Notice that the function call ends with a semicolon, which tells the compiler that the function call is an executable statement.

When a `void` function is called, the arguments are substituted for the formal parameters, and the statements in the function body are executed. For example, a call to the `void` function `showResults`, which we gave earlier in this section, will cause some output to be written to the screen. One way to think of a call to a `void` function is to imagine that the body of the function definition is copied into the program in place of the function call. When the function is called, the arguments are substituted for the formal parameters, and then it is just as if the body of the function were lines in the program. (Chapter 4 describes the process of substituting arguments for formal parameters in detail. Until then, we will use only simple examples that should be clear enough without a formal description of the substitution process.)

Function Declaration (Function Prototype)

A function declaration (function prototype) tells you all you need to know to write a call to the function. A function declaration (or the full function definition) must appear in your code prior to a call to the function. Function declarations are normally placed before the main part of your program.

SYNTAX

```
Type_Returned_Or_void FunctionName (Parameter_List);
```

Do not forget
this semicolon.

where the `Parameter_List` is a comma-separated list of parameters:

```
Type_1 Formal_Parameter_1, Type_2 Formal_Parameter_2, . . .
                Type_Last Formal_Parameter_Last
```

EXAMPLES

```
double totalWeight(int number, double weightOfOne);
//Returns the total weight of number items that
//each weigh weightOfOne.

void showResults(double fDegrees, double cDegrees);
//Displays a message saying fDegrees Fahrenheit
//is equivalent to cDegrees Celsius.
```

functions with no arguments

It is perfectly legal, and sometimes useful, to have a function with no arguments. In that case there simply are no formal parameters listed in the function declaration and no arguments are used when the function is called. For example, the `void` function initializeScreen, defined next, simply sends a newline command to the screen:

```
void initializeScreen( )
{
    cout << endl;
}
```

If your program includes the following call to this function as its first executable statement, then the output from the previously run program will be separated from the output for your program:

```
initializeScreen( );
```

Be sure to notice that even when there are no parameters to a function, you still must include the parentheses in the function declaration and in a call to the function.

Placement of the function declaration (function prototype) and the function definition is the same for void functions as what we described for functions that return a value.

return Statements in void Functions

void functions and return statements

Both void functions and functions that return a value can have return statements. In the case of a function that returns a value, the return statement specifies the value returned. In the case of a void function, the return statement does not include any expression for a value returned. A return statement in a void function simply ends the function call. Every function that returns a value must end by executing a return statement. However, a void function need not contain a return statement. If it does not contain a return statement, it will end after executing the code in the function body. It is as if there were an implicit return statement just before the final closing brace, }, at the end of the function body.

The fact that there is an implicit return statement before the final closing brace in a function body does not mean that you never need a return statement in a void function. For example, the function definition in Display 3.7 might be used as part of a restaurant-management program. That function outputs instructions for dividing a given amount of ice cream among the people at a table. If there are no people at the table (that is, if number equals 0), then the return statement within the if statement terminates the function call and avoids a division by zero. If number is not 0, then the function call ends when the last cout statement is executed at the end of the function body.

Preconditions and Postconditions

precondition

postcondition

One good way to write a function declaration comment is to break it down into two kinds of information called the *precondition* and the *postcondition*. The **precondition** states what is assumed to be true when the function is called. The function should not be used and cannot be expected to perform correctly unless the precondition holds. The **postcondition** describes the effect of the function call; that is, the postcondition tells what will be true after the function is executed in a situation in which the precondition holds. For a function that returns a value, the postcondition will describe the value returned by the function. For a function that changes the value of some argument variables, the postcondition will describe all the changes made to the values of the arguments.

Display 3.7 Use of return in a void Function

```
 1  #include <iostream>
 2  using namespace std;

 3  void iceCreamDivision(int number, double totalWeight);
 4  //Outputs instructions for dividing totalWeight ounces of ice cream
 5  //among number customers. If number is 0, only an error
    //message is output.

 6  int main( )
 7  {
 8      int number;
 9      double totalWeight;

10      cout << "Enter the number of customers: ";
11      cin >> number;
12      cout << "Enter weight of ice cream to divide (in ounces): ";
13      cin >> totalWeight;

14      iceCreamDivision(number, totalWeight);

15      return 0;
16  }

17  void iceCreamDivision(int number, double totalWeight)
18  {
19      double portion;

20      if (number == 0)
21      {
22          cout << "Cannot divide among zero customers.\n";
23          return;          ──────────  If number is 0, then the
24      }                                 function execution ends here.
25      portion = totalWeight/number;
26      cout << "Each one receives "
27          << portion << " ounces of ice cream." << endl;
28  }
```

Sample Dialogue

```
Enter the number of customers: 0
Enter weight of ice cream to divide (in ounces): 12
Cannot divide among zero customers.
```

For example, the following is a function declaration with precondition and postcondition:

```
void showInterest(double balance, double rate);
//Precondition: balance is a nonnegative savings account balance.
//rate is the interest rate expressed as a percentage, such as 5
//for 5%.
//Postcondition: The amount of interest on the given balance
//at the given rate is shown on the screen.
```

You do not need to know the definition of the function showInterest in order to use this function. All that you need to know in order to use this function is given by the precondition and postcondition.

When the only postcondition is a description of the value returned, programmers usually omit the word Postcondition, as in the following example:

```
double celsius(double fahrenheit);
//Precondition: fahrenheit is a temperature in degrees
//Fahrenheit.
//Returns the equivalent temperature expressed in degrees
//Celsius.
```

Some programmers choose not to use the words *precondition* and *postcondition* in their function comments. However, whether you use the words or not, you should always think in terms of precondition and postcondition when designing a function and when deciding what to include in the function comment.

main Is a Function

As we already noted, the main part of a program is actually the definition of a function called main. When the program is run, the function main is automatically called; it, in turn, may call other functions. Although it may seem that the return statement in the main part of a program should be optional, practically speaking it is not. The C++ standard says that you can omit the return 0 statement in the main part of the program, but many compilers still require it and almost all compilers allow you to include it. For the sake of portability, you should include a return 0 statement in the main function. You should consider the main part of a program to be a function that returns a value of type int and thus requires a return statement. Treating the main part of your program as a function that returns an integer may sound strange, but that is the tradition which many compilers enforce.

Although some compilers may allow you to get away with it, you should not include a call to main in your code. Only the system should call main, which it does when you run your program.

Recursive Functions

C++ does allow you to define recursive functions. Recursive functions are covered in Chapter 13. If you do not know what recursive functions are, there is no need to be concerned until you reach that chapter. If you want to read about recursive functions early, you can read Sections 13.1 and 13.2 of Chapter 13 after you complete Chapter 4. Note that the main function should not be called recursively.

Self-Test Exercises

15. What is the output of the following program?

```
#include <iostream>
using namespace std;
void friendly( );
void shy(int audienceCount);
int main( )
{
    friendly( );
    shy(6);
    cout << "One more time:\n";
    shy(2);
    friendly( );
    cout << "End of program.\n";
    return 0;
}
void friendly( )
{
    cout << "Hello\n";
}
void shy(int audienceCount)
{
    if (audienceCount < 5)
        return;
    cout << "Goodbye\n";
}
```

16. Suppose you omitted the return statement in the function definition for iceCreamDivision in Display 3.7. What effect would it have on the program? Would the program compile? Would it run? Would the program behave any differently?

17. Write a definition for a void function that has three arguments of type int and that outputs to the screen the product of these three arguments. Put the definition in a complete program that reads in three numbers and then calls this function.

18. Does your compiler allow void main( ) and int main( )? What warnings are issued if you have int main( ) and do not supply a return 0; statement? To find out, write several small test programs and perhaps ask your instructor or a local guru.

19. Give a precondition and a postcondition for the predefined function sqrt, which returns the square root of its argument.

3.3 Scope Rules

Let the end be legitimate, let it be within the scope of the constitution, ...

JOHN MARSHALL, Chief Justice U.S. Supreme Court,
McCulloch v. Maryland (1819)

VideoNote
**Scope
Walkthrough**

Functions should be self-contained units that do not interfere with other functions—or any other code for that matter. To achieve this you often need to give the function variables of its own that are distinct from any other variables that are declared outside the function definition and that may have the same names as the variables that belong to the function. These variables that are declared in a function definition are called *local variables* and are the topic of this section.

Local Variables

Look back at the program in Display 3.1. It includes a call to the predefined function `sqrt`. We did not need to know anything about the details of the function definition for `sqrt` in order to use this function. In particular, we did not need to know what variables were declared in the definition of `sqrt`. A function that you define is no different. Variable declarations within a function definition are the same as if they were variable declarations in a predefined function or in another program. If you declare a variable in a function definition and then declare another variable of the same name in the `main` function of the program (or in the body of some other function definition), then these two variables are two different variables, even though they have the same name. Let's look at an example.

The program in Display 3.8 has two variables named `averagePea`; one is declared and used in the function definition for the function `estimateOfTotal`, and the other is declared and used in the `main` function of the program. The variable `averagePea` in the function definition for `estimateOfTotal` and the variable `averagePea` in the `main` function are two different variables. It is the same as if the function `estimateOfTotal` were a predefined function. The two variables named `averagePea` will not interfere with each other any more than two variables in two completely different programs would. When the variable `averagePea` is given a value in the function call to `estimateOfTotal`, this does not change the value of the variable in the `main` function that is also named `averagePea`.

Variables that are declared within the body of a function definition are said to be **local** to that function or to have that function as their **scope**. If a variable is local to some function, we sometimes simply call it a *local variable*, without specifying the function.

Another example of local variables can be seen in Display 3.5. The definition of the function `totalCost` in that program begins as follows:

local
variable
scope

```
double totalCost(int numberParameter, double priceParameter)
{
    const double TAXRATE = 0.05; //5% sales tax
    double subtotal;
```

Display 3.8   Local Variables (part 1 of 2)

```
1    //Computes the average yield on an experimental pea growing patch.
2    #include <iostream>
3    using namespace std;
4    double estimateOfTotal(int minPeas, int maxPeas, int podCount);
5    //Returns an estimate of the total number of peas harvested.
6    //The formal parameter podCount is the number of pods.
7    //The formal parameters minPeas and maxPeas are the minimum
8    //and maximum number of peas in a pod.
9    int main( )
10   {
11       int maxCount, minCount, podCount;
12       double averagePea, yield;                      This variable named
                                                        averagePea is local to the
                                                        main function.
13       cout << "Enter minimum and maximum number of peas in a pod: ";
14       cin >> minCount >> maxCount;
15       cout << "Enter the number of pods: ";
16       cin >> podCount;
17       cout << "Enter the weight of an average pea (in ounces): ";
18       cin >> averagePea;
19       yield =
20           estimateOfTotal(minCount, maxCount, podCount) * averagePea;

21       cout.setf(ios::fixed);
22       cout.setf(ios::showpoint);
23       cout.precision(3);
24       cout << "Min number of peas per pod = " << minCount << endl
25            << "Max number of peas per pod = " << maxCount << endl
26            << "Pod count = " << podCount << endl
27            << "Average pea weight = "
28            << averagePea << " ounces" << endl
29            << "Estimated average yield = " << yield << " ounces"
30            << endl;

31       return 0;
32   }

33
34   double estimateOfTotal(int minPeas, int maxPeas, int podCount)
35   {
36       double averagePea;                      This variable named
                                                 averagePea is local to
                                                 the function estimateOfTotal.
37       averagePea = (maxPeas + minPeas)/2.0;
38       return (podCount * averagePea);
39   }
```

Display 3.8   Local Variables (part 2 of 2)

Sample Dialogue

```
Enter minimum and maximum number of peas in a pod: 4 6
Enter the number of pods: 10
Enter the weight of an average pea (in ounces): 0.5
Min number of peas per pod = 4
Max number of peas per pod = 6
Pod count = 10
Average pea weight = 0.500 ounces
Estimated average yield = 25.000 ounces
```

The variable subtotal is local to the function totalCost. The named constant TAXRATE is also local to the function totalCost. (A named constant is in fact nothing but a variable that is initialized to a value and that cannot have that value changed.)

Local Variables

Variables that are declared within the body of a function definition are said to be *local to that function* or to have that function as their *scope*. If a variable is local to a function, then you can have another variable (or other kind of item) with the same name that is declared in another function definition; these will be two different variables, even though they have the same name. (In particular, this is true even if one of the functions is the main function.)

Procedural Abstraction

A person who uses a program should not need to know the details of how the program is coded. Imagine how miserable your life would be if you had to know and remember the code for the compiler you use. A program has a job to do, such as compiling your program or checking the spelling of words in your paper. You need to know *what* the program's job is so that you can use the program, but you do not (or at least should not) need to know *how* the program does its job. A function is like a small program and should be used in a similar way. A programmer who uses a function in a program needs to know *what* the function does (such as calculate a square root or convert a temperature from degrees Fahrenheit to degrees Celsius), but should not need to know *how* the function accomplishes its task. This is often referred to as treating the function like a *black box*.

black box   Calling something a **black box** is a figure of speech intended to convey the image of a physical device that you know how to use but whose method of operation is a mystery because it is enclosed in a black box that you cannot see inside of (and cannot pry open).

**information
hiding**

**procedural
abstraction**

If a function is well designed, the programmer can use the function as if it were a black box. All the programmer needs to know is that if he or she puts appropriate arguments into the black box, then it will take some appropriate action. Designing a function so that it can be used as a black box is sometimes called **information hiding** to emphasize the fact that the programmer acts as if the body of the function were hidden from view.

Writing and using functions as if they were black boxes is also called **procedural abstraction**. When programming in C++ it might make more sense to call it *functional abstraction*. However, *procedure* is a more general term than *function* and computer scientists use it for all "function-like" sets of instructions, and so they prefer the term *procedural abstraction*. The term *abstraction* is intended to convey the idea that when you use a function as a black box, you are abstracting away the details of the code contained in the function body. You can call this technique the *black box principle* or the *principle of procedural abstraction* or *information hiding*. The three terms mean the same thing. Whatever you call this principle, the important point is that you should use it when designing and writing your function definitions.

Procedural Abstraction

When applied to a function definition, the principle of *procedural abstraction* means that your function should be written so that it can be used like a *black box*. This means that the programmer who uses the function should not need to look at the body of the function definition to see how the function works. The function declaration and the accompanying comment should be all the programmer needs to know in order to use the function. To ensure that your function definitions have this important property, you should strictly adhere to the following rules:

HOW TO WRITE A BLACK-BOX FUNCTION DEFINITION

■ The function declaration comment should tell the programmer any and all conditions that are required of the arguments to the function and should describe the result of a function invocation.

■ All variables used in the function body should be declared in the function body. (The formal parameters do not need to be declared, because they are listed in the function heading.)

Global Constants and Global Variables

As we noted in Chapter 1, you can and should name constant values using the `const` modifier. For example, in Display 3.5 we used the `const` modifier to give a name to the rate of sales tax with the following declaration:

```
const double TAXRATE = 0.05; //5% sales tax
```

If this declaration is inside the definition of a function, as in Display 3.5, then the name TAXRATE is local to the function definition, which means that outside the definition of the function that contains the declaration, you can use the name TAXRATE for another named constant, or variable, or anything else.

On the other hand, if this declaration were to appear at the beginning of your program, outside the body of all the functions (and outside the body of the main part of your program), then the named constant is said to be a **global named constant** and the named constant can be used in any function definition that follows the constant declaration.

Display 3.9 shows a program with an example of a global named constant. The program asks for a radius and then computes both the area of a circle and the volume of a sphere with that radius, using the following formulas:

```
area = π × (radius)²
volume = (4/3) × π × (radius)³
```

Both formulas include the constant π, which is approximately equal to 3.14159. The symbol π is the Greek letter called "pi." The program thus uses the following global named constant,

```
const double PI = 3.14159;
```

which appears outside the definition of any function (including outside the definition of main).

The compiler allows you wide latitude in where you place the declarations for your global named constants. To aid readability, however, you should place all your include directives together, all your global named constant declarations together in another group, and all your function declarations (function prototypes) together. We will follow standard practice and place all our global named constant declarations after our include and using directives and before our function declarations.

Placing all named constant declarations at the start of your program can aid readability even if the named constant is used by only one function. If the named constant might need to be changed in a future version of your program, it will be easier to find if it is at the beginning of your program. For example, placing the constant declaration for the sales tax rate at the beginning of an accounting program will make it easy to revise the program should the tax rate change.

It is possible to declare ordinary variables, without the const modifier, as **global variables**, which are accessible to all function definitions in the file. This is done similar to the way it is done for global named constants, except that the modifier const is not used in the variable declaration. However, there is seldom any need to use such global variables. Moreover, global variables can make a program harder to understand and maintain, so we urge you to avoid using them.

global named constant

global variable

Display 3.9   A Global Named Constant (part 1 of 2)

```
1    //Computes the area of a circle and the volume of a sphere.
2    //Uses the same radius for both calculations.
3    #include <iostream>
4    #include <cmath>
5    using namespace std;

6    const double PI = 3.14159;

7    double area(double radius);
8    //Returns the area of a circle with the specified radius.

9    double volume(double radius);
10   //Returns the volume of a sphere with the specified radius.

11   int main( )
12   {
13       double radiusOfBoth, areaOfCircle, volumeOfSphere;

14       cout << "Enter a radius to use for both a circle\n"
15            << "and a sphere (in inches): ";
16       cin >> radiusOfBoth;

17       areaOfCircle = area(radiusOfBoth);
18       volumeOfSphere = volume(radiusOfBoth);

19       cout << "Radius = " << radiusOfBoth << " inches\n"
20            << "Area of circle = " << areaOfCircle
21            << " square inches\n"
22            << "Volume of sphere = " << volumeOfSphere
23            << " cubic inches\n";

24       return 0;
25   }

26   double area(double radius)
27   {
28
29       return (PI * pow(radius, 2));
30   }

31   double volume(double radius)
32   {
33       return ((4.0/3.0) * PI * pow(radius, 3));
34   }
```

Display 3.9   A Global Named Constant (part 2 of 2)

Sample Dialogue

```
Enter a radius to use for both a circle
and a sphere (in inches) : 2
Radius = 2 inches
Area of circle = 12.5664 square inches
Volume of sphere = 33.5103 cubic inches
```

Self-Test Exercises

20. If you use a variable in a function definition, where should you declare the variable? In the function definition? In the main function? Any place that is convenient?

21. Suppose a function named function1 has a variable named sam declared within the definition of function1, and a function named function2 also has a variable named sam declared within the definition of function2. Will the program compile (assuming everything else is correct)? If the program will compile, will it run (assuming that everything else is correct)? If it runs, will it generate an error message when run (assuming everything else is correct)? If it runs and does not produce an error message when run, will it give the correct output (assuming everything else is correct)?

22. What is the purpose of the comment that accompanies a function declaration?

23. What is the principle of procedural abstraction as applied to function definitions?

24. What does it mean when we say the programmer who uses a function should be able to treat the function like a black box? (This question is very closely related to the previous question.)

Blocks

block

A variable declared inside a compound statement (that is, inside a pair of braces) is local to the compound statement. The name of the variable can be used for something else, such as the name of a different variable, outside the compound statement.

A compound statement with declarations is usually called a **block**. Actually, *block* and *compound statement* are two terms for the same thing. However, when we focus on variables declared within a compound statement, we normally use the term *block* rather than *compound statement* and we say that the variables declared within the block are *local to the block*.

If a variable is declared in a block, then the definition applies from the location of the declaration to the end of the block. This is usually expressed by saying that the *scope* of the declaration is from the location of the declaration to the end of the block. So if a variable is declared at the start of a block, its scope is the entire block. If the variable is declared part way through the block, the declaration does not take effect until the program reaches the location of the declaration (see Self-Test Exercise 25).

Notice that the body of a function definition is a block. Thus, a variable that is local to a function is the same thing as a variable that is local to the body of the function definition (which is a block).

Blocks

A *block* is some C++ code enclosed in braces. The variables declared in a block are local to the block, and so the variable names can be used outside the block for something else (such as being reused as the names for different variables).

Nested Scopes

Suppose you have one block nested inside another block, and suppose that one identifier is declared as a variable in each of these two blocks. These are two different variables with the same name. One variable exists only within the inner block and cannot be accessed outside that inner block. The other variable exists only in the outer block and cannot be accessed in the inner block. The two variables are distinct, so changes made to one of these variables will have no effect on the other of these two variables.

Scope Rule for Nested Blocks

If an identifier is declared as a variable in each of two blocks, one within the other, then these are two different variables with the same name. One variable exists only within the inner block and cannot be accessed outside of the inner block. The other variable exists only in the outer block and cannot be accessed in the inner block. The two variables are distinct, so changes made to one of these variables will have no effect on the other of these two variables.

TIP: Use Function Calls in Branching and Loop Statements

The `switch` statement and the `if-else` statement allow you to place several different statements in each branch. However, doing so can make the `switch` statement or `if-else` statement difficult to read. Rather than placing a compound statement in a branching statement, it is usually preferable to convert the compound statement to a

(continued)

TIP: (continued)

function definition and place a function call in the branch. Similarly, if a loop body is large, it is preferable to convert the compound statement to a function definition and make the loop body a function call. ■

Variables Declared in a for Loop

A variable may be declared in the heading of a `for` statement so that the variable is both declared and initialized at the start of the `for` statement. For example,

```
for (int n = 1; n <= 10; n++)
    sum = sum + n;
```

The ANSI/ISO C++ standard requires that a C++ compiler that claims compliance with the standard treat any declaration in a `for` loop initializer as if it were local to the body of the loop. Earlier C++ compilers did not do this. You should determine how your compiler treats variables declared in a `for` loop initializer. If portability is critical to your application, you should not write code that depends on this behavior. Eventually, all widely used C++ compilers will likely comply with this rule, but compilers presently available may or may not comply.

Self-Test Exercise

25. Though we urge you not to program using this style, we are providing an exercise that uses nested blocks to help you understand the scope rules. State the output that this code fragment would produce if embedded in an otherwise complete, correct program.

```
{
    int x = 1;
    cout << x << endl;
    {
        cout << x << endl;
        int x = 2;
        cout << x << endl;
        {
            cout << x << endl;
            int x = 3;
            cout << x << endl;
        }
        cout << x << endl;
    }
    cout << x << endl;
}
```

Chapter Summary

- There are two kinds of functions in C++: functions that return a value and `void` functions.

- A function should be defined so that it can be used as a black box. The programmer who uses the function should not need to know any details about how the function is coded. All the programmer should need to know is the function declaration and the accompanying comment that describes the value returned. This rule is sometimes called the principle of procedural abstraction.

- A good way to write a function declaration comment is to use a precondition and a postcondition. The precondition states what is assumed to be true when the function is called. The postcondition describes the effect of the function call; that is, the postcondition tells what will be true after the function is executed in a situation in which the precondition holds.

- A variable that is declared in a function definition is said to be local to the function.

- A formal parameter is a kind of placeholder that is filled in with a function argument when the function is called. The details on this "filling in" process are covered in Chapter 4.

Answers to Self-Test Exercises

1. a. `4.0    4.0    8.0`
   b. `8.0    8.0    1.21`
   c. `3      3      0`
   d. `3.0    3.5    3.5`
   e. `6.0    6.0    5.0`
   f. `5.0    4.5    4.5`
       `3      3.0    3.0`

2. a. `sqrt(x + y)`
   b. `pow(x, y + 7)`
   c. `sqrt(area + fudge)`
   d. `sqrt(time+tide)/nobody`
   e. `(-b + sqrt(b*b - 4*a*c))/(2*a)`
   f. `abs(x - y)` or `labs(x - y)` or `fabs(x - y)`

3. ```
   #include <iostream>
   #include <cmath>
   using namespace std;
   int main( )
   {
       int i;
   ```
   ```

```
    for (i = 1; i <= 10; i++)
        cout << "The square root of " << i
             << " is " << sqrt(i) << endl;

    return 0;
}
```

4. The argument is given to the operating system. As far as your C++ program is concerned, you can use any int value as the argument. By convention, however, 1 is used for a call to exit that is caused by an error, and 0 is used in other cases.

5. `(5 + (rand( ) % 6))`

6.
```
#include <iostream>
#include <cstdlib>
using namespace std;

int main( )
{
    cout << "Enter a nonnegative integer to use as the\n"
         << "seed for the random number generator: ";

    unsigned int seed;

    cin >> seed;
    srand(seed);

    cout << "Here are ten random probabilities:\n";
    int i;
    for (i = 0; i < 10; i++)
    cout << ((RAND_MAX - rand( ))/static_cast<double>(RAND_MAX))
         << endl;

    return 0;
}
```

7. Wow

8. The function declaration is

```
int sum(int n1, int n2, int n3);
//Returns the sum of n1, n2, and n3.
```

The function definition is

```
int sum(int n1, int n2, int n3)
{
    return (n1 + n2 + n3);
}
```

9. The function declaration is

```
char positiveTest(double number);
//Returns 'P' if number is positive.
//Returns 'N' if number is negative or zero.
```

The function definition is

```
char positiveTest(double number)
{
    if (number > 0)
        return 'P';
    else
        return 'N';
}
```

10. No, a function definition cannot appear inside the body of another function definition.
11. Predefined functions and user-defined functions are invoked (called) in the same way.
12.
```
bool inOrder(int n1, int n2, int n3)
{
    return ((n1 <= n2) && (n2 <= n3));
}
```
13.
```
bool even(int n)
{
    return ((n % 2) == 0);
}
```
14.
```
bool isDigit(char ch)
{
    return ('0' <= ch) && (ch <= '9');
}
```
15.
```
Hello
Goodbye
One more time:
Hello
Hello
End of program.
```
16. If you omitted the return statement in the function definition for iceCreamDivision in Display 3.7, the program would compile and run. However, if you input zero for the number of customers, then the program would produce a run-time error because of a division by zero.

17.
```
#include <iostream>
using namespace std;
void productOut(int n1, int n2, int n3);
int main( )
{
    int num1, num2, num3;
    cout << "Enter three integers: ";
    cin >> num1 >> num2 >> num3;
    productOut(num1, num2, num3);
    return 0;
}
```

```
void productOut(int n1, int n2, int n3)
{
    cout << "The product of the three numbers "
         << n1 << ", " << n2 << ", and "
         << n3 << " is " << (n1*n2*n3) << endl;
}
```

18. These answers are system-dependent.

19. `double sqrt(double n);`
    `//Precondition: n >= 0.`
    `//Returns the square root of n.`

    You can rewrite the second comment line as follows if you prefer, but the previous version is the usual form used for a function that returns a value:

    `//Postcondition: Returns the square root of n.`

20. If you use a variable in a function definition, you should declare the variable in the body of the function definition.

21. Everything will be fine. The program will compile (assuming everything else is correct). The program will run (assuming that everything else is correct). The program will not generate an error message when run (assuming everything else is correct). The program will give the correct output (assuming everything else is correct).

22. The comment explains what action the function takes, including any value returned, and gives any other information that you need to know in order to use the function.

23. The principle of procedural abstraction says that a function should be written so that it can be used like a black box. This means that the programmer who uses the function need not look at the body of the function definition to see how the function works. The function declaration and accompanying comment should be all the programmer needs in order to use the function.

24. When we say that the programmer who uses a function should be able to treat the function like a black box, we mean the programmer should not need to look at the body of the function definition to see how the function works. The function declaration and accompanying comment should be all the programmer needs in order to use the function.

25. It helps to slightly change the code fragment to understand to which declaration each usage resolves. The code has three different variables named x. In the following we have renamed these three variables x1, x2, and x3. The output is given in the comments.

```
int x1 = 1; // output in this column
cout << x1 << endl; // 1<new line>
{
    cout << x1 << endl; // 1<new line>
    int x2 = 2;
```

```
    cout << x2 << endl; // 2<new line>
    {
        cout << x2 << endl; // 2<new line>
        int x3 = 3;
        cout << x3 << endl; // 3<new line>
    }
    cout << x2 << endl; // 2<new line>
}
    cout << x1 << endl; // 1<new line>
}
```

Programming Projects

Visit www.myprogramminglab.com to complete select exercises online and get instant feedback.

1. A liter is 0.264179 gallons. Write a program that will read in the number of liters of gasoline consumed by the user's car and the number of miles traveled by the car and will then output the number of miles per gallon the car delivered. Your program should allow the user to repeat this calculation as often as the user wishes. Define a function to compute the number of miles per gallon. Your program should use a globally defined constant for the number of liters per gallon.

2. Write a program to gauge the rate of inflation for the past year. The program asks for the price of an item (such as a hot dog or a one-carat diamond) both one year ago and today. It estimates the inflation rate as the difference in price divided by the year-ago price. Your program should allow the user to repeat this calculation as often as the user wishes. Define a function to compute the rate of inflation. The inflation rate should be a value of type double giving the rate as a percentage, for example 5.3 for 5.3%.

3. Enhance your program from the previous exercise by having it also print out the estimated price of the item in one and in two years from the time of the calculation. The increase in cost over one year is estimated as the inflation rate times the price at the start of the year. Define a second function to determine the estimated cost of an item in a specified number of years, given the current price of the item and the inflation rate as arguments.

4. The gravitational attractive force between two bodies with masses m_1 and m_2 separated by a distance d is given by the following formula,

$$F = \frac{Gm_1m_2}{d^2}$$

where G is the universal gravitational constant:

$$G = 6.673 \times 10^{-8} \text{ cm}^3/(\text{g} \cdot \text{sec}^2)$$

Write a function definition that takes arguments for the masses of two bodies and the distance between them and returns the gravitational force between them.

Since you will use the previous formula, the gravitational force will be in dynes. One dyne equals a

$$g \bullet \text{cm/sec}^2$$

You should use a globally defined constant for the universal gravitational constant. Embed your function definition in a complete program that computes the gravitational force between two objects given suitable inputs. Your program should allow the user to repeat this calculation as often as the user wishes.

5. Write a program that asks for the user's height, weight, and age, and then computes clothing sizes according to the following formulas.

- Hat size = weight in pounds divided by height in inches and all that multiplied by 2.9.

- Jacket size (chest in inches) = height times weight divided by 288 and then adjusted by adding one-eighth of an inch for each 10 years over age 30. (Note that the adjustment only takes place after a full 10 years. So, there is no adjustment for ages 30 through 39, but one-eighth of an inch is added for age 40.)

- Waist in inches = weight divided by 5.7 and then adjusted by adding one-tenth of an inch for each 2 years over age 28. (Note that the adjustment only takes place after a full 2 years. So, there is no adjustment for age 29, but one-tenth of an inch is added for age 30.)

Use functions for each calculation. Your program should allow the user to repeat this calculation as often as he or she wishes.

6. Write a function that computes the average and standard deviation of four scores. The standard deviation is defined to be the square root of the average of the four values: $(s_i - a)^2$, where a is the average of the four scores s_1, s_2, s_3, and s_4. The function will have six parameters and will call two other functions. Embed the function in a program that allows you to test the function again and again until you tell the program you are finished.

7. In cold weather, meteorologists report an index called the *wind chill factor*, which takes into account the wind speed and the temperature. The index provides a measure of the chilling effect of wind at a given air temperature. Wind chill may be approximated by the following formula,

$$w = 33 - \frac{(10\sqrt{v} - v + 10.5)(33 - t)}{23.1}$$

where

$v =$ wind speed in m/sec

$t =$ temperature in degrees Celsius: $t <= 10$

$W =$ wind chill index (in degrees Celsius)

Write a function that returns the wind chill index. Your code should ensure that the restriction on the temperature is not violated. Look up some weather reports in back issues of a newspaper in your library and compare the wind chill index you calculate with the result reported in the newspaper.

8. Write a program that outpus all 99 stanzas of the "Ninety-Nine Bottles of Beer on the Wall" song. Your program should print the number of bottles in English, not as a number:

Ninety-nine bottles of beer on the wall,

Ninety-nine bottles of beer,

Take one down, pass it around,

Ninety-eight bottles of beer on the wall.

...

One bottle of beer on the wall,

One bottle of beer,

Take one down, pass it around,

Zero bottles of beer on the wall.

Your program should not use ninety-nine different output statements!

9. In the game of craps, a "Pass Line" bet proceeds as follows. The first roll of the two, six-sided dice in a craps round is called the "come out roll." The bet immediately wins when the come out roll is 7 or 11, and loses when the come out roll is 2, 3, or 12. If 4, 5, 6, 8, 9, or 10 is rolled on the come out roll, that number becomes "the point." The player keeps rolling the dice until either 7 or the point is rolled. If the point is rolled first, then the player wins the bet. If the player rolls a 7 first, then the player loses.

Write a program that plays craps using those rules so that it simulates a game without human input. Instead of asking for a wager, the program should calculate whether the player would win or lose. Create a function that simulates rolling the two dice and returns the sum. Add a loop so that the program plays 10,000 games. Add counters that count how many times the player wins, and how many times the player loses. At the end of the 10,000 games, compute the probability of winning, as Wins / (Wins + Losses), and output this value. Over the long run, who is going to win more games of craps, you or the house?

10. One way to estimate the height of a child is to use the following formula, which uses the height of the parents:

$$H_{male\_child} = ((H_{mother} \cdot 13/12) + H_{father})/2$$

$$H_{female\_child} = ((H_{father} \cdot 12/13) + H_{mother})/2$$

All heights are in inches. Write a function that takes as input parameters the gender of the child, height of the mother in inches, and height of the father in inches, and outputs the estimated height of the child in inches. Embed your function in a program that allows you to test the function over and over again until telling the program to exit. The user should be able to input the heights in feet and inches, and the program should output the estimated height of the child in feet and inches. Use the integer data type to store the heights.

11. The game of Pig is a simple two player dice game in which the first player to reach 100 or more points wins. Players take turns. On each turn a player rolls a six-sided die:

   • If the player rolls a 2–6 then he or she can either

      — ROLL AGAIN or

      — HOLD. At this point the sum of all rolls made this turn is added to the player's total score and it becomes the other player's turn.

   • If the player rolls a 1 then the player loses his or her turn. The player gets no new points and it becomes the opponent's turn.

   If a player reaches 100 or more points after holding then the player wins.

   Write a program that plays the game of Pig, where one player is a human and the other is the computer. Allow the human to input "r" to roll again or "h" to hold.

   The computer program should play according to the following rule: Keep rolling on the computer's turn until it has accumulated 20 or more points, then hold. Of course, if the computer wins or rolls a 1 then the turn ends immediately. Allow the human to roll first.

   Write your program using at least two functions:

   ```
   int humanTurn(int humanTotalScore);
   int computerTurn(int computerTotalScore);
   ```

   These functions should perform the necessary logic to handle a single turn for either the computer or the human. The input parameter is the total score for the human or computer. The functions should return the turn total to be added to the total score upon completion of the turn. For example, if the human rolls a 3 and 6 and then holds, then humanTurn should return 9. However, if the human rolls a 3 and 6 and then a 1, then the function should return 0.

12. Write a program that inputs a date (e.g., July 4, 2008) and outputs the day of the week that corresponds to that date. The following algorithm is from http://en.wikipedia.org/wiki/Calculating_the_day_of_the_week. The implementation will require several functions:

   ```
   bool isLeapYear(int year);
   ```

   This function should return true if year is a leap year and false if it is not. Here is pseudocode to determine a leap year:

      leap_year = ((year divisible by 400) or (year divisible by 4 and year not divisible by 100))

   ```
   int getCenturyValue(int year);
   ```

   This function should take the first two digits of the year (i.e., the century), divide by 4, and save the remainder. Subtract the remainder from 3 and return this value multiplied by 2. For example, the year 2008 becomes (20/4) = 5 remainder 0. 3 − 0 = 3. Return 3 * 2 = 6.

   ```
   int getYearValue(int year);
   ```

This function computes a value based on the years since the beginning of the century. First, extract the last two digits of the year. For example, 08 is extracted for 2008. Next, factor in leap years. Divide the value from the previous step by 4 and discard the remainder. Add the two results together and return this value. For example, from 2008 we extract 08. Then (8/4) = 2 remainder 0. Return 2 + 8 = 10.

`int getMonthValue(int month, int year);`

This function should return a value based on the following table and will require invoking the `isLeapYear` function:

MONTH	RETURN VALUE
January	0 (6 if year is a leap year)
February	3 (2 if year is a leap year)
March	3
April	6
May	1
June	4
July	6
August	2
September	5
October	0
November	3
December	5

Finally, to compute the day of the week, compute the sum of the date's day plus the values returned by getMonthValue, getYearValue, and getCenturyValue. Divide the sum by 7 and compute the remainder. A remainder of 0 corresponds to Sunday, 1 corresponds to Monday, etc.—up to 6—which corresponds to Saturday. For example, the date July 4, 2008 should be computed as (day of month) + (getMonthValue) + (getYearValue) + (getCenturyValue) = 4 + 6 + 10 + 6 = 26. 26/7 = 3 remainder 5. The fifth day of the week corresponds to Friday.

Your program should allow the user to enter any date and output the corresponding day of the week in English.

13. You have four identical prizes to give away and a pool of 25 finalists. The finalists are assigned numbers from 1 to 25. Write a program to randomly select the numbers of 4 finalists to receive a prize. Make sure not to pick the same number twice. For example, picking finalists 3, 15, 22, and 14 would be valid but picking 3, 3, 31, and 17 would be invalid, because finalist number 3 is listed twice and 31 is not a valid finalist number.

14. Programming Project 2.9 asked you to implement the Babylonian Algorithm to compute the square root of a number.

Put this algorithm into a function and test it by using it to calculate the square root of several numbers. The function should return the square root as a double and also process the number **n** as a double.

Parameters and Overloading 4

Parameters and Overloading

Introduction

This chapter discusses the details of the mechanisms used by C++ for plugging in arguments for parameters in function calls. It also discusses overloading, which is a way to give two (or more) different function definitions to the same function name. Finally, it goes over some basic techniques for testing functions.

4.1   Parameters

You can't put a square peg in a round hole.

Common saying

This section describes the details of the mechanisms used by C++ for plugging in an argument for a formal parameter when a function is invoked. There are two basic kinds of parameters and therefore two basic plugging-in mechanisms in C++. The two basic kinds of parameters are *call-by-value parameters* and *call-by-reference parameters*. All the parameters that appeared before this point in the book were call-by-value parameters. With **call-by-value parameters**, only the value of the argument is plugged in. With **call-by-reference parameters**, the argument is a variable and the variable itself is plugged in; therefore, the variable's value can be changed by the function invocation. A call-by-reference parameter is indicated by appending the ampersand sign, &, to the parameter type, as illustrated by the following function declarations:

```
void getInput(double& variableOne, int& variableTwo);
```

A call-by-value parameter is indicated by not using the ampersand. The details on call-by-value and call-by-reference parameters are given in the following subsections.

Call-by-Value Parameters

Call-by-value parameters are more than just blanks that are filled in with the argument values for the function. A call-by-value parameter is actually a local variable. When the function is invoked, the value of a call-by-value argument is computed and the corresponding call-by-value parameter, which is a local variable, is initialized to this value.

In most cases, you can think of a call-by-value parameter as a kind of blank, or placeholder, that is filled in by the value of its corresponding argument in the function invocation. However, in some cases it is handy to use a call-by-value parameter as a local variable and change the value of the parameter within the body of the function

call-by-value parameter

call-by-reference parameter

definition. For example, the program in Display 4.1 illustrates a call-by-value parameter used as a local variable whose value is changed in the body of the function definition. Notice the formal parameter minutesWorked in the definition of the function fee. It is used as a variable and has its value changed by the following line, which occurs within the function definition:

```
minutesWorked = hoursWorked*60 + minutesWorked;
```

Display 4.1 Formal Parameter Used as a Local Variable (part 1 of 2)

```
1   //Law office billing program.
2   #include <iostream>
3   using namespace std;

4   const double RATE = 150.00; //Dollars per quarter hour.

5   double fee(int hoursWorked, int minutesWorked);
6   //Returns the charges for hoursWorked hours and
7   //minutesWorked minutes of legal services.

8   int main( )
9   {
10      int hours, minutes;
11      double bill;

12      cout << "Welcome to the law office of\n"
13           << "Dewey, Cheatham, and Howe.\n"
14           << "The law office with a heart.\n"
15           << "Enter the hours and minutes"
16           << " of your consultation:\n";
17      cin >> hours >> minutes;

18      bill = fee(hours, minutes);

19      cout.setf(ios::fixed);
20      cout.setf(ios::showpoint);
21      cout.precision(2);
22      cout << "For " << hours << " hours and " << minutes
23           << " minutes, your bill is $" << bill << endl;

24      return 0;
25  }
26  double fee(int hoursWorked, int minutesWorked)
27  {
28      int quarterHours;

29      minutesWorked = hoursWorked*60 + minutesWorked;
30      quarterHours = minutesWorked/15;
31      return (quarterHours*RATE);
32  }
```

The value of minutes is not changed by the call to fee.

minutesWorked is a local variable initialized to the value of minutes.

(continued)

Display 4.1   Formal Parameter Used as a Local Variable (part 2 of 2)

Sample Dialogue

```
Welcome to the law office of
Dewey, Cheatham, and Howe.
The law office with a heart.
Enter the hours and minutes of your consultation:
5 46
For 5 hours and 46 minutes, your bill is $3450.00
```

Call-by-value parameters are local variables just like the variables you declare within the body of a function. However, you should not add a variable declaration for the formal parameters. Listing the formal parameter `minutesWorked` in the function heading also serves as the variable declaration. The following is the *wrong way* to start the function definition for `fee` because it declares `minutesWorked` twice:

```
double fee(int hoursWorked, int minutesWorked)
{
    int quarterHours;
    int minutesWorked;  ◄──── minutesWorked
                              is a parameter!
                                    Do not do this when
                                    minutesWorked
                                    is a parameter!
```

. . .

Self-Test Exercises

1. Carefully describe the call-by-value parameter mechanism.

2. The following function is supposed to take as arguments a length expressed in feet and inches and to return the total number of inches in that many feet and inches. For example, `totalInches(1, 2)` is supposed to return 14, because 1 foot and 2 inches is the same as 14 inches. Will the following function perform correctly? If not, why not?

```
double totalInches(int feet, int inches)
{
    inches = 12*feet + inches;
    return inches;
}
```

A First Look at Call-by-Reference Parameters

The call-by-value mechanism that we used until now is not sufficient for all tasks you might want a function to perform. For example, one common task for a function is to obtain an input value from the user and set the value of an argument variable to this input value. With the call-by-value formal parameters that we have used until now,

ampersand, &

a corresponding argument in a function call can be a variable, but the function takes only the value of the variable and does not change the variable in any way. With a call-by-value formal parameter only the *value* of the argument is substituted for the formal parameter. For an input function, you want the *variable* (not the value of the variable) to be substituted for the formal parameter. The call-by-reference mechanism works in just this way. With a call-by-reference formal parameter, the corresponding argument in a function call must be a variable, and this argument variable is substituted for the formal parameter. It is almost as if the argument variable were literally copied into the body of the function definition in place of the formal parameter. After the argument is substituted in, the code in the function body is executed and can change the value of the argument variable.

A call-by-reference parameter must be marked in some way so that the compiler will know it from a call-by-value parameter. The way that you indicate a call-by-reference parameter is to attach the **ampersand sign**, &, to the end of the type name in the formal parameter list. This is done in both the function declaration (function prototype) and the header of the function definition. For example, the following function definition has one formal parameter, receiver, which is a call-by-reference parameter:

```
void getInput(double& receiver)
{
    cout << "Enter input number:\n";
    cin >> receiver;
}
```

In a program that contains this function definition, the following function call will set the double variable inputNumber equal to a value read from the keyboard:

```
getInput(inputNumber);
```

C++ allows you to place the ampersand either with the type name or with the parameter name, so you will sometimes see

```
void getInput(double &receiver);
```

which is equivalent to

```
void getInput(double& receiver);
```

Display 4.2 demonstrates call-by-reference parameters. The program reads in two numbers and writes the same numbers out, but in the reverse order. The parameters in the functions getNumbers and swapValues are call-by-reference parameters. The input is performed by the function call

```
getNumbers(firstNum, secondNum);
```

The values of the variables firstNum and secondNum are set by this function call. After that, the following function call reverses the values in the two variables firstNum and secondNum:

```
swapValues(firstNum, secondNum);
```

Display 4.2   Call-by-Reference Parameters

```
1   //Program to demonstrate call-by-reference parameters.
2   #include <iostream>
3   using namespace std;

4   void getNumbers(int& input1, int& input2);
5   //Reads two integers from the keyboard.

6   void swapValues(int& variable1, int& variable2);
7   //Interchanges the values of variable1 and variable2.

8   void showResults(int output1, int output2);
9   //Shows the values of output1 and output2, in that order.

10  int main( )
11  {
12      int firstNum, secondNum;

13      getNumbers(firstNum, secondNum);
14      swapValues(firstNum, secondNum);
15      showResults(firstNum, secondNum);
16      return 0;
17  }

18  void getNumbers(int& input1, int& input2)
19  {
20      cout << "Enter two integers: ";
21      cin >> input1
22          >> input2;
23  }

24  void swapValues(int& variable1, int& variable2)
25  {
26      int temp;

27      temp = variable1;
28      variable1 = variable2;
29      variable2 = temp;
30  }

31  void showResults(int output1, int output2)
32  {
33      cout << "In reverse order the numbers are: "
34          << output1 << " " << output2 << endl;
35          << output1 << " " << output2 << endl;
36  }
```

Sample Dialogue

```
Enter two integers: 5 6
In reverse order the numbers are: 6 5
```

The next few subsections describe the call-by-reference mechanism in more detail and also explain the particular functions used in Display 4.2.

Call-by-Reference Parameters

To make a formal parameter a call-by-reference parameter, append the ampersand sign, &, to its type name. The corresponding argument in a call to the function should then be a variable, not a constant or other expression. When the function is called, the corresponding variable argument (not its value) will be substituted for the formal parameter. Any change made to the formal parameter in the function body will be made to the argument variable when the function is called. The exact details of the substitution mechanisms are given in the text of this chapter.

EXAMPLE

```
void getData(int& firstInput, double& secondInput);
```

Call-by-Reference Mechanism in Detail

In most situations the call-by-reference mechanism works as if the name of the variable given as the function argument were literally substituted for the call-by-reference formal parameter. However, the process is a bit more subtle than that. In some situations, this subtlety is important, so we need to examine more details of this call-by-reference substitution process.

Program variables are implemented as memory locations. Each memory location has a unique **address** that is a number. The compiler assigns one memory location to each variable. For example, when the program in Display 4.2 is compiled, the variable firstNum might be assigned location 1010, and the variable secondNum might be assigned 1012. For all practical purposes, these memory locations are the variables. For example, consider the following function declaration from Display 4.2:

```
void getNumbers(int& input1, int& input2);
```

The call-by-reference formal parameters input1 and input2 are placeholders for the actual arguments used in a function call.

Now consider a function call like the following from the same program:

```
getNumbers(firstNum, secondNum);
```

When the function call is executed, the function is *not* given the argument names firstNum and secondNum. Instead, it is given a list of the memory locations associated with each name. In this example, the list consists of the locations

```
1010
1012
```

which are the locations assigned to the argument variables firstNum and secondNum, *in that order*. It is these memory locations that are associated with the formal parameters.

address

The first memory location is associated with the first formal parameter, the second memory location is associated with the second formal parameter, and so forth. Diagrammatically, in this case, the correspondence is

```
firstNum   ⟶ 1010 ⟶ input1
secondNum  ⟶ 1012 ⟶ input2
```

When the function statements are executed, whatever the function body says to do to a formal parameter is actually done to the variable in the memory location associated with that formal parameter. In this case, the instructions in the body of the function getNumbers say that a value should be stored in the variable in the formal parameter input1 using a cin statement, and so that value is stored in the variable in memory location 1010 (which happens to be the variable firstNum). Similarly, the instructions in the body of the function getNumbers say that another value should then be stored in the formal parameter input2 using a cin statement, and so that value is stored in the variable in memory location 1012 (which happens to be the variable secondNum). Thus, whatever the function instructs the computer to do to input1 and input2 is actually done to the variables firstNum and secondNum.

It may seem that there is an extra level of detail, or at least an extra level of verbiage. If firstNum is the variable with memory location 1010, why do we insist on saying "the variable at memory location 1010" instead of simply saying "firstNum?" This extra level of detail is needed if the arguments and formal parameters contain some confusing coincidence of names. For example, the function getNumbers has formal parameters named input1 and input2. Suppose you want to change the program in Display 4.2 so that it uses the function getNumbers with arguments that are also named input1 and input2, and suppose that you want to do something less than obvious. Suppose you want the first number typed in to be stored in a variable named input2, and the second number typed in to be stored in the variable named input1—perhaps because the second number will be processed first or because it is the more important number. Now, let's suppose that the variables input1 and input2, which are declared in the main part of your program, have been assigned memory locations 1014 and 1016. The function call could be as follows:

```
int input1, input2;
getNumbers(input2, input1); ⟵
```

Notice the order
of the arguments.

In this case if you say "input1," we do not know whether you mean the variable named input1 that is declared in the main part of your program or the formal parameter input1. However, if the variable input1 declared in the main function of your program is assigned memory location 1014, the phrase "the variable at memory location 1014" is unambiguous. Let's go over the details of the substitution mechanisms in this case.

In this call the argument corresponding to the formal parameter input1 is the variable input2, and the argument corresponding to the formal parameter input2 is the variable input1. This can be confusing to us, but it produces no problem at all for the computer, since the computer never does actually "substitute input2 for input1" or "substitute input1 for input2." The computer simply deals with memory locations. The computer substitutes "the variable at memory location 1016" for the formal parameter input1, and "the variable at memory location 1014" for the formal parameter input2.

Constant Reference Parameters

We place this subsection here for reference value. If you are reading this book in order, you may as well skip this section. The topic is explained in more detail later in the book.

If you place a const before a call-by-reference parameter's type, you get a call-by-reference parameter that cannot be changed. For the types we have seen so far, this has no advantages. However, it will turn out to be an aid to efficiency with array and class type parameters. We will discuss these constant parameters when we discuss arrays and when we discuss classes.

EXAMPLE: The swapValues Function

The function swapValues defined in Display 4.2 interchanges the values stored in two variables. The description of the function is given by the following function declaration and accompanying comment:

```
void swapValues(int& variable1, int& variable2);
//Interchanges the values of variable1 and variable2.
```

To see how the function is supposed to work, assume that the variable firstNum has the value 5 and the variable secondNum has the value 6 and consider the following function call:

```
swapValues(firstNum, secondNum);
```

After this function call, the value of firstNum will be 6 and the value of secondNum will be 5.

As shown in Display 4.2, the definition of the function swapValues uses a local variable called temp. This local variable is needed. You might be tempted to think the function definition could be simplified to the following:

```
void swapValues(int& variable1, int& variable2)
{
    variable1 = variable2;              This does not work!
    variable2 = variable1;
}
```

To see that this alternative definition cannot work, consider what would happen with this definition and the function call

```
swapValues(firstNum, secondNum);
```

(continued)

EXAMPLE: (continued)

The variables `firstNum` and `secondNum` would be substituted for the formal parameters `variable1` and `variable2` so that with this incorrect function definition, the function call would be equivalent to the following:

```
firstNum = secondNum;
secondNum = firstNum;
```

This code does not produce the desired result. The value of `firstNum` is set equal to the value of `secondNum`, just as it should be. But then, the value of `secondNum` is set equal to the changed value of `firstNum`, which is now the original value of `secondNum`. Thus, the value of `secondNum` is not changed at all. (If this is unclear, go through the steps with specific values for the variables `firstNum` and `secondNum`.) What the function needs to do is save the original value of `firstNum` so that value is not lost. This is what the local variable `temp` in the correct function definition is used for. That correct definition is the one in Display 4.2. When that correct version is used and the function is called with the arguments `firstNum` and `secondNum`, the function call is equivalent to the following code, which works correctly:

```
temp = firstNum;
firstNum = secondNum;
secondNum = temp;
```

TIP: Think of Actions, Not Code

Although we can explain how a function call works in terms of substituting code for the function call, that is not the way you should normally think about a function call. You should instead think of a function call as an action. For example, consider the function `swapValues` in Display 4.2 and an invocation such as

```
swapValues(firstNum, secondNum);
```

It is easier and clearer to think of this function call as the action of swapping the values of its two arguments. It is much less clear to think of it as the code

```
temp = firstNum;
firstNum = secondNum;
secondNum = temp;
```
■

Self-Test Exercises

3. What is the output of the following program?

```
#include <iostream>
using namespace std;
```

Self-Test Exercises (continued)

```
void figureMeOut(int& x, int y, int& z);

int main( )
{
    int a, b, c;
    a = 10;
    b = 20;
    c = 30;
    figureMeOut(a, b, c);
    cout << a << " " << b << " " << c << endl;
    return 0;
}
void figureMeOut(int& x, int y, int& z)
{
    cout << x << " " << y << " " << z << endl;
    x = 1;
    y = 2;
    z = 3;
    cout << x << " " << y << " " << z << endl;
}
```

4. What would be the output of the program in Display 4.2 if you omitted the ampersands (&) from the first parameter in the function declaration and function heading of swapValues? The ampersand is not removed from the second parameter. Assume the user enters numbers as in the sample dialogue in Display 4.2.

5. Write a void function definition for a function called zeroBoth that has two call-by-reference parameters, both of which are variables of type int, and sets the values of both variables to 0.

6. Write a void function definition for a function called addTax. The function addTax has two formal parameters: taxRate, which is the amount of sales tax expressed as a percentage; and cost, which is the cost of an item before tax. The function changes the value of cost so that it includes sales tax.

Mixed Parameter Lists

Whether a formal parameter is a call-by-value parameter or a call-by-reference parameter is determined by whether there is an ampersand attached to its type specification. If the ampersand is present, the formal parameter is a call-by-reference parameter. If there is no ampersand associated with the formal parameter, it is a call-by-value parameter.

mixing
call-by-
reference
and
call-by-value
parameters

It is perfectly legitimate to mix call-by-value and call-by-reference formal parameters in the same function. For example, the first and last of the formal parameters in the following function declaration are call-by-reference formal parameters, and the middle one is a call-by-value parameter:

```
void goodStuff(int& par1, int par2, double& par3);
```

Call-by-reference parameters are not restricted to `void` functions. You can also use them in functions that return a value. Thus, a function with a call-by-reference parameter could both change the value of a variable given as an argument and return a value.

Parameters and Arguments

All the different terms that have to do with parameters and arguments can be confusing. However, if you keep a few simple points in mind, you will be able to easily handle these terms.

1. The *formal parameters* for a function are listed in the function declaration and are used in the body of the function definition. A formal parameter (of any sort) is a kind of blank or placeholder that is filled in with something when the function is called.

2. An *argument* is something that is used to fill in a formal parameter. When you write down a function call, the arguments are listed in parentheses after the function name. When the function call is executed, the arguments are plugged in for the formal *parameters*.

3. The terms *call-by-value* and *call-by-reference* refer to the mechanism that is used in the plugging-in process. In the *call-by-value* method only the value of the argument is used. In this call-by-value mechanism, the formal parameter is a local variable that is initialized to the value of the corresponding argument. In the *call-by-reference* mechanism the argument is a variable and the entire variable is used. In the call-by-reference mechanism the argument variable is substituted for the formal parameter so that any change that is made to the formal parameter is actually made to the argument variable.

TIP: What Kind of Parameter to Use

Display 4.3 illustrates the differences between how the compiler treats call-by-value and call-by-reference formal parameters. The parameters par1Value and par2Ref are both assigned a value inside the body of the function definition. Because they are different kinds of parameters, however, the effect is different in the two cases. par1Value is a call-by-value parameter, so it is a local variable. When the function is called as follows,

```
doStuff(n1, n2);
```

the local variable par1Value is initialized to the value of n1. That is, the local variable par1Value is initialized to 1 and the variable n1 is then ignored by the function. As you can see from the sample dialogue, the formal parameter par1Value (which

TIP: (continued)

is a local variable) is set to 111 in the function body, and this value is output to the screen. However, the value of the argument n1 is not changed. As shown in the sample dialogue, n1 has retained its value of 1.

On the other hand, par2Ref is a call-by-reference parameter. When the function is called, the variable argument n2 (not just its value) is substituted for the formal parameter par2Ref. So when the following code is executed,

```
par2Ref = 222;
```

it is the same as if the following were executed:

```
n2 = 222;
```

Thus, the value of the variable n2 is changed when the function body is executed, so, as the dialogue shows, the value of n2 is changed from 2 to 222 by the function call. If you keep in mind the lesson of Display 4.3, it is easy to decide which parameter mechanism to use. If you want a function to change the value of a variable, then the corresponding formal parameter must be a call-by-reference formal parameter and must be marked with the ampersand sign, &. In all other cases, you can use a call-by-value formal parameter. ∎

Display 4.3   Comparing Argument Mechanisms (part 1 of 2)

```
1   //Illustrates the difference between a call-by-value
2   //parameter and a call-by-reference parameter.
3   #include <iostream>
4   using namespace std;

5   void doStuff(int par1Value, int& par2Ref);
6   //par1Value is a call-by-value formal parameter and
7   //par2Ref is a call-by-reference formal parameter.

8   int main( )
9   {
10      int n1, n2;

11
12      n1 = 1;
13      n2 = 2;

14      doStuff(n1, n2);
15      cout << "n1 after function call = " << n1 << endl;
16      cout << "n2 after function call = " << n2 << endl;
17      return 0;
18  }

19  void doStuff(int par1Value, int& par2Ref)
20  {
21      par1Value = 111;
```

(continued)

Display 4.3 Comparing Argument Mechanisms (part 2 of 2)

```
22      cout << "par1Value in function call = "
23           << par1Value << endl;
24      par2Ref = 222;
25      cout << "par2Ref in function call = "
26           << par2Ref << endl;
27  }
```

Sample Dialogue

```
par1Value in function call = 111
par2Ref in function call = 222
n1 after function call = 1
n2 after function call = 222
```

PITFALL: Inadvertent Local Variables

If you want a function to change the value of a variable, the corresponding formal parameter must be a call-by-reference parameter and therefore must have the ampersand, &, attached to its type. If you carelessly omit the ampersand, the function will have a call-by-value parameter where you meant to have a call-by-reference parameter. When the program is run, you will discover that the function call does not change the value of the corresponding argument, because a formal call-by-value parameter is a local variable. If the parameter has its value changed in the function, then, as with any local variable, that change has no effect outside the function body. This is an error that can be very difficult to see because the code *looks* right.

For example, the program in Display 4.4 is similar to the program in Display 4.2 except that the ampersands were mistakenly omitted from the function swapValues. As a result, the formal parameters variable1 and variable2 are local variables. The argument *variables* firstNum and secondNum are never substituted in for variable1 and variable2; variable1 and variable2 are instead initialized to *the values of* firstNum and secondNum. Then, the values of variable1 and variable2 are interchanged, but the values of firstNum and secondNum are left unchanged. The omission of two ampersands has made the program completely wrong, yet it looks almost identical to the correct program and will compile and run without any error messages. ■

Display 4.4 Inadvertent Local Variable (part 1 of 2)

```
1   //Program to demonstrate call-by-reference parameters.
2   #include <iostream>
3   using namespace std;

4   void getNumbers(int& input1, int& input2);
5   //Reads two integers from the keyboard.
```

Display 4.4   Inadvertent Local Variable (part 2 of 2)

```
                                                Forgot the & here
6    void swapValues(int variable1, int variable2);
7    //Interchanges the values of variable1 and variable2.

8    void showResults(int output1, int output2);
9    //Shows the values of variable1 and variable2, in that order.

10   int main( )
11   {
12       int firstNum, secondNum;

13       getNumbers(firstNum, secondNum);
14       swapValues(firstNum, secondNum);
15       showResults(firstNum, secondNum);
16       return 0;
17   }
                                                Forgot the & here
18   void swapValues(int variable1, int variable2)
19   {
20       int temp;                              Inadvertent
                                                local variables
21       temp = variable1;
22       variable1 = variable2;
23       variable2 = temp;
24   }

25                   The definitions of getNumbers and
26                   showResults are the same as in Display 4.2.
```

Sample Dialogue

```
Enter two integers: 5  6
In reverse order the numbers are: 5  6
```

Error due to
inadvertent local
variables

TIP: Choosing Formal Parameter Names

Functions should be self-contained modules that are designed separately from the rest of the program. On large programming projects, different programmers may be assigned to write different functions. The programmer should choose the most meaningful names he or she can find for formal parameters. The arguments that will be substituted for the formal parameters may well be variables in another function or in the main function. These variables should also be given meaningful names, often chosen by someone other than the programmer who writes the function definition. This makes it likely that some or all arguments will have the same names as some of the formal parameters. This is perfectly acceptable. No matter what names are chosen for the variables that will be used as arguments, these names will not produce any confusion with the names used for formal parameters. ■

EXAMPLE: Buying Pizza

The large "economy" size of an item is not always a better buy than the smaller size. This is particularly true when buying pizzas. Pizza sizes are given as the diameter of the pizza in inches. However, the quantity of pizza is determined by the area of the pizza, and the area is not proportional to the diameter. Most people cannot easily estimate the difference in area between a ten-inch pizza and a twelve-inch pizza and so cannot easily determine which size is the best buy—that is, which size has the lowest price per square inch. Display 4.5 shows a program that a consumer can use to determine which of two sizes of pizza is the better buy.

Note that the functions getData and giveResults have the same parameters, but since getData will change the values of its arguments, its parameters are call-by-reference. On the other hand, giveResults only needs the values of its arguments, and so its parameters are call-by-value.

Also note that giveResults has two local variables and that its function body includes calls to the function unitPrice. Finally, note that the function unitPrice has both local variables and a locally defined constant.

Self-Test Exercise

7. What would be the output of the program in Display 4.3 if you changed the function declaration for the function doStuff to the following and you changed the function header to match, so that the formal parameter par2Ref were changed to a call-by-value parameter?

```
void doStuff (int par1Value, int par2Ref);
```

Display 4.5   Buying Pizza (part 1 of 3)

```
1   //Determines which of two pizza sizes is the best buy.
2   #include <iostream>
3   using namespace std;

4   void getData(int& smallDiameter,    double& priceSmall,
5                int& largeDiameter,    double& priceLarge);

6   void giveResults(int smallDiameter, double priceSmall,
7                int largeDiameter,    double priceLarge);

8   double unitPrice(int diameter, double price);
9   //Returns the price per square inch of a pizza.
10  //Precondition: The diameter parameter is the diameter of the pizza
11  //in inches. The price parameter is the price of the pizza.
```

Display 4.5   Buying Pizza (part 2 of 3)

```cpp
12  int main( )
13  {
14      int diameterSmall, diameterLarge;
15      double priceSmall, priceLarge;

16      getData(diameterSmall, priceSmall, diameterLarge, priceLarge);
17      giveResults(diameterSmall, priceSmall, diameterLarge, priceLarge);

18      return 0;
19  }

20  void getData(int& smallDiameter, double& priceSmall,
21               int& largeDiameter, double& priceLarge)
22  {
23      cout << "Welcome to the Pizza Consumers Union.\n";
24      cout << "Enter diameter of a small pizza (in inches): ";
25      cin >> smallDiameter;
26      cout << "Enter the price of a small pizza: $";
27      cin >> priceSmall;
28      cout << "Enter diameter of a large pizza (in inches): ";
29      cin >> largeDiameter;
30      cout << "Enter the price of a large pizza: $";
31      cin >> priceLarge;
32  }

33
34  void giveResults(int smallDiameter, double priceSmall,
35                   int largeDiameter, double priceLarge)
36  {
37      double unitPriceSmall, unitPriceLarge;

38      unitPriceSmall = unitPrice(smallDiameter, priceSmall);
39      unitPriceLarge = unitPrice(largeDiameter, priceLarge);
40      cout.setf(ios::fixed);
41      cout.setf(ios::showpoint);
42      cout.precision(2);
43      cout << "Small pizza:\n"
44           << "Diameter = " << smallDiameter << " inches\n"
45           << "Price = $" << priceSmall
46           << " Per square inch = $" << unitPriceSmall << endl
47           << "Large pizza:\n"
48           << "Diameter = " << largeDiameter << " inches\n"
49           << "Price = $" << priceLarge
50           << " Per square inch = $" << unitPriceLarge << endl;
51      if (unitPriceLarge < unitPriceSmall)
52          cout << "The large one is the better buy.\n";
```

The variables `diameterSmall`,
`diameterLarge`, `priceSmall`, *and*
`priceLarge` *are used to carry data from*
the function `getData` *to the function*
`giveResults`.

One function called
within another
function

(continued)

Display 4.5   Buying Pizza (part 3 of 3)

```
53      else
54          cout << "The small one is the better buy.\n";
55          cout << "Buon Appetito!\n";
56  }

57  double unitPrice(int diameter, double price)
58  {
59      const double PI = 3.14159;
60      double radius, area;

61      radius = diameter/static_cast<double>(2);
62      area = PI * radius * radius;
63      return (price/area);
64  }
```

Sample Dialogue

```
Welcome to the Pizza Consumers Union.
Enter diameter of a small pizza (in inches): 10
Enter the price of a small pizza: $7.50
Enter diameter of a large pizza (in inches): 13
Enter the price of a large pizza: $14.75
Small pizza:
Diameter = 10 inches
Price = $7.50 Per square inch = $0.10
Large pizza:
Diameter = 13 inches
Price = $14.75 Per square inch = $0.11
The small one is the better buy.
Buon Appetito!
```

4.2   Overloading and Default Arguments

"…and that shows that there are three hundred and sixty-four days when you might get un-birthday presents—"

"Certainly," said Alice.

"And only one for birthday presents, you know. There's glory for you!"

"I don't know what you mean by glory,' " Alice said.

Humpty Dumpty smiled contemptuously, "Of course you don't—till I tell you. I mean 'there's a nice knock-down argument for you!"

"But 'glory' doesn't mean 'a nice knock-down argument,' " Alice objected.

"When I use a word," Humpty Dumpty said, in rather a scornful tone, "it means just what I choose it to mean—neither more nor less."

"The question is," said Alice, "whether you can make words mean so many different things."

"The question is," said Humpty Dumpty, "which is to be master—that's all."

LEWIS CARROLL, *Through the Looking-Glass*

overloading

C++ allows you to give two or more different definitions to the same function name, which means you can reuse names that have strong intuitive appeal across a variety of situations. For example, you could have three functions called max: one that computes the larger of two numbers, another that computes the largest of three numbers, and yet another that computes the largest of four numbers. Giving two (or more) function definitions for the same function name is called **overloading** the function name.

Introduction to Overloading

Suppose you are writing a program that requires you to compute the average of two numbers. You might use the following function definition:

```
double ave (double n1,  double n2)
{
    return ((n1 + n2)/2.0);
}
```

Now suppose your program also requires a function to compute the average of three numbers. You might define a new function called ave3 as follows:

```
double ave3 (double n1,  double n2,  double n3)
{
    return ((n1 + n2 + n3)/3.0);
}
```

This will work, and in many programming languages you have no choice but to do something like this. However, C++ overloading allows for a more elegant solution. In

C++ you can simply use the same function name ave for both functions. In C++ you can use the following function definition in place of the function definition ave3

```
double ave(double n1, double n2, double n3)
{
    return ((n1 + n2 + n3) / 3.0);
}
```

so that the function name ave then has two definitions. This is an example of overloading. In this case we have overloaded the function name ave. Display 4.6 embeds these two function definitions for ave into a complete sample program. Be sure to notice that each function definition has its own declaration (prototype).

The compiler can tell which function definition to use by checking the number and types of the arguments in a function call. In the program in Display 4.6, one of the functions called ave has two arguments and the other has three arguments. When there are two arguments in a function call, the first definition applies. When there are three arguments in a function call, the second definition applies.

Overloading a Function Name

If you have two or more function definitions for the same function name, that is called *overloading*. When you overload a function name, the function definitions must have different numbers of formal parameters or some formal parameters of different types. When there is a function call, the compiler uses the function definition whose number of formal parameters and types of formal parameters match the arguments in the function call.

Whenever you give two or more definitions to the same function name, the various function definitions must have different specifications for their arguments; that is, any two function definitions that have the same function name must use different numbers of formal parameters or have one or more parameters of different types (or both). Notice that when you overload a function name, the declarations for the two different definitions must differ in their formal parameters. *You cannot overload a function name by giving two definitions that differ only in the type of the value returned. You cannot overload a function name* based on any difference other than the number or types of parameters. You cannot overload based solely on const or solely on call-by-value versus call-by-reference parameters.[1]

You already saw a kind of overloading in Chapter 1 (reviewed here) with the division operator, /. If both operands are of type int, as in 13/2, then the value returned is the result of integer division, in this case, 6. On the other hand, if one or both operands are of type double, then the value returned is the result of regular division; for example, 13/2.0 returns the value 6.5. There are two definitions for the

determining
which
definition
applies

---

[1] Some compilers will, in fact, allow you to overload on the basis of const versus no const, but you should not count on this. The C++ standard says it is not allowed.

division operator, /, and the two definitions are distinguished not by having different numbers of operands but rather by requiring operands of different types. The only difference between overloading of / and overloading function names is that the C++ language designers have already done the overloading of /, whereas you must program the overloading of your function names yourself. Chapter 8 discusses how to overload operators such as +, −, and so on.

Display 4.6   Overloading a Function Name

```
1   //Illustrates overloading the function name ave.
2   #include <iostream>
3   using namespace std;

4   double ave(double n1, double n2);
5   //Returns the average of the two numbers n1 and n2.
6
7   double ave(double n1, double n2, double n3);
8   //Returns the average of the three numbers n1, n2, and n3.

9   int main( )
10  {
11      cout << "The average of 2.0, 2.5, and 3.0 is "
12           << ave(2.0, 2.5, 3.0) << endl;

13      cout << "The average of 4.5 and 5.5 is "
14           << ave(4.5, 5.5) << endl;

15      return 0;
16  }

17  double ave(double n1, double n2)
18  {
19      return ((n1 + n2)/2.0);
20  }

21  double ave(double n1, double n2, double n3)
22  {
23      return ((n1 + n2 + n3)/3.0);
24  }
```

Two arguments

Three arguments

Sample Dialogue

```
The average of 2.0, 2.5, and 3.0 is 2.5
The average of 4.5 and 5.5 is 5.0
```

A function's **signature** is the function's name with the sequence of types in the parameter list, not including the const keyword and not including the ampersand, &. When you overload a function name, the two definitions of the function name must have different signatures using this definition of signature. (Some authorities include the const and/or ampersand as part of the signature, but we wanted a definition that works for explaining overloading.)

Signature

PITFALL: Automatic Type Conversion and Overloading

Suppose that the following function definition occurs in your program and that you have *not* overloaded the function name mpg (so this is the only definition of a function called mpg).

```
double mpg(double miles, double gallons)
//Returns miles per gallon.
{
    return (miles / gallons);
}
```

If you call the function mpg with arguments of type int, then C++ will automatically convert any argument of type int to a value of type double. Hence, the following will output 22.5 miles per gallon to the screen:

```
cout << mpg(45, 2) << " miles per gallon";
```

C++ converts the 45 to 45.0 and the 2 to 2.0 and then performs the division 45.0/2.0 to obtain the value returned, which is 22.5.

If a function requires an argument of type double and you give it an argument of type int, C++ will automatically convert the int argument to a value of type double. This is so useful and natural that we hardly give it a thought. However, overloading can interfere with this automatic type conversion. Let us look at an example.

Suppose you had (foolishly) overloaded the function name mpg so that your program contained the following definition of mpg as well as the one previous:

interaction of overloading and type conversion

```
int mpg(int goals, int misses)
//Returns the Measure of Perfect Goals
//which is computed as (goals - misses).
{
    return (goals - misses);
}
```

In a program that contains both of these definitions for the function name mpg, the following will (unfortunately) output 43 miles per gallon (since 43 is 45 - 2):

```
cout << mpg(45, 2) << " miles per gallon";
```

PITFALL: (continued)

When C++ sees the function call `mpg(45, 2)`, which has two arguments of type `int`, C++ *first* looks for a function definition of `mpg` that has two formal parameters of type `int`. If it finds such a function definition, C++ uses that function definition. C++ does not convert an `int` argument to a value of type `double` unless that is the only way it can find a matching function definition.

The `mpg` example illustrates one more point about overloading: You should not use the same function name for two unrelated functions. Such careless use of function names is certain to eventually produce confusion. ∎

Self-Test Exercises

8. Suppose you have two function definitions with the following declarations:

```
double score(double time, double distance);
int score(double points);
```

Which function definition would be used in the following function call and why would it be the one used? (`x` is of type `double`.)

```
double finalScore = score(x);
```

9. Suppose you have two function definitions with the following declarations:

```
double theAnswer(double data1, double data2);
double theAnswer(double time, int count);
```

Which function definition would be used in the following function call and why would it be the one used? (`x` and `y` are of type `double`.)

```
x = theAnswer(y, 6.0);
```

Rules for Resolving Overloading

If you use overloading to produce two definitions of the same function name with similar (but not identical) parameter lists, then the interaction of overloading and automatic type conversion can be confusing. The rules that the compiler uses for resolving which of multiple overloaded definitions of a function name to apply to a given function call are as follows:

1. *Exact match*: If the number and types of arguments exactly match a definition (without any automatic type conversion), then that is the definition used.

2. *Match using automatic type conversion:* If there is no exact match but there is a match using automatic type conversion, then that match is used.

If two matches are found at stage 1 or if no matches are found at stage 1 and two matches are found at stage 2, then there is an ambiguous situation and an error message will be issued.

For example, the following overloading is dubious style, but is perfectly valid:

```
void f(int n, double m);
void f(double n, int m);
```

However, if you also have the invocation

```
f(98, 99);
```

then the compiler does not know which of the two `int` arguments to convert to a value of type `double`, and an error message is generated.

To see how confusing and dangerous the situation can be, suppose you add the following third overloading:

```
void f(int n, int m);
```

With this third overloading added, you no longer get an error message, since there is now an exact match. Obviously, such confusing overloading is to be avoided.

The previous two rules will work in almost all situations. In fact, if you need more precise rules, you should rewrite your code to be more straightforward. However, the exact rules are even a bit more complicated. For reference value, we give the exact rules here. Some of the terms may not make sense until you read more of this book, but do not be concerned. The simple two rules given previously will serve you well until you do understand the more complete rules.

1. Exact match as described earlier.
2. Matches using promotion within integer types or within floating-point types, such as `short` to `int` or `float` to `double`. (Note that `bool-to-int` and `char-to-int` conversions are considered promotions within integer types.)
3. Matches using other conversions of predefined types, such as `int` to `double`.
4. Matches using conversions of user-defined types (see Chapter 8).
5. Matches using ellipses ... (This is not covered in this book, and if you do not use it, it will not be an issue.)

If two matches are found at the first stage that a match is found, then there is an ambiguous situation and an error message will be issued.

EXAMPLE: Revised Pizza-Buying Program

The Pizza Consumers Union has been very successful with the program that we wrote for it in Display 4.5. In fact, now everybody always buys the pizza that is the best buy. One disreputable pizza parlor used to make money by fooling consumers into buying the more expensive pizza, but our program has put an end to its evil practices. However, the owners wish to continue their despicable behavior and have come up with a new way to fool consumers. They now offer both round pizzas and rectangular pizzas. They know that the program we wrote cannot deal with rectangular-shaped pizzas, so they hope they can again confuse consumers. Display 4.7 is another version of our program that compares a round pizza and a rectangular pizza. Note that the function name unitPrice has been overloaded so that it applies to both round and rectangular pizzas.

Display 4.7   Revised Pizza Program (part 1 of 3)

```
1   //Determines whether a round pizza or a rectangular pizza is the best
    //buy.
2   #include <iostream>
3   using namespace std;

4   double unitPrice(int diameter, double price);
5   //Returns the price per square inch of a round pizza.
6   //The formal parameter named diameter is the diameter of the pizza
7   //in inches. The formal parameter named price is the price of the pizza.

8   double unitPrice(int length, int width, double price);
9   //Returns the price per square inch of a rectangular pizza
10  //with dimensions length by width inches.
11  //The formal parameter price is the price of the pizza.
12  int main( )
13  {
14      int diameter, length, width;
15      double priceRound, unitPriceRound,
16             priceRectangular, unitPriceRectangular;

17      cout << "Welcome to the Pizza Consumers Union.\n";
18      cout << "Enter the diameter in inches"
19           << " of a round pizza: ";
20      cin >> diameter;
21      cout << "Enter the price of a round pizza: $";
22      cin >> priceRound;
23      cout << "Enter length and width in inches\n"
24           << "of a rectangular pizza: ";
25      cin >> length >> width;
26      cout << "Enter the price of a rectangular pizza: $";
```

(continued)

Display 4.7   Revised Pizza Program (part 2 of 3)

```cpp
27     cin >> priceRectangular;
28     unitPriceRectangular =
29            unitPrice(length, width, priceRectangular);
30     unitPriceRound = unitPrice(diameter, priceRound);

31     cout.setf(ios::fixed);
32     cout.setf(ios::showpoint);
33     cout.precision(2);
34     cout << endl
35          << "Round pizza: Diameter = "
36          << diameter << " inches\n"
37          << "Price = $" << priceRound
38          << " Per square inch = $" << unitPriceRound
39          << endl
40          << "Rectangular pizza: Length = "
41          << length << " inches\n"
42          << "Rectangular pizza: Width = "
43          << width << " inches\n"
44          << "Price = $" << priceRectangular
45          << " Per square inch = $" << unitPriceRectangular
46          << endl;
47     if (unitPriceRound < unitPriceRectangular)
48         cout << "The round one is the better buy.\n";
49     else
50         cout << "The rectangular one is the better buy.\n";
51     cout << "Buon Appetito!\n";

52     return 0;
53 }

54 double unitPrice(int diameter, double price)
55 {
56     const double PI = 3.14159;
57     double radius, area;

58     double radius, area;
59     radius = diameter/double(2);
60     area = PI * radius * radius;
61     return (price/area);
62 }

63 double unitPrice(int length, int width, double price)
64 {
65     double area = length * width;
66     return (price/area);
67 }
```

Display 4.7   Revised Pizza Program (part 3 of 3)

Sample Dialogue

```
Welcome to the Pizza Consumers Union.
Enter the diameter in inches of a round pizza: 10
Enter the price of a round pizza: $8.50
Enter length and width in inches
of a rectangular pizza: 6 4
Enter the price of a rectangular pizza: $7.55

Round pizza: Diameter = 10 inches
Price = $8.50 Per square inch = $0.11
Rectangular pizza: Length = 6 inches
Rectangular pizza: Width = 4 inches
Price = $7.55 Per square inch = $0.31
The round one is the better buy.
Buon Appetito!
```

Default Arguments

default argument

You can specify a **default argument** for one or more call-by-value parameters in a function. If the corresponding argument is omitted, then it is replaced by the default argument. For example, the function volume in Display 4.8 computes the volume of a box from its length, width, and height. If no height is given, the height is assumed to be 1. If neither a width nor a height is given, they are both assumed to be 1.

Note that in Display 4.8 the default arguments are given in the function declaration but not in the function definition. A default argument is given the first time the function is declared (or defined, if that occurs first). Subsequent declarations or a following definition should not give the default arguments again because some compilers will consider this an error even if the arguments given are consistent with the ones given previously.

You may have more than one default argument, but all the default argument positions must be in the rightmost positions. Thus, for the function volume in Display 4.8, we could have given default arguments for the last one, last two, or all three parameters, but any other combinations of default arguments are not allowed.

If you have more than one default argument, then when the function is invoked, you must omit arguments starting from the right. For example, note that in Display 4.8 there are two default arguments. When only one argument is omitted, it is assumed to be the last argument. There is no way to omit the second argument in an invocation of volume without also omitting the third argument.

Default arguments are of limited value, but sometimes they can be used to reflect your way of thinking about arguments. Default arguments can only be used with call-by-value parameters. They do not make sense for call-by-reference parameters. Anything you can do with default arguments can be done using overloading, although the default argument version will probably be shorter than the overloading version.

Display 4.8 Default Arguments

```
1   #include <iostream>
2   using namespace std;
3
4   void showVolume(int length, int width = 1, int height = 1);
5   //Returns the volume of a box.
6   //If no height is given, the height is assumed to be 1.
7   //If neither height nor width is given, both are assumed to be 1.
8
9   int main( )
10  {
11      showVolume(4, 6, 2);
12      showVolume(4, 6);
13      showVolume(4);
14
15      return 0;
16  }
17
18  void showVolume(int length, int width, int height)
19  {
20      cout << "Volume of a box with \n"
21           << "Length = " << length << ", Width = " << width << endl
22           << "and Height = " << height
23           << "is " << length*width*height << endl;
24  }
```

Default arguments

A default argument should not be given a second time.

Sample Dialogue

```
Volume of a box with
Length = 4, Width = 6
and Height = 2 is 48
Volume of a box with
Length = 4, Width = 6
and Height = 1 is 24
Volume of a box with
Length = 4, Width = 1
and Height = 1 is 4
```

Self-Test Exercise

10. This question has to do with the programming example entitled "Revised Pizza-Buying Program." Suppose the evil pizza parlor that is always trying to fool customers introduces a square pizza. Can you overload the function unitPrice so that it can compute the price per square inch of a square pizza as well as the price per square inch of a round pizza? Why or why not?

4.3   Testing and Debugging Functions

I beheld the wretch —the miserable monster whom I had created.

MARY WOLLSTONECRAFT SHELLEY, *Frankenstein*

This section reviews some general guidelines for testing programs and functions.

The assert Macro

assertion

An **assertion** is a statement that is either true or false. Assertions are used to document and check the correctness of programs. Preconditions and postconditions, which we discussed in Chapter 3, are examples of assertions. When expressed precisely and in the syntax of C++, an assertion is simply a Boolean expression. If you convert an assertion to a Boolean expression, then the predefined macro assert can be used to check whether or not your code satisfies the assertion. (A **macro** is very similar to an inline function and is used just like a function is used.)

macro

The assert macro is used like a void function that takes one call-by-value parameter of type bool. Since an assertion is just a Boolean expression, this means that the argument to assert is an assertion. When the assert macro is invoked, its assertion argument is evaluated. If it evaluates to true, then nothing happens. If the argument evaluates to false, then the program ends and an error message is issued. Thus, calls to the assert macro are a compact way to include error checks within your program.

For example, the following function declaration is taken from Programming Project 4.3:

```
void computeCoin(int coinValue, int& number, int& amountLeft);
//Precondition: 0 < coinValue < 100; 0 <= amountLeft < 100.
//Postcondition: number has been set equal to the maximum number
//of coins of denomination coinValue cents that can be obtained
//from amountLeft cents. amountLeft has been decreased by the
//value of the coins, that is, decreased by number*coinValue.
```

You can check that the precondition holds for a function invocation, as shown by the following example:

```
assert((0 < currentCoin) && (currentCoin < 100)
    && (0 <= currentAmountLeft) && (currentAmountLeft < 100));
computeCoin(currentCoin, number, currentAmountLeft);
```

If the precondition is not satisfied, your program will end and an error message will be output.

The assert macro is defined in the library cassert, so any program that uses the assert macro must contain the following:

```
#include <cassert>
```

VideoNote
Using an
Integrated
Debugger

turning off assert

One advantage of using `assert` is that you can turn `assert` invocations off. You can use `assert` invocations in your program to debug your program, and then turn them off so that users do not get error messages that they might not understand. Doing so reduces the overhead performed by your program. To turn off all the `assert` invocations in your program, add `#define NDEBUG` before the `#include` directive, as follows:

#define NDEBUG

```
#define NDEBUG
#include <cassert>
```

Thus, if you insert `#define NDEBUG` in your program after it is fully debugged, all `assert` invocations in your program will be turned off. If you later change your program and need to debug it again, you can turn the `assert` invocations back on by deleting the `#define NDEBUG` line (or commenting it out).

Not all comment assertions can easily be translated into C++ Boolean expressions. Preconditions are more likely to translate easily than postconditions are. Thus, the `assert` macro is not a cure-all for debugging your functions, but it can be very useful.

Stubs and Drivers

Each function should be designed, coded, and tested as a separate unit from the rest of the program. When you treat each function as a separate unit, you transform one big task into a series of smaller, more manageable tasks. But how do you test a function outside the program for which it is intended? One way is to write a special program to do the testing. For example, Display 4.9 shows a program to test the function `unitPrice` that was used in the program in Display 4.5. Programs like this one are called **driver programs**. These driver programs are temporary tools and can be quite minimal. They need not have fancy input routines. They need not perform all the calculations the final program will perform. All they need do is obtain reasonable values for the function arguments in as simple a way as possible—typically from the user—then execute the function and show the result. A loop, as in the program shown in Display 4.9, will allow you to retest the function on different arguments without having to rerun the program.

driver program

If you test each function separately, you will find most of the mistakes in your program. Moreover, you will find out which functions contain the mistakes. If you were to test only the entire program, you would probably find out if there were a mistake, but you may have no idea where the mistake is. Even worse, you may think you know where the mistake is, but be wrong.

Once you have fully tested a function, you can use it in the driver program for some other function. Each function should be tested in a program in which it is the only untested function. However, it is fine to use a fully tested function when testing some other function. If a bug is found, you know the bug is in the untested function.

It is sometimes impossible or inconvenient to test a function without using some other function that has not yet been written or has not yet been tested. In this case, you can use a simplified version of the missing or untested function. These simplified functions are called **stubs**. These stubs will not necessarily perform the correct calculation, but they will deliver values that suffice for testing, and they are

stub

simple enough that you can have confidence in their performance. For example, the following is a possible stub for the function unitPrice:

```
//A stub. The final function definition must still be written.
double unitPrice(int diameter, double price)
{
    return (9.99);//Not correct but good enough for a stub.
}
```

Display 4.9   Driver Program (part 1 of 2)

```
1
2   //Driver program for the function unitPrice.
3   #include <iostream>
4   using namespace std;
5   double unitPrice(int diameter, double price);
6   //Returns the price per square inch of a pizza.
7   //Precondition: The diameter parameter is the diameter of the pizza
8   //in inches. The price parameter is the price of the pizza.
9   int main( )
10  {
11      double diameter, price;
12      char ans;
13      do
14      {
15          cout << "Enter diameter and price:\n";
16          cin >> diameter >> price;
17          cout << "unit Price is $"
18               << unitPrice(diameter, price) << endl;
19          cout << "Test again? (y/n)";
20          cin >> ans;
21          cout << endl;
22      } while (ans == 'y' || ans == 'Y');
23      return 0;
24  }
25
26  double unitPrice(int diameter, double price)
27  {
28      const double PI = 3.14159;
29      double radius, area;
30      radius = diameter/static_cast<double>(2);
31      area = PI * radius * radius;
32      return (price/area);
33  }
```

(continued)

Display 4.9   Driver Program (part 2 of 2)

Sample Dialogue

```
Enter diameter and price:
13 14.75
Unit price is: $0.111126
Test again? (y/n): y
Enter diameter and price:
2 3.15
Unit price is: $1.00268
Test again? (y/n): n
```

Using a program outline with stubs allows you to test and then flesh out the basic program outline, rather than write a completely new program to test each function. For this reason, a program outline with stubs is usually the most efficient method of testing. A common approach is to use driver programs to test some basic functions, such as input and output, and then use a program with stubs to test the remaining functions. The stubs are replaced by functions one at a time: One stub is replaced by a complete function and tested; once that function is fully tested, another stub is replaced by a full function definition, and so forth, until the final program is produced.

> ### The Fundamental Rule for Testing Functions
>
> Every function should be tested in a program in which every other function in that program has already been fully tested and debugged.

Self-Test Exercises

11. What is the fundamental rule for testing functions? Why is this a good way to test functions?

12. What is a driver program?

13. What is a stub?

14. Write a stub for the function whose declaration is given next. Do not write a whole program, only the stub that would go in a program. (*Hint:* It will be very short.)

```
double rainProb(double pressure, double humidity, double temp);
//Precondition: pressure is the barometric pressure in inches
//of mercury, humidity is the relative humidity as a
//percentage, and temp is the temperature in degrees
//Fahrenheit. Returns the probability of rain, which is a
//number between 0 and 1. 0 means no chance of rain. 1 means
//rain is 100% certain.
```

Chapter Summary

- A formal parameter is a kind of placeholder that is filled in with a function argument when the function is called. In C++, there are two methods of performing this substitution, call by value and call by reference, and so there are two basic kinds of parameters: call-by-value parameters and call-by-reference parameters.

- A call-by-value formal parameter is a local variable that is initialized to the value of its corresponding argument when the function is called. Occasionally, it is useful to use a formal call-by-value parameter as a local variable.

- In the call-by-reference substitution mechanism, the argument should be a variable, and the entire variable is substituted for the corresponding argument.

- The way to indicate a call-by-reference parameter in a function definition is to attach the ampersand sign, &, to the type of the formal parameter. (A call-by-value parameter is indicated by the absence of an ampersand.)

- An argument corresponding to a call-by-value parameter cannot be changed by a function call. An argument corresponding to a call-by-reference parameter can be changed by a function call. If you want a function to change the value of a variable, then you must use a call-by-reference parameter.

- You can give multiple definitions to the same function name, provided that the different functions with the same name have different numbers of parameters or some parameter position with differing types, or both. This is called overloading the function name.

- You can specify a default argument for one or more call-by-value parameters in a function. Default arguments are always in the rightmost argument positions.

- The assert macro can be used to help debug your program by checking whether or not assertions hold.

- Every function should be tested in a program in which every other function in that program has already been fully tested and debugged.

Answers to Self-Test Exercises

1. A call-by-value parameter is a local variable. When the function is invoked, the value of a call-by-value argument is computed and the corresponding call-by-value parameter (which is a local variable) is initialized to this value.

2. The function will work fine. That is the entire answer, but here is some additional information: The formal parameter inches is a call-by-value parameter and, as discussed in the text, is therefore a local variable. Thus, the value of the argument will not be changed.

3. 10 20 30
1 2 3
1 20 3

4. Enter two integers: **5 10**
In reverse order the numbers are: 5 5

5. void zeroBoth(int& n1, int& n2)
{
    n1 = 0;
    n2 = 0;
}

6. void addTax(double taxRate, double& cost)
{
    cost = cost + (taxRate/100.0)*cost;
}

7. par1Value in function call = 111
par2Ref in function call = 222
n1 after function call = 1
n2 after function call = 2   ⟵――――― Different

The division by 100 is to convert a percentage to a fraction. For example, 10% is 10/100.0, or one-tenth of the cost.

8. The one with one parameter would be used because the function call has only one parameter.

9. The first one would be used because it is an exact match, namely, two parameters of type double.

10. This cannot be done (at least not in any nice way). The natural ways to represent a square and a round pizza are the same. Each is naturally represented as one number, which is the radius for a round pizza and the length of a side for a square pizza. In either case the function unitPrice would need to have one formal parameter of type double for the price and one formal parameter of type int for the size (either radius or side). Thus, the two function declarations would have the same number and types of formal parameters. (Specifically, they would both have one formal parameter of type double and one formal parameter of type int.) Thus, the compiler would not be able to decide which definition to use. You can still defeat this evil pizza parlor's strategy by defining two functions, but they will need to have different names.

11. The fundamental rule for testing functions is that every function should be tested in a program in which every other function in that program has already been fully tested and debugged. This is a good way to test a function because if you follow this rule, then when you find a bug, you will know which function contains the bug.

12. A driver program is a program written for the sole purpose of testing a function.

13. A stub is a simplified version of a function that is used in place of the function so that other functions can be tested.

```
14. //THIS IS JUST A STUB.
    double rainProb(double pressure,
                    double humidity, double temp)
    {
        return 0.25; //Not correct,
                     //but good enough for some testing.
    }
```

Programming Projects

Visit www.myprogramminglab.com to complete select exercises online and get instant feedback.

1. Write a program that converts from 24-hour notation to 12-hour notation. For example, it should convert 14:25 to 2:25 P.M. The input is given as two integers. There should be at least three functions: one for input, one to do the conversion, and one for output. Record the A.M./P.M. information as a value of type char, 'A' for A.M. and 'P' for P.M. Thus, the function for doing the conversions will have a call-by-reference formal parameter of type char to record whether it is A.M. or P.M. (The function will have other parameters as well.) Include a loop that lets the user repeat this computation for new input values again and again until the user says he or she wants to end the program.

2. The area of an arbitrary triangle can be computed using the formula

$$Area = \sqrt{s(s-a)(s-b)(s-c)}$$

where a, b, and c are the lengths of the sides, and s is the semiperimeter.

$$s = (a + b + c)/2$$

Write a void function that uses five parameters: three value parameters that provide the lengths of the edges, and two reference parameters that compute the area and perimeter (*not the semiperimeter*). Make your function robust. Note that not all combinations of a, b, and c produce a triangle. Your function should produce correct results for legal data and reasonable results for illegal combinations.

3. Write a program that tells what coins to give out for any amount of change from 1 cent to 99 cents. For example, if the amount is 86 cents, the output would be something like the following:

```
86 cents can be given as

3 quarter(s) 1 dime(s) and 1 penny(pennies)
```

Use coin denominations of 25 cents (quarters), 10 cents (dimes), and 1 cent (pennies). Do not use nickel and half-dollar coins. Your program will use the following function (among others):

```
void computeCoin(int coinValue, int& number, int& amountLeft);
//Precondition: 0 < coinValue < 100; 0 <= amountLeft < 100.
//Postcondition: number has been set equal to the maximum number
//of coins of denomination coinValue cents that can be obtained
```

```
//from amountLeft cents. amountLeft has been decreased by the
//value of the coins, that is, decreased by number*coinValue.
```

For example, suppose the value of the variable amountLeft is 86. Then, after the following call, the value of number will be 3 and the value of amountLeft will be 11 (because if you take three quarters from 86 cents, that leaves 11 cents):

```
computeCoins(25, number, amountLeft);
```

Include a loop that lets the user repeat this computation for new input values until the user says he or she wants to end the program. (*Hint:* Use integer division and the % operator to implement this function.)

4. Write a program that will read in a length in feet and inches and output the equivalent length in meters and centimeters. Use at least three functions: one for input, one or more for calculating, and one for output. Include a loop that lets the user repeat this computation for new input values until the user says he or she wants to end the program. There are 0.3048 meters in a foot, 100 centimeters in a meter, and 12 inches in a foot.

5. Write a program like that of the previous exercise that converts from meters and centimeters into feet and inches. Use functions for the subtasks.

6. (You should do the previous two programming projects before doing this one.) Write a program that combines the functions in the previous two programming projects. The program asks the user if he or she wants to convert from feet and inches to meters and centimeters or from meters and centimeters to feet and inches. The program then performs the desired conversion. Have the user respond by typing the integer 1 for one type of conversion and 2 for the other conversion. The program reads the user's answer and then executes an if-else statement. Each branch of the if-else statement will be a function call. The two functions called in the if-else statement will have function definitions that are very similar to the programs for the previous two programming projects. Thus, they will be fairly complicated function definitions that call other functions. Include a loop that lets the user repeat this computation for new input values until the user says he or she wants to end the program.

7. Write a program that will read in a weight in pounds and ounces and will output the equivalent weight in kilograms and grams. Use at least three functions: one for input, one or more for calculating, and one for output. Include a loop that lets the user repeat this computation for new input values until the user says he or she wants to end the program. There are 2.2046 pounds in a kilogram, 1000 grams in a kilogram, and 16 ounces in a pound.

8. Write a program like that of the previous exercise that converts from kilograms and grams into pounds and ounces. Use functions for the subtasks.

9. (You should do the previous two programming projects before doing this one.) Write a program that combines the functions of the previous two programming projects. The program asks the user if he or she wants to convert from pounds and ounces to kilograms and grams or from kilograms and grams to pounds and ounces. The program then performs the desired conversion. Have the user respond by typing the integer 1 for one type of conversion and 2 for the other. The program

VideoNote
Solution to
Programming
Project 4.4

reads the user's answer and then executes an `if-else` statement. Each branch of the `if-else` statement will be a function call. The two functions called in the `if-else` statement will have function definitions that are very similar to the programs for the previous two programming projects. Thus, they will be fairly complicated function definitions that call other functions in their function bodies. Include a loop that lets the user repeat this computation for new input values until the user says he or she wants to end the program.

10. (You should do Programming Projects 4.6 and 4.9 before doing this programming project.) Write a program that combines the functions of Programming Projects 4.6 and 4.9. The program asks the user if he or she wants to convert lengths or weights. If the user chooses lengths, then the program asks the user if he or she wants to convert from feet and inches to meters and centimeters or from meters and centimeters to feet and inches. If the user chooses weights, a similar question about pounds, ounces, kilograms, and grams is asked. The program then performs the desired conversion. Have the user respond by typing the integer 1 for one type of conversion and 2 for the other. The program reads the user's answer and then executes an `if-else` statement. Each branch of the `if-else` statement will be a function call. The two functions called in the `if-else` statement will have function definitions that are very similar to the programs for Programming Projects 4.6 and 4.9. Thus, these functions will be fairly complicated function definitions that call other functions; however, they will be very easy to write by adapting the programs you wrote for Programming Projects 4.6 and 4.9. Notice that your program will have `if-else` statements embedded inside of `if-else` statements, but only in an indirect way. The outer `if-else` statement will include two function calls, as its two branches. These two function calls will each in turn include an `if-else` statement, but you need not think about that. They are just function calls and the details are in a black box that you create when you define these functions. If you try to create a four-way branch, you are probably on the wrong track. You should only need to think about two-way branches (even though the entire program does ultimately branch into four cases). Include a loop that lets the user repeat this computation for new input values until the user says he or she wants to end the program.

11. You are a contestant on a game show and have won a shot at the grand prize. Before you are three doors. $1,000,000 in cash has randomly been placed behind one door. Behind the other two doors are the consolation prizes of dishwasher detergent. The game show host asks you to select a door, and you randomly pick one. However, before revealing the prize behind your door, the game show host reveals one of the other doors that contains a consolation prize. At this point, the game show host asks if you would like to stick with your original choice or to switch to the remaining door.

Write a function to simulate the game show problem. Your function should randomly select locations for the prizes, select a door at random chosen by the contestant, and then determine whether the contestant would win or lose by sticking with the original choice or switching to the remaining door. You may wish to create additional functions invoked by this function.

Next, modify your program so that it simulates playing 10,000 games. Count the number of times the contestant wins when switching versus staying. If you are the contestant, what choice should you make to optimize your chances of winning the cash, or does it not matter?

12. In the land of Puzzlevania, Aaron, Bob, and Charlie had an argument over which one of them was the greatest puzzle-solver of all time. To end the argument once and for all, they agreed on a duel to the death. Aaron was a poor shot and only hit his target with a probability of 1/3. Bob was a bit better and hit his target with a probability of 1/2. Charlie was an expert marksman and never missed. A hit means a kill and the person hit drops out of the duel.

To compensate for the inequities in their marksmanship skills, the three decided that they would fire in turns, starting with Aaron, followed by Bob, and then by Charlie. The cycle would repeat until there was one man standing. That man would be remembered for all time as the Greatest Puzzle-Solver of All Time.

An obvious and reasonable strategy is for each man to shoot at the most accurate shooter still alive, on the grounds that this shooter is the deadliest and has the best chance of hitting back.

Write a program to simulate the duel using this strategy. Your program should use random numbers and the probabilities given in the problem to determine whether a shooter hits his target. You will likely want to create multiple subroutines and functions to complete the problem. Once you can simulate a duel, add a loop to your program that simulates 10,000 duels. Count the number of times that each contestant wins and print the probability of winning for each contestant (e.g., for Aaron your program might output "Aaron won 3595/10,000 duels or 35.95%").

An alternate strategy is for Aaron to intentionally miss on his first shot. Modify the program to accommodate this new strategy and output the probability of winning for each contestant. What strategy is better for Aaron, to intentionally miss on the first shot or to try and hit the best shooter?

13. You would like to know how fast you can run in miles per hour. Your treadmill will tell you your speed in terms of a pace (minutes and seconds per mile, such as "5:30 mile") or in terms of kilometers per hour (kph).

Write an overloaded function called convertToMPH. The first definition should take as input two integers that represent the pace in minutes and seconds per mile and return the speed in mph as a double. The second definition should take as input one double that represents the speed in kph and return the speed in mph as a double. One mile is approximately 1.61 kilometers. Write a driver program to test your function.

14. Your time machine is capable of going forward in time up to 24 hours. The machine is configured to jump ahead in minutes. To enter the proper number of minutes into your machine, you would like a program that can take a start time and an end time and calculate the difference in minutes between them. The end time will

always be within 24 hours of the start time. Use military notation for both the start and end times (e.g., 0000 for midnight and 2359 for one minute before midnight).

Write a function that takes as input a start time and an end time represented as an `int`, using military notation. The function should return the difference in minutes as an integer. Write a driver program that calls your subroutine with times entered by the user.

Hint: Be careful of time intervals that start before midnight and end the following day.

15. Write a function named `convertToLowestTerms` that inputs two integer parameters by reference named `numerator` and `denominator`. The function should treat these variables as a fraction and reduce them to lowest terms. For example, if `numerator` is 20 and `denominator` is 60, then the function should change the variables to 1 and 3, respectively. This will require finding the greatest common divisor for the numerator and denominator then dividing both variables by that number. If the denominator is zero, the function should return `false`, otherwise the function should return `true`. Write a test program that uses `convertToLowestTerms` to reduce and output several fractions.

16. Consider a text file named `scores.txt` that contains player scores for a game. A possible sample is shown here where Ronaldo's best score is 10400, Didier's best score is 9800, etc.

```
Ronaldo
10400
Didier
9800
Pele
12300
Kaka
8400
Cristiano
8000
```

Write a function named `getHighScore` that takes a string reference parameter and an integer reference parameter. The function should scan through the file and set the reference parameters to the name of the player with the highest score and the corresponding score.

17. Write a function named `sort` that takes three integer parameters by reference. The function should rearrange the parameter values so that the first parameter gets set to the smallest value, the second parameter gets set to the second smallest value, and the third parameter gets set to the largest value. For example, given the variable assignments `a = 30; b = 10; c = 20;` then the function call `sort(a,b,c)` should result in `a = 10, b = 20, and c = 30`. Note that the array construct covered in Chapter 5 will give you a way to solve this problem for an arbitrary number of items instead of only for three items.

Arrays 5

It is a capital mistake to theorize before one has data.

SIR ARTHUR CONAN DOYLE, *Scandal in Bohemia* (Sherlock Holmes)

Introduction

An *array* is used to process a collection of data all of which is of the same type, such as a list of temperatures or a list of names. This chapter introduces the basics of defining and using arrays in C++ and presents many of the basic techniques used when designing algorithms and programs that use arrays.

You may skip this chapter and read Chapter 6 and most of Chapter 7, which cover classes, before reading this chapter. The only material in those chapters that uses material from this chapter is Section 7.3, which introduces vectors.

5.1 Introduction to Arrays

Suppose we wish to write a program that reads in five test scores and performs some manipulations on these scores. For instance, the program might compute the highest test score and then output the amount by which each score falls short of the highest. The highest score is not known until all five scores are read in. Hence, all five scores must be retained in storage so that after the highest score is computed each score can be compared with it. To retain the five scores, we will need something equivalent to five variables of type `int`. We could use five individual variables of type `int`, but five variables are hard to keep track of, and we may later want to change our program to handle 100 scores; certainly, 100 variables are impractical. An array is the perfect solution. An **array** behaves like a list of variables with a uniform naming mechanism that can be declared in a single line of simple code. For example, the names for the five individual variables we need might be `score[0]`, `score[1]`, `score[2]`, `score[3]`, and `score[4]`. The part that does not change, in this case `score`, is the name of the array. The part that can change is the integer in the square brackets, [ ].

Declaring and Referencing Arrays

array

In C++, an array consisting of five variables of type `int` can be declared as follows:

```
int score[5];
```

This declaration is like declaring the following five variables to all be of type `int`:

```
score[0], score[1], score[2], score[3], score[4]
```

These individual variables that together make up the array are referred to in a variety of different ways. We will call them **indexed variables**, though they are also sometimes called **subscripted variables** or **elements** of the array. The number in square brackets is called an **index** or a **subscript**. In C++, *indexes are numbered starting with* 0, *not starting with* 1 *or any other number except* 0. The number of indexed variables in an array is called the **declared size** of the array, or sometimes simply the **size** of the array. When an array is declared, the size of the array is given in square brackets after the array name. The indexed variables are then numbered (also using square brackets), starting with 0 and ending with the integer that is one less than the size of the array.

In our example, the indexed variables were of type int, but an array can have indexed variables of any type. For example, to declare an array with indexed variables of type double, simply use the type name double instead of int in the declaration of the array. All the indexed variables for one array, however, are of the same type. This type is called the **base type** of the array. Thus, in our example of the array score, the base type is int.

You can declare arrays and regular variables together. For example, the following declares the two int variables next and max in addition to the array score:

```
int next, score[5], max;
```

An indexed variable such as score[3] can be used anyplace that an ordinary variable of type int can be used.

Do not confuse the two ways to use the square brackets, []], with an array name. When used in a declaration, such as

```
int score[5];
```

the number enclosed in the square brackets specifies how many indexed variables the array has. When used anywhere else, the number enclosed in the square brackets tells which indexed variable is meant. For example, score[0] through score[4] are indexed variables of the array previously declared.

The index inside the square brackets need not be given as an integer constant. You can use any expression in the square brackets as long as the expression evaluates to one of the integers ranging from 0 through the integer one less than the size of the array. For example, the following will set the value of score[3] equal to 99:

```
int n = 2;
score[n + 1] = 99;
```

Although they may look different, score[n + 1] and score[3] are the same indexed variable in the previous code, because n + 1 evaluates to 3.

The identity of an indexed variable, such as score[i], is determined by the value of its index, which in this instance is i. Thus, you can write programs that say things like "do such and such to the ith indexed variable," where the value of i is computed by the program. For example, the program in Display 5.1 reads in scores and processes them in the way described at the start of this chapter.

indexed variable, subscripted variable, or element

index or subscript

declared size

base type

VideoNote
Array
Walkthrough

Display 5.1   Program Using an Array

```
1    //Reads in five scores and shows how much each
2    //score differs from the highest score.
3    #include <iostream>
4    using namespace std;

5    int main( )
6    {
7        int i, score[5], max;

8        cout << "Enter 5 scores:\n";
9        cin >> score[0];
10       max = score[0];
11       for (i = 1; i < 5; i++)
12       {
13           cin >> score[i];
14           if (score[i] > max)
15               max = score[i];
16           //max is the largest of the values score[0],...., score[i].
17       }

18       cout << "The highest score is " << max << endl
19            << "The scores and their\n"
20            << "differences from the highest are:\n";
21       for (i = 0; i < 5; i++)
22           cout << score[i] << " off by "
23                << (max - score[i]) << endl;
24       return 0;
25   }
```

Sample Dialogue

```
Enter 5 scores:
5 9 2 10 6
The highest score is 10
The scores and their
differences from the highest are:
5 off by 5
9 off by 1
2 off by 8
10 off by 0
6 off by 4
```

TIP: Use for Loops with Arrays

The second `for` loop in Display 5.1 illustrates a common way to step through an array:

```
for (i = 0; i < 5; i++)
    cout << score[i] << " off by "
         << (max - score[i]) << endl;
```

The `for` statement is ideally suited to array manipulations. ■

PITFALL: Array Indexes Always Start with Zero

The indexes of an array always start with 0 and end with the integer that is one less than the size of the array. ■

TIP: Use a Defined Constant for the Size of an Array

Look again at the program in Display 5.1. It only works for classes that have exactly five students. Most classes do not have exactly five students. One way to make a program more versatile is to use a defined constant for the size of each array. For example, the program in Display 5.1 could be rewritten to use the following defined constant:

```
const int NUMBER_OF_STUDENTS = 5;
```

The line with the array declaration would then be

```
int i, score[NUMBER_OF_STUDENTS], max;
```

Of course, all places in the program that have a 5 for the size of the array should also be changed to have NUMBER_OF_STUDENTS instead of 5. If these changes are made to the program (or better still, if the program had been written this way in the first place), then the program can be revised to work for any number of students by simply changing the one line that defines the constant NUMBER_OF_STUDENTS.

You may be tempted to use a variable for the array size, such as the following:

```
cout << "Enter number of students:\n";
cin >> number;
int score[number]; //ILLEGAL ON MANY COMPILERS!
```

Some but not all compilers will allow you to specify an array size with a variable in this way. However, for the sake of portability you should not do so, even if your compiler permits it. (In Chapter 10 we will discuss a different kind of array whose size can be determined when the program is run.) ■

Array Declaration

SYNTAX

Type_Name Array_Name[*Declared_Size*];

EXAMPLES

```
int bigArray[100];
double a[3];
double b[5];
char grade[10], oneGrade;
```

An array declaration of the form shown here will define *Declared_Size* index variables, namely, the indexed variables *Array_Name*[0] through *Array_Name*[*Declared_Size*−1]. Each index variable is a variable of type *Type_Name*.

The array a consists of the indexed variables a[0], a[1], and a[2], all of type double. The array b consists of the indexed variables b[0], b[1], b[2], b[3], and b[4], also all of type double. You can combine array declarations with the declaration of simple variables, such as the variable oneGrade shown here.

Arrays in Memory

Before discussing how arrays are represented in a computer's memory, let us first see how a simple variable, such as a variable of type int or double, is represented in the computer's memory. A computer's memory consists of a list of numbered locations called *bytes*.[1] The number of a byte is known as its **address**. A simple variable is implemented as a portion of memory consisting of some number of consecutive bytes. The number of bytes is determined by the type of the variable. Thus, a simple variable in memory is described by two pieces of information: an address in memory (giving the location of the first byte for that variable) and the type of the variable, which tells how many bytes of memory the variable requires. When we speak of the *address of a variable*, it is this address we are talking about. When your program stores a value in the variable, what really happens is that the value (coded as zeros and ones) is placed in those bytes of memory that are assigned to that variable. Similarly, when a variable is given as a (call-by-reference) argument to a function, it is the address of the variable that is actually given to the calling function. Now let us move on to discuss how arrays are stored in memory.

Array indexed variables are represented in memory the same way as ordinary variables, but with arrays there is a little more to the story. The locations of the various array indexed variables are always placed next to one another in memory. For example, consider the following:

```
int a[6];
```

[1] A byte consists of eight bits, but the exact size of a byte is not important to this discussion.

When you declare this array, the computer reserves enough memory to hold six variables of type int. Moreover, the computer always places these variables one after the other in memory. The computer then remembers the address of indexed variable a[0], but it does not remember the address of any other indexed variable. When your program needs the address of some other indexed variable in this array, the computer calculates the address for this other indexed variable from the address of a[0]. For example, if you start at the address of a[0] and count past enough memory for three variables of type int, then you will be at the address of a[3]. To obtain the address of a[3], the computer starts with the address of a[0] (which is a number). The computer then adds the number of bytes needed to hold three variables of type int to the number for the address of a[0]. The result is the address of a[3]. This implementation is diagrammed in Display 5.2. Many of the peculiarities of arrays in C++ can only be understood in terms of these details about memory. For example, in the next Pitfall section, we use these details to explain what happens when your program uses an illegal array index.

Display 5.2   An Array in Memory

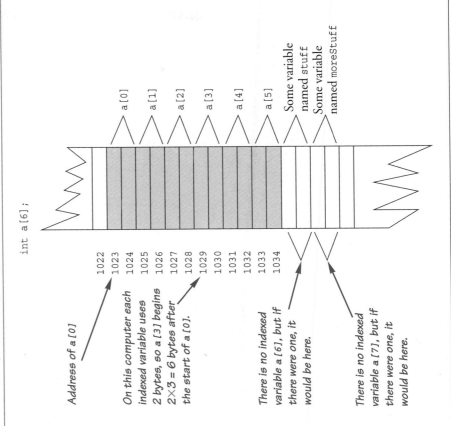

```
int a[6];
```

Address of a[0]

1022
1023
1024
1025
1026
1027
1028
1029
1030
1031
1032
1033
1034

a[0]
a[1]
a[2]
a[3]
a[4]
a[5]

Some variable named stuff
Some variable named moreStuff

On this computer each indexed variable uses 2 bytes, so a[3] begins 2×3 = 6 bytes after the start of a[0].

There is no indexed variable a[6], but if there were one, it would be here.

There is no indexed variable a[7], but if there were one, it would be here.

PITFALL: Array Index out of Range

The most common programming error made when using arrays is attempting to reference a nonexistent array index. For example, consider the following array declaration:

```
int a[6];
```

When using the array a, every index expression must evaluate to one of the integers 0 through 5. For example, if your program contains the indexed variable a[i], the i must evaluate to one of the six integers 0, 1, 2, 3, 4, or 5. If i evaluates to anything else, that is an error. When an index expression evaluates to some value other than those allowed by the array declaration, the index is said to be **out of range** or simply **illegal**. On most systems, the result of an illegal array index is that your program will simply do something wrong, possibly disastrously wrong, and will do so without giving you any warning.

For example, suppose your system is typical, the array a is declared as shown, and your program contains the following:

```
a[i] = 238;
```

illegal array index

Now, suppose the value of i, unfortunately, happens to be 7. The computer proceeds as if a[7] were a legal indexed variable. The computer calculates the address where a[7] would be (if only there were an a[7]) and places the value 238 in that location in memory. However, there is no indexed variable a[7] and the memory that receives this 238 probably belongs to some other variable, maybe a variable named moreStuff. So the value of moreStuff has been unintentionally changed. This situation is illustrated in Display 5.2.

Array indexes most commonly get out of range at the first or last iteration of a loop that processes the array. Thus, it pays to carefully check all array processing loops to be certain that they begin and end with legal array indexes. ■

Initializing Arrays

An array can be initialized when it is declared. When initializing the array, the values for the various indexed variables are enclosed in braces and separated with commas. For example, consider the following:

```
int children[3] = {2, 12, 1};
```

The previous declaration is equivalent to the following code:

```
int children[3];
children[0] = 2;
children[1] = 12;
children[2] = 1;
```

If you list fewer values than there are indexed variables, those values will be used to initialize the first few indexed variables, and the remaining indexed variables will be initialized to a zero of the array base type. In this situation, indexed variables not provided with initializers are initialized to zero. However, arrays with no initializers and other variables declared within a function definition, including the main function of a program, are not initialized. Although array indexed variables (and other variables) may sometimes be automatically initialized to zero, you cannot and should not count on it.

If you initialize an array when it is declared, you can omit the size of the array, and the array will automatically be declared to have the minimum size needed for the initialization values. For example, the following declaration

```
int b[] = {5, 12, 11};
```

is equivalent to

```
int b[3] = {5, 12, 11};
```

Self-Test Exercises

1. Describe the difference in the meaning of int a[5]; and the meaning of a[4]. What is the meaning of the [5] and [4] in each case?

2. In the array declaration

```
double score[5];
```

identify the following:

a. The array name

b. The base type

c. The declared size of the array

d. The range of values an index accessing this array can have

e. One of the indexed variables (or elements) of this array

3. Identify any errors in the following array declarations.

a. int x[4] = { 8, 7, 6, 4, 3 };

b. int x[] = { 8, 7, 6, 4 };

c. const int SIZE = 4;
   int x[SIZE];

4. What is the output of the following code?

```
char symbol [3] = {'a', 'b', 'c'};
for (int index = 0; index < 3; index++)
    cout << symbol [index];
```

(continued)

Self-Test Exercises (continued)

5. What is the output of the following code?

```
double a[3] = {1.1, 2.2, 3.3};
cout << a[0] << " " << a[1] << " " << a[2] << endl;
a[1] = a[2];
cout << a[0] << " " << a[1] << " " << a[2] << endl;
```

6. What is the output of the following code?

```
int i, temp[10];
for (i = 0; i < 10; i++)
    temp[i] = 2*i;
for (i = 0; i < 10; i++)
    cout << temp[i] << " ";
cout << endl;
for (i = 0; i < 10; i = i + 2)
    cout << temp[i] << " ";
```

7. What is wrong with the following piece of code?

```
int sampleArray[10];
for (int index = 1; index <= 10; index++)
    sampleArray[index] = 3*index;
```

8. Suppose we expect the elements of the array a to be ordered so that

```
a[0] ≤ a[1] ≤ a[2] ≤ ...
```

However, to be safe we want our program to test the array and issue a warning in case it turns out that some elements are out of order. The following code is supposed to output such a warning, but it contains a bug. What is it?

```
double a[10];
    <Some code to fill the array a goes here.>
for (int index = 0; index < 10; index++)
    if (a[index] > a[index + 1])
        cout << "Array elements " << index << " and "
             << (index + 1) << " are out of order.";
```

9. Write some C++ code that will fill an array a with 20 values of type int read in from the keyboard. You need not write a full program, just the code to do this, but do give the declarations for the array and for all variables.

Self-Test Exercises (continued)

10. Suppose you have the following array declaration in your program:

    ```
    int yourArray[7];
    ```

    Also, suppose that in your implementation of C++, variables of type int use two bytes of memory. When you run your program, how much memory will this array consume? Suppose that, when you run your program, the system assigns the memory address 1000 to the indexed variable yourArray[0]. What will be the address of the indexed variable yourArray[3]?

5.2   Arrays in Functions

You can use both array indexed variables and entire arrays as arguments to functions. We first discuss array indexed variables as arguments to functions.

Indexed Variables as Function Arguments

An indexed variable can be an argument to a function in exactly the same way that any variable of the array base type can be an argument. For example, suppose a program contains the following declarations:

```
double i, n, a[10];
```

If myFunction takes one argument of type double, then the following is legal:

```
myFunction(n);
```

Since an indexed variable of the array a is also a variable of type double, just like n, the following is equally legal:

```
myFunction(a[3]);
```

An indexed variable can be a call-by-value argument or a call-by-reference argument. One subtlety applies to indexed variables used as arguments, however. For example, consider the following function call:

```
myFunction(a[i]);
```

If the value of i is 3, then the argument is a[3]. On the other hand, if the value of i is 0, then this call is equivalent to the following:

```
myFunction(a[0]);
```

The indexed expression is evaluated in order to determine exactly which indexed variable is given as the argument.

Self-Test Exercises

11. Consider the following function definition:

```
void tripler(int& n)
{
    n = 3 * n;
}
```

Which of the following are acceptable function calls?

```
int a[3] = {4, 5, 6}, number = 2;
tripler(a[2]);
tripler(a[3]);
tripler(a[number]);
tripler(a);
tripler(number);
```

12. What (if anything) is wrong with the following code? The definition of tripler is given in Self-Test Exercise 11.

```
int b[5] = {1, 2, 3, 4, 5};
for (int i = 1; i <= 5; i++)
    tripler(b[i]);
```

Entire Arrays as Function Arguments

A function can have a formal parameter for an entire array so that when the function is called, the argument that is plugged in for this formal parameter is an entire array. However, a formal parameter for an entire array is neither a call-by-value parameter nor a call-by-reference parameter; it is a new kind of formal parameter referred to as an **array parameter.** Let's start with an example.

The function defined in Display 5.3 has one array parameter, a, which will be replaced by an entire array when the function is called. It also has one ordinary call-by-value parameter (size) that is assumed to be an integer value equal to the size of the array. This function fills its array argument (that is, fills all the array's indexed variables) with values typed in from the keyboard; the function then outputs a message to the screen telling the index of the last array index used.

The formal parameter int a[] is an array parameter. The square brackets, with no index expression inside, are what C++ uses to indicate an array parameter. An array parameter is not quite a call-by-reference parameter, but for most practical purposes it behaves very much like a call-by-reference parameter. Let us go through this example in detail to see how an array argument works in this case. (An **array argument** is, of course, an array that is plugged in for an array parameter, such as a[].)

Display 5.3 Function with an Array Parameter

Function Declaration

```
void fillUp(int a[], int size);
//Precondition: size is the declared size of the array a.
//The user will type in size integers.
//Postcondition: The array a is filled with size integers
//from the keyboard.
```

Function Definition

```
void fillUp(int a[], int size)
{
    cout << "Enter " << size << " numbers:\n";
    for (int i = 0; i < size; i++)
        cin >> a[i];
    cout << "The last array index used is " << (size - 1) << endl;
}
```

When the function fillUp is called, it must have two arguments: The first gives an array of integers, and the second should give the declared size of the array. For example, the following is an acceptable function call:

```
int score[5], numberOfScores = 5;
fillUp(score, numberOfScores);
```

This call to fillUp will fill the array score with five integers typed in at the keyboard. Notice that the formal parameter a[] (which is used in the function declaration and the heading of the function definition) is given with square brackets but no index expression. (You may insert a number inside the square brackets for an array parameter, but the compiler will simply ignore the number, so we will not use such numbers in this book.) On the other hand, the argument given in the function call (score, in this example) is given without any square brackets or any index expression.

What happens to the array argument score in this function call? Very loosely speaking, the argument score is plugged in for the formal array parameter a in the body of the function, and then the function body is executed. Thus, the function call

```
fillUp(score, numberOfScores);
```

is equivalent to the following code:

```
{
    size = 5;
    cout << "Enter " << size << " numbers:\n";
    for (int i = 0; i < size; i++)
        cin >> score[i];
    cout << "The last array index used is " << (size - 1) << endl;
}
```

5 is the value of
numberOfScores

when to use []

The formal parameter a is a different kind of parameter from the ones we have seen before now. The formal parameter a is merely a placeholder for the argument score. When the function fillUp is called with score as the array argument, the computer behaves as if a were replaced with the corresponding argument score. When an array is used as an argument in a function call, any action that is performed on the array parameter is performed on the array argument, so the values of the indexed variables of the array argument can be changed by the function. If the formal parameter in the function body is changed (for example, with a cin statement), then the array argument will be changed.

So far it looks as if an array parameter is simply a call-by-reference parameter for an array. That is close to being true, but an array parameter is slightly different from a call-by-reference parameter. To help explain the difference, let us review some details about arrays.

Recall that an array is stored as a contiguous chunk of memory. For example, consider the following declaration for the array score:

arrays in memory

```
int score[5];
```

When you declare this array, the computer reserves enough memory to hold five variables of type int, which are stored one after the other in the computer's memory. The computer does not remember the addresses of each of these five indexed variables; it remembers only the address of the indexed variable score[0]. The computer also remembers that score has a total of five indexed variables, all of type int. It does not remember the address in memory of any indexed variable other than score[0]. For example, when your program needs score[3], the computer calculates the address of score[3] from the address of score[0]. The computer knows that score[3] is located three int variables past score[0]. Thus, to obtain the address of score[3], the computer takes the address of score[0] and adds a number that represents the amount of memory used by three int variables; the result is the address of score[3].

Viewed this way, an array has three parts: the address (location in memory) of the first indexed variable, the base type of the array (which determines how much memory each indexed variable uses), and the size of the array (that is, the number of indexed variables). When an array is used as an array argument to a function, only the first of these three parts is given to the function. When an array argument is plugged in for its corresponding formal parameter, all that is plugged in is the address of the array's first indexed variable. The base type of the array argument must match the base type of the formal parameter, so the function also knows the base type of the array. *However, the array argument does not tell the function the size of the array.* When the code in the function body is executed, the computer knows where the array starts in memory and how much memory each indexed variable uses, but (unless you make special provisions) it does not know how many indexed variables the array has. That is why it is critical that you always have another int argument telling the function the size of the array. (That is also why an array parameter is *not* the same as a call-by-reference parameter. You can think of an array parameter as a weak form of call-by-reference parameter in which everything about the array is told to the function except for the size of the array.)[2]

These array parameters may seem a little strange, but they have at least one very nice property as a direct result of their seemingly strange definition. This advantage is best illustrated by again looking at our example of the function `fillUp` given in Display 5.3. *That same function can be used to fill an array of any size,* as long as the base type of the array is `int`. For example, suppose you have the following array declarations:

```
int score[5], time[10];
```

The first of the following calls to `fillUp` fills the array `score` with five values, and the second fills the array `time` with ten values:

```
fillUp(score, 5);
fillUp(time, 10);
```

You can use the same function for array arguments of different sizes, because the size is a separate argument.

Different size array arguments can be plugged in for the same array parameter

---

Array Formal Parameters and Arguments

An argument to a function may be an entire array, but an argument for an entire array is neither a call-by-value argument nor a call-by-reference argument. It is a new kind of argument known as an *array argument*. When an array argument is plugged in for an *array parameter*, all that is given to the function is the address in memory of the first indexed variable of the array argument (the one indexed by 0). The array argument does not tell the function the size of the array. Therefore, when you have an array parameter to a function, you normally must also have another formal parameter of type `int` that gives the size of the array (as in the following example).

An array argument is like a call-by-reference argument in the following way: If the function body changes the array parameter, then when the function is called, that change is actually made to the array argument. Thus, a function can change the values of an array argument (that is, can change the values of its indexed variables).

The syntax for a function declaration with an array parameter is as follows.

SYNTAX

Type_Returned Function_Name(..., *Base_Type Array_Name*[ ],...);

EXAMPLE

```
void sumArray(double& sum, double a[ ], int size);
```

---

[2]If you have heard of pointers, this will sound like pointers and indeed an array argument is passed by passing a pointer to its first (zeroth) index variable. We will discuss this in Chapter 10. If you have not yet learned about pointers, you can safely ignore this footnote.

const

constant
array
parameter

The const Parameter Modifier

When you use an array argument in a function call, the function can change the values stored in the array. This is usually fine. However, in a complicated function definition, you might write code that inadvertently changes one or more of the values stored in an array even though the array should not be changed at all. As a precaution, you can tell the compiler that you do not intend to change the array argument, and the computer will then check to make sure your code does not inadvertently change any of the values in the array. To tell the compiler that an array argument should not be changed by your function, insert the modifier const before the array parameter for that argument position. An array parameter that is modified with a const is called a **constant array parameter.**

For example, the following function outputs the values in an array but does not change the values in the array:

```
void showTheWorld(int a[], int sizeOfa)
//Precondition: sizeOfa is the declared size of the array a.
//All indexed variables of a have been given values.
//Postcondition: The values in a have been written to the screen.
{
    cout << "The array contains the following values:\n";
    for (int i = 0; i < sizeOfa; i++)
        cout << a[i] << " ";
    cout << endl;
}
```

This function will work fine. However, as an added safety measure, you can add the modifier const to the function heading as follows:

```
void showTheWorld(const int a[], int sizeOfa)
```

With the addition of this modifier const, the computer will issue an error message if your function definition contains a mistake that changes any of the values in the array argument. For example, the following is a version of the function showTheWorld that contains a mistake that inadvertently changes the value of the array argument. Fortunately, this version of the function definition includes the modifier const, so that an error message will tell us that the array a has been changed. This error message will help to explain the mistake:

```
void showTheWorld(const int a[], int sizeOfa)
//Precondition: sizeOfa is the declared size of the array a.
//All indexed variables of a have been given values.
//Postcondition: The values in a have been written to the screen.
{
    cout << "The array contains the following values:\n";
    for (int i = 0; i < sizeOfa; a[i]++)
        cout << a[i] << " ";                    ← Mistake, but the compiler
    cout << endl;                                  will not catch it unless you
}                                                  use the const modifier.
```

If we had not used the `const` modifier in the previous function definition and if we made the mistake shown, the function would compile and run with no error messages. However, the code would contain an infinite loop that continually increments `a[0]` and writes its new value to the screen.

The problem with this incorrect version of `showTheWorld` is that the wrong item is incremented in the `for` loop. The indexed variable `a[i]` is incremented, but it should be the index `i` that is incremented. In this incorrect version, the index `i` starts with the value `0` and that value is never changed. But `a[i]`, which is the same as `a[0]`, is incremented. When the indexed variable `a[i]` is incremented, that changes a value in the array, and since we included the modifier `const`, the computer will issue a warning message. That error message should serve as a clue to what is wrong.

You normally have a function declaration in your program in addition to the function definition. When you use the `const` modifier in a function definition, you must also use it in the function declaration so that the function heading and the function declaration are consistent.

The modifier `const` can be used with any kind of parameter, but it is normally used only with array parameters and call-by-reference parameters for classes, which are discussed in Chapters 6 and 7.

PITFALL: Inconsistent Use of const Parameters

The `const` parameter modifier is an all-or-nothing proposition. If you use it for one array parameter of a particular type, then you should use it for every other array parameter that has that type and that is not changed by the function. The reason has to do with function calls within function calls. Consider the definition of the function `showDifference`, which is given here along with the declaration of a function used in the definition:

```
double computeAverage(int a[], int numberUsed);
//Returns the average of the elements in the first numberUsed
//elements of the array a. The array a is unchanged.

void showDifference(const int a[], int numberUsed)
{
    double average = computeAverage(a, numberUsed);
    cout << "Average of the " << numberUsed
         << " numbers = " << average << endl
         << "The numbers are:\n";
    for (int index = 0; index < numberUsed; index++)
        cout << a[index] << " differs from average by "
             << (a[index] - average) << endl;
}
```

The code shown will give an error message or warning message with most compilers. The function `computeAverage` does not change its parameter a. However, when the

(continued)

PITFALL: (continued)

compiler processes the function definition for `showDifference`, it will think that `computeAverage` does (or at least might) change the value of its parameter a. This is because when it is translating the function definition for `showDifference`, all the compiler knows about the function `computeAverage` is the function declaration for `computeAverage`, which does not contain a `const` to tell the compiler that the parameter a will not be changed. Thus, if you use `const` with the parameter a in the function `showDifference`, then you should also use the modifier `const` with the parameter a in the function `computeAverage`. The function declaration for `computeAverage` should be as follows:

```
double computeAverage(const int a[], int numberUsed);
```

Functions That Return an Array

A function may not return an array in the same way that it returns a value of type `int` or `double`. There is a way to obtain something more or less equivalent to a function that returns an array. The thing to do is return a pointer to the array. We will discuss this topic when we discuss the interaction of arrays and pointers in Chapter 10. Until you learn about pointers, you have no way to write a function that returns an array. ∎

EXAMPLE: Production Graph

Display 5.4 contains a program that uses an array and a number of array parameters. This program for the Apex Plastic Spoon Manufacturing Company displays a bar graph showing the productivity of each of its four manufacturing plants for any given week. Plants keep separate production figures for each department, such as the teaspoon department, soup spoon department, plain cocktail spoon department, colored cocktail spoon department, and so forth. Moreover, each of the four plants has a different number of departments.

As you can see from the sample dialogue in Display 5.4, the graph uses one asterisk for each 1000 production units. Since output is in units of 1000, it must be scaled by dividing it by 1000. This presents a problem because the computer must display a whole number of asterisks. It cannot display 1.6 asterisks for 1600 units. We therefore round to the nearest thousand. Thus, 1600 will be the same as 2000 and will produce two asterisks.

The array `production` holds the total production for each of the four plants. In C++, array indexes always start with 0. But since the plants are numbered 1 through 4, rather than 0 through 3, we have placed the total production for plant number n in indexed variable `production[n-1]`. The total output for plant number 1 will be held in `production[0]`, the figures for plant 2 will be held in `production[1]`, and so forth.

EXAMPLE: (continued)

Since the output is in thousands of units, the program will scale the values of the array elements. If the total output for plant number 3 is 4040 units, then the value of `production[2]` will initially be set to 4040. This value of 4040 will then be scaled to 4 so that the value of `production[2]` is changed to 4 and four asterisks will be output to represent the output for plant number 3. This scaling is done by the function `scale`, which takes the entire array production as an argument and changes the values stored in the array.

The function round rounds its argument to the nearest integer. For example, `round(2.3)` returns 2, and `round(2.6)` returns 3. The function round was discussed in Chapter 3, in the programming example entitled "A Rounding Function."

Display 5.4 Production Graph Program (part 1 of 4)

```
1  //Reads data and displays a bar graph showing productivity for each plant.

2  #include <iostream>
3  #include <cmath>
4  using namespace std;
5  const int NUMBER_OF_PLANTS = 4;

6  void inputData(int a[], int lastPlantNumber);
7  //Precondition: lastPlantNumber is the declared size of the array a.
8  //Postcondition: For plantNumber = 1 through lastPlantNumber:
9  //a[plantNumber-1] equals the total production for plant number
   //plantNumber.

10 void scale(int a[], int size);
11 //Precondition: a[0] through a[size-1] each has a nonnegative value.
12 //Postcondition: a[i] has been changed to the number of 1000s (rounded to
13 //an integer) that were originally in a[i], for all i such that 0 <= i
   //<= size-1.

14 void graph(const int asteriskCount[], int lastPlantNumber);
15 //Precondition: a[0] through a[lastPlantNumber-1] have nonnegative values.
16 //Postcondition: A bar graph has been displayed saying that plant
17 //number N has produced a[N-1] 1000s of units, for each N such that
18 //1 <= N <= lastPlantNumber

19 void getTotal(int& sum);
20 //Reads nonnegative integers from the keyboard and
21 //places their total in sum.

22 int round(double number);
23 //Precondition: number >= 0.
24 //Returns number rounded to the nearest integer.
```

(continued)

Display 5.4   Production Graph Program (part 2 of 4)

```
25    void printAsterisks(int n);
26    //Prints n asterisks to the screen.

27    int main( )
28    {
29        int production[NUMBER_OF_PLANTS];

30        cout << "This program displays a graph showing\n"
31             << "production for each plant in the company.\n";

32        inputData(production, NUMBER_OF_PLANTS);
33        scale(production, NUMBER_OF_PLANTS);
34        graph(production, NUMBER_OF_PLANTS);
35        return 0;
36    }

37    void inputData(int a[], int lastPlantNumber)
38    {
39        for (int plantNumber = 1;
40                 plantNumber <= lastPlantNumber; plantNumber++)
41        {
42            cout << endl
43                 << "Enter production data for plant number "
44                 << plantNumber << endl;
45            getTotal(a[plantNumber - 1]);
46        }
47    }

48    void getTotal(int& sum)
49    {
50        cout << "Enter number of units produced by each department.\n"
51             << "Append a negative number to the end of the list.\n";

52        sum = 0;
53        int next;
54        cin >> next;
55        while (next >= 0)
56        {
57            sum = sum + next;
58            cin >> next;
59        }

60        cout << "Total = " << sum << endl;
61    }

62
63    void scale(int a[], int size)
64    {
```

Display 5.4   Production Graph Program (part 3 of 4)

```
65        for (int index = 0; index < size; index++)
66            a[index] = round(a[index]/1000.0);
67    }

68    int round(double number)
69    {
70        return static_cast<int>(floor(number + 0.5));
71    }

72    void graph(const int asteriskCount[], int lastPlantNumber)
73    {
74        cout << "\nUnits produced in thousands of units:\n\n";
75        for (int plantNumber = 1;
76                 plantNumber <= lastPlantNumber; plantNumber++)
77        {
78            cout << "Plant #" << plantNumber << " ";
79            printAsterisks(asteriskCount[plantNumber - 1]);
80            cout << endl;
81        }
82    }

83    void printAsterisks(int n)
84    {
85        for (int count = 1; count <= n; count++)
86            cout << "*";
87    }
```

Sample Dialogue

```
This program displays a graph showing
Production for each plant in the company.

Enter production data for plant number 1
Enter number of units produced by each department.
Append a negative number to the end of the list.
2000 3000 1000 -1

Total = 6000

Enter production data for plant number 2
Enter number of units produced by each department.
Append a negative number to the end of the list.
2050 3002 1300 -1

Total = 6352
```

(continued)

Display 5.4   Production Graph Program (part 4 of 4)

```
Enter production data for plant number 3
Enter number of units produced by each department.
Append a negative number to the end of the list.
5000 4020 500 4348 -1
Total = 13868

Enter production data for plant number 4
Enter number of units produced by each department.
Append a negative number to the end of the list.
2507 6050 1809 -1
Total = 10366

Units produced in thousands of units:

Plant #1 ******
Plant #2 ******
Plant #3 ***********
Plant #4 **********
```

Self-Test Exercises

13. Write a function definition for a function called oneMore, which has a formal parameter for an array of integers and increases the value of each array element by 1. Add any other formal parameters that are needed.

14. Consider the following function definition:

```
void too2(int a[], int howMany)
{
    for (int index = 0; index < howMany; index++)
        a[index] = 2;
}
```

Which of the following are acceptable function calls?

```
int myArray[29];
too2(myArray, 29);
too2(myArray, 10);
too2(myArray, 55);
"Hey too2. Please come over here."
int yourArray[100];
too2(yourArray, 100);
too2(myArray[3], 29);
```

Self-Test Exercises (continued)

15. Insert const before any of the following array parameters that can be changed to constant array parameters.

```
void output(double a[], int size);
//Precondition: a[0] through a[size - 1] have values.
//Postcondition: a[0] through a[size - 1] have been written out.

void dropOdd(int a[], int size);
//Precondition: a[0] through a[size - 1] have values.
//Postcondition: All odd numbers in a[0] through a[size - 1]
//have been changed to 0.
```

16. Write a function named outOfOrder that takes as parameters an array of double and an int parameter named size and returns a value of type int. This function will test this array for being out of order, meaning that the array violates the following condition:

```
a[0] <= a[1] <= a[2] <= ...
```

The function returns −1 if the elements are not out of order; otherwise, it will return the index of the first element of the array that is out of order. For example, consider the declaration

```
double a[10] = {1.2, 2.1, 3.3, 2.5, 4.5,
                7.9, 5.4, 8.7, 9.9, 1.0};
```

In the previous array, a[2] and a[3] are the first pair out of order and a[3] is the first element out of order, so the function returns 3. If the array were sorted, the function would return −1.

5.3   Programming with Arrays

Never trust to general impressions, my boy, but concentrate yourself upon details.

SIR ARTHUR CONAN DOYLE, *A Case of Identity* (Sherlock Holmes)

This section discusses partially filled arrays and gives a brief introduction to sorting and searching of arrays. This section includes no new material about the C++ language, but does include more practice with C++ array parameters.

Partially Filled Arrays

Often the exact size needed for an array is not known when a program is written, or the size may vary from one run of the program to another. One common and easy way to handle this situation is to declare the array to be of the largest size the program could possibly need. The program is then free to use as much or as little of the array as is needed.

Partially filled arrays require some care. The program must keep track of how much of the array is used and must not reference any indexed variable that has not been given a value. The program in Display 5.5 illustrates this point. The program reads in a list of golf scores and shows how much each score differs from the average. This program will work for lists as short as one score, as long as ten scores, and of any length in between. The scores are stored in the array score, which has ten indexed variables, but the program uses only as much of the array as it needs. The variable numberUsed keeps track of how many elements are stored in the array. The elements (that is, the scores) are stored in positions score[0] through score[numberUsed-1]. The details are very similar to what they would be if numberUsed were the declared size of the array and the entire array were used. In particular, the variable numberUsed usually must be an argument to any function that manipulates the partially filled array. Since the argument numberUsed (when used properly) can often ensure that the function will not reference an illegal array index, this sometimes (but not always) eliminates the need for an argument that gives the declared size of the array. For example, the functions showDifference and computeAverage use the argument numberUsed to ensure that only legal array indexes are used. However, the function fillArray needs to know the maximum declared size for the array so that it does not overfill the array.

TIP: Do Not Skimp on Formal Parameters

Notice the function fillArray in Display 5.5. When fillArray is called, the declared array size MAX_NUMBER_SCORES is given as one of the arguments, as shown in the following function call from Display 5.5:

```
fillArray(score,  MAX_NUMBER_SCORES,  numberUsed);
```

You might protest that MAX_NUMBER_SCORES is a globally defined constant and so it could be used in the definition of fillArray without the need to make it an argument. You would be correct, and if we did not use fillArray in any program other than the one in Display 5.5, we could get by without making MAX_NUMBER_SCORES an argument to fill Array. However, fillArray is a generally useful function that you may want to use in several different programs. We do in fact also use the function fillArray in the program in Display 5.6, discussed in the next subsection. In the program in Display 5.6 the argument for the declared array size is a different named global constant. If we had written the global constant MAX_NUMBER_SCORES into the body of the function fillArray, we would not have been able to reuse the function in the program in Display 5.6.

Even if we used fillArray in only one program, it can still be a good idea to make the declared array size an argument to fillArray. Displaying the declared size of the array as an argument reminds us that the function needs this information in a critically important way. ■

Display 5.5   Partially Filled Array (part 1 of 2)

```
1   //Shows the difference between each of a list of golf scores and
    //their average.

2   #include <iostream>
3   using namespace std;
4   const int MAX_NUMBER_SCORES = 10;

5   void fillArray(int a[], int size, int& numberUsed);
6   //Precondition: size is the declared size of the array a.
7   //Postcondition: numberUsed is the number of values stored in a.
8   //a[0] through a[numberUsed-1] have been filled with
9   //nonnegative integers read from the keyboard.

10  double computeAverage(const int a[], int numberUsed);
11  //Precondition: a[0] through a[numberUsed-1] have values;
    //numberUsed > 0.
12  //Returns the average of numbers a[0] through a[numberUsed-1].

13  void showDifference(const int a[], int numberUsed);
14  //Precondition: The first numberUsed indexed variables of a have values.
15  //Postcondition: Gives screen output showing how much each of the first
16  //numberUsed elements of the array a differs from their average.

17  int main( )
18  {
19      int score[MAX_NUMBER_SCORES], numberUsed;
20      cout << "This program reads golf scores and shows\n"
21           << "how much each differs from the average.\n";

22      cout << "Enter golf scores:\n";

23      fillArray(score, MAX_NUMBER_SCORES, numberUsed);
24      showDifference(score, numberUsed);

25      return 0;
26  }

27  void fillArray(int a[], int size, int& numberUsed)
28  {
29      cout << "Enter up to " << size << " nonnegative whole numbers.\n"
30           << "Mark the end of the list with a negative number.\n";
31      int next, index = 0;
32      cin >> next;
33      while ((next >= 0) && (index < size))
34      {
35          a[index] = next;
36          index++;
37          cin >> next;
38      }
```

(continued)

Display 5.5   Partially Filled Array (part 2 of 2)

```
39      numberUsed = index;
40  }

41  double computeAverage(const int a[], int numberUsed)
42  {
43      double total = 0;
44      for (int index = 0; index < numberUsed; index++)
45          total = total + a[index];
46      if (numberUsed > 0)
47      {
48          return (total/numberUsed);
49      }
50      else
51      {
52          cout << "ERROR: number of elements is 0 in computeAverage.\n"
53               << "computeAverage returns 0.\n";
54          return 0;
55      }
56  }

57  void showDifference(const int a[], int numberUsed)
58  {
59      double average = computeAverage(a, numberUsed);
60      cout << "Average of the " << numberUsed
61           << " scores = " << average << endl
62           << "The scores are:\n";
63      for (int index = 0; index < numberUsed; index++)
64          cout << a[index] << " differs from average by "
65               << (a[index] - average) << endl;
66  }
```

Sample Dialogue

```
This program reads golf scores and shows
how much each differs from the average.
Enter golf scores:
Enter up to 10 nonnegative whole numbers.
Mark the end of the list with a negative number.
69 74 68 -1
Average of the 3 scores = 70.3333
The scores are:
69 differs from average by -1.33333
74 differs from average by 3.66667
68 differs from average by -2.33333
```

EXAMPLE: Searching an Array

A common programming task is to search an array for a given value. For example, the array may contain the student numbers for all students in a given course. To tell whether a particular student is enrolled, the array is searched to see if it contains the student's number. The simple program in Display 5.6 fills an array and then searches the array for values specified by the user. A real application program would be much more elaborate, but this shows all the essentials of the sequential search algorithm. The sequential search is the most straightforward searching algorithm you could imagine: The program looks at the array elements in order, first to last, to see if the target number is equal to any of the array elements.

In Display 5.6 the function search is used to search the array. When searching an array, you often want to know more than simply whether or not the target value is in the array. If the target value is in the array, you often want to know the index of the indexed variable holding that target value, since the index may serve as a guide to some additional information about the target value. Therefore, we designed the function search to return an index giving the location of the target value in the array, provided the target value is, in fact, in the array. If the target value is not in the array, search returns −1. Let's look at the function search in a little more detail.

The function search uses a while loop to check the array elements one after the other to see whether any of them equals the target value. The variable found is used as a flag to record whether or not the target element has been found. If the target element is found in the array, found is set to true, which in turn ends the while loop.

Display 5.6   Searching an Array (part 1 of 3)

```
1   //Searches a partially filled array of nonnegative integers.
2   #include <iostream>
3   using namespace std;
4   const int DECLARED_SIZE = 20;

5   void fillArray(int a[], int size, int& numberUsed);
6   //Precondition: size is the declared size of the array a.
7   //Postcondition: numberUsed is the number of values stored in a.
8   //a[0] through a[numberUsed-1] have been filled with
9   //nonnegative integers read from the keyboard.

10  int search(const int a[], int numberUsed, int target);
11  //Precondition: numberUsed is <= the declared size of a.
12  //Also, a[0] through a[numberUsed -1] have values.
13  //Returns the first index such that a[index] == target,
14  //provided there is such an index; otherwise, returns -1.
```

(continued)

Display 5.6   Searching an Array (part 2 of 3)

```
15   int main( )
16   {
17       int arr[DECLARED_SIZE], listSize, target;

18       fillArray(arr, DECLARED_SIZE, listSize);

19       char ans;
20       int result;
21       do
22       {
23           cout << "Enter a number to search for: ";
24           cin >> target;

25           result = search(arr, listSize, target);
26           if (result == -1)
27               cout << target << " is not on the list.\n";
28           else
29               cout << target << " is stored in array position "
30                    << result << endl
31                    << "(Remember: The first position is 0.)\n";

32           cout << "Search again?(y/n followed by Return): ";
33           cin >> ans;
34       } while ((ans != 'n') && (ans != 'N'));
35       cout << "End of program.\n";
36       return 0;
37   }

38   void fillArray(int a[], int size, int& numberUsed)
39   <The rest of the definition of fillArray is given in Display 5.5>
40   int search(const int a[], int numberUsed, int target)
41   {
42       int index = 0;
43       bool found = false;
44       while ((!found) && (index < numberUsed))
45           if (target == a[index])
               found = true;
47           else
48               index++;

49       if (found)
50           return index;
51       else
52           return -1;
53   }
```

Display 5.6   Searching an Array (part 3 of 3)

Sample Dialogue

```
Enter up to 20 nonnegative whole numbers.
Mark the end of the list with a negative number.
10 20 30 40 50 60 70 80 -1
Enter a number to search for: 10
10 is stored in array position 0
(Remember: The first position is 0.)
Search again?(y/n followed by Return): y
Enter a number to search for: 40
40 is stored in array position 3
(Remember: The first position is 0.)
Search again?(y/n followed by Return): y
Enter a number to search for: 42
42 is not on the list.
Search again?(y/n followed by Return): n
End of program.
```

EXAMPLE: Sorting an Array

One of the most widely encountered programming tasks, and certainly the most thoroughly studied, is sorting a list of values, such as a list of sales figures that must be sorted from lowest to highest or from highest to lowest, or a list of words that must be sorted into alphabetical order. This example describes a function called sort that will sort a partially filled array of numbers so that they are ordered from smallest to largest.

The procedure sort has one array parameter, a. The array a will be partially filled, so there is an additional formal parameter called numberUsed that tells how many array positions are used. Thus, the declaration and precondition for the function sort are as follows:

```
void sort(int a[], int numberUsed);
    //Precondition: numberUsed <= declared size of the array a.
    //The array elements a[0] through a[numberUsed-1] have values.
```

The function sort rearranges the elements in array a so that after the function call is completed the elements are sorted as follows:

$$a[0] \leq a[1] \leq a[2] \leq \ldots \leq a[numberUsed - 1]$$

The algorithm we use to do the sorting is called *selection sort*. It is one of the easiest of the sorting algorithms to understand.

(continued)

EXAMPLE: (continued)

One way to design an algorithm is to rely on the definition of the problem. In this case the problem is to sort an array a from smallest to largest. That means rearranging the values so that a[0] is the smallest, a[1] the next smallest, and so forth. That definition yields an outline for the **selection sort** algorithm:

```
for (int index = 0; index < numberUsed; index++)
    Place the indexth smallest element in a[index]
```

There are many ways to realize this general approach. The details could be developed using two arrays and copying the elements from one array to the other in sorted order, but one array should be both adequate and economical. Therefore, the function sort uses only the one array containing the values to be sorted. The function sort rearranges the values in the array a by interchanging pairs of values. Let us go through a concrete example so that you can see how the algorithm works.

Consider the array shown in Display 5.7. The algorithm will place the smallest value in a[0]. The smallest value is the value in a[3], so the algorithm interchanges the values of a[0] and a[3]. The algorithm then looks for the next-smallest element. The value in a[0] is now the smallest element, and so the next-smallest element is the smallest of the remaining elements a[1], a[2], a[3], ..., a[9]. In the example in Display 5.7 the next-smallest element is in a[5], so the algorithm interchanges the values of a[1] and a[5]. This positioning of the second-smallest element is illustrated in the fourth and fifth array pictures in Display 5.7. The algorithm then positions the third-smallest element, and so forth. As the sorting proceeds, the beginning array elements are set equal to the correct sorted values. The sorted portion of the array grows by adding elements one after the other from the elements in the unsorted end of the array. Notice that the algorithm need not do anything with the value in the last indexed variable, a[9]. Once the other elements are positioned correctly, a[9] must also have the correct value. After all, the correct value for a[9] is the smallest value left to be moved, and the only value left to be moved is the value that is already in a[9].

The definition of the function sort, included in a demonstration program, is given in Display 5.8. sort uses the function indexOfSmallest to find the index of the smallest element in the unsorted end of the array, and then it does an interchange to move this next-smallest element down into the sorted part of the array.

The function swapValues, shown in Display 5.8, is used to interchange the values of indexed variables. For example, the following call will interchange the values of a[0] and a[3]:

```
swapValues(a[0], a[3]);
```

The function swapValues was explained in Chapter 4.

Display 5.7   Selection Sort

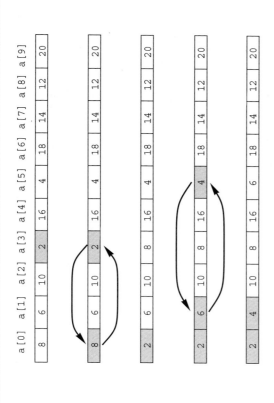

Display 5.8   Sorting an Array (part 1 of 3)

```
1   //Tests the procedure sort.
2   #include <iostream>
3   using namespace std;

4   void fillArray(int a[], int size, int& numberUsed);
5   //Precondition: size is the declared size of the array a.
6   //Postcondition: numberUsed is the number of values stored in a.
7   //a[0] through a[numberUsed - 1] have been filled with
8   //nonnegative integers read from the keyboard.

9   void sort(int a[], int numberUsed);
10  //Precondition: numberUsed <= declared size of the array a.
11  //The array elements a[0] through a[numberUsed - 1] have values.
12  //Postcondition: The values of a[0] through a[numberUsed - 1] have
13  //been rearranged so that a[0] <= a[1] <= ... <= a[numberUsed - 1].

14  void swapValues(int& v1, int& v2);
15  //Interchanges the values of v1 and v2.

16  int indexOfSmallest(const int a[ ], int startIndex, int numberUsed);
17  //Precondition: 0 <= startIndex < numberUsed. Reference array elements
18  //have values. Returns the index i such that a[i] is the smallest of the
19  //values a[startIndex], a[startIndex + 1], ..., a[numberUsed - 1].
```

(continued)

Display 5.8   Sorting an Array (part 2 of 3)

```
20    int main( )
21    {
22        cout << "This program sorts numbers from lowest to highest.\n";

23        int sampleArray[10], numberUsed;
24        fillArray(sampleArray, 10, numberUsed);
25        sort(sampleArray, numberUsed);

26        cout << "In sorted order the numbers are:\n";
27        for (int index = 0; index < numberUsed; index++)
28            cout << sampleArray[index] << " ";
29        cout << endl;

30        return 0;
31    }

32    void fillArray(int a[], int size, int& numberUsed)
33        <The rest of the definition of fillArray is given in Displays 5.5.>

34    void sort(int a[], int numberUsed)
35    {
36        int indexOfNextSmallest;
37        for (int index = 0; index < numberUsed - 1; index++)
38        {//Place the correct value in a[index]:
39            indexOfNextSmallest =
40                indexOfSmallest(a, index, numberUsed);
41            swapValues(a[index], a[indexOfNextSmallest]);
42            //a[0] <= a[1] <=...<= a[index] are the smallest of the
43            //original array elements. The rest of the
44            //elements are in the remaining positions.
45        }
46    }

47    void swapValues(int& v1, int& v2)
48    {
49        int temp;
50        temp = v1;
51        v1 = v2;
52        v2 = temp;
53    }

54    int indexOfSmallest(const int a[], int startIndex, int numberUsed)
55    {
56        int min = a[startIndex],
57            indexOfMin = startIndex;
```

Display 5.8   Sorting an Array (part 3 of 3)

```
58      for (int index = startIndex + 1; index < numberUsed; index++)
59          if (a[index] < min)
60          {
61              min = a[index];
62              indexOfMin = index;
63              //min is the smallest of a[startIndex] through a[index]
64          }
65      return indexOfMin;
66  }
```

Sample Dialogue

```
This program sorts numbers from lowest to highest.
Enter up to 10 nonnegative whole numbers.
Mark the end of the list with a negative number.
80 30 50 70 60 90 20 30 40 -1
In sorted order the numbers are:
20 30 30 40 50 60 70 80 90
```

Self-Test Exercises

17. Write a program that will read up to ten nonnegative integers into an array called numberArray and then write the integers back to the screen. For this exercise you need not use any functions. This is just a toy program and can be very minimal.

18. Write a program that will read up to ten letters into an array and write the letters back to the screen in the reverse order. For example, if the input is

     abcd.

     then the output should be

     dcba

     Use a period as a sentinel value to mark the end of the input. Call the array letterBox. For this exercise you need not use any functions. This is just a toy program and can be very minimal.

19. Following is the declaration for an alternative version of the function search defined in Display 5.6. In order to use this alternative version of the search function we would need to rewrite the program slightly, but for this

(continued)

Self-Test Exercises (continued)

exercise all you need do is write the function definition for this alternative version of search.

```
bool search(const int a[], int numberUsed,
                 int target, int& where);
//Precondition: numberUsed is <= the declared size of the
//array a. Also, a[0] through a[numberUsed -1] have values.
//Postcondition: If target is one of the elements a[0]
//through a[numberUsed - 1], then this function returns
//true and sets the value of where so that a[where] ==
//target; otherwise, this function returns false and the
//value of where is unchanged.
```

5.4 Multidimensional Arrays

C++ allows you to declare arrays with more than one index. This section describes these multidimensional arrays.

Multidimensional Array Basics

It is sometimes useful to have an array with more than one index, and this is allowed in C++. The following declares an array of characters called page. The array page has two indexes: The first index ranges from 0 to 29 and the second from 0 to 99.

array declarations

```
char page[30][100];
```

The indexed variables for this array each have two indexes. For example, page[0][0], page[15][32], and page[29][99] are three of the indexed variables for this array. Note that each index must be enclosed in its own set of square brackets. As was true of the one-dimensional arrays we have already seen, each indexed variable for a multidimensional array is a variable of the base type.

indexed variables

An array may have any number of indexes, but perhaps the most common number of indexes is two. A two-dimensional array can be visualized as a two-dimensional display with the first index giving the row and the second index giving the column. For example, the array indexed variables of the two-dimensional array page can be visualized as follows:

```
page[0][0],   page[0][1],   ...,  page[0][99]
page[1][0],   page[1][1],   ...,  page[1][99]
page[2][0],   page[2][1],   ...,  page[2][99]
             .
             .
             .
page[29][0],  page[29][1],  ...,  page[29][99]
```

You might use the array page to store all the characters on a page of text that has 30 lines (numbered 0 through 29) and 100 characters on each line (numbered 0 through 99).

In C++, a two-dimensional array, such as page, is actually an array of arrays. The array page shown is actually a one-dimensional array of size 30, whose base type is a one-dimensional array of characters of size 100. Normally, this need not concern you, and you can usually act as if the array page were actually an array with two indexes (rather than an array of arrays, which is harder to keep track of). There is, however, at least one situation in which a two-dimensional array looks very much like an array of arrays, namely, when you have a function with an array parameter for a two-dimensional array, which is discussed in the next subsection.

Multidimensional Array Declaration

SYNTAX

Type Array_Name[Size_Dim_1][Size_Dim_2]...[Size_Dim_Last];

EXAMPLES

```
char page[30] [100] ;
int matrix[2] [3] ;
double threeDPicture[10] [20] [30] ;
```

An array declaration of the form shown here will define one indexed variable for each combination of array indexes. For example, the second of the previous sample declarations defines the following six indexed variables for the array matrix:

```
matrix[0] [0], matrix[0] [1], matrix[0] [2],
matrix[1] [0], matrix[1] [1], matrix[1] [2]
```

Multidimensional Array Parameters

The following declaration of a two-dimensional array actually declares a one-dimensional array of size 30 whose base type is a one-dimensional array of characters of size 100.

```
char page[30] [100] ;
```

Viewing a two-dimensional array as an array of arrays will help you to understand how C++ handles parameters for multidimensional arrays.

For example, the following is a function that takes an array, like page, and prints it to the screen:

```
void displayPage(const char p[] [100] , int sizeDimension1)
{
    for (int index1 = 0; index1 < sizeDimension1; index1++)
    { //Printing one line:
        for (int index2 = 0; index2 < 100; index2++)
            cout << p[index1] [index2] ;
        cout << endl;
    }
}
```

Notice that with a two-dimensional array parameter, the size of the first dimension is not given, so we must include an int parameter to give the size of this first dimension. (As with ordinary arrays, the compiler will allow you to specify the first dimension by placing a number within the first pair of square brackets. However, such a number is only a comment; the compiler ignores the number.) The size of the second dimension (and all other dimensions if there are more than two) is given after the array parameter, as shown for the parameter

```
const char p[][100]
```

If you realize that a multidimensional array is an array of arrays, then this rule begins to make sense. Since the two-dimensional array parameter

```
const char p[][100]
```

is a parameter for an array of arrays, the first dimension is really the index of the array and is treated just like an array index for an ordinary, one-dimensional array. The second dimension is part of the description of the base type, which is an array of characters of size 100.

Multidimensional Array Parameters

When a multidimensional array parameter is given in a function heading or function declaration, the size of the first dimension is not given, but the remaining dimension sizes must be given in square brackets. Since the first dimension size is not given, you usually need an additional parameter of type int that gives the size of this first dimension. The following is an example of a function declaration with a two-dimensional array parameter p:

```
void getPage(char p[][100], int sizeDimension1);
```

EXAMPLE: Two-Dimensional Grading Program

Display 5.9 contains a program that uses a two-dimensional array named grade to store and then display the grade records for a small class. The class has four students, and the records include three quizzes. Display 5.10 illustrates how the array grade is used to store data. The first array index is used to designate a student, and the second array index is used to designate a quiz. Since the students and quizzes are numbered starting with 1 rather than 0, we must subtract 1 from the student number and subtract 1 from the quiz number to obtain the indexed variable that stores a particular quiz score. For example, the score that student number 4 received on quiz number 1 is recorded in grade[3][0].

Our program also uses two ordinary one-dimensional arrays. The array stAve will be used to record the average quiz score for each of the students. For example, the program will set stAve[0] equal to the average of the quiz scores received by student 1, stAve[1] equal to the average of the quiz scores received by student 2,

EXAMPLE: (continued)

and so forth. The array quizAve will be used to record the average score for each quiz. For example, the program will set quizAve[0] equal to the average of all the student scores for quiz 1, quizAve[1] will record the average score for quiz 2, and so forth. Display 5.10 illustrates the relationship between the arrays grade, stAve, and quizAve. This display shows some sample data for the array grade. These data, in turn, determine the values that the program stores in stAve and in quizAve. Display 5.11 also shows these values, which the program computes for stAve and quizAve.

The complete program for filling the array grade and then computing and displaying both the student averages and the quiz averages is shown in Display 5.9. In that program we have declared array dimensions as global named constants. Since the procedures are particular to this program and cannot be reused elsewhere, we have used these globally defined constants in the procedure bodies, rather than having parameters for the size of the array dimensions. Since it is routine, the display does not show the code that fills the array.

Display 5.9   Two-Dimensional Array (part 1 of 3)

```
1    //Reads quiz scores for each student into the two-dimensional array
2    //grade (but the input code is not shown in this display).
3    //Computes the average score for each student and the average score
     //for each quiz. Displays the quiz scores and the averages.
4    #include <iostream>
5    #include <iomanip>
6    using namespace std;
7    const int NUMBER_STUDENTS = 4, NUMBER_QUIZZES = 3;
8    void computeStAve(const int grade[] [NUMBER_QUIZZES], double stAve[]);
9    //Precondition: Global constants NUMBER_STUDENTS and NUMBER_QUIZZES
10   //are the dimensions of the array grade. Each of the indexed variables
11   //grade[stNum-1, quizNum-1] contains the score for student stNum on
     //quiz quizNum.
12   //Postcondition: Each stAve[stNum-1] contains the average for student
     //number stNum.
13
14   void computeQuizAve(const int grade[] [NUMBER_QUIZZES],
                         double quizAve[]);
15   //Precondition: Global constants NUMBER_STUDENTS and NUMBER_QUIZZES
16   //are the dimensions of the array grade. Each of the indexed variables
17   //grade[stNum-1, quizNum-1] contains the score for student stNum on
     //quiz quizNum.
18   //Postcondition: Each quizAve[quizNum-1] contains the average for
19   //quiz numbered quizNum.
```

(continued)

Display 5.9   Two-Dimensional Array (part 2 of 3)

```
20    void display(const int grade[] [NUMBER_QUIZZES],
21                      const double stAve[],
                        const double quizAve[]);

22    //Precondition: Global constants NUMBER_STUDENTS and NUMBER_QUIZZES
23    //are the dimensions of the array grade. Each of the indexed variables
24    //grade[stNum-1, quizNum-1] contains the score for student stNum on
25    //quiz quizNum. Each stAve[stNum-1] contains the average for student
26    //stNum. Each quizAve[quizNum-1] contains the average for quiz
27    //numbered quizNum.
28    //Postcondition: All the data in grade, stAve, and quizAve have been
      //output.

29    int main( )
30    {
31        int grade[NUMBER_STUDENTS][NUMBER_QUIZZES];
32        double stAve[NUMBER_STUDENTS];
33        double quizAve[NUMBER_QUIZZES];

      <The code for filling the array grade goes here, but is not shown.>

34        computeStAve(grade, stAve);
35        computeQuizAve(grade, quizAve);
36        display(grade, stAve, quizAve);
37        return 0;
38    }

39

40    void computeStAve(const int grade[] [NUMBER_QUIZZES], double stAve[])
41    {
42        for (int stNum = 1; stNum <= NUMBER_STUDENTS; stNum++)
43        {//Process one stNum:
44            double sum = 0;
45            for (int quizNum = 1; quizNum <= NUMBER_QUIZZES; quizNum++)
46                sum = sum + grade[stNum-1][quizNum-1];
47            //sum contains the sum of the grades for student number stNum.
48            stAve[stNum-1] = sum/NUMBER_QUIZZES;
49            //Average for student stNum is the value of stAve[stNum-1]
50        }
51    }

52    void computeQuizAve(const int grade[] [NUMBER_QUIZZES],
                          double quizAve[])
53    {
54        for (int quizNum = 1; quizNum <= NUMBER_QUIZZES; quizNum++)
55        {//Process one quiz (for all students):
56            double sum = 0;
57            for (int stNum = 1; stNum <= NUMBER_STUDENTS; stNum++)
```

Display 5.9   Two-Dimensional Array (part 3 of 3)

```
58            sum = sum + grade[stNum-1][quizNum-1];
59        //sum contains the sum of all student scores on quiz number
          //quizNum.
60        quizAve[quizNum-1] = sum/NUMBER_STUDENTS;
61        //Average for quiz quizNum is the value of quizAve[quizNum-1]
62    }
63 }

64 void display(const int grade[][NUMBER_QUIZZES],
65                const double stAve[], const double quizAve[])
66 {
67    cout.setf(ios::fixed);
68    cout.setf(ios::showpoint);
69    cout.precision(1);

70    cout << setw(10) << "Student"
71         << setw(5) << "Ave"
72         << setw(15) << "Quizzes\n";
73    for (int stNum = 1; stNum <= NUMBER_STUDENTS; stNum++)
74    {//Display for one stNum:
75        cout << setw(10) << stNum
76             << setw(5) << stAve[stNum-1] << " ";
77        for (int quizNum = 1; quizNum <= NUMBER_QUIZZES; quizNum++)
78            cout << setw(5) << grade[stNum-1][quizNum-1];
79        cout << endl;
80    }

81    cout << "Quiz averages = ";
82    for (int quizNum = 1; quizNum <= NUMBER_QUIZZES; quizNum++)
83        cout << setw(5) << quizAve[quizNum-1];
84    cout << endl;
85 }
```

Sample Dialogue

<The dialogue for filling the array grade is not shown.>

Student	Ave	Quizzes			
1	10.0	10	10	10	
2	1.0	2	0	1	
3	7.7	8	6	9	
4	7.3	8	4	10	
Quiz Average =		7.0	5.0	7.5	

Display 5.10   The Two-Dimensional Array grade

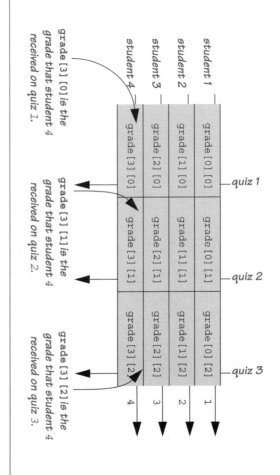

grade[3][0] is the
grade that student 4
received on quiz 1.

grade[3][1] is the
grade that student 4
received on quiz 2.

grade[3][2] is the
grade that student 4
received on quiz 3.

Display 5.11   The Two-Dimensional Array grade

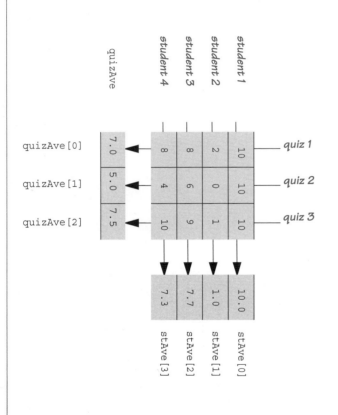

Self-Test Exercises

20. What is the output produced by the following code?

```
int myArray[4] , index1, index2;
for (index1 = 0; index1 < 4; index1++)
    for (index2 = 0; index2 < 4; index2++)
        myArray[index1][index2] = index2;
for (index1 = 0; index1 < 4; index1++)
{
    for(index2 = 0; index2 < 4; index2++)
        cout << myArray[index1][index2] << " ";
    cout << endl;
}
```

21. Write code that will fill the array a (declared next) with numbers typed in at the keyboard. The numbers will be input five per line, on four lines (although your solution need not depend on how the input numbers are divided into lines).

```
int a[4][5];
```

22. Write a function definition for a void function called echo such that the following function call will echo the input described in Self-Test Exercise 21, and will echo it in the same format as we specified for the input (that is, four lines of five numbers per line):

```
echo(a, 4);
```

Chapter Summary

- An array can be used to store and manipulate a collection of data that is all of the same type.

- The indexed variables of an array can be used just like any other variables of the base type of the array.

- A for loop is a good way to step through the elements of an array and perform some program action on each indexed variable.

- The most common programming error made when using arrays is attempting to access a nonexistent array index. Always check the first and last iterations of a loop that manipulates an array to make sure it does not use an index that is illegally small or illegally large.

- An array formal parameter is neither a call-by-value parameter nor a call-by-reference parameter, but a new kind of parameter. An array parameter is similar to a call-by-reference parameter in that any change that is made to the formal parameter in the body of the function will be made to the array argument when the function is called.

- The indexed variables for an array are stored next to each other in the computer's memory so that the array occupies a contiguous portion of memory. When the array is passed as an argument to a function, only the address of the first indexed variable (the one numbered 0) is given to the calling function. Therefore, a function with an array parameter usually needs another formal parameter of type `int` to give the size of the array.

- When using a partially filled array, your program needs an additional variable of type `int` to keep track of how much of the array is being used.

- To tell the compiler that an array argument should not be changed by your function, you can insert the modifier `const` before the array parameter for that argument position. An array parameter that is modified with a `const` is called a constant array parameter.

- If you need an array with more than one index, you can use a multidimensional array.

Answers to Self-Test Exercises

1. The statement `int a[5];` is a declaration, in which 5 is the number of array elements. The expression `a[4]` is an access into the array defined by the previous statement. The access is to the element having index 4, which is the fifth (and last) array element.

2. a. `score`

   b. `double`

   c. 5

   d. 0 through 4

   e. Any of `score[0]`, `score[1]`, `score[2]`, `score[3]`, `score[4]`

3. a. One too many initializers

   b. Correct. The array size is 4.

   c. Correct. The array size is 4.

4. `abc`

5. `1.1  1.2  2.2  3.3`

   `1.1  3.3  3.3`

   (Remember that the indexes start with 0, not 1.)

6. `0  2  4  6  8  10  12  14  16  18`

   `0  4  8  12  16`

7. The indexed variables of `sampleArray` are `sampleArray[0]` through `sampleArray[9]`, but this piece of code tries to fill `sampleArray[1]` through `sampleArray[10]`. The index 10 in `sampleArray[10]` is out of range.

8. There is an index out of range. When index is equal to 9, index + 1 is equal to 10, so a[index + 1], which is the same as a[10], has an illegal index. The loop should stop with one fewer iteration. To correct the code, change the first line of the for loop to

```
for (int index = 0; index < 9; index++)
```

9. ```
   int i, a[20];
   cout << "Enter 20 numbers:\n";
   for (i = 0; i < 20; i++)
       cin >> a[i];
   ```

10. The array will consume 14 bytes of memory. The address of the indexed variable yourArray[3] is 1006.

11. The following function calls are acceptable:

```
tripler(a[2]);
tripler(a[number]);
tripler(number);
```

The following function calls are incorrect:

```
tripler(a[3]);
tripler(a);
```

The first one has an illegal index. The second has no indexed expression at all. You cannot use an entire array as an argument to tripler, as in the second call. The section "Entire Arrays as Function Arguments" discusses a different situation in which you can use an entire array as an argument.

12. The loop steps through indexed variables b[1] through b[5], but 5 is an illegal index for the array b. The indexes are 0, 1, 2, 3, and 4. The correct version of the code is given here:

```
int b[5] = {1, 2, 3, 4, 5};
for (int i = 0; i < 5; i++)
    tripler(b[i]);
```

13. ```
    void oneMore(int a[], int size)
    //Precondition: size is the declared size of the array a.
    //a[0] through a[size-1] have been given values.
    //Postcondition: a[index] has been increased by 1
    //for all indexed variables of a.
    {
        for (int index = 0; index < size; index++)
            a[index] = a[index] + 1;
    }
    ```

14. The following function calls are all acceptable:

```
too2(myArray, 29);
too2(myArray, 10);
too2(yourArray, 100);
```

The call

```
too2(myArray, 10);
```

is legal, but will fill only the first ten indexed variables of myArray. If that is what is desired, the call is acceptable.

The following function calls are all incorrect:

```
too2(myArray, 55);
"Hey too2. Please come over here."
too2(myArray[3], 29);
```

The first of these is incorrect because the second argument is too large, the second because it is missing a final semicolon (and for other reasons), and the third because it uses an indexed variable for an argument where it should use the entire array.

15. You can make the array parameter in output a constant parameter, since there is no need to change the values of any indexed variables of the array parameter. You cannot make the parameter in dropOdd a constant parameter because it may have the values of some of its indexed variables changed.

```
void output(const double a[], int size);
//Precondition: a[0] through a[size - 1] have values.
//Postcondition: a[0] through a[size - 1] have been written out.

void dropOdd(int a[], int size);
//Precondition: a[0] through a[size - 1] have values.
//Postcondition: All odd numbers in a[0] through a[size - 1]
//have been changed to 0.
```

16.
```
int outOfOrder(double array[], int size)
{
    for(int i = 0; i < size - 1; i++)
        if(array[i] > array[i+1])//fetch a[i+1] for each i.
            return i+1;
    return -1;
}
```

17.
```
#include <iostream>
using namespace std;
const int DECLARED_SIZE = 10;
int main( )
{
    cout << "Enter up to ten nonnegative integers.\n"
         << "Place a negative number at the end.\n";
    int numberArray[DECLARED_SIZE], next, index = 0;
    cin >> next;
    while( (next >= 0) && (index < DECLARED_SIZE) )
```

```
        {
            numberArray[index] = next;
            index++;
            cin >> next;
        }

        int numberUsed = index;
        cout << "Here they are back at you:";
        for (index = 0; index < numberUsed; index++)
            cout << numberArray[index] << " ";

        cout << endl;
        return 0;
    }

18. #include <iostream>
    using namespace std;
    const int DECLARED_SIZE = 10;
    int main( )
    {
        cout << "Enter up to ten letters"
             << " followed by a period:\n";
        char letterBox[DECLARED_SIZE], next;
        int index = 0;
        cin >> next;
        while ( (next != '.') && (index < DECLARED_SIZE) )
        {
            letterBox[index] = next;
            index++;
            cin >> next;
        }

        int numberUsed = index;
        cout << "Here they are backwards:\n";
        for (index = numberUsed-1; index >= 0; index--)
            cout << letterBox[index];

        cout << endl;
        return 0;
    }

19. bool search(const int a[], int numberUsed,
                             int target, int& where)
    {
        int index = 0;
        bool found = false;
        while ((!found) && (index < numberUsed))
            if (target == a[index])
                found = true;
            else
                index++;
```

```
        //If target was found, then
        //found == true and a[index] == target.
        if (found)
            where = index;
        return found;
    }
```

20. 0 1 2 3
    0 1 2 3
    0 1 2 3
    0 1 2 3

21. int a[4][5];
    int index1, index2;
    for (index1 = 0; index1 < 4; index1++)
        for (index2 = 0; index2 < 5; index2++)
            cin >> a[index1][index2];

22. void echo(const int a[][5], int sizeOfa)
    //Outputs the values in the array a on sizeOfa lines
    //with 5 numbers per line.
    {
        for (int index1 = 0; index1 < sizeOfa; index1++)
        {
            for (int index2 = 0; index2 < 5; index2++)
                cout << a[index1][index2] << " ";
            cout << endl;
        }
    }

Programming Projects

Visit www.myprogramminglab.com to complete select exercises online and get instant feedback.

1. Write a program that reads in the average monthly rainfall for a city for each month of the year and then reads in the actual monthly rainfall for each of the previous 12 months. The program then prints out a nicely formatted table showing the rainfall for each of the previous 12 months as well as how much above or below average the rainfall was for each month. The average monthly rainfall is given for the months January, February, and so forth, in order. To obtain the actual rainfall for the previous 12 months, the program first asks what the current month is and then asks for the rainfall figures for the previous 12 months. The output should correctly label the months. There are a variety of ways to deal with the month names. One straightforward method is to code the months as integers and then do a conversion before doing the output. A large switch statement is acceptable in an output function. The month input can be handled in any manner you wish, as long as it is relatively easy and pleasant for the user.

MyProgrammingLab™

After you have completed the previous program, produce an enhanced version that also outputs a graph showing the average rainfall and the actual rainfall for each of the previous 12 months. The graph should be similar to the one shown in Display 5.4, except that there should be two bar graphs for each month and they should be labeled as the average rainfall and the rainfall for the most recent month. Your program should ask the user whether he or she wants to see the table or the bar graph, and then should display whichever format is requested. Include a loop that allows the user to see either format as often as the user wishes until the user requests that the program end.

2. Write a function called deleteRepeats that has a partially filled array of characters as a formal parameter and that deletes all repeated letters from the array. Since a partially filled array requires two arguments, the function will actually have two formal parameters: an array parameter and a formal parameter of type int that gives the number of array positions used. When a letter is deleted, the remaining letters are moved forward to fill in the gap. This will create empty positions at the end of the array so that less of the array is used. Since the formal parameter is a partially filled array, a second formal parameter of type int will tell how many array positions are filled. This second formal parameter will be a call-by-reference parameter and will be changed to show how much of the array is used after the repeated letters are deleted. For example, consider the following code:

```
char a[10];
a[0] = 'a';
a[1] = 'b';
a[2] = 'a';
a[3] = 'c';
int size = 4;
deleteRepeats(a, size);
```

After this code is executed, the value of a[0] is 'a', the value of a[1] is 'b', the value of a[2] is 'c', and the value of size is 3. (The value of a[3] is no longer of any concern, since the partially filled array no longer uses this indexed variable.) You may assume that the partially filled array contains only lowercase letters. Embed your function in a suitable test program.

3. The standard deviation of a list of numbers is a measure of how much the numbers deviate from the average. If the standard deviation is small, the numbers are clustered close to the average. If the standard deviation is large, the numbers are scattered far from the average. The standard deviation, S, of a list of N numbers x_i is defined as follows,

$$S = \sqrt{\dfrac{\displaystyle\sum_{i=1}^{N} (x_i - \bar{x})^2}{N}}$$

where $\bar{x}$ is the average of the N numbers $x_1, x_2, \ldots$. Define a function that takes a partially filled array of numbers as its argument and returns the standard deviation of the numbers in the partially filled array. Since a partially filled array requires two arguments, the function will actually have two formal parameters: an array parameter and a formal parameter of type int that gives the number of array positions used. The numbers in the array will be of type double. Embed your function in a suitable test program.

4. Write a program that reads in an array of type int. You may assume that there are fewer than 50 entries in the array. Your program determines how many entries are used. The output is to be a two-column list. The first column is a list of the distinct array elements; the second column is the count of the number of occurrences of each element. The list should be sorted on entries in the first column, largest to smallest.
For the array values

-12 3 -12 4 1 1 -12 1 -1 1 2 3 4 2 3 -12

the output should be

```
N    Count
4    2
3    3
2    2
1    4
-1   1
-12  4
```

5. An array can be used to store large integers one digit at a time. For example, the integer 1234 could be stored in the array a by setting a[0] to 1, a[1] to 2, a[2] to 3, and a[3] to 4. However, for this exercise you might find it more useful to store the digits backward, that is, place 4 in a[0], 3 in a[1], 2 in a[2], and 1 in a[3]. In this exercise you will write a program that reads in two positive integers that are 20 or fewer digits in length and then outputs the sum of the two numbers. Your program will read the digits as values of type char so that the number 1234 is read as the four characters '1', '2', '3', and '4'. After they are read into the program, the characters are changed to values of type int. The digits will be read into a partially filled array, and you might find it useful to reverse the order of the elements in the array after the array is filled with data from the keyboard. (Whether or not you reverse the order of the elements in the array is up to you. It can be done either way, and each way has its advantages and disadvantages.) Your program will perform the addition by implementing the usual paper-and-pencil addition algorithm. The result of the addition is stored in an array of size 20 and the result is then written to the screen. If the result of the addition is an integer with more than the maximum number of digits (that is, more than 20 digits), then your program should issue a message saying that it has encountered "integer overflow." You should be able to change the maximum length of the integers by changing only one globally defined constant. Include a loop that allows the user to continue to do more additions until the user says the program should end.

6. In the sport of diving, seven judges award a score between 0 and 10, where each score may be a floating-point value. The highest and lowest scores are thrown out and the remaining scores are added together. The sum is then multiplied by

the degree of difficulty for that dive. The degree of difficulty ranges from 1.2 to 3.8 points. The total is then multiplied by 0.6 to determine the diver's score.

Write a computer program that inputs a degree of difficulty and seven judges' scores, and outputs the overall score for that dive. The program should ensure that all inputs are within the allowable data ranges.

7. Generate a text-based histogram for a quiz given to a class of students. The quiz is graded on a scale from 0 to 5. Write a program that allows the user to enter grades for each student. As the grades are being entered, the program should count, using an array, the number of 0's, the number of 1's, the number of 2's, the number of 3's, the number of 4's, and the number of 5's. The program should be capable of handling an arbitrary number of student grades.

You can do this by making an array of size 6, where each array element is initialized to zero. Whenever a zero is entered, increment the value in the array at index 0. Whenever a one is entered, increment the value in the array at index 1, and so on, up to index 5 of the array.

Output the histogram count at the end. For example, if the input grades are 3, 0, 1, 3, 3, 5, 5, 4, 5, 4, then the program should output

1 grade(s) of 0
1 grade(s) of 1
0 grade(s) of 2
3 grade(s) of 3
2 grade(s) of 4
3 grade(s) of 5

8. The birthday paradox is that there is a surprisingly high probability that two people in the same room happen to share the same birthday. By birthday, we mean the same day of the year (ignoring leap years), but not the exact birthday including the birth year or time of day. Write a program that approximates the probability that two people in the same room have the same birthday, for 2 to 50 people in the room.

The program should use simulation to approximate the answer. Over many trials (say, 5000), randomly assign birthdays to everyone in the room. Count up the number of times at least two people have the same birthday, and then divide by the number of trials to get an estimated probability that two people share the same birthday for a given room size.

Your output should look something like the following. It will not be exactly the same due to the random numbers:

For 2 people, the probability of two birthdays is about 0.002
For 3 people, the probability of two birthdays is about 0.0082
For 4 people, the probability of two birthdays is about 0.0163

. . .

For 49 people, the probability of two birthdays is about 0.9654
For 50 people, the probability of two birthdays is about 0.969

VideoNote
Solution to
Programming
Project 5.7

9. Write a program that will allow two users to play tic-tac-toe. The program should ask for moves alternately from player X and player O. The program displays the game positions as follows:

```
1   2   3
4   5   6
7   8   9
```

The players enter their moves by entering the position number they wish to mark. After each move, the program displays the changed board. A sample board configuration is as follows:

```
X   X   O
4   5   6
O   8   9
```

10. Write a program to assign passengers seats in an airplane. Assume a small airplane with seat numbering as follows:

```
1   A   B   C   D
2   A   B   C   D
3   A   B   C   D
4   A   B   C   D
5   A   B   C   D
6   A   B   C   D
7   A   B   C   D
```

The program should display the seat pattern, with an 'X' marking the seats already assigned. For example, after seats 1A, 2B, and 4C are taken, the display should look like this:

```
1   X   B   C   D
2   A   X   C   D
3   A   B   C   D
4   A   B   X   D
5   A   B   C   D
6   A   B   C   D
7   A   B   C   D
```

After displaying the seats available, the program prompts for the seat desired, the user types in a seat, and then the display of available seats is updated. This continues until all seats are filled or until the user signals that the program should end. If the user types in a seat that is already assigned, the program should say that that seat is occupied and ask for another choice.

11. Write a program that accepts input like the program in Display 5.4 and that outputs a bar graph like the one in that program, except that your program will output the bars vertically rather than horizontally. A two-dimensional array may be useful.

12. The mathematician John Horton Conway invented the "Game of Life." Though not a "game" in any traditional sense, it provides interesting behavior that is

specified with only a few rules. This project asks you to write a program that allows you to specify an initial configuration. The program follows the rules of Life (listed shortly) to show the continuing behavior of the configuration.

LIFE is an organism that lives in a discrete, two-dimensional world. While this world is actually unlimited, we do not have that luxury, so we restrict the array to 80 characters wide by 22 character positions high. If you have access to a larger screen, by all means use it.

This world is an array with each cell capable of holding one LIFE cell. Generations mark the passing of time. Each generation brings births and deaths to the LIFE community. The births and deaths follow this set of rules:

1. We define each cell to have eight neighbor cells. The neighbors of a cell are the cells directly above, below, to the right, to the left, diagonally above to the right and left, and diagonally below, to the right and left.

2. If an occupied cell has zero or one neighbor, it dies of loneliness. If an occupied cell has more than three neighbors, it dies of overcrowding.

3. If an empty cell has exactly three occupied neighbor cells, there is a birth of a new cell to replace the empty cell.

4. Births and deaths are instantaneous and occur at the changes of generation. A cell dying for whatever reason may help cause birth, but a newborn cell cannot resurrect a cell that is dying, nor will a cell's death prevent the death of another, say, by reducing the local population.

Examples: ``*** becomes * then becomes *** again, and so on.``

```
    *
*** becomes *   then becomes  ***
    *
```

Notes: Some configurations grow from relatively small starting configurations. Others move across the region. It is recommended that for text output you use a rectangular char array with 80 columns and 22 rows to store the LIFE world's successive generations. Use an * to indicate a living cell and use a blank to indicate an empty (or dead) cell. If you have a screen with more rows than that, by all means make use of the whole screen.

Suggestions: Look for stable configurations. That is, look for communities that repeat patterns continually. The number of configurations in the repetition is called the *period.* There are configurations that are fixed, that is, that continue without change. A possible project is to find such configurations.

Hints: Define a void function named generation that takes the array we call world, an 80-column by 22-row array of type char, which contains the initial configuration. The function scans the array and modifies the cells, marking the cells with births and deaths in accord with the rules listed previously. This involves examining each cell in turn and either killing the cell, letting it live, or, if the cell is empty, deciding whether a cell should be born. There should be a function display that accepts the array world and displays the array on the screen. Some sort of time delay is appropriate between calls to generation and display. To do this, your program should generate and display the next generation when you press Return. You are at liberty to automate this, but automation is not necessary for the program.

13. A common memory matching game played by young children is to start with a deck of cards that contains identical pairs. For example, given six cards in the deck, two might be labeled "1", two might be labeled "2", and two might be labeled "3". The cards are shuffled and placed facedown on the table. The player then selects two cards that are facedown, turns them faceup, and if they match they are left faceup. If the two cards do not match, they are returned to their original position facedown. The game continues in this fashion until all cards are faceup.

Write a program that plays the memory matching game. Use 16 cards that are laid out in a 4×4 square and are labeled with pairs of numbers from 1 to 8. Your program should allow the player to specify the cards through a coordinate system.

For example, in the following layout

	1	2	3	4
1	8	*	*	*
2	*	*	*	*
3	*	8	*	*
4	*	*	*	*

all of the cards are facedown except for the pair of 8's, which has been located at coordinates (1,1) and (2,3). To hide the cards that have been temporarily placed faceup, output a large number of newlines that force the old board off the screen.

Hint: Use a 2D array for the arrangement of cards and another 2D array that indicates whether a card is faceup or facedown. Write a function that "shuffles" the cards in the array by repeatedly selecting two cards at random and swapping them.

14. You have collected reviews from four movie reviewers where the reviewers are numbered 0–3. Each reviewer has rated six movies where the movies are numbered 100–105. The ratings range from 1 (terrible) to 5 (excellent).

The reviews are shown in the following table:

	100	101	102	103	104	105
0	3	1	5	2	1	5
1	4	2	1	4	2	4
2	3	1	2	4	4	1
3	5	1	4	2	4	2

Write a program that stores this data using a 2D array. Based on this information your program should allow the user to enter ratings for any three movies. The program should then find the reviewer whose ratings most closely match the ratings input by the user. It should then predict the user's interest in the other movies by outputting the ratings by the reviewer for the movies that were not rated by the user. Use the Cartesian distance as the metric to determine how close the reviewer's movie ratings are to the ratings input by the user. This technique is a simple version of the **nearest neighbor** classification algorithm.

For example, if the user inputs a rating of 5 for movie 102, 2 for movie 104, and 5 for movie 105, then the closest match is reviewer 0 with a distance of $\sqrt{}$ $((5 - 5)^2 + (2 - 1)^2 + (5 - 5)^2) = 1$. The program would then predict a rating of 3 for movie 100, a rating of 1 for movie 101, and a rating of 2 for movie 103.

15. Traditional password entry schemes are susceptible to "shoulder surfing" in which an attacker watches an unsuspecting user enter their password or PIN number and uses it later to gain access to the account. One way to combat this problem is with a randomized challenge-response system. In these systems, the user enters different information every time based on a secret in response to a randomly generated challenge. Consider the following scheme in which the password consists of a five-digit PIN number (00000 to 99999). Each digit is assigned a random number that is 1, 2, or 3. The user enters the random numbers that correspond to their PIN instead of their actual PIN numbers.

For example, consider an actual PIN number of 12345. To authenticate, the user would be presented with a screen such as

```
PIN:  0 1 2 3 4 5 6 7 8 9
NUM:  3 2 3 1 1 3 2 2 1 3
```

The user would enter 23113 instead of 12345. This does not divulge the password even if an attacker intercepts the entry because 23113 could correspond to other PIN numbers, such as 69440 or 70439. The next time the user logs in, a different sequence of random numbers would be generated, such as

```
PIN:  0 1 2 3 4 5 6 7 8 9
NUM:  1 1 2 3 1 2 2 3 3 3
```

Your program should simulate the authentication process. Store an actual PIN number in your program. The program should use an array to assign random numbers to the digits from 0 to 9. Output the random digits to the screen, input the response from the user, and output whether or not the user's response correctly matches the PIN number.

16. Do Programming Project 5.14 except instead of only four reviewers allow for up to 1000 reviewers and store the reviews in a text file. While your program should support up to 1000 reviewers, the actual number of reviewers stored in the file could vary from 1 to 1000. The only movies that are reviewed are numbered from 100 to 105 as in Programming Project 14. You are welcome to design the format used to store the reviews in the text file. After the reviews are read from the text file the program should input three movies and make predictions for the remaining two movies as in Programming Project 5.14.

17. Programming Project 2.12 asked you to explore Benford's Law. An easier way to write the program is to use an array to store the digit counts. That is, count[0] might store the number of times 0 is the first digit (if that is possible in your data set), count[1] might store the number of times 1 is the first digit, and so forth. Redo Programming Project 2.12 using arrays.

VideoNote
Solution to
Programming
Project 5.15

18. This project is an extension of Programming Project 4.16. Consider a text file named scores.txt that contains player scores for a game. A possible sample is shown next where Ronaldo's best score is 10400, Didier's best score is 9800, etc. Put at least five names and scores in the file.

```
Ronaldo
10400
Didier
9800
Pele
12300
Kaka
8400
Cristiano
8000
```

Write a function named getHighScores that takes two array parameters, an array of strings and an array of integers. The function should scan through the file and set the string array entry at index 0 to the name of the player with the highest score and set the integer array entry at index 0 to the score of the player with the highest score. The string array entry at index 1 should be set to the name of the player with the second highest score and the integer array entry at index 1 should be set to the score of the player with the second highest score. Do the same for the entries at index 2. Together, these two arrays give you the names and scores of the top three players. In your main function, test the getHighScores function by calling it and ouputting the top three players and scores.

Structures and Classes 6

6 Structures and Classes

structure

Introduction

Classes are perhaps the single most significant feature that separates the C++ language from the C language. A *class* is a type whose values are called *objects*. Objects have both data and member functions. These objects are the objects of object-oriented programming, a very popular and powerful programming philosophy.

We will introduce classes in two steps. We first tell you how to give a type definition for a structure. A **structure** (of the kind discussed here) can be thought of as an object without any member functions.[1] The important property of structures is that the data in a structure can be a collection of data items of diverse types. After you learn about structures it will be a natural extension to define classes.

You do not need the material on arrays given in Chapter 5 in order to read Chapter 6, and most of Chapters 7 and 8, which cover classes.

6.1 Structures

Sometimes it is useful to have a collection of values of different types and to treat the collection as a single item. For example, consider a bank certificate of deposit, which is often called a CD. A CD is a bank account that does not allow withdrawals for a specified number of months. A CD naturally has three pieces of data associated with it: the account balance, the interest rate for the account, and the term, which is the number of months until maturity. The first two items can be represented as values of type `double`, and the number of months can be represented as a value of type `int`.

---

[1] A structure actually can have member functions in C++, but that is not the approach we will take. This detail is explained later in the chapter. This footnote is only to let readers who feel they have found an error know that we are aware of the official definition of a structure. Most readers should ignore this footnote.

Display 6.1 shows the definition of a structure called `CDAccountV1` that can be used for this kind of account. (The `V1` stands for version 1. We will define an improved version later in this chapter.)

Display 6.1   A Structure Definition (part 1 of 2)

```
1   //Program to demonstrate the CDAccountV1 structure type.
2   #include <iostream>
3   using namespace std;

4   //Structure for a bank certificate of deposit:          An improved version of this
5   struct CDAccountV1                                        structure will be given later in
6   {                                                         this chapter.
7       double balance;
8       double interestRate;
9       int term; //months until maturity
10  };

11  void getData(CDAccountV1& theAccount);
12  //Postcondition: theAccount.balance, theAccount.interestRate, and
13  //theAccount.term have been given values that the user entered at the
14  //keyboard.

14  int main( )
15  {
16      CDAccountV1 account;
17      getData(account);

18      double rateFraction, interest;
19      rateFraction = account.interestRate/100.0;
20      interest = account.balance*(rateFraction*(account.term/12.0));
21      account.balance = account.balance + interest;

22      cout.setf(ios::fixed);
23      cout.setf(ios::showpoint);
24      cout.precision(2);
25      cout << "When your CD matures in "
26           << account.term << " months,\n"
27           << "it will have a balance of $"
28           << account.balance << endl;

29      return 0;
30  }
31  //Uses iostream:
32  void getData(CDAccountV1& theAccount)
33  {
34      cout << "Enter account balance: $";
35      cin  >> theAccount.balance;
```

(continued)

Display 6.1   A Structure Definition (part 2 of 2)

```
36    cout << "Enter account interest rate: ";
37    cin >> theAccount.interestRate;
38    cout << "Enter the number of months until maturity: ";
39    cin >> theAccount.term;
40    }
```

Sample Dialogue

```
Enter account balance: $100.00
Enter account interest rate: 10.0
Enter the number of months until maturity: 6
When your CD matures in 6 months,
it will have a balance of $105.00
```

Structure Types

The structure definition in Display 6.1 is as follows:

```
struct CDAccountV1
{
    double balance;
    double interestRate;
    int term;//months until maturity
};
```

struct

The keyword **struct** announces that this is a structure-type definition. The identifier CDAccountV1 is the name of the structure type, which is known as the **structure tag.**

structure tag The structure tag can be any legal identifier that is not a keyword. Although this is not required by the C++ language, structure tags are usually spelled starting with an uppercase letter. The identifiers declared inside the braces, {}, are called **member names.** As illustrated in this example, a structure type definition ends with both a brace, }, and a semicolon.

member name

where to place a structure definition

A structure definition is usually placed outside any function definition (in the same way that globally defined constant declarations are placed outside all function definitions.) The structure type is then a global definition that is available to all the code that follows the structure definition.

Once a structure type definition has been given, the structure type can be used just like the predefined types int, char, and so forth. Note that in Display 6.1 the structure type CDAccountV1 is used to declare a variable in the function main and is used as the name of the parameter type for the function getData.

structure value

A structure variable can hold values just like any other variable can. A **structure value** is a collection of smaller values called **member values.** There is one member value for each member name declared in the structure definition. For example, a value of the type CDAccountV1 is a collection of three member values, two of type double and one of type int. The member values that together make up the structure value are stored in member variables, which we discuss next.

member value

member variable

Each structure type specifies a list of member names. In Display 6.1 the structure CDAccountV1 has three member names: balance, interestRate, and term. Each of these member names can be used to pick out one smaller variable that is a part of the larger structure variable. These smaller variables are called **member variables**. Member variables are specified by giving the name of the structure variable followed by a dot and then the member name. For example, if account is a structure variable of type CDAccountV1 (as declared in Display 6.1), then the structure variable account has the following three member variables:

```
account.balance
account.interestRate
account.term
```

The first two member variables are of type double, and the last is of type int. As illustrated in Display 6.1, these member variables can be used just like any other variables of those types. For example, the following line from the program in Display 6.1 will add the value contained in the member variable account.balance and the value contained in the ordinary variable interest and will then place the result in the member variable account.balance:

```
account.balance = account.balance + interest;
```

reusing member names

Two or more structure types may use the same member names. For example, it is perfectly legal to have the following two type definitions in the same program:

```
struct FertilizerStock
{
    double quantity;
    double nitrogenContent;
};
```

and

```
struct CropYield
{
    int quantity;
    double size;
};
```

The Dot Operator

The **dot operator** is used to specify a member variable of a structure variable.

SYNTAX

Structure_Variable_Name.Member_Variable_Name

Dot operator

EXAMPLES

```
struct StudentRecord
{
    int studentNumber;
    char grade;
};

int main( )
{
    StudentRecord yourRecord;
    yourRecord.studentNumber = 2001;
    yourRecord.grade = 'A';
```

Some writers call the dot operator the *structure member access operator*, although we will not use that term.

This coincidence of names will produce no problems. For example, if you declare the following two structure variables,

```
FertilizerStock superGrow;
CropYield apples;
```

then the quantity of superGrow fertilizer is stored in the member variable superGrow. quantity and the quantity of apples produced is stored in the member variable apples.quantity. The dot operator and the structure variable specify which quantity is meant in each instance.

A structure value can be viewed as a single (complex) value (that just happens to be made up of member values). Since a structure value can be viewed as a single value, structure values and structure variables can be used in the same ways that you use simple values and simple variables of the predefined types such as int. In particular, you can assign structure values using the equal sign. For example, if apples and oranges are structure variables of the type CropYield defined earlier, then the following is perfectly legal:

```
apples = oranges;
```

The previous assignment statement is equivalent to

```
apples.quantity = oranges.quantity;
apples.size = oranges.size;
```

structure variables in assignment statements

A structure value can be viewed as a collection of member values. A structure value can also be viewed as a single (complex) value (that just happens to be made up of member values).

Simple Structure Types

You define a structure type as shown here. The *Structure_Tag* is the name of the structure type.

SYNTAX

```
struct Structure_Tag
{
    Type_1 Member_Variable_Name_1;
    Type_2 Member_Variable_Name_2;
            .
            .
            .
    Type_Last Member_Variable_Name_Last;
};          Do not forget this semicolon.
```

EXAMPLE

```
struct Automobile
{
    int year;
    int doors;
    double horsePower;
    char model;
};
```

Although we will not use this feature, you can combine member names of the same type into a single list separated by commas. For example, the following is equivalent to the previous structure definition:

```
struct Automobile
{
    int year, doors;
    double horsePower;
    char model;
};
```

Variables of a structure type can be declared in the same way as variables of other types. For example,

```
Automobile myCar, yourCar;
```

The member variables are specified using the dot operator. For example, myCar.year, myCar.doors, myCar.horsePower, and myCar.model.

PITFALL: Forgetting a Semicolon in a Structure Definition

When you add the final brace, }, to a structure definition, it feels like the structure definition is finished, but it is not. You must also place a semicolon after that final brace. There is a reason for this, even though the reason is a feature that we will have no occasion to use. A structure definition is more than a definition. It can also be used to declare structure variables. You are allowed to list structure variable names between that final brace and that final semicolon. For example, the following defines a structure called WeatherData and declares two structure variables, dataPoint1 and dataPoint2, both of type WeatherData:

```
struct WeatherData
{
    double temperature;
    double windVelocity;
} dataPoint1, dataPoint2;
```

■

Structures as Function Arguments

structure arguments

A function can have call-by-value parameters of a structure type or call-by-reference parameters of a structure type, or both. The program in Display 6.1, for example, includes a function named getData that has a call-by-reference parameter with the structure type CDAccountV1.

functions can return structures

A structure type can also be the type for the value returned by a function. For example, the following defines a function that takes one argument of type CDAccountV1 and returns a different structure of type CDAccountV1. The structure returned will have the same balance and term as the argument, but will pay double the interest rate that the argument pays.

```
CDAccountV1 doubleInterest(CDAccountV1 oldAccount)
{
    CDAccountV1 temp;
    temp = oldAccount;
    temp.interestRate = 2*oldAccount.interestRate;
    return temp;
}
```

Notice the local variable temp of type CDAccountV1; temp is used to build up a complete structure value of the desired kind, which is then returned by the function. If myAccount is a variable of type CDAccountV1 that has been given values for its member variables, then the following will give yourAccount values for an account with double the interest rate of myAccount:

```
CDAccountV1 yourAccount;
yourAccount = doubleInterest(myAccount);
```

TIP: Use Hierarchical Structures

Sometimes it makes sense to have structures whose members are themselves smaller structures. For example, a structure type called `PersonInfo` that can be used to store a person's height, weight, and birth date can be defined as follows:

```
struct Date
{
        int month;
        int day;
        int year;
};

struct PersonInfo
{
        double height; //in inches
        int weight; //in pounds
        Date birthday;
};
```

A structure variable of type `PersonInfo` is declared in the usual way:

```
PersonInfo person1;
```

If the structure variable `person1` has had its value set to record a person's birth date, then the year the person was born can be output to the screen as follows:

```
cout << person1.birthday.year;
```

The way to read such expressions is left to right, and very carefully. Starting at the left end, `person1` is a structure variable of type `PersonInfo`. To obtain the member variable with the name `birthday`, you use the dot operator as follows:

```
person1.birthday
```

This member variable is itself a structure variable of type `Date`. Thus, this member variable itself has member variables. A member variable of the structure variable `person1.birthday` is obtained by adding a dot and the member variable name, such as `year`, which produces the expression `person1.birthday.year` shown previously.

In Display 6.2 we have rewritten the class for a certificate of deposit from Display 6.1. This new version has a member variable of the structure type `Date` that holds the date of maturity. We have also replaced the single `balance` member variable with two new member variables giving the initial balance and the balance at maturity. ■

Display 6.2   A Structure with a Structure Member (part 1 of 2)

```
1    //Program to demonstrate the CDAccount structure type.
2    #include <iostream>
3    using namespace std;
4
5    struct Date
6    {
7        int month;
8        int day;
9        int year;
10   };
11
12   //Improved structure for a bank certificate of deposit:
13   struct CDAccount
14   {
15       double initialBalance;
16       double interestRate;
17       int term; //months until maturity
18       Date maturity; //date when CD matures
19       double balanceAtMaturity;
20   };
```

This is an improved version of the structure CDAccountV1 defined in Display 6.1.

```
19   void getCDData(CDAccount& theAccount);
20   //Postcondition: theAccount.initialBalance, theAccount.interestRate,
21   //theAccount.term, and theAccount.maturity have been given values
22   //that the user entered at the keyboard.
23
24   void getDate(Date& theDate);
25   //Postcondition: theDate.month, theDate.day, and theDate.year
26   //have been given values that the user entered at the keyboard.
27
28   int main( )
29   {
30       CDAccount account;
31       cout << "Enter account data on the day account was opened:\n";
32       getCDData(account);
33       double rateFraction, interest;
34       rateFraction = account.interestRate / 100.0;
35       interest = account.initialBalance*(rateFraction*(account.term /
                                                          12.0));
36       account.balanceAtMaturity = account.initialBalance + interest;
37
38       cout.setf(ios::fixed);
40       cout.precision(2);
41       cout << "When the CD matured on "
44            << "it had a balance of $"
45            << account.balanceAtMaturity << endl;
46
47       return 0;
```

```
35   account.balanceAtMaturity = account.initialBalance + interest;
36   cout.setf(ios::fixed);
37   cout.setf(ios::showpoint);
38   cout.precision(2);
39   cout << "When the CD matured on "
40        << account.maturity.month << "-" << account.maturity.day
41        << "-" << account.maturity.year << endl
42        << "it had a balance of $"
43        << account.balanceAtMaturity << endl;
44   return 0;
```

Display 6.2   A Structure with a Structure Member (part 2 of 2)

```
45   }
46   //uses iostream:
47   void getCDData(CDAccount& theAccount)
48   {
49       cout << "Enter account initial balance: $";
50       cin >> theAccount.initialBalance;
51       cout << "Enter account interest rate: ";
52       cin >> theAccount.interestRate;
53       cout << "Enter the number of months until maturity: ";
54       cin >> theAccount.term;
55       cout << "Enter the maturity date:\n";
56       getDate(theAccount.maturity);
57   }

58   //uses iostream:
59   void getDate(Date& theDate)
60   {
61       cout << "Enter month: ";
62       cin >> theDate.month;
63       cout << "Enter day: ";
64       cin >> theDate.day;
65       cout << "Enter year: ";
66       cin >> theDate.year;
67   }
```

Sample Dialogue

```
Enter account data on the day account was opened:
Enter account initial balance: $100.00
Enter account interest rate: 10.0
Enter the number of months until maturity: 6
Enter the maturity date:
Enter month: 2
Enter day: 14
Enter year: 1899
When the CD matured on 2-14-1899
it had a balance of $105.00
```

Initializing Structures

You can initialize a structure at the time that it is declared. To give a structure variable a value, follow it by an equal sign and a list of the member values enclosed in braces. For example, the following definition of a structure type for a date was given in the previous subsection:

```
struct Date
{
    int month;
```

```
    int day;
    int year;
};
```

Once the type Date is defined, you can declare and initialize a structure variable called dueDate as follows:

```
Date dueDate = {12, 31, 2012};
```

The initializing values must be given in the order that corresponds to the order of member variables in the structure-type definition. In this example, dueDate.month receives the first initializing value of 12, dueDate.day receives the second value of 31, and dueDate.year receives the third value of 2012.

It is an error if there are more initializer values than struct members. If there are fewer initializer values than struct members, the provided values are used to initialize data members, in order. Each data member without an initializer is initialized to a zero value of an appropriate type for the variable.

Self-Test Exercises

1. Given the following structure and structure variable declaration,

```
struct CDAccountV2
{
    double balance;
    double interestRate;
    int term;
    char initial1;
    char initial2;
};
CDAccountV2 account;
```

what is the type of each of the following? Mark any that are not correct.

a. account.balance
b. account.interestRate
c. CDAccountV1.term
d. account.initial2
e. account

2. Consider the following type definition:

```
struct ShoeType
{
    char style;
    double price;
};
```

Self-Test Exercises (continued)

Given the previous structure-type definitions, what will be the output produced by the following code?

```
ShoeType shoe1, shoe2;
shoe1.style = 'A';
shoe1.price = 9.99;
cout << shoe1.style << " $" << shoe1.price << endl;
shoe2 = shoe1;

shoe2.price = shoe2.price/9;
cout << shoe2.style << " $" << shoe2.price << endl;
```

3. What is the error in the following structure definition?

```
struct Stuff
{
    int b;
    int c;
}

int main( )
{
    Stuff x;
    // other code
}
```

4. Given the following struct definition,

```
struct A
{
    int member b;
    int member c;
};
```

declare x to have this structure type. Initialize the members of x, member b and member c, to the values 1 and 2, respectively.

5. Here is an initialization of a structure type. State what happens with each initialization. Note any problems with these initializations.

```
struct Date
{
    int month;
    int day;
    int year;
};
```

a. Date dueDate = {12, 21};
b. Date dueDate = {12, 21, 1995};
c. Date dueDate = {12, 21, 19, 95};

(continued)

Self-Test Exercises (continued)

6. Write a definition for a structure type for records consisting of a person's wage rate, accrued vacation (which is some whole number of days), and status (which is either hourly or salaried). Represent the status as one of the two char values 'H' and 'S'. Call the type `EmployeeRecord`.

7. Give a function definition corresponding to the following function declaration. (The type `ShoeType` is given in Self-Test Exercise 2.)

```
void readShoeRecord(ShoeType& newShoe);
//Fills newShoe with values read from the keyboard.
```

8. Give a function definition corresponding to the following function declaration. (The type `ShoeType` is given in Self-Test Exercise 2.)

```
ShoeType discount(ShoeType oldRecord);
//Returns a structure that is the same as its argument,
//but with the price reduced by 10%.
```

6.2   Classes

We all know—the Times knows—but we pretend we don't.

VIRGINIA WOOLF, *Monday or Tuesday*

A class is basically a structure with member functions as well as member data. Classes are central to the programming methodology known as *object-oriented programming*.

Defining Classes and Member Functions

class   A **class** is a type that is similar to a structure type, but a class type normally has member functions as well as member variables. An overly simple, but illustrative, example of a class called `DayOfYear` is given in Display 6.3. This class has one member function named `output`, as well as the two member variables `month` and `day`. The term `public:` is called an access specifier. It simply means that there are no restrictions on the members that follow. We will discuss `public:` and its alternatives after going through this simple example. The type `DayOfYear` defined in Display 6.3 is a class definition for objects whose values are dates, such as January 1 or July 4.

object   The value of a variable of a class type is also often called an **object** (therefore, when speaking loosely, a variable of a class type is also often called an *object*). An object has both data members and function members. When programming with classes, a program is viewed as a collection of interacting objects. The objects can interact because they are capable of actions, namely, invocations of member functions. Variables of a class type hold objects as values. Variables of a class type are declared in the same way as variables of the predefined types and in the same way as structure variables.

member function

For the moment ignore the word public: shown in Display 6.3. The rest of the definition of the class DayOfYear is very much like a structure definition, except that it uses the keyword class instead of struct and it lists the member function output (as well as the member variables month and day). Notice that the member function output is listed by giving its declaration (prototype). A class definition normally contains only the declaration for its member functions. The definitions for the member functions are usually given elsewhere. In a C++ class definition, you can intermix the ordering of the member variables and member functions in any way you wish, but the style we will follow has a tendency to list the member functions before the member variables.

Display 6.3   Class with a Member Function (part 1 of 3)

```
1   //Program to demonstrate a very simple example of a class.
2   //A better version of the class DayOfYear will be given in Display 6.4.
3   #include <iostream>
4   using namespace std;
5   class DayOfYear
6   {
7   public:
8       void output( );
9       int month;
10      int day;
11   };
12  int main( )
13  {
14      DayOfYear today, birthday;
15      cout << "Enter today's date:\n";
16      cout << "Enter month as a number: ";
17      cin >> today.month;
18      cout << "Enter the day of the month: ";
19      cin >> today.day;
20      cout << "Enter your birthday:\n";
21      cout << "Enter month as a number: ";
22      cin >> birthday.month;
23      cout << "Enter the day of the month: ";
24      cin >> birthday.day;
25      cout << "Today's date is ";
26      today.output( );
27      cout << endl;
28      cout << "Your birthday is ";
29      birthday.output( );
30      cout << endl;
31      if (today.month == birthday.month && today.day == birthday.day)
32          cout << "Happy Birthday!\n";
```

Normally, member variables are private and not public, as in this example. This is discussed a bit later in this chapter.

Member function declaration

Calls to the member function output

(continued)

Display 6.3   Class with a Member Function (part 2 of 3)

```
33      else
34          cout << "Happy Unbirthday!\n";
35      return 0;
36  }

37  //Uses iostream:
38  void DayOfYear::output( )      ◀——————— Member function definition
39  {
40      switch (month)
41      {
42      case 1:
43          cout << "January "; break;
44      case 2:
45          cout << "February "; break;
46      case 3:
47          cout << "March "; break;
48      case 4:
49          cout << "April "; break;
50      case 5:
51          cout << "May "; break;
52      case 6:
53          cout << "June "; break;
54      case 7:
55          cout << "July "; break;
56      case 8:
57          cout << "August "; break;
58      case 9:
59          cout << "September "; break;
60      case 10:
61          cout << "October "; break;
62      case 11:
63          cout << "November "; break;
64      case 12:
65          cout << "December "; break;
66      default:
67          cout << "Error in DayOfYear::output. ";
68      }
69
70      cout << day;
71  }
```

Display 6.3   Class with a Member Function (part 3 of 3)

Sample Dialogue

```
Enter today's date:
Enter month as a number: 10
Enter the day of the month: 15
Enter your birthday:
Enter month as a number: 2
Enter the day of the month: 21
Today's date is October 15
Your birthday is February 21
Happy Unbirthday!
```

calling member functions

Member variables for an object of a class type are specified using the dot operator in the same way that the dot operator is used to specify member variables of a structure. For example, if today is a variable of the class type DayOfYear defined in Display 6.3, then today.month and today.day are the two member variables of the object today.

Member functions for classes that you define are invoked using the dot operator in a way that is similar to how you specify a member variable. For example, the program in Display 6.3 declares two objects of type DayOfYear in the following way:

DayOfYear today, birthday;

The member function output is called with the object today as follows,

today.output ( ) ;

and the member function output is called with the object birthday as follows:

birthday.output ( ) ;

defining member functions

When a member function is defined, the definition must include the class name because there may be two or more classes that have member functions with the same name. In Display 6.3 there is only one class definition, but in other situations you may have many class definitions, and more than one class may have member functions with the same name. The definition for the member function output of the class DayOfYear is shown in part 2 of Display 6.3. The definition is similar to an ordinary function definition except that you must specify the class name in the heading of the function definition.

The heading of the function definition for the member function output is as follows:

void DayOfYear::output ( )

scope resolution operator

The operator :: is called the **scope resolution operator** and serves a purpose similar to that of the dot operator. Both the dot operator and the scope resolution operator are used to tell what a member function is a member of. However, the scope resolution operator :: is used with a class name, whereas the dot operator is used with objects

type qualifier

(that is, with class variables). The scope resolution operator consists of two colons with no space between them. The class name that precedes the scope resolution operator is often called a **type qualifier**, because it specializes ("qualifies") the function name to one particular type.

Member Function Definition

A member function is defined similar to any other function except that the `Class_Name` and the scope resolution operator, `::`, are given in the function heading.

SYNTAX

```
Returned_Type Class_Name:: Function_Name(Parameter_List)
{
    Function_Body_Statements
}
```

EXAMPLE

See Display 6.3. Note that the member variables (month and day) are not preceded by an object name and dot when they occur in a member function definition.

member variables in function definitions

Look at the definition of the member function `DayOfYear::output` given in Display 6.3. Notice that in the function definition of `DayOfYear::output`, we used the member names `month` and `day` by themselves without first giving the object and dot operator. That is not as strange as it may at first appear. At this point we are simply defining the member function `output`. This definition of `output` will apply to all objects of type `DayOfYear`, but at this point we do not know the names of the objects of type `DayOfYear` that we will use, so we cannot give their names. When the member function is called, as in

```
today.output( );
```

all the member names in the function definition are specialized to the name of the calling object. So, the previous function call is equivalent to the following:

```
{
    switch (today.month)
    {
        case 1:
        .
        .
        .
    }

    cout << today.day;
}
```

In the function definition for a member function, you can use the names of all members of that class (both the data members and the function members) without using the dot operator.

The Dot Operator and the Scope Resolution Operator

Both the dot operator and the scope resolution operator are used with member names to specify of what thing they are a member. For example, suppose you have declared a class called DayOfYear and you declare an object called today as follows:

```
DayOfYear today;
```

You use the dot operator to specify a member of the object today. For example, output is a member function for the class DayOfYear (defined in Display 6.3), and the following function call will output the data values stored in the object today:

```
today.output( );
```

You use the scope resolution operator, ::, to specify the class name when giving the function definition for a member function. For example, the heading of the function definition for the member function output would be as follows:

```
void DayOfYear::output( )
```

Remember, the scope resolution operator, ::, is used with a class name, whereas the dot operator is used with an object of that class.

A Class Is a Full-Fledged Type

A class is a type just like the types int and double. You can have variables of a class type, you can have parameters of a class type, a function can return a value of a class type, and more generally, you can use a class type like any other type.

Self-Test Exercises

9. Here we have redefined the class DayOfYear from Display 6.3 so that it now has one additional member function called input. Write an appropriate definition for the member function input.

```
class DayOfYear
{
public:
    void input( );
    void output( );
    int month;
    int day;

};
```

(continued)

Self-Test Exercises (continued)

10. Given the following class definition, write an appropriate definition for the member function set. ⟳

```
class Temperature
{
public:
    void set(double newDegrees, char newScale);
    //Sets the member variables to the values given as
    //arguments.
    double degrees;
    char scale; ///'F' for Fahrenheit or 'C' for Celsius.
};
```

11. Carefully distinguish between the meaning and use of the dot operator and the scope resolution operator, ::.

Encapsulation

A data type, such as the type int, has certain specified values, such as 0, 1, -1, 2, and so forth. You tend to think of the data type as being these values, but the operations on these values are just as important as the values. Without the operations, you could do nothing of interest with the values. The operations for the type int consist of +, -, *, /, %, and a few other operators and predefined library functions. You should not think of a data type as being simply a collection of values. **A data type** consists of a collection of values *together with* a set of basic operations defined on these values. A data type is called an **abstract data type** (abbreviated **ADT**) if the programmers who use the type do not have access to the details of how the values and operations are implemented. The predefined types, such as int, are ADTs. You do not know how the operations, such as + and *, are implemented for the type int. Even if you did know, you could not use this information in any C++ program. Classes, which are programmer-defined types, should also be ADTs; that is, the details of how the "operations" are implemented should be hidden from, or at least irrelevant to, any programmer who uses the class. The operations of a class are the (public) member functions of the class. A programmer who uses a class should not need to even look at the definitions of the member functions. The member function declarations, given in the class definition, and a few comments should be all the programmer needs in order to use the class.

A programmer who uses a class also should not need to know how the data of the class is implemented. The implementation of the data should be as hidden as the implementation of the member functions. In fact, it is close to impossible to distinguish between hiding the implementation of the member functions and the implementation of the data. To a programmer, the class DayOfYear (Display 6.3) has dates as data, not numbers. The programmer should not know or care whether the month March is implemented as the int value 3, the quoted string "March", or in some other way.

Defining a class so that the implementation of the data in objects are not known, or is at least irrelevant, to the

encapsulation

programmer who uses the class is known by a number of different terms. The most common terms used are **information hiding**, **data abstraction**, and **encapsulation**, each of which means that the details of the implementation of a class are hidden from the programmer who uses the class. This principle is one of the main tenets of object-oriented programming (OOP). When discussing OOP, the term that is used most frequently is *encapsulation*. One of the ways to apply this principle of encapsulation to your class definitions is to make all member variables private, which is what we discuss in the next subsection.

Public and Private Members

Look back at the definition of the type DayOfYear given in Display 6.3. In order to use that class, you need to know that there are two member variables of type int that are named month and day. This violates the principle of encapsulation (information hiding) that we discussed in the previous subsection. Display 6.4 is a rewritten version of the class DayOfYear that better conforms to this encapsulation principle.

private:

Notice the words private: and public: in Display 6.4. All the items that follow the word private: (in this case the member variables month and day) are said to be **private**

private member variable

, which means that they cannot be referenced by name anyplace except within the definitions of the member functions of the class DayOfYear. For example, with this changed definition of the class DayOfYear, the following two assignments and other indicated code are no longer permitted in the main function of the program and are not permitted in any other function definition, except for member functions of the class DayOfYear:

```
DayOfYear today; //This line is OK.
today.month = 12; //ILLEGAL
today.day = 25; //ILLEGAL
cout << today.month; //ILLEGAL
cout << today.day; //ILLEGAL
if (today.month == 1) //ILLEGAL
    cout << "January";
```

Display 6.4   Class with Private Members (part 1 of 3)

```
1   #include <iostream>
2   #include <cstdlib>
3   using namespace std;

4   class DayOfYear
5   {
6   public:
7       void input( );
8       void output( );
9       void set(int newMonth, int newDay);
10      //Precondition: newMonth and newDay form a possible date.
11      void set(int newMonth);
12      //Precondition: 1 <= newMonth <= 12
```

This is an improved version of the class DayOfYear that we gave in Display 6.3.

(continued)

Display 6.4   Class with Private Members (part 2 of 3)

```
13    //Postcondition: The date is set to the first day of the given month.

14    int getMonthNumber( );  //Returns 1 for January, 2 for February, etc.
15    int getDay( );
16  private:
17    int month;
18    int day;
19  };

20  int main( )
21  {
22    DayOfYear today, bachBirthday;
23    cout << "Enter today's date:\n";
24    today.input( );
25    cout << "Today's date is ";
26    today.output( );
27    cout << endl;

28    bachBirthday.set(3, 21);
29    cout << "J. S. Bach's birthday is ";
30    bachBirthday.output( );
31    cout << endl;
32    if ( today.getMonthNumber( ) == bachBirthday.getMonthNumber( ) &&
33              today.getDay( ) == bachBirthday.getDay( ) )
34        cout << "Happy Birthday Johann Sebastian!\n";
35    else
36        cout << "Happy Unbirthday Johann Sebastian!\n";

37
38    return 0;
39  }

40  //Uses iostream and cstdlib:
41  void DayOfYear::set(int newMonth, int newDay)
42  {
43    if ((newMonth >= 1) && (newMonth <= 12))
44        month = newMonth;
45    else
46    {
47        cout << "Illegal month value! Program aborted.\n";
48        exit(1);
49    }
50    if ((newDay >= 1) && (newDay <= 31))
51        day = newDay;
52    else
53    {
54        cout << "Illegal day value! Program aborted.\n";
55        exit(1);
56    }
57  }
```

Private members (arrows pointing to lines 17–18: `int month;` `int day;`)

Mutator function (pointing to line 41)

Note that the function name set is overloaded. You can overload a member function just like you can overload any other function.

Display 6.4   Class with Private Members (part 3 of 3)

```
58   //Uses iostream and cstdlib:                          Mutator function
59   void DayOfYear::set(int newMonth)
60   {
61       if ((newMonth >= 1) && (newMonth <= 12))
62           month = newMonth;
63       else
64       {
65           cout << "Illegal month value! Program aborted.\n";
66           exit(1);
67       }
68       day = 1;
69   }
70
71   int DayOfYear::getMonthNumber( )                       Accessor functions
72   {
73       return month;
74   }
75
76   int DayOfYear::getDay( )
77   {
78       return day;
79   }
80
81   //Uses iostream and cstdlib:
82   void DayOfYear::input( )
83   {
84       cout << "Enter the month as a number: ";
85       cin >> month;                                      Private members may
86       cout << "Enter the day of the month: ";            be used in member
87       cin >> day;                                        function definitions
88       if ((month < 1) || (month > 12) || (day < 1) || (day > 31))   (but not elsewhere).
89       {
90           cout << "Illegal date! Program aborted.\n";
91           exit(1);
92       }
93   }
```

```
58   //Uses iostream and cstdlib:                          Mutator function
59   void DayOfYear::set(int newMonth)
60   {
61       if ((newMonth >= 1) && (newMonth <= 12))
62           month = newMonth;
63       else
64       {
65           cout << "Illegal month value! Program aborted.\n";
66           exit(1);
67       }
68       day = 1;
69   }
70
71   int DayOfYear::getMonthNumber( )                       Accessor functions
72   {
73       return month;
74   }
75
76   int DayOfYear::getDay( )
77   {
78       return day;
79   }
80
81   //Uses iostream and cstdlib:
82   void DayOfYear::input( )
83   {
84       cout << "Enter the month as a number: ";
85       cin >> month;                                      Private members may
86       cout << "Enter the day of the month: ";            be used in member
87       cin >> day;                                        function definitions
                                                            (but not elsewhere).
88       if ((month < 1) || (month > 12) || (day < 1) || (day > 31))
89       {
90           cout << "Illegal date! Program aborted.\n";
91           exit(1);
92       }
93   }
```

```
92   void DayOfYear::output( )
93       <The rest of the definition of DayOfYear::output is given in Display 6.3.>
```

Sample Dialogue

```
Enter today's date:
Enter the month as a number: 3
Enter the day of the month: 21
Today's date is March 21
J. S. Bach's birthday is March 21
Happy Birthday Johann Sebastian!
```

Once you make a member variable a private member variable, there is no way to change its value (or to reference the member variable in any other way) except by using one of the member functions. That means that the compiler will enforce the hiding of the implementation of the data for the class DayOfYear. If you look carefully at the program in Display 6.4, you will see that the only place the member variable names month and day are used is in the definitions of the member functions. There is no reference to today.month, today.day, bachBirthday.month, or bachBirthday.day anyplace outside the definitions of member functions.

All the items that follow the word public: (in this case the member functions) are said to be **public**, which means that they can be referenced by name anyplace. There are no restrictions on the use of public members.

Any member variables can be either public or private. Any member functions can be public or private. However, normal good programming practices require that *all* member variables be private and that typically most member functions be public.

You can have any number of occurrences of public and private access specifiers in a class definition. Every time you insert the label

    public:

the list of members changes from private to public. Every time you insert the label

    private:

the list of members changes back to being private members. You need not have just one public and one private group of members. However, it is common to have just one public section and one private section.

There is no universal agreement about whether the public members should be listed first or the private members should be listed first. The majority seem to prefer listing the public members first. This allows for easy viewing of the portions programmers using the class actually get to use. You can make your own decision on what you wish to place first, but the examples in the book usually list the public members before the private members.

In one sense C++ seems to favor placing the private members first. If the first group of members has neither the public: nor the private: specifier, then members of that group will automatically be private. You will see this default behavior used in code and should be familiar with it. However, we will not use it in this book.

Accessor and Mutator Functions

You should always make all member variables in a class private. You may sometimes need to do something with the data in a class object, however. The member functions will allow you to do many things with the data in an object, but sooner or later you will want or need to do something with the data for which there is no member function. How can you do anything new with the data in an object? The answer is that you can do anything you might reasonably want, provided you equip your classes with suitable accessor and mutator functions. These are member functions that allow you to access and change the data in an object in a very general way. **Accessor functions** allow you to read the data. In Display 6.4, the member functions

---

public

public
member
variable

accessor
function

accessor
function

getMonthNumber and getDay are accessor functions. The accessor functions need not literally return the values of each member variable, but they must return something equivalent to those values. For example, for a class like DayOfYear, you might have an accessor function return the name of the month as some sort of string value, rather than return the month as a number.

mutator function

Mutator functions allow you to change the data. In Display 6.4, the two functions named set are mutator functions. It is traditional to use names that include the word get for accessor functions and names that include the word set for mutator functions. (The functions input and output in Display 6.4 are really mutator and accessor functions, respectively, but I/O is such a special case that they are usually just called *I/O functions* rather than accessor or mutator functions.)

Your class definitions should always provide an adequate collection of accessor and mutator functions.

It may seem that accessor and mutator functions defeat the purpose of making member variables private, but that is not so. Notice the mutator function set in Display 6.4. It will not allow you to set the month member variable to 13 or to any number that does not represent a month. Similarly, it will not allow you to set the day member variable to any number that is not in the range 1 to 31 (inclusive). If the variables were public you could set the data to values that do not make sense for a date. (As it is, you can still set the data to values that do not represent a real date, such as February 31, but it would be easy to exclude these dates as well. We did not exclude these dates to keep the example simple.) With mutator functions, you can control and filter changes to the data.

Self-Test Exercises

12. Suppose your program contains the following class definition,

```
class Automobile
{
    public:
        void setPrice(double newPrice);
        void setProfit(double newProfit);
        double getPrice();
    private:
        double price;
        double profit;
        double getProfit();
};
```

and suppose the main function of your program contains the following declaration and that the program somehow sets the values of all the member variables to some values:

```
Automobile hyundai, jaguar;
```

(continued)

Self-Test Exercises (continued)

Which of the following statements are then allowed in the main function of your program?

```
hyundai.price = 4999.99;
jaguar.setPrice(30000.97);
double aPrice, aProfit;
aPrice = jaguar.getPrice();
aProfit = jaguar.getProfit();
aProfit = hyundai.getProfit();
hyundai = jaguar;
```

13. Suppose you change Self-Test Exercise 12 so that in the definition of the class Automobile all member variables are public instead of private. How would this change your answer to the question in Self-Test Exercise 12?

14. Explain what public: and private: mean in a class definition.

15. a. How many public: sections are required in a class for the class to be useful?

    b. How many private: sections are required in a class?

TIP: Separate Interface and Implementation

The principle of encapsulation says that you should define classes so that a programmer who uses the class need not be concerned with the details of how the class is implemented. The programmer who uses the class need only know the rules for how to use the class. The rules for how to use the class are known as the **interface** or **API**. There is some disagreement on exactly what the initials API stand for, but it is generally agreed that they stand for something like *application programmer interface* or *abstract programming interface* or something similar. In this book we will call these rules the *interface* for the class. It is important to keep in mind a clear distinction between the interface and the implementation of a class. If your class is well designed, then any programmer who uses the class need only know the interface for the class and need not know any details of the implementation of the class. A class whose interface and implementation are separated in this way is sometimes called an *abstract data type (ADT)* or a nicely encapsulated class. In Chapter 11 we will show you how to separate the interface and implementation by placing them in different files, but the important thing is to keep them conceptually separated.

For a C++ class, the *interface* consists of two sorts of things: the comments, usually at the beginning of the class definition, that tell what the data of the object is supposed to represent, such as a date or bank account or state of a simulated car wash; and the public member functions of the class along with the comments that tell how to use these public member functions. In a well-designed class, the interface of the class should be all you need to know in order to use the class in your program.

interface
API

mplementation

TIP: (continued)

The **implementation** of a class tells how the class interface is realized as C++ code. The implementation consists of the private members of the class and the definitions of both the public and private member functions. Although you need the implementation in order to run a program that uses the class, you should not need to know anything about the implementation in order to write the rest of a program that uses the class; that is, you should not need to know anything about the implementation in order to write the main function of the program and to write any nonmember functions or other classes used by the main function.

The most obvious benefit you derive from cleanly separating the interface and implementation of your classes is that you can change the implementation without having to change the other parts of your program. On large programming projects this division between interface and implementation will facilitate dividing the work among different programmers. If you have a well-designed interface, then one programmer can write the implementation for the class while other programmers write the code that uses the class. Even if you are the only programmer working on a project, you have divided one larger task into two smaller tasks, which makes your program easier to design and to debug. ■

TIP: A Test for Encapsulation

If your class definition produces an ADT (that is, if it properly separates the interface and the implementation), then you can change the implementation of the class (that is, change the data representation and/or change the implementation of some member functions) without needing to change any (other) code for any program that uses the class definition. This is a sure test for whether you have defined an ADT or just some class that is not properly encapsulated.

For example, you can change the implementation of the class DayOfYear in Display 6.4 to the following and no program that uses this class definition would need any changes:

```
class DayOfYear
{
public:
    void input( );
    void output( );

    void set(int newMonth, int newDay);
    //Precondition: newMonth and newDay form a possible date.
    //Postcondition: The date is reset according to the
    //arguments.

    void set(int newMonth);
    //Precondition: 1 <= newMonth <= 12
    //Postcondition: The date is set to first day of the month.
                                                    (continued)
```

TIP: (continued)

```
    int getMonthNumber ( );
    //Returns 1 for January, 2 for February, etc.
    int getDay ( );
private:
    char firstLetter;//of month
    char secondLetter;//of month
    char thirdLetter;//of month
    int day;
};
```

In this version, a month is represented by the first three letters in its name, such as 'J', 'a', and 'n' for January. The member functions should also be rewritten, of course, but they can be rewritten to behave *exactly* as they did before. For example, the definition of the function getMonthNumber might start as follows:

```
int DayOfYear::getMonthNumber ( )
{
    if (firstLetter == 'J' && secondLetter == 'a'
        && thirdLetter == 'n')
        return 1;
    if (firstLetter == 'F' && secondLetter == 'e'
        && thirdLetter == 'b')
        return 2;
    ...
```

This would be rather tedious, but not difficult. ■

Structures versus Classes

Structures are normally used with all member variables public and with no member functions. However, in C++ a structure can have private member variables and both public and private member functions. Aside from some notational differences, a C++ structure can do anything a class can do. Having said this and satisfied the "truth in advertising" requirement, we advocate that you forget this technical detail about structures. If you take this technical detail seriously and use structures in the same way that you use classes, then you will have two names (with different syntax rules) for the same concept. On the other hand, if you use structures as we described them, then you will have a meaningful difference between structures (as you use them) and classes; and your usage will be the same as that of most other programmers.

One difference between a structure and a class is that they differ in how they treat an initial group of members that has neither a public nor a private access specifier. If the first group of members in a definition is not labeled with either public: or private:, then a structure assumes the group is public, whereas a class would assume the group is private.

Classes and Objects

A class is a type whose variables can have both member variables and member functions.
The syntax for a class definition is given as follows.

SYNTAX

```
class Class_Name
{
public:
        Member_Specification_N+1
        Member_Specification_N+2        Public members
            .
            .
            .
private:
        Member_Specification_1
        Member_Specification_2          Private members
            .
            .
            .
        Member_Specification_N
};                      Do not forget this semicolon.
```

Each `Member_Specification_i` is either a member variable declaration or a member
function declaration (prototype).

Additional `public:` and `private:` sections are permitted. If the first group of members
does not have either a `public:` or a `private:` label, then it is the same as if there were a
`private:` before the first group.

EXAMPLE

```
class Bicycle
{
public:
        char getColor( );
        int numberOfSpeeds( );
        void set(int theSpeeds, char theColor);
private:
        int speeds;
        char color;
};
```

Once a class is defined, an object variable (variable of the class type) can be declared in the
same way as variables of any other type. For example, the following declares two object
variables of type Bicycle:

```
Bicycle myBike, yourBike;
```

TIP: Thinking Objects

If you have not programmed with classes before, it can take a little while to get the feel of programming with them. When you program with classes, data rather than algorithms take center stage. It is not that there are no algorithms. However, the algorithms are made to fit the data, as opposed to designing the data to fit the algorithms. It is a difference in point of view. In the extreme case, which is considered by many to be the best style, you have no global functions at all, only classes with member functions. In this case, you define objects and how the objects interact, rather than algorithms that operate on data. We will discuss the details of how you accomplish this throughout this book. Of course, you can ignore classes completely or relegate them to a minor role, but then you are really programming in C, not C++. ■

Self-Test Exercises

16. When you define a C++ class, should you make the member variables public or private? Should you make the member functions public or private?

17. When you define a C++ class, what items are considered part of the interface? What items are considered part of the implementation?

Chapter Summary

- A structure can be used to combine data of different types into a single (compound) data value.

- A class can be used to combine data and functions into a single (compound) object.

- A member variable or a member function for a class can be either public or private. If it is public, it can be used outside the class. If it is private, it can be used only in the definition of a member function.

- A function can have formal parameters of a class or structure type. A function can return values of a class or structure type.

- A member function for a class can be overloaded in the same way as ordinary functions are overloaded.

- When defining a C++ class, you should separate the interface and implementation so that any programmer who uses the class need only know the interface and need not even look at the implementation. This is the principle of encapsulation.

Answers to Self-Test Exercises

1. a. `double`

   b. `double`

   c. illegal—cannot use a structure tag instead of a structure variable

   d. `char`

   e. `CDAccountV2`

2. A `$9.99`

   A `$1.11`

3. A semicolon is missing from the end of the definition of `stuff`.

4. `A x = {1,2};`

5. a. Too few initializers; not a syntax error. After initialization, `month==12`, `day==21`, and `year==0`. Member variables not provided an initializer are initialized to a zero of the appropriate type.

   b. Correct after initialization. `12==month`, `21==day`, and `1995==year`.

   c. Error: too many initializers.

6. ```
   struct EmployeeRecord
   {
       double wageRate;
       int vacation;
       char status;
   };
   ```

7. ```
   void readShoeRecord(ShoeType& newShoe)
   {
       cout << "Enter shoe style (one letter): ";
       cin >> newShoe.style;
       cout << "Enter shoe price $";
       cin >> newShoe.price;
   }
   ```

8. ```
   ShoeType discount(ShoeType oldRecord)
   {
       ShoeType temp;
       temp.style = oldRecord.style;
       temp.price = 0.90*oldRecord.price;
       return temp;
   }
   ```
   ```

9.
```
void DayOfYear::input( )
{
    cout << "Enter month as a number: ";
    cin >> month;
    cout << "Enter the day of the month: ";
    cin >> day;
}
```

10.
```
void Temperature::set(double newDegrees, char newScale)
{
    degrees = newDegrees;
    scale = newScale;
}
```

11. Both the dot operator and the scope resolution operator are used with member names to specify of what class or structure the member name is a member. If class DayOfYear is as defined in Display 6.3 and today is an object of the class DayOfYear, then the member month may be accessed with the dot operator: today. month. When we give the definition of a member function, the scope resolution operator is used to tell the compiler that this function is the one declared in the class.

12.
```
hyundai.price = 4999.99; //ILLEGAL. price is private.
jaguar.setPrice(30000.97); //LEGAL
double aPrice, aProfit; //LEGAL
aPrice = jaguar.getPrice( ); //LEGAL
aProfit = jaguar.getProfit( ); //ILLEGAL. getProfit is
                                         //private.
aProfit = hyundai.getProfit( ); //ILLEGAL. getProfit is
                                          //private.

hyundai = jaguar; //LEGAL
```

13. After the change, they would all be legal.

14. All members (member variables and member functions) that are marked private: can only be accessed by name in the definitions of member functions (both public and private) of the same class. Members marked public: have no restrictions on where they can be used.

15. a. Only one. The compiler warns if you have no public: members in a class (or struct, for that matter).

b. None, but we normally expect to find at least one private: section in a class.

16. The member variables should all be private. The member functions that are part of the interface should be public. You may also have auxiliary (helping) functions that are only used in the definitions of other member functions. These auxiliary functions should be private.

17. All the declarations of private member variables are part of the implementation. (There should be no public member variables.) All the declarations for public member functions of the class (which are listed in the class definitions), as well as the explanatory comments for these declarations, are parts of the interface.

All the declarations for private member functions are parts of the implementation. All member function definitions (whether the function is public or private) are parts of the implementation.

Programming Projects

Visit www.myprogramminglab.com to complete select exercises online and get instant feedback.

1. Write a grading program for a class with the following grading policies:

    a. There are two quizzes, each graded on the basis of 10 points.

    b. There is one midterm exam and one final exam, each graded on the basis of 100 points.

    c. The final exam counts for 50% of the grade, the midterm counts for 25%, and the two quizzes together count for a total of 25%. (Do not forget to normalize the quiz scores. They should be converted to a percentage before they are averaged in.)

   Any grade of 90 or more is an A, any grade of 80 or more (but less than 90) is a B, any grade of 70 or more (but less than 80) is a C, any grade of 60 or more (but less than 70) is a D, and any grade below 60 is an F. The program will read in the student's scores and output the student's record, which consists of two quiz and two exam scores as well as the student's average numeric score for the entire course and final letter grade. Define and use a structure for the student record.

2. Define a class for a type called `CounterType`. An object of this type is used to count things, so it records a count that is a nonnegative whole number. Include a mutator function that sets the counter to a count given as an argument. Include member functions to increase the count by one and to decrease the count by one. Be sure that no member function allows the value of the counter to become negative. Also, include a member function that returns the current count value and one that outputs the count. Embed your class definition in a test program.

3. The type `Point` is a fairly simple data type, but under another name (the template class `pair`) this data type is defined and used in the C++ Standard Template Library, although you need not know anything about the Standard Template Library to do this exercise. Write a definition of a class named `Point` that might be used to store and manipulate the location of a point in the plane. You will need to declare and implement the following member functions:

    a. A member function `set` that sets the private data after an object of this class is created.

    b. A member function to move the point by an amount along the vertical and horizontal directions specified by the first and second arguments.

    c. A member function to rotate the point by 90 degrees clockwise around the origin.

    d. Two `const` inspector functions to retrieve the current coordinates of the point.

Document these functions with appropriate comments. Embed your class in a test program that requests data for several points from the user, creates the points, then exercises the member functions.

4. Write the definition for a class named `GasPump` to be used to model a pump at an automobile service station. Before you go further with this programming exercise, write down the behavior you expect from a gas pump from the point of view of the purchaser.

The following are listed things a gas pump might be expected to do. If your list differs, and you think your list is as good or better than these, then consult your instructor. You and your instructor should jointly decide what behavior you are to implement. Then implement and test the agreed upon design for a gas pump class.

a. A display of the amount dispensed

b. A display of the amount charged for the amount dispensed

c. A display of the cost per gallon, liter, or other unit of volume that is used where you reside

d. Before use, the gas pump must reset the amount dispensed and amount charged to zero.

e. Once started, a gas pump continues to dispense fuel, keep track of the amount dispensed, and compute the charge for the amount dispensed until stopped.

f. A stop dispensing control of some kind is needed.

Implement the behavior of the gas pump as declarations of member functions of the gas pump class, then write implementations of these member functions. You will have to decide if there is data the gas pump has to keep track of that the user of the pump should not have access to. If so, make these private member variables.

5. Define a class for a type called `Fraction`. This class is used to represent a ratio of two integers. Include mutator functions that allow the user to set the numerator and the denominator. Also include a member function that returns the value of the numerator divided by the denominator as a double. Include an additional member function that outputs the value of the fraction reduced to lowest terms. For example, instead of outputting 20/60 the function should output 1/3. This will require finding the greatest common divisor for the numerator and denominator, and then dividing both by that number. Embed your class in a test program.

6. Define a class called `Odometer` that will track fuel and mileage for an automotive vehicle. The class should have member variables to track the miles driven and the fuel efficiency of the vehicle in miles per gallon. Include a mutator function to reset the odometer to zero miles, a mutator function to set the fuel efficiency, a mutator function that accepts miles driven for a trip and adds it to the odometer's total, and an accessor function that returns the number of gallons of gasoline that the vehicle has consumed since the odometer was last reset.

Use your class with a test program that creates several trips with different fuel efficiencies. You should decide which variables should be public, if any.

VideoNote

Solution to
Programming
Project 6.5

7. Define a class called Pizza that has member variables to track the type of pizza (either deep dish, hand tossed, or pan) along with the size (either small, medium, or large) and the number of pepperoni or cheese toppings. You can use constants to represent the type and size. Include mutator and accessor functions for your class. Create a void function, outputDescription( ), that outputs a textual description of the pizza object. Also include a function, computePrice( ), that computes the cost of the pizza and returns it as a double according to the following rules:

   Small pizza = $10 + $2 per topping

   Medium pizza = $14 + $2 per topping

   Large pizza = $17 + $2 per topping

   Write a suitable test program that creates and outputs a description and price of various pizza objects.

8. Define a class named Money that stores a monetary amount. The class should have two private integer variables, one to store the number of dollars and another to store the number of cents. Add accessor and mutator functions to read and set both member variables. Add another function that returns the monetary amount as a double. Write a program that tests all of your functions with at least two different Money objects.

9. Do Programming Project 6.8, except remove the two private integer variables and use a single variable of type double to store the monetary value in their place. The rest of the functions should have the same headers. For several functions, this will require code to convert from an integer format to appropriately modify the double. For example, if the monetary amount stored in the double is 4.55 (representing $4.55) and if the function to set the dollar amount is invoked with the value 13, then the double should be changed to 13.55. While this will take some work, the code in your test program from Programming Project 6.8 should still work without requiring any changes. This is the benefit of encapsulating the member variables.

10. Create a Temperature class that internally stores a temperature in degrees Kelvin. Create functions named setTempKelvin, setTempFahrenheit, and setTempCelsius that take an input temperature in the specified temperature scale, convert the temperature to Kelvin, and store that temperature in the class member variable. Also, create functions that return the stored temperature in degrees Kelvin, Fahrenheit, or Celsius. Write a main function to test your class. Use the equations shown next to convert between the three temperature scales.

   Kelvin = Celsius + 273.15

   Celsius = (5.0/9) × (Fahrenheit − 32)

11. Do Programming Project 5.18 except use only one array as a parameter instead of two arrays. The single array should be of type Player where Player is a class that you create. The Player class should have a member variable of type string to store the player's name and a member variable of type int to score the player's score. Encapsulate these variables appropriately. Upon return from your function the array entry at index 0 should be set to the name and score of the player with the best score, the entry at index 1 should be set to the name and score of the player with the second best score, etc.

VideoNote
**Solution to
Programming
Project 6.9**

12. Your Community Supported Agriculture (CSA) farm delivers a box of fresh fruits and vegetables to your house once a week. For this Programming Project, define the class BoxOfProduce that contains exactly three bundles of fruits or vegetables. You can represent the fruits or vegetables as an array of type string. Add accessor and mutator functions to get or set the fruits or vegetables stored in the array. Also write an output function that displays the complete contents of the box on the console.

Next, write a main function that creates a BoxOfProduce with three items randomly selected from this list:

```
Broccoli
Tomato
Kiwi
Kale
Tomatillo
```

This list should be stored in a text file that is read in by your program. For now you can assume that the list contains exactly five types of fruits or vegetables.

Do not worry if your program randomly selects duplicate produce for the three items. Next, the main function should display the contents of the box and allow the user to substitute any one of the five possible fruits or vegetables for any of the fruits or vegetables selected for the box. After the user is done with substitutions output the final contents of the box to be delivered.

Constructors and Other Tools 7

7 Constructors and Other Tools

Give us the tools, and we will finish the job.

WINSTON CHURCHILL, *Radio broadcast (February 9, 1941)*

Introduction

This chapter presents a number of important tools to use when programming with classes. The most important of these tools are class constructors, a kind of function used to initialize objects of the class.

Section 7.3 introduces *vectors* as an example of classes and as a preview of the Standard Template Library (STL). Vectors are similar to arrays but can grow and shrink in size. The STL is an extensive library of predefined classes. Section 7.3 may be covered now or later. The material in Chapters 8 through 18 does not require the material in Section 7.3, so you may postpone covering vectors (Section 7.3) if you wish.

Sections 7.1 and 7.2 do not use the material in Chapter 5 but do use the material in Chapter 6. Section 7.3 requires Chapters 1 through 6 as well as Section 7.1.

7.1   Constructors

Well begun is half done.

Proverb

Often you want to initialize some or all the member variables for an object when you declare the object. As we will see later in this book, there are other initializing actions you might also want to take, but initializing member variables is the most common sort of initialization. C++ includes special provisions for such initializations. When you define a class you can define a special kind of member function known as a **constructor**. A constructor is a member function that is automatically called when an object of that class is declared. A constructor is used to initialize the values of some or all member variables and to do any other sort of initialization that may be needed.

Constructor Definitions

You define a constructor the same way that you define any other member function, except for two points:

1. A constructor must have the same name as the class. For example, if the class is named BankAccount, then any constructor for this class must be named BankAccount.

2. A constructor definition cannot return a value. Moreover, no type, not even void, can be given at the start of the function declaration or in the function header.

constructor

For example, suppose we wanted to add a constructor for initializing the month and day for objects of type DayOfYear, which we gave in Display 6.4 and redefine in what follows so it includes a constructor. (We have omitted some of the comments to save space, but they should be included in an actual program.)

```
class DayOfYear
{
public:
    DayOfYear(int monthValue, int dayValue); ←——— Constructor
    //Initializes the month and day to arguments.

    void input( );
    void output( );
    void set(int newMonth, int newDay);
    void set(int newMonth);
    int getMonthNumber( );
    int getDay( );
private:
    int month;
    int day;
};
```

Notice that the constructor is named DayOfYear, which is the name of the class. Also notice that the declaration (prototype) for the constructor DayOfYear does not start with void or any other type name. Finally, notice that the constructor is placed in the public section of the class definition. Normally, you should make your constructors public member functions. If you were to make all your constructors private members, then you would not be able to declare any objects of that class type, which would make the class completely useless.

With the redefined class DayOfYear, two objects of type DayOfYear can be declared and initialized as follows:

```
DayOfYear date1(7, 4), date2(5, 5);
```

Assuming that the definition of the constructor performs the initializing action that we promised, the previous declaration will declare the object date1, set the value of date1.month to 7, and set the value of date1.day to 4. Thus, the object date1 is initialized so that it represents the date July 4. Similarly, date2 is initialized so that it represents the date May 5. What happens is that the object date1 is declared, and then the constructor DayOfYear is called with the two arguments 7 and 4. Similarly, date2 is declared, and then the constructor DayOfYear is called with the arguments 5 and 5. The result is conceptually equivalent to the following (although you cannot write it this way in C++):

```
DayOfYear date1, date2; //PROBLEMS—BUT FIXABLE
date1.DayOfYear(7, 4); //VERY ILLEGAL
date2.DayOfYear(5, 5); //VERY ILLEGAL
```

As the comments indicate, you cannot place the three lines shown in your program. The first line can be made to be acceptable, but the two calls to the constructor `DayOfYear` are illegal. A constructor cannot be called in the same way as an ordinary member function is called. Still, it is clear what we want to happen when we write those three lines, and that happens automatically when you declare the objects `date1` and `date2` as follows:

```
DayOfYear date1(7, 4), date2(5, 5);
```

The definition of a constructor is given in the same way as any other member function. For example, if you revise the definition of the class `DayOfYear` by adding the constructor just described, you need to also add a definition of the constructor, which might be as follows:

```
DayOfYear::DayOfYear(int monthValue, int dayValue)
{
    month = monthValue;
    day = dayValue;
}
```

Since the class and the constructor function have the same name, the name `DayOfYear` occurs twice in the function heading; the `DayOfYear` before the scope resolution operator `::` is the name of the class, and the `DayOfYear` after the scope resolution operator is the name of the constructor function. Also notice that no return type is specified in the heading of the constructor definition, not even the type `void`. Aside from these points, a constructor can be defined in the same way as an ordinary member function.

Constructor

A *constructor* is a member function of a class that has the same name as the class. A constructor is called automatically when an object of the class is declared. Constructors are used to initialize objects. A constructor must have the same name as the class of which it is a member.

As we just illustrated, a constructor can be defined just like any other member function. However, there is an alternative way of defining constructors that is preferable to use. The previous definition of the constructor `DayOfYear` is completely equivalent to the following version:

```
DayOfYear::DayOfYear(int monthValue, int dayValue)
                    : month(monthValue), day(dayValue)
{/*Body intentionally empty*/}
```

initialization section

The new element shown on the second line of the constructor definition is called the **initialization section**. As this example shows, the initialization section goes after the parenthesis that ends the parameter list and before the opening brace of the function body. The initialization section consists of a colon followed by a list of some or all the member variables separated by commas. Each member variable is followed by its initializing value in parentheses. Notice that the initializing values can be given in terms of the constructor parameters.

The function body in a constructor definition with an initialization section need not be empty as in the previous example. For example, the following improved version of the constructor definition checks to see that the arguments are appropriate:

```
DayOfYear::DayOfYear(int monthValue, int dayValue)
                            : month(monthValue), day(dayValue)
{
    if ((month < 1) || (month > 12))
    {
        cout << "Illegal month value!\n";
        exit(1);
    }
    if ((day < 1) || (day > 31))
    {
        cout << "Illegal day value!\n";
        exit(1);
    }
}
```

You can overload a constructor name like DayOfYear, just as you can overload any other member function name. In fact, constructors usually are overloaded so that objects can be initialized in more than one way. For example, in Display 7.1 we have redefined the class DayOfYear so that it has three versions of its constructor. This redefinition overloads the constructor name DayOfYear so that it can have two arguments (as we just discussed), one argument, or no arguments.

Notice that in Display 7.1, two constructors call the member function testDate to check that their initialized values are appropriate. The member function testDate is private since it is only intended to be used by other member functions and so is part of the hidden implementation details.

We have omitted the member function set from this revised class definition of DayOfYear. Once you have a good set of constructor definitions, there is no need for any other member functions to set the member variables of the class. You can use the constructor DayOfYear in Display 7.1 for the same purposes that you would use the member function set (which we included in the old version of the class shown in Display 6.4).

Display 7.1 Class with Constructors (part 1 of 2)

```
1   #include <iostream>
2   #include <cstdlib>  //for exit
3   using namespace std;
4   class DayOfYear
5   {
6   public:
7       DayOfYear(int monthValue, int dayValue);
8       //Initializes the month and day to arguments.
9       DayOfYear(int monthValue);
10      //Initializes the date to the first of the given month.
11      DayOfYear( );
12      //Initializes the date to January 1.
13      void input( );
14      void output( );
15      int getMonthNumber( );
16      //Returns 1 for January, 2 for February, etc.
17      int getDay( );
18  private:
19      int month;
20      int day;
21      void testDate( );
22  };
23  int main( )
24  {
25      DayOfYear date1(2, 21), date2(5), date3;
26      cout << "Initialized dates:\n";
27      date1.output( ); cout << endl;
28      date2.output( ); cout << endl;
29      date3.output( ); cout << endl;
30      date1 = DayOfYear(10, 31);
31      cout << "date1 reset to the following:\n";
32      date1.output( ); cout << endl;
33      return 0;
34  }
35
36  DayOfYear::DayOfYear(int monthValue, int dayValue)
37                        : month(monthValue), day(dayValue)
38  {
39      testDate( );
40  }
```

This definition of DayOfYear is an improved version of the class DayOfYear given in Display 6.4.

← default constructor

This causes a call to the default constructor. Notice that there are no parentheses.

an explicit call to the constructor
DayOfYear::DayOfYear

Display 7.1   Class with Constructors (part 2 of 2)

```
41  DayOfYear::DayOfYear(int monthValue) : month(monthValue), day(1)
42  {
43      testDate( );
44  }

45  DayOfYear::DayOfYear( ) : month(1), day(1)
46  {/*Body intentionally empty.*/}

47  //uses iostream and cstdlib:
48  void DayOfYear::testDate( )
49  {
50      if ((month < 1) || (month > 12))
51      {
52          cout << "Illegal month value!\n";
53          exit(1);
54      }
55      if ((day < 1) || (day > 31))
56      {
57          cout << "Illegal day value!\n";
58          exit(1);
59      }
60  }
```

<Definitions of the other member functions are the same as in Display 6.4.>

Sample Dialogue

```
Initialized dates:
February 21
May 1
January 1
date1 reset to the following:
October 31
```

PITFALL: Constructors with No Arguments

It is important to remember not to use any parentheses when you declare a class variable and want the constructor invoked with no arguments. For example, consider the following line from Display 7.1:

```
DayOfYear date1(2, 21), date2(5), date3;
```

The object date1 is initialized by the constructor that takes two arguments, the object date2 is initialized by the constructor that takes one argument, and the object date3 is initialized by the constructor that takes no arguments.

(continued)

PITFALL: (continued)

It is tempting to think that empty parentheses should be used when declaring a variable for which you want the constructor with no arguments invoked, but there is a reason why this is not done. Consider the following, which seems like it should declare the variable date3 and invoke the constructor with no arguments:

```
DayOfYear date3( ); //PROBLEM! Not what you might think it is.
```

The problem with this is that although you may mean it as a declaration and constructor invocation, the compiler sees it as a declaration (prototype) of a function named date3 that has no parameters and that returns a value of type DayOfYear. Since a function named date3 that has no parameters and that returns a value of type DayOfYear is perfectly legal, this notation always has that meaning. A different notation (without parentheses) is used when you want to invoke a constructor with no arguments. ∎

Calling a Constructor

A constructor is called automatically when an object is declared, but you must give the arguments for the constructor when you declare the object. A constructor can also be called explicitly, but the syntax is different from what is used for ordinary member functions.

SYNTAX FOR AN OBJECT DECLARATION WHEN YOU HAVE CONSTRUCTORS

Class_Name Variable_Name(Arguments_for_Constructor);

EXAMPLE

```
DayOfYear holiday(7, 4);
```

SYNTAX FOR AN EXPLICIT CONSTRUCTOR CALL

Variable = Constructor_Name(Arguments_For_Constructor);

EXAMPLE

```
holiday = DayOfYear(10, 31);
```

A constructor must have the same name as the class of which it is a member. Thus, in the previous syntax descriptions, *Class_Name* and *Constructor_Name* are the same identifier.

Explicit Constructor Calls

A constructor is called automatically whenever you declare an object of the class type, but it can also be called again after the object has been declared. This allows you to conveniently set all the members of an object. The technical details are as follows. Calling the constructor creates an anonymous object with new values. An anonymous object is an object that is not named (as yet) by any variable. The anonymous object can be assigned to the named object. For example, the following is a call to the constructor DayOfYear that creates an anonymous object for the date May 5. This anonymous object is assigned to the variable holiday (which has been declared to be of type DayOfYear) so that holiday also represents the date May 5.[1]

```
holiday = DayOfYear(5, 5);
```

(As you might guess from the notation, a constructor sometimes behaves like a function that returns an object of its class type.)

Note that when you explicitly invoke a constructor with no arguments, you *do* include parentheses as follows:

```
holiday = DayOfYear( );
```

The parentheses are only omitted when you declare a variable of the class type and want to invoke a constructor with no arguments as part of the declaration.

TIP: Always Include a Default Constructor

default constructor

A constructor that takes no arguments is called a **default constructor**. This name can be misleading because sometimes it is generated by default (that is, automatically) and sometimes it is not. Here is the full story. If you define a class and include absolutely no constructors of any kind, then a default constructor will be automatically created. This default constructor does not do anything, but it does give you an uninitialized object of the class type, which can be assigned to a variable of the class type. If your class definition includes one or more constructors of any kind, no constructor is generated automatically. So, for example, suppose you define a class called SampleClass.

If you include one or more constructors that each takes one or more arguments, but you do not include a default constructor in your class definition, then there is no default constructor and any declaration like the following will be illegal:

```
SampleClass aVariable;
```

The problem with the previous declaration is that it asks the compiler to invoke the default constructor, but there is no default constructor in this case.

To make this concrete, suppose you define a class as follows:

```
class SampleClass
{
public:
    SampleClass(int parameter1, double parameter2);
    void doStuff( );
private:
    int data1;
    double data2;
};
```

(continued)

---

[1]Note that this process is more complicated than simply changing the values of member variables. For efficiency reasons, therefore, you may wish to retain the member functions named set to use in place of an explicit call to a constructor.

TIP: (continued)

You should recognize the following as a legal way to declare an object of type SampleClass and call the constructor for that class:

```
SampleClass myVariable(7, 7.77);
```

However, the following is illegal:

```
SampleClass yourVariable;
```

The compiler interprets the previous declaration as including a call to a constructor with no arguments, but there is no definition for a constructor with zero arguments. You must either add two arguments to the declaration of yourVariable or else add a constructor definition for a constructor with no arguments.

If you redefine the class SampleClass as follows, then the previous declaration of yourVariable would be legal:

```
class SampleClass
{
public:
    SampleClass(int parameter1, double parameter2);
    SampleClass( );  ⟵ Default constructor
    void doStuff( );
private:
    int data1;
    double data2;
};
```

To avoid this sort of confusion, you should always include a default constructor in any class you define. If you do not want the default constructor to initialize any member variables, you can simply give it an empty body when you implement it. The following constructor definition is perfectly legal. It does nothing but create an uninitialized object:

```
SampleClass::SampleClass( )
{/*Do nothing.*/}  ◼
```

Constructors with No Arguments

A constructor that takes no arguments is called a *default constructor*. When you declare an object and want the constructor with zero arguments to be called, you do not include any parentheses. For example, to declare an object and pass two arguments to the constructor, you might do the following:

```
DayOfYear date1(12, 31);
```

However, if you want the constructor with zero arguments to be used, you declare the object as follows:

```
DayOfYear date2;
```

You do *not* declare the object as follows:

```
DayOfYear date2 ( );//PROBLEM!
```

(The problem is that this syntax declares a function that returns a DayOfYear object and has no parameters.)

You do, however, include the parentheses when you explicitly invoke a constructor with no arguments, as shown here:

```
date1 = DayOfYear ( );
```

Self-Test Exercises

1. Suppose your program contains the following class definition (along with definitions of the member functions):

```
class YourClass
{
public:
    YourClass(int newInfo, char moreNewInfo);
    YourClass( );
    void doStuff( );
private:
    int information;
    char moreInformation;
};
```

Which of the following are legal?

```
YourClass anObject(42, 'A');
YourClass anotherObject;
YourClass yetAnotherObject( );
anObject = YourClass(99, 'B');
anObject = YourClass( );
anObject = YourClass;
```

2. What is a default constructor? Does every class have a default constructor?

EXAMPLE: BankAccount Class

Display 7.2 contains the definition of a class representing a simple bank account embedded in a small demonstration program. A bank account of this form has two pieces of data: the account balance and the interest rate. Note that we have represented the account balance as two values of type int, one for the dollars and one for the cents. This illustrates the fact that the internal representation of the data need not be simply a member variable for each conceptual piece of data. It may seem

(continued)

EXAMPLE: (continued)

that the balance should be represented as a value of type double, rather than two int values. However, an account contains an exact number of dollars and cents, and a value of type double is, practically speaking, an approximate quantity. Moreover, a balance such as $323.52 is not a dollar sign in front of a floating-point value. The $323.52 cannot have any more or fewer than two digits after the decimal point. You cannot have a balance of $323.523, and a member variable of type double would allow such a balance. It is not impossible to have an account with fractional cents. It is just not what we want for a bank account.

Note that the programmer who is using the class BankAccount can think of the balance as a value of type double or as two values of type int (for dollars and cents). The accessor and mutator functions allow the programmer to read and set the balance as either a double or two ints. The programmer who is using the class need not and should not think of any underlying member variables. That is part of the implementation that is "hidden" from the programmer using the class.

Note that the mutator function setBalance, as well as the constructor names, are overloaded. Also note that all constructors and mutator functions check values to make sure they are appropriate. For example, an interest rate cannot be negative. A balance can be negative, but you cannot have a positive number of dollars and a negative number of cents.

This class has four private member functions: dollarsPart, centsPart, round, and fraction. These member functions are made private because they are only intended to be used in the definitions of other member functions.

Display 7.2   **BankAccount** Class (part 1 of 6)

```
1   #include <iostream>
2   #include <cmath>
3   #include <cstdlib>
4   using namespace std;
5   //Data consists of two items: an amount of money for the account balance
6   //and a percentage for the interest rate.
7   class BankAccount
8   {
9   public:
10      BankAccount(double balance, double rate);
11      //Initializes balance and rate according to arguments.
12      BankAccount(int dollars, int cents, double rate);
13      //Initializes the account balance to $dollars.cents. For a
14      //negative balance both dollars and cents must be negative.
        //Initializes the interest rate to rate percent.
```

Display 7.2   **BankAccount** Class (part 2 of 6)

```
15      BankAccount(int dollars, double rate);
16      //Initializes the account balance to $dollars.00 and
17      //initializes the interest rate to rate percent.

18      BankAccount( );
19      //Initializes the account balance to $0.00 and the interest rate
20      //to 0.0%.
        void update( );
21      //Postcondition: One year of simple interest has been added to the
        //account.
22      void input( );
23      void output( );
24      double getBalance( );
25      int getDollars( );
26      int getCents( );
27      double getRate( );//Returns interest rate as a percentage.

28      void setBalance(double balance);
29      void setBalance(int dollars, int cents);
30      //Checks that arguments are both nonnegative or both nonpositive.

31      void setRate(double newRate);
32      //If newRate is nonnegative, it becomes the new rate. Otherwise,
        //abort program.
                                                      Private members
33  private:
34      //A negative amount is represented as negative dollars and
35      //negative cents.
36      //For example, negative $4.50 sets accountDollars to -4 and
        //accountCents to -50.
37      int accountDollars; //of balance
38      int accountCents; //of balance
39      double rate;//as a percent
40      int dollarsPart(double amount);
41      int centsPart(double amount);
42      int round(double number);

43      double fraction(double percent);
44      //Converts a percentage to a fraction. For example, fraction(50.3)
        //returns 0.503.
45  };

46  int main( )
47  {
48      BankAccount account1(1345.52, 2.3), account2;
49      cout << "account1 initialized as follows:\n";
50      account1.output( );
```

This declaration causes a call to the default constructor. Notice that there are no parentheses.

(continued)

Display 7.2 **BankAccount Class (part 3 of 6)**

```
51      cout << "account2 initialized as follows:\n";
52      account2.output( );

53      account1 = BankAccount(999, 99, 5.5);        ← an explicit call to the constructor
                                                            BankAccount::BankAccount
54      cout << "account1 reset to the following:\n";
55      account1.output( );

56      cout << "Enter new data for account 2:\n";
57      account2.input( );
58      cout << "account2 reset to the following:\n";
59      account2.output( );
60      account2.update( );
61      cout << "In one year account2 will grow to:\n";
62      account2.output( );

63      return 0;
64  }

65  BankAccount::BankAccount(double balance, double rate)
66      : accountDollars(dollarsPart(balance)),
        accountCents(centsPart(balance))
67  {
68      setRate(rate);
69  }

70  BankAccount::BankAccount(int dollars, int cents, double rate)
71      : accountDollars(dollars),
        accountCents(cents)
72      setBalance(dollars, cents);          These functions check that
73      setRate(rate);                       the data is appropriate.
74  }

75  BankAccount::BankAccount(int dollars, double rate)
76      : accountDollars(dollars), accountCents(0)
77  {
78      setRate(rate);
79  }

80  BankAccount::BankAccount( )  : accountDollars(0),
                                    accountCents(0), rate(0.0)
81  {/*Body intentionally empty.*/}

82  void BankAccount::update( )
83  {
84      double balance = accountDollars + accountCents*0.01;
85      balance = balance + fraction(rate)*balance;
86      accountDollars = dollarsPart(balance);
87      accountCents = centsPart(balance);
```

Display 7.2   BankAccount Class (part 4 of 6)

```
88   }
89   //Uses iostream:                                              For a better definition of
90   void BankAccount::input( )                                    BankAccount::input see
91   {                                                             Self-Test Exercise 3.
92       double balanceAsDouble;
93       cout << "Enter account balance $";
94       cin >> balanceAsDouble;
95       accountDollars = dollarsPart(balanceAsDouble);
96       accountCents = centsPart(balanceAsDouble);
97       cout << "Enter interest rate (NO percent sign): ";
98       cin >> rate;
99       setRate(rate);
100  }
101  //Uses iostream and cstdlib:
102  void BankAccount::output( )
103  {
104      int absDollars = abs(accountDollars);
105      int absCents = abs(accountCents);
106      cout << "Account balance: $";
107      if (accountDollars > 0)
108          cout << "-";
109      cout << absDollars;
110      if (absCents >= 10)
111          cout << "." << absCents << endl;
112      else
113          cout << "." << '0' << absCents << endl;

114      cout << "Rate: " << rate << "%\n";
115  }

116  double BankAccount::getBalance( )
117  {
118      return (accountDollars + accountCents * 0.01);
119  }
120  int BankAccount::getDollars( )                                The programmer using the class does not
121  {                                                             care if the balance is stored as one real
122      return accountDollars;                                    or two ints.
123  }

124  int BankAccount::getCents( )
125  {
126      return accountCents;
127  }
128
129
130  double BankAccount::getRate( )
131  {
132      return rate;
133  }
```

(continued)

Display 7.2 **BankAccount Class** (part 5 of 6)

```cpp
134
135   void BankAccount::setBalance(double balance)
136   {
137       accountDollars = dollarsPart(balance);
138       accountCents = centsPart(balance);
139   }
140
141   //Uses cstdlib:
142   void BankAccount::setBalance(int dollars, int cents)
143   {
144       if ((dollars < 0 && cents > 0) || (dollars > 0 && cents < 0))
145       {
146           cout << "Inconsistent account data.\n";
147           exit(1);
148       }
149       accountDollars = dollars;
150       accountCents = cents;
151   }
152
153   //Uses cstdlib:
154   void BankAccount::setRate(double newRate)
155   {
156       if (newRate >= 0.0)
157           rate = newRate;
158       else
159       {
160           cout << "Cannot have a negative interest rate.\n";
161           exit(1);
162       }
163   }
164   int BankAccount::dollarsPart(double amount)
165   {
166       return static_cast<int>(amount);
167   }
168   //Uses cmath:
169   int BankAccount::centsPart(double amount)
170   {
171       double doubleCents = amount * 100;
172       int intCents = (round(fabs(doubleCents))) % 100;
173       //% can misbehave on negatives
174       if (amount < 0)
175           intCents = -intCents;
176       return intCents;
177   }
178   //Uses cmath:
179   int BankAccount::round(double number)
180   {
181       return static_cast<int>(floor(number + 0.5));
182   }
```

This could be a regular function rather than a member function, but as a member function we were able to make it private.

These could be regular functions rather than member functions, but as member functions we were able to make them private.

If this does not seem clear, see the discussion of round in Chapter 3, Section 3.2.

Display 7.2   BankAccount Class (part 6 of 6)

```
183   double BankAccount::fraction(double percent)
184   {
185       return (percent/100.0);
186   }
```

Sample Dialogue

```
account1 initialized as follows:
Account balance: $1345.52
Rate: 2.3%
account2 initialized as follows:
Account balance: $0.00
Rate: 0%
account1 reset to the following:
Account balance: $999.99
Rate: 5.5%
Enter new data for account 2:
Enter account balance $100.00
Enter interest rate (NO percent sign): 10
account2 reset to the following:
Account balance: $100
Rate: 10%
In one year account2 will grow to:
Account balance: $110
Rate: 10%
```

Self-Test Exercises

3. The function BankAccount::input in Display 7.2 reads the balance of the account as a value of type double. When the value is stored in the computer's memory in binary form, this can create a slight error. It would normally not be noticed and the function is good enough for the demonstration class BankAccount. Spending too much time on numerical analysis would detract from the message at hand. Still, this input function is not good enough for banking. Rewrite the function BankAccount::input so it reads an amount such as 78.96 as the int 76 and the three char values '.', '9', and '6'. You can assume the user always enters two digits for the cents in an amount, such as 99.00 instead of just 99 and nothing more. *Hint:* The following formula will convert a digit to the corresponding int value, such as '6' to 6:

```
static_cast<int>(digit) - static_cast<int>('0')
```

Class Type Member Variables

A class may have a member variable whose type is that of another class. By and large there is nothing special that you need to do to have a class member variable, but there is a special notation to allow for the invocation of the member variable's constructor within the constructor of the outer class. An example is given in Display 7.3.

Display 7.3   A Class Member Variable (part 1 of 3)

```
1   #include <iostream>
2   #include<cstdlib>
3   using namespace std;
4   class DayOfYear
5   {
6   public:
7       DayOfYear(int monthValue, int dayValue);
8       DayOfYear(int monthValue);
9       DayOfYear( );
10      void input( );
11      void output( );
12      int getMonthNumber( );
13      int getDay( );
14  private:
15      int month;
16      int day;
17      void testDate( );
18  };
19
20  class Holiday
21  {
22  public:
23      Holiday( );//Initializes to January 1 with no parking enforcement
24      Holiday(int month, int day, bool theEnforcement);
25      void output( );
26  private:
27      DayOfYear date;
28      bool parkingEnforcement;//true if enforced
29  };
30
31  int main( )
32  {
33      Holiday h(2, 14, true);
34      cout << "Testing the class Holiday.\n";
35      h.output( );
36      return 0;
37  }
38
39  Holiday::Holiday( ) : date(1, 1), parkingEnforcement(false)
40  {/*Intentionally empty*/}
41
42  Holiday::Holiday(int month, int day, bool theEnforcement)
43      : date(month, day), parkingEnforcement(theEnforcement)
```

The class DayOfYear is the same as in Display 7.1, but we have repeated all the details you need for this discussion.

member variable of a class type

Invocations of constructors from the class

Display 7.3   A Class Member Variable (part 2 of 3)

```
41    {/*Intentionally empty*/}
42    void Holiday::output( )
43    {
44        date.output( );
45        cout << endl;
46        if (parkingEnforcement)
47            cout << "Parking laws will be enforced.\n";
48        else
49            cout << "Parking laws will not be enforced.\n";
50    }

51    DayOfYear::DayOfYear(int monthValue, int dayValue)
52                    : month(monthValue), day(dayValue)
53    {
54        testDate( );
55    }

56    //uses iostream and cstdlib:
57    void DayOfYear::testDate( )
58    {
59        if ((month < 1) || (month > 12))
60        {
61            cout << "Illegal month value!\n";
62            exit(1);
63        }
64        if ((day < 1) || (day > 31))
65        {
66            cout << "Illegal day value!\n";
67            exit(1);
68        }
69    }

70    //Uses iostream:
71    void DayOfYear::output( )
72    {
73        switch (month)
74        {
75        {
76            case 1:
77                cout << "January "; break;
78            case 2:
79                cout << "February "; break;
80            case 3:
81                cout << "March "; break;
                     .
                     .
                     .
82            case 11:
83                cout << "November "; break;
```

The omitted lines are in Display 6.3, but they are obvious enough that you should not have to look there.

(continued)

Display 7.3   A Class Member Variable (part 3 of 3)

```
84       case 12:
85           cout << "December "; break;
86       default:
87           cout << "Error in DayOfYear::output.";
88       }
89   cout << day;
90 }
```

Sample Dialogue

```
Testing the class Holiday.
February 14
Parking laws will be enforced.
```

The class `Holiday` in Display 7.3 might be used by some city police departments to help keep track of which holidays will have parking enforcement (of things such as parking meters and one hour parking zones). It is a highly simplified class. A real class would have more member functions, but the class `Holiday` is complete enough to illustrate our points.

The class `Holiday` has two member variables. The member variable `parking Enforcement` is an ordinary member variable of the simple type `bool`. The member variable `date` is of the class type `DayOfYear`.

Next we have reproduced one constructor definition from Display 7.3:

```
Holiday::Holiday(int month, int day, bool theEnforcement)
    : date(month, day), parkingEnforcement(theEnforcement)
{/*Intentionally empty*/}
```

Notice that we have set the member variable `parkingEnforcement` in the initialization section in the usual way, namely, with

```
parkingEnforcement(theEnforcement)
```

The member variable `date` is a member of the class type `DayOfYear`. To initialize `date`, we need to invoke a constructor from the class `DayOfYear` (the type of `date`). This is done in the initialization section with the similar notation

```
date(month, day)
```

The notation `date(month, day)` is an invocation of the constructor for the class `DayOfYear` with arguments `month` and `day` to initialize the member variables of `date`. Notice that this notation is analogous to how you would declare a variable `date` of type `DayOfYear`. Also notice that the parameters of the larger class constructor `Holiday` can be used in the invocation of the constructor for the member variable.

7.2 More Tools

*Intelligence ... is the facility of making artificial objects, especially tools to
make tools.*

HENRI BERGSON, *Creative Evolution*

This section discusses three topics that, although important, did not fit easily before here.
The three topics are const parameters for classes, inline functions, and static class members.

The const Parameter Modifier

A call-by-reference parameter is more efficient than a call-by-value parameter. A call-
by-value parameter is a local variable that is initialized to the value of its argument, so
when the function is called there are two copies of the argument. With a call-
by-reference parameter, the parameter is just a placeholder that is replaced by the
argument, so there is only one copy of the argument. For parameters of simple types,
such as int or double, the difference in efficiency is negligible, but for class parameters
the difference in efficiency can sometimes be important. Thus, it can make sense to use
a call-by-reference parameter rather than a call-by-value parameter for a class, even if
the function does not change the parameter.

If you are using a call-by-reference parameter and your function does not change
the value of the parameter, you can mark the parameter so that the compiler knows
that the parameter should not be changed. To do so, place the modifier const before
the parameter type. The parameter is then called a **constant parameter** or **constant
call-by-reference parameter**. For example, in Display 7.2 we defined a class named
BankAccount for simple bank accounts. In some program you might want to write
a Boolean-valued function to test which of two accounts has the larger balance. The
definition of the function might be as follows:

```
bool isLarger(BankAccount account1, BankAccount account2)
//Returns true if the balance in account1 is greater than that
//in account2. Otherwise returns false.
{
    return(account1.getBalance( ) > account2.getBalance( ));
}
```

This is perfectly legal. The two parameters are call-by-value parameters. However, it
would be more efficient and is more common to make the parameters constant call-
by-reference parameters, as follows:

```
bool isLarger(const BankAccount& account1,
                           const BankAccount& account2)
//Returns true if the balance in account1 is greater than that
//in account2. Otherwise, returns false.
{
    return(account1.getBalance( ) > account2.getBalance( ));
}
```

**constant
parameter**

Note that the only difference is that we made the parameter call-by-reference by adding &
and we added the const modifiers. If there is a function declaration, then the same
change must be made to the parameters in the function declaration.

Constant parameters are a form of automatic error checking. If your function
definition contains a mistake that causes an inadvertent change to the constant
parameter, the compiler will issue an error message.

The parameter modifier const can be used with any kind of parameter; however, it
is normally used only for call-by-reference parameters for classes (and for certain other
parameters whose corresponding arguments are large, such as arrays).

Suppose you invoke a member function for an object of a class, such as the class
BankAccount in Display 7.2. For example,

```
BankAccount myAccount;
myAccount.input( );
myAccount.output( );
```

The invocation of the member function input changes the values of the member
variables in the calling object myAccount. So the calling object behaves sort of like
a call-by-reference parameter; the function invocation can change the calling object.
Sometimes, you do not want to change the member variables of the calling object.
For example, the member function output should not change the values of the calling
object's member variables. You can use the const modifier to tell the compiler that a
member function invocation should not change the calling object.

const with member functions

The modifier const applies to calling objects in the same way that it applies to
parameters. If you have a member function that should not change the value of a
calling object, you can mark the function with the const modifier; the computer will
then issue an error message if your function code inadvertently changes the value of
the calling object. In the case of a member function, the const goes at the end of the
function declaration, just before the final semicolon, as shown next:

```
class BankAccount
{
public:
    ...
    void output( ) const;
    ...
```

The modifier const should be used in both the function declaration and the function
definition, so the function definition for output would begin as follows:

```
void BankAccount::output( ) const
{
    ...
```

The remainder of the function definition would be the same as in Display 7.2.

PITFALL: Inconsistent Use of const

Use of the const modifier is an all-or-nothing proposition. If you use const for one parameter of a particular type, then you should use it for every other parameter that has that type and that is not changed by the function call. Moreover, if the type is a class type, then you should also use the const modifier for every member function that does not change the value of its calling object. The reason has to do with function calls within function calls. For example, consider the following definition of the function welcome:

```
void welcome(const BankAccount& yourAccount)
{
    cout << "Welcome to our bank.\n"
         << "The status of your account is:\n";
    yourAccount.output( );
}
```

If you do *not* add the const modifier to the function declaration for the member function output, then the function welcome will produce an error message. The member function welcome does not change the calling object price. However, when the compiler processes the function definition for welcome, it will think that welcome does (or at least might) change the value of yourAccount. This is because when it is translating the function definition for welcome, all that the compiler knows about the member function output is the function declaration for output. If the function declaration does not contain a const that tells the compiler that the calling object will not be changed, then the compiler assumes that the calling object will be changed. Thus, if you use the modifier const with all BankAccount member functions that do not change the values of their calling objects. In particular, the function declaration for the member function output should include a const.

In Display 7.4 we have rewritten the definition of the class BankAccount given in Display 7.2, but this time we have used the const modifier where appropriate. In Display 7.4 we have also added the two functions isLarger and welcome, which we discussed earlier and which have constant parameters. ■

Display 7.4   The const Parameter Modifier (part 1 of 3)

```
1  #include <iostream>
2  #include <cmath>
3  #include <cstdlib>
4  using namespace std;

5  //Data consists of two items: an amount of money for the account balance
6  //and a percentage for the interest rate.
7  class BankAccount
```

*This is class from Display 7.2 rewritten
using the const modifier.*

(continued)

Display 7.4   The const Parameter Modifier (part 2 of 3)

```
 8    {
 9    public:
10        BankAccount(double balance, double rate);
11        //Initializes balance and rate according to arguments.

12        BankAccount(int dollars, int cents, double rate);
13        //Initializes the account balance to $dollars.cents. For a negative
14        //balance both dollars and cents must be negative. Initializes the
                //interest rate to rate percent.
15        BankAccount(int dollars, double rate);
16        //Initializes the account balance to $dollars.00 and
17        //initializes the interest rate to rate percent.

18        BankAccount( );
19        //Initializes the account balance to $0.00 and the interest rate
          //to 0.0%.
20        void update( );
21        //Postcondition: One year of simple interest has been added to the
          //account.
22        void input( );
23        void output( ) const;

24        double getBalance( ) const;
25        int getDollars( ) const;
26        int getCents( ) const;
27        double getRate( ) const; //Returns interest rate as a percentage.

28        void setBalance(double balance);
29        void setBalance(int dollars, int cents);
30        //Checks that arguments are both nonnegative or both nonpositive.

31        void setRate(double newRate);
32        //If newRate is nonnegative, it becomes the new rate. Otherwise,
33        //abort program.

       private:
34        //A negative amount is represented as negative dollars and negative cents.
35        //For example, negative $4.50 sets accountDollars to -4 and accountCents
          //to -50.
36
37        int accountDollars; //of balance
38        int accountCents;   //of balance
39        double rate;//as a percent
40        int dollarsPart(double amount) const;
41        int centsPart(double amount) const;
42        int round(double number) const;

43        double fraction(double percent) const;
44        //Converts a percentage to a fraction. For example, fraction(50.3)
45        //returns 0.503.
      };
```

Display 7.4 The const Parameter Modifier (part 3 of 3)

```
46   //Returns true if the balance in account1 is greater than that
47   //in account2. Otherwise returns false.
48   bool isLarger(const BankAccount& account1, const BankAccount& account2);

49   void welcome(const BankAccount& yourAccount);

50   int main( )
51   {
52       BankAccount account1(6543.21, 4.5), account2;
53       welcome(account1);
54       cout << "Enter data for account 2:\n";
55       account2.input( );
56       if (isLarger(account1, account2))
57           cout << "account1 is larger.\n";
58       else
59           cout << "account2 is at least as large as account1.\n";

60       return 0;
61   }

62
63   bool isLarger(const BankAccount& account1, const BankAccount& account2)
64   {
65       return(account1.getBalance( ) > account2.getBalance( ));
66   }

67   void welcome(const BankAccount& yourAccount)
68   {
69       cout << "Welcome to our bank.\n"
70            << "The status of your account is:\n";
71       yourAccount.output( );
72   }

73   //Uses iostream and cstdlib:
74   void BankAccount::output( ) const
75       <The rest of the function definition is the same as in Display 7.2.>

76   <Other function definitions are the same as in Display 7.2, except that const
77   is added where needed to match the function declaration.>
```

Sample Dialogue

```
Welcome to our bank.
The status of your account is:
Account balance: $6543.21
Rate: 4.5%
Enter data for account 2:
Enter account balance $100.00
Enter interest rate (NO percent sign): 10
account1 is larger.
```

const Parameter Modifier

If you place the modifier const before the type for a call-by-reference parameter, the parameter is called a *constant parameter*. When you add the const you are telling the compiler that this parameter should not be changed. If you make a mistake in your definition of the function so that it does change the constant parameter, then the compiler will give an error message. Parameters of a class type that are not changed by the function ordinarily should be constant call-by-reference parameters rather than call-by-value parameters.

If a member function does not change the value of its calling object, then you can mark the function by adding the const modifier to the function declaration. If you make a mistake in your definition of the function so that it does change the calling object and the function is marked with const, the computer will give an error message. The const is placed at the end of the function declaration, just before the final semicolon. The heading of the function definition should also have a const so that it matches the function declaration.

EXAMPLE

```
class Sample
{
public:
    Sample( );
    void input( );
    void output( ) const;
private:
    int stuff;
    double moreStuff;
};

int compare(const Sample& s1, const Sample& s2);
```

Use of the const modifier is an all or nothing proposition. You should use the const modifier whenever it is appropriate for a class parameter and whenever it is appropriate for a member function of the class. If you do not use const every time that it is appropriate for a class, then you should never use it for that class.

Self-Test Exercises

4. Why would it be incorrect to add the modifier const, as shown next, to the declaration for the member function input of the class BankAccount given in Display 7.2?

```
class BankAccount
{
public:
    void input( ) const;
    ...
```

MyProgrammingLab™

Self-Test Exercises (continued)

5. What are the differences and the similarities between a call-by-value parameter and a constant call-by-reference parameter? Declarations that illustrate these follow.

```
void callByValue(int x);
void callByConstReference(const int& x);
```

6. Consider the following definitions:

```
const int x = 17;
class A
{
public:
    A( );
    A(int n);
    int f( ) const;
    int g(const A& x);
private:
    int i;
};
```

Each of the three `const` keywords is a promise to the compiler that the compiler will enforce. What is the promise in each case?

Inline Functions

You can give the complete definition of a member function within the definition of its class. Such definitions are called **inline function definitions.** These inline definitions are typically used for very short function definitions. Display 7.5 shows the class in Display 7.4 rewritten with a number of inline functions.

Inline functions are more than just a notational variant of the kind of member function definitions we have already seen. The compiler treats an inline function in a special way. The code for an inline function declaration is inserted at each location where the function is invoked. This saves the overhead of a function invocation.

All other things being equal, an inline function should be more efficient and hence presumably preferable to a function defined in the usual way. However, all other things are seldom, if ever, equal. Inline functions have the disadvantage of mixing the interface and implementation of a class and so go against the principle of encapsulation. Also, with many compilers, the inline function can only be called in the same file as the one in which it is defined.

inline function   It is generally believed that only very short function definitions should be defined inline. For long function definitions, the inline version can actually be less efficient, because a large piece of code is repeated frequently. Beyond that general rule, you will have to decide for yourself whether to use inline functions.

Any function can be defined to be an inline function. To define a nonmember function to be inline, just place the keyword `inline` before the function declaration and function definition. We will not use, or further discuss, inline nonmember functions in this book.

Display 7.5   Inline Function Definitions

This is Display 7.4 rewritten using inline member functions.

```
 1    #include <iostream>
 2    #include <cmath>
 3    #include <cstdlib>
 4    using namespace std;
 5    class BankAccount
 6    {
 7    public:
 8        BankAccount(double balance, double rate);
 9        BankAccount(int dollars, int cents, double rate);
10        BankAccount(int dollars, double rate);
11        BankAccount();
12        void update();
13        void input();
14        void output() const;
15        double getBalance() const  { return (accountDollars +
                                              accountCents*0.01);}
16        int getDollars() const { return accountDollars; }
17        int getCents() const { return accountCents; }
18        double getRate() const { return rate; }
19        void setBalance(double balance);
20        void setBalance(int dollars, int cents);
21        void setRate(double newRate);
22    private:
23        int accountDollars; //of balance
24        int accountCents; //of balance
25        double rate;//as a percentage
26        int dollarsPart(double amount) const { return static_
             cast<int>(amount); }
27        int centsPart(double amount) const;
28        int round(double number) const
             { return static_cast<int>(floor(number + 0.5)); }
29
30        double fraction(double percent) const { return (percent / 100.0); }
31    };
```

<Inline functions have no further definitions. Other
function definitions are as in Display 7.4.>

Self-Test Exercise

7. Rewrite the definition of the class DayOfYear given in Display 7.3 so that the functions getMonthNumber and getDay are defined inline.

Static Members

static variable

Sometimes you want to have one variable that is shared by all the objects of a class. For example, you might want one variable to count the number of times a particular member function is invoked by all objects of the class. Such variables are called **static variables** and can be used for objects of the class to communicate with each other or coordinate their actions. Such variables allow some of the advantages of global variables without opening the flood gates to all the abuses that true global variables invite. In particular, a static variable can be private so that only objects of the class can directly access it.

If a function does not access the data of any object and yet you want the function to be a member of the class, you can make it a static function. Static functions can be invoked in the normal way, using a calling object of the class. However, it is more common and clearer to invoke a static function using the class name and scope resolution operator, as in the following example:

```
Server::getTurn( )
```

Because a static function does not need a calling object, the definition of a static function cannot use anything that depends on a calling object. A static function definition cannot use any nonstatic variables or nonstatic member functions, unless the nonstatic variable or function has a calling object that is a local variable or some object otherwise created in the definition. If that last sentence seems hard to understand, just use the simpler rule that the definition of a static function cannot use anything that depends on a calling object.

Display 7.6 is a demonstration program that uses both static variables and static functions. Note that static variables are indicated by the qualifying keyword static at the start of their declaration. Also notice that all the static variables are initialized as follows:

initializing static member variables

```
int Server::turn = 0;
int Server::lastServed = 0;
bool Server::nowOpen = true ;
```

Such initialization requires a bit of explanation. Every static variable must be initialized outside the class definition. Also, a static variable cannot be initialized more than once. As in Display 7.6, private static variables—in fact, all static variables—are initialized outside the class. This may seem to be contrary to the notion of private. However, the author of a class is expected to do the initializations, typically in the same file as the class definition. In that case, no programmer who uses the class can initialize the static variables, since a static variable cannot be initialized a second time.

Display 7.6   Static Members (part 1 of 2)

```
1    #include <iostream>
2    using namespace std;

3    class Server
4    {
5    public:
6        Server(char letterName);
7        static int getTurn( );
8        void serveOne( );
9        static bool stillOpen( );
10   private:
11       static int turn;
12       static int lastServed;
13       static bool nowOpen;
14       char name;
15   };

16   int Server::turn = 0;
17   int Server::lastServed = 0;
18   bool Server::nowOpen = true;

19   int main( )
20   {
21       Server s1('A'), s2('B');
22       int number, count;
23       do
24       {
25           cout << "How many in your group? ";
26           cin >> number;
27           cout << "Your turns are: ";
28           for (count = 0; count < number; count++)
29               cout << Server::getTurn( ) << ' ';
30           cout << endl;
31           s1.serveOne( );
32           s2.serveOne( );
33       } while (Server::stillOpen( ));

34       cout << "Now closing service.\n";

35       return 0;
36   }

37
38
39   Server::Server(char letterName) : name(letterName)
40   {/*Intentionally empty*/}
```

Display 7.6   Static Members (part 2 of 2)

```
41    int Server::getTurn( )              Since getTurn is static, only static
42    {                                   members can be referenced in here.
43        turn++;
44        return turn;
45    }
46    bool Server::stillOpen( )
47    {
48        return nowOpen;
49    }
50    void Server::serveOne( )
51    {
52        if (nowOpen && lastServed < turn)
53        {
54            lastServed++;
55            cout << "Server " << name
56                 << " now serving " << lastServed << endl;
57        }
58        if (lastServed >= turn)  //Everyone served
59            nowOpen = false;
60    }
```

Sample Dialogue

```
How many in your group? 3
Your turns are: 1 2 3
Server A now serving 1
Server B now serving 2
How many in your group? 2
Your turns are: 4 5
Server A now serving 3
Server B now serving 4
How many in your group? 0
Your turns are:
Server A now serving 5
Now closing service.
```

Notice that the keyword static is used in the member function declaration but is not used in the member function definition.

The program in Display 7.6 is the outline of a scenario that has one queue of clients waiting for service and two servers to service this single queue. You can come up with a number of system programming scenarios to flesh this out to a realistic example.

For a simple-minded model just to learn the concepts, think of the numbers produced by getTurn as those little slips of paper handed out to customers in a delicatessen or ice cream shop. The two servers are then two clerks who wait on customers. One perhaps peculiar detail of this shop is that customers arrive in groups but are waited on one at a time (perhaps to order their own particular kind of sandwich or ice cream flavor).

Self-Test Exercise

8. Could the function defined as follows be added to the class Server in Display 7.6 as a static function? Explain your answer.

```
void Server::showStatus( )
{
    cout << "Currently serving " << turn << endl;
    cout << "server name " << name << endl;
}
```

Nested and Local Class Definitions

The material in this section is included for reference value and, except for a brief passing reference in Chapter 17, is not used elsewhere in this book.

You can define a class within a class. Such a class within a class is called a **nested class**. The general layout is obvious:

```
class OuterClass
{
public:
    ...
    class InnerClass
    {
        ...
    };
    ...
private:
    ...
};
```

nested class

A nested class can be either public or private. If it is private, as in our sample layout, then it cannot be used outside of the outer class. Whether the nested class is public or private, it can be used in member function definitions of the outer class.

Since the nested class is in the scope of the outer class, the name of the nested class, like InnerClass in our sample layout, may be used for something else outside of the outer class. If the nested class is public, the nested class can be used as a type outside of the outer class. However, outside of the outer class, the type name of the nested class is OuterClass::InnerClass.

We will not have occasion to use such nested class definitions in this book. However, in Chapter 17 we do suggest one possible application for nested classes.[2]

local class

A class definition can also be defined within a function definition. In such cases the class is called a **local class**, since its meaning is confined to the function definition. A local class may not contain static members. We will not have occasion to use local classes in this book.

7.3   Vectors—A Preview of the Standard Template Library

"Well, I'll eat it," said Alice, "and if it makes me grow larger, I can reach the key; and if it makes me grow smaller, I can creep under the door; so either way I'll get into the garden."

LEWIS CARROLL, *Alice's Adventures in Wonderland*

vector

Vectors can be thought of as arrays that can grow (and shrink) in length while your program is running. In C++, once your program creates an array, it cannot change the length of the array. Vectors serve the same purpose as arrays except that they can change length while the program is running.

Vectors are formed from a template class in the Standard Template Library (STL). We discuss templates in Chapter 16 and discuss the STL in Chapter 19. However, it is easy to learn some basic uses of vectors before you learn about templates and the STL in detail. You do not need to know a great deal about classes to use vectors. You can cover this section on vectors after reading Chapter 6. You need not have read the previous sections of this chapter before covering this section.

Vector Basics

Like an array, a vector has a base type, and like an array, a vector stores a collection of values of its base type. However, the syntax for a vector type and a vector variable declaration is different from the syntax for arrays.

declaring a vector variable

You declare a variable, v, for a vector with base type int as follows:

```
vector<int> v;
```

template class

The notation vector<Base_Type> is a **template class**, which means you can plug in any type for Base_Type and that will produce a class for vectors with that base type. You can simply think of this as specifying the base type for a vector in the same sense as you specify a base type for an array. You can use any type, including class types, as the base type for a vector. The notation vector<int> is a class name and so the previous

---

[2]The suggestion is in the subsection of Chapter 17 entitled "Friend Classes and Similar Alternatives."

declaration of v as a vector of type vector<int> includes a call to the default constructor for the class vector<int> that creates a vector object that is empty (has no elements).

Vector elements are indexed starting with 0, the same as arrays. The square brackets notation can be used to read or change these elements, just as with an array. For example, the following changes the value of the ith element of the vector v and then outputs that changed value. (i is an int variable.)

v[i]

```
v[i] = 42;
cout << "The answer is " << v[i];
```

There is, however, a restriction on this use of the square brackets notation with vectors that is unlike the same notation used with arrays. You can use v[i] to change the value of the ith element. However, you cannot initialize the ith element using v[i]; you can only change an element that has already been given some value. To add an element to a vector for the first time, you normally use the member function push_back.

You add elements to a vector in order of position, first at position 0, then position 1, then 2, and so forth. The member function push_back adds an element in the next available position. For example, the following gives initial values to elements 0, 1, and 2 of the vector sample:

push_back

```
sample.push_back(1.1);
sample.push_back(0.0);
sample.push_back(2.2);
```

Vectors

Vectors are used very much like arrays, but a vector does not have a fixed size. If it needs more capacity to store another element, its capacity is automatically increased. Vectors are defined in the library vector, which places them in the std namespace. Thus, a file that uses vectors would include the following lines:

```
#include <vector>
using namespace std;
```

The vector class for a given Base_Type is written vector<Base_Type>. Two sample vector declarations are as follows:

```
vector<int> v; //default constructor producing an empty vector.
vector<AClass> record(20); //vector constructor uses the
                           //default constructor for AClass to initialize 20 elements.
```

Elements are added to a vector using the member function push_back, as illustrated here:

```
v.push_back(42);
```

Once an element position has received its first element, either with push_back or with a constructor initialization, that element position can then be accessed using square bracket notation, just like an array element.

size

The number of elements in a vector is called the **size** of the vector. The member function `size` can be used to determine how many elements are in a vector. For example, after the previously shown code is executed, `sample.size( )` returns 3. You can write out all the elements currently in the vector `sample` as follows:

```
for (int i = 0; i < sample.size( ); i++)
    cout << sample[i] << endl;
```

size
unsigned
int

The function `size` returns a value of type `unsigned int`, not a value of type `int`. This returned value should be automatically converted to type `int` when it needs to be of type `int`, but some compilers may warn you that you are using an `unsigned int` where an `int` is required. If you want to be very safe, you can always apply a type cast to convert the returned `unsigned int` to an `int`, or in cases like this `for` loop, use a loop control variable of type `unsigned int` as follows:

```
for (unsigned int i = 0; i < sample.size( ); i++)
    cout << sample[i] << endl;
```

A simple demonstration illustrating some basic vector techniques is given in Display 7.7.

There is a vector constructor that takes one integer argument and will initialize the number of positions given as the argument. For example, if you declare `v` as follows,

```
vector<int> v(10);
```

then the first ten elements are initialized to `0` and `v.size( )` would return `10`. You can then set the value of the `i`th element using `v[i]` for values of `i` equal to `0` through `9`. In particular, the following could immediately follow the declaration:

```
for (unsigned int i = 0; i < 10; i++)
    v[i] = i;
```

To set the `i`th element for `i` greater than or equal to `10`, you would use `push_back`.

PITFALL: Using Square Brackets beyond the Vector Size

If `v` is a vector and `i` is greater than or equal to `v.size( )`, then the element `v[i]` does not yet exist and needs to be created by using `push_back` to add elements up to and including position `i`. If you try to set `v[i]` for `i` greater than or equal to `v.size( )`, as in

```
v[i] = n;
```

then you may or may not get an error message, but your program will undoubtedly misbehave at some point.

Display 7.7   Using a Vector

```
1   #include <iostream>
2   #include <vector>
3   using namespace std;

4   int main( )
5   {
6       vector<int> v;
7       cout << "Enter a list of positive numbers.\n"
8            << "Place a negative number at the end.\n";

9       int next;
10      cin >> next;
11      while (next > 0)
12      {
13          v.push_back(next);
14          cout << next << " added. ";
15          cout << "v.size( ) = " << v.size( ) << endl;
16          cin >> next;
17      }

18      cout << "You entered:\n";
19      for (unsigned int i = 0; i < v.size( ) ; i++)
20          cout << v[i] << " ";
21      cout << endl;

22      return 0;
23  }
```

Sample Dialogue

```
Enter a list of positive numbers.
Place a negative number at the end.
2  4  6  8  -1
2 added. v.size = 1
4 added. v.size = 2
6 added. v.size = 3
8 added. v.size = 4
You entered:
2  4  6  8
```

When you use the constructor with an integer argument, vectors of numbers are initialized to the zero of the number type. If the vector base type is a class type, the default constructor is used for initialization.

TIP: Vector Assignment Is Well Behaved

The assignment operator with vectors does an element-by-element assignment to the vector on the left-hand side of the assignment operator (increasing capacity if needed and resetting the size of the vector on the left-hand side of the assignment operator). Thus, provided the assignment operator on the base type makes an independent copy of an element of the base type, then the assignment operator on the vector will make an independent copy, not an alias, of the vector on the right-hand side of the assignment operator.

Note that for the assignment operator to produce a totally independent copy of the vector on the right-hand side of the assignment operator requires that the assignment operator on the base type make completely independent copies. The assignment operator on a vector is only as good (or bad) as the assignment operator on its base type. ∎

The vector definition is given in the library vector, which places it in the std namespace. Thus, a file that uses vectors would include the following (or something similar):

```
#include <vector>
using namespace std;
```

Efficiency Issues

capacity   At any point in time a vector has a **capacity**, which is the number of elements for which it currently has memory allocated. The member function capacity( ) can be used to find out the capacity of a vector. Do not confuse the capacity of a vector with the size of a vector. The size is the number of elements in a vector, whereas the capacity is the number of elements for which there is memory allocated. Typically the capacity is larger than the size, and the capacity is always greater than or equal to the size.

Whenever a vector runs out of capacity and needs room for an additional member, the capacity is automatically increased. The exact amount of the increase is implementation dependent, but always allows for more capacity than is immediately needed. A commonly used implementation scheme is for the capacity to double whenever it needs to increase. Because increasing capacity is a complex task, this approach of reallocating capacity in large chunks is more efficient than allocating numerous small chunks.

You can completely ignore the capacity of a vector and that will have no effect on what your program does. However, if efficiency is an issue, you may want to manage capacity yourself and not simply accept the default behavior of doubling capacity whenever more is needed. You can use the member function reserve to explicitly increase the capacity of a vector. For example,

```
v.reserve(32);
```

sets the capacity to at least 32 elements, and

```
v.reserve(v.size( ) + 10);
```

sets the capacity to at least 10 more than the number of elements currently in the vector. Note that you can rely on v.reserve to increase the capacity of a vector, but it does not necessarily decrease the capacity of a vector if the argument is smaller than the current capacity.

You can change the size of a vector using the member function resize. For example, the following resizes a vector to 24 elements:

```
v.resize(24);
```

If the previous size were less than 24, then the new elements are initialized as we described for the constructor with an integer argument. If the previous size were greater than 24, then all but the first 24 elements are lost. The capacity is automatically increased if need be. Using resize and reserve, you can shrink the size and capacity of a vector when there is no longer any need for some elements or some capacity.

Size and Capacity

The *size* of a vector is the number of elements in the vector. The *capacity* of a vector is the number of elements for which it currently has memory allocated. For a vector v, the size and capacity can be recovered with the member functions v.size( ) and v.capacity( ).

Self-Test Exercises

9. Is the following program legal? If so, what is the ouput?

```
#include <iostream>
#include <vector>
using namespace std;

int main( )
{
    vector<int> v(10);
    int i;

    for (i = 0; i < v.size( ); i++)
        v[i] = i;
    vector<int> copy;
    copy = v;
    v[0] = 42;

    for (i = 0; i < copy.size( ); i++)
        cout << copy[i] << " ";
    cout << endl;

    return 0;
}
```

10. What is the difference between the size and the capacity of a vector?

Chapter Summary

- A *constructor* is a member function of a class that is called automatically when an object of the class is declared. A constructor must have the same name as the class of which it is a member.

- A *default constructor* is a constructor with no parameters. You should always define a default constructor for your classes.

- A member variable for a class may itself be of a class type. If a class has a class member variable, then the member variable constructor can be invoked in the initialization section of the outer class constructor.

- A *constant call-by-reference parameter* is more efficient than a call-by-value parameter for class type parameters.

- Making very short function definitions inline can improve the efficiency of your code.

- *Static member variables* are variables that are shared by all objects of a class.

- *Vector* classes have objects that behave very much like arrays whose capacity to hold elements will automatically increase if more capacity is needed.

Answers to Self-Test Exercises

1.
```
YourClass anObject(42, 'A'); //LEGAL
YourClass anotherObject; //LEGAL
YourClass yetAnotherObject( ); //PROBLEM
anObject = YourClass(99, 'B'); //LEGAL
anObject = YourClass( ); //LEGAL
anObject = YourClass; //ILLEGAL
```

The statement marked //PROBLEM is not strictly illegal, but it does not mean what you might think it means. If you mean this to be a declaration of an object called yetAnotherObject, then it is wrong. It is a correct declaration for a function called yetAnotherObject that takes zero arguments and that returns a value of type YourClass, but that is not usually the intended meaning. As a practical matter, you can probably consider it illegal. The correct way to declare an object called yetAnotherObject so that it will be initialized with the default constructor is as follows:

```
YourClass yetAnotherObject;
```

2. A default constructor is a constructor that takes no arguments. Not every class has a default constructor. If you define absolutely no constructors for a class, then a default constructor will be automatically provided. On the other hand, if you define one or more constructors but do not define a default constructor, then your class will have no default constructor.

3. The definition is easier to give if you also add a private helping function named
`BankAccount::digitToInt`, as shown, to the class `BankAccount`.

```
//Uses iostream:
void BankAccount::input( )
{
    int dollars;
    char point, digit1, digit2;
    cout <<
        "Enter account balance (include cents even if .00) $";
    cin >> dollars;
    cin >> point >> digit1 >> digit2;
    accountDollars = dollars;
    accountCents = digitToInt(digit1)*10 + digitToInt(digit2);
    if (accountDollars < 0)
        accountCents = -accountCents;
    cout << "Enter interest rate (NO percent sign) : ";
    cin >> rate;
    setRate(rate);
}

int BankAccount::digitToInt(char digit)
{
    return (static_cast<int>(digit) - static_cast<int>('0'));
}
```

4. The member function input changes the value of its calling object, and so the
compiler will issue an error message if you add the const modifier.

5. Similarities: Each parameter call method protects the caller's argument from
change. Differences: If the type is a large structure or class object, a call by value
makes a copy of the caller's argument and thus uses more memory than a call by
constant reference.

6. In `const int x = 17;`, the const keyword promises the compiler that code written by the author will not change the value of x.

In the `int f( ) const;` declaration, the const keyword is a promise to the compiler that code written by the author to implement function f will not change
anything in the calling object.

In `int g(const A& x);`, the const keyword is a promise to the compiler that
code written by the class author will not change the argument plugged in for x.

7. `class DayOfYear`
```
{
public:
    DayOfYear(int monthValue, int dayValue);
    DayOfYear(int monthValue);
    DayOfYear( );
```

```
    void input( );
    void output( );
    int getMonthNumber( ) { return month; }
    int getDay( ) { return day; }
private:
    int month;
    int day;
    void testDate( );
};
```

8. No, it cannot be a static member function because it requires a calling object for the member variable name.

9. The program is legal. The output is

```
0 1 2 3 4 5 6 7 8 9
```

Note that changing v does not change copy. A true independent copy is made with the assignment.

```
copy = v;
```

10. The size is the number of elements in a vector, while the capacity is number of elements for which there is memory allocated. Typically the capacity is larger than the size.

Programming Projects

Visit www.myprogramminglab.com to complete select exercises online and get instant feedback.

1. Define a class called Month that is an abstract data type for a month. Your class will have one member variable of type int to represent a month (1 for January, 2 for February, and so forth). Include all the following member functions: a constructor to set the month using the first three letters in the name of the month as three arguments, a constructor to set the month using an integer as an argument (1 for January, 2 for February, and so forth), a default constructor, an input function that reads the month as an integer, an input function that reads the month as the first three letters in the name of the month, an output function that outputs the month as an integer, an output function that outputs the month as the first three letters in the name of the month, and a member function that returns the next month as a value of type Month. Embed your class definition in a test program.

2. Redefine the implementation of the class Month described in Programming Project 7.1 (or do the definition for the first time, but do the implementation as described here). This time the month is implemented as three member variables of type char that store the first three letters in the name of the month. Embed your definition in a test program.

VideoNote

Solution to
Programming
Project 7.4

3. My mother always took a little red counter to the grocery store. The counter was used to keep tally of the amount of money she would have spent so far on that visit to the store if she bought everything in the basket. The counter had a four-digit display, increment buttons for each digit, and a reset button. An overflow indicator came up red if more money was entered than the $99.99 it would register. (This was a *long* time ago.)

Write and implement the member functions of a class Counter that simulates and slightly generalizes the behavior of this grocery store counter. The constructor should create a Counter object that can count up to the constructor's argument. That is, Counter(9999) should provide a counter that can count up to 9999. A newly constructed counter displays a reading of 0. The member function void reset( ) sets the counter's number to 0. The member function void incr1( ) increments the units digits by 1, void incr10( ) increments the tens digit by 1, and void incr100( ) increments the next two digits, respectively. Accounting for any carrying when you increment should require no further action than adding an appropriate number to the private data member. A member function bool overflow( ) detects overflow. (Overflow is the result of incrementing the counter's private data member beyond the maximum entered at counter construction.)

Use this class to provide a simulation of my mother's little red clicker. Even though the display is an integer, in the simulation, the rightmost (lower order) two digits are always thought of as cents and tens of cents, the next digit is dollars, and the fourth digit is tens of dollars.

Provide keys for cents, dimes, dollars, and tens of dollars. Unfortunately, no choice of keys seems particularly mnemonic. One choice is to use the keys asdfo: a for cents, followed by a digit 1 to 9; s for dimes, followed by a digit 1 to 9; d for dollars, followed by a digit 1 to 9; and f for tens of dollars, again followed by a digit 1 to 9. Each entry (one of asdf followed by 1 to 9) is followed by pressing the Return key. Any overflow is reported after each operation. Overflow can be requested by pressing the o key.

4. You operate several hot dog stands distributed throughout town. Define a class named HotDogStand that has a member variable for the hot dog stand's ID number and a member variable for how many hot dogs the stand sold that day. Create a constructor that allows a user of the class to initialize both values.

Also create a function named JustSold that increments the number of hot dogs the stand has sold by one. This function will be invoked each time the stand sells a hot dog so that you can track the total number of hot dogs sold by the stand. Add another function that returns the number of hot dogs sold.

Finally, add a static variable that tracks the total number of hot dogs sold by all hot dog stands and a static function that returns the value in this variable. Write a main function to test your class with at least three hot dog stands that each sell a variety of hot dogs.

5. In an ancient land, the beautiful princess Eve had many suitors. She decided on the following procedure to determine which suitor she would marry. First, all of the suitors would be lined up one after the other and assigned numbers. The first

suitor would be number 1, the second number 2, and so on up to the last suitor, number *n*. Starting at the first suitor she would then count three suitors down the line (because of the three letters in her name) and the third suitor would be eliminated from winning her hand and removed from the line. Eve would then continue, counting three more suitors, and eliminating every third suitor. When she reached the end of the line she would continue counting from the beginning.

For example, if there were six suitors then the elimination process would proceed as follows:

123456	initial list of suitors, start counting from 1
12456	suitor 3 eliminated, continue counting from 4
1245	suitor 6 eliminated, continue counting from 1
125	suitor 4 eliminated, continue counting from 5
15	suitor 2 eliminated, continue counting from 5
1	suitor 5 eliminated, 1 is the lucky winner

Write a program that uses a vector to determine which position you should stand in to marry the princess if there are *n* suitors. You will find the following function from the Vector class useful:

```
v.erase(iter);
// Removes element at position iter
```

For example, to use this function to erase the fourth element from the beginning of a vector variable named theVector, use

```
theVector.erase(theVector.begin( ) + 3);
```

The number 3 is used because the first element in the vector is at index position 0.

6. This Programming Project requires you to first complete Programming Project 6.7 from Chapter 6, which is an implementation of a Pizza class. Add an Order class that contains a private vector of type Pizza. This class represents a customer's entire order, where the order may consist of multiple pizzas. Include appropriate functions so that a user of the Order class can add pizzas to the order (type is deep dish, hand tossed, or pan; size is small, medium, or large; number of pepperoni or cheese toppings). You can use constants to represent the type and size. Also write a function that outputs everything in the order along with the total price. Write a suitable test program that adds multiple pizzas to an order(s).

7. Do Programming Project 6.8, the definition of a Money class, except create a default constructor that sets the monetary amount to 0 dollars and 0 cents, and create a second constructor with input parameters for the amount of the dollars and cents variables. Modify your test code to invoke the constructors.

VideoNote
Solution to
Programming
Project 7.7

8. Write a program that outputs a histogram of grades for an assignment given to a class of students. The program should input each student's grade as an integer and store the grade in a vector. Grades should be entered until the user enters −1 for a grade. The program should then scan through the vector and compute the histogram. In computing the histogram, the minimum value of a grade is 0, but your program should determine the maximum value entered by the user. Output the histogram to the console. See Programming Project 5.7 for information on how to compute a histogram.

9. Prior to 2009 the bar code on an envelope used by the U.S. Postal Service represented a five (or more) digit zip code using a format called POSTNET. The bar code consists of long and short bars as shown here:

For this program, we will represent the bar code as a string of digits. The digit 1 represents a long bar, and the digit 0 represents a short bar. Therefore, the bar code shown would be represented in our program as follows:

11010010100101011010000010011

The first and last digits of the bar code are always 1. Removing these leave 25 digits. If these 25 digits are split into groups of five digits each then we have the following:

10100 10100 01010 11000 01001

Next, consider each group of five digits. There always will be exactly two 1's in each group of digits. Each digit stands for a number. From left to right, the digits encode the values 7, 4, 2, 1, and 0. Multiply the corresponding value with the digit and compute the sum to get the final encoded digit for the zip code. The following table shows the encoding for 10100.

Bar Code Digits	1	0	1	0	0
Value	7	4	2	1	0
Product of Digit * Value	7	0	2	0	0

Zip Code Digit = 7 + 0 + 2 + 0 + 0 = **9**

Repeat this for each group of five digits and concatenate to get the complete zip code. There is one special value. If the sum of a group of five digits is 11, then this represents the digit 0 (this is necessary because with two digits per group it is not possible to represent zero). The zip code for the sample bar code decodes to 99504. While the POSTNET scheme may seem unnecessarily complex, its design allows machines to detect if errors have been made in scanning the zip code.

Write a `zip code` class that encodes and decodes five-digit bar codes used by the U.S. Postal Service on envelopes. The class should have two constructors. The first constructor should input the zip code as an integer, and the second constructor should input the zip code as a bar code string consisting of 0's and 1's as described above. Although you have two ways to input the zip code, internally, the class should only store the zip code using one format. (You may choose to store it as a bar code string or as a zip code number.) The class also should have at least two `public` member functions: one to return the zip code as an integer and the other to return the zip code in bar code format as a string. All helper functions should be declared `private`. Embed your class definition in a suitable test program.

10. First, complete Programming Project 6.12. Modify the main function with a loop so that the user determines how many `BoxOfProduce` objects are created. Each box should contain three bundles of fruits or vegetables selected randomly from this list: tomatillo, broccoli, tomato, kiwi, and kale. Add a menu so the user can decide when to stop creating boxes. The menu should allow the user to make substitutions for the randomly selected items in a box.

You would like to throw in a free recipe flyer for salsa verde if the box contains tomatillos. However, there are only 5 recipe flyers. Add a static member variable to the `BoxOfProduce` class that counts the number of recipe flyers remaining and initialize it to 5. Also add a member variable that indicates whether or not the box contains a recipe flyer and modify the `output` function to also print "salsa verde recipe" if the box contains a recipe flyer. Finally, add logic inside the class so that if the box contains at least one order of tomatillos then it automatically gets a recipe flyer until all of the recipe flyers are gone. Note that a box should only get one recipe flyer even if there are multiple orders of tomatillos.

Test your class by creating boxes with tomatillos from your menu until all of the flyers are gone.

Operator Overloading, Friends, and References

8 Operator Overloading, Friends, and References

Eternal truths will be neither true nor eternal unless they have fresh meaning for every new social situation.

FRANKLIN D. ROOSEVELT, *Address at the University of Pennsylvania* [September 20, 1940]

Introduction

This chapter discusses a number of tools to use when defining classes. The first tool is operator overloading, which allows you to overload operators, such as + and ==, so that they apply to objects of the classes you define. The second tool is the use of friend functions which are functions that are not members of a class but still have access to the private members of the class. This chapter also discusses how to provide automatic type conversion from other data types to the classes you define.

If you have not yet covered arrays (Chapter 5) you should skip the subsection of 8.3 entitled "Overloading the Array Operator [ ]". It covers a topic that may not make sense unless you know about array basics.

8.1 Basic Operator Overloading

He's a smooth operator.

Line from a song by Sade (written by Sade Adu and Ray St. John)

Operators such as +, -, %, ==, and so forth are nothing but functions that are used with a slightly different syntax. We write x + 7 rather than +(x, 7), but the + operator is a function that takes two arguments (often called **operands** rather than arguments) and returns a single value. As such, operators are not really necessary. We could make do with +(x, 7) or even add(x, 7). Operands are an example of what is often called **syntactic sugar**, meaning a slightly different syntax that people like. However, people are very comfortable with the usual operator syntax, x + 7, that C++ uses for types such as int and double. And one way to view a high-level language, such as C++, is as a way to make people comfortable with programming computers. Thus, this syntactic sugar is probably a good idea; at the least, it is a well-entrenched idea. In C++ you can overload the operators, such as + and ==, so that they work with operands in the classes you define. The way to overload an operator is very similar to the way you overload a function name. The details are best explained through an example.

operators and functions

operand

syntactic sugar

Overloading Basics

how to overload an operator

Display 8.1 contains the definition of a class whose values are amounts of U.S. money, such as $9.99 or $1567.29. The class has a lot in common with the BankAccount class we defined in Display 7.2. It represents amounts of money in the same way, as two ints for the dollars and cents parts. It has the same private helping functions. Its constructors and accessor and mutator functions are similar to those of the class BankAccount. What is truly new about this Money class is that we have overloaded the plus sign and the minus sign so they can be used to add or subtract two objects of the class Money, and we have overloaded the == sign so it can be used to compare two objects of the class Money to see if they represent the same amount of money. Let us look at these overloaded operators.

You can overload the operator + (and many other operators) so that it will accept arguments of a class type. The difference between overloading the + operator and defining an ordinary function involves only a slight change in syntax: You use the symbol + as the function name and precede the + with the keyword operator. The operator declaration (function declaration) for the plus sign is as follows:

```
const Money operator +(const Money& amount1, const Money& amount2);
```

The operands (arguments) are both constant reference parameters of type Money. The operands can be of any type, as long as at least one is a class type. In the general case, operands may be call-by-value or call-by-reference parameters and may have the const modifier or not. However, for efficiency reasons, constant call by reference is usually used in place of call by value for classes. In this case the value returned is of type Money, but in the general case the value returned can be of any type, including void. The const before the returned type Money will be explained later in this chapter. For now, you can safely ignore that const.

Note that the overloaded binary operators + and - are not member operators (member functions) of the class Money and therefore do not have access to the private members of the class Money. That is why the definition for the overloaded operators uses accessor and mutator functions. Later in this chapter we will see other ways of overloading an operand, including overloading it as a member operator. Each of the different ways of overloading an operator has its advantages and disadvantages.

The definitions of the overloaded binary operators + and - are perhaps a bit more complicated than you might expect. The extra details are there to cope with the fact that amounts of money can be negative.

The unary minus sign operator - is discussed in the subsection "Overloading Unary Operators," later in this chapter.

The operator == is also overloaded so that it can be used to compare two objects of the class Money. Note that the type returned is bool so that == can be used to make comparisons in the usual ways, such as in an if-else statement.

If you look at the main function in the demonstration program in Display 8.1, you will see that the overloaded binary operators +, -, and = are used with objects of the class Money in the same way that +, -, and == are used with the predefined types, such as int and double.

Display 8.1   Operator Overloading (part 1 of 5)

```
1    #include <iostream>
2    #include <cstdlib>
3    #include <cmath>
4    using namespace std;

5    //Class for amounts of money in U.S. currency
6    class Money
7    {
8    public:
9        Money( );
10       Money(double amount);
11       Money(int theDollars, int theCents);
12       Money(int theDollars);
13       double getAmount( ) const;
14       int getDollars( ) const;
15       int getCents( ) const;
16       void input( );    //Reads the dollar sign as well as the amount number.
17       void output( ) const;
18   private:
19       int dollars;    //A negative amount is represented as negative
                         //dollars and
20       int cents;      //negative cents. Negative $4.50 is represented
                         //as -4 and -50.
21       int dollarsPart(double amount) const;
22       int centsPart(double amount) const;
23       int round(double number) const;
24   };

25   const Money operator +(const Money& amount1, const Money& amount2);
26   const Money operator -(const Money& amount1, const Money& amount2);
27   bool operator ==(const Money& amount1, const Money& amount2);
28   const Money operator -(const Money& amount);

29   int main( )
30   {
31       Money yourAmount, myAmount(10, 9);
32       cout << "Enter an amount of money: ";
33       yourAmount.input( );
34       cout << "Your amount is ";
35       yourAmount.output( );
36       cout << endl;
37       cout << "My amount is ";
38       myAmount.output( );
39       cout << endl;
```

This is a unary operator and is discussed in the subsection "Overloading Unary Operators."

For an explanation of a const on a returned type see the subsection "Returning by const Value."

Display 8.1 Operator Overloading (part 2 of 5)

```
40      if (yourAmount == myAmount)
41          cout << "We have the same amounts.\n";
42      else
43          cout << "One of us is richer.\n";

44      Money ourAmount = yourAmount + myAmount;
45      yourAmount.output( ); cout << " + "; myAmount.output( );
46      cout << " equals "; ourAmount.output(); cout << endl;

47      Money diffAmount = yourAmount - myAmount;
48      yourAmount.output( ); cout << " - "; myAmount.output( );
49      cout << " equals "; diffAmount.output(); cout << endl;

50      return 0;
51  }

52  const Money operator +(const Money& amount1,  const Money& amount2)
53  {
54      int allCents1 = amount1.getCents( ) + amount1.getDollars( )*100;
55      int allCents2 = amount2.getCents( ) + amount2.getDollars( )*100;
56      int sumAllCents = allCents1 + allCents2;
57      int absAllCents = abs(sumAllCents); //Money can be negative.
58      int finalDollars = absAllCents / 100;
59      int finalCents = absAllCents % 100;

60      if (sumAllCents < 0)
61      {
62          finalDollars = -finalDollars;
63          finalCents = -finalCents;
64      }

65      return Money(finalDollars, finalCents);
66  }

67  //Uses cstdlib:
68  const Money operator -(const Money& amount1,  const Money& amount2)
69  {
70      int allCents1 = amount1.getCents( ) + amount1.getDollars( )*100;
71      int allCents2 = amount2.getCents( ) + amount2.getDollars( )*100;
72      int diffAllCents = allCents1 - allCents2;
73      int absAllCents = abs(diffAllCents);
74      int finalDollars = absAllCents / 100;
75      int finalCents = absAllCents % 100;

76      if (diffAllCents < 0)
77      {
78          finalDollars = -finalDollars;
```

Note that we need to use accessor and mutator functions.

If the return statements puzzle you, see the tip entitled "A Constructor Can Return an Object."

(continued)

Display 8.1 Operator Overloading (part 3 of 5)

```
79          finalCents = -finalCents;
80      }
81      return Money(finalDollars, finalCents);
82  }

83  bool operator ==(const Money& amount1, const Money& amount2)
84  {
85      return ((amount1.getDollars( ) == amount2.getDollars( ))
86          && (amount1.getCents( ) == amount2.getCents( )));
87  }

88  const Money operator -(const Money& amount)
89  {
90      return Money(-amount.getDollars( ), -amount.getCents( ));
91  }

92  Money::Money( ) : dollars(0), cents(0)
93  {/*Body intentionally empty.*/}

94  Money::Money(double amount)
95              : dollars(dollarsPart(amount)), cents(centsPart(amount))
96  {/*Body intentionally empty*/}

97  Money::Money(int theDollars)
98              : dollars(theDollars), cents(0)
99  {/*Body intentionally empty*/}

100 //Uses cstdlib:
101 Money::Money(int theDollars, int theCents)
102 {
103     if ((theDollars < 0 && theCents > 0) ||
104         (theDollars > 0 && theCents < 0))
105     {
106         cout << "Inconsistent money data.\n";
107         exit(1);
108     }
109     dollars = theDollars;
110     cents = theCents;
111 }

112 double Money::getAmount( ) const
113 {
114     return (dollars + cents*0.01);
115 }
```

If you prefer, you could make these short constructor definitions inline function definitions as discussed in Chapter 7.

Display 8.1   Operator Overloading (part 4 of 5)

```
116   int Money::getDollars( ) const
117   {
118       return dollars;
119   }

120   int Money::getCents( ) const
121   {
122       return cents;
123   }

124   //Uses iostream and cstdlib:
125   void Money::output( ) const
126   {
127       int absDollars = abs(dollars);
128       int absCents = abs(cents);
129       if (dollars < 0 || cents < 0)
                          //accounts for dollars == 0 or cents == 0
130           cout << "$-";
131       else
132           cout << '$';
133       cout << absDollars;
134
135       if (absCents >= 10)
136           cout << '.' << absCents;
137       else
138           cout << '.' << '0' << absCents;
139   }

140   //Uses iostream and cstdlib:
141   void Money::input( )
142   {
143       char dollarSign;
144       cin >> dollarSign; //hopefully
145       if (dollarSign != '$')
146       {
147           cout << "No dollar sign in Money input.\n";
148           exit(1);
149       }

150       double amountAsDouble;
151       cin >> amountAsDouble;
152       dollars = dollarsPart(amountAsDouble);
153       cents = centsPart(amountAsDouble);
154   }

155   int Money::dollarsPart(double amount) const
156   <The rest of the definition is the same as BankAccount::dollarsPart in Display 7.2.>
```

For a better definition of the input function, see Self-Test Exercise 3 in Chapter 7.

(continued)

Display 8.1   Operator Overloading (part 5 of 5)

```
157    int Money::centsPart(double amount) const
158        <The rest of the definition is the same as BankAccount::centsPart in Display 7.2.>

159    int Money::round(double number) const
160        <The rest of the definition is the same as BankAccount::round in Display 7.2.>
```

Sample Dialogue

```
Enter an amount of money: $123.45
Your amount is $123.45
My amount is $10.09.
One of us is richer.
$123.45 + $10.09 equals $133.54
$123.45 - $10.09 equals $113.36
```

You can overload most but not all operators. One major restriction on overloading an operator is that at least one operand must be of a class type. So, for example, you can overload the % operator to apply to two objects of type Money or to an object of type Money and a double, but you cannot overload % to combine two doubles.

Operator Overloading

A (binary) operator, such as +, -, /, %, and so forth, is simply a function that is called using a different syntax for listing its arguments. With a binary operator, the arguments are listed before and after the operator; with a function the arguments are listed in parentheses after the function name. An operator definition is written similar to a function definition, except that the operator definition includes the reserved word operator before the operator name. The predefined operators, such as +, -, and so forth, can be overloaded by giving them a new definition for a class type. An example of overloading the +, -, and == operators is given in Display 8.1.

TIP: A Constructor Can Return an Object

We often think of a constructor as if it were a void function. However, constructors are special functions with special properties, and sometimes it makes more sense to think of them as returning a value. Notice the return statement in the definition of the overloaded + operator in Display 8.1, which we repeat here:

```
return Money(finalDollars, finalCents);
```

TIP: (continued)

The expression that is returned is an invocation of the constructor for Money. Although we sometimes think of a constructor as a void function, a constructor constructs an object and can also be thought of as returning an object of the class. If you feel uncomfortable with this use of the constructor, it may help to know that this return statement is equivalent to the following, more cumbersome and less efficient, code:

```
Money temp;
temp = Money(finalDollars, finalCents);
return temp;
```

anonymous object

An expression, such as Money(finalDollars, finalCents), is sometimes called an **anonymous object**, since it is not named by any variable. However, it is still a full-fledged object. You can even use it as a calling object, as in the following:

```
Money(finalDollars, finalCents).getDollars()
```

The previous expression returns the int value of finalDollars. ■

Self-Test Exercises

1. What is the difference between a (binary) operator and a function?

2. Suppose you wish to overload the operator < so that it applies to the type Money defined in Display 8.1. What do you need to add to the definition of Money given in Display 8.1?

3. Is it possible using operator overloading to change the behavior of + on integers? Why or why not?

Returning by const Value

Notice the returned types in the declarations for overloaded operators for the class Money in Display 8.1. For example, the following is the declaration for the overloaded plus operator as it appears in Display 8.1:

```
const Money operator +(const Money& amount1,
                       const Money& amount2);
```

This subsection explains the const at the start of the line. But before we discuss that first const, let us make sure we understand all the other details about returning a value. So, let us first consider the case where that const does not appear in either the declaration or definition of the overloaded plus operator. Let us suppose that the declaration reads as follows:

```
Money operator +(const Money& amount1, const Money& amount2);
```

and let us see what we can do with the value returned.

When an object is returned, for example, (m1 + m2), where m1 and m2 are of type Money, the object can be used to invoke a member function, which may or may not change the value of the member variables in the object (m1 + m2). For example,

```
(m1 + m2).output( );
```

is perfectly legal. In this case, it does not change the object (m1 + m2). However, if we omitted the const before the type returned for the plus operator, then the following would be legal and would change the values of the member variables of the object (m1 + m2):

```
(m1 + m2).input( );
```

So, objects can be changed, even when they are not associated with any variable. One way to make sense of this is to note that objects have member variables and thus have some kinds of variables that can be changed.

Now let us assume that everything is as shown in Display 8.1; that is, there is a const before the returned type of each operator that returns an object of type Money. For example, following is the declaration for the overloaded plus operator as it appears in Display 8.1:

```
const Money operator +(const Money& amount1, const Money& amount2);
```

The first const on the line is a new use of the const modifier. This is called **returning a value as const** or **returning by const value** or **returning by constant value**. What the const modifier means in this case is that the returned object cannot be changed. For example, consider the following code:

```
Money m1(10.99), m2(23.57);

(m1 + m2).output();
```

The invocation of output is perfectly legal because it does not change the object (m1 + m2). However, with that const before the returned type, the following will produce a compiler error message:

```
(m1 + m2).input( );
```

Why would you want to return by const value? It provides a kind of automatic error checking. When you construct (m1 + m2), you normally do not want to inadvertently change it. In this case changing the object (m1 + m2) probably does not matter, but if the returned object is a reference to an existing object then this can cause problems. References are covered in Section 8.3.

At first this protection from changing an object may seem like too much protection, since you can have

```
Money m3;
m3 = (m1 + m2);
```

and you very well may want to change m3. No problem—the following is perfectly legal:

```
m3 = (m1 + m2);
m3.input( );
```

return by constant value

The values of m3 and (m1 + m2) are two different objects. The assignment operator does not make m3 the same as the object (m1 + m2). Instead, it copies the values of the member variables of (m1 + m2) into the member variables of m3. *With objects of a class, the default assignment operator does not make the two objects the same object; it only copies values of member variables from one object to another object.*

This distinction is subtle but important. It may help you understand the details if you recall that a variable of a class type and an object of a class type are not the same thing. An object is a value of a class type and may be stored in a variable of a class type, but the variable and the object are not the same thing. In the code

```
m3 = (m1 + m2);
```

the variable m3 and its value (m1 + m2) are different things, just as n and 5 are different things in

```
int n = 5;
```

or in

```
int n = (2 + 3);
```

It may take you a while to become comfortable with this notion of return by const value. In the meantime, a good rule of thumb is to always return class types by const value unless you have an explicit reason not to do so. For most simple programs this will have no effect on your program other than to flag some subtle errors.

Note that although it is legal, it is pointless to return basic types, such as int, by const value. The const has no effect in the case of the basic types. When a function or operator returns a value of one of the basic types, such as int, double, or char, it returns the value, such as 5, 5.5, or 'A'. It does not return a variable or anything like a variable. Unlike a variable, the value cannot be changed—you cannot change 5. Values of a basic type cannot be changed whether there is a const before the returned type or not. On the other hand, values of a class type—that is, objects—can be changed, since they have member variables, and so the const modifier has an effect on the object returned.

Self-Test Exercise

4. Suppose you omit the const at the beginning of the declaration and definition of the overloaded plus operator for the class Money, so that the value is not returned by const value. Is the following legal?

```
Money m1(10.99), m2(23.57), m3(12.34);
(m1 + m2) = m3;
```

Is it legal if the definition of the class Money is as shown in Display 8.1, so that the plus operator returns its value by const value?

Overloading Unary Operators

In addition to the binary operators, such as + in x + y, C++ has unary operators, such as the operator - when it is used to mean negation. A **unary operator** is an operator that takes only one operand (one argument). In the following statement, the unary operator - is used to set the value of a variable x equal to the negative of the value of the variable y:

```
x = -y;
```

unary operator

The increment and decrement operators, ++ and --, are other examples of unary operators.

You can overload unary operators as well as binary operators. For example, we have overloaded the minus operator - for the type Money (Display 8.1) so that it has both a unary and a binary operator version of the subtraction/negation operator -. For example, suppose your program contains this class definition and the following code:

```
Money amount1(10), amount2(<), amount3;
```

Then the following sets the value of amount3 to amount1 minus amount2:

```
amount3 = amount1 - amount2;
```

The following will, then, output $4.00 to the screen:

```
amount3.output( );
```

On the other hand, the following will set amount3 equal to the negative of amount1:

```
amount3 = -amount1;
amount3.output( );
```

++ and --

You can overload the ++ and -- operators in ways similar to how we overloaded the negation operator in Display 8.1. If you overload the ++ and -- operators following the example of the minus sign - in Display 8.1, then the overloading definition will apply to the operator when it is used in prefix position, as in ++x and --x. Later in this chapter we will discuss overloading ++ and -- more fully and will then explain how to overload these operators for use in the postfix position.

Overloading as Member Functions

In Display 8.1 we overloaded operators as standalone functions defined outside the class. It is also possible to overload an operator as a member operator (member function). This is illustrated in Display 8.2.

Note that when a binary operator is overloaded as a member operator, there is only one parameter, not two. The calling object serves as the first parameter. For example, consider the following code:

```
Money cost(1, 50), tax(0, 15), total;
total = cost + tax;
```

When + is overloaded as a member operator, then in the expression cost + tax the variable cost is the calling object and tax is the single argument to +.

The definition of the member operator + is given in Display 8.2. Notice the following line from that definition:

```
int allCents1 = cents + dollars * 100;
```

The expressions `cents` and `dollars` are member variables of the calling object, which in this case is the first operand. If this definition is applied to

```
cost + tax
```

then `cents` means `cost.cents` and `dollars` means `cost.dollars`.

Note that since the first operand is the calling object, you should, in most cases, add the `const` modifier to the end of the operator declaration and to the end of the operator definition. Whenever the operator invocation does not change the calling object (which is the first operand), good style dictates that you add the `const` to the end of the operator declaration and to the end of the operator definition, as illustrated in Display 8.2.

Overloading an operator as a member variable can seem strange at first, but it is easy to get used to the new details. Many experts advocate always overloading operators as member operators rather than as nonmembers (as in Display 8.1): It is more in the spirit of object-oriented programming and is a bit more efficient, since the definition can directly reference member variables and need not use accessor and mutator functions. However, as we will discover in Section 8.2, overloading an operator as a member also has a significant disadvantage.

Display 8.2   Overloading Operators as Members (part 1 of 2)

This is Display 8.1 redone with the overloaded operators as member functions.

```
1  #include <iostream>
2  #include <cstdlib>
3  #include <cmath>
4  using namespace std;

5  //Class for amounts of money in U.S. currency
6  class Money
7  {
8  public:
9      Money( );
10     Money(double amount);
11     Money(int dollars, int cents);
12     Money(int dollars);
13     double getAmount( ) const;
14     int getDollars( ) const;
15     int getCents( ) const;
16     void input( ); //Reads the dollar sign as well as the amount number.
17     void output( ) const;
18     const Money operator +(const Money& amount2) const;
19     const Money operator -(const Money& amount2) const;       The calling object is
20     bool operator ==(const Money& amount2) const;             the first operand.
21     const Money operator -( ) const;
```

(continued)

Display 8.2   Overloading Operators as Members (part 2 of 2)

```
22    private:
23        int dollars;  //A negative amount is represented as negative
                         //dollars and
24        int cents;     //negative cents. Negative $4.50 is represented as
                         //-4 and -50.
25        int dollarsPart(double amount) const;
26        int centsPart(double amount) const;
27        int round(double number) const;
28    };
29    int main( )
30    {
31        <If the main function is the same as in Display 8.1, then the screen dialogue
          will be the same as shown in Display 8.1.>
32    }
33
34    const Money Money::operator +(const Money& secondOperand) const
35    {
36        int allCents1 = cents + dollars * 100;
37        int allCents2 = secondOperand.cents + secondOperand.dollars * 100;
38        int sumAllCents = allCents1 + allCents2;
39        int absAllCents = abs(sumAllCents); //Money can be negative.
40        int finalDollars = absAllCents / 100;
41        int finalCents = absAllCents % 100;
42        if (sumAllCents < 0)
43        {
44            finalDollars = -finalDollars;
45            finalCents = -finalCents;
46        }
47        return Money(finalDollars, finalCents);
48    }
49    const Money Money::operator -(const Money& secondOperand) const
50        <The rest of this definition is Self-Test Exercise 5.>
51    bool Money::operator ==(const Money& secondOperand) const
52    {
53        return ((dollars == secondOperand.dollars)
54                && (cents == secondOperand.cents));
55    }
56    const Money Money::operator -( ) const
57    {
58        return Money(-dollars, -cents);
59    }
60        <Definitions of all other member functions are the same as in Display 8.1.>
```

TIP: A Class Has Access to All Its Objects

When defining a member function or operator, you may access any private member variable (or function) of the calling object. However, you are allowed even more than that. You may access any private member variable (or private member function) of any object of the class being defined.

For example, consider the following few lines that begin the definition of the plus operator for the class Money in Display 8.2:

```
const Money Money::operator +(const Money& secondOperand) const
{
    int allCents1 = cents + dollars*100;
    int allCents2 = secondOperand.cents + secondOperand.dollars
                                         * 100
```

In this case, the plus operator is being defined as a member operator, so the variables cents and dollars, in the first line of the function body, are the member variables of the calling object (which happens to be the first operand). However, it is also legal to access by name the member variables of the object secondOperand, as in the following line:

```
int allCents2 = secondOperand.cents + secondOperand.dollars * 100;
```

This is legal because secondOperand is an object of the class Money and this line is in the definition of a member operator for the class Money. Many novice programmers mistakenly think they only have direct access to the private members of the calling object and do not realize that they have direct access to all objects of the class being defined. ■

Self-Test Exercise

5. Complete the definition of the member binary operator in Display 8.2.

Overloading Function Application ( )

The function call operator ( ) must be overloaded as a member function. It allows you to use an object of the class as if it were a function. If class AClass has overloaded the function application operator to have one argument of type int and anObject is an object of AClass, then anObject(42) invokes the overloaded function call operator ( ) with calling object anObject and argument 42. The type returned may be void or any other type.

The function call operator ( ) is unusual in that it allows any number of arguments. So, you can define several overloaded versions of the function call operator ( ).

PITFALL: Overloading &&, ||, and the Comma Operator

The predefined versions of && and || that work for the type bool use short-circuit evaluation. However, when overloaded these operators perform complete evaluation. This is so contrary to what most programmers expect that it inevitably causes problems. It is best to just not overload these two operators.

The comma operator also presents problems. In its normal use the comma operator guarantees left-to-right evaluations. When overloaded no such guarantee is given. The comma operator is another operator it is safest to avoid overloading. ■

8.2   Friend Functions and Automatic Type Conversion

Trust your friends.

Common advice

Friend functions are nonmember functions that have all the privileges of member functions. Before we discuss friend functions in any detail, we discuss automatic type conversion via constructors, since that helps to explain one of the advantages of overloading operators (or any functions) as friend functions.

Constructors for Automatic Type Conversion

If your class definition contains the appropriate constructors, the system will perform certain type conversions automatically. For example, if your program contains the definition of the class Money either as given in Display 8.1 or as given in Display 8.2, you could use the following in your program:

```
Money baseAmount(100, 60), fullAmount;
fullAmount = baseAmount + 25;
fullAmount.output( );
```

The output would be

```
$125.60
```

The previous code may look simple and natural enough, but there is one subtle point. The 25 (in the expression baseAmount + 25) is not of the appropriate type. In Display 8.1 we only overloaded the operator + so that it could be used with two values of type Money. We did not overload + so that it could be used with a value of type Money and an integer. The constant 25 can be considered to be of type int, but 25 cannot be used as a value of type Money unless the class definition somehow tells the system how to convert an integer to a value of type Money. The only way that the system knows that 25 means $25.00 is that we included a constructor that takes a single argument of type int. When the system sees the expression

```
baseAmount + 25
```

it first checks to see if the operator + has been overloaded for the combination of a value of type Money and an integer. Since there is no such overloading, the system next looks to see if there is a constructor that takes a single argument that is an integer. If it finds a constructor that takes a single integer argument, it uses that constructor to convert the integer 25 to a value of type Money. The one-argument constructor says that 25 should be converted to an object of type Money whose member variable dollars is equal to 25 and whose member variable cents is equal to 0. In other words, the constructor converts 25 to an object of type Money that represents $25.00. (The definition of the constructor is in Display 8.1.)

Note that this type conversion will not work unless there is a suitable constructor. If the class Money did not contain a constructor with one parameter of type int (or of some other number type, such as long or double), then the expression

```
baseAmount + 25
```

would produce an error message.

These automatic type conversions (produced by constructors) seem most common and compelling with overloaded numeric operators such as + and -. However, these automatic conversions apply in exactly the same way to arguments of ordinary functions, arguments of member functions, and arguments of other overloaded operators.

PITFALL: Member Operators and Automatic Type Conversion

When you overload a binary operator as a member operator, the two arguments are no longer symmetric. One is a calling object, and only the second "argument" is a true argument. This is not only unaesthetic but also has a very practical shortcoming. Any automatic type conversion will only apply to the second argument. So, for example, as we noted in the previous subsection, the following would be legal:

```
Money baseAmount(100, 60), fullAmount;
fullAmount = baseAmount + 25;
```

This is because Money has a constructor with one argument of type int, and so the value 25 will be considered an int value that is automatically converted to a value of type Money.

However, if you overload + as a member operator (as in Display 8.2), then you cannot reverse the two arguments to +. The following is illegal,

```
fullAmount = 25 + baseAmount;
```

because 25 cannot be a calling object. Conversion of int values to type Money works for arguments but not for calling objects.

(continued)

PITFALL: (continued)

On the other hand, if you overload + as a nonmember (as in Display 8.1), then the following is perfectly legal:

```
fullAmount = 25 + baseAmount;
```

This is the biggest advantage of overloading an operator as a nonmember. Overloading an operator as a nonmember gives you automatic type conversion of all arguments. Overloading an operator as a member gives you the efficiency of bypassing accessor and mutator functions and directly accessing member variables. There is a way to overload an operator (and certain functions) that offers both of these advantages. It is called *overloading as a friend function* and is our next topic. ■

Friend Functions

If your class has a full set of accessor and mutator functions, you can use the accessor and mutator functions to define nonmember overloaded operators (as in Display 8.1 as opposed to Display 8.2). However, although this may give you access to the private member variables, it may not give you efficient access to them. Look again at the definition of the overloaded addition operator + given in Display 8.1. Rather than just reading four member variables, it must incur the overhead of two invocations of getCents and two invocations of getDollars. This adds a bit of inefficiency and also can make the code harder to understand. The alternative of overloading + as a member gets around this problem at the price of losing automatic type conversion of the first operand. Overloading the + operator as a friend will allow us to both directly access member variables and have automatic type conversion for all operands.

A **friend function** of a class is not a member function of the class, but it has access to the private members of that class (to both private member variables and private member functions) just as a member function does. To make a function a friend function, you must name it as a friend in the class definition. For example, in Display 8.3 we have rewritten the definition of the class Money yet another time. This time we have overloaded the operators as friends. You make an operator or function a friend of a class by listing the operator or function declaration in the definition of the class and placing the keyword friend in front of the operator or function declaration.

A friend operator or friend function has its declaration listed in the class definition, just as you would list the declaration of a member function, except that you precede the declaration by the keyword friend. However, a friend is *not* a member function; rather, it really is an ordinary function with extraordinary access to the data members of the class. The friend is defined exactly like the ordinary function it is. In particular, the operator definitions shown in Display 8.3 do not include the qualifier Money:: in the function heading. Also, you do not use the keyword friend in the function definition (only in the function declaration). The friend operators in Display 8.3 are invoked just like the nonfriend, nonmember operators in Display 8.1, and they have automatic type conversion of all arguments just like the nonfriend, nonmember operators in Display 8.1.

The most common kinds of friend functions are overloaded operators. However, any kind of function can be made a friend function.

A function (or overloaded operator) can be a friend of more than one class. To make it a friend of multiple classes, just give the declaration of the friend function in each class for which you want it to be a friend.

Many experts consider friend functions (and operators) to be in some sense not "pure." They feel that in the true spirit of object-oriented programming all operators and functions should be member functions. On the other hand, overloading operators as friends provides the pragmatic advantage of automatic type conversion in all arguments, and since the operator declaration is inside the class definitions, it provides at least a bit more encapsulation than nonmember, nonfriend operators. We have shown you three ways to overload operators: as nonmember nonfriends, as members, and as friends. You can decide for yourself which technique you prefer.

Display 8.3   Overloading Operators as Friends (part 1 of 2)

```
1   #include <iostream>
2   #include <cstdlib>
3   #include <cmath>
4   using namespace std;

5   //Class for amounts of money in U.S. currency
6   class Money
7   {
8   public:
9       Money( );
10      Money(double amount);
11      Money(int dollars, int cents);
12      Money(int dollars);
13      double getAmount( ) const;
14      int getDollars( ) const;
15      int getCents( ) const;
16      void input( ); //Reads the dollar sign as well as the amount number.
17      void output( ) const;
18      friend const Money operator +(const Money& amount1,
                                      const Money& amount2);
19      friend const Money operator -(const Money& amount1,
                                      const Money& amount2);
20      friend bool operator ==(const Money& amount1, const Money& amount2);
21      friend const Money operator -(const Money& amount);
22  private:
23      int dollars; //A negative amount is represented as negative
                     //dollars and
24      int cents; //negative cents. Negative $4.50 is represented
                   //as -4 and -50.
```

(continued)

Display 8.3 Overloading Operators as Friends (part 2 of 2)

```
25      int dollarsPart(double amount) const;
26      int centsPart(double amount) const;
27      int round(double number) const;
28  };
29
30  int main( )
31  {
```
       <If the main function is the same as in Display 8.1, then the screen dialogue
       will be the same as shown in Display 8.1.>

```
32  }
33
34  const Money operator +(const Money& amount1, const Money& amount2)
35  {
36      int allCents1  = amount1.cents + amount1.dollars*100;
37      int allCents2  = amount2.cents + amount2.dollars*100;
38      int sumAllCents = allCents1 + allCents2;
39      int absAllCents = abs(sumAllCents); //Money can be negative.
40      int finalDollars = absAllCents/100;
41      int finalCents = absAllCents%100;
```
       Note that friends have
       direct access to
       member variables.
```
42      if (sumAllCents < 0)
43      {
44          finalDollars = -finalDollars;
45          finalCents = -finalCents;
46      }
47      return Money(finalDollars, finalCents);
48  }
49  const Money operator -(const Money& amount1, const Money& amount2)
50      <The complete definition is Self-Test Exercise 7.>
51  bool operator ==(const Money& amount1, const Money& amount2)
52  {
53      return ((amount1.dollars == amount2.dollars)
54          && (amount1.cents == amount2.cents));
55  }
56  const Money operator -(const Money& amount)
57  {
58      return Money(-amount.dollars, -amount.cents);
59  }
60
```
       <Definitions of all other member functions are the same as in Display 8.1.>

Friend Classes

friend class

A class can be a **friend** of another class in the same way that a function can be a friend of a class. If the class F is a friend of the class C, then every member function of the class F is a friend of the class C. To make one class a friend of another, you must declare the friend class as a friend within the other class.

forward declaration

When one class is a friend of another class, it is typical for the classes to reference each other in their class definitions. This requires that you include a **forward declaration** to the class defined second, as illustrated in the outline that follows this paragraph. Note that the forward declaration is just the heading of the class definition followed by a semicolon.

Friend Functions

A friend function of a class is an ordinary function except that it has access to the private members of objects of that class. To make a function a friend of a class, you must list the function declaration for the friend function in the class definition. The function declaration is preceded by the keyword friend. The function declaration may be placed in either the private section or the public section, but it will be a public function in either case, so it is clearer to list it in the public section.

SYNTAX OF A CLASS DEFINITION WITH FRIEND FUNCTIONS

```
class Class_Name
{
public:
    friend Declaration_for_Friend_Function_1
    friend Declaration_for_Friend_Function_2
              .
              .
              .
    Member_Function_Declarations
private:
    Private_Member_Declarations
};
```

You need not list the friend functions first. You can intermix the order of these declarations.

EXAMPLE

```
class FuelTank
{
public:
    friend void fillLowest(FuelTank& t1, FuelTank& t2);
    //Fills the tank with the lowest fuel level, or t1 if a tie.

    FuelTank(double theCapacity, double theLevel);
    FuelTank( );
```

(continued)

```
    void input( );
    void output( ) const;
private:
    double capacity;//in liters
    double level;
};
```

A friend function is *not* a member function. A friend function is defined and called the same way as an ordinary function. You do not use the dot operator in a call to a friend function, and you do not use a type qualifier in the definition of a friend function.

If you want the class F to be a friend of the class C, the general outline of how you set things up is as follows:

```
class F;//forward declaration

class C
{
public:
    . . .
    friend class F;
    . . .
};
class F
{
    . . .
```

Complete examples using friend classes are given in Chapter 17. We will not be using friend classes until then.

PITFALL: Compilers without Friends

On some C++ compilers friend functions simply do not work as they are supposed to work. Worst of all, they may work sometimes and not work at other times. On these compilers friend functions do not always have access to private members of the class as they are supposed to. Presumably, this will be fixed in later releases of these compilers. In the meantime, you will have to work around this problem. If you have one of these compilers for which friend functions do not work, you must either use accessor functions to define nonmember functions and overloaded operators or you must overload operators as members. ∎

Rules on Overloading Operators

- When overloading an operator, at least one parameter (one operand) of the resulting overloaded operator must be of a class type.

- Most operators can be overloaded as a member of the class, a friend of the class, or a nonmember, nonfriend.

- The following operators can only be overloaded as (nonstatic) members of the class: =, [], ->, and ().

- You cannot create a new operator. All you can do is overload existing operators such as +, -, *, /, %, and so forth.

- You cannot change the number of arguments that an operator takes. For example, you cannot change % from a binary to a unary operator when you overload %; you cannot change ++ from a unary to a binary operator when you overload it.

- You cannot change the precedence of an operator. An overloaded operator has the same precedence as the ordinary version of the operator. For example, x*y + z always means (x*y) + z, even if x, y, and z are objects and the operators + and * have been overloaded for the appropriate classes.

- The following operators cannot be overloaded: the dot operator (.), the scope resolution operator (::), sizeof, ?:, and the operator .*, which is not discussed in this book.

- An overloaded operator cannot have default arguments.

Self-Test Exercises

6. What is the difference between a friend function for a class and a member function for a class?

7. Complete the definition of the friend subtraction operator - in Display 8.3.

8. Suppose you wish to overload the operator < so that it applies to the type Money defined in Display 8.3. What do you need to add to the definition of Money given in Display 8.3?

8.3   References and More Overloaded Operators

Do not mistake the pointing finger for the moon.

Zen saying

This section covers some specialized, but important, overloading topics, including overloading the assignment operator and the <<, >>, [], ++, and -- operators. Because you need to understand returning a reference to correctly overload some of these operators, we also discuss this topic.

References

A **reference** is the name of a storage location[1]. You can have a standalone reference, as in the following:

```
int robert;
int& bob = robert;
```

This makes bob a reference to the storage location for the variable robert, which makes bob an alias for the variable robert. Any change made to bob will also be made to robert. Stated this way, it sounds like a standalone reference is just a way to make your code confusing and get you in trouble. In most instances, a standalone reference is just trouble, although there a few cases where it can be useful. We will not discuss standalone references anymore, nor will we use them.

As you may suspect, references are used to implement the call-by-reference parameter mechanism. So, the concept is not completely new to this chapter, although the phrase *a reference* is new.

We are interested in references here because returning a reference will allow you to overload certain operators in a more natural way. Returning a reference can be viewed as something like returning a variable or, more precisely, an alias to a variable. The syntactic details are simple. You add an & to the return type. For example,

```
double& sampleFunction(double& variable);
```

Since a type like double& is a different type from double, you must use the & in both the function declaration and the function definition. The return expression must be something with a reference, such as a variable of the appropriate type. It cannot be an expression, such as x + 5. Although many compilers will let you do it (with unfortunate results), you also should not return a local variable because you would be generating an alias to a variable and immediately destroying the variable. A trivial example of the function definition is

```
double& sampleFunction(double& variable)
{
    return variable;
}
```

Of course, this is a pretty useless, even troublesome, function, but it illustrates the concept. For example, the following code will output 99 and then 42:

```
double m = 99;
cout << sampleFunction(m) << endl;
sampleFunction(m) = 42;
cout << m << endl;
```

---

[1] If you know about pointers, you will notice that a reference sounds like a pointer. A reference is essentially, but not exactly, a constant pointer. There are differences between pointers and references, and they are not completely interchangeable.

We will only be returning a reference when defining certain kinds of overloaded operators.

L-Values and R-Values

The term **l-value** is used for something that can appear on the left-hand side of an assignment operator. The term **r-value** is used for something that can appear on the right-hand side of an assignment operator.

If you want the object returned by a function to be an l-value, it must be returned by reference.

TIP: Returning Member Variables of a Class Type

When returning a member variable of a class type, in almost all cases it is important to return the member value by const value. To see why, suppose you do not, as in the example outlined in what follows:

```
class Employee
{
public:
    Money& getSalary( ) { return salary; }
    ...
private:
    Money salary;
    ...
};
```

In this example, salary is a private member variable that should not be changeable except by using some accessor function of the class Employee. The getSalary function returns the variable salary which is of type Money. If we do not return salary by reference then a new, temporary copy of salary will be created and returned. We might wish to avoid this overhead by returning a reference to salary as indicated in the example. However, even though salary is declared as private, this privateness is easily circumvented as follows:

```
Employee joe;
(joe.getSalary( )).input( );
```

The lucky employee named joe can now enter any salary she wishes!

On the other hand, suppose getSalary returns its value by const value, as follows:

```
class Employee
{
public:
    const Money& getSalary( ) { return salary; }
    ...
```

(continued)

TIP: (continued)

```
    private:
        Money salary;
    . . .
};
```

In this case, the following will give a compiler error message.

```
(joe.getSalary( )).input( );
```

(The declaration for getSalary should ideally be

```
const Money& getSalary( ) const { return salary; }
```

but we did not want to confuse the issue with another kind of const.)

In general, when a member function returns a member variable and that member variable is of some class type, then it should normally not be returned by reference to avoid external access to a private member variable. If you want to return by reference for efficiency reasons then adding const to the return value can help protect access to the member variable. ■

Overloading >> and <<

The operators >> and << can be overloaded so that you can use them to input and output objects of the classes you define. The details are not that different from what we have already seen for other operators, but there are some new subtleties.

The insertion operator << that we used with cout is a binary operator very much like + or -. For example, consider the following:

<< is an operator

```
cout << "Hello out there.\n";
```

The operator is <<, the first operand is the predefined object cout (from the library iostream), and the second operand is the string value "Hello out there.\n". The predefined object cout is of type ostream, and so when you overload <<, the parameter that receives cout will be of type ostream. You can change either of the two operands to <<. When we cover file I/O in Chapter 12 you will see how to create an object of type ostream that sends output to a file. (These file I/O objects as well as the objects cin and cout are called **streams**, which is why the library name is ostream.) The overloading that we create, with cout in mind, will turn out to also work for file output without any changes in the definition of the overloaded <<.

streams

In our previous definitions of the class Money (Display 8.1 through Display 8.3) we used the member function output to output values of type Money. This is adequate, but it would be nicer if we could simply use the insertion operator << to output values of type Money, as in the following,

overloading <<

```
Money amount(100);
cout << "I have " << amount << " in my purse.\n";
```

instead of having to use the member function output as shown here:

```
Money amount (100);
cout << "I have ";
amount.output ( );
cout << " in my purse.\n";
```

One problem in overloading the operator `<<` is deciding what value, if any, should be returned when `<<` is used in an expression like the following:

```
cout << amount
```

The two operands in the previous expression are cout and amount, and evaluating the expression should cause the value of amount to be written to the screen. But if `<<` is an operator like + or –, then the previous expression should also return some value. After all, expressions with other operands, such as n1 + n2, return values. But what does `cout << amount` return? To obtain the answer to that question, we need to look at a more complicated expression involving `<<`.

chains of <<

Let us consider the following expression, which involves evaluating a chain of expressions using `<<`:

```
cout << "I have " << amount << " in my purse.\n";
```

If you think of the operator `<<` as being analogous to other operators, such as +, then the latter expression should be (and in fact is) equivalent to the following:

```
( (cout << "I have ") << amount ) << " in my purse.\n";
```

What value should `<<` return to make sense of the previous expression? The first thing evaluated is the subexpression:

```
(cout << "I have ")
```

If things are to work out, then the previous subexpression had better return cout so that the computation can continue as follows:

```
( cout << amount ) << " in my purse.\n";
```

And if things are to continue to work out, (cout << amount) had better also return cout so that the computation can continue as follows:

```
cout << " in my purse.\n";
```

This is illustrated in Display 8.4. The operator `<<` should return its first argument, which is of type ostream (the type of cout).

<< returns a stream

Thus, the declaration for the overloaded operator `<<` (to use with the class Money) should be as follows:

```
class Money
{
public:
    . . .
    friend ostream& operator <<(ostream& outs,
                                const Money& amount);
```

Display 8.4 << as an Operator

```
cout << "I have " << amount << " in my purse.\n";
```

means the same as

```
((cout << "I have ") << amount) << " in my purse.\n";
```

and is evaluated as follows:

First evaluate (cout << "I have "), which returns cout:

```
((cout << "I have ")
      << amount) << " in my purse.\n";
```
The string `"I have"` *is output.*

```
(cout << amount) << " in my purse.\n";
```

Then evaluate (cout << amount), which returns cout:

```
(cout << amount) <<
      " in my purse.\n";
```
The value of `amount` *is output.*

```
cout << " in my purse.\n";
```

Then evaluate cout << " in my purse.\n", which returns cout:

```
cout << " in my purse.\n";
```
The string `"in my purse.\n"` *is output.*

```
cout ;
```
Since there are no more << *operators, the process ends.*

Once we have overloaded the insertion (output) operator <<, we will no longer need the member function output and will delete output from our definition of the class Money. The definition of the overloaded operator << is very similar to the member function output. In outline form, the definition for the overloaded operator is as follows:

```
ostream& operator <<(ostream& outputStream, const Money& amount)
{
    /*This part is the same as the body of
    Money::output which is given in Display 8.1 (except that
    dollars is replaced with amount.dollars
    and cents is replaced by amount.cents).*/

    return outputStream;
}
```

**<< and >>
return a
reference**

Note that the operator returns a reference.

The extraction operator >> is overloaded in a way that is analogous to what we described for the insertion operator <<. However, with the extraction (input) operator >>, the second argument will be the object that receives the input value, so the second parameter must be an ordinary call-by-reference parameter. In outline form the definition for the overloaded extraction operator >> is as follows:

```
istream& operator >>(istream& inputStream, Money& amount)
{

    /*This part is the same as the body of
      Money::input, which is given in Display 8.1 (except that
      dollars is replaced with amount.dollars
      and cents is replaced by amount.cents).*/

    return inputStream;
}
```

The complete definitions of the overloaded operators << and >> are given in Display 8.5, where we have rewritten the class Money yet again. This time we have rewritten the class so that the operators << and >> are overloaded to allow us to use these operators with values of type Money.

Note that you cannot realistically overload >> or << as member operators. If << and >> are to work as we want, then the first operand (first argument) must be cout or cin (or some file I/O stream). But if we want to overload the operators as members of, say, the class Money, then the first operand would have to be the calling object and so would have to be of type Money, and that will not allow you to define the operators so they behave in the normal way for >> and <<.

Display 8.5 Overloading << and >> (part 1 of 3)

```
1   #include <iostream>
2   #include <cstdlib>
3   #include <cmath>
4   using namespace std;

5   //Class for amounts of money in U.S. currency
6   class Money
7   {
8   public:
9       Money( );
10      Money(double amount);
11      Money(int theDollars, int theCents);
12      Money(int theDollars);
13      double getAmount( ) const;
14      int getDollars( ) const;
15      int getCents( ) const;
```

(continued)

Display 8.5 Overloading << and >> (part 2 of 3)

```
16      friend const Money operator + (const Money& amount1,
                                        const Money& amount2);
17      friend const Money operator - (const Money& amount1,
                                        const Money& amount2);
18      friend bool operator == (const Money& amount1,
                                 const Money& amount2);
19      friend const Money operator - (const Money& amount2);
20      friend ostream& operator << (ostream& outputStream,
                                      const Money& amount);
21      friend istream& operator >> (istream& inputStream, Money& amount);
22  private:
23      //A negative amount is represented as negative dollars
        //and negative cents. Negative $4.50 is represented as
        //-4 and -50.
24      int dollars, cents;
25      int dollarsPart(double amount) const;
26      int centsPart(double amount) const;
27      int round(double number) const;
28  };
29  int main()
30  {
31      Money yourAmount, myAmount(10, 9);
32      cout << "Enter an amount of money: ";
33      cin >> yourAmount;
34      cout << "Your amount is " << yourAmount << endl;
35      cout << "My amount is " << myAmount << endl;
36
37      if (yourAmount == myAmount)
38          cout << "We have the same amounts.\n";
39      else
40          cout << "One of us is richer.\n";
41
42      Money ourAmount = yourAmount + myAmount;
43      cout << yourAmount << " + " << myAmount
44          << " equals " << ourAmount << endl;
45      Money diffAmount = yourAmount - myAmount;
46      cout << yourAmount << " - " << myAmount
47          << " equals " << diffAmount << endl;
48  }
        return 0;
    }
```

Since << returns a reference, you can chain << like this. You can chain >> in a similar way.

< Definitions of other member functions are as in Display 8.1.
Definitions of other overloaded operators are as in Display 8.3. >

Display 8.5   Overloading `<<` and `>>`   (part 3 of 3)

```
49   ostream& operator <<(ostream& outputStream, const Money& amount)
50   {
                                                    In the main function, cout is plugged
                                                    in for outputStream.
51       int absDollars = abs(amount.dollars);
52       int absCents = abs(amount.cents);
53       if (amount.dollars < 0 || amount.cents < 0)
54           //accounts for dollars == 0 or cents == 0
55           outputStream << "$-";
56       else                                       For an alternate input
57           outputStream << '$';                   algorithm, see Self-Test
58           outputStream << absDollars;            Exercise 3 in Chapter 7.
59       if (absCents >= 10)
60           outputStream << '.' << absCents;
61       else
62           outputStream << '.' << '0' << absCents;
63       return outputStream;                       Returns a reference
64   }
65
66   //Uses iostream and cstdlib:
67   istream& operator >>(istream& inputStream, Money& amount)
68   {
                                                    In the main function, cin is
                                                    plugged in for inputStream.
69       char dollarSign;
70       inputStream >> dollarSign; //hopefully
71       if (dollarSign != '$')
72       {
73           cout << "No dollar sign in Money input.\n";
74           exit(1);
75       }
                                                    Since this is not a member operator,
                                                    you need to specify a calling object
                                                    for member functions of Money.
76       double amountAsDouble;
77       inputStream >> amountAsDouble;
78       amount.dollars = amount.dollarsPart(amountAsDouble);
79       amount.cents = amount.centsPart(amountAsDouble);
80       return inputStream;                        Returns a reference
81   }
```

Sample Dialogue

```
Enter an amount of money: $123.45
Your amount is $123.45
My amount is $10.09.
One of us is richer.
$123.45 + $10.09 equals $133.54
$123.45 - $10.09 equals $113.36
```

MyProgrammingLab™

Self-Test Exercises

9. In Display 8.5, the definition of the overloaded operator `<<` contains lines like the following:

```
outputStream << "$-";
```

Is this not circular? Are we not defining `<<` in terms of `<<`?

10. Why can we not overload `<<` or `>>` as member operators?

11. Following is the definition for a class called `Percent`. Objects of type `Percent` represent percentages such as 10% or 99%. Give the definitions of the overloaded operators `>>` and `<<` so that they can be used for input and output with objects of the class `Percent`. Assume that input always consists of an integer followed by the character '`%`', such as 25%. All percentages are whole numbers and are stored in the `int` member variable named `value`. You do not need to define the other overloaded operators and do not need to define the constructor. You only have to define the overloaded operators `>>` and `<<`.

```
#include <iostream>
using namespace std;
class Percent
{
public:
    friend bool operator ==(const Percent& first,
                            const Percent& second);
    friend bool operator <(const Percent& first,
                           const Percent& second);
    Percent( );
    friend istream& operator >>(istream& inputStream,
                                Percent& aPercent);
    friend ostream& operator <<(ostream& outputStream,
                                const Percent& aPercent);
    //There would normally also be other members and friends.
private:
    int value;
};
```

TIP: What Mode of Returned Value to Use

A function can return a value of type `T` in four different ways:

- By plain old value, as in the function declaration `T f( );`
- By constant value, as in the function declaration `const T f( );`
- By reference, as in the function declaration `T& f( );`
- By `const` reference, as in the function declaration `const T& f( );`

TIP: (continued)

There is not unanimous agreement on which to use when. So, do not expect too much consistency in usage. Even when an author or programmer has a clear policy, they seldom manage to follow it without exception. Still, some points are clear.

If you are returning a simple type, like int or char, there is no point in using a const when returning by value or by reference. So programmers typically do not use a const on the return type when it is a simple type. If you want the simple value returned to be allowed as an l-value, that is to be allowed on the left-hand side of an assignment statement, then return by reference; otherwise return the simple type by plain old value. Class types are not so simple. The rest of this discussion applies to returning an object of a class type.

The decision on whether or not to return by reference has to do with whether or not you want to be able to use the returned object as an l-value. If you want to return something that can be used as an l-value, that is, that can be used on the left-hand side of an assignment operator, you must return by reference and so must use an ampersand & on the returned type.

Returning a local variable (or other short-lived object) by reference, with or without a const, can produce problems and should be avoided.

For class types, the two returned type specifications const T and const T& are very similar. They both mean that you cannot change the returned object by invoking some mutator function directly on the returned object, as in

```
f().mutator( );
```

The returned value can still be copied to another variable with an assignment operator and that other variable can have the mutator function applied to it. If you cannot decide between the const T& and const T, use const T (without the ampersand). A const T& is perhaps a bit more efficient than a const T.[2] However, the difference is not typically that important and most programmers use const T rather than const T& as a returned type specification. As noted earlier, const T& can sometimes cause problems.

The following summary may be of help. T is assumed to be a class type. Copy constructors are not covered until Chapter 10, but we include details about them here for reference value. If you have not yet read Chapter 10, simply ignore all references to copy constructors.

If a public member function returns a private class member variable, it should always have a const on the returned type, as we explained in the Tip section of this chapter entitled "Returning Member Variables of a Class Type." (One exception to this rule is that programmers normally always return a value of type string by ordinary value, not by const value. This is presumably because the type string is thought of as a simple type like int and char, even though string is a class type.)

(continued)

---

[2] This is because const T& does not call the copy constructor while const T does call the copy constructor. Copy constructors are discussed in Chapter 10.

TIP: (continued)

The following summary may be of help. `T` is assumed to be a class type.

Simple returning by value, as in the function declaration `T f( );` Cannot be used as an l-value, and the returned value can be changed directly as in `f( ).mutator( ).` Calls the copy constructor.

Returning by constant value, as in `const T f( );` This case is the same as the previous case, but the returned value cannot be changed directly as in `f( ).mutator( ).`

Returning by reference as in `T& f( );` Can be used as an l-value, and the returned value can be changed directly as in `f( ).mutator( ).` Does not call the copy constructor.

Returning by constant reference, as in `const T& f( );` Cannot be used as an l-value, and the returned value cannot be changed directly as in `f( ).mutator( ).` Does not call the copy constructor. ∎

Overloading >> and <<

The input and output operators `>>` and `<<` can be overloaded just like any other operators. If you want the operators to behave as expected for `cin`, `cout`, and file I/O, then the value returned should be of type `istream` for input and `ostream` for output, and the value should be returned by reference.

DECLARATIONS

```
class Class_Name
{
public:
    . . .
    friend istream& operator >>(istream& Parameter_1,
                                Class_Name& Parameter_2);
    friend ostream& operator <<(ostream& Parameter_3,
                                const Class_Name& Parameter_4);
    . . .
```

The operators do not need to be friends but cannot be members of the class being input or output.

DEFINITIONS

```
istream& operator >>(istream& Parameter_1,
                     Class_Name& Parameter_2)
{
    .
    .
    .
}

ostream& operator <<(ostream& Parameter_3,
                     const Class_Name& Parameter_4)
{
    .
    .
    .
}
```

If you have enough accessor and mutator functions, you can overload >> and << as nonfriend functions. However, it is natural and more efficient to define them as friends.

The Assignment Operator

If you overload the assignment operator =, you must overload it as a member operator. If you do not overload the assignment operator =, then you automatically get an assignment operator for your class. This default assignment operator copies the values of member variables from one object of the class to the corresponding member variables of another object of the class. For simple classes, that is usually what you want. When we discuss pointers, this default assignment operator will not be what we want, and we will discuss overloading the assignment operator at that point.

Overloading the Increment and Decrement Operators

prefix and postfix

The increment and decrement operators ++ and -- each have two versions. They can do different things depending on whether they are used in prefix notation, ++x, or postfix (suffix) notation, x++. Thus, when overloading these operators, you need to somehow distinguish between the prefix and postfix versions so that you can have two versions of the overloaded operator. In C++ this distinction between prefix and postfix versions is handled in a way that at first reading (and maybe even on second reading) seems a bit contrived. If you overload the ++ operator in the regular way (as a nonmember operator with one parameter or as a member operator with no parameters), then you have overloaded the prefix form. To obtain the postfix version, x++ or x--, you add a second parameter of type int. This is just a marker for the compiler; you do not give a second int argument when you invoke x++ or x--.

For example, Display 8.6 contains the definition of a class whose data is pairs of integers. The increment operator ++ is defined so it works in both prefix and postfix notation. We have defined ++ so that it has the intuitive spirit of ++ on int variables. This is the best way to define ++, but you are free to define it to return any kind of type and perform any kind of action.

The definition of the postfix version ignores that `int` parameter, as shown in Display 8.6. When the compiler sees `a++`, it treats it as an invocation of `IntPair::operator++(int)`, with a as the calling object.

The increment and decrement operator on simple types, such as `int` and `char`, return by reference in the prefix form and by value in the postfix form. If you want to emulate what happens with simple types when you overload these operators for your class types, then you would return by reference for the prefix form and by value for the postfix form. However, we find it opens the door to too many problems to return by reference with increment or decrement operators, and so we always simply return by value for all versions of the increment and decrement operators.

return by reference

Self-Test Exercise

12. Is the following legal? Explain your answer. (The definition of `IntPair` is given in Display 8.6.)

```
IntPair a(1,2);
(a++)++;
```

Display 8.6   Overloading ++ (part 1 of 3)

```
1   #include <iostream>
2   #include <cstdlib>
3   using namespace std;
4
5   class IntPair
6   {
7   public:
8       IntPair(int firstValue, int secondValue);
9       IntPair operator++();       //Prefix version
10      IntPair operator++(int);    //Postfix version
11      void setFirst(int newValue);
12      void setSecond(int newValue);
13      int getFirst( ) const;
14      int getSecond( ) const;
15  private:
16      int first;
17      int second;
18  };
19
20  int main( )
21  {
        IntPair a(1,2);
        cout << "Postfix a++: Start value of object a: ";
```

You need not give a parameter name in a function or operator declaration.

For ++ it makes sense to give no parameter since the parameter is not used.

Display 8.6   Overloading ++ (part 2 of 3)

```cpp
22        cout << a.getFirst( ) << " " << a.getSecond( ) << endl;
23        IntPair b = a++;
24        cout << "Value returned: ";
25        cout << b.getFirst( ) << " " << b.getSecond( ) << endl;
26        cout << "Changed object: ";
27        cout << a.getFirst( ) << " " << a.getSecond( ) << endl;

28        a = IntPair(1, 2);
29        cout << "Prefix ++a: Start value of object a: ";
30        cout << a.getFirst( ) << " " << a.getSecond( ) << endl;
31        IntPair c = ++a;
32        cout << "Value returned: ";
33        cout << c.getFirst( ) << " " << c.getSecond( ) << endl;
34        cout << "Changed object: ";
35        cout << a.getFirst( ) << " " << a.getSecond( ) << endl;
36        return 0;
37
38   }

39   IntPair::IntPair(int firstValue, int secondValue)
40                    : first(firstValue), second(secondValue)
41   {/*Body intentionally empty*/}
42   IntPair IntPair::operator++(int ignoreMe)  //Postfix version
43   {
44        int temp1 = first;
45        int temp2 = second;
46        first++;
47        second++;
48        return IntPair(temp1, temp2);
49   }

50   IntPair IntPair::operator++( )  //Prefix version
51   {
52        first++;
53        second++;
54        return IntPair(first, second);
55   }

56   void IntPair::setFirst(int newValue)
57   {
58        first = newValue;
59   }

60   void IntPair::setSecond(int newValue)
61   {
62        second = newValue;
63   }
```

(continued)

Display 8.6 Overloading ++ (part 3 of 3)

```
64    int IntPair::getFirst( ) const
65    {
66        return first;
67    }
68    int IntPair::getSecond( ) const
69    {
70        return second;
71    }
```

Sample Dialogue

```
Postfix a++: Start value of object a: 1 2
Value returned: 1 2
Changed object: 2 3
Prefix ++a: Start value of object a: 1 2
Value returned: 2 3
Changed object: 2 3
```

Overloading the Array Operator []

You can overload the square brackets, [], for a class so that they can be used with objects of the class. If you want to use [] in an expression on the left-hand side of an assignment operator, then the operator must be defined to return a reference. When overloading [], the operator [] *must* be a member function.

It may help to review the syntax for the operator [], since it is different from any other operator we have seen. Remember that [] is overloaded as a member operator; therefore one thing in an expression using [] must be the calling object. In the expression a[2], a is the calling object and 2 is the argument to the member operator []. When overloading [], this "index" parameter must be an integer type, that is, enum, char, short, int, long, or an unsigned version of one of these types.

For example, in Display 8.7 we define a class called CharPair whose objects behave like arrays of characters with the two indexes 1 and 2 (*not* 0 and 1). Note that the expressions a[1] and a[2] behave just like array indexed variables. If you look at the definition of the overloaded operator [], you will see that a reference is returned and that it is a reference to a member variable, not to the entire CharPair object. This is because the member variable is analogous to an indexed variable of an array. When you change a[1] (in the sample code in Display 8.7), you want that to be a change to the member variable first. Note that this gives access to the private member variables to any program, for example, via a[1] and a[2] in the sample main function in Display 8.7. Although first and second are private members, the code is legal because it does not reference first and second by name but indirectly using the names a[1] and a[2].

Display 8.7   Overloading [] (part 1 of 2)

```
1   #include <iostream>
2   #include <cstdlib>
3   using namespace std;

4   class CharPair
5   {
6   public:
7       CharPair( ){/*Body intentionally empty*/}
8       CharPair(char firstValue, char secondValue)
9                   : first(firstValue), second(secondValue)
10      {/*Body intentionally empty*/}
11
12      char& operator[](int index);
13  private:
14      char first;
15      char second;
16  };

17  int main( )
18  {
19      CharPair a;
20      a[1] = 'A';
21      a[2] = 'B';
22      cout << "a[1] and a[2] are:\n";
23      cout << a[1] << a[2] << endl;

24      cout << "Enter two letters (no spaces):\n";
25      cin >> a[1] >> a[2];
26      cout << "You entered:\n";
27      cout << a[1] << a[2] << endl;

28      return 0;
29  }

30
31  //Uses iostream and cstdlib:
32  char& CharPair::operator[](int index)
33  {
34      if (index == 1)
35          return first;
36      else if (index == 2)
37          return second;
38      else
39      {
40          cout << "Illegal index value.\n";
41          exit(1);
42      }
43  }
```

Note that you return the member variable,
not the entire Pair object, because the
member variable is analogous to an indexed
variable of an array.

(continued)

Display 8.7   Overloading [] (part 2 of 2)

Sample Dialogue

```
a[1] and a[2] are:
AB
Enter two letters (no spaces):
CD
You entered:
CD
```

Overloading Based on L-Value versus R-Value

Although we will not be doing it in this book, you can overload a function name (or operator) so that it behaves differently when used as an l-value and when it is used as an r-value. (Recall that an l-value means it can be used on the left-hand side of an assignment statement.) For example, if you want a function f to behave differently depending on whether it is used as an l-value or an r-value, you can do so as follows:

```
class SomeClass
{
public:
    int& f( ); // will be used in any l-value invocation

    const int& f( ) const; // used in any r-value invocation

    . . .
};
```

The two parameter lists need not be empty, but they should be the same (or else you just get simple overloading). Be sure to notice that the second declaration of f has two occurrences of const. You must include both occurrences of const. The ampersand signs & are of course also required.

Chapter Summary

- Operators, such as + and ==, can be overloaded so that they can be used with objects of a class type that you define.

- An operator is just a function that uses a different syntax for invocations.

- A *friend function* of a class is an ordinary function except that it has access to the private members of the class, just like member functions do.

- When an operator is overloaded as a member of a class, the first operand is the calling object.

- If your classes each have a full set of accessor functions, then the only reason to make a function a friend is to make the definition of the friend function simpler and more efficient, but that is often reason enough.

- A *reference* is a way of naming a variable. It is essentially an alias for the variable.

- When overloading the >> or << operators, the type returned should be a stream type and should be a reference, which is indicated by appending an & to the name of the returned type.

Answers to Self-Test Exercises

1. The difference between a (binary) operator (such as +, *, or /) and a function involves the syntax of how they are called. In a function call, the arguments are given in parentheses after the function name. With an operator the arguments are given before and after the operator. Also, you must use the reserved word operator in the operator declaration and in the definition of an overloaded operator.

2. Add the following declaration and function definition:

```
bool operator <(const Money& amount1,  const Money& amount2);

bool operator <(const Money& amount1,  const Money& amount2)
{
    int dollars1 = amount1.getDollars( );
    int dollars2 = amount2.getDollars( );
    int cents1 = amount1.getCents( );
    int cents2 = amount2.getCents( );
    return ((dollars1 < dollars2) ||
            ((dollars1 == dollars2) && (cents1 < cents2)));
}
```

3. When overloading an operator, at least one of the arguments to the operator must be of a class type. This prevents changing the behavior of + for integers.

4. If you omit the const at the beginning of the declaration and definition of the overloaded plus operator for the class Money, then the following is legal:

```
(m1 + m2) = m3;
```

If the definition of the class Money is as shown in Display 8.1, so that the plus operator returns by const value, then it is not legal.

5.
```
const Money
    Money::operator -(const Money& secondOperand) const
{
    int allCents1 = cents + dollars*100;
    int allCents2 = secondOperand.cents
                    + secondOperand.dollars*100;
    int diffAllCents = allCents1 - allCents2;
    int absAllCents = abs(diffAllCents);
```

```
    int finalDollars = absAllCents/100;
    int finalCents = absAllCents%100;

    if (diffAllCents < 0)
    {
        finalDollars = -finalDollars;
        finalCents = -finalCents;
    }

    return Money(finalDollars, finalCents);
}
```

6. A friend function and a member function are alike in that they both can use any member of the class (either public or private) in their function definition. However, a friend function is defined and used just like an ordinary function; the dot operator is not used when you call a friend function and no type qualifier is used when you define a friend function. A member function, on the other hand, is called using an object name and the dot operator. Also, a member function definition includes a type qualifier consisting of the class name and the scope resolution operator, ::.

7. //Uses cstdlib:
```
const Money operator -(const Money& amount1,
                       const Money& amount2)
{
    int allCents1 = amount1.cents + amount1.dollars*100;
    int allCents2 = amount2.cents + amount2.dollars*100;
    int diffAllCents = allCents1 - allCents2;
    int absAllCents = abs(diffAllCents);

    int finalDollars = absAllCents/100;
    int finalCents = absAllCents%100;
    if (diffAllCents < 0)
    {
        finalDollars = -finalDollars;
        finalCents = -finalCents;
    }

    return Money(finalDollars, finalCents);
}
```

8. Add the following declaration and function definition:
```
friend bool operator <(const Money& amount1,
                       const Money& amount2);
bool operator <(const Money& amount1,
                const Money& amount2)
{
    return ((amount1.dollars < amount2.dollars) ||
           ((amount1.dollars == amount2.dollars) &&
            (amount1.cents < amount2.cents)));
}
```

9. To understand why it is not circular, you need to think about the basic message of overloading: A single function or operator name can have two or more definitions. That means that two or more different operators (or functions) can share a single name. In the line

```
outputStream << "$-";
```

the operator `<<` is the name of an operator defined in the library `iostream` to be used when the second argument is a quoted string. The operator named `<<` that we define in Display 8.5 is a different operator that works when the second argument is of type `Money`.

10. If `<<` and `>>` are to work as we want, then the first operand (first argument) must be `cout` or `cin` (or some file I/O stream). But if we want to overload the operators as members of, say, the class `Money`, then the first operand would have to be the calling object and so would have to be of type `Money`, and that is not what we want.

11. ```
//Uses iostream:
istream& operator >>(istream& inputStream,
                     Percent& aPercent)
{
    char percentSign;
    inputStream >> aPercent.value;
    inputStream >> percentSign;//Discards the % sign.
    return inputStream;
}
```

```
//Uses iostream:
ostream& operator <<(ostream& outputStream,
                     const Percent& aPercent)
{
    outputStream << aPercent.value << '%';
    return outputStream;
}
```

12. It is legal, but the meaning is not what you might want. `(a++)` increases the value of the member variables in a by one, but `(a++)++` raises the value of the member variables in `a++` by one, and `a++` is a different object from a. (It is possible to define the increment operator so that `(a++)++` will increase the value of the member variables by two but that requires use of the `this` pointer which is not discussed until Chapter 10.)

Programming Projects

Visit www.myprogramminglab.com to complete select exercises online and get instant feedback.

1. Modify the definition of the class `Money` shown in Display 8.5 so that the following are added:

   a. The operators `<`, `<=`, `>`, and `>=` have each been overloaded to apply to the type `Money`. (*Hint:* See Self-Test Exercise 8.)
```

b. The following member function has been added to the class definition. (We show the function declaration as it should appear in the class definition. The definition of the function itself will include the qualifier Money::.)

```
const Money percent(int percentFigure) const;
//Returns a percentage of the money amount in the calling
//object. For example, if percentFigure is 10, then the value
//returned is 10% of the amount of money represented by the
//calling object.
```

For example, if purse is an object of type Money whose value represents the amount $100.10; that is, it returns a value of type Money that represents the amount $10.01.

```
purse.percent(10);
```

returns 10% of $100.10; that is, it returns a value of type Money that represents the amount $10.01.

2. Define a class for rational numbers. A rational number is a number that can be represented as the quotient of two integers. For example, 1/2, 3/4, 64/2, and so forth are all rational numbers. (By 1/2 and so on we mean the everyday fraction, not the integer division this expression would produce in a C++ program.) Represent rational numbers as two values of type int, one for the numerator and one for the denominator. Call the class Rational. Include a constructor with two arguments that can be used to set the member variables of an object to any legitimate values. Also include a constructor that has only a single parameter of type int; call this single parameter wholeNumber and define the constructor so that the object will be initialized to the rational number wholeNumber/1. Include a default constructor that initializes an object to 0 (that is, to 0/1). Overload the input and output operators >> and <<. Numbers are to be input and output in the form 1/2, 15/32, 300/401, and so forth. Note that the numerator, the denominator, or both may contain a minus sign, so -1/2, 15/-32, and -300/-401 are also possible inputs. Overload all the following operators so that they correctly apply to the type Rational: ==, <, <=, >, >=, +, -, *, and /. Write a test program to test your class. *Hint:* Two rational numbers a/b and c/d are equal if a*d equals c*b. If b and d are *positive* rational numbers, a/b is less than c/d provided a*d is less than c*b. You should include a function to normalize the values stored so that, after normalization, the denominator is positive and the numerator and denominator are as small as possible. For example, after normalization 4/-8 would be represented the same as -1/2.

3. Define a class for complex numbers. A complex number is a number of the form

$$a + b*i$$

where for our purposes, *a* and *b* are numbers of type double, and *i* is a number that represents the quantity $\sqrt{-1}$. Represent a complex number as two values of type `double`. Name the member variables `real` and `imaginary`. (The variable for the number that is multiplied by i is the one called `imaginary`.) Call the class `Complex`. Include a constructor with two parameters of type `double` that can be used to set the member variables of an object to any values. Include a constructor that has only a single parameter of type `double`; call this parameter `realPart` and define the constructor so that the object will be initialized to `realPart + 0*i`. Include a default constructor that initializes an object to 0 (that is, to `0 + 0*i`). Overload all the following operators so that they correctly apply to the type `Complex`: `==`, `+`, `-`, `*`, `>>`, and `<<`. You should also write a test program to test your class. *Hints*: To add or subtract two complex numbers, add or subtract the two member variables of type `double`. The product of two complex numbers is given by the following formula:

$$(a + b*i)*(c + d*i) == (a*c - b*d) + (a*d + b*c)*i$$

In the interface file, you should define a constant `i` as follows:

```
const Complex i(0, 1);
```

This defined constant `i` will be the same as the i discussed above.

4. Cumulatively modify the example from Display 8.7 as follows.

a. In Display 8.7, replace the private `char` members `first` and `second` with an array of `char` of size `100` and a private data member named `size`.

Provide a default constructor that initializes `size` to `10` and sets the first `10` of the `char` positions to `'#'`. (This only uses 10 of the possible 100 slots.)

Provide an accessor function that returns the value of the private member `size`.

Test.

b. Add an `operator[]` member that returns a `char&` that allows the user to access or to set any member of the private data array using a non-negative index that is less than `size`.

Test.

c. Add a constructor that takes an `int` argument, `sz`, that sets the first `sz` members of the `char` array to `'#'`.

Test.

d. Add a constructor that takes an `int` argument, `sz`, and an array of `char` of size `sz`. The constructor should set the first `sz` members of the private data array to the `sz` members of the argument array of `char`.

Test.

NOTES: When you test, you should test with known good values, with data on boundaries and with deliberately bad values. You are not required to put checks for index out of bounds errors in your code, but that would be a nice touch. Error handling alternatives: Issue an error message then die (that is, call `exit(1)`) or give the user another chance to make a correct entry.

VideoNote

Solution to
Programming
Project 8.7

5. Write the definition for a class named Vector2D that stores information about a two-dimensional vector. The class should have functions to get and set the x and y components, where x and y are integers.

   Next, overload the * operator so that it returns the dot product of two vectors. The dot product of two-dimensional vectors **A** and **B** is equal to

$$(A_x \times B_x) + (A_y \times B_y).$$

   Finally, write a main subroutine that tests the * operation.

6. Define a class named MyInteger that stores an integer and has functions to get and set the integer's value. Then, overload the [] operator so that the index returns the digit in position i, where $i = 0$ is the least-significant digit. If no such digit exists then –1 should be returned.

   For example, if x is of type MyInteger and is set to 418, then x[0] should return 8, x[1] should return 1, x[2] should return 4, and x[3] should return –1.

7. Define a class named PrimeNumber that stores a prime number. The default constructor should set the prime number to 1. Add another constructor that allows the caller to set the prime number. Also, add a function to get the prime number. Finally, overload the prefix and postfix ++ and -- operators so they return a PrimeNumber object that is the next largest prime number (for ++) and the next smallest prime number (for --). For example, if the object's prime number is set to 13, then invoking ++ should return a PrimeNumber object whose prime number is set to 17. Create an appropriate test program for the class.

8. Do Programming Project 6.10, the definition of a Temperature class, except overload ==, <<, and >> as member operators. The == operator should return true if the two temperature values are identical, while << should output the temperature in Fahrenheit and >> should input the temperature in Fahrenheit. Create appropriate tests for the overloaded operators.

9. Programming Project 6.12 asked you to write a BoxOfProduce class that stored three bundles of fruits or vegetables (stored in an array of strings of size 3) to ship to a customer. Rewrite this class to use a vector instead of an array and add appropriate constructors, mutators, and accessors. The class should have a function to add additional fruits or vegetables to the box so there could be more than three bundles in one box. Overload the + operator to return a new BoxOfProduce object that combines the vector contents of both operand BoxOfProduce objects. Test your functions and + operator from the main function. You do not have to implement the rest of Programming Project 6.12 for this Programming Project, only the changes to the BoxOfProduce class.

Strings 9

9 Strings

Polonius: What do you read my lord? Hamlet: Words, words, words

WILLIAM SHAKESPEARE, *Hamlet*

Introduction

This chapter discusses two types whose values represent strings of characters, such as "Hello". One type is just an array with base type char that stores strings of characters in the array and marks the end of the string with the null character, '\0'. This is the older way of representing strings, which C++ inherited from the C programming language. These sorts of strings are called *C-strings*. Although C-strings are an older way of representing strings, it is difficult to do any sort of string processing in C++ without at least passing contact with C-strings. For example, quoted strings, such as "Hello", are implemented as C-strings in C++.

The ANSI/ISO C++ standard includes a more modern string handling facility in the form of the class string. The class string is the second string type that we will discuss in this chapter. If you have the choice between using a C-string or the class string then the general recommendation is to use the class string because it offers greater functionality and checks for error conditions that results in a more secure application. The full class string uses templates and so is similar to the template classes in the Standard Template Library (STL). Templates are covered in Chapter 16 and the STL is covered in Chapter 19. This chapter covers basic uses of the class string that do not require a knowledge of templates.

This material does not require extensive knowledge of arrays, but you should be familiar with basic array notation, such as a[i]. Section 5.1 of Chapter 5 covers more than enough material about arrays to allow you to read the material of this chapter. This material also does not require extensive knowledge of classes. Section 9.1 on C-strings and Section 9.2 on character manipulation can be covered before Chapters 6, 7, and 8, which cover classes. However, before reading Section 9.3 on the standard class string, you should read Chapter 6 and the following parts of Chapter 7: Section 7.1 and the subsection of Section 7.2 entitled "The const Parameter Modifier" along with its accompanying pitfall section.

9.1   An Array Type for Strings

In everything one must consider the end.

JEAN DE LA FONTAINE, *Fables, book III* (1668)

This section describes one way to represent strings of characters, which C++ inherited from the C language. Section 9.3 describes a string class that is a more modern way to represent strings. Although the string type described here may be a bit "old fashioned," it is still widely used and is an integral part of the C++ language.

C-String Values and C-String Variables

One way to represent a string is as an array with base type char. However, if the string is "Hello", it is handy to represent it as an array of characters with six indexed variables: five for the five letters in "Hello" plus one for the character '\0', which serves as an end marker. The character '\0' is called the **null character** and is used as an end marker because it is distinct from all the "real" characters. The end marker allows your program to read the array one character at a time and know that it should stop reading when it reads the '\0'. A string stored in this way (as an array of characters terminated with '\0') is called a **C-string**.

We spell '\0' with two symbols when we write it in a program, but just like the newline character '\n', the character '\0' is really only a single character value. Like any other character value, '\0' can be stored in one variable of type char or one indexed variable of an array of characters.

null character, '\0'

C-string

The Null Character, '\0'

The null character, '\0', is used to mark the end of a C-string that is stored in an array of characters. When an array of characters is used in this way, the array is often called a C-string variable. Although the null character '\0' is written using two symbols, it is a single character that fits in one variable of type char or one indexed variable of an array of characters.

You have already been using C-strings. In C++, a literal string, such as "Hello" is stored as a C-string, although you seldom need to be aware of this detail.

A **C-string variable** is just an array of characters. Thus, the following array declaration provides us with a C-string variable capable of storing a C-string value with nine or fewer characters:

```
char s[10];
```

The 10 is for the nine letters in the string plus the null character '\0' to mark the end of the string.

A C-string variable is a partially filled array of characters. Like any other partially filled array, a C-string variable uses positions starting at indexed variable 0 through as many as are needed. However, a C-string variable does not use an int variable to keep track of how much of the array is currently being used. Instead, a string variable places the special symbol '\0' in the array immediately after the last character of the C-string. Thus, if s contains the string "Hi Mom!", the array elements are filled as shown next:

C-string variables

s[0]	s[1]	s[2]	s[3]	s[4]	s[5]	s[6]	s[7]	s[8]	s[9]
H	i		M	o	m	!	\0	?	?

The character '\0' is used as a sentinel value to mark the end of the C-string. If you read the characters in the C-string starting at indexed variable s[0], proceed to s[1], then to s[2], and so forth, you know that when you encounter the symbol '\0' you have reached the end of the C-string. Since the symbol '\0' always occupies one element of the array, the length of the longest string that the array can hold is one less than the size of the array.

The thing that distinguishes a C-string variable from an ordinary array of characters is that a C-string variable must contain the null character '\0' at the end of the C-string value. This is a distinction regarding how the array is used rather than a distinction regarding what the array is. *A C-string variable is an array of characters, but it is used in a different way.*

C-String Variable Declaration

A C-string variable is the same thing as an array of characters, but it is used differently. A C-string variable is declared to be an array of characters in the usual way.

SYNTAX

```
char Array_Name[Maximum_C-string_Size + 1];
```

EXAMPLE

```
char myCstring[11];
```

The + 1 allows for the null character '\0', which terminates any C-string stored in the array. For example, the C-string variable myCstring in the previous example can hold a C-string that is ten or fewer characters long.

You can initialize a C-string variable when you declare it, as illustrated by the following example:

```
char myMessage[20] = "Hi there.";
```

Notice that the C-string assigned to the C-string variable need not fill the entire array. When you initialize a C-string variable, you can omit the array size and C++ will automatically make the size of the C-string variable one more than the length of the quoted string. (The one extra indexed variable is for '\0'.) For example,

```
char shortString[] = "abc";
```

is equivalent to

```
char shortString[4] = "abc";
```

Be sure you do not confuse the following initializations:

```
char shortString[] = "abc";
```

and

```
char shortString[] = {'a', 'b', 'c'};
```

They are *not equivalent*. The first of these two possible initializations places the null character '\0' in the array after the characters 'a', 'b', and 'c'. The second one does not put a '\0' anyplace in the array.

Initializing a C-String Variable

A C-string variable can be initialized when it is declared, as illustrated by the following example:

```
char yourString[11] = "Do Be Do";
```

Initializing in this way automatically places the null character, '\0', in the array at the end of the C-string specified.

If you omit the number inside the square brackets, [], then the C-string variable will be given a size one character longer than the length of the C-string. For example, the following declares myString to have nine indexed variables (eight for the characters of the C-string "Do Be Do" and one for the null character '\0'):

```
char myString[] = "Do Be Do";
```

A C-string variable is an array, so it has indexed variables that can be used just like those of any other array. For example, suppose your program contains the following C-string variable declaration:

```
char ourString[5] = "Hi";
```

With ourString declared as shown, your program has the following indexed variables: ourString[0], ourString[1], ourString[2], ourString[3], and ourString[4]. For example, the following will change the C-string value in ourString to a C-string of the same length consisting of all 'X' characters:

```
int index = 0;
while (ourString[index] != '\0')
{
    ourString[index] = 'X';
    index++;
}
```

indexed variables for C-string variables

Do not destroy the '\0'.

When manipulating these indexed variables you should be very careful not to replace the null character '\0' with some other value. If the array loses the value '\0' it will no longer behave like a C-string variable. For example, the following will change the array happyString so that it no longer contains a C-string:

```
char happyString[7] = "DoBeDo";
happyString[6] = 'Z';
```

After the previous code is executed, the array happyString will still contain the six letters in the C-string "DoBeDo", but happyString will no longer contain the null character '\0' to mark the end of the C-string. Many string-manipulating functions depend critically on the presence of '\0' to mark the end of the C-string value.

As another example, consider the above while loop that changes characters in the C-string variable ourString. That while loop changes characters until it encounters a '\0'. If the loop never encounters a '\0', then it could change a large chunk of memory to some unwanted values, which could make your program do strange things. As a safety feature, it would be wise to rewrite the previous while loop as follows, so that if the null character '\0' is lost, the loop will not inadvertently change memory locations beyond the end of the array:

```
{
    int index = 0;
    while ( (ourString[index] != "\0") && (index < SIZE) )
    {
        ourString[index] = "X";
        index++;
    }
}
```

SIZE is a defined constant equal to the declared size of the array ourString.

The <cstring> Library

You do not need any include directive or using statement to declare and initialize C-strings. However, when processing C-strings you inevitably will use some of the predefined string functions in the library <cstring>. Thus, when using C-strings, you will normally give the following include directive near the beginning of the file containing your code:

```
#include <cstring>
```

The definitions in <cstring> are placed in the global namespace, not in the std namespace, and so no using statement is required.

PITFALL: Using = and == with C-strings

C-string values and C-string variables are not like values and variables of other data types, and many of the usual operations do not work for C-strings. You cannot use a C-string variable in an assignment statement using =. If you use = to test C-strings for equality, you will not get the result you expect. The reason for these problems is that C-strings and C-string variables are arrays.

Assigning a value to a C-string variable is not as simple as it is for other kinds of variables. The following is illegal:

assigning a
C-string value

```
char aString[10];
aString = "Hello";        ←——————— Illegal!
```

Although you can use the equal sign to assign a value to a C-string variable when the variable is declared, you cannot do it anywhere else in your program. Technically, the use of the equal sign in a declaration, as in

```
char happyString[7] = "DoBeDo";
```

is an initialization, not an assignment. If you want to assign a value to a C-string variable, you must do something else.

There are a number of different ways to assign a value to a C-string variable. The easiest way is to use the predefined function strcpy as shown here:

```
strcpy(aString, "Hello");
```

This will set the value of aString equal to "Hello". Unfortunately, this version of the function strcpy does not check to make sure the copying does not exceed the size of the string variable that is the first argument. Many, but not all, versions of C++ also have a version of strcpy called strncpy (note the extra 'n') that takes a third argument which gives the maximum number of characters to copy. If this third parameter is set to one less than the size of the array variable in the first argument position, then you obtain a safe version of strncpy (provided your version of C++ allows this third argument). For example,

```
char anotherString[10];
strncpy(anotherString, aStringVariable, 9);
```

With this version of strncpy, at most nine characters (leaving room for '\0') will be copied from the C-string variable aStringVariable no matter how long the string in aStringVariable may be.

You also cannot use the operator == in an expression to test whether two C-strings are the same. (Things are actually much worse than that. You can use == with C-strings, but it does not test for the C-strings being equal. So if you use == to test two C-strings for equality, you are likely to get incorrect results, but no error message!)

To test whether two C-strings are the same, you can use the predefined function strcmp. For example,

```
if (strcmp(cString1, cString2))
    cout << "The strings are NOT the same.";
else
    cout << "The strings are the same.";
```

Note that the function strcmp works differently than you might guess. The comparison is true if the strings do not match. The function strcmp compares the characters in the C-string arguments a character at a time. If at any point the numeric encoding of the character from cString1 is less than the numeric encoding of the corresponding character from cString2, the testing stops at that point and a negative number is returned. If the character from cString1 is greater than the

(continued)

testing
C-strings
for equality

PITFALL: (continued)

character from cString2, a positive number is returned. (Some implementations of strcmp return the difference of the character encoding, but you should not depend on that.) If the C-strings are the same, a 0 is returned. The ordering relationship used for comparing characters is called **lexicographic order**. The important point to note is that if both strings are in all uppercase or all lowercase, then lexicographic order is just alphabetic order.

We see that strcmp returns a negative value, a positive value, or zero depending on whether the C-strings compare lexicographically as lesser, greater, or equal. If you use strcmp as a Boolean expression in an if or a looping statement to test C-strings for equality, then the nonzero value will be converted to true if the strings are different, and the zero will be converted to false. Be sure that you remember this inverted logic in your testing for C-string equality.

C++ compilers that are compliant with the standard have a safer version of strcmp that has a third argument that gives the maximum number of characters to compare.

The functions strcpy and strcmp are in the library with the header file <cstring>, so to use them you must insert the following near the top of the file:

```
#include <cstring>
```

The definitions of strcpy and strcmp are placed in the global namespace, not in the std namespace, and so no using directive is required. ■

Other Functions in <cstring>

Display 9.1 contains a few of the most commonly used functions from the library with the header file <cstring>. To use them, insert the following near the top of the file:

```
#include <cstring>
```

Note that <cstring> places all these definitions in the global namespace, not in the std namespace, and so no using statement is required.

We have already discussed strcpy and strcmp. The function strlen is easy to understand and use. For example, strlen("dobedo") returns 6 because there are six characters in "dobedo".

The function strcat is used to concatenate two C-strings; that is, to form a longer string by placing the two shorter C-strings end-to-end. The first argument must be a C-string variable. The second argument can be anything that evaluates to a C-string value, such as a quoted string. The result is placed in the C-string variable that is the first argument. For example, consider the following:

```
char stringVar[20] = "The rain";
strcat(stringVar, "in Spain");
```

This code will change the value of stringVar to "The rainin Spain". As this example illustrates, you need to be careful to account for blanks when concatenating

C-strings. If you look at the table in Display 9.1 you will see that there is a safer, three-argument version of the function strcat that is available in many, but not all, versions of C++.

C-String Arguments and Parameters

A C-string variable is an array, so a C-string parameter to a function is simply an array parameter.

As with any array parameter, whenever a function changes the value of a C-string parameter, it is safest to include an additional int parameter given the declared size of the C-string variable.

On the other hand, if a function only uses the value in a C-string argument but does not change that value, then there is no need to include another parameter to give either the declared size of the C-string variable or the amount of the C-string variable array that is filled. The null character, '\0', can be used to detect the end of the C-string value that is stored in the C-string variable.

Display 9.1   Some Predefined C-String Functions in `<cstring>` (part 1 of 2)

FUNCTION	DESCRIPTION	CAUTIONS
strcpy (Target_ String_Var, Src_String)	Copies the C-string value Src_ String into the C-string variable Target_String_Var.	Does not check to make sure Target_String_Var is large enough to hold the value Src_ String.
strncpy (Target_ String_Var, Src_String, Limit)	The same as the two-argument strcpy except that at most Limit characters are copied.	If Limit is chosen carefully, this is safer than the two-argument version of strcpy. Not implemented in all versions of C++.
strcat (Target_ String_Var, Src_String)	Concatenates the C-string value Src_String onto the end of the C-string in the C-string variable Target_String_Var.	Does not check to see that Target_String_Var is large enough to hold the result of the concatenation.
strncat (Target_ String_Var, Src_String, Limit)	The same as the two-argument strcat except that at most Limit characters are appended.	If Limit is chosen carefully, this is safer than the two-argument version of strcat. Not implemented in all versions of C++.
strlen (Src_ String)	Returns an integer equal to the length of Src_String. (The null character, '\0', is not counted in the length.)	

(continued)

Display 9.1 Some Predefined C-String Functions in `<cstring>` (part 2 of 2)

FUNCTION	DESCRIPTION	CAUTIONS
`strcmp` (`String_1,` `String_2`)	Returns 0 if `String_1` and `String_2` are the same. Returns a value < 0 if `String_1` is less than `String_2`. Returns a value > 0 if `String_1` is greater than `String_2` (that is, returns a nonzero value if `String_1` and `String_2` are different). The order is lexicographic.	If `String_1` equals `String_2`, this function returns 0, which converts to `false`. Note that this is the reverse of what you might expect it to return when the strings are equal.

`strncmp`
(`String_1,`
`String_2,`
`Limit`)
	The same as the two-argument `strcat` except that at most `Limit` characters are compared.	If `Limit` is chosen carefully, this is safer than the two-argument version of `strcmp`. Not implemented in all versions of C++.

EXAMPLE: Command-Line Arguments

So far, we have not specified any parameters for the `main` function. However, it is possible to specify input parameters for `main`. The input parameters match up with arguments given to the program when it is invoked from a command line. For example, on a UNIX machine the command

        ls /home

invokes the `ls` program with the command-line argument of `/home` to list the contents of the `/home` directory. To access the command-line arguments input to a C++ program, use the following header for `main`:

        int main(int argc, char *argv[])

The `argc` parameter is an integer that specifies how many arguments are given to the program. The name of the program counts, so `argc` will be at least 1.

The `argv` parameter is an array of C-strings. `argv[0]` holds the name of the program. `argv[1]` holds the name of the first parameter, `argv[2]` holds the name of the second parameter, and so on up to `argv[argc-1]`.

For example, if the program is named `getPalindromes` and is invoked from the command line as

        getPalindromes string1 string2

then inside main, `argc` = 3, `argv[0]` = "getPalindromes", `argv[1]` = "string1", and `argv[2]` = "string2".

EXAMPLE: (continued)

If your program intends to use the contents of argv, then it should verify that arguments were actually input by ensuring that argc is appropriately set. Otherwise, your program may produce incorrect results when accessing argv.

Self-Test Exercises

1. Which of the following declarations are equivalent?

```
char stringVar[10] = "Hello";
char stringVar[10] = {'H', 'e', 'l', 'l', 'o', '\0'};
char stringVar[10] = {'H', 'e', 'l', 'l', 'o'};
char stringVar[6] = "Hello";
char stringVar[] = "Hello";
```

2. What C-string will be stored in singingstring after the following code is run?

```
char singingString[20] = "DoBeDo";
strcat(singingString, " to you");
```

Assume that the code is embedded in a complete and correct program and that an include directive for <cstring> is in the program file.

3. What (if anything) is wrong with the following code?

```
char stringVar[] = "Hello";
strcat(stringVar, " and Good-bye.");
cout << stringVar;
```

Assume that the code is embedded in a complete program and that an include directive for <cstring> is in the program file.

4. Suppose the function strlen (which returns the length of its string argument) was not already defined for you. Give a function definition for strlen. Note that strlen has only one argument, which is a C-string. Do not add additional arguments; they are not needed.

5. What is the length (maximum) of a string that can be placed in the string variable declared by the following declaration? Explain.

```
char s[6];
```

6. How many characters are in each of the following character and string constants?

   a. '\n'
   b. "n"
   c. "Mary"
   d. "M"
   e. "Mary\n"

(continued)

Self-Test Exercises (continued)

7. Since character strings are just arrays of `char`, why does the text caution you not to confuse the following declaration and initialization?

   ```
   char shortString[] = "abc";
   char shortString[] = { 'a', 'b', 'c'};
   ```

8. Given the following declaration and initialization of the string variable, write a loop to assign 'X' to all positions of this string variable, keeping the length the same.

   ```
   char ourString[15] = "Hi there!";
   ```

9. Consider the following declaration of a C-string variable, where `SIZE` is a defined constant:

   ```
   char ourString[SIZE];
   ```

   The C-string variable `ourString` has been assigned in code not shown here. For correct C-string variables, the following loop reassigns all positions of `ourString` the value 'X', leaving the length the same as before. Assume this code fragment is embedded in an otherwise complete and correct program. Answer the questions following this code fragment.

   ```
   int index = 0;
   while (ourString[index] != '\0')
   {
       ourString[index] = 'X';
       index++;
   }
   ```

   a. Explain how this code can destroy the contents of memory beyond the end of the array.

   b. Modify this loop to protect against inadvertently changing memory beyond the end of the array.

10. Write code using a library function to copy the string constant "Hello" into the string variable declared next. Be sure to #include the necessary header file to get the declaration of the function you use.

    ```
    char aString[10];
    ```

11. What string will be output when this code is run? (Assume, as always, that this code is embedded in a complete, correct program.)

    ```
    char song[10] = "I did it";
    char franksSong[20];
    strcpy ( franksSong, song );
    strcat ( franksSong, "my way!");
    cout << franksSong << endl;
    ```

12. What is the problem (if any) with this code?

    ```
    char aString[20] = "How are you?";
    strcat (aString, "Good, I hope.");
    ```

C-String Input and Output

C-strings can be output using the insertion operator, <<. In fact, we have already been doing so with quoted strings. You can use a C-string variable in the same way. For example,

```
cout << news << "Wow.\n";
```

where news is a C-string variable.

It is possible to fill a C-string variable using the input operator >>, but there is one thing to keep in mind. As for all other types of data, all whitespace (blanks, tabs, and line breaks) are skipped when C-strings are read this way. Moreover, each reading of input stops at the next space or line break. For example, consider the following code:

```
char a[80], b[80];
cout << "Enter some input:\n";
cin >> a >> b;
cout << a << b << "END OF OUTPUT\n";
```

When embedded in a complete program, this code produces a dialogue like the following:

```
Enter some input:
Do be do to you!
DobeEND OF OUTPUT
```

The C-string variables a and b each receive only one word of the input: a receives the C-string value "Do" because the input character following Do is a blank; b receives "be" because the input character following be is a blank.

If you want your program to read an entire line of input, you can use the extraction operator, >>, to read the line one word at a time. This can be tedious and it still will not read the blanks in the line. There is an easier way to read an entire line of input and place the resulting C-string into a C-string variable: Just use the predefined member function getline, which is a member function of every input stream (such as cin or a file input stream). The function getline has two arguments. The first argument is a C-string variable to receive the input and the second is an integer that typically is the declared size of the C-string variable. The second argument specifies the maximum number of array elements in the C-string variable that getline will be allowed to fill with characters. For example, consider the following code:

```
getline
```

```
char a[80];
cout << "Enter some input:\n";
cin.getline(a, 80);
cout << a << "END OF OUTPUT\n";
```

When embedded in a complete program, this code produces a dialogue like the following:

```
Enter some input:
Do be do to you!
Do be do to you!END OF OUTPUT
```

With the function cin.getline, the entire line is read. The reading ends when the line ends, even though the resulting C-string may be shorter than the maximum number of characters specified by the second argument.

When getline is executed, the reading stops after the number of characters given by the second argument has been filled in the C-string array, even if the end of the line has not been reached. For example, consider the following code:

```
char shortString[5];
cout << "Enter some input:\n";
cin.getline(shortString, 5);
cout << shortString << "END OF OUTPUT\n";
```

When embedded in a complete program, this code produces a dialogue like the following:

```
Enter some input:
dobedowap
dobeEND OF OUTPUT
```

Notice that four, not five, characters are read into the C-string variable shortString, even though the second argument is 5. This is because the null character '\0' fills one array position. Every C-string is terminated with the null character when it is stored in a C-string variable, and this always consumes one array position.

The C-string input and output techniques we illustrated for cout and cin work the same way for input and output with files. The input stream cin can be replaced by an input stream that is connected to a file. The output stream cout can be replaced by an output stream that is connected to a file. (File I/O is discussed in Chapter 12.)

getline

The member function getline can be used to read a line of input and place the string of characters on that line into a C-string variable.

SYNTAX

```
cin.getline (String_Var, Max_Characters + 1);
```

One line of input is read from the stream Input_Stream and the resulting C-string is placed in String_Var. If the line is more than Max_Characters long, only the first Max_Characters on the line are read. (The +1 is needed because every C-string has the null character '\0' added to the end of the C-string and thus the string stored in String_Var is one longer than the number of characters read in.)

EXAMPLE

```
char oneLine[80];
cin.getline(oneLine, 80);
```

As you will see in Chapter 12, you can use an input stream connected to a text file in place of cin.

Self-Test Exercises

13. Consider the following code (and assume it is embedded in a complete and correct program and then run):

```
char a[80], b[80];
cout << "Enter some input:\n";
cin >> a >> b;
cout << a << '-' << b << "END OF OUTPUT\n";
```

If the dialogue begins as follows, what will be the next line of output?

```
Enter some input:
The
      time is now.
```

14. Consider the following code (and assume it is embedded in a complete and correct program and then run):

```
char myString[80];
cout << "Enter a line of input:\n";
cin.getline(myString, 6);
cout << myString << "<END OF OUTPUT";
```

If the dialogue begins as follows, what will be the next line of output?

```
Enter a line of input:
May the hair on your toes grow long and curly.
```

9.2 Character Manipulation Tools

They spell it Vinci and pronounce it Vinchy; foreigners always spell better than they pronounce.

MARK TWAIN, *The Innocents Abroad*

Any form of string is ultimately composed of individual characters. When your program outputs the number 10, it is really the two characters '1' and '0' that are output. Similarly, when the user wants to type in the number 10, he or she types in the character '1' followed by the character '0'. Whether the computer interprets this "10" as two characters or as the number 10 depends on how your program is written. But, however your program is written, the computer hardware is always reading the

Character I/O

All data is input and output as character data. When your program outputs the number 10, it is really the two characters '1' and '0' that are output. Similarly, when the user wants to type in the number 10, he or she types in the character '1' followed by the character '0'. Whether the computer interprets this "10" as two characters or as the number 10 depends on how your program is written. But, however your program is written, the computer hardware is always reading the characters '1' and '0', not the number 10. This conversion between characters and numbers is usually done automatically so that you need not think about such details; however, sometimes all this automatic help gets in the way. Therefore, C++ provides some low-level facilities for input and output of character data. These low-level facilities include no automatic conversions. This allows you to bypass the automatic facilities and do input/output in absolutely any way you want. You could even write input and output functions that can read and write int values in Roman numeral notation, if you wanted to be so perverse.

The Member Functions get and put

The function get allows your program to read in one character of input and store it in a variable of type char. Every input stream, whether it is an input-file stream or the stream cin, has get as a member function. We will describe get here as a member function of the object cin. (When we discuss file I/O in Chapter 12 we will see that it behaves exactly the same for input-file streams as it does for cin.)

Before now, we have used cin with the extraction operator, >>, in order to read a character of input (or any other input, for that matter). When you use the extraction operator >>, some things are done for you automatically, such as skipping over whitespace. But sometimes you do not want to skip over whitespace. The member function cin.get reads the next input character no matter whether the character is whitespace or not.

The member function get takes one argument, which should be a variable of type char. That argument receives the input character that is read from the input stream. For example, the following will read in the next input character from the keyboard and store it in the variable nextSymbol:

```
char nextSymbol;
cin.get(nextSymbol);
```

It is important to note that your program can read any character in this way. If the next input character is a blank, this code will read the blank character. If the next character is the newline character '\n' (that is, if the program has just reached the end of an input line), then the previous call to cin.get will set the value of nextSymbol equal to '\n'. For example, suppose your program contains the following code,

```
char c1, c2, c3;
cin.get(c1);
cin.get(c2);
cin.get(c3);
```

and suppose you type in the following two lines of input to be read by this code:

AB
CD

The value of c1 is set to 'A', the value of c2 is set to 'B', and the value of c3 is set to '\n'. The variable c3 is not set equal to 'C'.

One thing you can do with the member function get is to have your program detect the end of a line. The following loop will read a line of input and stop after passing the newline character '\n'. Any subsequent input will be read from the beginning of the next line. For this first example, we have simply echoed the input, but the same technique would allow you to do whatever you want with the input.

```
cout << "Enter a line of input and I will echo it:\n";
char symbol;
do
{
    cin.get(symbol);
    cout << symbol;
} while (symbol != '\n');
cout << "That's all for this demonstration.\n";
```

This loop will read any line of input and echo it exactly, including blanks. The following is a sample dialogue produced by this code:

```
Enter a line of input and I will echo it:
Do Be Do 1 2   34
Do Be Do 1 2   34
That's all for this demonstration.
```

Notice that the newline character '\n' is both read and output. Since '\n' is output, the string that begins with the word "That's" is on a new line.

'\n' and "\n"

'\n' and "\n" sometimes seem like the same thing. In a cout statement, they produce the same effect, but they cannot be used interchangeably in all situations. '\n' is a value of type char and can be stored in a variable of type char. On the other hand, "\n" is a string that happens to be made up of exactly one character. Thus, "\n" is not of type char and cannot be stored in a variable of type char.

The member function put is analogous to the member function get except that it is used for output rather than input. The function put allows your program to output one character. The member function cout.put takes one argument, which should be an expression of type char, such as a constant or a variable of type char. The value of the argument is output to the screen when the function is called. For example, the following will output the letter 'a' to the screen:

```
cout.put("a");
```

The function cout.put does not allow you to do anything you could not do with the insertion operator <<, but we include it for completeness. (When we discuss file I/O in Chapter 12, we will see that put can be used with an output stream connected to a text file and is not restricted to being used only with cout.)

The Member Function get

The function get can be used to read one character of input. Unlike the extraction operator, >>, get reads the next input character, no matter what that character is. In particular, get will read a blank or the newline character, '\n', if either of these are the next input character. The function get takes one argument, which should be a variable of type char. When get is called, the next input character is read and the argument variable has its value set equal to this input character.

EXAMPLE

```
char nextSymbol;
cin.get(nextSymbol);
```

As we will see in Chapter 12, if you wish to use get to read from a file, you use an input-file stream in place of the stream cin.

If your program uses cin.get or cout.put, then just as with other uses of cin and cout, your program should include one of the following (or something similar):

```
#include <iostream>
using namespace std;
```

or

```
#include <iostream>
using std::cin;
using std::cout;
```

EXAMPLE: Checking Input Using a Newline Function

The function getInt in Display 9.2 asks the user if the input is correct and asks for a new value if the user says the input is incorrect. The program in Display 9.2 is just a driver program to test the function getInt, but the function, or one very similar to it, can be used in just about any kind of program that takes its input from the keyboard.

Notice the call to the function newLine( ). The function newLine reads all the characters on the remainder of the current line but does nothing with them. This amounts to discarding the remainder of the current line. Thus, if the user types in No, then the program reads the first letter, which is N, and then calls the function newLine, which discards the rest of the input line. This means that if the user types 75 on the next input line, as shown in the sample dialogue, the program will read the number 75 and will not attempt to read the letter o in the word No. If the program did not include a call to the function newLine, then the next item read would be the o in the line containing No instead of the number 75 on the following line.

Display 9.2 Checking Input (part 1 of 2)

```
1    //Program to demonstrate the functions newLine and getInput
2    #include <iostream>
3    using namespace std;

4    void newLine( );
5    //Discards all the input remaining on the current input line.
6    //Also discards the '\n' at the end of the line.

7    void getInt(int& number);
8    //Sets the variable number to a
9    //value that the user approves of.

10   int main( )
11   {
12       int n;

13       getInt(n);
14       cout << "Final value read in = " << n << endl
15            << "End of demonstration.\n";

16       return 0;
17   }

18   //Uses iostream:
19   void newLine( )
20   {
21       char symbol;
22       do
23       {
24           cin.get(symbol);
25       } while (symbol != '\n');

26   }
27   //Uses iostream:
28   void getInt(int& number)
29   {
30       char ans;
31       do
32       {
33           cout << "Enter input number: ";
34           cin >> number;
35           cout << "You entered " << number
36                << " Is that correct? (yes/no): ";
37           cin >> ans;
38           newLine( );
39       } while ((ans == 'N') || (ans == 'n'));
40   }
```

(continued)

Display 9.2 Checking Input (part 2 of 2)

Sample Dialogue

```
Enter input number: 57
You entered 57 Is that correct? (yes/no): No No No!
Enter input number: 75
You entered 75 Is that correct? (yes/no): yes
Final value read in = 75
End of demonstration.
```

PITFALL: Unexpected '\n' in Input

When using the member function get you must account for every character of input, even the characters you do not think of as being symbols, such as blanks and the newline character, '\n'. A common problem when using get is forgetting to dispose of the '\n' that ends every input line. If there is a newline character in the input stream that is not read (and usually discarded), then when your program next expects to read a "real" symbol using the member function get, it will instead read the character '\n'. To clear the input stream of any leftover '\n', you can use the function newline, which we defined in Display 9.2 (or you can use the function ignore, which we discuss in the next subsection). Let us look at a concrete example.

It is legal to mix the different forms of cin. For example, the following is legal:

```
cout << "Enter a number:\n";
int number;
cin >> number;
cout << "Now enter a letter:\n";
char symbol;
cin.get(symbol);
```

However, this can produce problems, as illustrated by the following dialogue:

```
Enter a number:
21
Now enter a letter:
A
```

With this dialogue, the value of number will be 21 as you expect. However, if you expect the value of the variable symbol to be 'A', you will be disappointed. The value given to symbol is '\n'. After reading the number 21, the next character in the input stream is the newline character, '\n', and so that is read next. Remember, get does not skip over line breaks and spaces. (In fact, depending on what is in the rest of the program, you may not even get a chance to type in the A. Once the variable symbol is filled with the character '\n', the program proceeds to whatever statement is next in the program. If the next statement sends output to the screen, the screen will be filled with output before you get a chance to type in the A.)

PITFALL: (continued)

The following rewriting of the previous code will cause the previous dialogue to fill the variable number with 21 and fill the variable symbol with `'A'`:

```
cout << "Enter a number:\n";
int number;
cin >> number;
cout << "Now enter a letter:\n";
char symbol;
cin >> symbol;
```

Alternatively, you can use the function newLine, defined in Display 9.2, as follows:

```
cout << "Enter a number:\n";
int number;
cin >> number;
newLine( );
cout << "Now enter a letter:\n";
char symbol;
cin.get(symbol);
```

As this second rewrite indicates, you can mix the two forms of cin and have your program work correctly, but it does require some extra care.

As a third alternative, you could use the function ignore, which we discuss in the next subsection. ■

The putback, peek, and ignore Member Functions

Sometimes your program needs to know the next character in the input stream. However, after reading the next character, it might turn out that you do not want to process that character and so would like to "put it back." For example, if you want your program to read up to but not include the first blank it encounters, then your program must read that first blank in order to know when to stop reading—but then that blank is no longer in the input stream. Some other part of your program might need to read and process this blank. One way to deal with this situation is to use the member function cin.putback. The function cin.putback takes one argument of type char and places the value of that argument back in the input stream so that it will be the next character to be read. The argument can be any expression that evaluates to a value of type char. The character that is put back into the input stream with the member function putback need not be the last character read; it can be any character you wish.

The peek member function does what you might expect from its name. cin.peek( ) returns the next character to be read by cin, but it does not use up that character; the next read starts with that character. In other words, the peek function peeks ahead to tell your program what the next character to be read will be.

putback

peek

ignore

If you want to skip over input up to some designated character, such as the newline character '\n', you can use the ignore member function. For example, the following will skip over all input characters up to and including the newline character, '\n':

```
cin.ignore(1000, '\n');
```

The 1000 is the maximum number of characters to ignore. If the delimiter, in this case '\n', has not been found after 1000 characters, then no more characters are ignored. Of course, a different int argument can be used in place of 1000 and a different character argument can be used in place of '\n'.

As we will see in Chapter 12, the member functions putback, peek, and ignore can be used with cin replaced by a file input stream object for text file input.

Self-Test Exercises

15. Consider the following code (and assume that it is embedded in a complete and correct program and then run):

```
char c1, c2, c3, c4;
cout << "Enter a line of input:\n";
cin.get(c1);
cin.get(c2);
cin.get(c3);
cin.get(c4);
cout << c1 << c2 << c3 << c4 << "END OF OUTPUT";
```

If the dialogue begins as follows, what will be the next line of ouput?

```
Enter a line of input:
a b c d e f g
```

16. Consider the following code (and assume that it is embedded in a complete and correct program and then run):

```
char next;
int count = 0;
cout << "Enter a line of input:\n";
cin.get(next);
while (next != '\n')
{
    if ((count % 2) == 0)          ← True if count is even
        cout << next;
    count++;
    cin.get(next);
}
```

If the dialogue begins as follows, what will be the next line of ouput?

```
Enter a line of input:
abcdef gh
```

Self-Test Exercises (continued)

17. Suppose that the program described in Self-Test Exercise 16 is run and the dialogue begins as follows (instead of beginning as shown in Self-Test Exercise 16). What will be the next line of output?

```
Enter a line of input:
0 1 2 3 4 5 6 7 8 9 10 11
```

18. Consider the following code (and assume that it is embedded in a complete and correct program and then run):

```
char next;
int count = 0;
cout << "Enter a line of input:\n";
cin >> next;
while (next != '\n')
{
    if ((count % 2) == 0)
        cout << next;

    count++;
    cin >> next;
}
```

If the dialogue begins as follows, what will be the next line of output?

```
Enter a line of input:
0 1 2 3 4 5 6 7 8 9 10 11
```

Character-Manipulating Functions

In text processing you often want to convert lowercase letters to uppercase or vice versa. The predefined function toupper can be used to convert a lowercase letter to an uppercase letter. For example, toupper('a') returns 'A'. If the argument to the function toupper is anything other than a lowercase letter, toupper simply returns the argument unchanged. So toupper('A') returns 'A', and toupper('?') returns '?'. The function tolower is similar except that it converts an uppercase letter to its lowercase version.

The functions toupper and tolower are in the library with the header file <cctype>, so any program that uses these functions, or any other functions in this library, must contain the following:

```
#include <cctype>
```

Note that <cctype> places all these definitions in the global namespace, and so no using directive is required. Display 9.3 contains descriptions of some of the most commonly used functions in the library <cctype>.

The function isspace returns true if its argument is a whitespace character.
whitespace **Whitespace** characters are all the characters that are displayed as blank space on the screen, including the blank character, the tab character, and the newline character, '\n'. If the argument to isspace is not a whitespace character, then isspace returns false. Thus, isspace(' ') returns true and isspace('a') returns false.

Display 9.3   Some Functions in `<cctype>`   (part 1 of 2)

FUNCTION	DESCRIPTION	EXAMPLE

toupper (Char_Exp)	Returns the uppercase version of Char_Exp (as a value of type int).	`char c = toupper('a');`
		`cout << c;`
		Outputs: A

tolower (Char_Exp)	Returns the lowercase version of Char_Exp (as a value of type int).	`char c = tolower('A');`
		`cout << c;`
		Outputs: a

isupper (Char_Exp)	Returns true provided Char_Exp is an uppercase letter; otherwise, returns false.	`if (isupper(c))`
		`    cout << "Is uppercase.";`
		`else`
		`    cout << "Is not uppercase.";`

islower (Char_Exp)	Returns true provided Char_Exp is a lowercase letter; otherwise, returns false.	`char c = 'a';`
		`if (islower(c))`
		`    cout << c << " is lowercase.";`
		Outputs: a is lowercase.

isalpha (Char_Exp)	Returns true provided Char_Exp is a letter of the alphabet; otherwise, returns false.	`if (isalpha(c))`
		`    cout << "Is a letter.";`
		`else`
		`    cout << "Is not a letter.";`
		Outputs: Is not a letter.

isdigit (Char_Exp)	Returns true provided Char_Exp is one of the digits '0' through '9'; otherwise, returns false.	`if (isdigit('3'))`
		`    cout << "It's a digit.";`
		`else`
		`    cout << "It's not a digit.";`
		Outputs: It's a digit.

isalnum (Char_Exp)	Returns true provided Char_Exp is either a letter or a digit; otherwise, returns false.	`if (isalnum('3') && isalnum('a'))`
		`    cout << "Both alphanumeric.";`
		`else`
		`    cout << "One or more are not.";`
		Outputs: Both alphanumeric.

isspace (Char_Exp)	Returns true provided Char_Exp is a whitespace character, such as the blank or newline character; otherwise, returns false.	`//Skips over one "word" and sets c`
		`//equal to the first whitespace`
		`//character after the "word":`
		`do`
		`{`
		`    cin.get(c);`
		`}`
		`while (! isspace(c));`

ispunct (Char_Exp)	Returns true provided Char_Exp is a printing character other than whitespace, a digit, or a letter; otherwise, returns false.	`if (ispunct('?'))`
		`    cout << "Is punctuation.";`
		`else`
		`    cout << "Not punctuation.";`

Display 9.3   Some Functions in `<cctype>`   (part 2 of 2)

FUNCTION	DESCRIPTION	EXAMPLE
`isprint` (`Char_Exp`)	Returns true provided `Char_Exp` is a printing character; otherwise, returns false.	
`isgraph` (`Char_Exp`)	Returns true provided `Char_Exp` is a printing character other than whitespace; otherwise, returns false.	
`isctrl` (`Char_Exp`)	Returns true provided `Char_Exp` is a control character; otherwise, returns false.	

For example, the following will read a sentence terminated with a period and echo the string with all whitespace characters replaced with the symbol '-':

```
char next;
do
{
    cin.get(next);
    if (isspace(next))
        cout << '-';
    else
        cout << next;
} while (next != '.');
```

For example, if the previous code is given the following input,

Ahh do be do.

it will produce the following output:

Ahh--do-be-do.

PITFALL: `toupper` and `tolower` Return `int` Values

In many ways C++ considers characters to be whole numbers, similar to the numbers of type `int`. Each character is assigned a number. When the character is stored in a variable of type `char`, it is this number that is placed in the computer's memory. In C++ you can use a value of type `char` as a number, for example, by placing it in a variable of type `int`. You can also store a number of type `int` in a variable of type

(continued)

PITFALL: (continued)

char (provided the number is not too large). Thus, the type char can be used as the type for characters or as a type for small whole numbers. Usually you need not be concerned with this detail and can simply think of values of type char as being characters without worrying about their use as numbers. However, when using some of the functions in <cctype>, this detail can be important. The functions toupper and tolower actually return values of type int rather than values of type char; that is, they return the number corresponding to the character we think of them as returning, rather than the character itself. Thus, the following will not output the letter 'A' but will instead output the number that is assigned to 'A':

```
cout << toupper('A');
```

To get the computer to treat the value returned by toupper or tolower as a value of type char (as opposed to a value of type int), you need to indicate that you want a value of type char. One way to do this is to place the value returned in a variable of type char. The following will output the character 'A', which is usually what we want.

```
char c = toupper('a');
cout << c;
```

Another way to get the computer to treat the value returned by toupper or tolower as a value of type char is to use a type cast, as follows:

```
cout << static_cast<char>(toupper('a'));
```

∎

Self-Test Exercises

19. Consider the following code (and assume that it is embedded in a complete and correct program and then run):

```
cout << "Enter a line of input:\n";
char next;
do
{
    cin.get(next);
    cout << next;
} while ( (!isdigit(next)) && (next != '\n') );
cout << "<END OF OUTPUT>";
```

If the dialogue begins as follows, what will be the next line of output?

```
Enter a line of input:
I'll see you at 10:30 AM.
```

20. Write some C++ code that will read a line of text and echo the line with all uppercase letters deleted.

21. Rewrite the definition of the newline function in Display 9.2 but this time use the ignore member function.

9.3 The Standard Class string

*I try to catch every sentence, every word you and I say, and quickly lock all
these sentences and words away in my literary storehouse because they might
come in handy.*

ANTON CHEKHOV, *The Seagull*

Section 9.1 introduced C-strings. These C-strings are simply arrays of characters
terminated with the null character, '\0'. To manipulate these C-strings you need to
worry about all the details of handling arrays. For example, when you want to add
characters to a C-string and there is not enough room in the array, you must create
another array to hold this longer string of characters. In short, C-strings require that
you the programmer keep track of all the low-level details of how the C-strings are
stored in memory. This is a lot of extra work and a source of programmer errors. The
ANSI/ISO standard for C++ specified that C++ must now also have a class string that
allows the programmer to treat strings as a basic data type without needing to worry
about implementation details. This section introduces you to this string type.

Introduction to the Standard Class string

The class string is defined in the library whose name is also <string>, and the
definitions are placed in the std namespace. To use the class string, therefore, your
code must contain the following (or something more or less equivalent):

```
#include <string>
using namespace std;
```

The class string allows you to treat string values and string expressions very much
like values of a simple type. You can use the = operator to assign a value to a string
variable, and you can use the + sign to concatenate two strings. For example, suppose
s1, s2, and s3 are objects of type string and both s1 and s2 have string values. Then
s3 can be set equal to the concatenation of the string value in s1 followed by the
string value in s2 as follows:

```
s3 = s1 + s2;
```

There is no danger of s3 being too small for its new string value. If the sum of the
lengths of s1 and s2 exceeds the capacity of s3, then more space is automatically
allocated for s3.

As we noted earlier in this chapter, quoted strings are really C-strings and so they are
not literally of type string. However, C++ provides automatic type casting of quoted
strings to values of type string. Thus, you can use quoted strings as if they were literal
values of type string, and we (and most others) will often refer to quoted strings as if
they were values of type string. For example,

```
s3 = "Hello Mom!";
```

sets the value of the string variable s3 to a string object with the same characters as
in the C-string "Hello Mom!".

**+ does
concatenation**

constructors

The class string has a default constructor that initializes a string object to the empty string. The class string also has a second constructor that takes one argument that is a standard C-string and so can be a quoted string. This second constructor initializes the string object to a value that represents the same string as its C-string argument. For example,

```
string phrase;
string noun("ants");
```

The first line declares the string variable phrase and initializes it to the empty string. The second line declares the noun to be of type string and initializes it to a string value equivalent to the C-string "ants". Most programmers when talking loosely would say that "noun is initialized to "ants", but there really is a type conversion here. The quoted string "ants" is a C-string, not a value of type string. The variable noun receives a string value that has the same characters as "ants" in the same order as "ants", but the string value is not terminated with the null character '\0'. In theory, at least, you do not need to know or care whether the string value of noun is even stored in an array, as opposed to some other data structure.

There is an alternate notation for declaring a string variable and invoking the default constructor. The following two lines are exactly equivalent:

```
string noun("ants");
string noun = "ants";
```

These basic details about the class string are illustrated in Display 9.4. Note that, as illustrated there, you can output string values using the operator <<.

Display 9.4   Program Using the Class string

```
1    //Demonstrates the standard class string.
2    #include <iostream>
3    #include <string>
4    using namespace std;
5
6    int main( )
7    {
8        string phrase;
9        string adjective("fried"), noun("ants");
10       string wish = "Bon appetite!";
11
12       phrase = "I love" + adjective + " " + noun + "!";
13
14       cout << phrase << endl
15            << wish << endl;
16
17       return 0;
18   }
```

Initialized to the empty string

Two equivalent ways of initializing a string variable

Sample Dialogue

```
I love fried ants!
Bon appetite!
```

converting C-string constants to the type string

Consider the following line from Display 9.4:

```
phrase = "I love " + adjective + " " + noun + "!";
```

C++ must do a lot of work to allow you to concatenate strings in this simple and natural fashion. The string constant "I love " is not an object of type string. A string constant like "I love " is stored as a C-string (in other words, as a null-terminated array of characters). When C++ sees "I love " as an argument to +, it finds the definition (or overloading) of + that applies to a value such as "I love ". There are overloadings of the + operator that have a C-string on the left and a string on the right, as well as the reverse of this positioning. There is even a version that has a C-string on both sides of the + and produces a string object as the value returned. Of course, there is also the overloading you expect, with the type string for both operands.

C++ did not really need to provide all those overloading cases for +. If these overloadings were not provided, C++ would look for a constructor that can perform a type conversion to convert the C-string "I love " to a value for which + did apply. In this case, the constructor with the one C-string parameter would perform just such a conversion. However, the extra overloadings are presumably more efficient.

The class string is often thought of as a modern replacement for C-strings. However, in C++ you cannot easily avoid also using C-strings when you program with the class string.

The Class string

The class string can be used to represent values that are strings of characters. The class string provides more versatile string representation than the C-strings discussed in Section 9.1.

The class string is defined in the library that is also named <string>, and its definition is placed in the std namespace. Programs that use the class string should therefore contain one of the following (or something more or less equivalent):

```
#include <string>
using namespace std;
```

or

```
#include <string>
using std::string;
```

The class string has a default constructor that initializes the string object to the empty string, and a constructor that takes a C-string as arguments and initializes the string object to a value that represents the string given as the argument. For example,

```
string s1, s2("Hello");
```

I/O with the Class `string`

You can use the insertion operator `>>` and `cout` to output `string` objects just as you do for data of other types. This is illustrated in Display 9.4. Input with the class `string` is a bit more subtle.

The extraction operator, `>>`, and `cin` work the same for `string` objects as for other data, but remember that the extraction operator ignores initial whitespace and stops reading when it encounters more whitespace. This is as true for strings as it is for other data. For example, consider the following code:

```
string s1, s2;
cin >> s1;
cin >> s2;
```

If the user types in

```
May the hair on your toes grow long and curly!
```

then `s1` will receive the value "May" with any leading (or trailing) whitespace deleted. The variable `s2` receives the string "the". Using the extraction operator, `>>`, and `cin`, you can only read in words; you cannot read in a line or other string that contains a blank. Sometimes this is exactly what you want, but sometimes it is not at all what you want.

If you want your program to read an entire line of input into a variable of type `string`, you can use the function `getline`. The syntax for using `getline` with

getline

`string` objects is a bit different from what we described for C-strings in Section 9.1. You do not use `cin.getline`; instead, you make `cin` the first argument to `getline`. [1] (So, this version of `getline` is not a member function.)

When embedded in a complete program, this code produces a dialogue like the following:

```
string line;
cout << "Enter a line of input:\n";
getline(cin, line);
cout << line << "END OF OUTPUT\n";
```

```
Enter some input:
Do be do to you!
Do be do to you!END OF OUTPUT
```

If there were leading or trailing blanks on the line, they too would be part of the `string` value read by `getline`. This version of `getline` is in the library `<string>`. (As we will see in Chapter 12, you can use a `stream` object connected to a text file in place of `cin` to do input from a file using `getline`.)

---

[1] This is a bit ironic, since the class `string` was designed using more modern object-oriented techniques, and the notation it uses for `getline` is the old fashioned, less object-oriented notation. This is an accident of history. This `getline` function was defined after the `<iostream>` library was already in use, so the designers had little choice but to make this `getline` a standalone function.

You cannot use cin and >> to read in a blank character. If you want to read one character at a time, you can use cin.get, which we discussed in Section 9.2. The function cin.get reads values of type char, not of type string, but it can be helpful when handling string input. Display 9.5 contains a program that illustrates both getline and cin.get used for string input. The significance of the function newline is explained in the Pitfall entitled "Mixing cin >> variable; and getline."

I/O with string Objects

You can use the insertion operator << with cout to output string objects. You can input a string with the extraction operator >> and cin. When using >> for input, the code reads in a string delimited with whitespace. You can use the function getline to input an entire line of text into a string object.

EXAMPLES

```
string greeting("Hello"), response, nextLine;
cout << greeting;
cin >> response;
getline(cin, nextLine);
```

Display 9.5   Program Using the Class string   (part 1 of 2)

```
1   //Demonstrates getline and cin.get.
2   #include <iostream>
3   #include <string>
4   using namespace std;

5   void newLine( );
6   int main( )
7   {
8       string firstName, lastName, recordName;
9       string motto = "Your records are our records.";
10      cout << "Enter your first and last name:\n";
11      cin >> firstName >> lastName;
12      newLine( );

13      recordName = lastName + ", " + firstName;
14      cout << "Your name in our records is: ";
15      cout << recordName << endl;
16      cout << "Our motto is\n"
17           << motto << endl;
18      cout << "Please suggest a better (one line) motto:\n";
19      getline(cin, motto);
20      cout << "Our new motto will be:\n";
21      cout << motto << endl;
```

(continued)

Display 9.5   Program Using the Class string (part 2 of 2)

```
22      return 0;
23  }
24  //Uses iostream:
25  void newLine( )
26  {
27      char nextChar;
28      do
29      {
30          cin.get(nextChar);
31      } while (nextChar != '\n');
32  }
```

Sample Dialogue

```
Enter your first and last names:
    B'Elanna Torres
Your name in our records is: Torres, B'Elanna
Our motto is
Your records are our records.
Please suggest a better (one-line) motto:
Our records go where no records dared to go before.
Our new motto will be:
Our records go where no records dared to go before.
```

Self-Test Exercises

22. Consider the following code (and assume that it is embedded in a complete and correct program and then run):

```
string s1, s2;
cout << "Enter a line of input:\n";
cin >> s1 >> s2;
cout << s1 << "*" << s2 << "<END OF OUTPUT";
```

If the dialogue begins as follows, what will be the next line of output?

```
Enter a line of input:
A string is a joy forever!
```

23. Consider the following code (and assume that it is embedded in a complete and correct program and then run):

```
string s;
cout << "Enter a line of input:\n";
getline(cin, s);
cout << s << "<END OF OUTPUT";
```

Self-Test Exercises (continued)

If the dialogue begins as follows, what will be the next next line of output?

```
Enter a line of input:
A string is a joy forever!
```

TIP: More Versions of getline

So far, we have described the following way of using getline:

```
string line;
cout << "Enter a line of input:\n";
getline(cin, line);
```

This version stops reading when it encounters the end-of-line marker, '\n'. There is a version that allows you to specify a different character to use as a stopping signal. For example, the following will stop when the first question mark is encountered:

```
string line;
cout << "Enter some input:\n";
getline(cin, line, '?');
```

It makes sense to use getline as if it were a void function, but it actually returns a reference to its first argument, which is cin in the previous code. Thus, the following will read in a line of text into s1 and a string of non-whitespace characters into s2:

```
string s1, s2;
getline(cin, s1) >> s2;
```

The invocation getline(cin, s1) returns a reference to cin, so that after the invocation of getline, the next thing to happen is equivalent to

```
cin >> s2;
```

This kind of use of getline seems to have been designed for use in a C++ quiz show rather than to meet any actual programming need, but it can come in handy sometimes. ■

PITFALL: Mixing cin >> variable; and getline

Take care in mixing input using cin >> variable; with input using getline. For example, consider the following code:

```
int n;
string line;
cin >> n;
getline(cin, line);
```

VideoNote
Using cin and getline with the string class

(continued)

PITFALL: (continued)

When this code reads the following input, you might expect the value of `n` to be set to `42` and the value of `line` to be set to a string value representing `"Hello hitchhiker."`:

```
42
Hello hitchhiker.
```

However, while `n` is indeed set to the value of `42`, `line` is set equal to the empty string. What happened?

Using `cin >> n` skips leading whitespace on the input but leaves the rest of the line, in this case just `'\n'`, for the next input. A statement like

```
cin >> n;
```

always leaves something on the line for a following `getline` to read (even if it is just the `'\n'`). In this case, the `getline` sees the `'\n'` and stops reading, so `getline` reads an empty string. If you find your program appearing to mysteriously ignore input data, see if you have mixed these two kinds of input. You may need to use either the `newline` function from Display 9.5 or the function `ignore` from the library `iostream`. For example,

```
cin.ignore(1000, '\n');
```

With these arguments, a call to the `ignore` member function will read and discard the entire rest of the line up to and including the `'\n'` (or until it discards `1000` characters if it does not find the end of the line after `1000` characters).

Other baffling problems can appear with programs that use `cin` with both `>>` and `getline`. Moreover, these problems can come and go as you move from one C++ compiler to another. When all else fails, or if you want to be certain of portability, you can resort to character-by-character input using `cin.get`.

These problems can occur with any of the versions of `getline` that we discuss in this chapter. ■

getline for Objects of the Class string

The `getline` function for string objects has two versions:

```
istream& getline(istream& ins, string& strVar, char delimiter);
```

and

```
istream& getline(istream& ins, string& strVar);
```

The first version of this function reads characters from the `istream` object given as the first argument (always `cin` in this chapter), inserting the characters into the string variable `strVar` until an instance of the `delimiter` character is encountered. The `delimiter` character is removed from the input and discarded. The second version uses '\n' for the default value of delimiter; otherwise, it works the same.

These getline functions return their first argument (always cin in this chapter), but they are usually used as if they were void functions.

String Processing with the Class string

The class string allows you to perform the same operations that you can perform with the C-strings we discussed in Section 9.1 and more. (A lot more! There are well over 100 members and other functions associated with the standard string class.)

You can access the characters in a string object in the same way that you access array elements, so string objects have the advantages of arrays of characters plus a number of advantages that arrays do not have, such as automatically increasing their capacity.

If lastName is the name of a string object, then lastName[i] gives access to the ith character in the string represented by lastName. This use of array square brackets is illustrated in Display 9.6.

length Display 9.6 also illustrates the member function length. Every string object has a member function named length that takes no arguments and returns the length of the string represented by the string object. Thus, a string object not only can be used like an array, but the length member function makes it behave like a partially filled array that automatically keeps track of how many positions are occupied.

The array square brackets when used with an object of the class string do not check for illegal indexes. If you use an illegal index (that is, an index that is greater than or equal to the length of the string in the object), the results are unpredictable but are bound to be bad. You may just get strange behavior without any error message that tells you that the problem is an illegal index value. There is a member function named at that does check for an illegal index value. The member function named at behaves basically the same as the square brackets, except for two points:

Display 9.6 A string Object Can Behave Like an Array (part 1 of 2)

```
1   //Demonstrates using a string object as if it were an array.
2   #include <iostream>
3   #include <string>
4   using namespace std;

5   int main( )
6   {
7       string firstName, lastName;

8       cout << "Enter your first and last name:\n";
9       cin >> firstName >> lastName;

10      cout << "Your last name is spelled:\n";
11      int i;
```

(continued)

Display 9.6   A string Object Can Behave Like an Array (part 2 of 2)

```
12    for (i = 0; i < lastName.length( ); i++)
13    {
14        cout << lastName[i] << " ";
15        lastName[i] = '-';
16    }
17    cout << endl;
18    for (i = 0; i < lastName.length( ); i++)
19        cout << lastName[i] << " "; //Places a "-" under each letter.
20    cout << endl;

21    cout << "Good day " << firstName << endl;
22    return 0;
23    }
```

Sample Dialogue

```
Enter your first and last names:
John Crichton
Your last name is spelled:
C r i c h t o n
- - - - - - - -
Good day John
```

You use function notation with at, so instead of a[i], you use a.at(i), and the at member function checks to see if i evaluates to an illegal index. If the value of i in a.at(i) is an illegal index, you should get a runtime error message telling you what is wrong. In the following code fragment, the attempted access is out of range, yet, it probably will not produce an error message, although it will be accessing a nonexistent indexed variable:

```
        string str("Mary");
        cout << str[6] << endl;
```

The next example, however, will cause the program to terminate abnormally, so that you at least know something is wrong:

```
        string str("Mary");
        cout << str.at(6) << endl;
```

But, be warned that some systems give very poor error messages when a.at(i) has an illegal index i.

You can change a single character in the string by assigning a char value to the indexed variable, such as str[i]. Since the member function at returns a reference, this may also be done with the member function at. For example, to change the third character in the string object str to 'X', you can use either of the following code fragments:

```
str.at(2)='X';
```

or

```
str[2]='X';
```

As in an ordinary array of characters, character positions for objects of type string are indexed starting with 0, so that the third character in a string is in index position 2.

Display 9.7 gives a partial list of the member functions of the class string.

In many ways objects of the class string are better behaved than the C-strings we introduced in Section 9.1. In particular, the == operator on objects of the string class returns a result that corresponds to our intuitive notion of strings being equal; namely, it returns true if the two strings contain the same characters in the same order and returns false otherwise. Similarly, the comparison operators <, >, <=, and >= compare string objects using lexicographic ordering. (Lexicographic ordering is alphabetic ordering using the order of symbols given in the ASCII character set in Appendix 3. If the strings consist of all letters and are both either all uppercase or all lowercase letters, then for this case lexicographic ordering is the same as everyday alphabetical ordering.).

Display 9.7 Member Functions of the Standard Class string (part 1 of 2)

EXAMPLE	REMARKS
Constructors	
string str;	Default constructor, creates empty string object str.
string str("string");	Creates a string object with data "string".
string str(aString);	Creates a string object str that is a copy of aString. aString is an object of the class string.
Element access	
str[i]	Returns read/write reference to character in str at index i.
str.at(i)	Returns read/write reference to character in str at index i.
str.substr(position, length)	Returns the substring of the calling object starting at position and having length characters.
Assignment/Modifiers	
str1 = str2;	Allocates space and initializes it to str2's data, releases memory allocated for str1, and sets str1's size to that of str2.
str1 += str2;	Character data of str2 is concatenated to the end of str1; the size is set appropriately.
str.empty( )	Returns true if str is an empty string; returns false otherwise.

(continued)

Display 9.7   Member Functions of the Standard Class `string` (part 2 of 2)

EXAMPLE	REMARKS
`str1 + str2`	Returns a string that has `str2`'s data concatenated to the end of `str1`'s data. The size is set appropriately.
`str.insert(pos, str2)`	Inserts `str2` into `str` beginning at position `pos`.
`str.remove(pos, length)`	Removes substring of size `length`, starting at position `pos`.
Comparisons	
`str1 == str2  str1 != str2`	Compare for equality or inequality; returns a Boolean value.
`str1 < str2  str2 > str1`	Four comparisons. All are lexicographical comparisons.
`str1 <= str2  str1 >=`	
`str.find(str1)`	Returns index of the first occurrence of `str1` in `str`.
`str.find(str1, pos)`	Returns index of the first occurrence of string `str1` in `str`; the search starts at position `pos`.
`str.find_first_of (str1, pos)`	Returns the index of the first instance in `str` of any character in `str1`, starting the search at position `pos`.
`str.find_first_not_of (str1, pos)`	Returns the index of the first instance in `str` of any character not in `str1`, starting search at position `pos`.

== and == Are Different for `strings` and C-strings

The operators =, ==, !=, <, >, <=, and <=, when used with the standard C++ type `string`, produce results that correspond to our intuitive notion of how strings compare. They do not misbehave as they do with C-strings, as we discussed in Section 9.1.

EXAMPLE: Palindrome Testing

A palindrome is a string that reads the same front to back as it does back to front. The program in Display 9.8 tests an input string to see if it is a palindrome. Our palindrome test will disregard all spaces and punctuation and will consider uppercase

EXAMPLE: (continued)

and lowercase versions of a letter to be the same when deciding if something is a palindrome. Some palindrome examples are as follows:

```
Able was I 'ere I saw Elba.
I Love Me, Vol. I.
Madam, I'm Adam.
A man, a plan, a canal, Panama.
Rats live on no evil star.
radar
deed
mom
racecar
```

The removePunct function is of interest in that it uses the string member functions substr and find. The member function substr extracts a substring of the calling object, given the position and length of the desired substring. The first three lines of removePunct declare variables for use in the function. The for loop runs through the characters of the parameter s one at a time and tries to find them in the punct string. To do this, a string that is the substring of s, of length 1 at each character position, is extracted. The position of this substring in punct is determined using the find member function. If this one-character string is not in the punct string, then the one-character string is concatenated to the noPunct string that is to be returned.

Display 9.8   Palindrome Testing Program (part 1 of 3)

```
1   //Test for palindrome property.
2   #include <iostream>
3   #include <string>
4   #include <cctype>
5   using namespace std;
6   void swap(char& v1, char& v2);
7   //Interchanges the values of v1 and v2.
8   string reverse(const string& s);
9   //Returns a copy of s but with characters in reverse order.

10  string removePunct(const string& s, const string& punct);
11  //Returns a copy of s with any occurrences of characters
12  //in the string punct removed.

13  string makeLower (const string& s);
14  //Returns a copy of s that has all uppercase
15  //characters changed to lowercase, with other characters unchanged.

16  bool isPal(const string& s);
17  //Returns true if s is a palindrome; false otherwise.
```

(continued)

Display 9.8   Palindrome Testing Program (part 2 of 3)

```
18   int main( )
19   {
20       string str;
21       cout << "Enter a candidate for palindrome test\n"
22            << "followed by pressing Return.\n";
23       getline(cin, str);
24
25       if (isPal(str))
26           cout << "\"" << str + "\" is a palindrome.";
27       else
28           cout << "\"" << str + "\" is not a palindrome.";
29       cout << endl;
30
31       return 0;
32   }
33
34   void swap(char& v1, char& v2)
35   {
36       char temp = v1;
37       v1 = v2;
38       v2 = temp;
39   }
40
41   string reverse(const string& s)
42   {
43       int start = 0;
44       int end = s.length( );
45       string temp(s);
46
47       while (start < end)
48       {
49           end--;
50           swap(temp[start], temp[end]);
51           start++;
52       }
53
54       return temp;
57   //Uses <cctype> and <string>
58   string makeLower(const string& s)
60       string temp(s);
```

```
49   }
50
51   //Uses <cctype> and <string>
52   string makeLower(const string& s)
53   {
54       string temp(s);
55       for (int i = 0; i < s.length( ); i++)
56           temp[i] = tolower(s[i]);
57
58       return temp;
59   }
60
```

Display 9.8   Palindrome Testing Program (part 3 of 3)

```
61  string removePunct(const string& s, const string& punct)
62  {
63      string noPunct; //initialized to empty string
64      int sLength = s.length( );
65      int punctLength = punct.length( );
66      for (int i = 0; i < sLength; i++)
67      {
68          string aChar = s.substr(i,1); //A one-character string
69          int location = punct.find(aChar, 0);
70          //Find location of successive characters
71          //of src in punct.
72          if (location < 0 || location >= punctLength)
73              noPunct = noPunct + aChar; //aChar is not in punct, so keep it
74      }
75
76      return noPunct;
77  }
78  //uses functions makeLower, removePunct
79  bool isPal(const string& s)
80  {
81      string punct(",;:.?!'\" "); //includes a blank
82      string str(s);
83      str = makeLower(str);
84      string lowerStr = removePunct(str, punct);
85
86      return (lowerStr == reverse(lowerStr));
87  }
```

Sample Dialogues

Enter a candidate for palindrome test
followed by pressing Return.
Madam, I'm Adam.
"Madam, I'm Adam." is a palindrome.

Enter a candidate for palindrome test
followed by pressing Return.
Radar
"Radar" is a palindrome.

Enter a candidate for palindrome test
followed by pressing Return.
Am I a palindrome?
"Am I a palindrome?" is not a palindrome.

Self-Test Exercises

24. Consider the following code:

```
string s1, s2("Hello");
cout << "Enter a line of input:\n";
cin >> s1;
if (s1 == s2)
    cout << "Equal\n";
else
    cout << "Not equal\n";
```

If the dialogue begins as follows, what will be the next line of output?

```
Enter a line of input:
Hello friend!
```

25. What is the output produced by the following code?

```
string s1, s2("Hello");
s1 = s2;
s2[0] = 'J';
cout << s1 << " " << s2;
```

Converting between string Objects and C-Strings

You have already seen that C++ will perform an automatic type conversion to allow you to store a C-string in a variable of type string. For example, the following will work fine:

```
char aCString[] = "This is my C-string.";
string stringVariable;
stringVariable = aCString;
```

However, the following will produce a compiler error message:

```
aCString = stringVariable; //ILLEGAL
```

The following is also illegal:

```
strcpy(aCString, stringVariable); //ILLEGAL
```

strcpy cannot take a string object as its second argument and there is no automatic conversion of string objects to C-strings, which is the problem we cannot seem to get away from.

To obtain the C-string corresponding to a string object you must perform an explicit conversion. This can be done with the string member function c_str( ). The correct version of the copying we have been trying to do is the following:

```
strcpy(aCString, stringVariable.c_str()); //Legal
```

c_str( )

Note that you need to use the `strcpy` function to do the copying. The member function `c_str()` returns the C-string corresponding to the `string` calling object. As we noted earlier in this chapter, the assignment operator does not work with C-strings. So, just in case you thought the following might work, we should point out that it too is illegal.

```
aCString = stringVariable.c_str( ); //ILLEGAL
```

Chapter Summary

- A *C-string* variable is the same thing as an array of characters, but it is used in a slightly different way. A string variable uses the null character, `'\0'`, to mark the end of the string stored in the array.

- C-string variables usually must be treated like arrays rather than simple variables of the kind we used for numbers and single characters. In particular, you cannot assign a C-string value to a C-string variable using the equal sign, =, and you cannot compare the values in two C-string variables using the == operator. Instead, you must use special C-string functions to perform these tasks.

- The library `<cctype>` has a number of useful character-manipulating functions.

- You can use `cin.get` to read a single character of input without skipping over whitespace. The function `cin.get` reads the next character no matter what kind of character it is.

- Various versions of the `getline` function can be used to read an entire line of input from the keyboard.

- The ANSI/ISO standard `<string>` library provides a fully featured class called `string` that can be used to represent strings of characters.

- Objects of the class `string` are better behaved than C-strings. In particular, the assignment and equal operators, = and ==, have their intuitive meanings when used with objects of the class `string`.

Answers to Self-Test Exercises

1. The following two declarations are equivalent to each other (but not equivalent to any others):

```
char stringVar[10] = "Hello";
char stringVar[10] = {'H', 'e', 'l', 'l', 'o', '\0'};
```

The following two declarations are equivalent to each other (but not equivalent to any others):

```
char stringVar[6] = "Hello";
char stringVar[] = "Hello";
```

The following declaration is not equivalent to any of the others:

```
char stringVar[10] = {'H', 'e', 'l', 'l', 'o'};
```

2. `"DoBeDo to you"`

3. The declaration means that `stringVar` has room for only six characters (including the null character, `'\0'`). The declaration `strcat` does not check that there is room to add more characters to `stringVar`, so `strcat` will write all the characters in the string `" and Good-bye."` into memory, even though that requires more memory than has been assigned to `stringVar`. This means memory that should not be changed will be changed. The net effect is unpredictable, but bad.

4. If `strlen` were not already defined for you, you could use the following definition:

```
int strlen(const char str[])
//Precondition: str contains a string value terminated
//with '\0'.
//Returns the number of characters in the string str (not
//counting '\0').
{
    int index = 0;
    while (str[index] != '\0')
        index++;
    return index;
}
```

5. The maximum number of characters is five because the sixth position is needed for the null terminator (`'\0'`).

6. a. 1
   b. 1
   c. 5 (including the `'\0'`)
   d. 2 (including the `'\0'`)
   e. 6 (including the `'\0'`)

7. These are *not equivalent*. The first of these places the null character `'\0'` in the array after the characters `'a'`, `'b'`, and `'c'`. The second only assigns the successive positions `'a'`, `'b'`, and `'c'` but does not put a `'\0'` anywhere.

8.
```
int index = 0;
while (ourString[index] != '\0' )
{
    ourString[index] = "X";
    index++;
}
```

9. a. If the C-string variable does not have a null terminator, `'\0'`, the loop can run beyond the memory allocated for the C-string, destroying the contents of memory there. To protect memory beyond the end of the array, change the while condition as shown in b.

   b. `while ( ourString[index] != '\0' && index < SIZE )`

10. ```
    #include <cstring>
    //needed to get the declaration of strcpy
    ...
    strcpy(aString, "Hello");
    ```

11. `I did it my way!`

12. The string `"good, I hope."` is too long for `aString`. A chunk of memory that does not belong to the array `aString` will be overwritten.

13. The complete dialogue is as follows:

    ```
    Enter some input:
    The
        time is now.
    The-time<END OF OUTPUT
    ```

14. The complete dialogue is as follows:

    ```
    Enter a line of input:
    May the hair on your toes grow long and curly.
    May t<END OF OUTPUT
    ```

15. The complete dialogue is as follows:

    ```
    Enter a line of input:
    a b c d e f g
    a.b END OF OUTPUT
    ```

16. The complete dialogue is as follows:

    ```
    Enter a line of input:
    abcdef gh
    ace h
    ```

    Note that the output is simply every other character of the input, and note that the blank is treated just like any other character.

17. The complete dialogue is as follows:

    ```
    Enter a line of input:
    0 1 2 3 4 5 6 7 8 9 10 11
    01234567891 1
    ```

    Be sure to note that only the '1' in the input string 10 is output. This is because cin.get is reading characters, not numbers, and so it reads the input 10 as the two characters '1' and '0'. Since this code is written to echo only every other character, the '0' is not output. Since the '0' is not output, the next character, which is a blank, is output, and so there is one blank in the output. Similarly, only one of the two '1' characters in 11 is output. If this is unclear, write the input on a sheet of paper and use a small square for the blank character. Then, cross out every other character; the output shown previously is what is left.
    ```

18. This code contains an infinite loop and will continue as long as the user continues to give it input. The Boolean expression (`next != '\n'`) is always true because next is filled via the statement

```
cin >> next;
```

and this statement always skips the newline character, `'\n'` (as well as any blanks). The code will run, and if the user gives no additional input, the dialogue will be as follows:

```
Enter a line of input:
0 1 2 3 4 5 6 7 8 9 10 11
0246811
```

This code outputs every other *nonblank* character. The two `'1'` characters in the output are the first character in the input 10 and the first character in the input 11.

19. The complete dialogue is as follows:

```
Enter a line of input:
I'll see you at 10:30 AM.
I'll see you at 1<END OF OUTPUT
```

20. ```
cout << "Enter a line of input:\n";

char next;

do
{
    cin.get(next);
    if (!isupper(next))
        cout << next;
} while (next != '\n');
```

Note that you should use `!isupper(next)` and not use `islower(next)`. This is because `islower(next)` returns `false` if next contains a character that is not a letter (such as the blank or comma symbol).

21. ```
//Uses iostream:
void newLine( )
{
    cin.ignore(10000, '\n');
}
```

Of course, this only works for lines less than about 10,000 characters, but any lines longer than that would likely indicate some other unrelated problem.

22. `A*string<END OF OUTPUT`

23. `A string is a joy forever!<END OF OUTPUT`

24. The complete dialogue is as follows:

```
Enter a line of input:
Hello friend!
Equal
```

25. `Hello Jello`

Programming Projects

Visit www.myprogramminglab.com to complete select exercises online and get instant feedback.

1. Write a program that will read in a sentence of up to 100 characters and output the sentence with spacing corrected and with letters corrected for capitalization. In other words, in the output sentence all strings of two or more blanks should be compressed to a single blank. The sentence should start with an uppercase letter but should contain no other uppercase letters. Do not worry about proper names; if their first letter is changed to lowercase, that is acceptable. Treat a line break as if it were a blank in the sense that a line break and any number of blanks are compressed to a single blank. Assume that the sentence ends with a period and contains no other periods. For example, the input

    ```
    the     Answer  to life,  the  Universe,  and   everything
    IS 42.
    ```

    should produce the following output:

    ```
    The answer to life, the universe, and everything is 42.
    ```

2. Write a program that will read in a line of text and output the number of words in the line and the number of occurrences of each letter. Define a word to be any string of letters that is delimited at each end by either whitespace, a period, a comma, or the beginning or end of the line. You can assume that the input consists entirely of letters, whitespace, commas, and periods. When outputting the number of letters that occur in a line, be sure to count uppercase and lowercase versions of a letter as the same letter. Output the letters in alphabetical order and list only those letters that occur in the input line. For example, the input line

    ```
    I say Hi.
    ```

    should produce output similar to the following:

    ```
    3 words
    1 a
    1 h
    2 i
    1 s
    1 y
    ```

3. Write a program that reads a person's name in the following format: first name, then middle name or initial, and then last name. The program then outputs the name in the following format:

    ```
    Last_Name, First_Name, Middle_Initial.
    ```

    For example, the input

    ```
    Mary Average User
    ```

    should produce the output

    ```
    User, Mary A.
    ```

The input

Mary A. User

should also produce the output

    User, Mary A.

Your program should place a period after the middle initial even if the input did not contain a period. Your program should allow for users who give no middle name or middle initial. In that case, the output, of course, contains no middle name or initial. For example, the input

Mary User

should produce the output

    User, Mary

If you are using C-strings, assume that each name is at most 20 characters long. Alternatively, use the class string. (*Hint:* You may want to use three string variables rather than one large string variable for the input. You may find it easier to *not* use getline.)

4. Write a program that reads in a line of text and replaces all four-letter words with the word "love". For example, the input string

I hate you, you dodo!

should produce the following output:

    I love you, you love!

Of course, the output will not always make sense. For example, the input string

John will run home.

should produce the following output:

    Love love run love.

If the four-letter word starts with a capital letter, it should be replaced by "Love", not by "love". You need not check capitalization, except for the first letter of a word. A word is any string consisting of the letters of the alphabet and delimited at each end by a blank, the end of the line, or any other character that is not a letter. Your program should repeat this action until the user says to quit.

5. Write a program that can be used to train the user to use less sexist language by suggesting alternative versions of sentences given by the user. The program will ask for a sentence, read the sentence into a string variable, and replace all occurrences of masculine pronouns with gender-neutral pronouns. For example, it will replace "he" with "she or he". Thus, the input sentence

See an adviser, talk to him, and listen to him.

should produce the following suggested changed version of the sentence:

    See an adviser, talk to her or him, and listen to her or him.

Be sure to preserve uppercase letters for the first word of the sentence. The pronoun "his" can be replaced by "her(s)"; your program need not decide between "her" and "hers". Allow the user to repeat this for more sentences until the user says she or he is done. This will be a long program that requires a good deal of patience. Your program should not replace the string "he" when it occurs inside another word such as "here". A word is any string consisting of the letters of the alphabet and delimited at each end by a blank, the end of the line, or any other character that is not a letter. Allow your sentences to be up to 100 characters long.

6. There is a CD available for purchase that contains .jpeg and .gif images of music that is in the public domain. The CD includes a file consisting of lines containing the names, then composers of that title, one per line. The name of the piece is first, then zero or more spaces then a dash (-) character, then one or more spaces, then the composer's name. The composer name may be only the last name, an initial and one name, two names (first and last), or three names (first, middle, and last). There are a few tunes with "no author listed" as author. In the subsequent processing, "no author listed" should not be rearranged. Here is a very abbreviated list of the titles and authors.

1. Adagio "MoonLight" Sonata - Ludwig Van Beethoven
2. An Alexis - F.H. Hummel and J.N. Hummel
3. A La Bien Aimee - Ben Schutt
4. At Sunset - E. MacDowell
5. Angelus - J. Massenet
6. Anitra's Dance - Edward Grieg
7. Ase's Death - Edward Grieg
8. Au Matin- Benj. - Godard

...

37. The Dying Poet - L. Gottschalk
38. Dead March - G.F. Handel
39. Do They Think of Me At Home - Chas. W. Glover
40. The Dearest Spot - W.T. Wrighton

1. Evening - L. Van Beethoven
2. Embarrassment - Franz Abt
3. Erin is my Home - no author listed
4. Ellen Bayne - Stephen C. Foster

...

9. Alla Mazurka - A. Nemerowsky

...

1. The Dying Volunteer - A.E. Muse
2. Dolly Day - Stephen C. Foster
3. Dolcy Jones - Stephen C. Foster
4. Dickory, Dickory, Dock - no author listed

5. The Dear Little Shamrock - no author listed

6. Dutch Warbler - no author listed

...

The ultimate task is to produce an alphabetized list of composers followed by a list of pieces by them alphabetized on the title within composer. This exercise is easier if it is broken into pieces:

Write code to do the following:

a. Remove the lead numbers, any periods, and any spaces so that the first word of the title is the first word of the line.

b. Replace any multiple spaces with a single space.

c. A few titles may have several - characters, for example,

```
20.  Ba-  Be-  Bi-  Bo-  Bu  -  no  author  listed
```

Replace all dash - characters on any line before the end of the line by a space except the last one.

d. The last word in the title may have the - character with no space between it and the = character. Put the space in.

e. When alphabetizing the title, you do not want to consider an initial "A", "An", or "The" in the title. Write code to move such initial words to just before the - character. A comma after the last word in the title is not required, but that would be a nice touch. This can be done after the composer's names are moved to the front, but obviously the code will be different.

f. Move the composer's names to the beginning of the line, followed by the character, followed by the composition title.

g. Move any first initial, or first and second names of the composer to after the composer's last name. If the composer is "no author listed" this should not be rearranged, so test for this combination.

h. Alphabetize by composer using any sort routine you know. You may ignore any duplicate composer's last name, such as CPE Bach and JS Bach, but sorting by composer's second name would be a nice touch. You may use the insertion sort, or selection sort, or bubble sort, or other sorting algorithm.

i. If you have not already done so, move "A", "An", or "The" that may begin a title to the end of the title. Then alphabetize within each composer by composition title.

j. Keep a copy of your design and your code. You will be asked to do this over using the STL vector container.

7. One sign that the caps lock key may be inadvertently on is that the first letter of a word is lowercase and the remaining letters are uppercase, lIKE tHIS. Write a program that scans a string input by the user and outputs any words that appear to suffer from caps-lock syndrome.

The program should allow the user to input as many strings as desired, testing each string for potential caps-lock words, until the user enters a blank string.

8. Write a program that converts a sentence input by the user into pig latin. You can assume that the sentence contains no punctuation. The rules for pig latin are as follows:

   a. For words that begin with consonants, move the leading consonant to the end of the word and add "ay." Thus, "ball" becomes "allbay"; "button" becomes "uttonbay"; and so forth.

   b. For words that begin with vowels, add "way" to the end. Thus, "all" becomes "allway"; "one" becomes "oneway"; and so forth.

9. Write a function to compare two C-strings for equality. The function should return true if the strings are equal and false if they are not. Your function should ignore case, punctuation, and whitespace characters. Test your function with a variety of input strings.

10. Write a simple trivia quiz game. Start by creating a Trivia class that contains information about a single trivia question. The class should contain a string for the question, a string for the answer to the question, and an integer representing the dollar amount the question is worth (harder questions should be worth more). Add appropriate constructor and accessor functions. In your main function create either an array or a vector of type Trivia and hard-code at least five trivia questions of your choice. Your program should then ask each question to the player, input the player's answer, and check if the player's answer matches the actual answer. If so, award the player the dollar amount for that question. If the player enters the wrong answer your program should display the correct answer. When all questions have been asked display the total amount that the player has won.

11. Write a function that determines if two strings are anagrams. The function should not be case sensitive and should disregard any punctuation or spaces. Two strings are anagrams if the letters can be rearranged to form each other. For example, "Eleven plus two" is an anagram of "Twelve plus one". Each string contains one "v", three "e's", two "l's", etc. Test your function with several strings that are anagrams and non-anagrams. You may use either the string class or a C-style string.

12. Write a function that converts a string into an integer. For example, given the string "1234" the function should return the integer 1234. If you do some research, you will find that there is a function named atoi and also the stringstream class that can do this conversion for you. However, in this Programming Project, you should write your own code to do the conversion. Also write a suitable test program.

VideoNote
Solution to
Programming
Project 9.11

VideoNote

Solution to
Programming
Project 9.13

13. Some word games require the player to find words that can be formed using the letters of another word. For example, given the word SWIMMING then other words that can be formed using the letters include SWIM, WIN, WING, SING, MIMING, etc. Write a program that lets the user enter a word and then output all the words contained in the file words.txt (included on the website with this book) that can be formed from the letters of the entered word. One algorithm to do this is to compare the letter histograms for each word. Create an array that counts up the number of each letter in the entered word (e.g., one S, one W, two I, two M, etc.) and then creates a similar array for the current word read from the file. The two arrays can be compared to see if the word from the file could be created out of the letters from the entered word.

Pointers and Dynamic Arrays

10

Introduction

A *pointer* is a construct that gives you more control of the computer's memory. This chapter will show you how pointers are used with arrays and will introduce a new form of array called a *dynamically allocated array*. Dynamically allocated arrays (dynamic arrays for short) are arrays whose size is determined while the program is running, rather than being fixed when the program is written.

Before reading Sections 10.1 and 10.2 on pointers and dynamically allocated arrays you should first read Chapters 1 through 6 (omitting the coverage of vectors if you wish), but you need not read any of Chapters 7 through 9. You can even read Sections 10.1 and 10.2 after reading just Chapters 1 to 5, provided you ignore the few passages that mention classes.

Section 10.3 discusses some tools for classes that only become relevant once you begin to use pointers and dynamically allocated data (such as dynamically allocated arrays). Before covering Section 10.3, you should read Chapters 1 through 8, although you may omit the coverage of vectors if you wish.

You may cover this chapter, Chapter 11 on separate compilation and namespaces, Chapter 12 on file I/O, and Chapter 13 on recursion in any order. If you do not read the Chapter 11 section on namespaces before this chapter, you might find it profitable to review the section of Chapter 1 entitled "Namespaces".

10.1 Pointers

pointer

A **pointer** is the memory address of a variable. Recall from Chapter 5 that the computer's memory is divided into numbered memory locations (called *bytes*) and that variables are implemented as a sequence of adjacent memory locations. Recall also that sometimes the C++ system uses these memory addresses as names for the variables. If a variable is implemented as, say, three memory locations, then the address of the first of these memory locations is sometimes used as a name for that variable. For example, when the variable is used as a call-by-reference argument, it is this address, not the identifier name of the variable, that is passed to the calling function. An address that is used to name a variable in this way (by giving the address in memory where the variable starts) is called a *pointer* because the address can be thought of as "pointing" to the variable. The address "points" to the variable because it identifies the variable by telling *where* the variable is, rather than telling what the variable's name is.

You have already been using pointers in a number of situations. As noted in the previous paragraph, when a variable is a call-by-reference argument in a function call, the function is given this argument variable in the form of a pointer to the variable. As noted in Chapter 5, an array is given to a function (or to anything else, for that matter) by giving a pointer to the first array element. (At the time we called these pointers "memory addresses," but that is the same thing as a pointer.) These are two powerful uses for pointers, but they are handled automatically by the C++ system. This chapter shows you how to write programs that directly manipulate pointers rather than relying on the system to manipulate the pointers for you.

Pointer Variables

A pointer can be stored in a variable. However, even though a pointer is a memory address and a memory address is a number, you cannot store a pointer in a variable of type int or double. A variable to hold a pointer must be declared to have a pointer type. For example, the following declares p to be a pointer variable that can hold one pointer that points to a variable of type double:

```
double *p;
```

The variable p can hold pointers to variables of type double, but it cannot normally contain a pointer to a variable of some other type, such as int or char. Each variable type requires a different pointer type.[1]

In general, to declare a variable that can hold pointers to other variables of a specific type, you declare the pointer variable just as you would declare an ordinary variable of that type, but you place an asterisk in front of the variable name. For example, the following declares the variables p1 and p2 so they can hold pointers to variables of type int; it also declares two ordinary variables v1 and v2 of type int:

```
int *p1, *p2, v1, v2;
```

declaring pointer variables

There must be an asterisk before *each* of the pointer variables. If you omit the second asterisk in the previous declaration, then p2 will not be a pointer variable; it will instead be an ordinary variable of type int.

When discussing pointers and pointer variables, we usually speak of *pointing* rather than speaking of *addresses*. When a pointer variable, such as p1, contains the address of a variable, such as v1, the pointer variable is said to *point to the variable* v1 or to be *a pointer to the variable* v1.

---

[1]There are ways to get a pointer of one type into a pointer variable for another type, but it does not happen automatically and is very poor style anyway.

Pointer Variable Declarations

A variable that can hold pointers to other variables of type $Type\_Name$ is declared similar to the way you declare a variable of type $Type\_Name$, except that you place an asterisk at the beginning of the variable name.

SYNTAX

$Type\_Name$ *$Variable\_Name1$, *$Variable\_Name2$,...;

EXAMPLE

```
double *pointer1, *pointer2;
```

Addresses and Numbers

A pointer is an address, and an address is an integer, but a pointer is not an integer. That is not crazy—that is abstraction! C++ insists that you use a pointer as an address and that you not use it as a number. A pointer is not a value of type int or of any other numeric type. You normally cannot store a pointer in a variable of type int. If you try, most C++ compilers will give you an error message or a warning message. Also, you cannot perform the normal arithmetic operations on pointers. (As you will see later in this chapter, you can perform a kind of addition and a kind of subtraction on pointers, but they are not the usual integer addition and subtraction.)

the & operator

Pointer variables, like `p1` and `p2` declared previously, can contain pointers to variables like `v1` and `v2`. You can use the operator & to determine the address of a variable, and you can then assign that address to a pointer variable. For example, the following will set the variable `p1` equal to a pointer that points to the variable `v1`:

```
p1 = &v1;
```

the * operator

You now have two ways to refer to `v1`: You can call it `v1` or you can call it "the variable pointed to by `p1`." In C++, the way you say "the variable pointed to by `p1`" is `*p1`. This is the same asterisk that we used when we declared `p1`, but now it has yet another meaning. When the asterisk is used in this way it is called the **dereferencing operator**, and the pointer variable is said to be *dereferenced*.

dereferencing operator

Putting these pieces together can produce some surprising results. Consider the following code:

```
v1 = 0;
p1 = &v1;
*p1 = 42;
cout << v1 << endl;
cout << *p1 << endl;
```

Pointer Types

There is a bit of an inconsistency (or at least a potential for confusion) in how C++ names pointer types. If you want a parameter whose type is, for example, a pointer to variables of type int, then the type is written int*, as in the following example:

```
void manipulatePointer(int* p);
```

If you want to declare a variable of the same pointer type, the * goes with the variable, as in the following example:

```
int *p1, *p2;
```

In fact, the compiler does not care whether the * is attached to the int or the variable name, so the following are also accepted by the compiler and have the same meanings:

```
void manipulatePointer(int *p);//Accepted but not as nice.
int* p1, *p2;//Accepted but dangerous.
```

However, we find the first versions to be clearer. In particular, note that when declaring variables there must be one * for each pointer variable.

This code will output the following to the screen:

```
42
42
```

As long as p1 contains a pointer that points to v1, then v1 and *p1 refer to the same variable. So when you set *p1 equal to 42, you are also setting v1 equal to 42.

The symbol & that is used to obtain the address of a variable is the same symbol that you use in function declarations to specify a call-by-reference parameter. This is not a coincidence. Recall that a call-by-reference argument is implemented by giving the address of the argument to the calling function. So, these two uses of the symbol & are very closely related, although they are not exactly the same.

You can assign the value of one pointer variable to another pointer variable. For example, if p1 is still pointing to v1, then the following will set p2 so that it also points to v1:

```
p2 = p1;
```

Provided we have not changed v1's value, the following will also output 42 to the screen:

```
cout << *p2;
```

Be sure you do not confuse

```
p1 = p2;
```

and

```
*p1 = *p2;
```

pointers in assignment statements

The * and & Operators

The * operator in front of a pointer variable produces the variable to which it points. When used this way, the * operator is called the *dereferencing operator*.

The operator & in front of an ordinary variable produces the address of that variable; that is, it produces a pointer that points to the variable. The & operator is simply called the **addressof operator**.

For example, consider the declarations

```
double *p, v;
```

The following sets the value of p so that p points to the variable v:

```
p = &v;
```

*p produces the variable pointed to by p, so after the previous assignment, *p and v refer to the same variable. For example, the following sets the value of v to 9.99, even though the name v is never explicitly used:

```
*p = 9.99;
```

When you add the asterisk, you are not dealing with the pointers p1 and p2, but with the variables to which the pointers are pointing. This is illustrated in Display 10.1, in which variables are represented as boxes and the value of the variable is written inside the box. We have not shown the actual numeric addresses in the pointer variables because the numbers are not important. What is important is that the number is the address of some particular variable. So, rather than use the actual number of the address, we have merely indicated the address with an arrow that points to the variable with that address.

Pointer Variables Used with =

If p1 and p2 are pointer variables, then the statement

```
p1 = p2;
```

changes the value of p1 so that it is the memory address (pointer) in p2. A common way to think of this is that the assignment will change p1 so that it points to the same thing to which p2 is currently pointing.

Display 10.1   Uses of the Assignment Operator with Pointer Variables

`p1 = p2;`

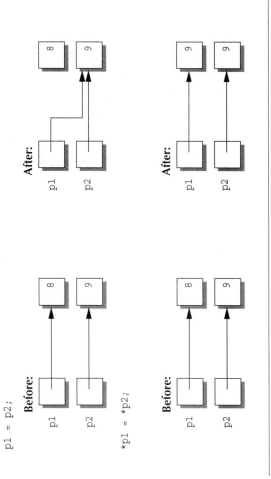

Since a pointer can be used to refer to a variable, your program can manipulate variables even if the variables have no identifiers to name them. The operator **new** can be used to create variables that have no identifiers to serve as their names. These nameless variables are referred to via pointers. For example, the following creates a new variable of type int and sets the pointer variable p1 equal to the address of this new variable (that is, p1 points to this new, nameless variable):

`p1 = new int;`

This new, nameless variable can be referred to as `*p1` (that is, as the variable pointed to by p1). You can do anything with this nameless variable that you can do with any other variable of type int. For example, the following code reads a value of type int from the keyboard into this nameless variable, adds 7 to the value, and then outputs this new value:

```
cin >> *p1;
*p1 = *p1 + 7;
cout << *p1;
```

The new operator produces a new, nameless variable and returns a pointer that points to this new variable. You specify the type for this new variable by writing the type name after the new operator. Variables that are created using the new operator are called **dynamically allocated variables** or simply **dynamic variables**, because they are created and destroyed while the program is running. The program in Display 10.2 demonstrates some simple operations on pointers and dynamic variables. Display 10.3 graphically illustrates the working of the program in Display 10.2.

new

dynamic variable

Display 10.2   Basic Pointer Manipulations

```
1   //Program to demonstrate pointers and dynamic variables.
2   #include <iostream>
3   using namespace std;

4   int main( )
5   {
6       int *p1, *p2;

7       p1 = new int;
8       *p1 = 42;
9       p2 = p1;
10      cout << "*p1 == " << *p1 << endl;
11      cout << "*p2 == " << *p2 << endl;

12      *p2 = 53;
13      cout << "*p1 == " << *p1 << endl;
14      cout << "*p2 == " << *p2 << endl;

15      p1 = new int;
16      *p1 = 88;
17      cout << "*p1 == " << *p1 << endl;
18      cout << "*p2 == " << *p2 << endl;

19      cout << "Hope you got the point of this example!\n";
20      return 0;
21  }
```

Sample Dialogue

```
*p1 == 42
*p2 == 42
*p1 == 53
*p2 == 53
*p1 == 88
*p2 == 53
Hope you got the point of this example!
```

Display 10.3   Explanation of Display 10.2

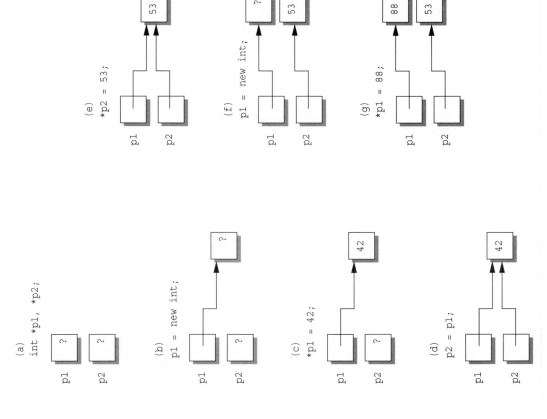

(a)
int *p1, *p2;

(b)
p1 = new int;

(c)
*p1 = 42;

(d)
p2 = p1;

(e)
*p2 = 53;

(f)
p1 = new int;

(g)
*p1 = 88;

When the new operator is used to create a dynamic variable of a class type, a constructor for the class is invoked. If you do not specify which constructor to use, the default constructor is invoked. For example, the following invokes the default constructor:

```
SomeClass *classPtr;
classPtr = new SomeClass;   //Calls default constructor.
```

The new Operator

The new operator creates a new dynamic variable of a specified type and returns a pointer that points to this new variable. For example, the following creates a new dynamic variable of type MyType and leaves the pointer variable p pointing to this new variable:

```
MyType *p;
p = new MyType;
```

If the type is a class type, the default constructor is called for the newly created dynamic variable. You can specify a different constructor by including arguments as follows:

```
MyType *mtPtr;
mtPtr = new MyType(32.0, 17); // calls MyType(double, int);
```

A similar notation allows you to initialize dynamic variables of nonclass types, as illustrated here:

```
int *n;
n = new int(17); // Initializes *n to 17
```

With earlier C++ compilers, if there was insufficient available memory to create the new variable, then new returned a special pointer named NULL. The C++ standard provides that if there is insufficient available memory to create the new variable, then the new operator, by default, terminates the program.

If you include constructor arguments, you can invoke a different constructor, as illustrated next:

```
classPtr = new SomeClass(32.0, 17);
            //Calls SomeClass(double, int).
```

A similar notation allows you to initialize dynamic variables of nonclass types, as illustrated next:

```
double *dPtr;
dPtr = new double(98.6); // Initializes *dPtr to 98.6.
```

pointer parameters

A pointer type is a full-fledged type and can be used in the same ways as other types. In particular, you can have a function parameter of a pointer type and you can have a function that returns a pointer type. For example, the following function has a parameter that is a pointer to an int variable and returns a (possibly different) pointer to an int variable:

```
int* findOtherPointer(int* p);
```

Self-Test Exercises

1. What is a pointer in C++?

2. Give at least three uses of the `*` operator. Name and describe each use.

3. What is the output produced by the following code?

```
int *p1, *p2;
p1 = new int;
p2 = new int;
*p1 = 10;
*p2 = 20;
cout << *p1 << " " << *p2 << endl;
p1 = p2;
cout << *p1 << " " << *p2 << endl;
*p1 = 30;
cout << *p1 << " " << *p2 << endl;
```

How would the output change if you were to replace

```
*p1 = 30;
```

with the following?

```
*p2 = 30;
```

4. What is the output produced by the following code?

```
int *p1, *p2;
p1 = new int;
p2 = new int;
*p1 = 10;
*p2 = 20;
cout << *p1 << " " << *p2 << endl;
*p1 = *p2; //This is different from Exercise 3
cout << *p1 << " " << *p2 << endl;
*p1 = 30;
cout << *p1 << " " << *p2 << endl;
```

Basic Memory Management

freestore or heap

A special area of memory, called the **freestore** or the **heap**, is reserved for dynamically allocated variables. Any new dynamic variable created by a program consumes some of the memory in the freestore. If your program creates too many dynamic variables, it will consume all the memory in the freestore. If this happens, any additional calls to `new` will fail. What happens when you use `new` after you have exhausted all the memory in the freestore (all the memory reserved for dynamically allocated variables) will depend on how up-to-date your compiler is. With earlier C++ compilers, if there was insufficient available memory to create the new variable, then new returned a special value named NULL. If you have a compiler that fully conforms to the newer C++ standard, then if there is insufficient available memory to create the new variable, the new operator terminates the program. Chapter 18 discusses ways to configure your program so that it can do things other than abort when new exhausts the freestore.[2]

If you have an older compiler, you can check to see if a call to new was successful by testing to see if NULL was returned by the call to new. For example, the following code tests to see if the attempt to create a new dynamic variable succeeded. The program will end with an error message if the call to new failed to create the desired dynamic variable:

```
int *p;
p = new int;
if (p == NULL)
{
    cout << "Error: Insufficient memory.\n";
    exit(1);
}

//If new succeeded, the program continues from here.
```

(Remember that since this code uses exit, you need an include directive for the library with header file <cstdlib> or, with some implementations, P<stdlib.h>.)

The constant NULL is actually the number 0, but we prefer to think of it and spell it as NULL to make it clear that you mean this special-purpose value which you can assign to pointer variables. We will discuss other uses for NULL later in this book. The definition of the identifier NULL is in a number of the standard libraries, such as <iostream> and <cstddef>, so you should use an include directive for either <iostream> or <cstddef> (or another suitable library) when you use NULL.

As we said, NULL is actually just the number 0. The definition of NULL is handled by the C++ preprocessor which replaces NULL with 0. Thus, the compiler never actually sees "NULL" and so there is no namespace issue and no using directive is needed for NULL.[3] While we prefer to use NULL rather than 0 in our code, we note that some authorities hold just the opposite view and advocate using 0 rather than NULL.

(Do not confuse the NULL pointer with the null character '\0' which is used to terminate C-strings. They are not the same. One is the integer 0 while the other is the character '\0'.)

Newer compilers do not require the previous explicit check to see if the new dynamic variable was created. On newer compilers, your program will automatically end with an error message if a call to new fails to create the desired dynamic variable. However, with any compiler, the previous check will cause no harm and will make your program more portable.

---

[2] Technically, the new operator throws an exception, which, if not caught, terminates the program. It is possible to catch the exception and handle the exception. Exception handling is discussed in Chapter 18.

[3] The details are as follows: The definition of NULL uses #define, a form of definition that was inherited from the C language and that is handled by the preprocessor.

delete

NULL

NULL is a special constant pointer value that is used to give a value to a pointer variable that would not otherwise have a value. NULL can be assigned to a pointer variable of any type. The identifier NULL is defined in a number of libraries, including <iostream>. (The constant NULL is actually the integer 0.)

The size of the freestore varies from one implementation of C++ to another. It is typically large, and a modest program is not likely to use all the memory in the freestore. However, even in modest programs it is a good practice to recycle any freestore memory that is no longer needed. If your program no longer needs a dynamic variable, the memory used by that dynamic variable can be returned to the **freestore manager** which recycles the memory to create other dynamic variables. The **delete** operator eliminates a dynamic variable and returns the memory that the dynamic variable occupied to the freestore manager so that the memory can be reused. Suppose that p is a pointer variable that is pointing to a dynamic variable. The following will destroy the dynamic variable pointed to by p and return the memory used by the dynamic variable to the freestore manager for reuse:

```
delete p;
```

The delete Operator

The delete operator eliminates a dynamic variable and returns the memory that the dynamic variable occupied to the freestore. The memory can then be reused to create new dynamic variables. For example, the following eliminates the dynamic variable pointed to by the pointer variable p:

```
delete p;
```

After a call to delete, the value of the pointer variable, like p shown, is undefined. (A slightly different version of delete, discussed later in this chapter, is used when the dynamically allocated variable is an array.)

PITFALL: Dangling Pointers

When you apply delete to a pointer variable, the dynamic variable to which it is pointing is destroyed. At that point, the value of the pointer variable is undefined, which means that you do not know where it is pointing. Moreover, if some other pointer variable was pointing to the dynamic variable that was destroyed, then this other pointer variable is also undefined. These undefined pointer variables are called **dangling pointers.** If p is a dangling pointer and your program applies the dereferencing operator * to p (to produce the expression *p), the result is unpredictable and usually disastrous. Before you apply the dereferencing operator * to a pointer variable, you should be certain that the pointer variable points to some variable.

**dangling
pointer**

C++ has no built-in test to check whether a pointer variable is a dangling pointer. One way to avoid dangling pointers is to set any dangling pointer variable equal to NULL. Then your program can test the pointer variable to see if it is equal to NULL before applying the dereferencing operator * to the pointer variable. When you use this technique, you follow a call to delete by code that sets all dangling pointers equal to NULL. Remember, other pointer variables may become dangling pointers besides the one pointer variable used in the call to delete, so be sure to set *all* dangling pointers to NULL. It is up to the programmer to keep track of dangling pointers and set them to NULL or otherwise ensure that they are not dereferenced. ■

Dynamic Variables and Automatic Variables

Variables created with the new operator are called **dynamic variables** (or **dynamically allocated variables**) because they are created and destroyed while the program is running. Local variables—that is, variables declared within a function definition—also have a certain dynamic characteristic, but they are not called dynamic variables. If a variable is local to a function, then the variable is created by the C++ system when the function is called and is destroyed when the function call is completed. Since the main part of a program is really just a function called main, this is even true of the variables declared in the main part of your program. (Since the call to main does not end until the program ends, the variables declared in main are not destroyed until the program ends, but the mechanism for handling local variables is the same for main as for any other function.) These local variables are sometimes called **automatic variables** because their dynamic properties are controlled automatically for you. They are automatically created when the function in which they are declared is called and automatically destroyed when the function call ends.

**automatic
variable**

Variables declared outside any function or class definition, including outside main, are called **global variables.** These global variables are sometimes called **statically allocated variables,** because they are truly static in contrast to dynamic and automatic variables. We discussed global variables briefly in Chapter 3. As it turns out, we have no need for global variables and have not used them.[4]

**global
variable**

---

[4] Variables declared within a class using the modifier static are static in a different sense than the dynamic/static contrast we are discussing in this section.

TIP: Define Pointer Types

You can define a pointer type name so that pointer variables can be declared like other variables without the need to place an asterisk in front of each pointer variable. For example, the following defines a type called `IntPtr`, which is the type for pointer variables that contain pointers to `int` variables:

```
typedef int* IntPtr;
```

Thus, the following two pointer variable declarations are equivalent:

```
IntPtr p;
```

and

```
int *p;
```

You can use `typedef` to define an alias for any type name or definition. For example, the following defines the type name `Kilometers` to mean the same thing as the type name `double`:

```
typedef double Kilometers;
```

Once you have given this type definition, you can define a variable of type `double` as follows:

```
Kilometers distance;
```

Renaming existing types this way can occasionally be useful. However, our main use of `typedef` will be to define types for pointer variables.

Keep in mind that a `typedef` does not produce a new type but is simply an alias for the type definition. For example, given the previous definition of `Kilometers`, a variable of type `Kilometers` may be substituted for a parameter of type `double`. `Kilometers` and `double` are two names for the same type.

There are two advantages to using defined pointer type names, such as `IntPtr` defined previously. First, it avoids the mistake of omitting an asterisk. Remember, if you intend `p1` and `p2` to be pointers, then the following is a mistake:

```
int *p1, p2;
```

Since the `*` was omitted from the `p2`, the variable `p2` is just an ordinary `int` variable, not a pointer variable. If you get confused and place the `*` on the `int`, the problem is the same but is more difficult to notice. C++ allows you to place the `*` on the type name, such as `int`, so that the following is legal:

```
int* p1, p2;
```

(continued)

TIP: (continued)

Although this is legal, it is misleading. It looks like both p1 and p2 are pointer variables, but in fact only p1 is a pointer variable; p2 is an ordinary int variable. As far as the C++ compiler is concerned, the * that is attached to the identifier int may as well be attached to the identifier p1. One correct way to declare both p1 and p2 to be pointer variables is

```
int *p1, *p2;
```

An easier and less error-prone way to declare both p1 and p2 to be pointer variables is to use the defined type name IntPtr as follows:

```
IntPtr p1, p2;
```

The second advantage of using a defined pointer type, such as IntPtr, is seen when you define a function with a call-by-reference parameter for a pointer variable. Without the defined pointer type name, you would need to include both an * and an & in the declaration for the function, and the details can get confusing. If you use a type name for the pointer type, then a call-by-reference parameter for a pointer type involves no complications. You define a call-by-reference parameter for a defined pointer type just like you define any other call-by-reference parameter. Here is an example:

```
void sampleFunction(IntPtr& pointerVariable);
```

■

MyProgrammingLab™

Self-Test Exercises

5. What unfortunate misinterpretation can occur with the following declaration?

    ```
    int* intPtr1, intPtr2;
    ```

6. Suppose a dynamic variable were created as follows:

    ```
    char *p;
    p = new char ;
    ```

    Assuming that the value of the pointer variable p has not changed (so it still points to the same dynamic variable), how can you destroy this new dynamic variable and return the memory it uses to the freestore manager so that the memory can be reused to create other new dynamic variables?

7. Write a definition for a type called NumberPtr that will be the type for pointer variables that hold pointers to dynamic variables of type double. Also, write a declaration for a pointer variable called myPoint, which is of type NumberPtr.

8. Describe the action of the new operator. What does the new operator return? What are the indications of errors?

Type Definitions

You can assign a name to a type definition and then use the type name to declare variables. This is done with the keyword typedef. These type definitions are normally placed outside the body of the main part of your program and outside the body of other functions, typically near the start of a file. That way the typedef is global and available to your entire program. We will use type definitions to define names for pointer types, as shown in the example here.

SYNTAX

typedef *Known_Type_Definition New_Type_Name;*

EXAMPLE

typedef int* IntPtr;

The type name IntPtr can then be used to declare pointers to dynamic variables of type int, as in the following example:

IntPtr pointer1, pointer2;

PITFALL: Pointers as Call-by-Value Parameters

When a call-by-value parameter is of a pointer type, its behavior can occasionally be subtle and troublesome. Consider the function call shown in Display 10.4. The parameter temp in the function sneaky is a call-by-value parameter, and hence it is a local variable. When the function is called, the value of temp is set to the value of the argument p and the function body is executed. Since temp is a local variable, no changes to temp should go outside the function sneaky. In particular, the value of the pointer variable p should not be changed. Yet the sample dialogue makes it look like the value of the pointer variable p has changed. Before the call to the function sneaky, the value of *p was 77, and after the call to sneaky the value of *p is 99. What has happened?

The situation is diagrammed in Display 10.5. Although the sample dialogue may make it look as if p were changed, the value of p was not changed by the function call to sneaky. Pointer p has two things associated with it: p's pointer value and the value stored where p points. But the value of p is the pointer (that is, a memory address). After the call to sneaky, the variable p contains the same pointer value (that is, the same memory address). The call to sneaky has changed the value of the variable pointed to by p, but it has not changed the value of p itself.

If the parameter type is a class or structure type that has member variables of a pointer type, the same kind of surprising changes can occur with call-by-value arguments of the class type. However, for class types, you can avoid (and control) these surprise changes by defining a copy constructor, as described later in this chapter. ■

Display 10.4   A Call-by-Value Pointer Parameter

```
1    //Program to demonstrate the way call-by-value parameters
2    //behave with pointer arguments.
3    #include <iostream>
4    using namespace std;

5    typedef int* IntPointer;

6    void sneaky(IntPointer temp);

7    int main( )
8    {
9        IntPointer p;

10       p = new int;
11       *p = 77;
12       cout << "Before call to function *p == "
13            << *p << endl;

14       sneaky(p);

15       cout << "After call to function *p == "
16            << *p << endl;

17       return 0;
18   }

19   void sneaky(IntPointer temp)
20   {
21       *temp = 99;
22       cout << "Inside function call *temp == "
23            << *temp << endl;
24   }
```

Sample Dialogue

```
Before call to function *p == 77
Inside function call *temp == 99
After call to function *p == 99
```

Uses for Pointers

Chapter 17 discusses ways to use pointers to create a number of useful data structures. This chapter only discusses one use of pointers, namely, to reference arrays, and in particular to create and reference a kind of array known as a *dynamically allocated array*. Dynamically allocated arrays are the topic of Section 10.2.

Display 10.5   The Function Call sneaky (p) ;

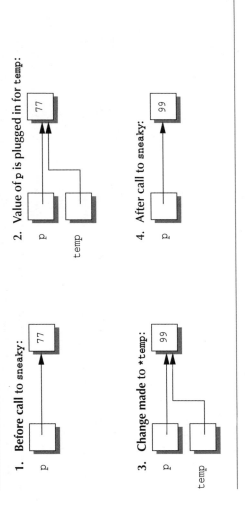

1. **Before call to sneaky:**

   p → 77

2. **Value of p is plugged in for temp:**

   p
   temp
   77

3. **Change made to *temp:**

   p
   temp
   99

4. **After call to sneaky:**

   p
   99

10.2   Dynamic Arrays

In this section you will see that array variables are actually pointer variables. You will also find out how to write programs with dynamically allocated arrays. A **dynamically allocated array** (also called simply a **dynamic array**) is an array whose size is not specified when you write the program, but is determined while the program is running.

Array Variables and Pointer Variables

Chapter 5 described how arrays are kept in memory. At that point we discussed arrays in terms of memory addresses. But a memory address is a pointer. So, in C++ an array variable is actually a kind of pointer variable that points to the first indexed variable of the array. Given the following two variable declarations, p and a are both pointer variables:

```
int a[10];
typedef int* IntPtr;
IntPtr p;
```

The fact that a and p are both pointer variables is illustrated in Display 10.6. Since a is a pointer that points to a variable of type int (namely, the variable a[0]), the value of a can be assigned to the pointer variable p as follows:

```
p = a;
```

After this assignment, p points to the same memory location that a points to. Thus, p[0], p[1], ... p[9] refer to the indexed variables a[0], a[1], ... a[9]. The square bracket notation you have been using for arrays applies to pointer variables as long as the pointer variable points to an array in memory. After the previous assignment, you can treat the identifier p as if it were an array identifier. You can also treat the identifier a as if it were a pointer variable, but there is one important reservation: *You cannot change the pointer value in an array variable.* If the pointer variable p2 has a value, you might be tempted to think the following is legal, but it is not:

a = p2; //ILLEGAL. You cannot assign a different address to a.

The underlying reason why this assignment does not work is that an array variable is not of type int*, but its type is a const version of int*. An array variable, like a, is a pointer variable with the modifier const, which means that its value cannot be changed.

Display 10.6   Arrays and Pointer Variables

```
1    //Program to demonstrate that an array variable is a kind of pointer
     //variable.
2    #include <iostream>
3    using namespace std;

4    typedef int* IntPtr;

5    int main( )
6    {
7        IntPtr p;
8        int a[10];
9        int index;

10       for (index = 0; index < 10; index++)
11           a[index] = index;

12       p = a;

13       for (index = 0; index < 10; index++)
14           cout << p[index] << " ";
15       cout << endl;

16       for (index = 0; index < 10; index++)
17           p[index] = p[index] + 1;

18       for (index = 0; index < 10; index++)            Note that changes
19           cout << a[index] << " ";                    to the array p
20       cout << endl;                                   are also changes
                                                         to the array a.
21       return 0;
22   }
```

Sample Dialogue

```
0 1 2 3 4 5 6 7 8 9
1 2 3 4 5 6 7 8 9 10
```

Creating and Using Dynamic Arrays

One problem with the kinds of arrays we discussed in Chapter 5 is that you must specify the size of the array when you write the program—but you may not know what size array you need until the program is run. For example, an array might hold a list of student identification numbers, but the size of the class may be different each time the program is run. With the kinds of arrays you have used thus far, you must estimate the largest possible size you may need for the array and hope that size is large enough. There are two problems with this. First, you may estimate too low, and then your program will not work in all situations. Second, since the array might have many unused positions, this can waste computer memory. Dynamically allocated arrays avoid these problems. If your program uses a dynamically allocated array for student identification numbers, then the number of students can be entered as input to the program and the dynamically allocated array can be created to have a size exactly equal to the number of students.

Dynamically allocated arrays are created using the new operator. The creation and use of dynamically allocated arrays is surprisingly simple. Since array variables are pointer variables, you can use the new operator to create dynamically allocated variables that are arrays and can treat these dynamically allocated arrays as if they were ordinary arrays. For example, the following creates a dynamically allocated array variable with ten array elements of type double:

creating a dynamic array

```
typedef double* DoublePtr;
DoublePtr d;
d = new double[10];
```

To obtain a dynamically allocated array of elements of any other type, simply replace double with the desired type. In particular, you can replace the type double with a struct or class type. To obtain a dynamically allocated array variable of any other size, simply replace 10 with the desired size.

There are also a number of less-obvious things to notice about this example. First, the pointer type that you use for a pointer to a dynamically allocated array is the same as the pointer type you would use for a single element of the array. For instance, the pointer type for an array of elements of type double is the same as the pointer type you would use for a simple variable of type double. The pointer to the array is actually a pointer to the first indexed variable of the array. In the previous example, an entire array with ten indexed variables is created, and the pointer d is left pointing to the first of these ten indexed variables.

Second, notice that when you call new, the size of the dynamically allocated array is given in square brackets after the type, which in this example is the type double. This tells the computer how much storage to reserve for the dynamic array. If you omitted the square brackets and the 10 in this example, the computer would allocate enough storage for only one variable of type double, rather than for an array of ten indexed variables of type double.

Display 10.7 contains a program that illustrates the use of a dynamically allocated array. The program searches a list of numbers stored in a dynamically allocated array. The size of the array is determined when the program is run. The user is asked how many numbers there will be, and then the new operator creates a dynamically allocated array of that size. The size of the dynamic array is given by the variable arraySize. The size of a dynamic array need not be given by a constant. It can, as in Display 10.7, be given by a variable whose value is determined when the program is run.

Display 10.7   A Dynamically Allocated Array (part 1 of 2)

```
 1    //Searches a list of numbers entered at the keyboard.
 2    #include <iostream>
 3    using namespace std;

 4    typedef int* IntPtr;

 5    void fillArray(int a[], int size);
 6    //Precondition: size is the size of the array a.
 7    //Postcondition: a[0] through a[size-1] have been
 8    //filled with values read from the keyboard.

 9    int search(int a[], int size, int target);
10    //Precondition: size is the size of the array a.
11    //The array elements a[0] through a[size-1] have values.
12    //If target is in the array, returns the first index of target.
13    //If target is not in the array, returns -1.

14    int main( )
15    {
16        cout << "This program searches a list of numbers.\n";

17        int arraySize;
18        cout << "How many numbers will be on the list? ";
19        cin >> arraySize;
20        IntPtr a;
21        a = new int [arraySize];

22        fillArray(a, arraySize);

23        int target;
24        cout << "Enter a value to search for: ";
25        cin >> target;
26        int location = search(a, arraySize, target);
27        if (location == -1)
28            cout << target << " is not in the array.\n";
29        else
30            cout << target << " is element " << location << " in the
                     array.\n";

31        delete [] a;

32
33
34        return 0;
35    }
```

(arrows pointing to lines 6-7 and 11-12) Ordinary array parameters

(arrow pointing to line 21) The dynamic array a is used like an ordinary array.

Display 10.7   A Dynamically Allocated Array (part 2 of 2)

```
36   //Uses the library <iostream>:
37   void fillArray(int a[], int size)
38   {
39       cout << "Enter " << size << " integers.\n";
40       for (int index = 0; index < size; index++)
41           cin >> a[index];
42   }

43   int search(int a[ ], int size, int target)
44   {
45       int index = 0;
46       while ((a[index] != target) && (index < size))
47           index++;
48       if (index == size)//if target is not in a.
49           index = -1;
50       return index;
51   }
```

Sample Dialogue

```
This program searches a list of numbers.
How many numbers will be on the list? 5
Enter 5 integers.
1 2 3 4 5
Enter a value to search for: 3
3 is element 2 in the array.
```

Notice the delete statement, which destroys the dynamically allocated array pointed to by a in Display 10.7. Since the program is about to end anyway, we did not really need this delete statement; if the program went on to do other things, however, you would want such a delete statement so that the memory used by this dynamically allocated array would be returned to the freestore manager. The delete statement for a dynamically allocated array is similar to the delete statement you saw earlier, except that with a dynamically allocated array you must include an empty pair of square brackets like so:

    delete [] a;

delete []   The square brackets tell C++ that a dynamically allocated array variable is being eliminated, so the system checks the size of the array and removes that many indexed variables. If you omit the square brackets you will not be eliminating the entire array. For example,

    delete a;

is not legal, but the error is not detected by most compilers. The C++ standard says that what happens when you do this is "undefined." That means the author of the compiler can have this do anything that is convenient (for the compiler writer, not for you). Always use the

```
delete [] arrayPtr;
```

syntax when you are deleting memory that was allocated with something like

```
arrayPtr = new MyType[37];
```

Also note the position of the square brackets in the `delete` statement

```
delete [] arrayPtr;  //Correct
delete arrayPtr[];   //ILLEGAL!
```

You create a dynamically allocated array with a call to `new` using a pointer, such as the pointer a in Display 10.7. After the call to `new`, you should not assign any other pointer value to this pointer variable because that can confuse the system when the memory for the dynamic array is returned to the freestore manager with a call to `delete`.

Dynamically allocated arrays are created using `new` and a pointer variable. When your program is finished using a dynamically allocated array, you should return the array memory to the freestore manager with a call to `delete`. Other than that, a dynamically allocated array can be used just like any other array.

EXAMPLE: A Function That Returns an Array

In C++ an array type is not allowed as the return type of a function. For example, the following is illegal:

```
int [] someFunction( );  //ILLEGAL
```

If you want to create a function similar to this, you must return a pointer to the array base type and have the pointer point to the array. So, the function declaration would be as follows:

```
int* someFunction( );  //Legal
```

An example of a function that returns a pointer to an array is given in Display 10.8.

Display 10.8   Returning a Pointer to an Array

```
 1  #include <iostream>
 2  using namespace std;

 3  int* doubler(int a[], int size);
 4  //Precondition: size is the size of the array a.
 5  //All indexed variables of a have values.
 6  //Returns: a pointer to an array of the same size as a in which
 7  //each indexed variable is double the corresponding element in a.

 8  int main()
 9  {
10      int a[] = {1, 2, 3, 4, 5};
11      int* b;

12      b = doubler(a, 5);

13      int i;
14      cout << "Array a:\n";
15      for (i = 0; i < 5; i++)
16          cout << a[i] << " ";
17      cout << endl;
18      cout << "Array b:\n";
19      for (i = 0; i < 5; i++)
20          cout << b[i] << " ";
21      cout << endl;

22      delete [] b;
23      return 0;
24  }

25  int* doubler(int a[], int size)
26  {
27      int* temp = new int[size];

28      for (int i =0; i < size; i++)
29          temp[i] = 2*a[i];

30      return temp;
31  }
```

This call to delete is not really needed since the program is ending, but in another context it could be important to include this delete.

Sample Dialogue

```
Array a:
1 2 3  4  5
Array b:
2 4 6  8  10
```

Self-Test Exercises

9. Write a type definition for pointer variables that will be used to point to dynamically allocated arrays. The array elements are to be of type char. Call the type CharArray.

10. Suppose your program contains code to create a dynamically allocated array as follows,

    ```
    int *entry;
    entry = new int[10];
    ```

    so that the pointer variable entry is pointing to this dynamically allocated array. Write code to fill this array with ten numbers typed in at the keyboard.

11. Suppose your program contains code to create a dynamically allocated array as in Self-Test Exercise 10, and suppose the pointer variable entry has not had its (pointer) value changed. Write code to destroy this dynamically allocated array and return the memory it uses to the freestore manager.

12. What is the output of the following code fragment?

    ```
    int a[10];
    int arraySize = 10;
    int *p = a;
    int i;
    for (i = 0; i < arraySize; i++)
        a[i] = i;
    for (i = 0; i < arraySize; i++)
        cout << p[i] << " ";
    cout << endl;
    ```

Pointer Arithmetic

You can perform a kind of arithmetic on pointers, but it is an arithmetic of addresses, not an arithmetic of numbers. For example, suppose your program contains the following code:

```
typedef double* DoublePtr;
DoublePtr d;
d = new double[10];
```

addresses, not numbers

After these statements, d contains the address of the indexed variable d[0]. The expression d + 1 evaluates to the address of d[1], d + 2 is the address of d[2], and so forth. Notice that although the value of d is an address and an address is a number, d + 1 does not simply add 1 to the number in d. If a variable of type double requires eight bytes (eight memory locations) and d contains the address 2000, then d + 1 evaluates to the memory address 2008. Of course, the type double can be replaced by any other type, and then pointer addition moves in units of variables for that type.

This pointer arithmetic gives you an alternative way to manipulate arrays. For example, if arraySize is the size of the dynamically allocated array pointed to by d, then the following will output the contents of the dynamic array:

```
for (int i = 0; i < arraySize; i++)
    cout << *(d + i)<< " ";
```

The previous is equivalent to the following:

```
for (int i = 0; i < arraySize; i++)
    cout << d[i] << " ";
```

++ and --

You may not perform multiplication or division of pointers. All you can do is add an integer to a pointer, subtract an integer from a pointer, or subtract two pointers of the same type. When you subtract two pointers, the result is the number of indexed variables between the two addresses. Remember, for subtraction of two pointer values, *these values must point into the same array!* It makes little sense to subtract a pointer that points into one array from another pointer that points into a different array.

You can also use the increment and decrement operators, ++ and --, to perform pointer arithmetic. For example, d++ will advance the value of d so that it contains the address of the next indexed variable, and d-- will change d so that it contains the address of the previous indexed variable.

Multidimensional Dynamic Arrays

You can have multidimensional dynamic arrays. You just need to remember that multidimensional dynamic arrays are arrays of arrays or arrays of arrays of arrays and so forth. For example, to create a two-dimensional dynamic array you must remember that it is an array of arrays. To create a two-dimensional dynamic array of integers, you first create a one-dimensional dynamic array of pointers of type int*, which is the type for a one-dimensional dynamic array of ints. Then you create a dynamic array of ints for each element of the array.

A type definition may help to keep things straight. The following is the variable type for an ordinary one-dimensional dynamic array of ints:

```
typedef int* IntArrayPtr;
```

To obtain a three-by-four array of ints, you want an array whose base type is IntArrayPtr. For example,

```
IntArrayPtr *m = new IntArrayPtr[3];
```

This is an array of three pointers, each of which can name a dynamic array of ints, as follows:

```
for (int i = 0; i < 3; i++)
    m[i] = new int[4];
```

The resulting array m is a three-by-four dynamic array. A simple program to illustrate this is given in Display 10.9.

How to Use a Dynamic Array

- *Define a pointer type:* Define a type for pointers to variables of the same type as the elements of the array. For example, if the dynamic array is an array of `double`s, you might use the following:

  ```
  typedef double* DoubleArrayPtr;
  ```

- *Declare a pointer variable:* Declare a pointer variable of this defined type. The pointer variable will point to the dynamically allocated array in memory and will serve as the name of the dynamic array.

  ```
  DoubleArrayPtr a;
  ```

  (Alternatively, without a defined pointer type, use `double *a;`).

- *Call new:* Create a dynamic array using the new operator:

  ```
  a = new double[arraySize];
  ```

  The size of the dynamic array is given in square brackets as in the previous example. The size can be given using an `int` variable or other `int` expression. In the previous example, `arraySize` can be a variable of type `int` whose value is determined while the program is running.

- *Use like an ordinary array:* The pointer variable, such as `a`, is used just like an ordinary array. For example, the indexed variables are written in the usual way: `a[0]`, `a[1]`, and so forth. The pointer variable should not have any other pointer value assigned to it, but should be used like an array variable.

- *Call* `delete[]`: When your program is finished with the dynamically allocated array variable, use `delete` and empty square brackets along with the pointer variable to eliminate the dynamic array and return the storage that it occupies to the freestore manager for reuse. For example,

  ```
  delete [] a;
  ```

`delete []`　　Be sure to notice the use of `delete` in Display 10.9. Since the dynamic array `m` is an array of arrays, each of the arrays created with `new` in the `for` loop on lines 13 and 14 must be returned to the freestore manager with a call to `delete []`; then, the array `m` itself must be returned to the freestore manager with another call to `delete []`. There must be a call to `delete []` for each call to `new` that created an array. (Since the program ends right after the calls to `delete []`, we could safely omit the calls to `delete []`, but we wanted to illustrate their usage.)

Display 10.9   A Two-Dimensional Dynamic Array

```
1    #include <iostream>
2    using namespace std;

3    typedef int* IntArrayPtr;

4    int main( )
5    {
6        int d1, d2;
7        cout << "Enter the row and column dimensions of the array:\n"
8        cin >> d1 >> d2;

9        IntArrayPtr *m = new IntArrayPtr[d1];
10       int i, j;
11       for (i = 0; i < d1; i++)
12           m[i] = new int[d2];
13       //m is now a d1-by-d2 array.

14       cout << "Enter " << d1 << " rows of "
15           << d2 << " integers each:\n";
16       for (i = 0; i < d1; i++)
17           for (j = 0; j < d2; j++)
18               cin >> m[i][j];

19       cout << "Echoing the two-dimensional array:\n";
20       for (i = 0; i < d1; i++)
21       {
22           for (j = 0; j < d2; j++)
23               cout << m[i][j] << " ";
24           cout << endl;
25       }

26
27       for (i = 0; i < d1; i++)
28           delete[] m[i];
29       delete[] m;

30       return 0;
31   }
```

Note that there must be one call to delete[] *for each call to* new *that created an array.*
(These calls to delete[] *are not really needed since the program is ending, but in another context it could be important to include them.)*

Sample Dialogue

```
Enter the row and column dimensions of the array:
3 4
Enter 3 rows of 4 integers each:
1 2 3 4
5 6 7 8
9 0 1 2
Echoing the two-dimensional array:
1 2 3 4
5 6 7 8
9 0 1 2
```

10.3 Classes, Pointers, and Dynamic Arrays

The combinations are endless.

A dynamically allocated array can have a base type that is a class. A class can have a member variable that is a dynamically allocated array. You can combine classes and dynamically allocated arrays in just about any combination. There are a few more things to worry about when using classes and dynamically allocated arrays, but the basic techniques are the ones that you have already used. Many of the techniques presented in this section apply to all dynamically allocated structures, such as those we will discuss in Chapter 17, and not just to classes involving dynamically allocated arrays.

The -> Operator

C++ has an operator that can be used with a pointer to simplify the notation for specifying the members of a `struct` or a class. The **arrow operator,** `->`, combines the actions of a dereferencing operator, `*`, and a dot operator to specify a member of a dynamic `struct` or class object that is pointed to by a given pointer. For example, suppose you have the following definition:

```
struct Record
{
    int number;
    char grade;
};
```

The following creates a dynamically allocated variable of type `Record` and sets the member variables of the dynamic `struct` variable to `2001` and `'A'`.

```
Record *p;
p = new Record;
p->number = 2001;
p->grade = 'A';
```

The notations

```
p->grade
```

and

```
(*p).grade
```

have the same meaning. However, the first is more convenient and is almost always the notation used.

arrow operator

The this Pointer

When defining member functions for a class, you sometimes want to refer to the calling object. The this pointer is a predefined pointer that points to the calling object. For example, consider a class like the following:

```
class Sample
{
public:
    . . .
    void showStuff( ) const;
    . . .
private:
    int stuff;
    . . .
};
```

The following two ways of defining the member function showStuff are equivalent:

```
void Sample::showStuff( ) const
{
    cout << stuff;
}

//Not good style, but this illustrates the this pointer:
void Sample::showStuff( )
{
    cout << this->stuff;
}
```

Notice that this is not the name of the calling object, but is the name of a pointer that points to the calling object. The this pointer cannot have its value changed; it always points to the calling object.

As our earlier comment indicated, you normally have no need for the pointer this. However, in a few situations it is handy. One place where the this pointer is commonly used is in overloading the assignment operator, =, which we discuss next.

Since the this pointer points to the calling object, you cannot use this in the definition of any static member functions. A static member function normally has no calling object to which the pointer this can point.

Overloading the Assignment Operator

In this book we usually use the assignment operator as if it were a void function. However, the predefined assignment operator returns a reference that allows for some specialized uses.

With the predefined assignment operator, you can chain assignment operators as follows: a = b = c;, which means a = (b = c);. The first operation, b = c, returns the new version of b. So, the action of

```
a = b = c;
```

is to set a as well as b equal to c. To ensure that your overloaded versions of the assignment operator can be used in this way, you need to define the assignment operator so it returns something of the same type as its left-hand side. As you will see shortly, the this pointer will allow you to do this. (No pun intended.) However, while this requires that the assignment operator return something of the type of its left-hand side, it does not require that it return a reference. Another use of the assignment operator explains why a reference is returned.

The reason that the predefined assignment operator returns a reference is so that you can invoke a member function with the value returned, as in

```
(a = b).f( );
```

where f is a member function. If you want your overloaded versions of the assignment operator to allow for invoking member functions in this way, then you should have them return a reference. This is not a very compelling reason for returning a reference, since this is a pretty minor property that is seldom used. However, it is traditional to return a reference, and it is not significantly more difficult to return a reference than to simply return a value.

For example, consider the following class (which might be used for some specialized string handling that is not easily handled by the predefined class string):

```
class StringClass
{
public:
    . . .
    void someProcessing( );
    . . .
    StringClass& operator=(const StringClass& rtSide);
    . . .
private:
    char *a; //Dynamic array for characters in the string
    int capacity; //size of dynamic array a
    int length; //Number of characters in a
};
```

As noted in Chapter 8, when you overload the assignment operator it must be a member of the class; it cannot be a friend of the class. That is why the previous definition has only one parameter for operator. For example, consider the following:

```
s1 = s2; //s1 and s2 in the class StringClass
```

In the previous call, s1 is the calling object and s2 is the argument to the member operator =.

The following definition of the overloaded assignment operator can be used in chains of assignments like

```
s1 = s2 = s3;
```

and can be used to invoke member functions as follows:

```
(s1 = s2).someProcessing( );
```

The definition of the overloaded assignment operator uses the `this` pointer to return the object on the left side of the = sign (which is the calling object):

```
//This version does not work in all cases.
StringClass& StringClass::operator=(const StringClass& rtSide)
{
    capacity = rtSide.capacity;
    length = rtSide.length;
    delete [] a;
    a = new char[capacity];
    for (int i = 0; i < length; i++)
        a[i] = rtSide.a[i];

    return *this;
}
```

This version has a problem when used in an assignment with the same object on both sides of the assignment operator, like the following:

```
s = s;
```

When this assignment is executed, the following statement is executed:

```
delete [] a;
```

But the calling object is s, so this means

```
delete [] s.a;
```

The pointer `s.a` is then undefined. The assignment operator has corrupted the object `s` and this run of the program is probably ruined.

For many classes, the obvious definition for overloading the assignment operator does not work correctly when the same object is on both sides of the assignment operator. You should always check this case and be careful to write your definition of the overloaded assignment operator so that it also works in this case.

To avoid the problem we had with our first definition of the overloaded assignment operator, you can use the `this` pointer to test this special case as follows:

```
//Final version with bug fixed:
StringClass& StringClass::operator=(const StringClass& rtSide)
{
    if (this == &rtSide)
        //if the right side is the same as the left side
    {
        return *this;
    }
    else
    {
        capacity = rtSide.capacity;
        length = rtSide.length;
        delete [] a;
        a = new char[capacity];
```

```
        for (int i = 0; i < length; i++)
            a[i] = rtSide.a[i] ;

        return *this ;
    }
}
```

A complete example with an overloaded assignment operator is given in the next programming example.

Display 10.10   Definition of a Class with a Dynamic Array Member

```
 1  //Objects of this class are partially filled arrays of doubles.
 2  class PFArrayD
 3  {
 4  public:
 5      PFArrayD( ) ;
 6      //Initializes with a capacity of 50.

 7      PFArrayD(int capacityValue) ;

 8      PFArrayD(const PFArrayD& pfaObject) ;              Copy constructor

 9      void addElement(double element) ;
10      //Precondition: The array is not full.
11      //Postcondition: The element has been added.

12      bool full( ) const { return (capacity == used) ; }
13      //Returns true if the array is full, false otherwise.

14      int getCapacity( ) const { return capacity; }

15      int getNumberUsed( ) const { return used; }

16      void emptyArray( ){ used = 0; }
17      //Empties the array.

18      double& operator[] (int index) ;
19      //Read and change access to elements 0 through numberUsed - 1.

20      PFArrayD& operator =(const PFArrayD& rightSide) ;      Overloaded
                                                              assignment

21      ~PFArrayD( ) ;                          Destructor

22  private:
23      double *a; //For an array of doubles
24      int capacity; //For the size of the array
25      int used; //For the number of array positions currently in use

26  };
```

Display 10.11   Member Function Definitions for **PFArrayD** Class (part 1 of 2)

```
1    //These are the definitions for the member functions for the class
     //PFArrayD.
2    //They require the following include and using directives:
3    //#include <iostream>
4    //using std::cout;

5    PFArrayD::PFArrayD( ) :capacity(50), used(0)
6    {
7        a = new double[capacity];
8    }

9    PFArrayD::PFArrayD(int size) :capacity(size), used(0)
10   {
11       a = new double[capacity];
12   }

13   PFArrayD::PFArrayD(const PFArrayD& pfaObject)
14   :capacity(pfaObject.getCapacity( )), used(pfaObject.getNumberUsed( ))
15   {
16       a = new double[capacity];
17       for (int i = 0; i < used; i++)
18           a[i] = pfaObject.a[i];
19   }

20   void PFArrayD::addElement(double element)
21   {
22       if (used >= capacity)
23       {
24           cout << "Attempt to exceed capacity in PFArrayD.\n";
25           exit(0);
26       }
27       a[used] = element;
28       used++;
29   }

30
31   double& PFArrayD::operator[](int index)
32   {
33       if (index >= used)
34       {
35           cout << "Illegal index in PFArrayD.\n";
36           exit(0);
37       }

38       return a[index];
39   }
```

(continued)

Display 10.11   Member Function Definitions for PFArrayD Class (part 2 of 2)

```
40   PFArrayD& PFArrayD::operator =(const PFArrayD& rightSide)
41   {
42       if (capacity != rightSide.capacity)
43       {
44           delete [] a;
45           a = new double[rightSide.capacity];
46       }
47       capacity = rightSide.capacity;
48       used = rightSide.used;
49       for (int i = 0; i < used; i++)
50           a[i] = rightSide.a[i];
51
52       return *this;
53   }
54
55   PFArrayD::~PFArrayD( )
56   {
57       delete [] a;
58   }
```

Note that this also checks for the case of having the same object on both sides of the assignment operator.

Display 10.12   Demonstration Program for PFArrayD (part 1 of 2)

```
1    //Program to demonstrate the class PFArrayD
2    #include <iostream>
3    using namespace std;

4    class PFArrayD
5    {
6        <The rest of the class definition is the same as in Display 10.10.>
7    };

8    void testPFArrayD( );
9    //Conducts one test of the class PFArrayD.

10   int main( )
11   {
12       cout << "This program tests the class PFArrayD.\n";
13       char ans;
14       do
15       {
16           testPFArrayD( );
17           cout << "Test again? (y/n) ";
18           cin >> ans;
19       } while ((ans == 'y') || (ans == 'Y'));

20       return 0;
21   }
```

In Section 11.1 of Chapter 11 we show you how to divide this long file into three shorter files corresponding roughly to Displays 10.10, 10.11, and this display without the code from Displays 10.10 and 10.11.

Display 10.12   Demonstration Program for PFArrayD   (part 2 of 2)

```
22      <The definitions of the member functions for the class PFArrayD go here.>
23      void testPFArrayD( )
24      {
25          int cap;
26          cout << "Enter capacity of this super array: ";
27          cin >> cap;
28          PFArrayD temp(cap);

29          cout << "Enter up to " << cap << " nonnegative numbers.\n";
30          cout << "Place a negative number at the end.\n";

31          double next;
32          cin >> next;
33          while ((next >= 0) && (!temp.full( )))
34          {
35              temp.addElement(next);
36              cin >> next;
37          }

38          cout << "You entered the following "
39               << temp.getNumberUsed( ) << " numbers:\n";
40          int index;
41          int count = temp.getNumberUsed( );
42          for (index = 0; index < count; index++)
43              cout << temp[index] << " ";
44          cout << endl;
45          cout << "(plus a sentinel value.)\n";
46      }
```

Sample Dialogue

```
This program tests the class PFArrayD.
Enter capacity of this super array: 10
Enter up to 10 nonnegative numbers.
Place a negative number at the end.
1.1
2.2
3.3
4.4
-1
You entered the following 4 numbers:
1.1 2.2 3.3 4.4
(plus a sentinel value.)
Test again? (y/n) n
```

EXAMPLE: A Class for Partially Filled Arrays

The class PFArrayD in Displays 10.10 and 10.11 is a class for a partially filled array of doubles.[5] As shown in the demonstration program in Display 10.12, an object of the class PFArrayD can be accessed using the square brackets just like an ordinary array, but the object also automatically keeps track of how much of the array is in use. Thus, it functions like a partially filled array. The member function getNumberUsed returns the number of array positions used and can thus be used in a for loop as in the following sample code:

```
PFArrayD stuff(cap);  //cap is an int variable.
<some code to fill object stuff with elements.>
for (int index = 0; index < stuff.getNumberUsed( ) ; index++)
    cout << stuff[index] << " ";
```

An object of the class PFArrayD has a dynamic array as a member variable. This member variable array stores the elements. The dynamic array member variable is actually a pointer variable. In each constructor, this member variable is set to point at a dynamic array. There are also two member variables of type int: The member variable capacity records the size of the dynamic array, and the member variable used records the number of array positions that have been filled so far. As is customary with partially filled arrays, the elements must be filled in order, going first into position 0, then 1, then 2, and so forth.

An object of the class PFArrayD can be used as a partially filled array of doubles. It has some advantages over an ordinary array of doubles or a dynamic array of doubles. Unlike the standard arrays, this array gives an error message if an illegal array index is used. Also, an object of the class PFArrayD does not require an extra int variable to keep track of how much of the array is used. (You may protest that "There is such an int variable. It's a member variable." However, that member variable is a private member variable in the implementation, and a programmer who uses the class PFArrayD need never be aware of that member variable.)

An object of the class PFArrayD only works for storing values of type double. When we discuss templates in Chapter 16, you will see that it would be easy to convert the definition to a template class that would work for any type, but for now we will settle for storing elements of type double.

Most of the details in the definition of the class PFArrayD use only items covered before now, but there are three new items: a copy constructor, a destructor, and an overloading of the assignment operator. We explain the overloaded assignment operator next and discuss the copy constructor and destructor in the next two subsections.

---

[5] If you have already read the section of Chapter 7 on vectors, you will notice that the class defined here is a weak version of a vector. Even though you can use a vector any place that you would use this class, this is still an instructive example using many of the techniques we discussed in this chapter. Moreover, this example will give you some insight into how a vector class might be implemented.

EXAMPLE: (continued)

To see why you want to overload the assignment operator, suppose that the overloading of the assignment operator was omitted from Displays 10.10 and 10.11. Suppose list1 and list2 are then declared as follows:

```
PFArrayD list1(10), list2(20);
```

If list2 has been given a list of numbers with invocations of list2.addElement, then even though we are assuming that there is no overloading of the assignment operator, the following assignment statement is still defined, but its meaning may not be what you would like it to be:

```
list1 = list2;
```

With no overloading of the assignment operator, the default predefined assignment operator is used. As usual, this predefined version of the assignment operator copies the value of each of the member variables of list2 to the corresponding member variables of list1. Thus, the value of list1.a is changed to be the same as list2.a, the value of list1.capacity is changed to be the same as list2.capacity, and the value of list1.used is changed to be the same as list2.used. But this can cause problems.

The member variable list1.a contains a pointer, and the assignment statement sets this pointer equal to the same value as list2.a. Both list1.a and list2.a therefore point to the same place in memory. Thus, if you change the array list1.a, you will also change the array list2.a. Similarly, if you change the array list2.a, you will also change the array list1.a. This is not what we normally want. We usually want the assignment operator to produce a completely independent copy of the thing on the right-hand side. The way to fix this is to overload the assignment operator so that it does what we want it to do with objects of the class PFArrayD. This is what we have done in Displays 10.10 and 10.11.

The definition of the overloaded assignment operator in Display 10.11 is reproduced next:

```
PFArrayD& PFArrayD::operator =(const PFArrayD& rightSide)
{
    if (capacity != rightSide.capacity)
    {
        delete [] a;
        a = new double[rightSide.capacity];
    }

    capacity = rightSide.capacity;
    used = rightSide.used;
    for (int i = 0; i < used; i++)
        a[i] = rightSide.a[i];

    return *this;
}
```

(continued)

EXAMPLE: (continued)

When you overload the assignment operator it must be a member of the class; it cannot be a friend of the class. That is why the previous definition has only one parameter. For example, consider the following:

```
list1 = list2;
```

In the previous call, list1 is the calling object and list2 is the argument to the member operator =.

Notice that the capacities of the two objects are checked to see if they are equal. If they are not equal, then the array member variable a of the left side (that is, of the calling object) is destroyed using delete and a new array with the appropriate capacity is created using new. This ensures that the object on the left side of the assignment operator will have an array of the correct size, but also does something else that is very important: It ensures that if the same object occurs on both sides of the assignment operator, then the array named by the member variable a will not be deleted with a call to delete. To see why this is important, consider the following alternative and simpler definition of the overloaded assignment operator:

```
//This version has a bug:
PFArrayD& PFArrayD::operator =(const PFArrayD& rightSide)
{
    delete [] a;
    a = new double [rightSide.capacity];

    capacity = rightSide.capacity;
    used = rightSide.used;
    for (int i = 0; i < used; i++)
        a[i] = rightSide.a[i];

    return *this;
}
```

This version has a problem when used in an assignment with the same object on both sides of the assignment operator, like the following:

```
myList = myList;
```

When this assignment is executed, the first statement executed is

```
delete [] a;
```

But the calling object is myList, so this means

```
delete [] myList.a;
```

The pointer myList.a is then undefined. The assignment operator has corrupted the object myList. This problem cannot happen with the definition of the overloaded assignment operator we gave in Display 10.11.

Shallow Copy and Deep Copy

When defining an overloaded assignment operator or a copy constructor, if your code simply copies the contents of member variables from one object to the other that is known as a *shallow copy*. The default assignment operator and the default copy constructor perform shallow copies. If there are no pointers or dynamically allocated data involved, this works fine. If some member variable names a dynamic array (or points to some other dynamic structure), then you normally do not want a shallow copy. Instead, you want to create a copy of what each member variable is pointing to, so that you get a separate but identical copy, as illustrated in Display 10.11. This is called a *deep copy* and is what we normally do when overloading the assignment operator or defining a copy constructor.

Destructors

Dynamically allocated variables have one problem: They do not go away unless your program makes a suitable call to delete. Even if the dynamic variable was created using a local pointer variable and the local pointer variable goes away at the end of a function call, the dynamic variable will remain unless there is a call to delete. If you do not eliminate dynamic variables with calls to delete, the dynamic variables will continue to occupy memory space, which may cause your program to abort by using up all the memory in the freestore manager. Moreover, if the dynamic variable is embedded in the implementation details of a class, the programmer who uses the class may not know about the dynamic variable and cannot be expected to perform the calls to delete. In fact, since the data members are normally private members, the programmer normally *cannot* access the needed pointer variables and so *cannot* call delete with these pointer variables. To handle this problem, C++ has a special kind of member function called a *destructor*.

destructor   A **destructor** is a member function that is called automatically when an object of the class passes out of scope. If your program contains a local variable that names an object from a class with a destructor, then when the function call ends, the destructor will be called automatically. If the destructor is defined correctly, the destructor will call delete to eliminate all the dynamically allocated variables created by the object. This may be done with a single call to delete or it may require several calls to delete. You may also want your destructor to perform some other clean-up details as well, but returning memory to the freestore manager for reuse is the main job of the destructor.

destructor name   The member function ~PFArrayD is the destructor for the class PFArrayD shown in Display 10.10. Like a constructor, a destructor always has the same name as the class of which it is a member, but the destructor has the tilde symbol, ~, at the beginning of its name (so you can tell that it is a destructor and not a constructor). Like a constructor, a destructor has no type for the value returned, not even the type void. A destructor has no parameters. Thus, a class can have only one destructor; you cannot overload the destructor for a class. Otherwise, a destructor is defined just like any other member function.

Notice the definition of the destructor ~PFArrayD given in Display 10.11. ~PFArrayD calls delete to eliminate the dynamically allocated array pointed to by the member pointer variable a. Look again at the function testPFArrayD in the sample program shown in Display 10.12. The local variable `temp` contains a dynamic array pointed to by the member variable `temp.a`. If this class did not have a destructor, then after the call to `testPFArrayD` ended, this dynamic array would still be occupying memory, even though the dynamic array is useless to the program. Moreover, every iteration of the `do-while` loop would produce another useless dynamic array to clutter up memory. If the loop is iterated enough times, the function calls could consume all the memory in the freestore manager and your program would then end abnormally.

Destructor

The destructor of a class is a member function of a class that is called automatically when an object of the class goes out of scope. Among other things, this means that if an object of the class type is a local variable for a function, then the destructor is automatically called as the last action before the function call ends. Destructors are used to eliminate any dynamically allocated variables that have been created by the object so that the memory occupied by these dynamic variables is returned to the freestore manager for reuse. Destructors may perform other clean-up tasks as well. The name of a destructor must consist of the tilde symbol, ~, followed by the name of the class.

Copy Constructors

A **copy constructor** is a constructor that has one parameter that is of the same type as the class. The one parameter must be a call-by-reference parameter, and normally the parameter is preceded by the `const` parameter modifier, so it is a constant parameter. In all other respects a copy constructor is defined in the same way as any other constructor and can be used just like other constructors. For example, a program that uses the class `PFArrayD` defined in Display 10.10 might contain the following:

```
PFArrayD b(20);
for (int i = 0; i < 20; i++)
    b.addElement(i);
PFArrayD temp(b); //Initialized by the copy constructor
```

copy constructor

The object `b` is initialized with the constructor that has a parameter of type `int`. Similarly, the object `temp` is initialized by the constructor that has one argument of type `const PFArrayD&`. When used in this way a copy constructor is being used just like any other constructor.

A copy constructor should be defined so that the object being initialized becomes a complete, independent copy of its argument. So, in the declaration

```
PFArrayD temp(b);
```

the member variable `temp.a` should not be simply set to the same value as `b.a`; that would produce two pointers pointing to the same dynamic array. The definition of the copy constructor is shown in Display 10.11. Note that in the definition of the copy constructor, a new dynamic array is created and the contents of one dynamic array are copied to the other dynamic array. Thus, in the previous declaration, `temp` is initialized so that its array member variable is different from the array member variable of `b`. The two array member variables, `temp.a` and `b.a`, contain the same values of type `double`, but if a change is made to one of these array member variables, it has no effect on the other array member variable. Thus, any change that is made to `temp` will have no effect on `b`.

As you have seen, a copy constructor can be used just like any other constructor. A copy constructor is also called automatically in certain other situations. Roughly speaking, whenever C++ needs to make a copy of an object, it automatically calls the copy constructor. In particular, the copy constructor is called automatically in three circumstances:

1. When a class object is being declared and is initialized by another object of the same type given in parentheses. (This is the case of using the copy constructor like any other constructor.)
2. When a function returns a value of the class type.
3. Whenever an argument of the class type is "plugged in" for a call-by-value parameter. In this case, the copy constructor defines what is meant by "plugging in."

If you do not define a copy constructor for a class, C++ will automatically generate a copy constructor for you. However, this default copy constructor simply copies the contents of member variables and does not work correctly for classes with pointers or dynamic data in their member variables. Thus, if your class member variables involve pointers, dynamic arrays, or other dynamic data, you should define a copy constructor for the class.

why a copy constructor is needed

To see why you need a copy constructor, let us see what would happen if we did not define a copy constructor for the class `PFArrayD`. *Suppose we did not include the copy constructor in the definition of the class* `PFArrayD` *and* suppose we used a call-by-value parameter in a function definition, for example,

```
void showPFArrayD(PFArrayD parameter)
{
    cout << "The first value is: "
         << parameter[0] << endl;

}
```

Consider the following code, which includes a function call:

```
PFArrayD sample(2);
sample.addElement(5.5);
sample.addElement(6.6);
showPFArrayD(sample);
cout << "After call: " << sample[0] << endl;
```

Because no copy constructor is defined for the class `PFArrayD`, the class has a default copy constructor that simply copies the contents of member variables. Things then proceed as follows. When the function call is executed, the value of `sample` is copied to the local variable `parameter`, so `parameter.a` is set equal to `sample.a`. But these are pointer variables, so during the function call `parameter.a` and `sample.a` point to the same dynamic array, as follows:

sample.a   parameter.a

When the function call ends, the destructor for `PFArrayD` is called to return the memory used by `parameter` to the freestore manager so it can be reused. The definition of the destructor contains the following statement:

```
delete [] a;
```

Since the destructor is called with the object `parameter`, this statement is equivalent to

```
delete [] parameter.a;
```

which changes the picture to the following:

sample.a   parameter.a

Undefined

Since `sample.a` and `parameter.a` point to the same dynamic array, deleting `parameter.a` is the same as deleting `sample.a`. Thus, `sample.a` is undefined when the program reaches the statement

```
cout << "After call: " << sample[0] << endl;
```

so this `cout` statement is undefined. The `cout` statement may by chance give you the output you want, but sooner or later the fact that `sample.a` is undefined will produce problems. One major problem occurs when the object `sample` is a local variable in some function. In this case the destructor will be called with `sample` when the function call ends. That destructor call will be equivalent to

```
delete [] sample.a;
```

But, as we just saw, the dynamic array pointed to by `sample.a` has already been deleted once, and now the system is trying to delete it a second time. Calling `delete` twice to delete the same dynamic array (or any other variable created with `new`) can produce a serious system error that can cause your program to crash.

That was what would happen if there were no copy constructor. Fortunately, we included a copy constructor in our definition of the class `PFArrayD`, so the copy constructor is called automatically when the following function call is executed:

```
showPFArrayD(sample);
```

The copy constructor defines what it means to plug in the argument sample for the call-by-value parameter named parameter, so that now the picture is as follows:

| 5.5, 6.6 | | 5.5, 6.6 |
| sample.a | | parameter.a |

returned value

Thus, any change that is made to parameter.a has no effect on the argument sample, and there are no problems with the destructor. If the destructor is called for parameter and then called for sample, each call to the destructor deletes a different dynamic array.

When a function returns a value of a class type, the copy constructor is called automatically to copy the value specified by the return statement. If there is no copy constructor, problems similar to what we described for call-by-value parameters will occur.

when you need a copy constructor

If a class definition involves pointers and dynamically allocated memory using the new operator, you need to include a copy constructor. Classes that do not involve pointers or dynamically allocated memory do not need to define a copy constructor.

assignment statements

Contrary to what you might expect, the copy constructor is *not* called when you set one object equal to another using the assignment operator.[6] However, if you do not like what the default assignment operator does, you can redefine the assignment operator as we have done in Displays 10.10 and 10.11.

Copy Constructor

A copy constructor is a constructor that has one call-by-reference parameter that is of the same type as the class. The one parameter must be a call-by-reference parameter; normally, the parameter is also a constant parameter—that is, it is preceded by the const parameter modifier. The copy constructor for a class is called automatically whenever a function returns a value of the class type. The copy constructor is also called automatically whenever an argument is plugged in for a call-by-value parameter of the class type. A copy constructor can also be used in the same ways as other constructors.

Any class that uses pointers and the new operator should have a copy constructor.

---

[6]C++ makes a distinction between initialization (the three cases where the copy constructor is called) and assignment. Initialization uses the copy constructor to create a new object; the assignment operator takes an existing object and modifies it so that it is an identical copy (in all but location) of the right-hand side of the assignment.

The Big Three

The copy constructor, the = assignment operator, and the destructor are called the *big three* because experts say that if you need any of them, you need all three. If any of these is missing, the compiler will create it, but the created item might not behave as you want. Thus, it pays to define them yourself. The copy constructor and overloaded = assignment operator that the compiler generates for you will work fine if all member variables are of predefined types such as `int` and `double`. For any class that uses pointers and the new operator, it is safest to define your own copy constructor, overloaded =, and a destructor.

Self-Test Exercises

13. If a class is named `MyClass` and it has a constructor, what is the constructor named? If `MyClass` has a destructor what is the destructor named?

14. Suppose you change the definition of the destructor in Display 10.11 to the following. How would the sample dialogue in Display 10.12 change?

```
PFArrayD::~PFArrayD( )
{
    cout << "\nGood-bye cruel world! The short life of\n"
         << "this dynamic array is about to end.\n";
    delete [] a;
}
```

15. The following is the first line of the copy constructor definition for the class `PFArrayD`. The identifier `PFArrayD` occurs three times and means something slightly different each time. What does it mean in each of the three cases?

```
PFArrayD::PFArrayD(const PFArrayD& pfaobject)
```

16. Answer these questions about destructors.

 a. What is a destructor and what must the name of a destructor be?

 b. When is a destructor called?

 c. What does a destructor actually do?

 d. What *should* a destructor do?

17. a. Explain carefully why no overloaded assignment operator is needed when the only data consists of built-in types.

 b. Same as part a for a copy constructor.

 c. Same as part a for a destructor.

Chapter Summary

- A *pointer* is a memory address, so a pointer provides a way to indirectly name a variable by naming the address of the variable in the computer's memory.

- *Dynamic variables* (also called *dynamically allocated variables*) are variables that are created (and destroyed) while a program is running.

- Memory for dynamic variables is in a special portion of the computer's memory called the *freestore* manager. When a program is finished with a dynamic variable, the memory used by the dynamic variable can be returned to the freestore manager for reuse; this is done with a delete statement.

- A *dynamically allocated array* (also called simply a *dynamic array*) is an array whose size is determined when the program is running. A dynamic array is implemented as a dynamic variable of an array type.

- A *destructor* is a special kind of member function for a class. A destructor is called automatically when an object of the class passes out of scope. The main reason for destructors is to return memory to the freestore manager so the memory can be reused.

- A *copy constructor* is a constructor that has a single argument that is of the same type as the class. If you define a copy constructor, it will be called automatically whenever a function returns a value of the class type and whenever an argument is plugged in for a call-by-value parameter of the class type. Any class that uses pointers and the operator new should have a copy constructor.

- When overloading the assignment operator, it must be overloaded as a member operator. Be sure to check that your overloading works when the same variable is on both sides of the overloaded assignment operator.

Answers to Self-Test Exercises

1. A pointer is the memory address of a variable.

2.
```
int *p;    // This declares a pointer to an int variable.
*p = 17;   //Here, * is the dereferencing operator. This assigns
           //17 to the memory location pointed to by p.
void func(int* p); // Declares p to be a pointer value
                   // parameter.
```

3.
```
10 20
20 20
30 30
```

If you replace *p1 = 30; with *p2 = 30;, the output would be the same.

4. 10 20
   20 20
   30 20

5. To the unwary or to the neophyte, this looks like two objects of type pointer to int, that is, int*. Unfortunately, the * binds to the *identifier*, not to the type (that is, not to the int). The result is that this declaration declares intPtr1 to be an int pointer, while intPtr2 is an ordinary int variable.

6. delete p;

7. typedef double* NumberPtr;
   NumberPtr myPoint;

8. The new operator takes a type for its argument. new allocates space on the freestore manager for a variable of the type of the argument. It returns a pointer to that memory, provided there is enough space. If there is not enough space, the new operator may return NULL, or may abort the program, depending on how your particular compiler works.

9. typedef char* CharArray;

10. cout << "Enter 10 integers:\n";
    for (int i = 0; i < 10; i++)
        cin >> entry[i];

11. delete [] entry;

12. 0 1 2 3 4 5 6 7 8 9

13. The *constructor* is named MyClass, the same name as the name of the class. The *destructor* is named ~MyClass.

14. The dialogue would change to the following:

This program tests the class PFArrayD.
Enter capacity of this super array: 10
Enter up to 10 nonnegative numbers.
Place a negative number at the end.
1.1
2.2
3.3
4.4
-1
You entered the following 4 numbers:
1.1 2.2 3.3 4.4
(plus a sentinel value.)
Good-bye cruel world! The short life of
this dynamic array is about to end.
Test again? (y/n) **n**

15. The PFArrayD before the :: is the name of the class. The PFArrayD right after the :: is the name of the member function. (Remember, a constructor is a member function that has the same name as the class.) The PFArrayD inside the parentheses is the type for the parameter pfaObject.

16. a. A destructor is a member function of a class. A destructor's name always begins with a tilde, ~, followed by the class name.

 b. A destructor is called when a class object goes out of scope.

 c. A destructor actually does whatever the class author programs it to do!

 d. A destructor is *supposed* to delete dynamic variables that have been allocated by constructors for the class. Destructors may also do other clean-up tasks.

17. In the case of the assignment operator = and the copy constructor, if there are only built-in types for data, the copy mechanism is exactly what you want, so the default works fine. In the case of the destructor, no dynamic memory allocation is done (no pointers), so the default do-nothing action is again what you want.

Programming Projects

Visit www.myprogramminglab.com to complete select exercises online and get instant feedback.

1. Reread the code in Display 10.9. Then, write a class TwoD that implements the two-dimensional dynamic array of doubles using ideas from this display in its constructors. You should have a private member of type pointer to double to point to the dynamic array, and two int (or unsigned int) values that are MaxRows and MaxCols.

 You should supply a default constructor for which you are to choose a default maximum row and column sizes and a parameterized constructor that allows the programmer to set maximum row and column sizes.

 Further, you should provide a void member function that allows setting a particular row and column entry and a member function that returns a particular row and column entry as a value of type double.

 Remark: It is difficult or impossible (depending on the details) to overload [ ] so it works as you would like for two-dimensional arrays. So simply use accessor and mutator functions using ordinary function notation.

 Overload the + operator as a friend function to add two two-dimensional arrays. This function should return the TwoD object whose i[th] row, j[th] column element is the sum of the ith row, j[th] column element of the left-hand operand TwoD object and the ith row, j[th] column element of the right-hand operand TwoD object.

 Provide a copy constructor, an overloaded operator=, and a destructor.

 Declare class member functions that do not change the data as const members.

2. Using dynamic arrays, implement a polynomial class with polynomial addition, subtraction, and multiplication.

Discussion: A variable in a polynomial does nothing but act as a placeholder for the coefficients. Hence, the only interesting thing about polynomials is the array of coefficients and the corresponding exponent. Think about the polynomial

```
x*x*x + x + 1
```

Where is the term in x*x? One simple way to implement the polynomial class is to use an array of `doubles` to store the coefficients. The index of the array is the exponent of the corresponding term. If a term is missing, then it simply has a zero coefficient.

There are techniques for representing polynomials of high degree with many missing terms. These use so-called sparse matrix techniques. Unless you already know these techniques, or learn very quickly, do not use these techniques.

Provide a default constructor, a copy constructor, and a parameterized constructor that enables an arbitrary polynomial to be constructed.

Supply an overloaded operator = and a destructor.

Provide these operations:

polynomial + polynomial, constant + polynomial, polynomial + constant,
polynomial − polynomial, constant − polynomial, polynomial − constant,
polynomial * polynomial, constant * polynomial, polynomial * constant,

Supply functions to assign and extract coefficients, indexed by exponent.

Supply a function to evaluate the polynomial at a value of type `double`.

You should decide whether to implement these functions as members, friends, or standalone functions.

3. Write a program that accepts a C-string input from the user and reverses the contents of the string. Your program should work by using two pointers. The "head" pointer should be set to the address of the first character in the string, and the "tail" pointer should be set to the address of the last character in the string (i.e., the character before the terminating `null`). The program should swap the characters referenced by these pointers, increment "head" to point to the next character, decrement "tail" to point to the second-to-last character, and so on, until all characters have been swapped and the entire string reversed.

4. Create a class named `student` that has three member variables:

`name`	—	A string that stores the name of the student
`numClasses`	—	An integer that tracks how many courses the student is currently enrolled in
`classList`	—	A dynamic array of strings used to store the names of the classes that the student is enrolled in

Write appropriate constructor(s), mutator, and accessor functions for the class along with the following:

- A function that inputs all values from the user, including the list of class names. This function will have to support input for an arbitrary number of classes.
- A function that outputs the name and list of all courses.
- A function that resets the number of classes to 0 and the classList to an empty list.
- An overloaded assignment operator that correctly makes a new copy of the list of courses.
- A destructor that releases all memory that has been allocated.

Write a main function that tests all of your functions.

5. This programming project is based on Programming Projects 7.8 and 5.7. Write a program that outputs a histogram of grades for an assignment given to a class of students. The program should input each student's grade as an integer and store the grade in a vector. Grades should be entered until the user enters -1 for a grade. The program should then scan through the vector and compute the histogram. In computing the histogram, the minimum value of a grade is 0, but your program should determine the maximum value entered by the user. Use a dynamic array to store the histogram. Output the histogram to the console.

6. One problem with dynamic arrays is that once the array is created using the new operator the size cannot be changed. For example, you might want to add or delete entries from the array similar to the behavior of a vector. This project asks you to create a class called DynamicStringArray that includes member functions that allow it to emulate the behavior of a vector of strings.

The class should have the following:

- A private member variable called dynamicArray that references a dynamic array of type string.
- A private member variable called size that holds the number of entries in the array.
- A default constructor that sets the dynamic array to NULL and sets size to 0.
- A function that returns size.
- A function named addEntry that takes a string as input. The function should create a new dynamic array one element larger than dynamicArray, copy all elements from dynamicArray into the new array, add the new string onto the end of the new array, increment size, delete the old dynamicArray, and then set dynamicArray to the new array.
- A function named deleteEntry that takes a string as input. The function should search dynamicArray for the string. If not found, it returns false. If found, it creates a new dynamic array one element smaller than dynamicArray. It should copy all elements except the input string into the new array, delete dynamicArray, decrement size, and return true.

- A function named `getEntry` that takes an integer as input and returns the string at that index in `dynamicArray`. It should return NULL if the index is out of `dynamicArray`'s bounds.

- A copy constructor that makes a copy of the input object's dynamic array.

- Overload the assignment operator so that the dynamic array is properly copied to the target object.

- A destructor that frees up the memory allocated to the dynamic array.

Embed your class in a suitable test program.

Separate Compilation and Namespaces

11.1 SEPARATE COMPILATION   472

11.2 NAMESPACES   487

11 Separate Compilation and Namespaces

*From mine own library with volumes that
I prize above my dukedom.*

WILLIAM SHAKESPEARE, *The Tempest*

Introduction

This chapter covers two topics that have to do with how to organize a C++ program into separate parts. Section 11.1 on separate compilation discusses how a C++ program can be distributed across a number of files so that when some parts of the program change only those parts need to be recompiled and so that the separate parts can be more easily reused in other applications.

Section 11.2 discusses namespaces, which were introduced briefly in Chapter 1. Namespaces are a way of allowing you to reuse the names of classes, functions, and other items by qualifying the names to indicate different uses. Namespaces divide your code into sections so that the different sections may reuse the same names with differing meanings. They allow a kind of local meaning for names that is more general than local variables.

This chapter can be covered earlier than its location in the book. This chapter does not use any of the material from Chapters 5 (arrays), 9 (strings), 10 (pointers and dynamic arrays) or Section 7.3 (vectors) of Chapter 7.

11.1 Separate Compilation

Your "if" is the only peacemaker; much virtue in "if."

WILLIAM SHAKESPEARE, *As You Like It*

C++ has facilities for dividing a program into parts that are kept in separate files, compiled separately, and then linked together when (or just before) the program is run. You can place the definition for a class (and its associated function definitions) in files that are separate from the programs that use the class. In this way you can build up a library of classes so that many programs can use the same class. You can compile the class once and then use it in many different programs, just like you use the predefined libraries such as those with header files iostream and cstdlib. Moreover, you can define the class itself in two files so that the specification of what the class does is separate from how the class is implemented. If you only change the implementation of the class, then you need only recompile the file containing the class implementation. The other files, including the files containing the programs that use the class, need not be changed or even recompiled. This section tells you how to carry out this separate compilation of classes.

Encapsulation Reviewed

The principle of encapsulation says that you should separate the specification of how the class is used by a programmer from the details of how the class is implemented. The separation should be so complete that you can change the implementation without needing to change any program that uses the class. The way to ensure this separation can be summarized in three rules:

interface

1. Make all the member variables private members of the class.

2. Make each of the basic operations for the class either a public member function of the class, a friend function, an ordinary function, or an overloaded operator. Group the class definition and the function and operator declarations (prototypes) together. This group, along with its accompanying comments, is called the **interface** for the class. Fully specify how to use each such function or operator in a comment given with the class or with the function or operator declaration.

implementation

3. Make the implementation of the basic operations unavailable to the programmer who uses the class. The **implementation** consists of the function definitions and overloaded operator definitions (along with any helping functions or other additional items these definitions require).

interface file and implementation file

In C++, the best way to ensure that you follow these rules is to place the interface and the implementation of the class in separate files. As you might guess, the file that contains the interface is often called the **interface file**, and the file that contains the implementation is called the **implementation file**. The exact details of how to set up, compile, and use these files will vary slightly from one version of C++ to another, but the basic scheme is the same in all versions of C++. In particular, the details of what goes into the files are the same in all systems. The only things that vary are the commands used to compile and link these files. The details about what goes into these files are illustrated in the next subsection.

Private members are part of the implementation.

A typical class has private member variables. Private member variables (and private member functions) present a problem to our basic philosophy of placing the interface and the implementation of a class in separate files. The public part of the definition for a class is part of the interface for the class, but the private part is part of the implementation. This is a problem because C++ will not allow you to split the class definition across two files. Thus, some sort of compromise is needed. The only sensible compromise is to place the entire class definition in the interface file. Since a programmer who is using the class cannot use any of the private members of the class, the private members will, in effect, still be hidden from the programmer.

Header Files and Implementation Files

Display 11.1 contains the interface file for a class called DigitalTime. DigitalTime is a class whose values are times of day, such as 9:30. Only the public members of the class are part of the interface. The private members are part of the implementation, even though they are in the interface file. The label private: warns you that these private members are not part of the public interface. Everything that a programmer needs to know in order to use the class DigitalTime is explained in the comment at the start of the file and in the comments in the public section of the class definition. As noted in the comment at the top of the interface file, this class uses 24-hour notation, so, for instance, 1:30 P.M. is input and output as 13:30. This and the other details you must know in order to effectively use the class DigitalTime are included in the comments given with the member functions.

header files

We have placed the interface in a file named dtime.h. The suffix .h indicates that this is a **header file**. An interface file is always a header file and so always ends with the suffix .h. Any program that uses the class DigitalTime must contain an include directive like the following, which names this file:

```
#include "dtime.h"
```

include

When you write an include directive, you must indicate whether the header file is a predefined header file that is provided for you or is a header file that you wrote. If the header file is predefined, write the header file name in angular brackets, like <iostream>. If the header file is one that you wrote, write the header file name in quotes, like "dtime.h". This distinction tells the compiler where to look for the header file. If the header file name is in angular brackets, the compiler looks for the header file. If the header file name is in angular brackets, the compiler looks wherever the predefined header files are kept in your implementation of C++. If the header file name is in quotes, the compiler looks in the current directory or wherever programmer-defined header files are kept on your system.

Any program that uses our DigitalTime class must contain the previous include directive that names the header file dtime.h. That is enough to allow you to compile the program, but is not enough to allow you to run the program. In order to run the program you must write (and compile) the definitions of the member functions and the overloaded operators. We have placed these function and operator definitions in another file, which is called the *implementation file*. Although it is not required by most compilers, it is traditional to give the interface file and the implementation file the same name. The two files do, however, end in different suffixes. We have placed the interface for our class in the file named dtime.h and the implementation for our class in a file named dtime.cpp. The suffix you use for the implementation file depends on your version of C++. Use the same suffix for the implementation file as you normally use for files that contain C++ programs. (Other common suffixes are .cc and .cxx and .hxx.) The implementation file for our DigitalTime class is given in Display 11.2. After we explain how the various files for our class interact with each other, we will return to Display 11.2 and discuss the details of the definitions in this implementation file.

file names

Display 11.1   Interface File for the DigitalTime Class (part 1 of 2)

```
1  //This is the header file dtime.h. This is the interface for the class
2  //DigitalTime. Values of this type are times of day. The values are
3  //input and output in 24-hour notation, as in 9:30 for 9:30 AM and
4  //14:45 for 2:45 PM.
5  #include <iostream>
   using namespace std;
```

Display 11.1   Interface File for the DigitalTime Class (part 2 of 2)

```
6    class DigitalTime
7    {
8    public:
9        DigitalTime(int theHour, int theMinute);
10       DigitalTime( );
11       //Initializes the time value to 0:00 (which is midnight).

12       int getHour( ) const;
13       int getMinute( ) const;
14       void advance(int minutesAdded);
15       //Changes the time to minutesAdded minutes later.

16       void advance(int hoursAdded, int minutesAdded);
17       //Changes the time to hoursAdded hours plus minutesAdded minutes
18       //later.

18       friend bool operator ==(const DigitalTime& time1,
19                               const DigitalTime& time2);

20       friend istream& operator >>(istream& ins, DigitalTime& theObject);

21       friend ostream& operator <<(ostream& outs, const DigitalTime&
         theObject);
22   private:
```

These member variables and helping functions are part of the implementation. They are not part of the interface. The word private *indicates that they are not part of the public interface.*

```
23       int hour;
24       int minute;

25       static void readHour(int& theHour);
26       //Precondition: Next input to be read from the keyboard is
27       //a time in notation, like 9:45 or 14:45.
28       //Postcondition: theHour has been set to the hour part of the time.
29       //The colon has been discarded and the next input to be read is the
         //minute.

30       static void readMinute(int& theMinute);
31       //Reads the minute from the keyboard after readHour has read the
         //hour.

32       static int digitToInt(char c);
33       //Precondition: c is one of the digits '0' through '9'.
34       //Returns the integer for the digit; for example, digitToInt('3')
         //returns 3.

35
36   };
```

Display 11.2   Implementation File (part 1 of 3)

```
1   //This is the implementation file dtime.cpp of the class DigitalTime.
2   //The interface for the class DigitalTime is in the header file dtime.h.
3   #include <iostream>
4   #include <cctype>
5   #include <cstdlib>
6   using namespace std;
7   #include "dtime.h"
8   //Uses iostream and cstdlib:
9   DigitalTime::DigitalTime(int theHour, int theMinute)
10  {
11      if (theHour < 0 || theHour > 24 || theMinute < 0 || theMinute > 59)
12      {
13          cout << "Illegal argument to DigitalTime constructor.";
14          exit(1);
15      }
16      else
17      {
18          hour = theHour;
19          minute = theMinute;
20      }
21      if (hour == 24)
22          hour = 0; //Standardize midnight as 0:00
23  }

24  DigitalTime::DigitalTime( )
25  {
26      hour = 0;
27      minute = 0;
28  }

29  int DigitalTime::getHour( ) const
30  {
31      return hour;
32  }

33  int DigitalTime::getMinute( ) const
34  {
35      return minute;
36  }

37  void DigitalTime::advance(int minutesAdded)
38  {
39      int grossMinutes = minute + minutesAdded;
40      minute = grossMinutes % 60;
41  }
```

Display 11.2   Implementation File (part 2 of 3)

```
42        int hourAdjustment = grossMinutes / 60;
43        hour = (hour + hourAdjustment)%24;
44    }

45    void DigitalTime::advance(int hoursAdded, int minutesAdded)
46    {
47        hour = (hour + hoursAdded) % 24;
48        advance(minutesAdded);
49    }

50    bool operator ==(const DigitalTime& time1, const DigitalTime& time2)
51    {
52        return (time1.hour == time2.hour && time1.minute == time2.minute);
53    }

54    //Uses iostream:
55    ostream& operator <<(ostream& outs, const DigitalTime& theObject)
56    {
57        outs << theObject.hour << ':';
58        if (theObject.minute < 10)
59            outs << '0';
60        outs << theObject.minute;
61        return outs;
62    }

63
64    //Uses iostream:
65    istream& operator >>(istream& ins, DigitalTime& theObject)
66    {
67        DigitalTime::readHour(theObject.hour);
68        DigitalTime::readMinute(theObject.minute);
69        return ins;
70    }

71    int DigitalTime::digitToInt(char c)
72    {
73        return ( static_cast<int>(c) - static_cast<int>('0') );
74    }

75    //Uses iostream, cctype, and cstdlib:
76    void DigitalTime::readMinute(int& theMinute)
77    {
78        char c1, c2;
79        cin >> c1 >> c2;

80        if (!(isdigit(c1) && isdigit(c2)))
81        {
82            cout << "Error: illegal input to readMinute\n";
```

(continued)

Display 11.2   Implementation File (part 3 of 3)

```
83          exit(1);
84      }
85      theMinute = digitToInt(c1)*10 + digitToInt(c2);
86      if (theMinute < 0 || theMinute > 59)
87      {
88          cout << "Error: illegal input to readMinute\n";
89          exit(1);
90      }
91  }
92
93  //Uses iostream, cctype, and cstdlib:
94  void DigitalTime::readHour(int& theHour)
95  {
96      char c1, c2;
97      cin >> c1 >> c2;
98      if ( !( isdigit(c1) && (isdigit(c2) || c2 == ':' ) ) )
99      {
100         cout << "Error: illegal input to readHour\n";
101         exit(1);
102     }
103     if (isdigit(c1) && c2 == ':')
104     {
105         theHour = DigitalTime::digitToInt(c1);
106     }
107     else //((isdigit(c1) && isdigit(c2))
108     {
109         theHour = DigitalTime::digitToInt(c1)*10
                        + DigitalTime::digitToInt(c2);
110         cin >> c2; //discard ':'
111         if (c2 != ':')
112         {
113             cout << "Error: illegal input to readHour\n";
114             exit(1);
115         }
116     }
117     if ( theHour < 0 || theHour > 23 )
118     {
119         cout << "Error: illegal input to readHour\n";
120         exit(1);
121     }
122     if (theHour == 24)
123         theHour = 0; //Standardize midnight as 0:00
124 }
125 }
```

Any file that uses the class DigitalTime must contain the include directive

application file or driver file

```
#include "dtime.h"
```

Thus, both the implementation file and the program file must contain the include directive that names the interface file. The file that contains the program (that is, the file that contains the main function) is often called the **application file** or **driver file.** Display 11.3 contains an application file with a very simple program that uses and demonstrates the DigitalTime class.

compiling and running the program

The exact details of how to run this complete program, which is contained in three files, depend on what system you are using. However, the basic details are the same for all systems. You must compile the implementation file and you must compile the application file that contains the main function. You do not compile the interface file, which in this example is the file dtime.h given in Display 11.1. You do not need to compile the interface file because the compiler thinks the contents of this interface file are already contained in each of the other two files. Recall that both the implementation file and the application file contain the directive

```
#include "dtime.h"
```

Compiling your program automatically invokes a preprocessor that reads this include directive and replaces it with the text in the file dtime.h. Thus, the compiler sees the contents of dtime.h, and so the file dtime.h does not need to be compiled separately. (In fact, the compiler sees the contents of dtime.h twice: once when you compile the implementation file and once when you compile the application file.) This copying of the file dtime.h is only a conceptual copying. The compiler acts as if the contents of dtime.h were copied into each file that has the include directive. However, if you look in those files after they are compiled, you will only find the include directive; you will not find the contents of the file dtime.h.

linking

linker

Once the implementation file and the application file are compiled, you still need to connect these files so that they can work together. This is called **linking** the files and is done by a separate utility called a **linker.** The details of how to call the linker depends on what system you are using. Often, the command to run a program automatically invokes the linker, so you need not explicitly call the linker at all. After the files are linked, you can run your program.

make

project

This sounds like a complicated process, but many systems have facilities that manage much of this detail for you automatically or semiautomatically. On any system, the details quickly become routine. On UNIX systems, these details are handled by the **make** facility. In most **Integrated Development Environments (IDEs)** these various files are combined into a **project.**

Why separate files?

Displays 11.1, 11.2, and 11.3 contain one complete program divided into pieces and placed in three different files. You could instead combine the contents of these three files into one file, and then compile and run this one file without all this fuss about include directives and linking separate files. Why bother with three separate files? There are several advantages to dividing your program into separate files. Since you have the definition and the implementation of the class DigitalTime in files separate from the application file, you can use this class in many different programs without

Display 11.3   Application File Using `DigitalTime` Class

```
1    //This is the application file timedemo.cpp, which demonstrates use of
2    //DigitalTime.
3    #include <iostream>
4    #include "dtime.h"
5    using namespace std;
6
7    int main( )
8    {
9        DigitalTime clock, oldClock;
10
11       cout << "You may write midnight as either 0:00 or 24:00,\n"
12            << "but I will always write it as 0:00.\n"
13            << "Enter the time in 24-hour notation: ";
14       cin >> clock;
15
16       oldClock = clock;
17       clock.advance(15);
18       if (clock == oldClock)
19           cout << "Something is wrong.";
20       cout << "You entered " << oldClock << endl;
21       cout << "15 minutes later the time will be "
22            << clock << endl;
23
24       clock.advance(2, 15);
25       cout << "2 hours and 15 minutes after that\n"
26            << "the time will be "
27            << clock << endl;
28
29       return 0;
30   }
```

```
1    //This is the application file timedemo.cpp, which demonstrates use of
2    //DigitalTime.
3    #include <iostream>
4    #include "dtime.h"
5    using namespace std;
6
7    int main( )
8    {
9        DigitalTime clock, oldClock;
10
11       cout << "You may write midnight as either 0:00 or 24:00,\n"
12            << "but I will always write it as 0:00.\n"
13            << "Enter the time in 24-hour notation: ";
14       cin >> clock;
15
16       oldClock = clock;
17       clock.advance(15);
18       if (clock == oldClock)
19           cout << "Something is wrong.";
20       cout << "You entered " << oldClock << endl;
21       cout << "15 minutes later the time will be "
22            << clock << endl;
23
24       return 0;
25   }
```

Sample Dialogue

```
You may write midnight as either 0:00 or 24:00,
but I will always write it as 0:00.
Enter the time in 24-hour notation: 11:15
You entered 11:15
15 minutes later the time will be 11:30
2 hours and 15 minutes after that
the time will be 13:45
```

needing to rewrite the definition of the class in each of the programs. Moreover, you need to compile the implementation file only once, no matter how many programs use the class DigitalTime. But there are more advantages than that. Since you have separated the interface from the implementation of your DigitalTime class, you can change the implementation file and will not need to change any program that uses the class. In fact, you will not even need to recompile the program. If you change the implementation file, you only need to recompile the implementation file and relink the files. Saving a bit of recompiling time is nice, but the big advantage is avoiding the

Defining a Class in Separate Files: A Summary

You can define a class and place the definition of the class and the implementation of its member functions in separate files. You can then compile the class separately from any program that uses the class and you can use this same class in any number of different programs. The class is placed in files as follows:

1. Put the definition of the class in a header file called the *interface file*. The name of this header file ends in .h. The interface file also contains the declarations (prototypes) for any functions and overloaded operators that define basic class operations but that are not listed in the class definition. Include comments that explain how all these functions and operators are used.

2. The definitions of all the functions and overloaded operators mentioned previously (whether they are members or friends or neither) are placed in another file called the *implementation file*. This file must contain an include directive that names the interface file previously described. This include directive uses quotes around the file name, as in the following example:

   ```
   #include "dtime.h"
   ```

   The interface file and the implementation file traditionally have the same name, but end in different suffixes. The interface file ends in .h. The implementation file ends in the same suffix that you use for files that contain a complete C++ program. The implementation file is compiled separately before it is used in any program.

3. When you want to use the class in a program, you place the main part of the program (and any additional function definitions, constant declarations, and such) in another file called an *application file* or *driver file*. This file also must contain an include directive naming the interface file, as in the following example:

   ```
   #include "dtime.h"
   ```

   The application file is compiled separately from the implementation file. You can write any number of these application files to use with one pair of interface and implementation files. To run an entire program, you must first link the object code produced by compiling the application file and the object code produced by compiling the implementation file. (On some systems the linking may be done automatically or semiautomatically.)

If you use multiple classes in a program, then you simply have multiple interface files and multiple implementation files, each compiled separately.

need to rewrite code. You can use the class in many programs without writing the class code into each program. You can change the implementation of the class and you need not rewrite any part of any program that uses the class.

The details of the implementation of the class `DigitalTime` are discussed in the following example section.

EXAMPLE: `DigitalTime` Class

Previously we described how the files in Displays 11.1, 11.2, and 11.3 divide a program into three files: the interface for the class `DigitalTime`, the implementation of the class `DigitalTime`, and an application that uses the class. Here we discuss the details of the class implementation. There is no new material in this example section, but if some of the details in the implementation (Display 11.2) are not completely clear to you, this section may shed some light on your confusion.

Most of the implementation details are straightforward, but there are two things that merit comment. Notice that the member function name `advance` is overloaded so that it has two function definitions. Also notice that the definition for the overloaded extraction (input) operator `>>` uses two helping functions called `readHour` and `readMinute` and that these two helping functions themselves use a third helping function called `digitToInt`. Let us discuss these points.

The class `DigitalTime` (Displays 11.1 and 11.2) has two member functions called `advance`. One version takes a single argument, that is, an integer giving the number of minutes to advance the time. The other version takes two arguments, one for a number of hours and one for a number of minutes, and advances the time by that number of hours plus that number of minutes. Notice that the definition of the two-argument version of `advance` includes a call to the one-argument version. Look at the definition of the two-argument version that is given in Display 11.2. First the time is advanced by `hoursAdded` hours and then the single-argument version of `advance` is used to advance the time by an additional `minutesAdded` minutes. At first this may seem strange, but it is perfectly legal. The two functions named `advance` are two different functions that, as far as the compiler is concerned, just coincidentally happen to have the same name.

Now let us discuss the helping functions. The helping functions `readHour` and `readMinute` read the input one character at a time and then convert the input to integer values that are placed in the member variables `hour` and `minute`. The functions `readHour` and `readMinute` read the hour and minute one digit at a time, so they are reading values of type `char`. This is more complicated than reading the input as `int` values, but it allows us to perform error checking to see whether the input is correctly formed and to issue an error message if the input is not well formed. These helping functions `readHour` and `readMinute` use another helping function named `digitToInt`. The function `digitToInt` converts a digit, such as `'3'`, to a number, such as 3. This function was given previously in this book as the answer to Self-Test Exercise 3 in Chapter 7.

TIP: Reusable Components

A class developed and coded into separate files is a software component that can be used again and again in a number of different programs. A reusable component saves effort because it does not need to be redesigned, recoded, and retested for every application. A reusable component is also likely to be more reliable than a component that is used only once. It is likely to be more reliable for two reasons. First, you can afford to spend more time and effort on a component if it will be used many times. Second, if the component is used again and again, it is tested again and again. Every use of a software component is a test of that component. Using a software component many times in a variety of contexts is one of the best ways to discover any remaining bugs in the software. ■

Using #ifndef

We have given you a method for placing a program in three (or more) files: two for the interface and implementation of each class and one for the application part of the program. A program can be kept in more than three files. For example, a program might use several classes, and each class might be kept in a separate pair of files. Suppose you have a program spread across a number of files and that more than one file has an include directive for a class interface file such as the following:

```
#include "dtime.h"
```

Under these circumstances you can have files that include other files, and these other files may in turn include yet other files. This can easily lead to a situation in which a file, in effect, contains the definitions in dtime.h more than once. C++ does not allow you to define a class more than once, even if the repeated definitions are identical. Moreover, if you are using the same header file in many different projects, it becomes close to impossible to keep track of whether you included the class definition more than once. To avoid this problem, C++ provides a way of marking a section of code to say "if you have already included this stuff once before, do not include it again." The way this is done is quite intuitive, although the notation may look a bit weird until you get used to it. We will go through an example, explaining the details as we go.

The following directive **defines** DTIME_H:

#define
```
#define DTIME_H
```

What this means is that the compiler's preprocessor puts DTIME_H on a list to indicate that DTIME_H has been seen. *Defined* is perhaps not the best word for this, since DTIME_H is not defined to mean anything but merely put on a list. The important point is that you can use another directive to test whether DTIME_H has been defined and so test whether a section of code has already been processed. You can use any (nonkeyword) identifier in place of DTIME_H, but you will see that there are standard conventions for which identifier you should use.

The following directive tests to see whether DTIME_H has been defined:

#ifndef
```
#ifndef DTIME_H
```

If `DTIME_H` has already been defined, then everything between this directive and the first occurrence of the following directive is skipped:

```
#endif
```

An equivalent way to state this, which may clarify the way the directives are spelled, is the following: If `DTIME_H` is *not* defined, then the compiler processes everything up to the next `#endif`. The *not* is why there is an n in `#ifndef`. (This may lead you to wonder whether there is a `#ifdef` directive as well as a `#ifndef` directive. There is, and it has the obvious meaning, but we will have no occasion to use `#ifdef`.)

Now consider the following code:

```
#ifndef DTIME_H
#define DTIME_H
<a class definition>
#endif
```

If this code is in a file named `dtime.h`, then no matter how many times your program contains

```
#include "dtime.h"
```

the class will be defined only one time.

The first time

```
#include "dtime.h"
```

is processed, the flag `DTIME_H` is defined and the class is defined. Now, suppose the compiler again encounters

```
#include "dtime.h"
```

When the `include` directive is processed this second time, the directive

```
#ifndef DTIME_H
```

says to skip everything up to

```
#endif
```

and so the class is not defined again.

In Display 11.4 we have rewritten the header file `dtime.h` shown in Display 11.1, but this time we used these directives to prevent multiple definitions. With the version of `dtime.h` shown in Display 11.4, if a file contains the following `include` directive more than once, the class `DigitalTime` will still be defined only once:

```
#include "dtime.h"
```

You may use some other identifier in place of `DTIME_H`, but the normal convention is to use the name of the file written in all uppercase letters with the underscore used in place of the period. You should follow this convention so that others can more easily read your code and so that you do not have to remember the flag name. This way the flag name is determined automatically and there is nothing arbitrary to remember.

VideoNote
Avoiding
Multiple
Definition
with
`#ifndef`

These same directives can be used to skip over code in files other than header files, but we will not have occasion to use these directives except in header files.

Display 11.4   Avoiding Multiple Definitions of a Class

```
 1    //This is the header file dtime.h. This is the interface for the class
 2    //DigitalTime. Values of this type are times of day. The values are
 3    //input and output in 24-hour notation, as in 9:30 for 9:30 AM and
      //14:45 for 2:45 PM.

 4    #ifndef DTIME_H
 5    #define DTIME_H

 6    #include <iostream>
 7    using namespace std;

 8    class DigitalTime
 9    {
         <The definition of the class DigitalTime is the same as in Display 11.1.>

10    };

11    #endif //DTIME_H
```

#Ifndef

You can avoid multiple definitions of a class (or anything else) by using #ifndef in the header file (interface file), as illustrated in Display 11.4. If the file is included more than once, only one of the definitions included will be used.

TIP: Defining Other Libraries

You need not define a class in order to use separate compilation. If you have a collection of related functions that you want to make into a library of your own design, you can place the function declarations (prototypes) and accompanying comments in a header file and the function definitions in an implementation file, just as we outlined for classes. After that, you can use this library in your programs the same way you would use a class that you placed in separate files.

Self-Test Exercises

1. Suppose that you are defining a class and that you then want to use this class in a program. You want to separate the class and program parts into separate files as described in this chapter. State whether each of the following should be placed in the interface file, implementation file, or application file.

    a. The class definition

    b. The declaration for a function that is to serve as a class operation but that is neither a member nor a friend of the class

    c. The declaration for an overloaded operator that is to serve as a class operation but that is neither a member nor a friend of the class

    d. The definition for a function that is to serve as a class operation but that is neither a member nor a friend of the class

    e. The definition for a friend function that is to serve as a class operation

    f. The definition for a member function

    g. The definition for an overloaded operator that is to serve as a class operation but that is neither a member nor a friend of the class

    h. The definition for an overloaded operator that is to serve as a class operation and that is a friend of the class

    i. The `main` function of your program

2. Which of the following files has a name that ends in `.h`: the interface file for a class, the implementation file for the class, or the application file that uses the class?

3. When you define a class in separate files, there is an interface file and an implementation file. Which of these files needs to be compiled? (Both? Neither? Only one? If so, which one?)

4. Suppose you define a class in separate files and use the class in a program. Now suppose you change the class implementation file. Which of the following files, if any, needs to be recompiled: the interface file, the implementation file, and/or the application file?

5. Suppose you want to change the implementation of the class `DigitalTime` given in Displays 11.1 and 11.2. Specifically, you want to change the way the time is recorded. Instead of using the two private variables `hour` and `minute`, you want to use a single (private) `int` variable, which will be called `minutes`. In this new implementation the private variable `minutes` will record the time as the number of minutes since the time 0:00 (that is, since midnight). For example, 1:30 is recorded as 90 minutes, since it is 90 minutes past midnight. Describe how you need to change the interface and implementation files shown in Displays 11.1 and 11.2. You need not write out the files in their entirety; just indicate what items you need to change and how, in a very general way, you would change them.

11.2 Namespaces

What's in a name? That which we call a rose
By any other name would smell as sweet.

WILLIAM SHAKESPEARE, *Romeo and Juliet*

namespace

When a program uses different classes and functions written by different programmers there is a possibility that two programmers will use the same name for two different things. Namespaces are a way to deal with this problem. A **namespace** is a collection of name definitions, such as class definitions and variable declarations. A namespace can, in a sense, be turned on and off so that when some of its names would otherwise conflict with names in another namespace, it can be turned off.

Namespaces and using Directives

We have already been using the namespace that is named std. The std namespace contains all the names defined in many of the standard C++ library files (such as iostream). For example, when you place the following line at the start of a file,

```
#include <iostream>
```

it places all the name definitions (for names like cin and cout) into the std namespace. Your program does not know about names in the std namespace unless you specify that it is using the std namespace. To make all the definitions in the std namespace available to your code, insert the following using directive:

```
using namespace std;
```

A good way to see why you might want to include this using directive is to think about why you might want to *not* include it. If you do not include this using directive for the namespace std, then you can define cin and cout to have some meaning other than their standard meaning. (Perhaps you want to redefine cin and cout because you want them to behave a bit differently from the standard versions.) Their standard meaning is in the std namespace; without the using directive (or something like it), your code knows nothing about the std namespace, and so, as far as your code is concerned, the only definitions of cin and cout it knows are whatever definitions you give them.

global namespace

Every bit of code you write is in some namespace. If you do not place the code in some specific namespace, then the code is in a namespace known as the **global namespace**. So far we have not placed any code we wrote in any namespace and so all our code has been in the global namespace. The global namespace does not have a using directive because you are always using the global namespace. You could say there is always an implicit automatic using directive that says you are using the global namespace.

Note that you can use more than one namespace in the same program. For example, we are always using the global namespace and we are usually using the std namespace. What happens if a name is defined in two namespaces and you are using both namespaces?

This results in an error (either a compiler error or a run-time error, depending on the exact details). You can have the same name defined in two different namespaces, but if that is true, then you can only use one of those namespaces at a time. However, this does not mean you cannot use the two namespaces in the same program. You can use them each at different times in the same program.

For example, suppose NS1 and NS2 are two namespaces and suppose myFunction is a void function with no arguments that is defined in both namespaces but defined in different ways in the two namespaces. The following is then legal:

```
{
    using namespace NS1;
    myFunction( );
}

{
    using namespace NS2;
    myFunction( );
}
```

The first invocation would use the definition of myFunction given in the namespace NS1, and the second invocation would use the definition of myFunction given in the namespace NS2.

Recall that a *block* is a list of statements, declarations, and possibly other code enclosed in braces, {}. A using directive at the start of a block applies only to that block. Therefore the first using directive shown applies only in the first block, and the second using directive applies only in the second block. The usual way of phrasing this is to say that the **scope** of the NS1 using directive is the first block, whereas the scope of the NS2 using directive is the second block. Note that because of this scope rule, we are able to use two conflicting namespaces in the same program (such as in a program that contains the two blocks we discussed in the previous paragraph).

scope

Normally, you place a using directive at the start of a block. If you place it further down in the block, however, you need to know its precise scope. The scope of a using directive runs from the place where it occurs to the end of the block. You may have a using directive for the same namespace in more than one block, so the entire scope of a namespace may cover multiple disconnected blocks. When you use a using directive in a block, it is typically the block consisting of the body of a function definition.

If you place a using directive at the start of a file (as we have usually done so far), then the using directive applies to the entire file. A using directive should normally be placed near the start of a file (or the start of a block), but the precise scope rule is that the scope of a using directive that is outside all blocks is from the occurrence of the using directive to the end of the file.

Scope Rule for using Directives

The scope of a using directive is the block in which it appears (more precisely, from the location of the using directive to the end of the block). If the using directive is outside all blocks, then it applies to all of the file that follows the using directive.

Creating a Namespace

namespace grouping

To place some code in a namespace, you simply place it in a **namespace grouping** of the following form:

```
namespace Name_Space_Name
{
    Some_Code
}
```

When you include one of these groupings in your code, you are said to place the names defined in `Some_Code` into the namespace `Name_Space_Name`. These names (really, the definitions of these names) can be made available with the using directive

```
using namespace Name_Space_Name;
```

For example, the following, taken from Display 11.5, places a function declaration in the namespace `Space1`:

```
namespace Space1
{
    void greeting( );
}
```

If you look again at Display 11.5, you see that the definition of the function `greeting` is also placed in namespace `Space1`. That is done with the following additional namespace grouping:

```
namespace Space1
{
    void greeting( )
    {
        cout << "Hello from namespace Space1.\n";
    }
}
```

Note that you can have any number of these namespace groupings for a single namespace. In Display 11.5, we used two namespace groupings for namespace `Space1` and two other groupings for namespace `Space2`.

Every name defined in a namespace is available inside the namespace groupings, but the names can also be made available to code outside the namespace groupings. For example, the function declaration and function definition in the namespace `Space1` can be made available with the using directive

```
using namespace Space1
```

as illustrated in Display 11.5.

Display 11.5 Namespace Demonstration (part 1 of 2)

```
 1   #include <iostream>
 2
 3   using namespace std;
 4
 5   namespace Space1
 6   {
 7       void greeting( );
 8   }
 9
10   namespace Space2
11   {
12       void greeting( );
13   }
14
15   void bigGreeting( );
16
17   int main( )
18   {
19       {
20           using namespace Space2;
21           greeting( );
22       }
23
24       {
25           using namespace Space1;
26           greeting( );
27       }
28
29       bigGreeting( );
30
31       return 0;
32   }
33
34   namespace Space1
35   {
36       void greeting( )
37       {
38           cout << "Hello from namespace Space1.\n";
39       }
40   }
41
42   namespace Space2
43   {
44       void greeting( )
45       {
46           cout << "Greetings from namespace Space2.\n";
47       }
48   }
```

Names in this block use definitions in namespaces Space2, std, and the global namespace.

Names in this block use definitions in namespaces Space1, std, and the global namespace.

Names out here only use definitions in the namespace std and the global namespace.

Display 11.5   Namespace Demonstration (part 2 of 2)

```
41   void bigGreeting( )
42   {
43       cout << "A Big Global Hello!\n";
44   }
```

Sample Dialogue

```
Greetings from namespace Space2.
Hello from namespace Space1.
A Big Global Hello!
```

Putting a Definition in a Namespace

You place a name definition in a namespace by placing it in a *namespace grouping*, which has the following syntax:

```
namespace Namespace_Name
{
    Definition_1
    Definition_2
        .
        .
        .
    Definition_Last
}
```

You can have multiple namespace groupings (even in multiple files), and all the definitions in all the groupings will be in the same namespace.

Self-Test Exercises

6. Consider the program shown in Display 11.5. Could we use the name greeting in place of bigGreeting?

7. In Exercise 6, we saw that you could *not* add a definition for the following function to the global namespace:

    ```
    void greeting( );
    ```

    Can you add a definition for the following function declaration to the global namespace?

    ```
    void greeting(int howMany );
    ```

using Declarations

This subsection describes a way to qualify a single name so that you can make only one name from a namespace available to your program, rather than making all the names in a namespace available. We saw this technique in Chapter 1 and so this is a review and amplification of what we said in Chapter 1.

Suppose you are faced with the following situation. You have two namespaces, NS1 and NS2. You want to use the function fun1 defined in NS1 and the function fun2 defined in namespace NS2. The complication is that both NS1 and NS2 define a function myFunction. (Assume all functions in this discussion take no arguments, so overloading does not apply.) You cannot use

```
using namespace NS1;
using namespace NS2;
```

This would potentially provide conflicting definitions for myFunction. (If the name myFunction is never used, then the compiler will not detect the problem and will allow your program to compile and run.)

What you need is a way to say you are using fun1 in namespace NS1 and fun2 in namespace NS2 and nothing else in the namespaces NS1 and NS2. We have already been using a technique that can handle this situation. The following is your solution:

```
using NS1::fun1;
using NS2::fun2;
```

A qualification of the form

```
using Name_Space::One_Name;
```

using declaration

makes the (definition of the) name *One_Name* from the namespace *Name_Space* available, but does not make any other names in *Name_Space* available. This is called a **using declaration.**

Note that the scope resolution operator :: that we use in these using declarations is the same as the scope resolution operator we use when defining member functions. These two uses of the scope resolution operator have a similarity. For example, Display 11.2 had the following function definition:

```
void DigitalTime::advance(int hoursAdded, int minutesAdded)
{
    hour = (hour + hoursAdded) %24 ;
    advance (minutesAdded) ;
}
```

In this case the :: means that we are defining the function advance for the class DigitalTime, as opposed to any other function named advance in any other class. Similarly,

using NS1::fun1

```
using NS1::fun1;
```

means we are using the function named fun1 as defined in the namespace NS1, as opposed to any other definition of fun1 in any other namespace.

There are two differences between a *using declaration*, such as

```
using std::cout;
```

and a *using directive*, such as

```
using namespace std;
```

The differences are as follows:

1. A using declaration makes only one name in the namespace available to your code, while a using directive makes all the names in a namespace available.
2. A using declaration introduces a name (like cout) into your code so no other use of the name can be made. However, a using directive only potentially introduces the names in the namespace.

Point 1 is pretty obvious. Point 2 has some subtleties. For example, suppose the namespaces NS1 and NS2 both provide definitions for myFunction, but have no other name conflicts. Then the following will produce no problems *provided* that (within the scope of these directives) the conflicting name myFunction is never used in your code.

```
using namespace NS1;
using namespace NS2;
```

On the other hand, the following is illegal, even if the function myFunction is never used:

```
using NS1::myFunction;
using NS2::myFunction;
```

Sometimes this subtle point can be important, but it does not impinge on most **using directive** routine code. So, we will often use the term **using directive** loosely to mean either a using directive or a using declaration.

Qualifying Names

This section introduces a way to qualify names that we have not discussed before. Suppose that you intend to use the name fun1 as defined in the namespace NS1, but you only intend to use it one time (or a small number of times). You can name the function (or other item) using the name of the namespace and the scope resolution operator as follows:

```
NS1::fun1( );
```

This form is often used when specifying a parameter type. For example, consider

```
int getInput(std::istream inputStream)
    . . .
```

In the function `getInput`, the parameter `inputStream` is of type `istream`, where `istream` is defined as in the `std` namespace. If this use of the type name `istream` is the only name you need from the `std` namespace (or if all the names you need are similarly qualified with `std::`), then you do *not* need

```
using namespace std;
```

or

```
using std::istream;
```

Note that you can use `std::istream` even within the scope of a using directive for another namespace which also defines the name `istream`. In this case `std::istream` and `istream` will have different definitions. For example, consider

```
using namespace MySpace;
void someFunction(istream p1, std::istream p2);
```

Assuming `istream` is a type defined in the namespace `MySpace`, then `p1` will have the type `istream` as defined in `MySpace` and `p2` will have the type `istream` as defined in the `std` namespace.

Self-Test Exercises

8. What is the output produced by the following program?

```
#include <iostream>
using namespace std;

namespace Hello
{
    void message( );
}

namespace GoodBye
{
    void message( );
}

void message( );

int main( )
{
    using Hello::message;
    message( );
    GoodBye::message( );
}
```

Self-Test Exercises (continued)

```
        message( );

        return 0;
    }

    void message( )
    {
        cout << "Global message.\n";
    }

    namespace Hello
    {
        void message( )
        {
            cout << "Hello.\n";
        }
    }

    namespace GoodBye
    {
        void message( )
        {
            cout << "Good-Bye.\n";
        }
    }
```

9. Write the declaration (prototype) for a void function named wow. The function wow has two parameters, the first of type speed as defined in the speedway namespace and the second of type speed as defined in the indy500 namespace.

TIP: Choosing a Name for a Namespace

It is a good idea to include your last name or some other unique string in the names of your namespaces so as to reduce the chance that somebody else will use the same namespace name as you do. With multiple programmers writing code for the same project, it is important that namespaces that are meant to be distinct really do have distinct names. Otherwise, you can easily have multiple definitions of the same names in the same scope. That is why we included the name savitch in the namespace DtimeSavitch in Display 11.9. ■

EXAMPLE: A Class Definition in a Namespace

In Displays 11.6 and 11.7 we have again rewritten both the header file dtime.h for the class DigitalTime and the implementation file for the class DigitalTime. This time (no pun intended), we have placed the definition in a namespace called DTimeSavitch. Note that the namespace DTimeSavitch spans the two files dtime.h and dtime.cpp. A namespace can span multiple files.

If you rewrite the definition of the class DigitalTime as shown in Displays 11.6 and 11.7, then the application file in Display 11.3 needs to specify the namespace DTimeSavitch in some way, such as the following:

```
using namespace DTimeSavitch;
```

or

```
using DTimeSavitch::DigitalTime;
```

Display 11.6   Placing a Class in a Namespace (Header File)

```
1   //This is the header file dtime.h.
2   #ifndef DTIME_H
3   #define DTIME_H

4   #include <iostream>
5   using std::istream;
6   using std::ostream;

7   namespace DTimeSavitch
8   {
9       class DigitalTime                A better version of this class definition will be
10      {                                given in Displays 11.8 and 11.9.
11
12
13          <The definition of the class DigitalTime  is the same as in Display 11.1>
14
15      };
16  }// DTimeSavitch

17  #endif //DTIME_H
```

Note that the namespace DTimeSavitch spans two files. The other is shown in Display 11.7.

Unnamed Namespaces

compilation unit

A **compilation unit** is a file, such as a class implementation file, along with all the files that are #included in the file, such as the interface header file for the class. Every compilation unit has an unnamed namespace. A namespace grouping for the unnamed namespace is written in the same way as for any other namespace, but no name is given, as in the following example:

```
namespace
{
    void sampleFunction( )
        .
        .
        .
} //unnamed namespace
```

Display 11.7   Placing a Class in a Namespace (Implementation File)

```
1   //This is the implementation file dtime.cpp.
2   #include <iostream>
3   #include <cctype>
4   #include <cstdlib>
5   using std::istream;
6   using std::ostream;
7   using std::cout;
8   using std::cin;
9   #include "dtime.h"
10  namespace DTimeSavitch
11  {
12
13      <All the function definitions from Display 11.2 go here.>
14
15  }// DTimeSavitch
```

You can use the single using directive
using namespace std;
in place of these four using declarations.
However, the four using declarations are
a preferable style.

All the names defined in the unnamed namespace are local to the compilation unit, and so the names can be reused for something else outside the compilation unit. For example, Displays 11.8 and 11.9 show a rewritten (and final) version of the interface and implementation file for the class DigitalTime. Note that the helping functions readHour, readMinute, and digitToInt are all in the unnamed namespace; thus they are local to the compilation unit. As illustrated in Display 11.10, the names in the unnamed namespace can be reused for something else outside the compilation unit. In Display 11.10, the function name readHour is reused for a different function in the application program.

If you look again at the implementation file in Display 11.9, you will see that the helping functions digitToInt, readHour, and readMinute are used outside the unnamed namespace without any namespace qualifier. Any name defined in the unnamed namespace can be used without qualification anywhere in the compilation unit. (Of course, this needed to be so, since the unnamed namespace has no name to use for qualifying its names.)

Display 11.8 Hiding the Helping Functions in a Namespace (Interface File)

```
1   //This is the header file dtime.h. This is the interface for the class
2   //DigitalTime. Values of this type are times of day. The values are
3   //input and output in 24-hour notation, as in 9:30 for 9:30 AM and
4   //14:45 for 2:45 PM.
5   #ifndef DTIME_H
6   #define DTIME_H
7   #include <iostream>
8   using std::istream;
9   using std::ostream;

10  namespace DTimeSavitch
11  {
12      class DigitalTime
13      {
14      public:
15          DigitalTime(int theHour, int theMinute);
16          DigitalTime( );
17          //Initializes the time value to 0:00 (which is midnight).
18          int getHour( ) const;
19          int getMinute( ) const;
20          void advance(int minutesAdded);
21          //Changes the time to minutesAdded minutes later.
22          void advance(int hoursAdded, int minutesAdded);
23          //Changes the time to hoursAdded hours plus minutesAdded
24          //                                    minutes later.
25          friend bool operator ==(const DigitalTime& time1,
26                                   const DigitalTime& time2);
27          friend istream& operator >>(istream& ins,
28                                       DigitalTime& theObject);
29          friend ostream& operator <<(ostream& outs,
30                                       const DigitalTime& theObject);
31      private:
32          int hour;
33          int minute;
34      };
35  }  //DTimeSavitch
36  #endif //DTIME_H
```

This is our final version of the class DigitalTime.
This is the best version and the one you should use.
The implementation to use with this interface is
given in Display 11.9.

Note that the helping functions are not mentioned
in the interface file.

Display 11.9   Hiding the Helping Functions in a Namespace (Implementation File) (part 1 of 3)

```
1    //This is the implementation file dtime.cpp of the class DigitalTime.
2    //The interface for the class DigitalTime is in the header file dtime.h.
3    #include <iostream>
4    #include <cctype>
5    #include <cstdlib>
6    using std::istream;
7    using std::ostream;
8    using std::cout;
9    using std::cin;
10   #include "dtime.h"
```

                                 ⟵ Specifies the unnamed namespace

```
11   namespace
12   {
13       int digitToInt(char c)
14       {
15           return ( int(c) - int('0') );
16       }
```

                                              Names defined in the unnamed namespace
                                              are local to the compilation unit. So, these
                                              helping functions are local to the file
                                              dtime.cpp.

```
17       //Uses iostream, cctype, and cstdlib:
18       void readMinute(int& theMinute)
19       {
20           char c1, c2;
21           cin >> c1 >> c2;
22           if (!(isdigit(c1) && isdigit(c2)))
23           {
24               cout << "Error: illegal input to readMinute\n";
25               exit(1);
26           }
27           theMinute = digitToInt(c1)*10 + digitToInt(c2);
28           if (theMinute < 0 || theMinute > 59)
29           {
30               cout << "Error: illegal input to readMinute\n";
31               exit(1);
32           }
33       }
34       //Uses iostream, cctype, and cstdlib:
35       void readHour(int& theHour)
36       {
37           char c1, c2;
38           cin >> c1 >> c2;
39
```

                                                                                   (continued)

Display 11.9   Hiding the Helping Functions in a Namespace (Implementation File) (part 2 of 3)

```
40      if ( !( isdigit(c1) && (isdigit(c2) || c2 == ':') ) )
41      {
42          cout << "Error: illegal input to readHour\n";
43          exit(1);
44      }

45      if (isdigit(c1) && c2 == ':')
46      {
47          theHour = digitToInt(c1);
48      }
49      else//(isdigit(c1) && isdigit(c2))
50      {
51          theHour = digitToInt(c1)*10 + digitToInt(c2);
52          cin >> c2; //discard ':'
53          if (c2 != ':')
54          {
55              cout << "Error: illegal input to readHour\n";
56              exit(1);
57          }
58      }

59      if (theHour == 24)
60          theHour = 0; //Standardize midnight as 0:00.

61      if (theHour < 0 || theHour > 23)
62      {
63          cout << "Error: illegal input to readHour\n";
64          exit(1);
65      }
66  }

67  } //unnamed namespace

68
69  namespace DTimeSavitch
70  {
71      //Uses iostream:
72      istream& operator >>(istream& ins, DigitalTime& theObject)
73      {
74          readHour(theObject.hour);
75          readMinute(theObject.minute);
76          return ins;
77      }
78      ostream& operator <<(ostream& outs, const DigitalTime& theObject)
```

Within the compilation unit (in this case dtime.cpp),you can use names in the unnamed namespace without qualification.

<The body of the function definition is the same as in Display 11.2.>

Display 11.9 Hiding the Helping Functions in a Namespace (Implementation File) (part 3 of 3)

```
79      bool operator ==(const DigitalTime& time1, const DigitalTime& time2)
        <The body of the function definition is the same as in Display 11.2.>

80      DigitalTime::DigitalTime(int theHour, int theMinute)
        <The body of the function definition is the same as in Display 11.2.>

81      DigitalTime::DigitalTime( )
        <The body of the function definition is the same as in Display 11.2.>

82      int DigitalTime::getHour( ) const
        <The body of the function definition is the same as in Display 11.2.>

83      int DigitalTime::getMinute( ) const
        <The body of the function definition is the same as in Display 11.2.>

84      void DigitalTime::advance(int minutesAdded)
        <The body of the function definition is the same as in Display 11.2.>

85      void DigitalTime::advance(int hoursAdded, int minutesAdded)
        <The body of the function definition is the same as in Display 11.2.>

86  } //DTimeSavitch
```

Display 11.10 Hiding the Helping Functions in a Namespace (Application Program) (part 1 of 2)

```
1   //This is the application file timedemo.cpp. This program
2   //demonstrates hiding the helping functions in an unnamed namespace.

3   #include <iostream>
4   #include "dtime.h"

5   void readHour(int& theHour);

6   int main( )
7   {
8       using std::cout;
9       using std::cin;
10      using std::endl;

11      using DTimeSavitch::DigitalTime;
12      int theHour;
13      readHour(theHour);
```

If you place the using declarations here, then the program behavior will be the same. However, many authorities say that you should make the scope of each using declaration or using directive as small as is reasonable, and we wanted to give you an example of that technique.

This is a different function readHour than the one in the implementation file dtime.cpp (shown in Display 11.9)

(continued)

Display 11.10 Hiding the Helping Functions in a Namespace (Application Program) (part 2 of 2)

```
14      DigitalTime clock(theHour, 0), oldClock;

15      oldClock = clock;
16      clock.advance(15);
17      if (clock == oldClock)
18          cout << "Something is wrong.";
19      cout << "You entered " << oldClock << endl;
20      cout << "15 minutes later the time will be "
21          << clock << endl;

22      clock.advance(2, 15);
23      cout << "2 hours and 15 minutes after that\n"
24          << "the time will be "
25          << clock << endl;

26
27      return 0;
28  }

29  void readHour(int& theHour)
30  {
31      using std::cout;
32      using std::cin;

33
34      cout << "Let's play a time game.\n"
35          << "Let's pretend the hour has just changed.\n"
36          << "You may write midnight as either 0 or 24,\n"
37          << "but, I will always write it as 0.\n"
38          << "Enter the hour as a number (0 to 24): ";
39      cin >> theHour;
40  }
```

When we gave these using declarations before, they were in main, so their scope was main. Thus, we need to repeat them here in order to use cin and cout in readHour.

Sample Dialogue

```
Let's play a time game.
Let's pretend the hour has just changed.
You may write midnight as either 0 or 24,
but, I will always write it as 0.
Enter the hour as a number (0 to 24): 11
You entered 11:00
15 minutes later the time will be 11:15
2 hours and 15 minutes after that
the time will be 13:30
```

Unnamed Namespace

You can use the *unnamed namespace* to make a definition local to a compilation unit. Each compilation unit has one unnamed namespace. All the identifiers defined in the unnamed namespace are local to the compilation unit. You place a definition in the unnamed namespace by placing the definition in a namespace grouping with no namespace name, as shown next:

```
namespace
{
    Definition_1
    Definition_2
        .
        .
        .
    Definition_Last
}
```

You can use any name in the unnamed namespace without qualifiers anyplace in the compilation unit. See Displays 11.8, 11.9, and 11.10 for a complete example.

PITFALL: Confusing the Global Namespace and the Unnamed Namespace

Do not confuse the global namespace with the unnamed namespace. If you do not put a name definition in a namespace grouping, then it is in the global namespace. To put a name definition in the unnamed namespace, you must put it in a namespace grouping that starts out as follows, without a name:

```
namespace
{
```

Names in the global namespace and names in the unnamed namespace may both be accessed without a qualifier. However, names in the global namespace have global scope (all the program files), whereas names in an unnamed namespace are local to a compilation unit.

This confusion between the global namespace and the unnamed namespace does not arise very much in writing code, since there is a tendency to think of names in the global namespace as being "in no namespace," even though that is not technically correct. However, the confusion can easily arise when discussing code. ■

TIP: Unnamed Namespaces Replace the static Qualifier

Earlier versions of C++ used the qualifier static to make a name local to a file. This use of static is being phased out, and you should instead use the unnamed namespace to make a name local to a compilation unit. Note that this use of static has nothing to do with the use of static to make class members shared by all objects of a class (as discussed in the subsection "Static Members" of Chapter 7). So, since static is used to mean more than one thing, it is probably good that one use of the word is being phased out. ∎

TIP: Hiding Helping Functions

There are two good ways to hide a helping function for a class. You can make the function a private member function of the class or you can place the helping function in the unnamed namespace for the implementation file of the class. If the function naturally takes a calling object, then it should be made a private member function. If it does not naturally take a calling object, you can make it a static member function (for example, DigitalTime::readHour in Displays 11.1 and 11.2) or you can place it in the unnamed namespace of the implementation file (for example, readHour in Displays 11.8 and 11.9.)

If the helping function does not need a calling object, then placing the helping function in the unnamed namespace of the implementation file makes for cleaner code because it better separates interface and implementation into separate files and it avoids the need for so much function name qualification. For example, note that in Display 11.9 we can use the function name readHour unqualified since it is in the unnamed namespace, while in the version in Display 11.2 we need to use DigitalTime::readHour. ∎

It is interesting to note how unnamed namespaces interact with the C++ rule that you cannot have two definitions of a name in the same namespace. There is one unnamed namespace in each compilation unit. It is easily possible for compilation units to overlap. For example, both the implementation file for a class and an application program using the class would normally both include the header file (interface file) for the class. Thus, the header file is in two compilation units and hence participates in two unnamed namespaces. As dangerous as this sounds, it will normally produce no problems as long as each compilation unit's namespace makes sense when considered by itself. For example, if a name is defined in the unnamed namespace in the header file, it cannot be defined again in the unnamed namespace in either the implementation file or the application file. Thus, a name conflict is avoided.

Nested Namespaces

It is legal to nest namespaces. When qualifying a name from a nested namespace, you simply qualify twice. For example, consider

```
namespace S1
{
    namespace S2
    {
        void sample( )
        {
            .
            .
            .
        }
    }
}//S2

}//S1
```

TIP: What Namespace Specification Should You Use?

You have three ways to specify that your code uses the definition of a function (or other item) named f that was defined in a namespace named theSpace. You can insert

```
using namespace theSpace;
```

Alternatively, you can insert

```
using theSpace::f;
```

Finally, you could omit the using directive altogether, but always qualify the function name by writing theSpace::f instead of just plain f.

Which form should you use? All three methods can be made to work, and authorities differ on what they recommend as the preferred style. However, to obtain the full value of namespaces, it is good to avoid the form

```
using namespace theSpace;
```

Placing such a using directive at the start of a file is little different than placing all definitions in the global namespace, which is what earlier versions of C++ actually did. So, this approach gets no value from the namespace mechanism. (If you place such a using directive inside a block, however, then it only applies to that block. This is another alternative, which is both sensible and advocated by many authorities.)

We prefer to use the second method most of the time, inserting statements like the following at the start of files:

```
using theSpace::f;
```

(continued)

TIP: (continued)

This allows you to omit names that are in the namespace but that are not used. That in turn avoids potential name conflicts. Moreover, it nicely documents which names you use, and it is not as messy as always qualifying a name with notation of the form theSpace::f.

If your files are structured so that different namespaces are used in different locations, it may sometimes be preferable to place your using directives and using declarations inside blocks, such as the bodies of function definitions, rather than at the start of the file. ■

To invoke sample outside the namespace S1, you use

S1::S2::sample( ) ;

To invoke sample outside the namespace S2 but within namespace S1, you use

S2::sample( ) ;

Alternatively, you could use a suitable using directive.

Self-Test Exercises

10. Would the program in Display 11.10 behave any differently if you replaced the four using declarations

    ```
    using std::cout;
    using std::cin;
    using std::endl;
    using DTimeSavitch::DigitalTime;
    ```

    with the following two using directives?

    ```
    using namespace std;
    using namespace DTimeSavitch;
    ```

11. What is the output produced by the following program?

    ```
    #include <iostream>
    using namespace std;
    namespace Sally
    {
        void message( ) ;
    }
    namespace
    {
        void message( ) ;
    }
    ```

Self-Test Exercises (continued)

```cpp
int main( )
{
    message( );
    using Sally::message;
    message( );
}

    message( );

    return 0;
}

namespace Sally
{
    void message( )
    {
        cout << "Hello from Sally.\n";
    }
}

namespace
{
    void message( )
    {
        cout << "Hello from unnamed.\n";
    }
}
```

12. What is the output produced by the following program?

```cpp
#include <iostream>
using namespace std;

namespace Outer
{
    void message( );
    namespace Inner
    {
        void message( );
    }
}

int main( )
{
    Outer::message( );
    Outer::Inner::message( );

    using namespace Outer;
    Inner::message( );
```

(continued)

Self-Test Exercises (continued)

```
        return 0;
    }
    namespace Outer
    {
        void message( )
        {
            cout << "Outer.\n";
        }
        namespace Inner
        {
            void message( )
            {
                cout << "Inner.\n";
            }
        }
    }
```

Chapter Summary

- You can define a class and place the definition of the class and the implementation of its member functions in separate files. You can then compile the class separately from any program that uses it, and you can use this same class in any number of different programs.

- A *namespace* is a collection of name definitions, such as class definitions and variable declarations.

- There are three ways to use a name from a namespace: by making all the names in the namespace available with a *using directive*, by making the single name available with a *using declaration* for the one name, or by qualifying the name with the name of the namespace and the scope resolution operator.

- You place a definition in a namespace by placing the definition in a *namespace grouping* for that namespace.

- The unnamed namespace can be used to make a name definition local to a compilation unit.

Answers to Self-Test Exercises

1. Parts a, b, and c go in the interface file; parts d through h go in the implementation file. (All the definitions of class operations of any sort go in the implementation file.) Part i (that is, the main part of your program) goes in the application file.

2. The name of the interface file ends in .h.

3. Only the implementation file needs to be compiled. The interface file does not need to be compiled.

4. Only the implementation file needs to be recompiled. You do, however, need to relink the files.

5. You need to delete the private member variables hour and minute from the interface file shown in Display 11.1 and replace them with the member variable minutes (with an s). You do not need to make any other changes in the interface file. In the implementation file, you need to change the definitions of all the constructors and other member functions, as well as the definitions of the overloaded operators, so that they work for this new way of recording time. (In this case, you do not need to change any of the helping functions readHour, readMinute, or digitToInt, but that might not be true for some other class or even some other reimplementation of this class.) For example, the definition of the overloaded operator, >>, could be changed to the following:

```
istream& operator >>(istream& ins,
                      DigitalTime& theObject)
{
    int inputHour, inputMinute;
    DigitalTime::readHour(inputHour);
    DigitalTime::readMinute(inputMinute);
    theObject.minutes = inputMinute + 60*inputHour;
    return ins;
}
```

You need not change any application files for programs that use the class. However, since the interface file is changed (as well as the implementation file), you will need to recompile any application files, and of course you will need to recompile the implementation file.

6. No. If you replace bigGreeting with greeting in the global namespace, you will have a definition for the name greeting in the global namespace. There are parts of the program where all the name definitions in the namespace Space1 and all the name definitions in the global namespace are simultaneously available. In those parts of the program, there would be two distinct definitions for

```
void greeting( );
```

7. Yes. The additional definition would cause no problems because overloading is always allowed. When, for example, the namespace Space1 and the global namespace are available, the function name greeting would be overloaded. The problem in Self-Test Exercise 6 was that the function name greeting with greeting would sometimes be two definitions of the function name greeting with the same parameter lists.

8. Hello
Good-Bye
Good-Bye

9. `void wow(speedway::speed s1, indy500::speed s2);`

10. The program would behave exactly the same. However, most authorities favor using the using declaration, as we have done in Display 11.10. Note that with either, there are still two different functions named `readHour`. The one in Display 11.10 is different from the one defined in the unnamed namespace in Display 11.9.

11. `Hello from unnamed.`
    `Hello from Sally.`
    `Hello from unnamed.`

12. `Outer.`
    `Inner.`
    `Inner.`

Programming Projects

Visit www.myprogramminglab.com to complete select exercises online and get instant feedback.

1. This exercise is intended to illustrate namespaces and separate compilation in your development environment. You should use the development environment you regularly use in this course for this exercise. In a file `f.h`, place a declaration of `void f()` in namespace A. In a file `g.h`, place a declaration of `void g()` in namespace A. In files `f.cpp` and `g.cpp`, place the definitions of `void f()` and `void g()`, respectively. Place the definitions of `void f()` and `void g()` in namespace A. The functions can do anything you want, but to keep track of execution include something like

   ```
   cout << "Function_Name called" << endl;
   ```

   where *Function_Name* is the name of the particular function. In another file, `main.cpp`, put your main function, `#include` the minimum collection of files to provide access to the names from namespace A. In your main function call the functions `f` then `g`. Compile, link, and execute using your development environment. To provide access to names in namespaces, you may use local using declarations such as

   ```
   using std::cout;
   ```

   or use local using directives such as

   ```
   using namespace std;
   ```

   inside a block, or qualify names using the names of namespaces, such as `std::cout`. You may not use global namespace directives such as the following which are not in a block and apply to the entire file:

   ```
   using namespace std;
   ```

   Of course you must handle namespace A and function names `f` and `g`, in addition to possibly `std` and `cout`.

   After doing this, write a one page description of how to create and use namespaces and separate compilation in your environment.

2. Obtain the source code for the PFArrayD class and the demonstration program from Displays 11.10, 10.11, and 10.12. Modify this program to use namespaces and separate compilation. Put the class definition and other function declarations

in one file. Place the implementations in a separate file. Distribute the namespace definition across the two files. Place the demonstration program in a third file. To provide access to names in namespaces, you may use local using declarations such as

```
using std::cout;
```

or use local using directives such as

```
using namespace std;
```

inside a block, or qualify names using the names of namespaces, such as std::cout. You may not use global namespace directives such as the following which are not in a block and apply to the entire file:

```
using namespace std;
```

3. Extend Programming Project 10.1 from Chapter 10 in which you implemented a two dimensional array class by placing the class definition and implementation in a namespace, then providing access to the names in the namespace. Test your code. To provide access to names in namespaces, you may use local using declarations such as

```
using std::cout;
```

or use local using directives such as

```
using namespace std;
```

inside a block, or qualify names using the names of namespaces, such as std::cout. You may not use global namespace directives such as the following which are not in a block and apply to the entire file:

```
using namespace std;
```

4. You would like to verify the credentials of a user for your system. Listed next is a class named Security, which authenticates a user and password. (Note that this example is really not very secure. Typically passwords would be encrypted or stored in a database.)

```
class Security
{
public:
    static int validate(string username, string password);
};

// This subroutine hard-codes valid users and is not
// considered a secure practice.
// It returns 0 if the credentials are invalid,
//  1 if valid user, and
//  2 if valid administrator

int Security::validate(string username, string password)
{
    if ((username=="abbott") && (password=="monday")) return 1;
    if ((username=="costello") && (password=="tuesday")) return 2;
    return 0;
}
```

Break this class into two files, a file with the header `security.h` and a file with the implementation `Security.cpp`.

Next, create two more classes that use the Security class by including the header file. The first class should be named Administrator and contain a function named Login that returns true if a given username and password have administrator clearance. The second class should be named User and contain a function named Login that returns true if a given username and password have either user or administrator clearance.

Both the User and Administrator classes should be split into separate files for the header and implementation.

Finally, write a main function that invokes the Login function for both the User and Administrator classes to test if they work properly. The main function should be in a separate file. Be sure to use the `#ifndef` directive to ensure that no header file is included more than once.

5. This Programming Project explores how the unnamed namespace works. Listed are snippets from a program to perform input validation for a username and password. The code to input and validate the username is in a separate file than the code to input and validate the password.

File header `user.cpp`:

```
namespace Authenticate
{
    void inputUserName( )
    {
        do
        {
            cout << "Enter your username (8 letters only)" << endl;
            cin >> username;
        } while (!isValid( ));
    }

    string getUserName( )
    {
        return username;
    }
}
```

Define the username variable and the `isValid( )` function in the unnamed namespace so the code will compile. The `isValid( )` function should return `true` if username contains exactly eight letters. Generate an appropriate header file for this code.

VideoNote
Solution to
Programming
Project 11.5

Repeat the same steps for the file password.cpp, placing the password variable and the isValid( ) function in the unnamed namespace. In this case, the isValid( ) function should return true if the input password has at least eight characters including at least one non-letter:

File header password.cpp:

```
namespace Authenticate
{

    void inputPassword( )
    {

        do
        {

            cout << "Enter your password (at least 8 characters " <<
                    "and at least one non-letter)" << endl;

            cin >> password;
        } while (!isValid( ));
    }

    string getPassword( )
    {

        return password;
    }
}
```

At this point, you should have two functions named isValid( ), each in different unnamed namespaces. Place the following main function in an appropriate place. The program should compile and run.

```
int main( )
{

    inputUserName( );
    inputPassword( );
    cout << "Your username is " << getUserName( ) <<
            " and your password is: " <<
            getPassword( ) << endl;

    return 0;
}
```

Test the program with several invalid usernames and passwords.

Streams and File I/O 12

12.1 I/O STREAMS 517

12.2 TOOLS FOR STREAM I/O 533

12.3 STREAM HIERARCHIES: A PREVIEW OF INHERITANCE 547

12.4 RANDOM ACCESS TO FILES 556

Fish say, they have their stream and pond;
But is there anything beyond?

RUPERT BROOKE, *Heaven* (1913)

As a leaf is carried by a stream, whether the stream ends in a lake or in
the sea, so too is the output of your program carried by a stream not
knowing if the stream goes to the screen or to a file.

Washroom Wall of a Computer Science Department (1995)

Introduction

Input is delivered to your program and output from your program is delivered to the
output device via special objects known as *streams*. The term *stream* is supposed to
convey the idea that the output is streamed to or from your program without your
program being aware (or at least not very aware) of where the input data came from or
where the output data goes. This should, and does, mean that file input is handled in
essentially the same way as the keyboard input we have been using up to now and that
file output is handled in essentially the same way as screen output.

File I/O makes a small but essential use of inheritance, which is not covered until
Chapter 14. However, we have placed this chapter before the inheritance chapter
because programmers often want to start using file I/O early. Therefore this chapter
includes a brief introduction to what few inheritance details are needed for file I/O.

You may cover this chapter anytime after covering the material of Chapters 1 to 4
and 6 to 9; in other words, you may cover this chapter before Chapters 5, 10, and 11.
Although simple file input was given in Chapter 2, the same concepts are repeated here
for continuity. The basic elements of file I/O, which are discussed in Section 12.1,
may be covered anytime after reading Chapters 1 to 4, Chapter 6, and the subsection
of Chapter 9 entitled "The Member Functions get and put." That subsection is self-
contained and does not require reading any other parts of Chapter 9. All of Section 12.2,
except for the subsection entitled "File Names as Input" may also be read after reading
only Chapters 1 to 4, Chapter 6, and the subsection of Chapter 9 entitled "The Member
Functions get and put."

If you have not read Chapter 11 on namespaces, you may want to review the
subsection of Chapter 1 on namespaces.

12.1 I/O Streams

Good Heavens! For more than forty years I have been speaking prose without knowing it.

MOLIÈRE, *Le Bourgeois Gentilhomme*

stream

A **stream** is a flow of characters (or other kind of data). If the flow is into your program, the stream is called an **input stream**. If the flow is out of your program, the stream is called an **output stream**. If the input stream flows from the keyboard, then your program will take input from the keyboard. If the input stream flows from a file, then your program will take its input from that file. Similarly, an output stream can go to the screen or to a file.

input stream

output stream

cin and cout are streams

Although you may not realize it, you have already been using streams in your programs. The cin that you have already used is an input stream connected to the keyboard, and cout is an output stream connected to the screen. These two streams are automatically available to your program as long as it has both an include directive that names the header file <iostream> and a using directive for the std namespace. You can define other streams that come from or go to files; once you have defined them, you can use them in your program in the same way you use the streams cin and cout. For example, suppose your program defines a stream called inStream that comes from some file. (We will tell you how to define it shortly.) You can then fill an int variable named theNumber with a number from this file by using the following in your program:

```
int theNumber;
inStream >> theNumber;
```

Similarly, if your program defines an output stream named outStream that goes to another file, then you can output the value of the variable theNumber to this other file. The following will output the string "theNumber is " followed by the contents of the variable theNumber to the output file that is connected to the stream outStream:

```
outStream << "theNumber is " << theNumber << endl;
```

Once the streams are connected to the desired files, your program can do file I/O the same way it does I/O using the keyboard and screen.

File I/O

The files we will use for I/O in this chapter are text files; that is, they are the same kind of files as those that contain your C++ programs.

reading and writing

When your program takes input from a file, it is said to be **reading** from the file; when your program sends output to a file, it is said to be **writing** to the file. There are other ways of reading input from a file, but the method given in this subsection reads the file from the beginning to the end (or as far as the program gets before ending). Using this method, your program is not allowed to back up and read anything in the file a second time. This is exactly what happens when your program takes input from the keyboard, so it should not seem new or strange. (As we will see, your program can reread a file starting from the beginning of the file, but this is starting over, not backing up.) Similarly, for the method presented here, your program writes output into a file starting at the beginning of the file and proceeding forward. Your program is not allowed to back up and change any output that it has previously written to the file. This is exactly what happens when your program sends output to the screen: You can send more output to the screen, but you cannot back up and change the screen output. The way that you get input from a file into your program or send output from your program into a file is to connect your program to the file by means of a stream.

\<fstream\>

To send output to a file, your program must first connect the file to a (stream) object of the class ofstream. To read input from a file, your program must first connect the file to a (stream) object of the class ifstream. The classes ifstream and ofstream are defined in the <fstream> library and placed in the std namespace. Thus, to do both file input and file output, your program would contain

```
#include <fstream>
using namespace std;
```

or

```
#include <fstream>
using std::ifstream;
using std::ofstream;
```

declaring streams

A stream must be declared just as you would declare any other class variable. Thus, you can declare inStream to be an input stream for a file and outStream to be an output stream for another file as follows:

```
ifstream inStream;
ofstream outStream;
```

connecting a stream to a file

open

Stream variables, such as inStream and outStream declared previously, must each be connected to a file. This is called **opening the file** and is done with the member function named open. For example, suppose you want the input stream inStream connected to the file named infile.txt. Your program must then contain the following before it reads any input from this file:

```
inStream.open("infile.txt");
```

pathnames

You can specify a pathname (a directory or folder) when giving the file name. The details of how to specify a pathname vary a little from system to system, so consult with a local guru for the details (or do a little trial-and-error programming). In our examples we will use simple file names, which assumes that the file is in the same directory (folder) as the one in which your program is running.

Once you have declared an input stream variable and connected it to a file using the open function, your program can take input from the file using the extraction operator, `>>`, with the input stream variable used the same way as `cin`. For example, the following reads two input numbers from the file connected to `inStream` and places them in the variables `oneNumber` and `anotherNumber`:

```
int oneNumber, anotherNumber;
inStream >> oneNumber >> anotherNumber;
```

An output stream is opened (that is, connected to a file) in the same way as just described for input streams. For example, the following declares the output stream `outStream` and connects it to the file named `outfile.txt`:

```
ofstream outStream;
outStream.open("outfile.txt");
```

When used with a stream of type `ofstream`, the member function `open` will create the output file if it does not already exist. If the output file already exists, the member function `open` will discard the contents of the file so that the output file is empty after the call to `open`. (We will discuss other ways of opening a file a bit later in this chapter.)

After a file is connected to the stream `outStream` with a call to `open`, the program can send output to that file using the insertion operator `<<`. For example, the following writes two strings and the contents of the variables `oneNumber` and `anotherNumber` to the file that is connected to the stream `outStream` (which in this example is the file named `outfile.txt`):

```
outStream << "oneNumber = " << oneNumber
          << " anotherNumber = " << anotherNumber;
```

Overloading of `>>` and `<<` Applies to Files

As we pointed out in Chapter 8, if you overload `>>` and `<<`, then those overloadings apply to file input and output streams the same as they apply to `cin` and `cout`. (If you have not yet read Chapter 8, you can ignore this remark. It will be repeated for you in Chapter 8.)

external file name Notice that when your program is dealing with a file, it is as if the file had two names. One is the usual name for the file that is used by the operating system, which is the **external file name**. In our sample code the external file names were `infile.txt` and `outfile.txt`. The external file name is in some sense the "real name" for the file. The conventions for spelling these external file names vary from one system to another. The names `infile.txt` and `outfile.txt` that we used in our examples may or may not look like file names on your system. You should name your files following whatever conventions are used on your operating system. Although the external file name is the real name for the file, it is typically used only once in a program. The external file name is given as an argument to the function open, but after the file is opened, the file is always referred to by naming the stream that is connected to the file. Thus, within your program, the stream name serves as a second name for the file.

A File Has Two Names

Every input and every output file used by your program has two names. The external file name is the real name of the file, but it is used only in the call to the member function open, which connects the file to a stream. After the call to open, you always use the stream name as the name of the file.

The sample program in Display 12.1 reads three numbers from one file and writes their sum, as well as some text, to another file.

Every file should be **closed** when your program is finished getting input from the file or sending output to the file. Closing a file disconnects the stream from the file. A file is closed with a call to the function close. The following lines from the program in Display 12.1 illustrate how to use the function close:

```
inStream.close( );
outStream.close( );
```

close

Notice that the function close takes no arguments. If your program ends normally but without closing a file, the system will automatically close the file for you. However, it is good to get in the habit of closing files for at least two reasons. First, the system will only close files for you if your program ends normally. If your program ends abnormally due to an error, the file will not be closed and may be left in a corrupted state. If your program closes files as soon as it is finished with them, file corruption is less likely. Second, you may want your program to send output to a file and later read that output back into the program. To do this, your program should close the file after it is finished writing to the file, and then reopen the file with an input stream. (It is possible to open a file for both input and output, but this is done in a slightly different way.)

A less commonly used member function, but one you may eventually need, is flush, which is a member function of every output stream. For reasons of efficiency, output is often *buffered*—that is, temporarily stored someplace—before it is actually written to a file. The member function flush flushes the output stream so that all output that may have been buffered is physically written to the file. An invocation of

Display 12.1   Simple File Input/Output

```
1    //Reads three numbers from the file infile.txt, sums the numbers,
2    //and writes the sum to the file outfile.txt.
3    #include <fstream>                    A better version of this program
4    using std::ifstream;                  is given in Display 12.3.
5    using std::ofstream;
6    using std::endl;

7    int main( )
8    {
9        ifstream inStream;
10       ofstream outStream;

11       inStream.open("infile.txt");
12       outStream.open("outfile.txt");

13       int first, second, third;
14       inStream >> first >> second >> third;
15       outStream << "The sum of the first 3\n"
16                 << "numbers in infile.txt\n"
17                 << "is " << (first + second + third)
18                 << endl;

19       inStream.close( );
20       outStream.close( );

21       return 0;
22   }
```

Sample Dialogue

There is no output to the screen
and no input from the keyboard.

Infile.txt
(Not changed by program)

```
1
2
3
4
```

Outfile.txt
(After program is run)

```
The sum of the first 3
numbers in infile.txt
is 6
```

`close` automatically invokes `flush`, so you very seldom need to use `flush`. The syntax for `flush` is indicated by the following example:

```
outStream.flush( );
```

PITFALL: Restrictions on Stream Variables

You declare a stream variable (one of type `ifstream` or `ofstream`) in the usual way, but these variables cannot be used in some of the ways that other variables are used. You cannot use an assignment statement to assign a value to a stream variable. You can have a parameter of a stream type (`ifstream`, `ofstream`, or any other stream type), but it must be a call-by-reference parameter. It cannot be a call-by-value parameter. ■

Appending to a File

When sending output to a file, your code must first use the member function `open` to open a file and connect it to a stream of type `ofstream`. The way we have done this thus far, with a single argument for the file name always yields an empty file. If a file of the specified name already exists, its old contents are lost. There is an alternative way to open a file so that the output from your program will be appended to the file after any data already in the file.

To append your output to a file named `"important.txt"`, you would use a two-argument version of `open`, as illustrated by the following:

```
ofstream outStream;
outStream.open("important.txt", ios::app);
```

If the file `"important.txt"` does not exist, this will create an empty file with that name to receive your program's output; if the file already exists, then all the output from your program will be appended to the end of the file, so that old data in the file is not lost. This is illustrated in Display 12.2.

The second argument `ios::app` is a defined constant in the class `ios`. The class `ios` is defined in the `<iostream>` library (and also in some other stream libraries). The definition of the class `ios` is placed in the `std` namespace, so either of the following will make `ios` (and hence `ios::app`) available to your program:

```
#include <iostream>
using namespace std;
```

or

```
#include <iostream>
using std::ios;
```

`ios::app`

Display 12.2   Appending to a File

```
1   //Appends data to the end of the file alldata.txt.
2   #include <fstream>
3   #include <iostream>
4   using std::ofstream;
5   using std::cout;
6   using std::ios;
7   int main( )
8   {
9       cout << "Opening data.txt for appending.\n";
10      ofstream fout;
11      fout.open("data.txt", ios::app);
12      fout << "5 6 pick up sticks.\n"
13           << "7 8 ain't C++ great!\n";
14      fout.close( );
15      cout << "End of appending to file.\n";
16      return 0;
17  }
```

Sample Dialogue

Data.txt
(Before program is run)

```
1 2 buckle my shoe.
3 4 shut the door.
```

Data.txt
(After program is run)

```
1 2 buckle my shoe.
3 4 shut the door.
5 6 pick up sticks.
7 8 ain't C++ great!
```

Screen Output

```
Opening data.txt for appending.
End of appending to file
```

Appending to a File

If you want to append data to a file so that it goes after any existing contents of the file, open the file as follows.

SYNTAX

Output_Stream.open(*File_Name*, ios::app);

EXAMPLE

```
ofstream outStream;
outStream.open("important.txt", ios::app);
```

TIP: Another Syntax for Opening a File

Each of the classes ifstream and ofstream has constructors that allow you to specify a file name and sometimes other parameters for opening a file. A few examples will make the syntax clear.

The two statements

```
ifstream inStream;
inStream.open("infile.txt");
```

can be replaced by the following equivalent line:

```
ifstream inStream("infile.txt");
```

The two statements

```
ofstream outStream;
outStream.open("outfile.txt");
```

can be replaced by the following equivalent line:

```
ofstream outStream("outfile.txt");
```

As our final example, the two lines

```
ofstream outStream;
outStream.open("important.txt", ios::app);
```

are equivalent to the following:

```
ofstream outStream("important.txt", ios::app);
```

Display 12.3   File I/O with Checks on open

```
1   //Reads three numbers from the file infile.txt and writes the sum to the
2   //file outfile.txt.
3   #include <fstream>
4   #include <iostream>
5   #include <cstdlib> //for exit
6   using std::ifstream;
7   using std::ofstream;
8   using std::cout;
9   using std::endl;

10  int main( )
11  {
12      ifstream inStream;
13      ofstream outStream;

14      inStream.open("infile.txt");
15      if (inStream.fail( ))
16      {
17          cout << "Input file opening failed.\n";
18          exit(1);
19      }

20      outStream.open("outfile.txt");
21      if (outStream.fail( ))
22      {
23          cout << "Output file opening failed.\n";
24          exit(1);
25      }

26      int first, second, third;
27      inStream >> first >> second >> third;
28      outStream << "The sum of the first 3\n"
29                << "numbers in infile.txt\n"
30                << "is " << (first + second + third) << endl;

31      inStream.close( );
32      outStream.close( );
33      return 0;
34  }
```

Sample Dialogue (*if the file infile.txt does not exist*)

```
Input file opening failed.
```

TIP: Check That a File Was Opened Successfully

A call to open can be unsuccessful for a number of reasons. For example, if you try to open an input file and there is no file with the external name that you specified, then the call to open will fail. As another example, an attempt to open an output file could fail because the file exists and your program (that is, your account) does not have write permission for the file. When such things happen, you may not receive an error message and your program may simply proceed to do something unexpected. Thus, you should always follow a call to open with a test to see whether the call to open was successful, and end the program (or take some other appropriate action) if the call to open was unsuccessful.

the member function `fail`

You can use the member function named `fail` to test whether or not a stream operation has failed. There is a member function named `fail` for each of the classes `ifstream` and `ofstream`. The `fail` function takes no arguments and returns a `bool` value.

You should place a call to `fail` immediately after each call to `open`; if the call to `open` fails, the function `fail` will return `true`. For example, if the following call to open fails, then the program will output an error message and end; if the call succeeds, the `fail` function returns `false` and the program will continue.

```
inStream.open("stuff.txt");
if (inStream.fail())
{
    cout << "Input file opening failed.\n";
    exit(1);
}
```

Display 12.3 contains the program from Display 12.1 rewritten to include tests to see if the input and output files were opened successfully. It processes files in exactly the same way as the program in Display 12.1. In particular, assuming that the file `infile.txt` exists and has the contents shown in Display 12.1, the program in Display 12.3 will create the file `outfile.txt` that is shown in Display 12.1. However, if there were something wrong and one of the calls to open failed, then the program in Display 12.3 would end and send an appropriate error message to the screen. For example, if there were no file named `infile.txt`, then the call to `inStream.open` would fail, the program would end, and an error message would be written to the screen. Notice that we used `cout` to output the error message; this is because we want the error message to go to the screen, as opposed to going to a file. Since this program uses `cout` to output to the screen (as well as doing file I/O), we have added an `include` directive for the header file `<iostream>`. (Actually, your program does not need to have `#include <iostream>` when your program has `#include <fstream>`, but it causes no problems to include it, and it reminds you that the program is using screen output in addition to file I/O.)

Summary of File I/O Statements

In this example the input comes from a file with the name `infile.txt`, and the output goes to a file with the name `outfile.txt`.

- Place the following include directives in your program file:

```
#include <fstream>              For file I/O
#include <iostream>            For cout
#include <cstdlib>             For exit
```

Add the following using directives (or something similar):

```
using std::ifstream;
using std::ofstream;
using std::cout;
using std::endl;   //if endl is used.
```

- Choose a stream name for the input stream and declare it to be a variable of type `ifstream`. Choose a stream name for the output file and declare it to be of type `ofstream`. For example,

```
ifstream inStream;
ofstream outStream;
```

- Connect each stream to a file using the member function open with the external file name as an argument. Remember to use the member function fail to test that the call to open was successful:

```
inStream.open("infile.txt");
if (inStream.fail( ))
{
    cout << "Input file opening failed.\n";
    exit(1);
}

outStream.open("outfile.txt");
if (outStream.fail( ))
{
    cout << "Output file opening failed.\n";
    exit(1);
}
```

- Use the stream inStream to get input from the file infile.txt just like you use cin to get input from the keyboard. For example,

```
inStream >> someVariable >> someOtherVariable;
```

(continued)

Summary of File I/O Statements (continued)

■ Use the stream outStream to send output to the file outfile.txt just like you use cout to send output to the screen. For example,

```
outStream << "someVariable = "
          << someVariable << endl;
```

■ Close the streams using the function close:

```
inStream.close();
outStream.close();
```

Self-Test Exercises

1. Suppose you are writing a program that uses a stream called fin, which will be connected to an input file, and a stream called fout, which will be connected to an output file. How do you declare fin and fout? What include directive, if any, do you need to place in your program file?

2. Suppose you are continuing to write the program discussed in the previous exercise and you want your program to take its input from the file stuff1.txt and send its output to the file stuff2.txt. What statements do you need to place in your program in order to connect the stream fin to the file stuff1.txt and to connect the stream fout to the file stuff2.txt? Be sure to include checks to make sure that the openings were successful.

3. Suppose that you are still writing the same program that we discussed in the previous two exercises and you reach the point at which you no longer need to get input from the file stuff1.txt and no longer need to send output to the file stuff2.txt. How do you close these files?

4. Suppose you want to change the program in Display 12.1 so that it sends its output to the screen instead of the file outfile.txt. (The input should still come from the file infile.txt.) What changes do you need to make to the program?

5. A programmer has read half of the lines in a file. What must the programmer do to the file to enable reading the first line a second time?

Character I/O

Chapter 9 described character I/O from the keyboard with cin and to the screen with cout. Character I/O from a file works the same way as character I/O with the keyboard and screen. Just use an input stream connected to a file in place of cin or an output stream connected to a file in place of cout. In particular, get, getline, putback, peek, and ignore work the same for file input as they do for keyboard input;[1] put works the same for file output as it does for screen output.

Checking for the End of a File

eof member function

A common way of processing an input file is to use a loop that processes data from the file until the end of the file is reached. There are two standard ways to test for the end of a file. The most straightforward way is to use the eof member function.

Every input-file stream has a member function called eof that can be used to test for reaching the end of the input file. The function eof takes no arguments, so if the input stream is called fin, then a call to the function eof is written

```
fin.eof( )
```

This is a Boolean expression that can be used to control a while loop, do-while loop, or an if-else statement. This expression returns true if the program has read past the end of the input file; otherwise, it returns false.

Since we usually want to test that we are *not* at the end of a file, a call to the member function eof is typically used with a *not* in front of it. Recall that in C++ the symbol ! is used to express *not*. For example, the entire contents of the file connected to the input stream inStream can be written to the screen with the following while loop:

ending an input loop with the eof function

```
inStream.get(next);
while (! inStream.eof( ))
{
    cout << next;              *If you prefer, you can*
    inStream.get(next);       *use cout.put(next) here.*
}
```

The previous while loop reads each character from the input file into the char variable next using the member function get, and then it writes the character to the screen. After the program has passed the end of the file, the value of inStream.eof( ) changes from false to true. Thus,

```
(! inStream.eof( ))
```

changes from true to false and the loop ends.

Notice that inStream.eof( ) does not become true until the program attempts to read one character beyond the end of the file. For example, suppose the file contains the following (without any newline character after the c):

```
ab
c
```

---

[1]If you have not yet read about getline, putback, peek, or ignore, do not be concerned. They are not used in this chapter, except for one brief reference to ignore at the very end of this chapter. You can ignore that one reference to ignore.

This is actually the following list of four characters:

```
ab<the newline character '\n'>c
```

The loop shown will read an 'a' and write it to the screen, then read a 'b' and write it to the screen, then read the newline character '\n' and write it to the screen, and then read a 'c' and write it to the screen. At that point the loop will have read all the characters in the file. However, `inStream.eof( )` will still be `false`. The value of `inStream.eof( )` will not change from `false` to `true` until the program tries to read one more character. That is why the previous `while` loop tries to read until the program tries to read one more character. That is why the previous `while` loop ends with `inStream.get (next)`. The loop needs to read one extra character in order to end the loop.

There is a special end-of-file marker at the end of a file. The member function `eof` does not change from `false` to `true` until this end-of-file marker is read. That is why the previous `while` loop could read one character beyond what you think of as the last character in the file. However, this end-of-file marker is not an ordinary character and should not be manipulated like an ordinary character. You can read this end-of-file marker, but you should not write it out again. If you write out the end-of-file marker, the result is unpredictable. The system automatically places this end-of-file marker at the end of each file for you.

To complicate things, the implementation of `eof` on some compilers will return `true` without having to read the end-of-file marker, so you may need to check your compiler's documentation or write a short program to determine your compiler's behavior.

the macho way
to test for end
of file

The second way to check for the end of the file is to note (and use) the fact that a read with an extraction operator actually returns a Boolean value. The expression

```
(inStream >> next)
```

returns `true` if the read was successful and returns `false` when your code attempts to read beyond the end of the file. For example, the following will read all the numbers in a file of integers connected to the input stream `inStream` and compute their sum in the variable `sum`:

```
double next, sum = 0;
while (inStream >> next)
    sum = sum + next;
cout << "the sum is " << sum << endl;
```

The previous loop may look a bit peculiar, because `inStream >> next` reads a number from the stream `inStream` and returns a Boolean value. An expression involving the extraction operator `>>` is simultaneously both an action and a Boolean condition.[2] If there is another number to be input, then the number is read and the Boolean value `true` is returned, so the body of the loop is executed one more time.

---

[2] Technically, the Boolean condition works this way: The returned value of the operator `>>` is an input stream reference (`istream&` or `ifstream&`), as explained in Chapter 8. This stream reference is automatically converted to a `bool` value. The resulting value is `true` if the stream was able to extract data, and `false` otherwise.

If there are no more numbers to be read in, then nothing is input and the Boolean value false is returned, so the loop ends. In this example the type of the input variable next was double, but this method of checking for the end of the file works the same way for other data types, such as int and char.

This second method of testing for the end of a file is preferred by many C++ programmers for what appears to be a cultural reason. It was commonly used in C programming. It is also possible that, depending on implementation details, this second method might be a bit more efficient. In any event, whether you use this second method or not, you need to know it so you can understand other programmers' code.

An illustration of using the eof member function is given in Display 12.4.

Display 12.4   Checking for the End of a File (part 1 of 2)

```
1    //Copies story.txt to numstory.txt,
2    //but adds a number to the beginning of each line.
3    //Assumes story.txt is not empty.
4    #include <fstream>
5    #include <iostream>
6    #include <cstdlib>

7    using std::ifstream;
8    using std::ofstream;
9    using std::cout;

10   int main( )
11   {
12       ifstream fin;
13       ofstream fout;

14       fin.open("story.txt");
15       if (fin.fail( ))
16       {
17           cout << "Input file opening failed.\n";
18           exit(1);
19       }

20       fout.open("numstory.txt");
21       if (fout.fail( ))
22       {
23           cout << "Output file opening failed.\n";
24           exit(1);
25       }
```

(continued)

Display 12.4   Checking for the End of a File (part 2 of 2)

```
26        char next;
27        int n = 1;
28        fin.get(next);
29        fout << n << " ";
30        while (! fin.eof( ))
31        {
32            fout << next;
33            if (next == '\n')
34            {
35                n++;
36                fout << n << ' ';
37            }
38            fin.get(next);
39        }
40
41        fin.close( );
42        fout.close( );
43
44        return 0;
45    }
```

Notice that the loop ends with a read (fin.get).
The member function fin.eof does not return
true until your program tries to read one more
character after reading the last character in the file.

Sample Dialogue

┌─────────────────────────────────┐
│   *There is no output to the screen* │
│   *and no input from the keyboard.* │
└─────────────────────────────────┘

Story.txt
(Not changed by program)

┌─────────────────────────────────┐
│ The little green men had   │
│ pointed heads and orange   │
│ toes with one long curly   │
│ hair on each toe.   │
└─────────────────────────────────┘

Numstory.txt
(After program is run)

┌─────────────────────────────────┐
│ 1 The little green men had   │
│ 2 pointed heads and orange   │
│ 3 toes with one long curly   │
│ 4 hair on each toe.   │
└─────────────────────────────────┘

Self-Test Exercises

6. What output will be produced when the following lines are executed, assuming the file list.txt contains the data shown (and assuming the lines are embedded in a complete and correct program with the proper include and using directives)?

Self-Test Exercises (continued)

```
ifstream ins;
ins.open("list.txt");
int count = 0, next;
while (ins >> next)
{
    count++;
    cout << next << endl;
}
ins.close( );
cout << count;
```

The file list.txt contains the following three numbers (and nothing more):

```
1 2
3
```

7. Write the definition for a void function called toScreen. The function toScreen has one formal parameter called fileStream, which is of type ifstream. The precondition and postcondition for the function are given next.

```
//Precondition: The stream fileStream has been connected
//to a file with a call to the member function open. The
//file contains a list of integers (and nothing else).
//Postcondition: The numbers in the file connected to
//fileStream have been written to the screen one per line.
//(This function does not close the file.)
```

12.2 Tools for Stream I/O

You shall see them on a beautiful quarto page, where a neat rivulet of text shall meander through a meadow of margin.

RICHARD BRINSLEY SHERIDAN, *The School for Scandal*

File Names as Input

Thus far, we have written the literal file names for our input and output files into the code of our programs. We did this by giving the file name as the argument to a call to the function open, as in the following example:

```
instream.open("infile.txt");
```

You can instead read the file name in from the keyboard, as illustrated by the following:

```
char fileName[16];
ifstream inStream;
```

```
cout << "Enter file name (maximum of 15 characters):\n";
cin >> fileName;
inStream.open(fileName);
```

as a C-string

Note that our code reads the file name as a C-string. The member function `open` takes an argument that is a C-string. You cannot use a string variable as an argument to open, and there is no predefined type cast operator to convert from a `string` object to a C-string. However, as an alternative, you can read the file name into a `string` variable and use the `string` member function `c_str( )` to produce the corresponding C-string value for `open`. The code would be as follows:

```
string fileName;
ifstream inStream;
```

as a string object

```
cout << "Enter file name:\n";
getline(cin, filename);
inStream.open(fileName.c_str( ));
```

Note that when you use a `string` variable for the file name, there is essentially no limit to the size of the file name.[3]

Formatting Output with Stream Functions

You can control the format of your output to a file or to the screen with commands that determine such details as the number of spaces between items and the number of digits after the decimal point. For example, in Chapter 1 we gave the following "magic formula" to use for outputting amounts of money:

```
cout.setf(ios::fixed);
cout.setf(ios::showpoint);
cout.precision(2);
```

We are now in a position to explain these and other formulas for formatting output.

The first thing to note is that you can use these formatting commands on any output stream. Output streams connected to a file have these same member functions as the object cout. If `outStream` is a file output stream (of type `ofstream`), you can format output in the same way:

```
outStream.setf(ios::fixed);
outStream.setf(ios::showpoint);
outStream.precision(2);
```

To explain this magic formula, we will consider the member functions in reverse order.

---

[3]The lack of accommodation for the type `string` within the `iostream` library is because `iostream` was written before the `string` type was added to the C++ libraries.

precision

Every output stream has a member function named `precision`. When your program executes a call to `precision` such as the previous one for the stream `outStream`, then from that point on in your program, any number with a decimal point that is output to that stream will be written with a total of two significant figures or with two digits after the decimal point, depending on when your compiler was written. The following is some possible output from a compiler that sets two significant digits:

```
23.     2.2     6.9e-1     0.00069
```

The following is some possible output from a compiler that sets two digits after the decimal point:

```
23.56   2.26e7   0.69   0.69e-4
```

In this book, we assume the compiler sets two digits after the decimal point. Of course, you can use a different argument than 2 to obtain more or less precision.

setf

flag

Every output stream has a member function named **setf** that can be used to set certain flags. These **flags** are constants in the class `ios`, which is in the `std` namespace. When set with a call to `setf`, the flags determine certain behaviors of the output stream. Following are the two calls to the member function `setf` with the stream `outStream` as the calling object:

```
outStream.setf(ios::fixed);
outStream.setf(ios::showpoint);
```

Each of these flags is an instruction to format output in one of two possible ways. What it causes the stream to do depends on the flag.

ios::fixed

fixed-point notation

The flag `ios::fixed` causes the stream to output floating-point numbers in what is called **fixed-point notation**, which is a fancy phrase for the way we normally write numbers. If the flag `ios::fixed` is set (by a call to `setf`), then all floating-point numbers (such as numbers of type `double`) that are output to that stream will be written in ordinary everyday notation, rather than e-notation.

ios:: showpoint

The flag `ios::showpoint` tells the stream to always include a decimal point in floating-point numbers. If the number to be output has a value of `2.0`, then it will be output as `2.0` and not simply as `2`; that is, the output will include the decimal point even if all the digits after the decimal point are `0`. Some common flags and the actions they cause are described in Display 12.5.

You can set multiple flags with a single call to `setf`. Simply connect the various flags with '`|`' symbols, as illustrated:[4]

```
outStream.setf(ios::fixed | ios::showpoint | ios::right);
```

---

[4]The `|` operator is bitwise-or. You are literally or-ing a bitwise mask that indicates the flag settings, although you need not be aware of this low level detail.

Display 12.5 Formatting Flags for setf

FLAG	MEANING OF SETTING THE FLAG	DEFAULT
ios::fixed	Floating-point numbers are not written in e-notation. (Setting this flag automatically unsets the flag ios::scientific.)	Not set
ios::scientific	Floating-point numbers are written in e-notation. (Setting this flag automatically unsets the flag ios::fixed.) If neither ios::fixed nor ios::scientific is set, then the system decides how to output each number.	Not set
ios::showpoint	A decimal point and trailing zeros are always shown for floating-point numbers. If it is not set, a number with all zeros after the decimal point might be output without the decimal point and following zeros.	Not set
ios::showpos	A plus sign is output before positive integer values.	Not set
ios::right	If this flag is set and some field-width value is given with a call to the member function width, then the next item output will be at the right end of the space specified by width. In other words, any extra blanks are placed before the item output. (Setting this flag automatically unsets the flag ios::left.)	Set
ios::left	If this flag is set and some field-width value is given with a call to the member function width, then the next item output will be at the left end of the space specified by width. In other words, any extra blanks are placed after the item output. (Setting this flag automatically unsets the flag ios::right.)	Not set
ios::dec	Integers are output in decimal (base 10) notation.	Set
ios::oct	Integers are output in octal (base 8) notation.	Not set
ios::hex	Integers are output in hexadecimal (base 16) notation.	Not set
ios::uppercase	An uppercase E is used instead of a lowercase e in scientific notation for floating-point numbers. Hexadecimal numbers are output using uppercase letters.	Not set
ios::showbase	Shows the base of an output number (leading 0 for octal, leading 0x for hexadecimal).	Not set

width

Output streams have other member functions besides `precision` and `setf`. One very commonly used formatting function is `width`. For example, consider the following call to `width` made by the stream `cout`:

```
cout << "Start Now";
cout.width(4);
cout << 7 << endl;
```

This code will cause the following line to appear on the screen:

```
Start Now   7
```

This output has exactly three spaces between the letter `'w'` and the number `7`. The `width` function tells the stream how many spaces to use when giving an item as output. In this case the number `7` occupies only one space and `width` is set to use four spaces, so three of the spaces are blank. If the output requires more space than you specified in the argument to `width`, then as much additional space as is needed will be used. The entire item is always output, no matter what argument you give to `width`.

The Class `ios`

The class `ios` has a number of important defined constants, such as `ios::app` (used to indicate that you are appending to a file) and the flags listed in Display 12.5. The class `ios` is defined in libraries for output streams, such as `<iostream>` and `<fstream>`. One way to make the class `ios` and hence all these constants (all these flags) available to your code is the following:

```
#include <iostream> //or #include <fstream> or both
using std::ios;
```

unsetf

Any flag that is set may be unset. To unset a flag, use the function **unsetf**. For example, the following will cause your program to stop including plus signs on positive integers that are output to the stream `cout`:

```
cout.unsetf(ios::showpos);
```

When a flag is set, it remains set until it is unset. The effect of a call to `precision` stays in effect until the precision is reset. However, the member function `width` behaves differently. A call to `width` applies only to the next item that is output. If you want to output 12 numbers, using four spaces to output each number, then you must call to `width` 12 times. If this becomes a nuisance, you may prefer to use the manipulator `setw` that is described in the next subsection.

Manipulators

manipulator

A **manipulator** is a function that is called in a nontraditional way. Manipulators are placed after the insertion operator <<, just as if the manipulator function call were an item to be output. Like traditional functions, manipulators may or may not have arguments. We have already seen one manipulator, endl. This subsection discusses two manipulators called setw and setprecision.

setw

The manipulator setw and the member function width (which you have already seen) do exactly the same thing. You call the setw manipulator by writing it after the insertion operator, <<, as if it were to be sent to the output stream, and this in turn calls the member function width. For example, the following will output the numbers 10, 20, and 30, using the field widths specified:

```
cout << "Start" << setw(4) << 10
     << setw(4) << 20 << setw(6) << 30;
```

The preceding statement will produce the following output:

```
Start  10   20    30
```

(There are two spaces before the 10, two spaces before the 20, and four spaces before the 30.)

Like the member function width, a call to setw applies only to the next item output, but it is easier to include multiple calls to setw than it is to make multiple calls to width.

setprecision

The manipulator setprecision does the same thing as the member function precision (which you have already seen). However, a call to setprecision is written after the insertion operator, <<, in a manner similar to how you call the setw manipulator. For example, the following will output the numbers listed using the number of digits after the decimal point that are indicated by the call to setprecision:

```
cout.setf(ios::fixed);
cout.setf(ios::showpoint);
cout << "$" << setprecision(2) << 10.3 << endl
     << "$" << 20.5 << endl;
```

The previous statement will produce the following output:

```
$10.30
$20.50
```

When you set the number of digits after the decimal point using the manipulator setprecision, then just as was the case with the member function precision, the setting stays in effect until you reset it to some other number by another call to either setprecision or precision.

To use either of the manipulators setw or setprecision, you must include the following directive in your program:

<iomanip>

```
#include <iomanip>
using namespace std;
```

Or, you must use one of the other ways of specifying the names and namespace, such as the following:

```
#include <iomanip>
using std::setw;
using std::setprecision;
```

Saving Flag Settings

A function should not have unwanted or unexpected side effects. For example, a function to output amounts of money might contain

```
cout.setf(ios::fixed);
cout.setf(ios::showpoint);
cout.precision(2);
```

After the function invocation ends, these settings will still be in effect. If you do not want such side effects, you can save and restore the original settings.

The function precision has been overloaded so that with no arguments it returns the current precision setting so the setting can later be restored.

The flags set with setf are easy to save and restore. The member function flags is overloaded to provide a way to save and then restore the flag settings. The member function cout.flags( ) returns a value of type long that codes all the flag settings. The flags can be reset by using this long value as an argument to cout.flags. These techniques work the same for file output streams as they do for cout.

For example, a function to save and restore these settings could be structured as follows:

```
void outputStuff(ofstream& outStream)
{

    int precisionSetting = outStream.precision( );
    long flagSettings = outStream.flags( );
    outStream.setf(ios::fixed);
    outStream.setf(ios::showpoint);
    outStream.precision(2);

        //Do whatever you want here.
    outStream.precision(precisionSetting);
    outStream.flags(flagSettings);

}
```

Another way to restore settings is

```
cout.setf(0, ios::floatfield);
```

An invocation of the member function setf with these arguments will restore the default setf settings. Note that these are the default values, not necessarily the settings before the last time they were changed. Also note that the default setting values are implementation-dependent. Finally, note that this does not reset precision settings or any settings that are not set with setf.

More Output Stream Member Functions

Display 12.6 summarizes some of the formatting member functions for the class ostream and some of the manipulators. Remember that to use the manipulators you need the following (or something similar):

```
#include <iomanip>
using namespace std;
```

Display 12.6   Formatting Tools for the Class ostream

FUNCTION	DESCRIPTION	CORRESPONDING MANIPULATOR
setf(ios_Flag)	Sets flags as described in Display 12.5	setiosflags(ios_Flag)
unsetf(ios_Flag)	Unsets flag	resetiosflags(ios_Flag)
setf(0, ios::floatfield)	Restores default flag settings	None
precision(int)	Sets precision for floating-point number output	setprecision(int)
precision()	Returns the current precision setting	None
width(int)	Sets the output field width; applies only to the next item output	setw(int)
fill(char)	Specifies the fill character when the output field is larger than the value output; the default is a blank	setfill(char)

Self-Test Exercises

8. What output will be produced when the following lines are executed?

```
cout << "*";
cout.width(5);
cout << 123
     << "*" << 123 << "*" << endl;
cout << "*" << setw(5) << 123
     << "*" << 123 << "*" << endl;
```

Self-Test Exercises (continued)

9. What output will be produced when the following lines are executed?

```
cout << "*" << setw(5) << 123;
cout.setf(ios::left);
cout << "*" << setw(5) << 123;
cout.setf(ios::right);
cout << "*" << setw(5) << 123 << "*" << endl;
```

10. What output will be produced when the following lines are executed?

```
cout << "*" << setw(5) << 123 << "*"
     << 123 << "*" << endl;
cout.setf(ios::showpos);
cout << "*" << setw(5) << 123 << "*"
     << 123 << "*" << endl;
cout.unsetf(ios::showpos);
cout.setf(ios::left);
cout << "*" << setw(5) << 123 << "*"
     << setw(5) << 123 << "*" << endl;
```

11. What output will be sent to the file stuff.txt when the following lines are executed?

```
ofstream fout;
fout.open("stuff.txt");
fout << "*" << setw(5) << 123 << "*"
     << 123 << "*" << endl;
fout.setf(ios::showpos);
fout << "*" << setw(5) << 123 << "*"
     << 123 << "*" << endl;
fout.unsetf(ios::showpos);
fout.setf(ios::left);
fout << "*" << setw(5) << 123 << "*"
     << setw(5) << 123 << "*" << endl;
```

12. What output will be produced when the following line is executed (assuming the line is embedded in a complete and correct program with the proper include and using directives)?

```
cout << "*" << setw(3) << 12345 << "*" << endl;
```

EXAMPLE: Cleaning Up a File Format

The program in Display 12.7 takes its input from the file rawdata.dat and writes its output, in a neat format, both to the screen and to the file neat.txt. The program copies numbers from the file rawdata.txt to the screen and to the file neat.txt, but it uses formatting instructions to write them in a neat way. The numbers are written one per line in a field of width 12, which means that each number is preceded by enough blanks so that the blanks plus the number occupy 12 spaces. The numbers are written in ordinary notation; that is, they are not written in e-notation. Each number is written with five digits after the decimal point and with a plus or minus sign. The program uses a function, named makeNeat, that has formal parameters for the input-file stream and the output-file stream.

Display 12.7   Formatting Output (part 1 of 3)

```
1    //Reads all the numbers in the file rawdata.dat and writes the numbers
2    //to the screen and to the file neat.txt in a neatly formatted way.
3    #include <iostream>
4    #include <fstream>
5    #include <cstdlib>
6    #include <iomanip>                          ←——— Needed for setw
7    using std::ifstream;
8    using std::ofstream;
9    using std::cout;
10   using std::endl;
11   using std::ios;
12   using std::setw;
13   void makeNeat(ifstream& messyFile, ofstream& neatFile,
14               int numberAfterDecimalpoint, int fieldWidth);
                                                        Stream parameters must
                                                        be call-by-reference parameters.
15   //Precondition: The streams messyFile and neatFile have been
16   //connected to two different files. The file named messyFile contains
17   //only floating-point numbers.
18   //Postcondition: The numbers in the file connected to messyFile have
19   //been written to the screen and to the file connected to the stream
20   //neatFile. The numbers are written one per line, in fixed-point
21   //notation (that is, not in e-notation), with numberAfterDecimalpoint
22   //digits after the decimal point; each number is preceded by a plus or
23   //minus sign and each number is in a field of width fieldWidth. (This
24   //function does not close the file.)
     int main()
```

Display 12.7   Formatting Output (part 2 of 3)

```
25    {
26        ifstream fin;
27        ofstream fout;

28        fin.open("rawdata.txt");
29        if (fin.fail( ))
30        {
31            cout << "Input file opening failed.\n";
32            exit(1);
33        }

34
35        fout.open("neat.txt");
36        if (fout.fail( ))
37        {
38            cout << "Output file opening failed.\n";
39            exit(1);
40        }
41        makeNeat(fin, fout, 5, 12);

42        fin.close( );
43        fout.close( );
44        cout << "End of program.\n";
45        return 0;
46    }

47    //Uses <iostream>, <fstream>, and <iomanip>:
48    void makeNeat(ifstream& messyFile, ofstream& neatFile,
49                  int numberAfterDecimalpoint, int fieldWidth)
50    {
51        neatFile.setf(ios::fixed);
52        neatFile.setf(ios::showpoint);
53        neatFile.setf(ios::showpos);
54        neatFile.precision(numberAfterDecimalpoint);

55        cout.setf(ios::fixed);
56        cout.setf(ios::showpoint);
57        cout.setf(ios::showpos);
58        cout.precision(numberAfterDecimalpoint);

59        double next;
60        while (messyFile >> next)
61        {
62            cout     << setw(fieldWidth) << next << endl;
63            neatFile << setw(fieldWidth) << next << endl;
64        }
65    }
```

setf and precision behave the same for a file output stream as they do for cout.

Satisfied if there is a next number to read

Works the same for file output streams as it does for cout

(continued)

Display 12.7   Formatting Output (part 3 of 3)

Sample Dialogue

Rawdata.txt
(Not changed by program)

```
10.37    -9.89897
2.313  -8.950  15.0

7.33333  92.8765
-1.237568432e2
```

neat.txt
(After program is run)

```
+10.37000
-9.89897
+2.31300
-8.95000
+15.00000
+7.33333
+92.87650
-123.75684
```

Screen Output

```
+10.37000
-9.89897
-8.95000
+15.00000
+7.33333
+92.87650
-123.75684
End of program.
```

EXAMPLE: Editing a Text File

The program discussed here is a very simple example of text editing applied to files. This program can be used to automatically generate C++ advertising material from existing C advertising material (in a rather simplistic way). The program takes its input from a file that contains advertising copy that says good things about C and writes similar advertising copy about C++ in another file. The file that contains the C advertising copy is called cad.txt, and the new file that receives the C++ advertising copy is called cppad.txt. The program is shown in Display 12.8. The program simply reads every character in the file cad.txt and copies the characters to the file cppad.txt. Every character is copied unchanged, except that when the uppercase letter 'C' is read from the input file, the program writes the string "C++" to the output file. This program assumes that whenever the letter 'C' occurs in the input file, it names the C programming language; so this change is exactly what is needed to produce the updated advertising copy.

Notice that the line breaks are preserved when the program reads characters from the input file and writes the characters to the output file. The newline character '\n' is treated just like any other character. It is read from the input file with the member function get, and it is written to the output file using the insertion operator, <<. We must use the member function get to read the input (rather than the extraction operator, >>) because we want to read whitespace.

Display 12.8   Editing a File of Text (part 1 of 2)

```
1   //Program to create a file called cplusad.txt that is identical
2   //to the file cad.txt except that all occurrences of 'C' are replaced
3   //by "C++". Assumes that the uppercase letter 'C' does not occur in
4   //cad.txt except as the name of the C programming language.
5   #include <fstream>
6   #include <iostream>
7   #include <cstdlib>
8   using std::ifstream;
9   using std::ofstream;
10  using std::cout;

11  void addPlusPlus(ifstream& inStream, ofstream& outStream);
12  //Precondition: inStream has been connected to an input file with open.
13  //outStream has been connected to an output file with open.
14  //Postcondition: The contents of the file connected to inStream have been
15  //copied into the file connected to outStream, but with each 'C' replaced
16  //by "C++". (The files are not closed by this function.)

17  int main( )
18  {
19      ifstream fin;
20      ofstream fout;

21      cout << "Begin editing files.\n";

22      fin.open("cad.txt");
23      if (fin.fail( ))
24      {
25          cout << "Input file opening failed.\n";
26          exit(1);
27      }

28      fout.open("cppad.txt");
29      if (fout.fail( ))
30      {
31          cout << "Output file opening failed.\n";
32          exit(1);
33      }
```

(continued)

Display 12.8   Editing a File of Text (part 2 of 2)

```
34      addPlusPlus(fin, fout);
35      fin.close( );
36      fout.close( );

37      cout << "End of editing files.\n";
38      return 0;
39  }

40  void addPlusPlus(ifstream& inStream, ofstream& outStream)
41  {
42      char next;

43      inStream.get(next);
44      while (! inStream.eof( ))
45      {
46          if (next == 'C')
47              outStream << "C++";
48          else
49              outStream << next;

50          inStream.get(next);
51      }
52  }
```

Sample Dialogue

cad.txt
(Not changed by program)

```
C is one of the world's most modern
programming languages. There is no
language as versatile as C, and C
is fun to use.
```

cppad.txt
(After program is run)

```
C++ is one of the world's most
modern programming languages. There
is no language as versatile as C++,
and C++ is fun to use.
```

Screen Output

```
Begin editing files.
End of editing files.
```

12.3   Stream Hierarchies: A Preview of Inheritance

One very useful way to organize classes is by means of the "derived from" relationship. When we say that one class is *derived from* another class we mean that the derived class was obtained from the other class by adding features. For example, the class of input-*file* streams is derived from the class of *all* input streams by adding additional member functions such as open and close. The stream cin belongs to the class of all input streams, but does *not* belong to the class of input-file streams because cin has no member functions named open and close. This section introduces the notion of a derived class as a way to think about and organize the predefined stream classes. (Chapter 14 shows how to use the idea of a derived class to define classes of your own.)

Inheritance among Stream Classes

Both the predefined stream cin and an input-file stream are input streams. So in some sense they are similar. For example, you can use the extraction operator, >>, with either kind of stream. On the other hand, an input-file stream can be connected to a file using the member function open, but the stream cin has no member function named open. An input-file stream is a similar but different kind of stream than cin. An input-file stream is of type ifstream. The object cin is an object of the class istream (spelled without the 'f'). The classes ifstream and istream are different but closely related types. The class ifstream is a *derived class* of the class istream. Let us see what that means.

When we say that some class D is a **derived class** of some other class B, it means that class D has all the features of class B but it also has added features. For example, any stream of type istream (without the 'f') can be used with the extraction operator, >>. The class ifstream (with the 'f') is a derived class of the class istream, so an object of type ifstream can be used with the extraction operator, >>. An object of the class ifstream has all the properties of an object of type istream. In particular, an object of the class ifstream *is also an object of type* istream.

However, ifstream has added features so that you can do more with an object of type ifstream than you can with an object that is only of type istream. For example, one added feature is that a stream of type ifstream can be used with the function open. The stream cin is only of type istream and not of type ifstream. You cannot use cin with the function open. Notice that the relationship between the classes ifstream and istream is not symmetric. Every object of type ifstream is of type istream (a file input stream is an input stream), but an object of type istream need not be of type ifstream (the object cin is of type istream but not of type ifstream).

derived class   The idea of a derived class is really quite common. An example from everyday life may help to make the idea clearer. The class of all convertibles is a derived class of the class of all automobiles. Every convertible is an automobile, but a convertible is not just an automobile. A convertible is a special kind of automobile with special properties that other kinds of automobiles do not have. If you have a convertible, you can lower the top so that the car is open. (You might say that a convertible has an "open" function as an added feature.)

If D is a derived class of the class B, then every object of type D is also of type B. A convertible is also an automobile. A file input stream (object of the class ifstream) is also an input stream (also an object of the class istream). So, if we use istream as the type for a function parameter, rather than using ifstream, then more objects can be plugged in for the parameter. Consider the following two function definitions, which differ only in the type of the parameter (and the function name):

```
void twoSumVersion1(ifstream& sourceFile)  //ifstream with an 'f'
{
    int n1, n2;
    sourceFile >> n1 >> n2;
    cout << n1 << " + " << n2 << " = " << (n1 + n2) << endl;
}
```

and

```
void twoSumVersion2(istream& sourceFile)  //istream without an 'f'
{
    int n1, n2;
    sourceFile >> n1 >> n2;
    cout << n1 << " + " << n2 << " = " << (n1 + n2) << endl;
}
```

With twoSumVersion1, the argument must be of type ifstream. So if fileIn is a file input stream connected to a file, then

```
twoSumVersion1(fileIn);
```

is legal, but

```
twoSumVersion1(cin);  //ILLEGAL
```

is not legal, because cin is not of type ifstream. The object cin is only a stream and only of type istream; cin is not a file input stream.

The function twoSumVersion2 is more versatile. Both of the following are legal:

```
twoSumVersion2(fileIn);
twoSumVersion2(cin);
```

The moral is clear: Use istream, not ifstream, as a parameter type whenever you can. When choosing a parameter type, use the most general type you can. (To draw a real-life analogy consider the following: You might prefer to own a convertible, but you would not want a garage that could only hold a convertible. What if you borrowed a sedan from a friend? You'd still want to be able to park the sedan in your garage.)

You cannot always use the parameter type istream instead of the parameter type ifstream. If you define a function with a parameter of type istream, then that parameter can only use istream member functions. In particular, it cannot use the functions open and close. If you cannot keep all calls to the member functions open and close outside the function definition, then you must use a parameter of type ifstream.

So far we have discussed two classes for input streams: istream and its derived class ifstream. The situation with output streams is similar. Chapter 1 introduced the output streams cout and cerr, which are in the class ostream. This chapter introduced the file output streams, which are in the class ofstream (with an 'f'). The class ostream is the class of all output streams. The streams cout and cerr are of type ostream, but not of type ofstream. In contrast to cout or cerr, an output-file stream is declared to be of type ofstream. The class ofstream of output-file streams is a derived class of the class ostream. For example, the following function writes the word "Hello" to the output stream given as its argument.

```
void sayHello(ostream& anyOutStream)
{
    anyOutStream << "Hello";
}
```

The first of the following calls writes "Hello" to the screen; the second writes "Hello" to the file with the external file name afile.txt.

```
ofstream fout;
fout.open("afile.txt");
sayHello(cout);
sayHello(fout);
```

Note that an output-file stream is of type ofstream *and* of type ostream.

inheritance

child

parent

Derived classes are often discussed using the metaphor of inheritance and family relationships. If class D is a derived class of class B, then class D is called a **child of** class B and class B is called a **parent** of class D. The derived class is said to **inherit** the member functions of its parent class. For example, every convertible inherits the fact that it has four wheels from the class of all automobiles, and every input-file stream inherits the extraction operator, >>, from the class of all input streams. This is why the topic of derived classes is often called *inheritance*.

EXAMPLE: Another newLine Function

As an example of how you can make a stream function more versatile, consider the function newLine that we defined in Display 9.2. That function works only for input from the keyboard, which is input from the predefined stream cin. The function newLine in Display 9.2 has no arguments. Next we have rewritten the function newLine so that it has a formal parameter of type istream for the input stream.

```
//Uses <iostream>:
void newLine(istream& inStream)
{
    char symbol;
    do
    {
        inStream.get(symbol);
    } while (symbol != '\n');
}
```

(continued)

EXAMPLE: (continued)

Now, suppose your program contains this new version of the function `newLine`. If your program is taking input from an input stream called `fin` (which is connected to an input file), the following will discard all the input left on the line currently being read from the input file:

```
newLine(fin);
```

If your program is also reading some input from the keyboard, the following will discard the remainder of the input line that was typed in at the keyboard:

```
newLine(cin);
```

If your program has only the previous rewritten version of `newLine`, which takes a stream argument such as `fin` or `cin`, you must always give the stream name, even if the stream name is `cin`. But thanks to overloading, you can have both versions of the function `newLine` in the same program: the version with no arguments that is given in Display 9.2 and the version with one argument of type `istream` that we just defined. In a program with both definitions of `newLine`, the following two calls are equivalent:

```
newLine(cin);
```

and

```
newLine();
```

You do not really need two versions of the function `newLine`. The version with one argument of type `istream` can serve all your needs. However, many programmers find it convenient to have a version with no arguments for keyboard input, since keyboard input is used so frequently.

An alternative to having two overloaded versions of the `newLine` function is to use a default argument (as discussed in Chapter 4). In the following code, we have rewritten the `newLine` function a third time.

```
//Uses <iostream>:
void newLine(istream& inStream = cin)
{
    char symbol;
    do
    {
        inStream.get(symbol);
    } while (symbol != '\n');
}
```

EXAMPLE: (continued)

If we call this function as

```
newLine ( ) ;
```

the formal parameter takes the default argument `cin`. If we call this as

```
newLine(fin);
```

the formal parameter takes the argument `fin`.

An alternative to using this `newLine` function is to use the function `ignore`, which we discussed in Chapter 9. The function `ignore` is a member of every input file stream as well as a member of `cin`.

Making Stream Parameters Versatile

If you want to define a function that takes an input stream as an argument and you want that argument to be `cin` in some cases and an input-file stream in other cases, then use a formal parameter of type `istream` (without an `'f'`). However, an input-file stream, even if used as an argument of type `istream`, must still be declared to be of type `ifstream` (with an `'f'`).

Similarly, if you want to define a function that takes an output stream as an argument and you want that argument to be `cout` in some cases and an output-file stream in other cases, then use a formal parameter of type `ostream`. However, an output-file stream, even if used as an argument of type `ostream`, must still be declared to be of type `ofstream` (with an `'f'`). You cannot open or close a stream parameter of type `istream` or `ostream`. Open these objects before passing them to your function and close them after the function call.

The stream classes `istream` and `ostream` are defined in the `iostream` library and placed in the `std` namespace. One way to make them available to your code is the following:

```
#include <iostream>
using std::istream;
using std::ostream;
```

Self-Test Exercises

13. What is the type of the stream `cin`? What is the type of the stream `cout`?

14. Define a function called `copyChar` that takes one argument that is an input stream. When called, `copyChar` will read one character of input from the input stream given as its argument and will write that character to the screen. You should be able to call your function using either `cin` or an input-file stream as the argument to your function `copyChar`. (If the argument is an

(continued)

Self-Test Exercises (continued)

input-file stream, then the stream is connected to a file before the function is called, so `copyChar` will not open or close any files.) For example, the first of the following two calls to `copyChar` will copy a character from the file `stuff.txt` to the screen, and the second will copy a character from the keyboard to the screen:

```
ifstream fin;
fin.open("stuff.txt");
copyChar(fin);
copyChar(cin);
```

15. Define a function called `copyLine` that takes one argument that is an input stream. When called, `copyLine` reads one line of input from the input stream given as its argument and writes that line to the screen. You should be able to call your function using either `cin` or an input-file stream as the argument to your function `copyLine`. (If the argument is an input-file stream, then the stream is connected to a file before the function is called, so `copyLine` will not open or close any files.) For example, the first of the following two calls to `copyLine` will copy a line from the file `stuff.txt` to the screen, and the second will copy a line from the keyboard to the screen:

```
ifstream fin;
fin.open("stuff.txt");
copyLine(fin);
copyLine(cin);
```

16. Define a function called `sendLine` that takes one argument that is an output stream. When called, `sendLine` reads one line of input from the keyboard and outputs the line to the output stream given as its argument. You should be able to call your function using either `cout` or an output-file stream as the argument to your function `sendLine`. (If the argument is an output-file stream, then the stream is connected to a file before the function is called, so `sendLine` will not open or close any files.) For example, the first of the following two calls to `sendLine` will copy a line from the keyboard to the file `morestuf.txt`, and the second will copy a line from the keyboard to the screen:

```
ofstream fout;
fout.open("morestuf.txt");
cout << "Enter 2 lines of input:\n";
sendLine(fout);
sendLine(cout);
```

17. Is the following statement true or false? If it is false, correct it. In either event, explain it carefully.

A function written using a parameter of class `ifstream` or `ofstream` can be called with `istream` or `ostream` arguments, respectively.

Parsing Strings with the `stringstream` Class

We can look to the `stringstream` class for another example of inheritance. This class is derived from the `iostream` class which in turn is derived from the `istream` class. The `stringstream` class allows you to manipulate a string using the `>>` operator which is inherited from `istream`. This means that you can manipulate the string using the same format that you already learned to process files, keyboard input, and console output. The `stringstream` class is useful when you need to create a string from variables of other data types or when you need to read variables of other data types from a string. To use the class we first must include it:

```
#include <sstream>
using std::stringstream;
```

Next create an object of type stringstream:

```
stringstream ss;
```

If you want to clear and initialize the stringstream to an empty string then use the following two instructions. The `clear` function is necessary to clear out any error status that may be stored with the stringstream. The `str` function is used to set the stringstream to an initial string. In the following code we set the `stringstream` object to a blank string although you can initialize it to another string if you like.

```
ss.clear();
ss.str("");
```

To create a stringstream ss from other variables use the stream insertion operator as if you were outputting variables to cout. Instead of displaying the variables to the console they will be appended to the stringstream object. For example, given an int variable num set to 10 and a char variable c set to 'x' the following code inserts "x 10" into ss.

```
ss << c << " " << num;
```

We can use the `str()` method to return the value of the stringstream as a string.

```
string s;
s = ss.str(); // Sets s to the string "x 10"
```

To extract variables from a string, add the string to a stringstream object and then use the stream extraction operator as if you were reading variables from cin. Instead of reading the values from the keyboard they will be read from the string. For example, given the stringstream variable ss set to "x 10" we can read the variables back out with the following code:

```
// If ss = "x 10" then c is set to 'x' and num is set to 10
ss >> c >> num;
```

In its simplest form you can use a stringstream to convert a single numeric value to a string and vice versa.

An example using the stringstream class is given in Display 12.9. In this example we start with a string containing a person's name and the person's scores. For example, if Luigi has three scores that are 70, 100, and 90 then the string is "Luigi 70 100 90". The program uses the stringstream stream extraction operator to read the name and each score as an integer. The scores are added together, the average calculated, and then the name and average are put into a string using the stringstream stream insertion operator. In our example, the resulting string is "Name: Luigi Average: 86".

VideoNote

Walkthrough of the string-stream demo

Display 12.9   Demonstration of the stringstream Class (part 1 of 2)

```
1    //Demonstration of the stringstream class. This program takes
2    //a string with a name followed by scores. It uses a
3    //stringstream to extract the name as a string, the scores
4    //as integers, then calculates the average score. The name
5    //and average are placed into a new string.
6    #include <iostream>
7    #include <string>
8    #include <sstream>

9    using namespace std;

10   int main( )
11   {
12       stringstream ss;
13       string scores = "Luigi 70 100 90";

14       // Clear the stringstream
15       ss.str("");
16       ss.clear();

17       //Put the scores into the stringstream
18       ss << scores;

19
20       // Extract the name and average the scores
21       string name = "";
22       int total = 0, count = 0, average = 0;
23       int score;
24       ss >> name; //Read the name
25       while (ss >> score) // Read until the end of the string
26       {
27           count++;
28           total += score;
29       }
30       if (count > 0)
31       {
32           average = total / count;
33       }
```

Display 12.9   Demonstration of the stringstream Class (part 2 of 2)

```
34        // Clear the stringstream
35        ss.clear();
36        ss.str("");
37        // Put the name and average into the stringstream
38        ss << "Name: " << name << " Average: " << average;

39        // Output as a string
40        cout << ss.str() << endl;

41        return 0;
42    }
```

Sample Dialogue

```
Name: Luigi Average: 86
```

Self-Test Exercises

18. Given the statement int num = 10; use the stringstream class to convert num into a string variable named s.

19. Given the statement string s = 10; use the stringstream class to convert s into a int variable named num.

20. The following code is supposed to compute the total from a list of numbers stored in a string. This is accomplished by putting the string into a stringstream and then using the getline function to extract values separated by a comma. Another stringstream object is then used to convert the field from a string to a double. However, the code does not quite calculate the correct total. What is wrong?

```
stringstream ssList, ssNum;
string numbers = "1.1, 1.2, 1.3";

double total = 0;
double num;

ssList.clear();
ssList.str(numbers);

string field;
while (getline(ssList, field, ','))
{
    ssNum.str(field);
    ssNum >> num;
    total += num;
}
cout << total << endl;
```

12.4   Random Access to Files

Any time, any where.

Common response to a challenge for a confrontation

The streams for sequential access to files, which we discussed in the previous sections of this chapter, are the ones most often used for file access in C++. However, some applications that require very rapid access to records in very large databases require some sort of random access to particular parts of a file. Such applications might best be done with specialized database software. But perhaps you are given the job of writing such a package in C++, or perhaps you are just curious about how such things are done in C++. C++ does provide for random access to files so that your program can both read from and write to random locations in a file. This section gives a brief glimpse of this random access to files. This is not a complete tutorial on random access to files, but will let you know the name of the main stream class used and the important issues you will encounter.

If you want to be able to both read and write to a file in C++, you use the stream class `fstream` that is defined in the `<fstream>` library. The definition of `fstream` is placed in the `std` namespace.

Details about opening a file and connecting it to a stream in the class `fstream` are basically the same as discussed for the classes `ifstream` and `ofstream`, except that `fstream` has a second argument to `open`. This second argument specifies whether the stream is used for input, output, or both input and output. For example, a program that does both input and output to a file named `"stuff"` might start as follows:

```
#include <fstream>
using namespace std;

int main( )
{
    fstream rwStream;
    rwStream.open("stuff", ios::in | ios::out);
```

If you prefer, you may use the following in place of the last two of the previous lines:

```
fstream rwStream("stuff", ios::in | ios::out);
```

After this, your program can read from the file `"stuff"` using the stream `fstream` and can also write to the file `"stuff"` using the same stream. There is no need to close and reopen the file when you change from reading to writing or from writing to reading. Moreover, you have random access for reading and writing to any location in the file. However, there are other complications.

At least two complications arise when reading and writing with random access via an `fstream`: (1) You normally work in bytes using the type `char` or arrays of `char` and need to handle type conversions on your own, and (2) you typically need to position a pointer (indicating where the read or write begins) before each read or write.

Recursion 13

13 Recursion

*After a lecture on cosmology and the structure of the solar system,
William James was accosted by a little old lady.*

*"Your theory that the sun is the center of the solar system, and the
earth is a ball which rotates around it has a very convincing ring to it,
Mr. James, but it's wrong," I've got a better theory," said the little old lady.*

"And what is that, madam?" inquired James politely.

"That we live on a crust of earth which is on the back of a giant turtle."

*Not wishing to demolish this absurd little theory by bringing to bear the
masses of scientific evidence he had at his command, James decided
to gently dissuade his opponent by making her see some of the
inadequacies of her position.*

*"If your theory is correct, madam," he asked, "what does this turtle
stand on?"*

*"You're a very clever man, Mr. James, and that's a very good question"
replied the little old lady, "but I have an answer to it. And it is this: the
first turtle stands on the back of a second, far larger, turtle, who stands
directly under him."*

"But what does this second turtle stand on?" persisted James patiently.

*To this the little old lady crowed triumphantly. "It's no use, Mr. James—
it's turtles all the way down."*

J. R. ROSS, *Constraints on Variables in Syntax*

Introduction

A function definition that includes a call to itself is said to be *recursive*. Like most
modern programming languages, C++ allows functions to be recursive. If used with a
little care, recursion can be a useful programming technique. This chapter introduces
the basic techniques needed for defining successful recursive functions. There is
nothing in this chapter that is truly unique to C++. If you are already familiar with
recursion, you can safely skip this chapter.

This chapter uses material from Chapters 1 to 5 only. Sections 13.1 and 13.2 do not
use any material from Chapter 5, so you can cover recursion any time after Chapter 4.
If you have not read Chapter 11, you may find it helpful to review the section of
Chapter 1 on namespaces.

13.1 Recursive void Functions

I remembered too that night which is at the middle of the Thousand and One Nights when Scheherazade (through a magical oversight of the copyist) begins to relate word for word the story of the Thousand and One Nights, establishing the risk of coming once again to the night when she must repeat it, and thus to infinity.

JORGE LUIS BORGES, *The Garden of Forking Paths*

When you are writing a function to solve a task, one basic design technique is to break the task into subtasks. Sometimes it turns out that at least one of the subtasks is a smaller example of the same task. For example, if the task is to search a list for a particular value, you might divide this into the subtask of searching the first half of the list and the subtask of searching the second half of the list. The subtasks of searching the halves of the list are "smaller" versions of the original task. Whenever one subtask is a smaller version of the original task to be accomplished, you can solve the original task using a recursive function. We begin with a simple example to illustrate this technique.

Recursion

In C++ a function definition may contain a call to the function being defined. In such cases the function is said to be **recursive**.

EXAMPLE: Vertical Numbers

Display 13.1 contains a demonstration program for a recursive function named writeVertical that takes one (nonnegative) int argument and writes that int to the screen, with the digits going down the screen one per line. For example, the invocation

```
writeVertical(1234);
```

would produce the output

```
1
2
3
4
```

The task to be performed by writeVertical may be broken down into the following two cases:

■ *Simple case:* If n < 10, then write the number n to the screen.
  After all, if the number is only one digit long, the task is trivial.

(continued)

Display 13.1   A Recursive void Function

```
1    //Program to demonstrate the recursive function writeVertical.
2    #include <iostream>
3    using std::cout;
4    using std::endl;

5    void writeVertical(int n);
6    //Precondition: n >= 0.
7    //Postcondition: The number n is written to the screen vertically,
8    //with each digit on a separate line.

9    int main( )
10   {
11       cout << "writeVertical(3):" << endl;
12       writeVertical(3);

13       cout << "writeVertical(12):" << endl;
14       writeVertical(12);

15       cout << "writeVertical(123):" << endl;
16       writeVertical(123);

17       return 0;
18   }

19   //uses iostream:
20   void writeVertical(int n)
21   {
22       if (n < 10)
23       {
24           cout << n << endl;
25       }
26       else //n is two or more digits long:
27       {
28           writeVertical(n / 10);
29           cout << (n % 10) << endl;
30       }
31   }
```

Sample Dialogue

```
writeVertical(3):
3
writeVertical(12):
1
2
writeVertical(123):
1
2
3
```

EXAMPLE: (continued)

■ *Recursive case:* If `n >= 10`, then do two subtasks:

1. Output all the digits except the last digit.
2. Output the last digit.

For example, if the argument were `1234`, the first subtask would output

1
2
3

and the second subtask would output 4. This decomposition into subtasks can be used to derive the function definition.

Subtask 1 is a smaller version of the original task, so we can implement this subtask with a recursive call. Subtask 2 is just the simple case we listed previously. Thus, an outline of our algorithm for the function `writeVertical` with parameter `n` is given by the following pseudocode:

```
if (n < 10)
{
    cout << n << endl;
}
else //n is two or more digits long:
{
    writeVertical(the number n with the last digit removed);
    cout << the last digit of n << endl;
}
```

Recursive subtask

If you observe the following identities, it is easy to convert this pseudocode to a complete C++ function definition:

`n / 10` is the number `n` with the last digit removed.
`n % 10` is the last digit of `n`.

For example, `1234 / 10` evaluates to `123`, and `1234 % 10` evaluates to 4. The complete code for the function is as follows:

```
void writeVertical(int n)
{
    if (n < 10)
    {
        cout << n << endl;
    }
    else //n is two or more digits long:
    {
        writeVertical(n / 10);
        cout << (n % 10) << endl;
    }
}
```

Tracing a Recursive Call

Let's see exactly what happens when the following function call is made (as in Display 13.1):

```
writeVertical(123);
```

When this function call is executed, the computer proceeds just as it would with any function call. The argument 123 is substituted for the parameter n, and the body of the function is executed. After the substitution of 123 for n, the code to be executed is equivalent to the following:

```
if (123 < 10)
{
    cout << 123 << endl;
}
else //n is two or more digits long:
{
    writeVertical(123 / 10);  ←——— Computation will
    cout << (123 % 10) << endl;       stop here until the recursive
}                                     call returns.
```

Since 123 is not less than 10, the else part is executed. However, the else part begins with the function call

```
writeVertical(n / 10);
```

which (since n is equal to 123) is the call

```
writeVertical(123 / 10);
```

which is equivalent to

```
writeVertical(12);
```

The recursive call

```
writeVertical(12);
```

is handled just like any other function call. The argument 12 is substituted for the parameter n, and the body of the function is executed. After substituting 12 for n, there are two computations, one suspended and one active, as follows:

When execution reaches this recursive call, the current function computation is placed in suspended animation and the recursive call is executed. When this recursive call is finished, the execution of the suspended computation will return to this point and the suspended computation will continue from there.

```
if (123 < 10)
{
    cout <<
}
else //n i
{
    writeVe
    cout <<

        if (12 < 10)
        {
            cout << 12 << endl;
        }
        else //n is two or more digits long:
        {
            writeVertical(12 / 10);
            cout << (12 % 10) << endl;
        }
}
```

Computation will stop here until the recursive call returns.

Since 12 is not less than 10, the else part is executed. However, as you already saw, the else part begins with a recursive call. The argument for the recursive call is n / 10, which in this case is equivalent to 12 / 10. So this second computation of the function writeVertical is suspended and the following recursive call is executed:

writeVertical(12 / 10);

which is equivalent to

writeVertical(1);

At this point there are two suspended computations waiting to resume, and the computer begins to execute this new recursive call, which is handled just like all the previous recursive calls. The argument 1 is substituted for the parameter n, and the body of the function is executed. At this point, the computation looks like the following:

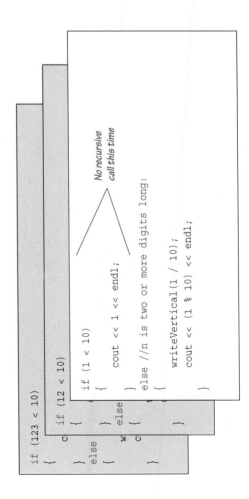

```
if (123 < 10)
{
    c
}
else
{
    w
    c

        if (12 < 10)
        {
            c
        }
        else
        {
            w
            c

                if (1 < 10)
                {
                    cout << 1 << endl;
                }
                else //n is two or more digits long:
                {
                    writeVertical(1 / 10);
                    cout << (1 % 10) << endl;
                }
        }
}
```

No recursive call this time

When the body of the function is executed this time, something different happens. Since 1 is less than 10, the Boolean expression in the if-else statement is true, so the statement before the else is executed. That statement is simply a cout statement that writes the argument 1 to the screen, and so the call writeVertical(1) writes 1 to the screen and ends without any recursive call.

When the call writeVertical(1) ends, the suspended computation that is waiting for it to end resumes where that suspended computation left off, as shown by the following:

```
if (123 < 10)
{
    c
    if (12 < 10)
    {
        cout << 12 << endl;
    }
    else
    {
    w
    c
    else //n is two or more digits long:
    {
        writeVertical(12 / 10);  ———— Computation resumes here.
        cout << (12 % 10) << endl;
    }
}
```

When this suspended computation resumes, it executes a cout statement that outputs the value 12 % 10, which is 2. That ends that computation, but there is yet another suspended computation waiting to resume.

When this last suspended computation resumes, the situation is as follows:

```
if (123 < 10)
{
    cout << 123 << endl;
}
else //n is two or more digits long:
{
    writeVertical(123 / 10);  ———— Computation resumes here.
    cout << (123 % 10) << endl;
}
```

This last suspended computation outputs the value 123%10, which is 3. The execution of the original function call then ends. And, sure enough, the digits 1, 2, and 3 have been written to the screen one per line, in that order.

A Closer Look at Recursion

The definition of the function writeVertical uses recursion. Yet we did nothing new or different in evaluating the function call writeVertical(123). We treated it just like any of the function calls we saw in previous chapters. We simply substituted the argument 123 for the parameter n and then executed the code in the body of the function definition. When we reached the recursive call

```
writeVertical(123 / 10);
```

we simply repeated this process one more time.

how recursion works

The computer keeps track of recursive calls in the following way. When a function is called, the computer plugs in the arguments for the parameter(s) and begins to execute the code. If it should encounter a recursive call, it temporarily stops its computation because it must know the result of the recursive call before it can proceed. It saves all the information it needs to continue the computation later on, and proceeds to evaluate the recursive call. When the recursive call is completed, the computer returns to finish the outer computation.

how recursion ends

The C++ language places no restrictions on how recursive calls are used in function definitions. However, in order for a recursive function definition to be useful, it must be designed so that any call of the function must ultimately terminate with some piece of code that does not depend on recursion. The function may call itself, and that recursive call may call the function again. The process may be repeated any number of times. However, the process will not terminate unless eventually one of the recursive calls does not depend on recursion in order to return a value. The general outline of a successful recursive function definition is as follows:

- One or more cases in which the function accomplishes its task by using one or more recursive calls to accomplish one or more smaller versions of the task.

- One or more cases in which the function accomplishes its task without the use of any recursive calls. These cases without any recursive calls are called **base cases** or **stopping cases.**

base case or stopping case

Often an if-else statement determines which of the cases will be executed. A typical scenario is for the original function call to execute a case that includes a recursive call. That recursive call may in turn execute a case that requires another recursive call. For some number of times each recursive call produces another recursive call, but eventually one of the stopping cases should apply. Every call of the function must eventually lead to a stopping case or else the function call will never end because of an infinite chain of recursive calls. (In practice, a call that includes an infinite chain of recursive calls will usually terminate abnormally rather than running forever.)

The most common way to ensure that a stopping case is eventually reached is to write the function so that some (positive) numeric quantity is decreased on each recursive call and to provide a stopping case for some "small" value. This is how we designed the function writeVertical in Display 13.1. When the function writeVertical is called, that call produces a recursive call with a smaller argument. This continues with each recursive call producing another recursive call until the argument is less than 10. When the argument is less than 10, the function call ends without producing any more recursive calls, and the process works its way back to the original call and then ends.

General Form of a Recursive Function Definition

The general outline of a successful recursive function definition is as follows:

- One or more cases that include one or more recursive calls to the function that did not involve recursion (that is, a stopping case was reached). If, on the other hand, every recursive call produces another recursive call, then a call to the function will, in theory, run forever. This is called **infinite recursion**. In practice, such a function will typically run until the computer runs out of resources and the program terminates abnormally.

- One or more cases that include no recursive calls. These cases without any recursive calls are called *base cases* or *stopping cases*.

PITFALL: Infinite Recursion

In the example of the function writeVertical discussed in the previous subsections, the series of recursive calls eventually reached a call of the function that did not involve recursion (that is, a stopping case was reached). If, on the other hand, every recursive call produces another recursive call, then a call to the function will, in theory, run forever. This is called **infinite recursion**. In practice, such a function will typically run until the computer runs out of resources and the program terminates abnormally.

Examples of infinite recursion are not hard to come by. The following is a syntactically correct C++ function definition that might result from an attempt to define an alternative version of the function writeVertical:

```
void newWriteVertical(int n)
{
    newWriteVertical(n / 10);
    cout << (n % 10) << endl;
}
```

If you embed this definition in a program that calls this function, the compiler will translate the function definition to machine code and you can execute the machine code. Moreover, the definition even has a certain reasonableness to it. It says that to output the argument to newWriteVertical, first output all but the last digit and then output the last digit. However, when called, this function will produce an infinite sequence of recursive calls. If you call newWriteVertical(12), that execution will stop to execute the recursive call newWriteVertical(12), that which is equivalent to newWriteVertical(1). The execution of that recursive call will, in turn, stop to execute the recursive call

```
newWriteVertical(1 / 10);
```

which is equivalent to

```
newWriteVertical(0);
```

PITFALL (continued)

That, in turn, will stop to execute the recursive call `newWriteVertical(0 / 10);` which is also equivalent to

```
newWriteVertical(0);
```

and that will produce another recursive call to again execute the same recursive function call `newWriteVertical(0);`, and so on, forever. Since the definition of `newWriteVertical` has no stopping case, the process will proceed forever (or until the computer runs out of resources). ■

Self-Test Exercises

1. What is the output of the following program?

```cpp
#include <iostream>
using std::cout;
void cheers(int n);

int main()
{
    cheers(3);
    return 0;
}
void cheers(int n)
{
    if (n == 1)
    {
        cout << "Hurray\n";
    }
    else
    {
        cout << "Hip ";
        cheers(n - 1);
    }
}
```

2. Write a recursive void function that has one parameter that is a positive integer and that writes out that number of asterisks (*) to the screen, all on one line.

3. Write a recursive void function that has one parameter that is a positive integer. When called, the function writes its argument to the screen backward. That is, if the argument is 1234, it outputs the following to the screen:

4321

(continued)

Self-Test Exercises (continued)

4. Write a recursive `void` function that takes a single `int` argument `n` and writes the integers 1, 2, . . . , `n`.

5. Write a recursive `void` function that takes a single `int` argument `n` and writes the integers `n`, `n-1`, . . . , 3, 2, 1. (*Hint:* Notice that you can get from the code for Self-Test Exercise 4 to that for this exercise, or vice versa, by an exchange of as little as two lines.)

Stacks for Recursion

To keep track of recursion (and a number of other things), most computer systems make use of a structure called a *stack*. A **stack** is a very specialized kind of memory structure that is analogous to a stack of paper. In this analogy, there is an inexhaustible supply of extra blank sheets of paper. To place some information in the stack, it is written on one of these sheets of paper and placed on top of the stack of papers. To place more information in the stack, a clean sheet of paper is taken, the information is written on it, and this new sheet of paper is placed on top of the stack. In this straightforward way, more and more information may be placed on the stack.

Getting information out of the stack is also accomplished by a very simple procedure. The top sheet of paper can be read, and when it is no longer needed, it is thrown away. There is one complication: Only the top sheet of paper is accessible. In order to read, say, the third sheet from the top, the top two sheets must be thrown away. Since the last sheet that is put on the stack is the first sheet taken off the stack, a stack is often called a **last-in/first-out** memory structure.

Using a stack, the computer can easily keep track of recursion. Whenever a function is called, a new sheet of paper is taken. The function definition is copied onto this sheet of paper, and the arguments are plugged in for the function parameters. Then the computer starts to execute the body of the function definition. When it encounters a recursive call, it stops the computation it is doing on that sheet in order to compute the value returned by the recursive call. But before computing the recursive call, it saves enough information so that when it does finally determine the value returned by the recursive call, it can continue the stopped computation. This saved information is written on a sheet of paper and placed on the stack. A new sheet of paper is used for the recursive call. The computer writes a second copy of the function definition on this new sheet of paper, plugs in the arguments for the function parameters, and starts to execute the recursive call. When it gets to a recursive call within the recursively called copy, it repeats the process of saving information on the stack and using a new sheet of paper for the new recursive call. This process is illustrated in the earlier subsection entitled "Tracing a Recursive Call." Even though we did not call it a stack at the time, the figures of computations placed one on top of the other illustrate the actions of the stack.

This process continues until some recursive call to the function completes its computation without producing any more recursive calls. When that happens, the

VideoNote
Recursion
and the Stack

last-in/first-out

stack

activation frame

computer turns its attention to the top sheet of paper on the stack. This sheet contains the partially completed computation that is waiting for the recursive computation that just ended. Thus, it is possible to proceed with that suspended computation. When that suspended computation ends, the computer discards that sheet of paper and the suspended computation that is below it on the stack becomes the computation on top of the stack. The computer turns its attention to the suspended computation that is now on the top of the stack, and so forth. The process continues until the computation on the bottom sheet is completed. Depending on how many recursive calls are made and how the function definition is written, the stack may grow and shrink in any fashion. Notice that the sheets in the stack can only be accessed in a last-in/first-out fashion, but that is exactly what is needed to keep track of recursive calls. Each suspended version is waiting for the completion of the version directly above it on the stack.

Needless to say, computers do not have stacks of paper. This is just an analogy. The computer uses portions of memory rather than pieces of paper. The content of one of these portions of memory ("sheets of paper") is called an **activation frame**. These activation frames are handled in the last-in/first-out manner we just discussed. (These activation frames do not contain a complete copy of the function definition, but merely reference a single copy of the function definition. However, an activation frame contains enough information to allow the computer to act as if the activation frame contained a complete copy of the function definition.)

Stack

A *stack* is a last-in/first-out memory structure. The first item referenced or removed from a stack is always the last item entered into the stack. Stacks are used by computers to keep track of recursion (and for other purposes).

PITFALL: Stack Overflow

stack overflow

There is always some limit to the size of the stack. If there is a long chain in which a function makes a recursive call to itself, and that call results in another recursive call, and that call produces yet another recursive call, and so forth, then each recursive call in this chain will cause another activation frame to be placed on the stack. If this chain is too long, the stack will attempt to grow beyond its limit. This is an error condition known as a **stack overflow**. If you receive an error message that says "stack overflow," it is likely that some function call has produced an excessively long chain of recursive calls. One common cause of stack overflow is infinite recursion. If a function is recursing infinitely, then it will eventually try to make the stack exceed any stack size limit. ■

Recursion versus Iteration

Recursion is not absolutely necessary. In fact, some programming languages do not allow it. Any task that can be accomplished using recursion can also be done in some other way without using recursion. For example, Display 13.2 contains a nonrecursive version of the function given in Display 13.1. The nonrecursive version of a function typically uses a loop (or loops) of some sort in place of recursion. For this reason, the nonrecursive version is usually referred to as an **iterative version.** If the definition of the function `writeVertical` given in Display 13.1 is replaced by the version given in Display 13.2, the output will be the same. As is true in this case, a recursive version of a function can sometimes be much simpler and more elegant than an iterative version so a gain in efficiency is not always preferable.

iterative version

Display 13.2   Iterative Version of the Function in Display 13.1

```
1    //Uses iostream:
2    void writeVertical(int n)
3    {
4        int nsTens = 1;
5        int leftEndPiece = n;
6        while (leftEndPiece > 9)
7        {
8            leftEndPiece = leftEndPiece / 10;
9            nsTens = nsTens * 10;
10       }
11       //nsTens is a power of ten that has the same number
12       //of digits as n. For example, if n is 2345, then
13       //nsTens is 1000.
14       for (int powerOf10 = nsTens;
15            powerOf10 > 0; powerOf10 = powerOf10 / 10)
16       {
17           cout << (n / powerOf10) << endl;
18           n = n % powerOf10;
19       }
20   }
```

Most modern compilers will convert certain simple recursive functions to equivalent iterative ones automatically for you. A function that uses **tail recursion** has the property that no further computation occurs after the recursive call; the function immediately returns. In the next section, when we cover recursive functions that return a value, then a function is tail recursive if the value of a recursive call is returned without modification. In such cases, a tail recursive function can be easily converted to an equivalent iterative solution. Check your compiler's documentation and optimization flags to see if this operation is available.

tail recursion

efficiency

A recursively written function that is not tail recursive will usually run slower and use more storage than an equivalent iterative version. The computer must do a good deal of work manipulating the stack in order to keep track of the recursion. However, since the system does all this for you automatically, using recursion can sometimes make your job as a programmer easier by producing code that is easier to understand.

Self-Test Exercises

6. If your program produces an error message that says "stack overflow," what is a likely source of the error?

7. Write an iterative version of the function cheers defined in Self-Test Exercise 1.

8. Write an iterative version of the function defined in Self-Test Exercise 2.

9. Write an iterative version of the function defined in Self-Test Exercise 3.

10. Trace the recursive solution you made to Self-Test Exercise 4.

11. Trace the recursive solution you made to Self-Test Exercise 5.

13.2 Recursive Functions That Return a Value

To iterate is human, to recurse divine.

ANONYMOUS

General Form for a Recursive Function That Returns a Value

The recursive functions you have seen thus far are all void functions, but recursion is not limited to void functions. A recursive function can return a value of any type. The technique for designing recursive functions that return a value is basically the same as that for void functions. An outline for a successful recursive function definition that returns a value is as follows:

- One or more cases in which the value returned is computed in terms of calls to the same function (that is, using recursive calls). As was the case with void functions, the arguments for the recursive calls should intuitively be "smaller."

- One or more cases in which the value returned is computed without the use of any recursive calls. These cases without any recursive calls are called *base cases* or *stopping cases* (just as they were with void functions).

This technique is illustrated in the next programming example.

EXAMPLE: Another Powers Function

Chapter 3 introduced the predefined function `pow` that computes powers. For example, `pow(2.0, 3.0)` returns $2.0^{3.0}$, so the following sets the variable `result` equal to 8.0:

```
double result = pow(2.0, 3.0);
```

The function `pow` takes two arguments of type `double` and returns a value of type `double`. Display 13.3 contains a recursive definition for a function that is similar but that works with the type `int` rather than `double`. This new function is called `power`. For example, the following will set the value of `result2` equal to 8, since 2^3 is 8:

```
int result2 = power(2, 3);
```

Our main reason for defining the function `power` is to have a simple example of a recursive function, but there are situations in which the function `power` would be preferable to the function `pow`. The function `pow` returns a value of type `double`, which is only an approximate quantity. The function `power` returns a value of type `int`, which is an exact quantity. In some situations, you might need the additional accuracy provided by the function `power`.

The definition of the function `power` is based on the following formula:

$$x^n \text{ is equal to } x^{n-1} * x$$

Translating this formula into C++ says that the value returned by `power(x, n)` should be the same as the value of the expression

```
power(x, n - 1)*x
```

The definition of the function `power` given in Display 13.3 does return the following value for `power`:

```
(x, n), provided n > 0.
```

The case where `n` is equal to 0 is the stopping case. If `n` is 0, then `power(x, n)` simply returns 1 (since x^0 is 1).

Let's see what happens when the function `power` is called with some sample values. First consider the following simple expression:

```
power(2, 0)
```

When the function is called, the value of `x` is set equal to 2, the value of `n` is set equal to 0, and the code in the body of the function definition is executed. Since the value of `n` is a legal value, the `if-else` statement is executed. Since this value of `n` is not greater than 0, the `return` statement after the `else` is used, so the function call returns 1. Thus, the following would set the value of `result3` equal to 1:

```
int result3 = power(2, 0);
```

Display 13.3   The Recursive Function power

```
1   //Program to demonstrate the recursive function power.
2   #include <iostream>
3   #include <cstdlib>
4   using std::cout;
5   using std::endl;

6   int power(int x, int n);
7   //Precondition: n >= 0.
8   //Returns x to the power n.

9   int main( )
10  {
11      for (int n = 0; n < 4; n++)
12          cout << "3 to the power " << n
13               << " is " << power(3, n) << endl;

14      return 0;
15  }

16  //uses iostream and cstdlib:
17  int power(int x, int n)
18  {
19      if (n < 0)
20      {
21          cout << "Illegal argument to power.\n";
22          exit(1);
23      }
24      if (n > 0)
25          return ( power(x, n - 1) * x );
26      else // n == 0
27          return (1);
28  }
```

Sample Dialogue

```
3 to the power 0 is 1
3 to the power 1 is 3
3 to the power 2 is 9
3 to the power 3 is 27
```

EXAMPLE: (continued)

Now let's look at an example that involves a recursive call. Consider the expression

```
power(2, 1)
```

When the function is called, the value of x is set equal to 2, the value of n is set equal to 1, and the code in the body of the function definition is executed. Since this value of n is greater than 0, the following return statement is used to determine the value returned:

```
return ( power(x, n - 1) * x );
```

which in this case is equivalent to

```
return ( power(2, 0) * 2 );
```

At this point, the computation of power(2, 1) is suspended, a copy of this suspended computation is placed on the stack, and the computer then starts a new function call to compute the value of power(2, 0). As you have already seen, the value of power(2, 0) is 1. After determining the value of power(2, 0), the computer replaces the expression power(2, 0) with its value of 1 and resumes the suspended computation. The resumed computation determines the final value for power(2, 1) from the preceding return statement as follows:

```
power(2, 0) * 2 is 1 * 2, which is 2.
```

Thus, the final value returned for power(2, 1) is 2. So, the following would set the value of result4 equal to 2:

```
int result4 = power(2, 1);
```

Larger numbers for the second argument will produce longer chains of recursive calls. For example, consider the statement

```
cout << power(2, 3);
```

The value of power(2, 3) is calculated as follows:

```
power(2, 3) is power(2, 2)*2
power(2, 2) is power(2, 1)*2
power(2, 1) is power(2, 0)*2
power(2, 0) is 1 (stopping case)
```

When the computer reaches the stopping case power(2, 0), there are three suspended computations. After calculating the value returned for the stopping case, it resumes the most recently suspended computations to determine the value of power(2, 1). After that, the computer completes each of the other suspended computations, using each value computed as a value to plug into another suspended computation, until it reaches and completes the computation for the original call, power(2, 3). The details of the entire computation are illustrated in Display 13.4.

Display 13.4 Evaluating the Recursive Function Call power(2, 3)

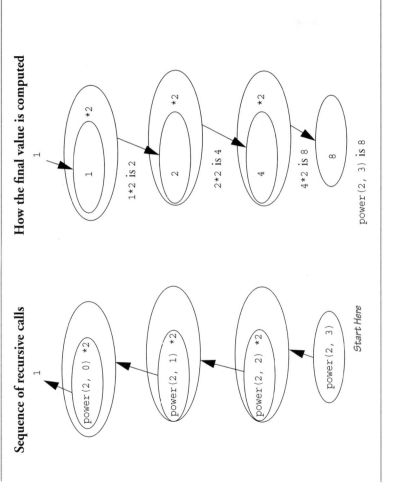

Sequence of recursive calls

How the final value is computed

power(2, 3) is 8

Start Here

Self-Test Exercises

12. What is the output of the following program?

```
#include <iostream>
using std::cout;
using std::endl;

int mystery(int n);
//Precondition n >= 1.

int main( )
{
    cout << mystery(3) << endl;
    return 0;
}
```

(continued)

Self-Test Exercises (continued)

```
int mystery(int n)
{
    if (n <= 1)
        return 1;
    else
        return ( mystery(n - 1) + n ) ;
}
```

13. What is the output of the following program? What well-known mathematical function is rose?

```
#include <iostream>
using std::cout;
using std::endl;

int rose(int n);
//Precondition: n >= 0.

int main( )
{
    cout << rose(4) << endl;
    return 0;
}

int rose(int n)
{
    if (n <= 0)
        return 1;
    else
        return ( rose(n - 1) * n ) ;
}
```

14. Redefine the function power so that it also works for negative exponents. In order to do this, you will also have to change the type of the value returned to double. The function declaration and header comment for the redefined version of power are as follows:

```
double power(int x, int n);
//Precondition: If n < 0, then x is not 0.
//Returns x to the power n.
```

Hint: x^{-n} is equal to $1/(x^n)$.

Mutual Recursion

mutual recursion

In our examples so far, the recursive function directly invoked the same function. However, it is possible to have a recursive function that indirectly invokes itself through another function. When two or more functions recursively call each other, it is called **mutual recursion.**

As a simple example, let's say that we are given a string consisting of 0s and 1s. We want to determine if there are an even number of 1s in the string. Our strategy is to examine the symbols in the string from left to right and end up in the function evenNumberOfOnes when the number of 1s encountered so far is even, and to end up in the function oddNumberOfOnes when the number of 1s encountered so far is odd. Initially we call the function evenNumberOfOnes. If the string is empty, then zero 1s is considered even, so the function returns true. On the other hand, if the string starts with a 1, then remove the 1 and call the function oddNumberOfOnes because the leading 1 just resulted in an odd number of 1s. Finally, if the string starts with a 0, then remove the 0 and call the function evenNumberOfOnes again because the leading 0 did not change the string from even to odd.

The function oddNumberOfOnes follows a similar strategy. If the string is empty, then the function returns false to indicate that the number of 1s is not even. If the string starts with a 1, then remove the 1 and call the function evenNumberOfOnes because the leading 1 just caused us to switch back to an even number of 1s. Finally, if the string starts with a 0, then remove the 0 and call the function oddNumberOfOnes again because the leading 0 did not change the string from odd to even.

For example, the input of "10011" is calculated as

```
evenNumberOfOnes("10011")
  oddNumberOfOnes("0011")
  oddNumberOfOnes("011")
  oddNumberOfOnes("11")
  evenNumberOfOnes("1")
  oddNumberOfOnes("")
  return false
```

Every time the leading character is a 1, we toggle between evenNumberOfOnes and oddNumberOfOnes. By ending up in the function oddNumberOfOnes after all the characters in the string have been examined, we can conclude that there is an odd number of 1s and false is returned back through the chain of recursive calls.

The mutually recursive functions are implemented in Display 13.5. The substr function is used to "remove" the first character of the string. By specifying a start index of 1 and no parameter for the length of the substring, the substr function returns everything in the string from index 1 to the end, skipping the character at index 0. This particular program would be easier to write iteratively, but the idea presented here can be extended to more sophisticated parsers that are easier to understand and implement using mutual recursion.

VideoNote
Walkthrough of Mutual Recursion

Display 13.5   Mutual Recursion to Determine if a String Has an Even Number of 1s

```
1   // uses iostream and string

2   // If the recursive calls end in this function with an empty string
3   // then we had an even number of 1s.
4   bool evenNumberOfOnes(string s)
5   {
6       if (s.length() == 0)
7           return true; // Is even
8       else if (s[0]=='1')
9           return oddNumberOfOnes(s.substr(1));
10      else
11          return evenNumberOfOnes(s.substr(1));
12  }

13  // if the recursive calls ends in this function with an empty string
14  // then we had an odd number of 1s.
15  bool oddNumberOfOnes(string s)
16  {
17      if (s.length() == 0)
18          return false; // Not even
19      else if (s[0]=='1')
20          return evenNumberOfOnes(s.substr(1));
21      else
22          return oddNumberOfOnes(s.substr(1));
23  }

24  int main ()
25  {
26      string s = "10011";
27
28      if (evenNumberOfOnes(s))
29          cout << "Even number of ones." << endl;
30      else
31          cout << "Odd number of ones." << endl;
32      return 0;
33  }
```

Sample Dialogue

```
Odd number of ones.
```

Self-Test Exercises

15. Are the functions in Display 13.5 tail recursive?

16. The function `even` should return `true` if the number is even, and it should return `false` if the number is odd, but it is incomplete. Write the function `odd` so that it works correctly.

```
bool even(int num)
{
    if (num == 0)
        return true;
    else
        return odd(num - 1);
}
```

13.3   Thinking Recursively

There are two kinds of people in the world, those who divide the world into two kinds of people and those who do not.

ANONYMOUS

Recursive Design Techniques

When defining and using recursive functions, you do not want to be continually aware of the stack and the suspended computations. The power of recursion comes from the fact that you can ignore that detail and let the computer do the bookkeeping for you. Consider the example of the function `power` in Display 13.3. The way to think of the definition of `power` is as follows:

```
power(x, n)
```

returns

```
power(x, n - 1)*x
```

Since x^n is equal to $x^{n-1}*x$, this is the correct value to return, provided that the computation will always reach and correctly compute a stopping case. So, after checking that the recursive part of the definition is correct, all you need to check is that the chain of recursive calls will always reach a stopping case and that the stopping case always returns the correct value.

When designing a recursive function, you need not trace out the entire sequence of recursive calls for the instances of that function in your program.

If the function returns a value, all you need do is check that the following three properties are satisfied:

1. *There is no infinite recursion.* (A recursive call may lead to another recursive call, which may lead to another, and so forth, but every such chain of recursive calls eventually reaches a stopping case.)

2. Each stopping case returns the correct value for that case.

3. For the cases that involve recursion: *If* all recursive calls return the correct value, *then* the final value returned by the function is the correct value.

For example, consider the function power in Display 13.3.

1. *There is no infinite recursion:* The second argument to power(x, n) is decreased by 1 in each recursive call, so any chain of recursive calls must eventually reach the case power(x, 0), which is the stopping case. Thus, there is no infinite recursion.

2. *Each stopping case returns the correct value for that case:* The only stopping case is power(x, 0). A call of the form power(x, 0) always returns 1, and the correct value for x^0 is 1. So the stopping case returns the correct value.

3. *For the cases that involve recursion, if all recursive calls return the correct value, then the final value returned by the function is the correct value:* The only case that involves recursion is when n > 1. When n > 1, power(x, n) returns

power(x, n - 1) * x

which is x^n, and that is the correct value for power(x, n).

To see that this is the correct value to return, note that *if* power(x, n - 1) returns the correct value, *then* power(x, n - 1) returns x^{n-1} and so power(x, n) returns $x^{n-1} * x$

which is x^n, and that is the correct value for power(x, n).

That is all you need to check to be sure that the definition of power is correct. (The preceding technique is known as *mathematical induction*, a concept that you may have heard about in a mathematics class. However, you do not need to be familiar with the term *mathematical induction* in order to use this technique.)

We gave you three criteria to use in checking the correctness of a recursive function that returns a value. Basically the same rules can be applied to a recursive void function. If you show that your recursive void function definition satisfies the following three criteria, then you will know that your void function performs correctly:

1. There is no infinite recursion.

2. Each stopping case performs the correct action for that case.

3. For each of the cases that involve recursion, *if* all recursive calls perform their actions correctly, *then* the entire case performs correctly.

Binary Search

This subsection develops a recursive function that searches an array to determine whether it contains a specified value. For example, the array may contain a list of numbers for credit cards that are no longer valid. A store clerk needs to search the list to see if a customer's card is valid or invalid.

The indexes of the array a are the integers 0 through finalIndex. To make the task of searching the array easier, we will assume that the array is sorted. Hence, we know the following:

```
a[0] ≤ a[1] ≤ a[2] ≤ ... ≤ a[finalIndex]
```

When searching an array, you are likely to want to know both whether the value is in the list and, if it is, where it is in the list. For example, if we are searching for a credit card number, then the array index may serve as a record number. Another array indexed by these same indexes may hold a phone number or other information to use for reporting the suspicious card. Hence, if the sought-after value is in the array, we will want our function to tell where that value is in the array.

Now let us proceed to produce an algorithm to solve this task. It will help to visualize the problem in very concrete terms. Suppose the list of numbers is so long that it takes a book to list them all. This is in fact how invalid credit card numbers are distributed to stores that do not have access to computers. If you are a clerk and are handed a credit card, you must check to see if it is on the list and hence invalid. How would you proceed? Open the book to the middle and see if the number is there. If it is not and it is smaller than the middle number, then work backward toward the beginning of the book. If the number is larger than the middle number, work your way toward the end of the book. This idea produces our first draft of an algorithm:

**algorithm—
first version**

```
found = false; //so far.
mid = approximate midpoint between 0 and finalIndex;
if (key == a[mid])
{
    found = true;
    location = mid;
}
else if (key < a[mid])
    search a[0] through a[mid - 1];
else if (key > a[mid])
    search a[mid + 1] through a[finalIndex];
```

Since the searchings of the shorter lists are smaller versions of the very task we are designing the algorithm to perform, this algorithm naturally lends itself to the use of recursion. The smaller lists can be searched with recursive calls to the algorithm itself.

Our pseudocode is a bit too imprecise to be easily translated into C++ code. The problem has to do with the recursive calls. There are two recursive calls shown:

```
search a[0] through a[mid - 1];
```

and

```
search a[mid + 1] through a[finalIndex];
```

To implement these recursive calls, we need two more parameters. A recursive call specifies that a subrange of the array is to be searched. In one case, it is the elements indexed by 0 through mid - 1. In the other case, it is the elements indexed by mid + 1 through finalIndex. The two extra parameters will specify the first and last indexes of the search, so we will call them first and last. Using these parameters for the lowest and highest indexes, instead of 0 and finalIndex, we can express the pseudocode more precisely, as follows:

algorithm— first refinement

```
To search a[first] through a[last] do the following:
found = false ;//so far.
mid = approximate midpoint between first and last;
if (key == a[mid])
{
    found = true ;
    location = mid;
}
else if (key < a[mid])
    search a[first] through a[mid - 1];
else if (key > a[mid])
    search a[mid + 1] through a[last] ;
```

To search the entire array, the algorithm would be executed with first set equal to 0 and last set equal to finalIndex. The recursive calls will use other values for first and last. For example, the first recursive call would set first equal to 0 and last equal to the calculated value mid - 1.

stopping case

As with any recursive algorithm, we must ensure that our algorithm ends rather than producing infinite recursion. If the sought-after number is found on the list, then there is no recursive call and the process terminates, but we need some way to detect when the number is not on the list. On each recursive call the value of first is increased or the value of last is decreased. If they ever pass each other and first actually becomes larger than last, we will know that there are no more indexes left to check and that the number key is not in the array. If we add this test to our pseudocode, we obtain a complete solution, as shown in Display 13.6.

algorithm— final version

Coding

Now we can routinely translate the pseudocode into C++ code. The result is shown in Display 13.7. The function search is an implementation of the recursive algorithm given in Display 13.6. A diagram of how the function performs on a sample array is given in Display 13.8.

Notice that the function search solves a more general problem than the original task. Our goal was to design a function to search an entire array, yet the search function will let us search any interval of the array by specifying the index bounds first and last. This is common when designing recursive functions. Frequently, it is necessary to solve a more general problem in order to be able to express the recursive algorithm. In this instance, we wanted only the answer in the case where first and last are set equal to 0 and finalIndex. However, the recursive calls will set them to values other than 0 and finalIndex.

Display 13.6   Pseudocode for Binary Search

```
int a[Some_Size_Value];
```

Algorithm to Search a[first] through a[last]

```
//Precondition:
//a[first] <= a[first + 1] <= a[first + 2] <=... <= a[last]
```

To locate the value key:

```
if (first > last) //A stopping case
    found = false;
else
{
    mid = approximate midpoint between first and last;
    if (key == a[mid]) //A stopping case
    {
        found = false;
        location = mid;
    }
    else if key < a[mid]  //A case with recursion
        search a[first] through a[mid - 1];
    else if key > a[mid]  //A case with recursion
        search a[mid + 1] through a[last];
}
```

Display 13.7   Recursive Function for Binary Search (part 1 of 2)

```
1  //Program to demonstrate the recursive function for binary search.
2  #include <iostream>
3  using std::cin;
4  using std::cout;
5  using std::endl;
6  const int ARRAY_SIZE = 10;

7  void search(const int a[], int first, int last,
8                  int key, bool& found, int& location);
9  //Precondition: a[first] through a[last] are sorted in increasing
   //order.
10 //Postcondition: if key is not one of the values a[first] through
   //a[last], then found == false; otherwise, a[location] == key
11 //and found == true.
12 int main()
13 {
14     int a[ARRAY_SIZE];
15     const int finalIndex = ARRAY_SIZE - 1;
```

(continued)

Display 13.7   Recursive Function for Binary Search (part 2 of 2)

This portion of the program contains some code to fill and sort the array a.
The exact details are irrelevant to this example.

```
16    int key, location;
17    bool found;
18    cout << "Enter number to be located: ";
19    cin >> key;
20    search(a, 0, finalIndex, key, found, location);
21
22    if (found)
23        cout << key << " is in index location "
24            << location << endl;
25    else
26        cout << key << " is not in the array." << endl;
27
28    return 0;
29    }

30    void search(const int a[], int first, int last,
31                int key, bool& found, int& location)
32    {
33        int mid;
34        if (first > last)
35        {
36            found = false;
37        }
38        else
39        {
40            mid = (first + last)/2;
41
42            if (key == a[mid])
43            {
44                found = true;
45                location = mid;
46            }
47            else if (key < a[mid])
48            {
49                search(a, first, mid - 1, key, found, location);
50            }
51            else if (key > a[mid])
52            {
53                search(a, mid + 1, last, key, found, location);
54            }
55        }
56    }
```

Display 13.8   Execution of the Function search

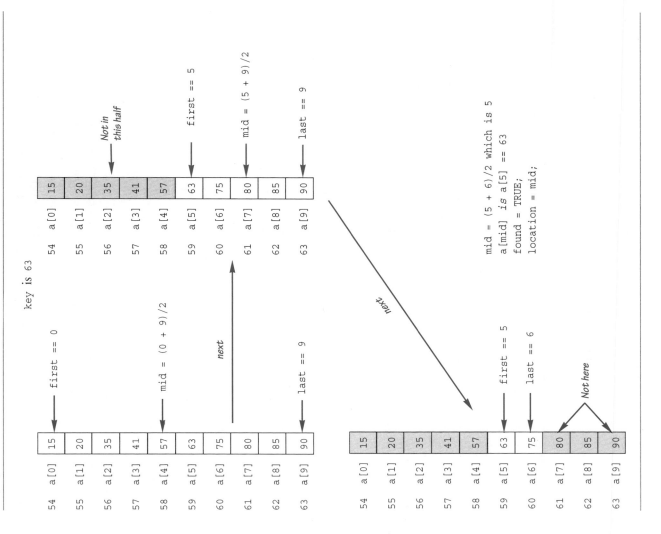

key is 63

first == 0

mid = (0 + 9)/2

last == 9

next

Not in
this half

first == 5

mid = (5 + 9)/2

last == 9

next

mid = (5 + 6)/2 which is 5
a[mid] is a[5] == 63
found = TRUE;
location = mid;

first == 5

last == 6

Not here

Checking the Recursion

The subsection entitled "Recursive Design Techniques" gave three criteria that you should check to ensure that a recursive void function definition is correct. Let's check these three things for the function search given in Display 13.7.

1. *There is no infinite recursion:* On each recursive call the value of first is increased or the value of last is decreased. If the chain of recursive calls does not end in some other way, then eventually the function will be called with first larger than last, which is a stopping case.

2. *Each stopping case performs the correct action for that case:* There are two stopping cases, when first > last and when key == a[mid]. Let's consider each case.

   If first > last, there are no array elements between a[first] and a[last] so key is not in this segment of the array. (Nothing is in this segment of the array!) So, if first > last, the function search correctly sets found equal to false.

   If key == a[mid], the algorithm correctly sets found equal to true and location equal to mid. Thus, both stopping cases are correct.

3. *For each of the cases that involve recursion, if all recursive calls perform their actions correctly, then the entire case performs correctly:* There are two cases in which there are recursive calls, when key < a[mid] and when key > a[mid]. We need to check each of these two cases.

   First, suppose key < a[mid]. In this case, since the array is sorted, we know that if key is anywhere in the array, then key is one of the elements a[first] through a[mid- 1]. Thus, the function needs only to search these elements, which is exactly what the recursive call

   search(a, first, mid - 1, key, found, location);

   does. So if the recursive call is correct, then the entire action is correct.

   Next, suppose key > a[mid]. In this case, since the array is sorted, we know that if key is anywhere in the array, then key is one of the elements a[mid + 1] through a[last]. Thus, the function needs only to search these elements, which is exactly what the recursive call

   search(a, mid + 1, last, key, found, location);

   does. So if the recursive call is correct, then the entire action is correct. Thus, in both cases the function performs the correct action (assuming that the recursive calls perform the correct action).

   The function search passes all three of our tests, so it is a good recursive function definition.

Efficiency

The binary search algorithm is extremely fast compared with an algorithm that simply tries all array elements in order. In the binary search, you eliminate about half the array from consideration right at the start. You then eliminate a quarter, then an eighth of the array, and so forth. These savings add up to a dramatically fast algorithm. For an array of 100 elements, the binary search will never need to compare more than 7 array elements to the key. A simple serial search could compare as many as 100 array elements to the key, and on the average will compare about 50 array elements to the key. Moreover, the larger the array is, the more dramatic the savings will be. On an array with 1000 elements, the binary search will need only to compare about 10 array elements to the key value, as compared to an average of 500 for the simple serial search algorithm.

An iterative version of the function search is given in Display 13.9. On some systems the iterative version will run more efficiently than the recursive version. The algorithm for the iterative version was derived by mirroring the recursive version. In the iterative version, the local variables first and last mirror the roles of the parameters in the recursive version, which are also named first and last. As this example illustrates, it often makes sense to derive a recursive algorithm even if you expect to later convert it to an iterative algorithm.

Display 13.9 Iterative Version of Binary Search (part 1 of 2)

Function Declaration

```
void search(const int a[ ], int lowEnd, int highEnd,
            int key, bool& found, int& location);
//Precondition: a[lowEnd] through a[highEnd] are sorted in
//increasing order.
//Postcondition: If key is not one of the values a[lowEnd]
//through a[highEnd], then found == false; otherwise,
//a[location] == key and found == true.
```

Function Definition

```
void search(const int a[ ], int lowEnd, int highEnd,
            int key, bool& found, int& location)
{
    int first = lowEnd;
    int last = highEnd;
    int mid;

    found = false;//so far
    while ((first <= last) && !(found) )
    {
        mid = (first + last)/2;
        if (key == a[mid])
        {
            found = true;
            location = mid;
```

(continued)

Display 13.9 Iterative Version of Binary Search (part 2 of 2)

```
        }
        else if (key < a[mid])
        {
            last = mid - 1;
        }
        else if (key > a[mid])
        {
            first = mid + 1;
        }
    }
}
```

Self-Test Exercises

17. Write a recursive function definition for the following function:

```
int squares(int n);
//Precondition: n >= 1
//Returns the sum of the squares of the numbers 1 through n.
```

For example, squares(3) returns 14 because $1^2 + 2^2 + 3^2$ is 14.

Chapter Summary

- If a problem can be reduced to smaller instances of the same problem, then a recursive solution is likely to be easy to find and implement.

- A recursive algorithm for a function definition normally contains two kinds of cases: one or more cases that include at least one recursive call and one or more *stopping cases* in which the problem is solved without any recursive calls.

- *Mutual recursion* occurs when two or more functions recursively call each other.

- When writing a recursive function definition, always check to see that the function will not produce *infinite recursion*.

- When you define a recursive function, use the three criteria given in the subsection "Recursive Design Techniques" to check that the function is correct.

- When designing a recursive function to solve a task, it is often necessary to solve a more general problem than the given task. This may be required to allow for the proper recursive calls, since the smaller problems may not be exactly the same problem as the given task. For example, in the binary search problem, the task was to search an entire array, but the recursive solution is an algorithm to search any portion of the array (either all of it or a part of it).

Answers to Self-Test Exercises

1. `Hip Hip Hurray`

2. ```
   using std::cout;
   void stars(int n)
   {
       cout << '*';
       if (n > 1)
           stars(n - 1);
   }
   ```

   The following is also correct, but is more complicated:

   ```
   void stars(int n)
   {
       if (n <= 1)
       {
           cout << '*';
       }
       else
       {
           stars(n - 1);
           cout << '*';
       }
   }
   ```

3. ```
   using std::cout;
   void backward(int n)
   {
       if (n < 10)
       {
           cout << n;
       }
       else
       {
           cout << (n%10); //write last digit
           backward(n/10); //write the other digits backward
       }
   }
   ```

4–5. The answer to Self-Test Exercise 4 is `writeUp;`. The answer to Self-Test Exercise 5 is `writeDown;`.

   ```
   #include<iostream>
   using std::cout;
   using std::endl;
   ```

```
void writeDown(int n)
{
    if (n >= 1)
    {
        cout << n << " "; //write while the
                          //recursion winds

        writeDown(n - 1);
    }
}

//5
void writeUp(int n)
{
    if (n >= 1)
    {
        writeUp(n - 1);
        cout << n << " "; //write while the
                          //recursion unwinds
    }
}

//testing code for both Self-Test Exercises 4 and 5
int main( )
{
    cout << "calling writeUp(" << 10 << ")\n";
    writeUp(10);
    cout << endl;
    cout << "calling writeDown(" << 10 << ")\n";
    writeDown(10);
    cout << endl;
    return 0;
}

/* Test results
calling writeUp(10)
1 2 3 4 5 6 7 8 9 10
calling writeDown(10)
10 9 8 7 6 5 4 3 2 1*/
```

6. An error message that says "stack overflow" is telling you that the computer has attempted to place more activation frames on the stack than are allowed on your system. A likely cause of this error message is infinite recursion.

7. `using std::cout;`

```
void cheers(int n)
{
    while (n > 1)
```

```
    {
        cout << "Hip ";
        n--;
    }
    cout << "Hurray\n";
}
```

8. ```
   using std::cout;
   void stars(int n)
   {
       for (int count = 1; count <= n; count++)
           cout << '*';
   }
   ```

9. ```
   using std::cout;
   void backward(int n)
   {
       while (n >= 10)
       {
           cout << (n%10);//write last digit
           n = n/10;//discard the last digit
       }
       cout << n;
   }
   ```

10. Trace for Self-Test Exercise 4. If n = 3, the code to be executed is
    ```
    if (3 >= 1)
    {
        writeDown(3 - 1);
    }
    ```

    On the next recursion, n = 2 and the code to be executed is
    ```
    if (2 >= 1)
    {
        writeDown(2 - 1)
    }
    ```

    On the next recursion, n = 1 and the code to be executed is
    ```
    if (1 >= 1)
    {
        writeDown(1 - 1)
    }
    ```

    On the final recursion, n = 0 and the true clause is not executed:
    ```
    if (0 >= 1) // condition false
    {
            // this clause is skipped
    }
    ```

The recursion unwinds, the `cout << n << " ";` line of code is executed for each recursive call that was on the stack, with n = 3, then n = 2, and finally n = 1. The output is 3 2 1.

11. Trace for Self-Test Exercise 5. If n = 3, the code to be executed is

```
if (3 >= 1)
{
    cout << 3 << " ";
    writeUp(3 - 1);
}
```

On the next recursion, n = 2 and the code to be executed is

```
if (2 >= 1)
{
    cout << 2 << " ";
    writeUp(2 - 1);
}
```

On the next recursion, n = 1 and the code to be executed is

```
if (1 >= 1)
{
    cout << 1 << " ";
    writeUp(1 - 1);
}
```

On the final recursion, n = 0 and the code to be executed is

```
if (0 >= 1) // condition false, body skipped
{
    // skipped
}
```

The recursions unwind; the output (obtained by working through the stack) is 1 2 3.

12. 6

13. The output is 24. The function is the factorial function, usually written *n!* and defined as follows:

n! is equal to n*(n - 1)*(n - 2)*...*1

14. //Uses iostream and cstdlib:
```
double power(int x, int n)
{
    if (n < 0 && x == 0)
    {
        cout << "Illegal argument to power.\n";
        exit(1);
    }
```

```
    if (n < 0)
        return (1/power(x, -n));
    else if (n > 0)
        return (power(x, n - 1)*x);
    else // n == 0
        return (1.0);
}
```

15. Yes, the functions simply return the recursive value with no further processing, which makes them tail recursive.

16.
```
bool odd(int num)
{
    if (num == 0)
        return false;
    else
        return even(num - 1);
}
```

17.
```
int squares(int n)
{
    if (n <= 1)
        return 1;
    else
        return (squares(n - 1) + n*n);
}
```

Programming Projects

Visit www.myprogramminglab.com to complete select exercises online and get instant feedback.

1. Write a recursive function definition for a function that has one parameter n of type int and that returns the nth Fibonacci number. The Fibonacci numbers are F_0 is 1, F_1 is 1, F_2 is 2, F_3 is 3, F_4 is 5, and in general

$$F_{i+2} = F_i + F_{i+1} \text{ for } i = 0, 1, 2, \ldots$$

2. The formula for computing the number of ways of choosing r different things from a set of *n* things is the following:

$$C(n, r) = n!/(r!*(n - r)!)$$

The factorial function *n!* is defined by

$$n! = n*(n-1)*(n-2)*\ldots*1$$

Discover a recursive version of the formula for $C(n, r)$ and write a recursive function that computes the value of the formula. Embed the function in a program and test it.

3. Write a recursive function that has an argument that is an array of characters and two arguments that are array indexes. The function should reverse the order of those entries in the array whose indexes are between the two bounds. For example, if the array is

a[1] == 'A' a[2] == 'B' a[3] == 'C' a[4] == 'D' a[5] == 'E'

and the bounds are 2 and 5, then after the function is run, the array elements should be

a[1] == 'A' a[2] == 'E' a[3] == 'D' a[4] == 'C' a[5] == 'B'

Embed the function in a program and test it. After you have fully debugged this function, define another function that takes a single argument that is an array that contains a string value; the function should reverse the spelling of the string value in the array argument. This function will include a call to the recursive definition you did for the first part of this project. Embed this second function in a program and test it.

4. Write an iterative version of the recursive function in the previous project. Embed it in a program and test it.

5. *Towers of Hanoi.* There is a story about Buddhist monks who are playing this puzzle with 64 stone disks. The story claims that when the monks finish moving the disks from one post to a second via the third post, time will end. Eschatology (concerns about the end of time) and theology will be left to those better qualified; our interest is limited to the recursive solution to the problem.

A stack of n disks of decreasing size is placed on one of three posts. The task is to move the disks one at a time from the first post to the second. To do this, any disk can be moved from any post to any other post, subject to the rule that you can never place a larger disk over a smaller disk. The (spare) third post is provided to make the solution possible. Your task is to write a recursive function that describes instructions for a solution to this problem. We do not have graphics available, so you should output a sequence of instructions that will solve the problem.

Hint. If you could move n−1 of the disks from the first post to the third post using the second post as a spare, the last disk could be moved from the first post to the second post. Then by using the same technique (whatever that may be), you can move the n−1 disks from the third post to the second post, using the first post as a spare. There! You have the puzzle solved. You have only to decide what the nonrecursive case is, what the recursive case is, and when to output instructions to move the disks.

6. (You need to have first completed Programming Project 13.1 to work on this project.) In this exercise, you will compare the efficiency of a recursive and an iterative function to compute the Fibonacci number.

   a. Examine the recursive function computation of Fibonacci numbers. Note that each Fibonacci number is recomputed many times. To avoid this recomputation, do Programming Project 13.1 iteratively, rather than recursively; that is, do the problem with a loop. You should compute each Fibonacci number once on the way to the number requested and discard the numbers when they are no longer needed.

b. Time the solution for Programming Project 13.1 and Part a of this project in finding the 1st, 3rd, 5th, 7th, 9th, 11th, 13th, and 15th Fibonacci numbers. Determine how long each function takes. Compare and comment on your results.

Hints: If you are running Linux, you can use the bash time utility. It gives real time (as in wall clock time), user time (time measured by cpu cycles devoted to your program), and sys time (cpu cycles devoted to tasks other than your program). If you are running in some other environment, you will have to read your manual, or ask your instructor, in order to find out how to measure the time a program takes to run.

7. (You need to have first completed Programming Project 13.6 to work on this project.) When computing a Fibonacci number using the most straightforward recursive function definition, the recursive solution recomputes each Fibonacci number too many times. To compute $F_{i+2} = F_i + F_{i+1}$, it computes all the numbers computed in Fi a second time in computing F_{i+1}. You can avoid this by saving the numbers in an array while computing F_i. Write another version of your recursive Fibonacci function based on this idea. In the recursive solution for calculating the Nth Fibonacci number, declare an array of size N. Array entry with index i stores the ith ($i \leq N$) Fibonacci number as it is computed the first time. Then use the array to avoid the second (redundant) recalculation of the Fibonacci numbers. Time this solution as you did in Programming Project 13.6, and compare it to your results for the iterative solution.

8. A savings account typically accrues savings using compound interest. If you deposit $1000 with a 10% interest rate per year, after one year you will have $1100. If you leave this money in the account for another year at 10% interest, you will have $1210. After three years you will have $1331, and so on.

Write a program that inputs the initial amount, an interest rate per year, and the number of years the money will accrue compound interest. Write a recursive function that calculates the amount of money that will be in the savings account using the input information.

To verify your function, the amount should be equal to $P(1+i)^n$, where P is the amount initially saved, i is the interest rate per year, and n is the number of years.

9. We have n people in a room, where n is an integer greater than or equal to 1. Each person shakes hands once with every other person. What is the total number, $h(n)$, of handshakes? Write a recursive function to solve this problem. To get you started, if there are only one or two people in the room, then

```
handshake(1) = 0
handshake(2) = 1
```

If a third person enters the room, he or she must shake hands with each of the two people already there. This is two handshakes in addition to the number of handshakes that would be made in a room of two people, or a total of three handshakes.

If a fourth person enters the room, he or she must shake hands with each of the three people already there. This is three handshakes in addition to the number of handshakes that would be made in a room of three people, or six handshakes.

If you can generalize this to n handshakes, you should be able to write the recursive solution.

10. Consider a frame of bowling pins, where each * represents a pin:

```
    *
   * *
  * * *
 * * * *
* * * * *
```

There are five rows and a total of fifteen pins. If we had only the top four rows, there would be a total of ten pins. If we had only the top three rows, there would be a total of six pins. If we had only the top two rows, there would be a total of three pins. If we had only the top row, there would be a total of one pin.

Write a recursive function that takes as input the number of rows, n, and outputs the total number of pins that would exist in a pyramid with n rows. Your program should allow for values of n that are larger than 5.

11. Write a recursive function named contains with the following header:

```
bool contains (char *haystack, char *needle)
```

The function should return true if the C-string needle is contained within the C-string haystack and false if needle is not in haystack. For example,

```
contains ("C++ programming", "ogra") should return true
contains ("C++ programming", "gramy") should return false
```

You are not allowed to use the string class substr or find functions to determine a match.

12. The following diagram is an example of a *deterministic finite state automaton*, or DFA. This particular DFA describes an algorithm to determine if a sequence of characters is a properly formatted monetary amount with commas. For example, "$1,000" and "$551,323,991,391" are properly formatted but "1,000" (no initial $) and "$1000" (missing comma) and "$5424,132" (missing comma) are not.

VideoNote
Solution to
Programming
Project 13.11

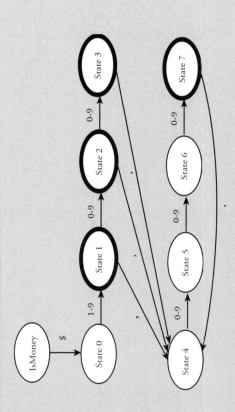

The DFA works by starting in the oval labeled IsMoney. This is the initial state. If the first character of the string is $, then we advance to the second character and move to state 0. Otherwise we conclude the string is not a proper monetary amount. In state 0, if the second character is a digit between 1 and 9, then we advance to the third character and move to state 1. Otherwise we conclude the string is not a proper monetary amount. In state 1, if we have no more characters left in the string, then we conclude that the string is a monetary amount. This is called a *final state* and is indicated by a bold oval. If the third character is a digit between 0 and 9, then we advance to the fourth character and move to state 2. Otherwise if the third character is a comma then we advance to the fourth character and move to state 4. Otherwise we conclude the string is not a proper monetary amount. The rest of the DFA behaves in a similar manner.

Write a program that uses recursion to implement the DFA. Your program should have a separate function for each state in the DFA. Each function should invoke the function corresponding to the next state indicated by the arrows in the diagram. There is mutual recursion because of the loop from state 7 to state 4. Test your solution with several strings and output whether each string is a properly formatted monetary amount.

This solution calls a function for every character in the string. However, the solution may be written in a tail-recursive manner, so it is possible that long strings will not exhaust the stack if your compiler is efficient.

13. A popular word game involves finding words from a grid of randomly generated letters. Words must be at least three letters long and formed from adjoining letters. Letters may not be reused and it is valid to move across diagonals. As an example, consider the following 4×4 grid of letters.

A	B	C	D
E	F	G	H
I	J	K	L
M	N	O	P

The word "FAB" is valid (letters in the upper left corner) and the word "KNIFE" is valid. The word "BABE" is not valid because the "B" may not be reused. The word "MINE" is not valid because the "E" is not adjacent to the "N".

Write a program that uses a 4×4 two-dimensional array to represent the game board. The program should randomly select letters for the board. You may wish to select vowels with a higher probability than consonants. You may also wish to always place a "U" next to a "Q" or to treat "QU" as a single letter. The program should read the words from the text file words.txt (included on the website with this book) and then use a recursive algorithm to determine if the word may be formed from the letters on the game board. The program should output all valid words from the file that are on the game board.

Inheritance 14

14.1 INHERITANCE BASICS 614

14.2 PROGRAMMING WITH INHERITANCE 636

14 Inheritance

Like mother, like daughter

Common saying

Introduction

Object-oriented programming is a popular and powerful programming technique. Among other things, it provides for a dimension of abstraction known as *inheritance*. This means that a very general form of a class can be defined and compiled. Later, more specialized versions of that class may be defined and can inherit the properties of the general class. This chapter covers inheritance in general and, more specifically, how it is realized in C++.

This chapter does not use any of the material presented in Chapter 12 (file I/O) or Chapter 13 (recursion). It also does not use the material in Section 7.3 of Chapter 7, which covers vectors. Section 14.1 also does not use any material from Chapter 10 (pointers and dynamic arrays).

14.1 Inheritance Basics

> *If there is anything that we wish to change in the child, we should first examine it and see whether it is not something that could better be changed in ourselves.*
>
> CARL GUSTAV JUNG, *The Integration of the Personality*

derived class
base class

Inheritance is the process by which a new class—known as a **derived class**—is created from another class, called the **base class**. A derived class automatically has all the member variables and all the ordinary member functions that the base class has, and can have additional member functions and additional member variables.

Derived Classes

Suppose we are designing a record-keeping program that has records for salaried employees and hourly employees. There is a natural hierarchy for grouping these classes. These are all classes of people who share the property of being employees.

Employees who are paid an hourly wage are one subset of employees. Another subset consists of employees who are paid a fixed wage each month or week. Although the program may not need any type corresponding to the set of all employees, thinking in terms of the more general concept of employees can be useful. For example, all employees have names and Social Security numbers, and the member functions for setting and changing names and Social Security numbers will be the same for salaried and hourly employees.

Within C++ you can define a class called Employee that includes all employees, whether salaried or hourly, and then use this class to define classes for hourly employees and salaried employees.

The class Employee will also contain member functions that manipulate the data fields of the class Employee. Displays 14.1 and 14.2 show one possible definition for the class Employee.

Display 14.1 Interface for the Base Class Employee

```
1   //This is the header file employee.h.
2   //This is the interface for the class Employee.
3   //This is primarily intended to be used as a base class to derive
4   //classes for different kinds of employees.
5   #ifndef EMPLOYEE_H
6   #define EMPLOYEE_H
7
8   #include <string>
9   using std::string;
10
11  namespace SavitchEmployees
12  {
13      class Employee
14      {
15      public:
16          Employee( );
17          Employee(const string& theName, const string& theSsn);
18          string getName( ) const;
19          string getSsn( ) const;
20          double getNetPay( ) const;
21          void setName(const string& newName);
22          void setSsn(const string& newSsn);
23          void setNetPay(double newNetPay);
24          void printCheck( ) const;
25      private:
26          string name;
27          string ssn;
28          double netPay;
29      };
30  }//SavitchEmployees
31
32  #endif //EMPLOYEE_H
```

Display 14.2 Implementation for the Base Class Employee (part 1 of 2)

```
1    //This is the file employee.cpp.
2    //This is the implementation for the class Employee.
3    //The interface for the class Employee is in the header file employee.h.
4    #include <string>
5    #include <cstdlib>
6    #include <iostream>
7    #include "employee.h"
8    using std::string;
9    using std::cout;
10
11   namespace SavitchEmployees
12   {
13       Employee::Employee( )  :  name("No name yet"),
                                    ssn("No number yet"), netPay(0)
14       {
15           //deliberately empty
16       }
17       Employee::Employee(const string& theName, const string& theNumber)
18       : name(theName), ssn(theNumber), netPay(0)
19       {
20           //deliberately empty
21       }
22       string Employee::getName( ) const
23       {
24           return name;
25       }
26       string Employee::getSsn( ) const
27       {
28           return ssn;
29       }
30       double Employee::getNetPay( ) const
31       {
32           return netPay;
33       }
34       void Employee::setName(const string& newName)
35       {
36           name = newName;
37       }
38       void Employee::setSsn(const string& newSsn)
```

Display 14.2   Implementation for the Base Class Employee (part 2 of 2)

```
40      {
41          ssn = newSsn;
42      }

43      void Employee::setNetPay (double newNetPay)
44      {
45          netPay = newNetPay;
46      }

47      void Employee::printCheck( ) const
48      {
49          cout << "\nERROR: printCheck FUNCTION CALLED FOR AN \n"
50               << "UNDIFFERENTIATED EMPLOYEE. Aborting the program.\n"
51               << "Check with the author of the program about this bug.\n";
52          exit(1);
53      }

54  }//SavitchEmployees
```

inherits

You can have an (undifferentiated) Employee object, but our reason for defining the class Employee is so that we can define derived classes for different kinds of employees. In particular, the function printCheck will always have its definition changed in derived classes so that different kinds of employees can have different kinds of checks. This is reflected in the definition of the function printCheck for the class Employee (Display 14.2). It makes little sense to print a check for such an (undifferentiated) Employee. We know nothing about this employee. Consequently, we implemented the function printCheck of the class Employee so that the program stops with an error message if printCheck is called for a base class Employee object. As you will see, derived classes will have enough information to redefine the function printCheck to produce meaningful employee checks.

A class that is derived from the class Employee will automatically have all the member variables of the class Employee (name, ssn, and netPay). A class that is derived from the class Employee will also have all the member functions of the class Employee, such as printCheck, getName, setName, and the other member functions listed in Display 14.1. This is usually expressed by saying that the derived class **inherits** the member variables and member functions.

The interface files with the class definitions of two derived classes of the class Employee are given in Displays 14.3 (HourlyEmployee) and 14.4 (SalariedEmployee). We have placed the class Employee and the two derived classes in the same namespace. C++ does not require that they be in the same namespace, but since they are related classes, it makes sense to put them in the same namespace. We will first discuss the derived class HourlyEmployee, given in Display 14.3.

Display 14.3   Interface for the Derived Class HourlyEmployee

```
1    //This is the header file hourlyemployee.h.
2    //This is the interface for the class HourlyEmployee.
3    #ifndef HOURLYEMPLOYEE_H
4    #define HOURLYEMPLOYEE_H
5
6    #include <string>
7    #include "employee.h"
8
9    using std::string;
10
11   namespace SavitchEmployees
12   {
13       class HourlyEmployee : public Employee
14       {
15       public:
16           HourlyEmployee( );
17           HourlyEmployee(const string& theName, const string& theSsn,
                             double theWageRate, double theHours);
18           void setRate(double newWageRate);
19           double getRate( ) const;
20           void setHours(double hoursWorked);
21           double getHours( ) const;
22           void printCheck( );          List only the declaration of an
                                          inherited member function if you
23       private:                         want to change the definition of
24           double wageRate;             the function.
25           double hours;
26       };
27   }//SavitchEmployees
     #endif //HOURLYEMPLOYEE_H
```

Note that the definition of a derived class begins like any other class definition but adds a colon, the reserved word public, and the name of the base class (such as Employee) to the first line of the class definition, as in the following (from Display 14.3):

```
class HourlyEmployee : public Employee
{
```

The derived class (such as HourlyEmployee) automatically receives all the member variables and member functions of the base class (such as Employee) and can add additional member variables and member functions.

The definition of the class HourlyEmployee does not mention the member variables name, ssn, and netPay, but every object of the class HourlyEmployee

Display 14.4   Interface for the Derived Class SalariedEmployee

```
1   //This is the header file salariedemployee.h.
2   //This is the interface for the class SalariedEmployee.
3   #ifndef SALARIEDEMPLOYEE_H
4   #define SALARIEDEMPLOYEE_H
5
6   #include <string>
7   #include "employee.h"
8
9   using std::string;
10
11  namespace SavitchEmployees
12  {
13      class SalariedEmployee : public Employee
14      {
15      public:
16          SalariedEmployee( );
17          SalariedEmployee (const string& theName, const string& theSsn,
18                                              double theWeeklySalary);
19          double getSalary( ) const;
20          void setSalary(double newSalary);
21          void printCheck( );
22      private:
23          double salary;//weekly
24      };
25  }//SavitchEmployees
26  #endif //SALARIEDEMPLOYEE_H
```

has member variables named name, ssn, and netPay. The member variables name, ssn, and netPay are inherited from the class Employee. The class HourlyEmployee declares two additional member variables named wageRate and hours. Thus, every object of the class HourlyEmployee has five member variables named name, ssn, netPay, wageRate, and hours. Note that the definition of a derived class (such as HourlyEmployee) lists only the added member variables. The member variables defined in the base class are not mentioned. They are provided automatically to the derived class.

Just as it inherits the member variables of the class Employee, so too the class HourlyEmployee inherits all the member functions from the class Employee. Thus, the class HourlyEmployee inherits the member functions getName, getSsn, getNetPay, setName, setSsn, setNetPay, and printCheck from the class Employee.

Inherited Members

A *derived class* automatically has all the member variables and all the ordinary member functions of the *base class*. (As discussed later in this chapter, there are some specialized member functions, such as constructors, that are not automatically inherited.) These members from the base class are said to be *inherited*. These inherited member functions and inherited member variables are, with one exception, not mentioned in the definition of the derived class but are automatically members of the derived class. As explained in the text, you do mention an inherited member function in the definition of the derived class if you want to change the definition of the inherited member function.

In addition to the inherited member variables and member functions, a derived class can add new member variables and new member functions. The new member variables and the declarations for the new member functions are listed in the class definition. For example, the derived class `HourlyEmployee` adds the two member variables `wageRate` and `hours` and adds the new member functions `setRate`, `getRate`, `setHours`, and `getHours`. This is shown in Display 14.3. Note that you do not give the declarations of the inherited member functions unless you want to change these definitions, which is a point that we will discuss shortly. For now, do not worry about the details of the constructor definition for the derived class. We will discuss constructors in the next subsection.

In the implementation file for the derived class, such as the implementation of `HourlyEmployee` in Display 14.5, give the definitions of all the added member functions. Note that you do not give definitions for the inherited member functions unless the definition of the member function is changed in the derived class, a point we discuss next.

Parent and Child Classes

When discussing derived classes, it is common to use terminology derived from family relationships. A base class is often called a **parent class**. A derived class is then called a **child class**. This makes the language of inheritance very smooth. For example, we can say that a child class inherits member variables and member functions from its parent class. This analogy is often carried one step further. A class that is a parent of a parent of a parent of another class (or some other number of "parent of" iterations) is often called an **ancestor class**. If class A is an ancestor of class B, then class B is often called a **descendant** of class A.

redefining

The definition of an inherited member function can be changed in the definition of a derived class so that it has a meaning in the derived class that is different from what it is in the base class. This is called **redefining** the inherited member function. For example, the member function `printCheck( )` is redefined in the definition of the derived class `HourlyEmployee`. To redefine a member function definition, simply list it in the class definition and give it a new definition, just as you would do with a member function that is added in the derived class. This is illustrated by the redefined function printCheck( ) of the class HourlyEmployee (Displays 14.3 and 14.5).

Display 14.5   Implementation for the Derived Class **HourlyEmployee**   (part 1 of 2)

```
1   //This is the file hourlyemployee.cpp.
2   //This is the implementation for the class HourlyEmployee.
3   //The interface for the class HourlyEmployee is in
4   //the header file hourlyemployee.h.
5   #include <string>
6   #include <iostream>
7   #include "hourlyemployee.h"
8   using std::string;
9   using std::cout;
10  using std::endl;
11  namespace SavitchEmployees
12  {
13      HourlyEmployee::HourlyEmployee( ) : Employee( ), wageRate(0), hours(0)
14      {
15          //deliberately empty
16      }
17      HourlyEmployee::HourlyEmployee(const string& theName,
18                          const string&theNumber, double theWageRate,
19                          double theHours)
                  : Employee(theName, theNumber), wageRate(theWageRate),
                          hours(theHours)
20      {
21          //deliberately empty
22      }
23      void HourlyEmployee::setRate(double newWageRate)
24      {
25          wageRate = newWageRate;
26      }
27      double HourlyEmployee::getRate( ) const
28      {
29          return wageRate;
30      }
31
32      void HourlyEmployee::setHours(double hoursWorked)
33      {
34          hours = hoursWorked;
```

(continued)

Display 14.5 Implementation for the Derived Class HourlyEmployee (part 2 of 2)

```
35    }
36
37    double HourlyEmployee::getHours( ) const
38    {
39        return hours;
40    }
41
42    void HourlyEmployee::printCheck( )
      {
          setNetPay(hours * wageRate);

43        cout << "\n";
44        cout << "Pay to the order of " << getName( ) << endl;
45        cout << "The sum of " << getNetPay( ) << " Dollars\n";
46        cout << "\n";
47        cout << "Check Stub: NOT NEGOTIABLE\n";
48        cout << "Employee Number: " << getSsn( ) << endl;
49        cout << "Hourly Employee. \nHours worked: " << hours
50        << " Rate: " << wageRate << " Pay: " << getNetPay( ) <<
          endl;
51        cout << "\n";
52        }
53    } //SavitchEmployee
```

We have chosen to set netPay as part of the printCheck function because that is when it is used. In any event, this is an accounting question, not a programming question.

But, note that C++ allows us to drop the const on the function printCheck when we redefine it in a derived class.

SalariedEmployee is another example of a derived class of the class Employee. The interface for the class SalariedEmployee is given in Display 14.4, and its implementation is given in Display 14.6. An object declared to be of type SalariedEmployee has all the member functions and member variables of Employee plus the new members given in the definition of the class SalariedEmployee. This is true even though the class SalariedEmployee lists none of the inherited variables and lists only one function from the class Employee—namely, the function printCheck, which will have its definition changed in SalariedEmployee. The class SalariedEmployee, nonetheless, has the three member variables name, ssn, and netPay, as well as the member variable salary. Notice that you do not have to declare the member variables and member functions of the class Employee, such as name and setName, in order for SalariedEmployee to have these members. The class SalariedEmployee gets these inherited members automatically without the programmer doing anything.

Note that the class Employee has all the code that is common to the two classes HourlyEmployee and SalariedEmployee. This saves you the trouble of writing identical code two times: once for the class HourlyEmployee and once for the class SalariedEmployee. Inheritance allows you to reuse the code in the class Employee.

Display 14.6   Implementation for the Derived Class `SalariedEmployee` (part 1 of 2)

```
1   //This is the file salariedemployee.cpp
2   //This is the implementation for the class SalariedEmployee.
3   //The interface for the class SalariedEmployee is in
4   //the header file salariedemployee.h.
5   #include <iostream>
6   #include <string>
7   #include "salariedemployee.h"
8   using std::string;
9   using std::cout;
10  using std::endl;
11
12  namespace SavitchEmployees
13  {
14      SalariedEmployee::SalariedEmployee( ) : Employee( ), salary(0)
15      {
16          //deliberately empty
17      }
18      SalariedEmployee::SalariedEmployee(const string& theName,
19                          const string& theNumber,
20                          double theWeeklyPay)
21                  : Employee(theName, theNumber), salary(theWeeklyPay)
22      {
23          //deliberately empty
24      }
25      double SalariedEmployee::getSalary( ) const
26      {
27          return salary;
28      }
29      void SalariedEmployee::setSalary(double newSalary)
30      {
31          salary = newSalary;
32      }
33      void SalariedEmployee::printCheck( )
34      {
35          setNetPay(salary);
36          cout << "\n";
37          cout << "Pay to the order of " << getName( ) << endl;
38          cout << "The sum of " << getNetPay( ) << " Dollars\n";
39          cout << "                                          \n";
40          cout << "Check Stub NOT NEGOTIABLE \n";
41          cout << "Employee Number: " << getSsn( ) << endl;
```

(continued)

Display 14.6 Implementation for the Derived Class `SalariedEmployee` (part 2 of 2)

```
42       cout << "Salaried Employee. Regular Pay: "
43            << salary << endl;
44       cout << "
45   }
46 }//SavitchEmployees
```

Constructors in Derived Classes

A constructor in a base class is not inherited in the derived class, but you can invoke a constructor of the base class within the definition of a derived class constructor, which is all you need or normally want. A constructor for a derived class uses a constructor from the base class in a special way. A constructor for a derived class initializes all the data inherited from the base class. Thus, a constructor for a derived class begins with an invocation of a constructor for the base class. The special syntax for invoking the base class constructor is illustrated in Display 14.5. In what follows we have reproduced (with minor changes in the line breaks to make it fit the text column) one of the constructor definitions for the class `HourlyEmployee` given in Display 14.5. In what follows we have reproduced (with definitions for the class `HourlyEmployee` taken from that display:

```
HourlyEmployee::HourlyEmployee(const string&theName,
       const string& theNumber, double theWageRate,
       double theHours)
: Employee(theName, theNumber),
       wageRate(theWageRate), hours(theHours)
{
       //deliberately empty
}
```

The portion after the colon is the initialization section of the constructor definition for the constructor `HourlyEmployee::HourlyEmployee`. The part `Employee(theName, theNumber)` is an invocation of the two-argument constructor for the base class `Employee`. Note that the syntax for invoking the base class constructor is analogous to the syntax used to set member variables: The entry `wageRate(theWageRate)` sets the value of the member variable `wageRate` to `theWageRate`; the entry `Employee(theName, theNumber)` invokes the base class constructor `Employee` with the arguments `theName` and `theNumber`. Since all the work is done in the initialization section, the body of the constructor definition is empty.

In the following, we reproduce the other constructor for the class `HourlyEmployee` from Display 14.5:

```
HourlyEmployee::HourlyEmployee( )  : Employee( ), wageRate(0),
                                           hours(0)
{
       //deliberately empty
}
```

An Object of a Derived Class Has More Than One Type

In everyday experience, an hourly employee is an employee. In C++ the same sort of thing holds. Since `HourlyEmployee` is a derived class of the class `Employee`, every object of the class `HourlyEmployee` can be used anyplace an object of the class `Employee` can be used. In particular, you can use an argument of type `HourlyEmployee` when a function requires an argument of type `Employee`. You can assign an object of the class `HourlyEmployee` to a variable of type `Employee`. (But be warned: You cannot assign a plain old `Employee` object to a variable of type `HourlyEmployee`. After all, an `Employee` is not necessarily an `HourlyEmployee`.) Of course, the same remarks apply to any base class and its derived class. You can use an object of a derived class anyplace that an object of its base class is allowed.

More generally, an object of a class type can be used anyplace that an object of any of its ancestor classes can be used. If class `Child` is derived from class `Ancestor` and class `Grandchild` is derived from class `Child`, then an object of class `Grandchild` can be used anyplace an object of class `Child` can be used, and the object of class `Grandchild` can also be used anyplace that an object of class `Ancestor` can be used.

In this constructor definition, the default (zero-argument) version of the base class constructor is called to initialize the inherited member variables. You should always include an invocation of one of the base class constructors in the initialization section of a derived class constructor.

If a constructor definition for a derived class does not include an invocation of a constructor for the base class, then the default (zero-argument) version of the base class constructor will be invoked automatically. So, the following definition of the default constructor for the class `HourlyEmployee` (with `Employee ( )` omitted) is equivalent to the version we just discussed:

```
HourlyEmployee::HourlyEmployee ( ) : wageRate(0), hours(0)
{
    //deliberately empty
}
```

However, we prefer to always explicitly include a call to a base class constructor, even if it would be invoked automatically.

A derived class object has all the member variables of the base class. When a derived class constructor is called, these member variables need to be allocated memory and should be initialized. This allocation of memory for the inherited member variables must be done by a constructor for the base class, and the base class constructor is the most convenient place to initialize these inherited member variables. That is why you should always include a call to one of the base class constructors when you define a constructor for a derived class. If you do not include a call to a base class constructor (in the initialization section of the definition of a derived class constructor), then the default (zero-argument) constructor of the base class is called automatically. (If there is no default constructor for the base class, an error occurs.)

order of
constructor
calls

The call to the base class constructor is the first action taken by a derived class constructor. Thus, if class B is derived from class A and class C is derived from class B, then when an object of class C is created, first a constructor for class A is called, then a constructor for B is called, and finally the remaining actions of the class C constructor are taken.

Constructors in Derived Classes

A derived class does not inherit the constructors of its base class. However, when defining a constructor for the derived class, you can and should include a call to a constructor of the base class (within the initialization section of the constructor definition).

If you do not include a call to a constructor of the base class, then the default (zero-argument) constructor of the base class will automatically be called when the derived class constructor is called.

PITFALL: Use of Private Member Variables from the Base Class

An object of the class `HourlyEmployee` (Displays 14.3 and 14.5) inherits a member variable called name from the class `Employee` (Displays 14.1 and 14.2). For example, the following would set the value of the member variable name of the object joe to "Josephine" (it also sets the member variable ssn to "123-45-6789" and both wageRate and hours to 0):

```
HourlyEmployee joe("Josephine", "123-45-6789", 0, 0);
```

If you want to change joe.name to "Mighty-Joe", you can do so as follows:

```
joe.setName("Mighty-Joe");
```

You must be a bit careful about how you manipulate inherited member variables such as name. The member variable name of the class `HourlyEmployee` was inherited from the class `Employee`, but the member variable name is a private member variable in the definition of the class `Employee`. That means that name can only be directly accessed within the definition of a member function in the class `Employee`. A member variable (or member function) that is private in a base class is not accessible *by name* in the definition of a member function for *any other class, not even in a member function definition of a derived class*. Thus, although the class `HourlyEmployee` does have a member variable named name (inherited from the base class `Employee`), it is illegal to directly access the member variable name in the definition of any member function in the class definition of `HourlyEmployee`.

PITFALL: (continued)

For example, the following are the first few lines from the body of the member function Hourly Employee::printCheck (taken from Display 14.5):

```
void HourlyEmployee::printCheck( )
{
    setNetPay(hours * wageRate);

    cout << "\n_____\n";
    cout << "Pay to the order of " << getName( ) << endl;
    cout << "The sum of " << getNetPay( ) << " Dollars\n";
```

You might have wondered why we needed to use the member function setNetPay to set the value of the netPay member variable. You might be tempted to rewrite the start of the member function definition as follows:

```
void HourlyEmployee::printCheck( )
{
    netPay = hours * wageRate;  Illegal use of netPay.
```

As the comment indicates, this will not work. The member variable netPay is a private member variable in the class Employee, and although a derived class like HourlyEmployee inherits the variable netPay, it cannot access it directly. It must use some public member function to access the member variable netPay. The correct way to accomplish the definition of printCheck in the class HourlyEmployee is the way we did it in Display 14.5 (part of which was displayed earlier).

The fact that name and netPay are inherited variables that are private in the base class also explains why we needed to use the accessor functions getName and getNetPay in the definition of HourlyEmployee::printCheck instead of simply using the variable names name and netPay. You cannot mention a private inherited member variable by name. You must instead use public accessor and mutator member functions (such as getName and setName) that were defined in the base class. (Recall that an *accessor function* is a function that allows you to access member variables of a class and a *mutator function* is one that allows you to change member variables of a class. Accessor and mutator functions are covered in Chapter 6.)

The fact that a private member variable of a base class cannot be accessed in the definition of a member function of a derived class often seems wrong to people. After all, if you are an hourly employee and you want to change your name, nobody says, "Sorry, name is a private member variable of the class Employee." If you are an hourly employee, you are also an employee. In Java, this is also true; an object of the class HourlyEmployee is also an object of the class Employee. However, if C++ allowed access to private member variables and private member functions from a derived class, then anytime you want to access a private member variable you could simply create a derived class and access it in a member function of that class. This

(continued)

PITFALL: (continued)

means that all private member variables would be accessible to anybody who wants to put in a little extra effort. This scenario illustrates the problem, but the bigger problem is unintentional errors rather than intentional subversion. If private member variables of a class are accessible in member function definitions of a derived class, then the member variables might be changed by mistake or in inappropriate ways. (Remember, accessor and mutator functions can guard against inappropriate changes to member variables.)

We will discuss one possible way to get around this restriction on private member variables of the base class in the subsection entitled "The `protected` Qualifier" a bit later in this chapter. ■

PITFALL: Private Member Functions Are Effectively Not Inherited

As noted in the previous Pitfall section, a member variable (or member function) that is private in a base class is not directly accessible outside the interface and implementation of the base class, *not even in a member function definition for a derived class.* Note that private member functions are just like private variables in terms of not being directly available. In the case of member functions, however, the restriction is more dramatic. A private variable can be accessed indirectly via an accessor or mutator member function. A private member function is simply not available. It is just as if the private member function were not inherited.

This should not be a problem. Private member functions should be used just as helping functions, and so their use should be limited to the class in which they are defined. If you want a member function to be used as a helping member function in a number of inherited classes, then it is not *just* a helping function, and you should make the member function public. ■

The `protected` Qualifier

As you have seen, you cannot access a private member variable or private member function in the definition or implementation of a derived class. There is a classification of member variables and functions that allows them to be accessed by name in a derived class, but not accessed anyplace else, such as in some class that is not a derived class. If you use the qualifier `protected`, rather than `private` or `public`, before a member variable or member function of a class, then for any class or function other than a derived class the effect is the same as if the member variable were labeled `private`; however, in a derived class the variable can be accessed by name.

protected

For example, consider the class HourlyEmployee, which was derived from the base class Employee. We were required to use accessor and mutator member functions to manipulate the inherited member variables in the definition of HourlyEmployee::printCheck. If all the private member variables in the class Employee were labeled with the keyword **protected** instead of private, the definition of HourlyEmployee::printCheck in the derived class Employee could be simplified to the following:

```
void HourlyEmployee::printCheck( )
//Only works if the member variables of Employee are marked
//protected instead of private.
{
    netPay = hours * wageRate;

    cout << "\n                                              \n";
    cout << "Pay to the order of " << name << endl;
    cout << "The sum of " << netPay << " Dollars\n";
    cout << "                                              \n";
    cout << "Check Stub: NOT NEGOTIABLE\n";
    cout << "Employee Number: " << ssn << endl;
    cout << "Hourly Employee. \nHours worked: " << hours
         << " Rate: " << wageRate << " Pay: " << netPay << endl;
    cout << "                                              \n";
}
```

In the derived class HourlyEmployee, the inherited member variables name, netPay, and ssn can be accessed by name in the base class Employee. However, in any class that is not derived from the class Employee, these member variables are treated as if they are marked private.

Member variables that are marked protected in the base class act as though they are also marked protected in any derived class. For example, suppose you define a derived class PartTimeHourlyEmployee of the class HourlyEmployee. The class PartTimeHourlyEmployee inherits all the member variables of the class HourlyEmployee, including the member variables that HourlyEmployee inherits from the class Employee. The class PartTimeHourlyEmployee will thus have the member variables netPay, name, and ssn. If these member variables are marked protected in the class Employee, then they can be used by name in the definitions of functions of the class PartTimeHourlyEmployee.

Except for derived classes (and derived classes of derived classes, etc.), a member variable that is marked protected is treated the same as if it were marked private.

We include this discussion of protected member variables primarily because you will see them used and should be familiar with them. Many, but not all, programming authorities say it is bad style to use protected member variables because doing so compromises the principle of hiding the class implementation. They say that all member variables should be marked private. If all member variables are marked private, the inherited member variables cannot be accessed by name in derived class function definitions. However, this is not as bad as it sounds. The inherited private member variables can be accessed indirectly by invoking inherited functions that either read or change the private inherited variables. Since authorities differ on whether you should use protected members, you will have to make your own decision on whether to utilize them.

Protected Members

If you use the qualifier protected (rather than private or public) before a member variable of a class, then for any class or function other than a derived class the effect is the same as if the member variable were labeled private. However, in the definition of a member function of a derived class, the variable can be accessed by name. Similarly, if you use the qualifier protected before a member function of a class, then for any class or function other than a derived class, the effect is the same as if the member variable were labeled private. However, in the definition of a member function of a derived class, the protected function can be used.

Protected members are inherited in the derived class as if they were marked protected in the derived class. In other words, if a member is marked as protected in a base class, then it can be accessed by name in the definitions of all descendant classes, not just in those classes directly derived from the base class.

Self-Test Exercises

1. Is the following program legal (assuming appropriate #include and using directives are added)?

```
void showEmployeeData(const Employee object);

int main( )
{
    HourlyEmployee joe("Mighty Joe",
                        "123-45-6789", 20.50, 40);
    SalariedEmployee boss("Mr. Big Shot",
                        "987-65-4321", 10500.50);

    showEmployeeData(joe);
    showEmployeeData(boss);

    return 0;
}

void showEmployeeData(const Employee object)
{
    cout << "Name: " << object.getName( ) << endl;
    cout << "Social Security Number: "
         << object.getSsn( ) << endl;
}
```

Self-Test Exercises (continued)

2. Give a definition for a class SmartBut that is a derived class of the base class Smart given in the following. Do not bother with #include directives or namespace details.

```
class Smart
{
public:
    Smart( );
    void printAnswer( ) const;
protected:
    int a;
    int b;
};
```

This class should have an additional data field, crazy, of type bool; one additional member function that takes no arguments and returns a value of type bool; and suitable constructors. The new function is named isCrazy. You do not need to give any implementations, just the class definition.

3. Is the following a legal definition of the member function isCrazy in the derived class SmartBut discussed in Self-Test Exercise 2? Explain your answer. (Remember, the question asks if it is legal, not if it is a sensible definition.)

```
bool SmartBut::isCrazy( ) const
{
    if (a > b)
        return crazy;
    else
        return true;
}
```

Redefinition of Member Functions

In the definition of the derived class HourlyEmployee (Display 14.3), we gave the declaration for the new member functions setRate, getRate, setHours, and getHours. We also gave the function declaration for only one of the member functions inherited from the class Employee. The inherited member functions whose function declarations were not given (such as setName and setSsn) are inherited unchanged. They have the same definition in the class HourlyEmployee as they do in the base class Employee. When you define a derived class like HourlyEmployee, you list only the function declarations for the inherited member functions whose definitions you want to change to have different definitions in the derived class. If you look at the implementation of the class HourlyEmployee (Display 14.5), you will see that we have redefined the inherited member function printCheck. The class SalariedEmployee also gives a new definition to the member function printCheck, as shown in Display 14.6. Moreover, the two classes give different definitions from each other. The function printCheck is *redefined* in the derived classes.

Display 14.7 gives a demonstration program that illustrates the use of the derived classes `HourlyEmployee` and `SalariedEmployee`.

Redefining an Inherited Function

A derived class inherits all the member functions (and member variables) that belong to the base class. However, if a derived class requires a different implementation for an inherited member function, the function may be redefined in the derived class. When a member function is redefined, you must list its declaration in the definition of the derived class, even though the declaration is the same as in the base class. If you do not wish to redefine a member function that is inherited from the base class, do not list it in the definition of the derived class.

Redefining versus Overloading

Do not confuse *redefining* a function definition in a derived class with *overloading* a function name. When you redefine a function definition, the new function definition given in the derived class has the same number and types of parameters. When you overload a function, the function in the derived class has a different number of parameters or a parameter of a different type from the function in the base class, and the derived class has both functions. For example, suppose we added a function with the following function declaration to the definition of the class `HourlyEmployee`:

```
void setName(string firstName, string lastName);
```

The class `HourlyEmployee` would have this two-argument function `setName` and would also inherit the following one-argument function `setName`:

```
void setName(string newName);
```

The class `HourlyEmployee` would have two functions named `setName`. This would be *overloading* the function name `setName`.

On the other hand, both the class `Employee` and the class `HourlyEmployee` define a function with the following function declaration:

```
void printCheck( );
```

In this case, the class `HourlyEmployee` has only one function named `printCheck`, but the definition of the function `printCheck` for the class `HourlyEmployee` is different from its definition for the class `Employee`. In this case, the function `printCheck` has been *redefined*.

If you get redefining and overloading confused, you do have one consolation: They are both legal. So, it is more important to learn how to use them than it is to learn to distinguish between them. Nonetheless, you should learn the difference between them.

Display 14.7   Using Derived Classes

```cpp
1   #include <iostream>
2   #include "hourlyemployee.h"
3   #include "salariedemployee.h"
4   using std::cout;
5   using std::endl;
6   using SavitchEmployees::HourlyEmployee;
7   using SavitchEmployees::SalariedEmployee;

8   int main( )
9   {
10      HourlyEmployee joe;
11      joe.setName("Mighty Joe");
12      joe.setSsn("123-45-6789");
13      joe.setRate(20.50);
14      joe.setHours(40);
15      cout << "Check for " << joe.getName( )
16           << " for " << joe.getHours( ) << " hours.\n";
17      joe.printCheck( );
18      cout << endl;

19      SalariedEmployee boss("Mr. Big Shot", "987-65-4321", 10500.50);
20      cout << "Check for " << boss.getName( ) << endl;
21      boss.printCheck( );

22      return 0;
23  }
```

The functions setName, setSsn, setRate, setHours, and getName are inherited unchanged from the class Employee. The function printCheck is redefined. The function getHours was added to the derived class HourlyEmployee.

Sample Dialogue

```
Check for Mighty Joe for 40 hours.

Pay to the order of Mighty Joe
The sum of 820 Dollars

Check Stub: NOT NEGOTIABLE
Employee Number: 123-45-6789
Hourly Employee.
Hours worked: 40  Rate: 20.5  Pay: 820

Check for Mr. Big Shot

Pay to the order of Mr. Big Shot
The sum of 10500.5 Dollars

Check Stub NOT NEGOTIABLE
Employee Number: 987-65-4321
Salaried Employee. Regular Pay: 10500.5
```

Signature

A function's **signature** is the function's name with the sequence of types in the parameter list, not including the const keyword and the ampersand, &. When you overload a function name, the two definitions of the function name must have different signatures using this definition of signature. (Some authorities include the const and/or ampersand as part of the signature, but we wanted a definition that works for explaining overloading.) A function that has the same name in a derived class as in the base class but has a different signature is overloaded, not redefined.

(As we noted in Chapter 4, some compilers will, in fact, allow you to overload on the basis of const versus no const, but you should not count on this. The C++ standard says it is not allowed.)

Access to a Redefined Base Function

Suppose you redefine a function so that it has a different definition in the derived class from what it had in the base class. The definition that was given in the base class is not completely lost to the derived class objects. However, if you want to invoke the version of the function given in the base class with an object in the derived class, you need some way to say "use the definition of this function as given in the base class (even though I am an object of the derived class)." The way you say this is to use the scope resolution operator with the name of the base class. An example should clarify the details.

Consider the base class `Employee` (Display 14.1) and the derived class `HourlyEmployee` (Display 14.3). The function `printCheck( )` is defined in both classes. Now suppose you have an object of each class, as in the following:

```
Employee JaneE;
HourlyEmployee SallyH;
```

Then

```
JaneE.printCheck( );
```

uses the definition of printCheck given in the class Employee, and

```
SallyH.printCheck( );
```

uses the definition of printCheck given in the class HourlyEmployee.

But suppose you want to invoke the version of printCheck given in the definition of the base class Employee with the derived class object SallyH as the calling object for printCheck. Do that as follows:

```
SallyH.Employee::printCheck( );
```

Of course, you are unlikely to want to use the version of printCheck given in the particular class Employee, but with other classes and other functions, you may occasionally want to use a function definition from a base class with a derived class object. An example is given in Self-Test Exercise 6.

Functions That Are Not Inherited

As a general rule, if Derived is a derived class with base class Base, then all "normal" functions in the class Base are usable inherited members of the class Derived. However, there are some special functions that are, for all practical purposes, not inherited. We have already seen that, as a practical matter, constructors and private member functions are not inherited. Destructors (discussed in Section 14.2) are also effectively not inherited.

The copy constructor is not inherited, but if you do not define a copy constructor in a derived class (or any class, for that matter), C++ will automatically generate a copy constructor for you. However, this default copy constructor simply copies the contents of member variables and does not work correctly for classes with pointers or dynamic data in their member variables. Thus, if your class member variables involve pointers, dynamic arrays, or other dynamic data, you should define a copy constructor for the class. This applies whether or not the class is a derived class.

The assignment operator = is also not inherited. If the base class Base defines the assignment operator, but the derived class Derived does not, then the class Derived will have an assignment operator, but it will be the default assignment operator that C++ creates (when you do not define =); it will not have anything to do with the base class assignment operator defined in Base. Techniques for defining the assignment operator are discussed in the subsection "Assignment Operators and Copy Constructors in Derived Classes" in Section 14.2.

It is natural that constructors, destructors, and the assignment operator are not inherited. In order to correctly perform their tasks, they need information that the base class does not possess; namely, they need to know about the new member variables introduced in the derived class.

Self-Test Exercises

4. The class SalariedEmployee inherits both of the functions getName and printCheck (among other things) from the base class Employee, yet only the function declaration for the function printCheck is given in the definition of the class SalariedEmployee. Why isn't the function declaration for the function getName given in the definition of SalariedEmployee?

(continued)

Self-Test Exercises (continued)

5. Give a definition for a class `TitledEmployee` that is a derived class of the base class `SalariedEmployee` given in Display 14.4. The class `TitledEmployee` has one additional member variable of type `string` called `title`. It also has two additional member functions: `getTitle`, which takes no arguments and returns a `string`, and `setTitle`, which is a `void` function that takes one argument of type `string`. It also redefines the member function `setName`. You do not need to give any implementations, just the class definition. However, do give all needed `#include` directives and all `using` namespace directives. Place the class `TitledEmployee` in the namespace `SavitchEmployees`.

6. Give the definitions of the constructors for the class `TitledEmployee` that you gave as the answer to Self-Test Exercise 5. Also, give the redefinition of the member function `setName`. The function `setName` should insert the title into the name. Do not bother with `#include` directives or namespace details.

7. You know that an overloaded assignment operator and a copy constructor are not inherited. Does this mean that if you do not define an overloaded assignment operator or a copy constructor for a derived class, then that derived class will have no assignment operator and no copy constructor?

14.2 Programming with Inheritance

The devil is in the details.

Common saying

This section presents some of the more subtle details regarding inheritance and gives another complete example, plus some discussion on inheritance and related programming techniques. The material in this section uses dynamic arrays (Chapter 10), and most of the topics are only relevant to classes that use dynamic arrays or pointers and other dynamic data.

Assignment Operators and Copy Constructors in Derived Classes

Overloaded assignment operators and constructors are not inherited. However, they can be used—and in almost all cases must be used—in the definitions of overloaded assignment operators and copy constructors in derived classes.

When overloading the assignment operator in a derived class, you normally use the overloaded assignment operator from the base class. To help understand the code outline we will give, remember that an overloaded assignment operator must be defined as a member function of the class.

If Derived is a class derived from Base, then the definition of the overloaded assignment operator for the class Derived would typically begin with something like the following:

```
Derived& Derived::operator =(const Derived& rightSide)
{
    Base::operator =(rightSide);
```

The first line of code in the body of the definition is a call to the assignment operator of the Base class. This takes care of the inherited member variables and their data. The definition of the overloaded assignment operator would then go on to set the new member variables that were introduced in the definition of the class Derived. A complete example that includes this technique is given in the programming example "Partially Filled Array with Backup" later in this chapter.

A similar situation holds for defining the copy constructor in a derived class. If Derived is a class derived from Base, then the definition of the copy constructor for the class Derived would typically use the copy constructor for the class Base to set the inherited member variables and their data. The code would normally begin with something like the following:

```
Derived::Derived(const Derived& Object)
         : Base(Object), <probably more initializations>
{
```

The invocation of the base class copy constructor Base(Object) sets the inherited member variables of the Derived class object being created. Note that since Object is of type Derived, it is also of type Base; therefore, Object is a legal argument to the copy constructor for the class Base. A complete example that includes a copy constructor in a base class is given in the programming example "Partially Filled Array with Backup," later in this chapter.

Of course, these techniques do not work unless you have a correctly functioning assignment operator and a correctly functioning copy constructor for the base class. This means that the base class definition must include a copy constructor and that either the default automatically created assignment operator works correctly for the base class or the base class has an overloaded definition of the assignment operator.

Destructors in Derived Classes

If a base class has a correctly functioning destructor, it is relatively easy to define a correctly functioning destructor in a class derived from the base class. When the destructor for the derived class is invoked, it automatically invokes the destructor of the base class, so there is no need for the explicit writing of a call to the base class destructor; it always happens automatically. The derived class destructor thus need only worry about using delete on the member variables (and any data they point to) that are added in the derived class. It is the job of the base class destructor to invoke delete on the inherited member variables.

If class B is derived from class A and class C is derived from class B, then when an object of class C goes out of scope, first the destructor for the class C is called, then the destructor for class B is called, and finally the destructor for class A is called. Note that the order of destructor calls is the reverse of the order in which constructors are called. We give an example of writing a destructor in a derived class in the programming example "Partially Filled Array with Backup."

EXAMPLE: Partially Filled Array with Backup

This example presents a derived class of the partially filled array class PFArrayD that we presented in Chapter 10 (Display 10.10). For reference, we repeat the header file for the base class PFArrayD in Display 14.8. We include as much as we will discuss of the implementation for the base class PFArrayD in Display 14.9. Note that we have made one important change to the definition presented in Chapter 10. We have changed the member variables from private to protected. This will allow member functions in the derived class to access the member variables by name.

We will define a derived class called PFArrayDBak using PFArrayD as a base class. An object of the derived class PFArrayDBak will have all the member functions of the base class PFArrayD and can be used just like an object of the class PFArrayD, but an object of the class PFArrayDBak will have the following added feature: There is a member function called backup that can make a backup copy of all the data in the partially filled array; at any later time the programmer can use the member function restore to restore the partially filled array to the state it was in just before the last invocation of backup. If the meaning of these added member functions is not clear, you should peek ahead to the sample demonstration program shown in Display 14.12.

The interface for the derived class PFArrayDBak is shown in Display 14.10. The class PFArrayDBak adds two member variables to hold a backed-up copy of the partially filled array: a member variable b of type double* that will point to a dynamic array with the backup version of the (inherited) working array, and an int member variable named usedB to indicate how much of the backed-up array b is filled with data. Since there is no way to change the capacity of a PFArrayD (or a PFArrayDBak), there is no need to back up the capacity value. All the basic functions for handling a partially filled array are inherited unchanged from the base class PFArrayD. These inherited functions manipulate the inherited array a and the inherited int variable used just as they did in the base class PFArrayD.

The implementation of the new member functions for the class PFArrayDBak is shown in Display 14.11. The constructors of the derived class PFArrayDBak rely on the constructors of the base class to set up the regular partially filled array (inherited member variables a, used, and capacity). Each constructor also creates a new dynamic array of the same size as the array a. This second array is the array b used for backing up the data in a.

EXAMPLE: (continued)

The member function `backup` copies data from the partially filled array (`a` and `used`) to the backup locations `b` and `usedB` with the following code:

```
usedB = used;
for (int i = 0; i < usedB; i++)
    b[i] = a[i];
```

You should note that the member variables `a` and `used` in the base class are protected and not private. Otherwise, the preceding code would be illegal because it accesses the inherited member variables `a` and `used` by name.

The member function `restore` simply reverses things and copies from `b` and `usedB` to `a` and `used`.

The definition of the overloaded assignment operator for the derived class `PFArrayDBak` begins with an invocation of the assignment operator for the base class `PFArrayD`. This copies all the data from the member variables `a`, `used`, and `capacity` from the object on the right-hand side of the assignment operator (from the parameter `rightSide`) to the object on the left-hand side of the assignment operator (the calling object). We are relying on the fact that this was done properly in the definition of the overloaded assignment operator in the base class. That is, we rely on the base class assignment operator to behave correctly when the same object (for the inherited part) occurs on both sides of the assignment operator, and we assume that the copying actions make an independent copy of the array `a`. The code in the body of the overloaded assignment operator for the derived class `PFArrayDBak` needs to create a similarly independent copy of the array `b`.

Since the objects on the right and left sides of the assignment operators may have different capacities, we must create a new array `b` (in most cases). This is done as follows:

```
if (oldCapacity != rightSide.capacity)
{
    delete [] b;
    b = new double [rightSide.capacity];
}
```

Note that the Boolean expression in the `if` statement ensures that `b` will not be deleted when the objects on either side of the assignment operator have the same capacity. In particular, this ensures that when the same object appears on both sides of the assignment operator, the array `b` is not deleted. After this, the copying of data is routine.

Note that the destructor for the class `PFArrayDBak` has no explicit mention of the inherited member variable `a`. It simply sends the `b` array memory back to the freestore for recycling with the following statement.

(continued)

EXAMPLE: (continued)

```
delete [] b;
```

The memory for the inherited array a is also sent back to the freestore, even though you do not see any mention of a in the destructor for the derived class PFArrayDBak. When the destructor for the derived class PFArrayDBak is invoked, it ends its action by automatically invoking the destructor for the base class PFArrayD; that destructor includes the following code to dispose of a:

```
delete [] a;
```

A demonstration program for our class PFArrayDBak is given in Display 14.12.

Display 14.8   Interface for the Base Class **PFArrayD** (part 1 of 2)

```
1    //This is the header file pfarrayd.h. This is the interface for the
2    //class PFArrayD. Objects of this type are partially filled arrays
3    //of doubles.
4    #ifndef PFARRAYD_H
5    #define PFARRAYD_H
6
7    class PFArrayD
8    {
9    public:
10       PFArrayD( );
11       //Initializes with a capacity of 50.

         PFArrayD(int capacityValue);

         PFArrayD(const PFArrayD& pfaObject);

12       void addElement(double element);
13       //Precondition: The array is not full.
14       //Postcondition: The element has been added.

15       bool full( ) const;
16       //Returns true if the array is full, false otherwise.

17       int getCapacity( ) const;

18       int getNumberUsed( ) const;
19       void emptyArray( );
20       //Resets the number used to zero, effectively emptying the array.

21       double& operator[](int index);
22       //Read and change access to elements 0 through numberUsed - 1.
```

This class is the same as the one in Display 10.10, except that we have made the member variables protected instead of private.

It would be good to place this class in a namespace, but we have not done so in order to keep the example simple.

Display 14.8   Interface for the Base Class **PFArrayD** (part 2 of 2)

```
23        PFArrayD& operator =(const PFArrayD& rightSide);

24        ~PFArrayD( );
25    protected:
26        double *a; //for an array of doubles.
27        int capacity; //for the size of the array.
28        int used; //for the number of array positions currently in use.
29    };

30    #endif //PFARRAYD_H
```

Display 14.9   Implementation for the Base Class **PFArrayD** (part 1 of 2)

*This is part of the implementation
file pfarrayd.cpp. The
complete implementation is given
in Display 10.11, but what is
shown here is all you need for this
chapter.*

```
1    #include <iostream>
2    using std::cout;
3    #include "pfarrayd.h"

4    PFArrayD::PFArrayD( ) : capacity( 50), used( 0)
5    {
6        a = new double[capacity];
7    }

8    PFArrayD::PFArrayD(int size) : capacity(size), used( 0)
9    {
10        a = new double[capacity];
11    }

12    PFArrayD::PFArrayD(const PFArrayD& pfaObject)
13        :capacity(pfaObject.getCapacity( )), used(pfaObject.getNumberUsed( ))
14    {
15        a = new double[capacity];
16        for (int i =0; i < used; i++)
17            a[i] = pfaObject.a[i];
18    }

19    double& PFArrayD:: operator[] (int index)
20    {
21        if (index >= used)
22        {
23            cout << "Illegal index in PFArrayD.\n";
24            exit(0);
25        }
26        return a[index];
27    }
28
```

(continued)

Display 14.9   Implementation for the Base Class PFArrayD (part 2 of 2)

```
29   PFArrayD& PFArrayD::operator =(const PFArrayD& rightSide)
30   {
31       if (capacity != rightSide.capacity)
32       {
33           delete [] a;
34           a = new double[rightSide.capacity];
35       }

36       capacity = rightSide.capacity;
37       used = rightSide.used;
38       for (int i = 0; i < used; i++)
39           a[i] = rightSide.a[i];
40       return *this;
41   }

42   PFArrayD::~PFArrayD( )
43   {
44       delete [] a;
45   }
```

Display 14.10   Interface for the Derived Class PFArrayDBak (part 1 of 2)

```
1    //This is the header file pfarraydbak.h. This is the interface for the
2    //class PFArrayDBak. Objects of this type are partially filled arrays
3    //of doubles.
4    //This version allows the programmer to make a backup copy and restore
5    //to the last saved copy of the partially filled array.
6    #ifndef PFARRAYDBAK_H
7    #define PFARRAYDBAK_H
8    #include "pfarrayd.h"

9    class PFArrayDBak : public PFArrayD
10   {
11   public:
12       PFArrayDBak( );
13       //Initializes with a capacity of 50.

14       PFArrayDBak(int capacityValue);

15       PFArrayDBak(const PFArrayDBak& Object);

16       void backup( );
17       //Makes a backup copy of the partially filled array.

18       void restore( );
19       //Restores the partially filled array to the last saved version.
```

Display 14.10   Interface for the Derived Class **PFArrayDBak** (part 2 of 2)

```
19        //If backup has never been invoked, this empties the partially
20        //filled array.
21        PFArrayDBak& operator =(const PFArrayDBak& rightSide);

22    private:
23        ~PFArrayDBak( );
24        double *b; //for a backup of main array.
25        int usedB; //backup for inherited member variable used.
26    };

27    #endif //PFARRAYD_H
```

Display 14.11   Implementation for the Derived Class **PFArrayDBak** (part 1 of 2)

```
1    //This is the file pfarraydbak.cpp.
2    //This is the implementation of the class PFArrayDBak.
3    //The interface for the class PFArrayDBak is in the file pfarraydbak.h.
4    #include "pfarraydbak.h"
5    #include <iostream>
6    using std::cout;

7    PFArrayDBak::PFArrayDBak( )  :  PFArrayD( ), usedB( 0)
8    {
9        b = new double[capacity];
10   }

11   PFArrayDBak::PFArrayDBak(int capacityValue) :
12                                PFArrayD(capacityValue), usedB(0)
13   {
14       b = new double[capacity];
15   }

16   PFArrayDBak::PFArrayDBak(const PFArrayDBak& oldObject)
17                        : PFArrayD(oldObject), usedB(0)
18   {
19       b = new double[capacity];
20       usedB = oldObject.usedB;
21       for (int i = 0; i < usedB; i++)
22           b[i] = oldObject.b[i];
23   }

24   void PFArrayDBak::backup( )
25   {
26       usedB = used;
27       for (int i = 0; i < usedB; i++)
28           b[i] = a[i];
29   }
30
```

Note that b is a copy of the array a.
We do not want to use b = a;.

(continued)

Display 14.11 Implementation for the Derived Class PFArrayDBak (part 2 of 2)

```
31  void PFArrayDBak::restore( )
32  {
33      used = usedB;
34      for (int i = 0; i < used; i++)
35          a[i] = b[i];
36  }

37  PFArrayDBak& PFArrayDBak::operator =(const PFArrayDBak& rightSide)
38  {
39      int oldCapacity = capacity;
40      PFArrayD::operator = (rightSide) ;
41      if (oldCapacity != rightSide.capacity)
42      {
43          delete [] b;
44          b = new double [rightSide.capacity] ;
45      }

46      usedB = rightSide.usedB;
47      for (int i = 0; i < usedB; i++)
48          b[i] = rightSide.b[i] ;

49      return *this ;
50  }

51  PFArrayDBak::~PFArrayDBak( )
52  {
53      delete [] b;
54  }
```

Use a call to the base class assignment operator in order to assign to the base class member variables.

The destructor for the base class PFArrayD is called automatically, and it performs delete [ ] a;.

Display 14.12 Demonstration Program for the Class PFArrayDBak (part 1 of 3)

```
1   //Program to demonstrate the class PFArrayDBak.
2   #include <iostream>
3   #include "pfarraydbak.h"
4   using std::cin;
5   using std::cout;
6   using std::endl;

7   void testPFArrayDBak( ) ;
8   //Conducts one test of the class PFArrayDBak.

9   int main( )
10  {
11      cout << "This program tests the class PFArrayDBak.\n";
```

Display 14.12   Demonstration Program for the Class **PFArrayDBak** (part 2 of 3)

```
12        char ans;
13        do
14        {
15            testPFArrayDBak( );
16            cout << "Test again? (y/n) ";
17            cin >> ans;
18        } while ((ans == 'y') || (ans == 'Y'));

19        return 0;
20    }

21    void testPFArrayDBak( )
22    {
23        int cap;
24        cout << "Enter capacity of this super array: ";
25        cin >> cap;
26        PFArrayDBak a(cap);

27        cout << "Enter up to " << cap << " nonnegative numbers.\n";
28        cout << "Place a negative number at the end.\n";

29        double next;

30        cin >> next;
31        while ((next >= 0) && (!a.full( )))
32        {
33            a.addElement(next);
34            cin >> next;
35        }
36        if (next >= 0)
37        {
38            cout << "Could not read all numbers.\n";
39            //Clear the unread input:
40            while (next >= 0)
41                cin >> next;
42        }
43        int count = a.getNumberUsed( );
44        cout << "The following " << count
45            << " numbers read and stored:\n";
46        int index;
47        for (index = 0; index < count; index++)
48            cout << a[index] << " ";
49        cout << endl;

50        cout << "Backing up array.\n";
51        a.backup( );
```

(continued)

Display 14.12 Demonstration Program for the Class PFArrayDBak (part 3 of 3)

```
52        cout << "Emptying array.\n";
53        a.emptyArray();
54        cout << a.getNumberUsed()
55             << " numbers are now stored in the array.\n";

56        cout << "Restoring array.\n";
57        a.restore();
58        count = a.getNumberUsed();
59        cout << "The following " << count
60             << " numbers are now stored:\n";
61        for (index = 0; index < count; index++)
62            cout << a[index] << " ";
63        cout << endl;
64    }
```

Sample Dialogue

```
This program tests the class PFArrayDBak.
Enter capacity of this super array: 10
Enter up to 10 nonnegative numbers.
Place a negative number at the end.
1 2 3 4 5 -1
The following 5 numbers read and stored:
1 2 3 4 5
Backing up array.
Emptying array.
0 numbers are now stored in the array.
Restoring array.
The following 5 numbers are now stored:
1 2 3 4 5
Test again? (y/n) Y
Enter capacity of this super array: 5
Enter up to 5 nonnegative numbers.
Place a negative number at the end.
1 2 3 4 5 6 7 -1
Could not read all numbers.
The following 5 numbers read and stored:
1 2 3 4 5
Backing up array.
Emptying array.
0 numbers are now stored in the array.
Restoring array.
The following 5 numbers are now stored:
1 2 3 4 5
Test again? (y/n) n
```

PITFALL: Same Object on Both Sides of the Assignment Operator

Whenever you overload an assignment operator, always make sure your definition works when the same object occurs on both sides of the assignment operator. In most cases, you will need to make this a special case with some code of its own. An example of this was given earlier in the programming example "Partially Filled Array with Backup." ■

Self-Test Exercises

8. Suppose `Child` is a class derived from the class `Parent` and that the class `Grandchild` is a class derived from the class `Child`. This question is concerned with the constructors and destructors for the three classes `Parent`, `Child`, and `Grandchild`. When a constructor for the class `Grandchild` is invoked, what constructors are invoked and in what order? When the destructor for the class `Grandchild` is invoked, what destructors are invoked and in what order?

9. Is the following alternative definition of the default constructor for the class `PFArrayDBak` (Displays 14.10 and 14.11) legal? (The invocation of the constructor from the base class has been omitted.) Explain your answer.

```
PFArrayDBak::PFArrayDBak( )  :  usedB(0)
{
    b = new double[capacity];
}
```

EXAMPLE: Alternate Implementation of `PFArrayDBak`

At first glance it may seem that we needed to make the member variables of the base class `PFArrayD` protected in order to give the definitions of the member functions for the derived class `PFArrayDBak`. After all, many of the member functions manipulate the inherited member variables `a`, `used`, and `capacity`. The implementation we gave in Display 14.11 does indeed refer to `a`, `used`, and `capacity` by name, and so those particular definitions do depend on these member variables being protected in the base class (as opposed to private). However, we have enough thinking, we can rewrite the implementation of the derived class `PFArrayDBak` so that it works even if all the member variables in the base class `PFArrayD` are private (rather than protected).

Display 14.13 shows an alternate implementation for the class `PFArrayDBak` that works fine even if all the member variables in the base class are private instead of protected. The parts that differ from our previous implementation are shaded. Most changes are obvious, but there are a few points that merit notice.

(continued)

EXAMPLE: (continued)

Consider the member function backup. In our previous implementation (Display 14.11), we copied the array entries from a to b. Since a is now private, we cannot access it by name, but we have overloaded the array square brackets operator (operator[]) so that it applies to objects of type PFArrayD, and this operator is inherited in PFArrayDBak. We simply use operator[] with the calling object. The net effect is to copy from the array a to the array b, but we never mention the private array a by name. The code is as follows:

```
usedB = getNumberUsed( );
for (int i = 0; i < usedB; i++)
    b[i] = operator[] (i);
```

Be sure to note the syntax for calling an operator of the class being defined. If superArray is an object of the class PFArrayDBak, then in the invocation superArray.backup( ), the notation operator[](i) means superArray[i].

We could have used the notation operator[](i) in our definition of the member function restore, but it is just as easy to empty the array a with the inherited member function emptyArray and then add the backed-up elements using addElement. This way, we also set the private member variable used in the process.

With this alternate implementation, the class PFArrayDBak is used just as it was with the previous implementation. In particular, the demonstration program in Display 14.12 works exactly the same for either implementation.

Display 14.13   Alternate Implementation of PFArrayDBak   (part 1 of 2)

```
1   //This is the file pfarraydbak.cpp.
2   //This is the implementation of the class PFArrayDBak.
3   //The interface for the class PFArrayDBak is in the file pfarraydbak.h.
4   #include "pfarraydbak.h"
5   #include <iostream>
6   using std::cout;
7   PFArrayDBak::PFArrayDBak( )  :  PFArrayD( ), usedB(0)
8   {
9       b = new double[getCapacity( )];
10  }
11  PFArrayDBak::PFArrayDBak(int capacityValue)  :  PFArrayD(capacityValue),
                                                      usedB(0)
12  {
13      b = new double[getCapacity( )];
14  }
```

Display 14.13   Alternate Implementation of **PFArrayDBak** (part 2 of 2)

```
15   PFArrayDBak::PFArrayDBak(const PFArrayDBak& oldObject)
16                 : PFArrayD(oldObject), usedB(0)
17   {
18       b = new double[getCapacity( )];          This implementation works even if all the
19       usedB = oldObject.usedB;                  member variables in the base class are
20       for (int i = 0; i < usedB; i++)           private (rather than protected).
21           b[i] = oldObject.b[i];
22   }
23   void PFArrayDBak::backup( )
24   {
25       usedB = getNumberUsed( );
26       for (int i = 0; i < usedB; i++)
27           b[i] = operator[] (i);                Invocation of the square brackets
28   }                                             operator with the calling object.
29
30   void PFArrayDBak::restore( )
31   {
32       emptyArray( );
33       for (int i = 0; i < usedB; i++)
34           addElement(b[i]);
35   }
36   PFArrayDBak& PFArrayDBak::operator =(const PFArrayDBak& rightSide)
37   {
38       int oldCapacity = getCapacity( );
39       PFArrayD::operator =(rightSide);
40       if (oldCapacity != rightSide.getCapacity( ))
41       {
42           delete [] b;
43           b = new double[rightSide.getCapacity( )];
44       }
45       usedB = rightSide.usedB;
46       for (int i = 0; i < usedB; i++)
47           b[i] = rightSide.b[i];
48       return *this;
49   }
50   PFArrayDBak::~PFArrayDBak( )
51   {
52       delete [] b;
53   }
```

TIP: A Class Has Access to Private Members of All Objects of the Class

Consider the following lines from the implementation of the overloaded assignment operator given in Display 14.13:

```
usedB = rightSide.usedB;
for (int i = 0; i < usedB; i++)
    b[i] = rightSide.b[i];
```

You might object that rightSide.usedB and rightSide.b[i] are illegal since usedB and b are private member variables of some object other than the calling object. Normally that objection would be correct. However, the object rightSide is of the same type as the class being defined, so this is legal.

In the definition of a class, you can access private members of any object of the class, not just private members of the calling object. ■

TIP: "Is a" versus "Has a"

Early in this chapter we defined a derived class called HourlyEmployee using the class Employee as the base class. In such a case an object of the derived class HourlyEmployee is also of type Employee. Stated more simply, an HourlyEmployee *is an* Employee. This is an example of the **"is a" relationship** between classes. It is one way to make a more complex class from a simpler class.

"is a" relationship

Another way to make a more complex class from a simpler class is known as the "has a" relationship. For example, if you have a class Date that records a date, then you might add a date of employment to the Employee class by adding a member variable of type Date to the Employee class. In this case, we say an Employee **"has a"** Date. As another example, if we have an appropriately named class to simulate a passenger airplane, and we are defining a class to simulate a passenger airplane, then we can give the PassengerAirPlane class one or more member variables of type JetEngine. In this case, we say that a PassengerAirPlane "has a" JetEngine.

"has a" relationship

In most situations, you can make your code work with either an "is a" relationship or a "has a" relationship. It seems silly (and it is silly) to make the PassengerAirPlane class a derived class of the JetEngine class, but it can be done and can be made to work (perhaps with difficulty). Fortunately, the best programming technique is to simply follow what sounds most natural in English. It makes more sense to say "A passenger airplane has a jet engine" than it does to say "A passenger airplane is a jet engine." So, it makes better programming sense to have JetEngine as a member variable of a PassengerAirPlane class. It makes little sense to make the PassengerAirPlane class a derived class of the JetEngine class. ■

Self-Test Exercises

10. Suppose you define a function with a parameter of type PFArrayD. Can you plug in an object of the class PFArrayDBak as an argument for this function?

11. Would the following be legal for the definition of a member function to add to the class Employee (Display 14.1)? (Remember, the question is whether it is legal, not whether it is sensible.)

```
void Employee::doStuff( )
{

    Employee object("Joe", "123-45-6789");
    cout << "Hello " << object.name << endl;

}
```

Protected and Private Inheritance

So far, all our definitions of derived classes included the keyword public in the class heading, as in the following:

```
class SalariedEmployee : public Employee
{
```

This may lead you to suspect that the word public can be replaced with either protected or private to obtain a different kind of inheritance. In this case, your suspicion would be correct. However, protected and private inheritance are seldom used. We include a brief description of them for the sake of completeness.

The syntax for protected and private inheritance is illustrated by the following:

```
class SalariedEmployee : protected Employee
{
```

If you use the keyword protected for inheritance, then members that are public in the base class are protected in the derived class when they are inherited. If you use the keyword private for inheritance, then all members of the base class (public, protected, and private) are inaccessible in the derived class; in other words, all members are inherited as if they were marked private in the base class.

Moreover, with protected and private inheritance, an object of the derived class cannot be used as an argument that has the type of the base class. If Derived is derived from Base using protected or private (instead of public), then an object of type Derived is not an object of type Base; the "is a" relationship does not hold with protected and private inheritance. The idea is that with protected and private inheritance the base class is simply a tool to use in defining the derived class. Although protected and private inheritance can be made to work for some purposes, they are, as you might suspect, seldom used, and any use they do have can be achieved in other ways. The details about protected and private inheritance are summarized in Display 14.14.

Display 14.14 Public, Protected, and Private Inheritance

ACCESS SPECIFIER IN BASE CLASS	TYPE OF INHERITANCE (SPECIFIER AFTER CLASS NAME IN DERIVED CLASS DEFINITION)		
	`public`	`protected`	`private`
`public`	Public	Protected	Private (Can only be used by name in definitions of member functions and friends)
`protected`	Protected	Protected	Private (Can only be used by name in definitions of member functions and friends)
`private`	Cannot be accessed by name in the derived class	Cannot be accessed by name in the derived class	Cannot be accessed by name in the derived class

Entries show how inherited members are treated in the derived class.

Note that protected and private inheritance are not inheritance in the sense we described for public inheritance. With protected or private inheritance, the base class is only a tool to be used in the derived class.

Multiple Inheritance

It is possible for a derived class to have more than one base class. The syntax is very simple: All the base classes are listed, separated by commas. However, the possibilities for ambiguity are numerous. What if two base classes have a function with the same name and parameter types? Which is inherited? What if two base classes have a member variable with the same name? All these questions can be answered, but these and other problems make multiple inheritance a very dangerous business. Some authorities consider multiple inheritance so risky that it should not be used at all. That may or may not be too extreme a position, but it is true that you should not seriously attempt multiple inheritance until you are a very experienced C++ programmer. At that point, you will realize that you can almost always avoid multiple inheritance by using some less dangerous technique. We will not discuss multiple inheritance in this book, but leave it for more advanced references.

Chapter Summary

- Inheritance provides a tool for code reuse by deriving one class from another, adding features to the derived class.

- *Derived class* objects inherit the members of the base class, and may add members.

- If a member variable is private in a *base class*, then it cannot be accessed by name in a derived class.

- Private member functions are not inherited.

- A member function may be redefined in a derived class so that it performs differently from how it performs in the base class. The declaration for a redefined member function must be given in the class definition of the derived class, even though it is the same as in the base class.

- A protected member in the base class can be accessed by name in the definition of a member function of a publicly derived class.

- An overloaded assignment operator is not inherited. However, the assignment operator of a base class can be used in the definition of an overloaded assignment operator of a derived class.

- Constructors are not inherited. However, a constructor of a base class can be used in the definition of a constructor for a derived class.

Answers to Self-Test Exercises

1. Yes. You can plug in an object of a derived class for a parameter of the base class type. An `HourlyEmployee` is an `Employee`. A `SalariedEmployee` is an `Employee`.

2. `class SmartBut : public Smart`

```
{
public:
    SmartBut( );
    SmartBut(int newA, int newB, bool newCrazy);
    bool isCrazy( ) const;
private:
    bool crazy;
};
```

3. It is legal because `a` and `b` are marked protected in the base class `Smart`, so they can be accessed by name in a derived class. If `a` and `b` had instead been marked private, then this would be illegal.

4. The declaration for the function `getName` is not given in the definition of `SalariedEmployee` because it is not redefined in the class `SalariedEmployee`. It is inherited unchanged from the base class `Employee`.

5.
```
#include <iostream>
#include "salariedemployee.h"
using namespace std;
namespace SavitchEmployees
{
    class TitledEmployee : public SalariedEmployee
    {
    public:
        TitledEmployee( );
        TitledEmployee(string theName, string theTitle,
                       string theSsn, double theSalary);
        string getTitle( ) const;
        void setTitle(string theTitle);
        void setName(string theName);
    private:
        string title;
    };
}//SavitchEmployees
```

6.
```
namespace SavitchEmployees
{
    TitledEmployee::TitledEmployee( )
        : SalariedEmployee( ), title("No title yet")
    {
        //deliberately empty
    }

    TitledEmployee::TitledEmployee(string theName,
                         string theTitle,
                         string theSsn, double theSalary)
        : SalariedEmployee(theName, theSsn, theSalary),
          title(theTitle)
    {
        //deliberately empty
    }

    void TitledEmployee::setName(string theName)
    {
        Employee::setName(title + theName);
    }
}//SavitchEmployees
```

7. No. If you do not define an overloaded assignment operator or a copy constructor for a derived class, then a default assignment operator and a default copy constructor will be defined for the derived class. However, if the class involves pointers, dynamic arrays, or other dynamic data, then it is almost certain that neither the default assignment operator nor the default copy constructor will behave as you want them to.

8. The constructors are called in the following order: first Parent, then Child, and finally Grandchild. The destructors are called in the reverse order: first Grandchild, then Child, and finally Parent.

9. Yes, it is legal and has the same meaning as the definition given in Display 14.11. If no base class constructor is called, then the default constructor for the base class is called automatically.

10. Yes. An object of a derived class is also an object of its base class. A PFArrayDBak is a PFArrayD.

11. Yes, it is legal. One reason you might think it illegal is that name is a private member variable. However, object is in the class Employee, which is the class that is being defined, so we have access to all member variables of all objects of the class Employee.

Programming Projects

Visit www.myprogramminglab.com to complete select exercises online and get instant feedback.

1. Write a program that uses the class SalariedEmployee given in Display 14.4. Your program is to define a derived class called Administrator, which is to be derived from the class SalariedEmployee. You are allowed to change private in the base class to protected. You are to supply the following additional data and function members:

   ■ A member variable of type string that contains the administrator's title, (such as Director or Vice President).

   ■ A member variable of type string that contains the company area of responsibility (such as Production, Accounting, or Personnel).

   ■ A member variable of type string that contains the name of this administrator's immediate supervisor.

   ■ A protected member variable of type double that holds the administrator's annual salary. It is possible for you to use the existing salary member if you changed private in the base class to protected.

   ■ A member function called setSupervisor, which changes the supervisor name.

   ■ A member function for reading in an administrator's data from the keyboard.

   ■ A member function called print, which outputs the object's data to the screen.

   ■ Finally, an overloading of the member function printCheck( ) with appropriate notations on the check.

2. Add temporary, administrative, permanent, and other classifications of employees to the hierarchy from Displays 14.1, 14.3, and 14.4. Implement and test this hierarchy. Test all member functions. A user interface with a menu would be a nice touch for your test program.

3. Give the definition of a class named Doctor whose objects are records for a clinic's doctors. This class will be a derived class of the class SalariedEmployee given

in Display 14.4. A Doctor record has the doctor's specialty (such as Pediatrician, Obstetrician, General Practitioner, etc., so use type string), and office visit fee (use type double). Be sure your class has a reasonable complement of constructors and accessor methods, an overloaded assignment operator, and a copy constructor. Write a driver program to test all your methods.

4. Create a base class called Vehicle that has the manufacturer's name (type string), number of cylinders in the engine (type int), and owner (type Person given in the code that follows). Then create a class called Truck that is derived from Vehicle and has additional properties, the load capacity in tons (type double since it may contain a fractional part) and towing capacity in pounds (type int). Be sure your classes have a reasonable complement of constructors and accessor methods, an overloaded assignment operator, and a copy constructor. Write a driver program that tests all your methods.

The definition of the class Person follows. The implementation of the class is part of this programming project.

```
class Person
{
public:
    Person( );
    Person(string theName);
    Person(const Person& theObject);
    string getName( ) const;
    Person& operator=(const Person& rtSide);
    friend istream& operator >>(istream& inStream,
                                Person& personObject);
    friend ostream& operator <<(ostream& outStream,
                                const Person& personObject);
private:
    string name;
};
```

5. Give the definition of two classes, Patient and Billing, whose objects are records for a clinic. Patient will be derived from the class Person given in Programming Project 14.4. A Patient record has the patient's name (inherited from the class Person) and primary physician, of type Doctor defined in Programming Project 14.3. A Billing object will contain a Patient object and a Doctor object, and an amount due of type double. Be sure your classes have a reasonable complement of constructors and accessor methods, an overloaded assignment operator, and a copy constructor. First write a driver program to test all your methods, then write a test program that creates at least two patients, at least two doctors, at least two Billing records, then prints out the total income from the Billing records.

6. Define a class named Payment that contains a member variable of type float that stores the amount of the payment and appropriate accessor and mutator functions. Also create a member function named paymentDetails that outputs an English sentence describing the amount of the payment.

Next, define a class named CashPayment that is derived from Payment. This class should redefine the paymentDetails function to indicate that the payment is in cash. Include appropriate constructor(s).

Define a class named CreditCardPayment that is derived from Payment. This class should contain member variables for the name on the card, expiration date, and credit card number. Include appropriate constructor(s). Finally, redefine the paymentDetails function to include all credit card information in the printout.

Create a main function that creates at least two CashPayment and two CreditCardPayment objects with different values and calls to paymentDetails for each.

7. Define a class named Document that contains a member variable of type string named text that stores any textual content for the document. Create a function named getText that returns the text field, a way to set this value, and an overloaded assignment operator.

Next, define a class for Email that is derived from Document and that includes member variables for the sender, recipient, and title of an e-mail message. Implement appropriate accessor and mutator functions. The body of the e-mail message should be stored in the inherited variable text. Also overload the assignment operator for this class.

Similarly, define a class for File that is derived from Document and that includes a member variable for the pathname. Implement appropriate accessor and mutator functions for the pathname and overload the assignment operator.

Finally, create several sample objects of type Email and File in your main function. Test your objects by passing them to the following subroutine, which will return true if the object contains the specified keyword in the text property.

```
bool ContainsKeyword(const Document& docObject, string keyword)
{
    if (docObject.getText().find(keyword) != string::npos)
        return true;

    return false;
}
```

For example, you might test to see whether an e-mail message contains the text "c++" with the call ContainsKeyword(emailObj, "c++");.

8. Create a class for a simple blog. The owner of the blog should be able to (a) post a new message, (b) numerically list and display all messages, and (c) select a specific message and delete it.

Viewers of the blog should only be able to numerically list and display all posted messages.

Create a class Viewer and a class Owner that uses inheritance to help implement the blog functionality. Store the data messages using any format you like (a vector of type string may be easiest). A menu function should be implemented for each class that outputs the legal choices for the type of user. To test your classes, the main function of the program should allow the user to invoke the menus from the Viewer and Owner objects.

VideoNote
**Solution to
Programming
Project 14.7**

9. Suppose that you are creating a fantasy role-playing game. In this game, we have four different types of creatures: humans, cyberdemons, balrogs, and elves. To represent one of these creatures, we might define a Creature class as follows:

```
class Creature
{
    private:
        int type;         // 0 human, 1 cyberdemon, 2 balrog, 3 elf
        int strength;     // How much damage we can inflict
        int hitpoints;    // How much damage we can sustain
        string getSpecies();  // Returns type of species

    public:
        Creature();
        // Initialize to human, 10 strength, 10 hit points

        Creature(int newType, int newStrength, int newHit);
        // Initialize creature to new type, strength, hit points

        // Also add appropriate accessor and mutator functions
        // for type, strength, and hit points

        int getDamage();
        // Returns amount of damage this creature
        // inflicts in one round of combat
};
```

Here is an implementation of the getSpecies() function:

```
string Creature::getSpecies()
{
    switch (type)
    {
        case 0: return "Human";
        case 1: return "Cyberdemon";
        case 2: return "Balrog";
        case 3: return "Elf";
    }
    return "Unknown";
}
```

The getDamage() function outputs and returns the damage this creature can inflict in one round of combat. The rules for calculating the damage are as follows:

- Every creature inflicts damage that is a random number r, where $0 < r \leq$ strength.

- Demons have a 5% chance of inflicting a demonic attack, which is an additional 50 damage points. Balrogs and Cyberdemons are demons.

- Elves have a 10% chance to inflict a magical attack that doubles the normal amount of damage.
- Balrogs are very fast, so they get to attack twice.

An implementation of getDamage( ) is given here:

```cpp
int Creature::getDamage( )
{
    int damage;

    // All creatures inflict damage, which is a
    // random number up to their strength
    damage = (rand( ) % strength) + 1;
    cout << getSpecies( ) << " attacks for " <<
        damage << " points!" << endl;

    // Demons can inflict damage of 50 with a 5% chance
    if ((type = 2) || (type == 1))
    {
        if ((rand( ) % 100) < 5)
        {
            damage = damage + 50;
            cout << "Demonic attack inflicts 50 "
                << " additional damage points!" << endl;
        }
    }

    // Elves inflict double magical damage with a 10% chance
    if (type == 3)
    {
        if ((rand( ) % 10)==0)
        {
            cout << "Magical attack inflicts " << damage <<
                " additional damage points!" << endl;
            damage = damage * 2;
        }
    }

    // Balrogs are so fast they get to attack twice
    if (type == 2)
    {
        int damage2 = (rand( ) % strength) + 1;
        cout << "Balrog speed attack inflicts " << damage2 <<
            " additional damage points!" << endl;
        damage = damage + damage2;
    }

    return damage;
}
```

One problem with this implementation is that it is unwieldy to add new creatures. Rewrite the class to use inheritance, which will eliminate the need for the variable type. The `Creature` class should be the base class. The classes `Demon`, `Elf`, and `Human` should be derived from `Creature`. The classes `Cyberdemon` and `Balrog` should be derived from `Demon`. You will need to rewrite the `getSpecies()` and `getDamage()` functions so they are appropriate for each class.

For example, the `getDamage()` function in each class should only compute the damage appropriate for that object. The total damage is then calculated by combining the results of `getDamage()` at each level of the inheritance hierarchy. As an example, invoking `getDamage()` for a `Balrog` object should invoke `getDamage()` for the `Demon` object, which should invoke `getDamage()` for the `Creature` object. This will compute the basic damage that all creatures inflict, followed by the random 5% damage that demons inflict, followed by the double damage that balrogs inflict.

Also include mutator and accessor functions for the private variables. Write a `main` function that contains a driver to test your classes. It should create an object for each type of creature and repeatedly outputs the results of `getDamage()`.

10. Define a `Pet` class that stores the pet's name, age, and weight. Add appropriate constructors, accessor functions, and mutator functions. Also define a function named `getLifespan` that returns a string with the value "unknown lifespan."

Next, define a `Dog` class that is derived from `Pet`. The `Dog` class should have a private member variable named `breed` that stores the breed of the dog. Add mutator and accessor functions for the breed variable and appropriate constructors. Redefine the `getLifespan` function to return "Approximately 7 years" if the dog's weight is over 100 pounds and "Approximately 13 years" if the dog's weight is under 100 pounds.

Next, define a `Rock` class that is derived from `Pet`. Redefine the `getLifespan` function to return "Thousands of years".

Finally, write a test program that creates instances of pet rocks and pet dogs that exercise the inherited and redefined functions.

Polymorphism and Virtual Functions

15.1 VIRTUAL FUNCTION BASICS 662

15.2 POINTERS AND VIRTUAL FUNCTIONS 674

I did it my way.

FRANK SINATRA

Introduction

Polymorphism refers to the ability to associate many meanings to one function name by means of a special mechanism known as *virtual functions* or *late binding*. Polymorphism is one of the fundamental mechanisms of a popular and powerful programming philosophy known as *object-oriented programming*. Wow, lots of fancy words! This chapter will explain them.

Section 15.1 does not require the material from Chapters 10 (pointers and dynamic arrays), 12 (file I/O), or 13 (recursion), but does require an understanding of Chapter 14 (inheritance). Section 15.2 does not require the material from Chapters 12 (file I/O) or 13 (recursion), but does require the material from Chapter 10 (pointers and dynamic arrays).

15.1 Virtual Function Basics

virtual adj. 1. Existing or resulting in essence or effect though not in actual fact, form, or name.

The American Heritage Dictionary of the English Language, Third Edition

A *virtual* function is so named because it may, in a sense to be made clear in this chapter, be used before it is defined. Virtual functions will prove to be another tool for software reuse.

Late Binding

Virtual functions are best explained by an example. Suppose you are designing software for a graphics package that has classes for several kinds of figures, such as rectangles, circles, ovals, and so forth. Each figure might be an object of a different class. For example, the Rectangle class might have member variables for a height, width, and center point, while the Circle class might have member variables for a center point and a radius. In a well-designed programming project, all of these classes would probably be descendants of a single parent class called, for example, Figure. Now, suppose you want a function to draw a figure on the screen. To draw a circle, you need different instructions from those you need to draw a rectangle. However, because the functions belong to the classes, they can all be called draw. If r is a Rectangle object and c is a `Circle` object, then `r.draw()` and `c.draw()` can be functions implemented with different code. All this is not news, but now we move on to something new: virtual functions defined in the parent class `Figure`.

The parent class `Figure` may have functions that apply to all figures. For example, it might have a function called `center` that moves a figure to the center of the screen by erasing it and then redrawing it in the center of the screen. The function `Figure::center` might use the function `draw` to redraw the figure in the center of the screen. When you think of using the inherited function `center` with figures of the classes `Rectangle` and `Circle`, you begin to see that there are complications here.

To make the point clear and more dramatic, let's suppose that the class `Figure` is already written and in use and that at some later time you add a class for a brand new kind of figure—say, the class `Triangle`. Now, `Triangle` can be a derived class of the class `Figure`, and so the function `center` will be inherited from the class `Figure`. The function `center` should therefore apply to (and perform correctly for) all `Triangle`s. But there is a complication. The function `center` uses `draw`, and the function `draw` is different for each type of figure. The inherited function `center` (if nothing special is done) will use the definition of the function `draw` given in the class `Figure`, and that function `draw` does not work correctly for `Triangle`s. We want the inherited member function `center` to use the function `Triangle::draw` rather than the function `Figure::draw`. But the class `Triangle`—and therefore the function `Triangle::draw`—was not even written when the function `center` (defined in the class `Figure`) was written and compiled! How can the function `center` possibly work correctly for `Triangle`s? The compiler did not know anything about `Triangle::draw` at the time that `center` was compiled! The answer is that it can apply provided `draw` is a *virtual function*.

virtual function

When you make a function **virtual**, you are telling the compiler "I do not know how this function is implemented. Wait until it is used in a program, and then get the implementation from the object instance." The technique of waiting until run time to determine the implementation of a procedure is often called **late binding** or **dynamic binding**. Virtual functions are the way C++ provides late binding. But, this is enough introduction. We need an example to make this come alive (and to teach you how to use virtual functions in your programs). To explain the details of virtual functions in C++, we will use a simplified example from an application area other than drawing figures.

**late binding
or dynamic
binding**

Virtual Functions in C++

Suppose you are designing a record-keeping program for an automobile parts store. You want to make the program versatile, but you are not sure you can account for all possible situations. For example, you want to keep track of sales, but you cannot anticipate all types of sales. At first, there will only be regular sales to retail customers who go to the store to buy one particular part. However, later you may want to add sales with discounts or mail order sales with a shipping charge. All these sales will be for an item with a basic price and ultimately will produce some bill. For a simple sale, the bill is just the basic price, but if you later add discounts, then some kinds of bills will also depend on the size of the discount. Your program will need to compute daily gross sales, which intuitively should just be the sum of all the individual sales bills. You may also want to calculate the largest and smallest sales of the day or the average sale for the day. All of these can be calculated from the individual bills, but many of the functions for computing the bills will not be added until later, when you decide what types of sales you will be dealing with. To accommodate this, we make the function for computing the bill a virtual function. (For simplicity in this first example, we assume that each sale is for just one item. Although, with derived classes and virtual functions we could account for sales of multiple items, but will not do that here.)

Displays 15.1 and 15.2 contain the interface and implementation for the class Sale. All types of sales will be derived classes of the class Sale. The class Sale corresponds to simple sales of a single item with no added discounts or charges. Notice the reserved word virtual in the declaration for the member function bill (Display 15.1). Notice (Display 15.2) that the member function savings and the overloaded operator, <, each use the function bill. Since bill is declared to be a virtual function, we can

Display 15.1   Interface for the Base Class Sale

```
1   //This is the header file sale.h.
2   //This is the interface for the class Sale.
3   //Sale is a class for simple sales.
4
5   #ifndef SALE_H
6   #define SALE_H
7
8   namespace SavitchSale
9   {
10      class Sale
11      {
12      public:
13          Sale( );
14          Sale(double thePrice);
15          double getPrice( ) const;
16          void setPrice(double newPrice);
17          virtual double bill( ) const;
18          double savings(const Sale& other) const;
19          //Returns the savings if you buy other instead of the calling object.
20          bool operator < (const Sale& first, const Sale& second);
21          //Compares two sales to see which is larger.
22      private:
23          double price;
24      };
25  }//SavitchSale
26  #endif // SALE_H
```

Display 15.2   Implementation of the Base Class Sale (part 1 of 2)

```
1   //This is the file sale.cpp.
2   //This is the implementation for the class Sale.
3   //The interface for the class Sale is in the file sale.h.
4
5   #include <iostream>
6   #include "sale.h"
7   using std::cout;
8
9   namespace SavitchSale
10  {
11      Sale::Sale( ) : price(0)
12      {
13          //Intentionally empty
14      }
15      Sale::Sale(double thePrice)
16      {
17          if (thePrice >= 0)
18              price = thePrice;
19          else
20          {
21              cout << "Error: Cannot have a negative price!\n";
22              exit(1);
23          }
24      }
25      double Sale::bill( ) const
26      {
27          return price;
28      }
29      double Sale::getPrice( ) const
30      {
31          return price;
32      }
33      void Sale::setPrice(double newPrice)
34      {
35          if (newPrice >= 0)
36              price = newPrice;
37          else
38          {
39              cout << "Error: Cannot have a negative price!\n";
40              exit(1);
41          }
42      }
43      double Sale::savings(const Sale&other) const
44      {
45          return (bill( ) - other.bill( ));
46      }
```

(continued)

Display 15.2   Implementation of the Base Class Sale (part 2 of 2)

```
47      bool operator < (const Sale& first, const Sale& second)
48      {
49          return (first.bill( ) < second.bill( ));
50      }
51  }//SavitchSale
```

later define derived classes of the class Sale and define their versions of the member function bill; the definitions of the member function savings and the overloaded operator, <, which we gave with the class Sale, will use the version of the member function bill that corresponds to the object of the derived class.

For example, Displays 15.3 and 15.4 show the derived class DiscountSale. Notice that the class DiscountSale requires a different definition for its version of the member function bill. Nonetheless, when the member function savings and the overloaded operator, <, are used with an object of the class DiscountSale, they will use the version of the function bill that was given with the class DiscountSale. This is indeed a pretty fancy trick for C++ to pull off. Consider the function call d1.savings(d2) for objects d1 and d2 of the class DiscountSale. The definition of the function savings (even for an object of the class DiscountSale) is given in the implementation file for the base class Sale, which was compiled before we even thought of the class DiscountSale. Yet, in the function call d1.savings(d2), the line that calls the function bill knows enough to use the definition of the function bill given for the class DiscountSale.

How does this work? In order to write C++ programs you can just assume it happens by magic, but the real explanation was given in the introduction to this section. When you label a function virtual, you are telling the C++ environment "Wait until this function is used in a program, and then get the implementation corresponding to the calling object."

Display 15.5 gives a sample program that illustrates how the virtual function bill and the functions that use bill work in a complete program.

Display 15.3   Interface for the Derived Class DiscountSale (part 1 of 2)

```
1   //This is the file discountsale.h.
2   //This is the interface for the class DiscountSale.
3
4   #ifndef DISCOUNTSALE_H
5   #define DISCOUNTSALE_H
6   #include "sale.h"
7
8   namespace SavitchSale
```

Display 15.3   Interface for the Derived Class `DiscountSale` (part 2 of 2)

```
8   {
9       class DiscountSale : public Sale
10      {
11      public:
12          DiscountSale( );
13          DiscountSale(double thePrice, double theDiscount);
14          //Discount is expressed as a percentage of the price.
15          //A negative discount is a price increase.
16          double getDiscount( ) const;
17          void setDiscount(double newDiscount);
18          double bill( ) const;      Since bill was declared virtual in the base class,
19      private:                       it is automatically virtual in the derived class
20          double discount;           DiscountSale. You can add the modifier virtual
                                       to the declaration of bill or omit it as here; in either
                                       case bill is virtual in the class DiscountSale.
                                       (We prefer to include the word virtual in all virtual
                                       function declarations, even if it is not required. We
21      };                             omitted it here to illustrate that it is not required.)
22  }//SavitchSale
23  #endif //DISCOUNTSALE_H
```

Display 15.4   Implementation for the Derived Class `DiscountSale` (part 1 of 2)

```
1   //This is the implementation for the class DiscountSale.
2   //This is the file discountsale.cpp.
3   //The interface for the class DiscountSale is in the header file
4   //discountsale.h.
5   #include "discountsale.h"
6
7   namespace SavitchSale
8   {
9       DiscountSale::DiscountSale( ) : Sale( ), discount(0)
10      {
11          //Intentionally empty
12      }
13      DiscountSale::DiscountSale(double thePrice, double theDiscount)
14                  : Sale(thePrice), discount(theDiscount)
15      {
16          //Intentionally empty
17      }
18      double DiscountSale::getDiscount( ) const
19      {
20          return discount;
21      }
```

(continued)

Display 15.4   Implementation for the Derived Class DiscountSale (part 2 of 2)

```
22    void DiscountSale::setDiscount(double newDiscount)
23    {
24        discount = newDiscount;
25    }

26    double DiscountSale::bill( ) const
27    {
28        double fraction = discount / 100;
29        return (1 - fraction) * getPrice( );
30    }

31    }//SavitchSale
```

You do not repeat the qualifier virtual in the function definition.

Display 15.5   Use of a Virtual Function

```
1    //Demonstrates the performance of the virtual function bill.
2    #include <iostream>
3    #include "sale.h"    //Not really needed, but safe due to ifndef.
4    #include "discountsale.h"
5    using std::cout;
6    using std::endl;
7    using std::ios;
8    using namespace SavitchSale;
9
10   int main( )
11   {
12       Sale simple(10.00);//One item at  $10.00.
13       DiscountSale discount(11.00, 10);
                      //One item at $11.00 with a 10% discount
14       cout.setf(ios::fixed);
15       cout.setf(ios::showpoint);
16       cout.precision(2);
17       if (discount < simple)
18       {
19           cout << "Discounted item is cheaper.\n";
20           cout << "Savings is $" << simple.savings(discount) << endl;
21       }
22       else
23           cout << "Discounted item is not cheaper.\n";
24       return 0;
25   }
```

The objects discount and simple use different code for the member function bill when the less-than comparison is made. Similar remarks apply to savings.

Sample Dialogue

```
Discounted item is cheaper.
Savings is $0.10
```

Virtual Function

A virtual function is indicated by including the modifier virtual in the member function declaration (which is given in the definition of the class).

If a function is virtual and a new definition of the function is given in a derived class, then for any object of the derived class, that object will always use the definition of the virtual function that was given in the derived class, even if the virtual function is used indirectly by being invoked in the definition of an inherited function. This method of deciding which definition of a virtual function to use is known as *late binding*.

Polymorphism

Polymorphism refers to the ability to associate many meanings to one function name by means of the late-binding mechanism. Thus, polymorphism, late binding, and virtual functions are really all the same topic.

Overriding

When a virtual function definition is changed in a derived class, programmers often say the function definition is **overridden**. In the C++ literature, a distinction is usually made between the terms *redefined* and *overridden*. Both terms refer to changing the definition of the function in a derived class. If the function is a virtual function, this act is called *overriding*. If the function is not a virtual function, it is called *redefining*. This may seem like a silly distinction to you the programmer, since you do the same thing in both cases, but the two cases are treated differently by the compiler.

TIP: The Virtual Property Is Inherited

The property of being a virtual function is inherited. For example, since bill was declared to be virtual in the base class Sale (Display 15.1), the function bill is automatically virtual in the derived class DiscountSale (Display 15.3). So, the following two declarations of the member function bill would be equivalent in the definition of the derived class DiscountSale:

```
double bill( ) const;
virtual double bill( ) const;
```

Thus, if SuperDiscountSale is a derived class of the class DiscountSale that inherits the function savings, and if the function bill is given a new definition for the class SuperDiscountSale, then all objects of the class SuperDiscountSale will use the definition of the function bill given in the definition of the class SuperDiscountSale. Even the inherited function savings (which includes a call to the function bill) will use the definition of bill given in SuperDiscountSale whenever the calling object is in the class SuperDiscountSale. ■

CHAPTER 15

TIP: When to Use a Virtual Function

There are clear advantages to using virtual functions and so far we have not seen any clear disadvantages. So, why not make all member functions virtual? In fact, why not define the C++ compiler so that (like some other languages, such as Java) all member functions are automatically virtual? The answer is that there is overhead to making a function virtual. Doing so uses more storage and makes your program run slower than if the function were not virtual. That is why the designers of C++ gave the programmer control over which member functions are virtual and which are not. If you expect to need the advantages of a virtual member function, then make that member function virtual. If you do not expect to need the advantages of a virtual function, then your program will run more efficiently if you do not make the member function virtual. ∎

Self-Test Exercises

1. Explain the difference among the terms *virtual function*, *late binding*, and *polymorphism*.

2. Suppose you modify the definitions of the class `Sale` (Display 15.1) by deleting the reserved word `virtual`. How would that change the output of the program in Display 15.5?

PITFALL: Omitting the Definition of a Virtual Member Function

It is wise to develop incrementally. This means code a little, then test a little, then code a little more and test a little more, and so forth. However, if you try to compile classes with `virtual` member functions but do not implement each member, you may run into some very-hard-to-understand error messages, even if you do not call the undefined member functions!

If any virtual member functions are not implemented before compiling, the compilation fails with error messages similar to this:

```
Undefined reference to Class_Name virtual table.
```

Even if there is *no derived class* and there is *only one* virtual member function, but that function does not have a definition, this kind of message still occurs.

What makes the error messages very hard to decipher is that without definitions for the functions declared `virtual`, there will be further error messages complaining about an undefined reference to default constructors, even if these constructors really are already defined.

Of course, you may use some trivial definition for a virtual function until you are ready to define the "real" version of the function.

This caution does not apply to *pure virtual functions*, which we discuss in the next section. As you will see, pure virtual functions are not supposed to have a definition. ∎

Abstract Classes and Pure Virtual Functions

You can encounter situations in which you want to have a class to use as a base class for a number of other classes, but you do not have any meaningful definition to give to one or more of its member functions. When we introduced virtual functions we discussed one such scenario. Let's review it now.

Suppose you are designing software for a graphics package that has classes for several kinds of figures, such as rectangles, circles, ovals, and so forth. Each figure might be an object of a different class, such as the Rectangle class or the Circle class. In a well-designed programming project, all of these classes would probably be descendants of a single parent class called, for example, Figure. Now, suppose you want a function to draw a figure on the screen. To draw a circle, you need different instructions from those you need to draw a rectangle. So, each class needs to have a different function to draw its kind of figure. If r is a Rectangle object and c is a Circle object, then r.draw() and c.draw() can be functions implemented with different code.

The parent class Figure may have a function called center that moves a figure to the center of the screen by erasing it and then redrawing it in the center of the screen. The function Figure::center might use the function draw to redraw the figure in the center of the screen. By making the member function draw a virtual function, you can write the code for the member function Figure::center in the class Figure and know that when it is used for a derived class—say, Circle—the definition of draw in the class Circle will be the definition used. You never plan to create an object of type Figure. You intend only to create objects of the derived classes, such as Circle and Rectangle. So, the definition that you give to Figure::draw will never be used. However, based only on what we covered so far, you would still need to give a definition for Figure::draw, even though it could be trivial.

pure virtual function

If you make the member function Figure::draw a **pure virtual function**, then you do not need to give any definition to that member function. The way to make a member function into a pure virtual function is to mark it as virtual and to add the annotation = 0 to the member function declaration, as in the following example:

```
virtual void draw() = 0;
```

Any kind of member can be made a pure virtual function. It need not be a void function with no parameters as in our example.

abstract class

A class with one or more pure virtual functions is called an **abstract class**. An abstract class can only be used as a base class to derive other classes. You cannot create objects of an abstract class, since it is not a complete class definition. An abstract class is a partial class definition because it can contain other member functions that are not pure virtual functions. An abstract class is also a type, so you can write code with parameters of the abstract class type and it will apply to all objects of classes that are descendants of the abstract class.

If you derive a class from an abstract class, the derived class will itself be an abstract class unless you provide definitions for all the inherited pure virtual functions (and also do not introduce any new pure virtual functions). If you do provide definitions for all the inherited pure virtual functions (and also do not introduce any new pure virtual functions), the resulting class is not an abstract class, which means you can create objects of the class.

EXAMPLE: An Abstract Class

In Display 15.6, we have slightly rewritten the class Employee from Display 14.1. This time we have made Employee an abstract class. The following line (highlighted in Display 15.6) is the only thing that is different from our previous definition of Employee (Display 14.1):

```
virtual void printCheck( ) const = 0;
```

The word virtual and the = 0 in the member function heading tell the compiler that this is a pure virtual function and that therefore the class Employee is now an abstract class. The implementation for the class Employee includes no definition for the class Employee::printCheck, but otherwise the implementation of the class Employee is the same as before (that is, the same as in Display 14.2).

It makes sense that there is no definition for the member function Employee:: printCheck, since you do not know what kind of check to write until you know with what kind of employee you are dealing. In our first definition of the class Employee (Displays 14.1 and 14.2), we were forced to give a definition to Employee::printCheck and so gave one that output an error message saying that the function should not be invoked. We now have a more elegant solution. By making Employee::printCheck a pure virtual function, we have set things up so that the compiler will enforce the ban against invoking Employee::printCheck.

Display 15.6   Interface for the Abstract Class Employee (part 1 of 2)

```
1   //This is the header file employee.h.
2   //This is the interface for the abstract class Employee.
3
4   #ifndef EMPLOYEE_H
5   #define EMPLOYEE_H
6
7   #include <string>
8   using std::string;
9
10  namespace SavitchEmployees
11  {
12      class Employee
13      {
14      public:
15          Employee( );
16          Employee(const string& theName, const string& theSsn);
17          string getName( ) const;
18          string getSsn( ) const;
          double getNetPay( ) const;
          void setName(const string& newName);
```

This is an improved version of the class Employee given in Display 14.1.

The implementation for this class is the same as in Display 14.2, except that no definition is given for the member function printCheck().

Display 15.6   Interface for the Abstract Class `Employee` (part 2 of 2)

```
19        void setSsn(const string& newSsn);
20        void setNetPay(double newNetPay);
21        virtual void printCheck( ) const = 0;    ← A pure virtual function.
22    private:
23        string name;
24        string ssn;
25        double netPay;
26    };
27  }//SavitchEmployees
28  #endif //EMPLOYEE_H
```

Self-Test Exercises

3. Is it legal to have an abstract class in which all member functions are pure virtual functions?

4. Given the definition of the class `Employee` in Display 15.6, which of the following are legal?

a. `Employee joe;`
   `joe = Employee( );`

b. `class HourlyEmployee :  public Employee`
   `{`
   `public:`
   `    HourlyEmployee( );`
   `<Some more legal member function definitions, none of which are`
   `pure virtual functions.>`
   `private:`
   `    double wageRate;`
   `    double hours;`
   `};`
   `    int main( )`
   `    {`
   `    Employee joe;`
   `    joe = HourlyEmployee( );`

c. `bool isBossOf(const Employee& e1,  const Employee& e2);`

15.2   Pointers and Virtual Functions

Beware lest you lose the substance by grasping at the shadow.

AESOP, *The Dog and the Shadow*

This section explores some of the more subtle points about virtual functions. To understand this material, you need to have covered the material on pointers given in Chapter 10.

Virtual Functions and Extended Type Compatibility

If Derived is a derived class of the base class Base, then you can assign an object of type Derived to a variable (or parameter) of type Base, but not the other way around. If you consider a concrete example, this becomes sensible. For example, DiscountSale is a derived class of Sale (Displays 15.1 and 15.3). You can assign an object of the class DiscountSale to a variable of type Sale, since a DiscountSale is a Sale. However, you cannot do the reverse assignment, since a Sale is not necessarily a DiscountSale. The fact that you can assign an object of a derived class to a variable (or parameter) of its base class is critically important for reuse of code via inheritance. However, it does have its problems.

For example, suppose a program or unit contains the following class definitions:

```
class Pet
{
public:
    string name;
    virtual void print( ) const;
};

class Dog : public Pet
{
public:
    string breed;
    virtual void print( ) const; //keyword virtual not needed,
                                 //but put here for clarity.
};

Dog vdog;
Pet vpet;
```

Now concentrate on the data members, name and breed. (To keep this example simple, we have made the member variables public. In a real application, they should be private and have functions to manipulate them.)

Anything that is a `Dog` is also a `Pet`. It would seem to make sense to allow programs to consider values of type `Dog` to also be values of type `Pet`, and hence the following should be allowed:

```
vdog.name = "Tiny";
vdog.breed = "Great Dane";
vpet = vdog;
```

slicing problem

C++ does allow this sort of assignment. You may assign a value, such as the value of vdog, to a variable of a parent type, such as vpet, but you are not allowed to perform the reverse assignment. Although the preceding assignment is allowed, the value that is assigned to the variable vpet loses its breed field. This is called the **slicing problem**. The following attempted access will produce an error message:

```
cout << vpet.breed;
    // Illegal: class Pet has no member named breed
```

You can argue that this makes sense, since once a `Dog` is moved to a variable of type `Pet` it should be treated like any other `Pet` and not have properties peculiar to `Dogs`. This makes for a lively philosophical debate, but it is usually just a nuisance when programming. The dog named Tiny is still a Great Dane, and we would like to refer to its breed, even if we treated it as a `Pet` someplace along the way.

Fortunately, C++ does offer us a way to treat a `Dog` as a `Pet` without throwing away the name of the breed. To do this, we use pointers to dynamic variables.

Suppose we add the following declarations:

```
Pet *ppet;
Dog *pdog;
```

If we use pointers and dynamic variables, we can treat Tiny as a `Pet` without losing his breed. The following is allowed.[1]

```
pdog = new Dog;
pdog->name = "Tiny";
pdog->breed = "Great Dane";
ppet = pdog;
```

Moreover, we can still access the breed field of the node pointed to by ppet. Suppose that

```
Dog::print( ) const;
```

has been defined as follows:

```
void Dog::print( ) const
{
    cout << "name:" << name << endl;
    cout << "breed:" << breed << endl;
}
```

---
[1]If you are not familiar with the `->` operator, see the subsection of Chapter 10 entitled "The `->` Operator."

The statement

```
ppet->print( );
```

will cause the following to be printed on the screen:

```
name: Tiny
breed: Great Dane
```

This nice output happens by virtue of the fact that print( ) is a virtual member function. (No pun intended.) We have included test code in Display 15.7.

Display 15.7   Defeating the Slicing Problem (part 1 of 2)

```
 1   //Program to illustrate use of a virtual function to defeat the slicing
 2   //problem.
 3   #include <string>
 4   #include <iostream>
 5   using std::string;
 6   using std::cout;
 7   using std::endl;

 8   class Pet
 9   {
10   public:
11       string name;
12       virtual void print( ) const;
13   };

14   class Dog : public Pet
15   {
16   public:
17       string breed;
18       virtual void print( ) const;
19   };

20   int main( )
21   {
22       Dog vdog;
23       Pet vpet;
24       vdog.name = "Tiny";
25       vdog.breed = "Great Dane";
26       vpet = vdog;
27       cout << "The slicing problem:\n";
28       //vpet.breed; is illegal since class Pet has no member named breed.
29       vpet.print( );
30       cout << "Note that it was print from Pet that was invoked.\n";
```

We have made the member variables public to keep the example simple. In a real application, they should be private and accessed via member functions.

Keyword virtual is not needed here, but we inserted it for clarity.

Display 15.7   Defeating the Slicing Problem (part 2 of 2)

```
31      cout << "The slicing problem defeated:\n";
32      Pet *ppet;
33      Dog *pdog;
34      pdog = new Dog;
35      pdog->name = "Tiny";
36      pdog->breed = "Great Dane";
37      ppet = pdog;
38      ppet->print( );
39      pdog->print( );
```

These two print the same output:

name: Tiny
breed: Great Dane

```
40      //The following, which accesses member variables directly
41      //rather than via virtual functions, would produce an error:
42      //cout << "name: " << ppet->name << " breed: "
43      //        << ppet->breed << endl;
44      //It generates an error message saying
45      //class Pet has no member named breed.

46      return 0;
47  }

48  void Dog::print( ) const
49  {
50      cout << "name: " << name << endl;
51      cout << "breed: " << breed << endl;
52  }

53  void Pet::print( ) const
54  {
55      cout << "name: " << name << endl;
56  }
```

Note that no breed is mentioned.

Sample Dialogue

```
The slicing problem:
name: Tiny
Note that it was print from Pet that was invoked.
The slicing problem defeated:
name: Tiny
breed: Great Dane
name: Tiny
breed: Great Dane
```

Object-oriented programming with dynamic variables is a very different way of viewing programming. This can all be bewildering at first. It will help if you keep two simple rules in mind:

1. If the domain type of the pointer pAncestor is an ancestor class for the domain type of the pointer pDescendant, then the following assignment of pointers is allowed:

```
pAncestor = pDescendant;
```

Moreover, none of the data members or member functions of the dynamic variable being pointed to by pDescendant will be lost.

2. Although all the extra fields of the dynamic variable are there, you will need virtual member functions to access them.

PITFALL: The Slicing Problem

Although it is legal to assign a derived class object to a base class variable, assigning a derived class object to a base class object slices off data. Any data members in the derived class object that are not also in the base class object will be lost in the assignment, and any member functions that are not defined in the base class are similarly unavailable to the resulting base class object.

For example, if Dog is a derived class of Pet, then the following is legal:

```
Dog vdog;
Pet vpet;
vpet = vdog;
```

However, vpet cannot be a calling object for a member function from Dog unless the function is also a member function of Pet, and all the member variables of vdog that are not inherited from the class Pet are lost. This is the slicing problem.

Note that simply making a member function virtual does not defeat the slicing problem. Note the following code from Display 15.7:

```
Dog vdog;
Pet vpet;

vdog.name = "Tiny";
vdog.breed = "Great Dane";
vpet = vdog;
  . . .
vpet.print ( );
```

Although the object in vdog is of type Dog, when vdog is assigned to the variable vpet (of type Pet) it becomes an object of type Pet. So, vpet.print ( ) invokes the version of print ( ) defined in Pet, not the version defined in Dog. This happens despite the fact that print ( ) is virtual. In order to defeat the slicing problem, the function must be virtual and you must use pointers and dynamic variables. ∎

Self-Test Exercises

5. Why can't you assign a base class object to a derived class variable?

6. What is the problem with the (legal) assignment of a derived class object to a base class variable?

7. Suppose the base class and the derived class each has a member function with the same signature. When you have a base class pointer to a derived class object and call a function member through the pointer, discuss what determines which function is actually called, the base class member function or the derived class member function.

TIP: Make Destructors Virtual

It is a good policy to always make destructors virtual, but before we explain why this is a good policy we need to say a word or two about how destructors and pointers interact and about what it means for a destructor to be virtual.

Consider the following code, where SomeClass is a class with a destructor that is not virtual:

```
SomeClass *p = new SomeClass;
    .
    .
    .
delete p;
```

When delete is invoked with p, the destructor of the class SomeClass is automatically invoked. Now, let's see what happens when a destructor is marked virtual.

The easiest way to describe how destructors interact with the virtual function mechanism is that destructors are treated as if all destructors had the same name (even though they do not really have the same name). For example, suppose Derived is a derived class of the class Base and that the destructor in the class Base is marked virtual. Now consider the following code:

```
Base *pBase = new Derived;
    .
    .
    .
delete pBase;
```

When delete is invoked with pBase, a destructor is called. Since the destructor in the class Base was marked virtual and the object pointed to is of type Derived, the destructor for the class Derived is called (and it in turn calls the destructor for the class Base). If the destructor in the class Base had not been declared as virtual, then only the destructor in the class Base would be called.

Another point to keep in mind is that when a destructor is marked virtual, then all destructors of derived classes are automatically virtual (whether or not they are marked virtual). Again, this behavior is as if all destructors had the same name (even though they do not).

(continued)

TIP: (continued)

Now we are ready to explain why all destructors should be virtual. Consider what happens when destructors are not declared as virtual in a base class. In particular, consider the base class `PFArrayD` (partially filled array of `doubles`) and its derived class `PFArrayDBak` (partially filled array of `doubles` with backup). We discussed these classes in Chapter 14, before we knew about virtual functions, and so the destructor in the base class `PFArrayD` was not marked `virtual`. In Display 15.8, we have summarized all the facts we need about the classes `PFArrayD` and `PFArrayDBak` so that you need not look back to Chapter 14.

Consider the following code:

```
PFArrayD *p = new PFArrayDBak;
  .  .  .
delete p;
```

Since the destructor in the base class is not marked `virtual`, only the destructor for the base class (`PFArrayD`) will be invoked. This will return the memory for the member array `a` (declared in `PFArrayD`) to the freestore, but the memory for the member array `b` (declared in `PFArrayDBak`) will never be returned to the freestore (until the program ends).

On the other hand, if (unlike Display 15.8) the destructor for the base class `PFArrayD` were marked `virtual`, then when `delete` is applied to `p`, the constructor for the class `PFArrayDBak` would be invoked (since the object pointed to is of type `PFArrayDBak`). The destructor for the class `PFArrayDBak` would delete the array `b` and then automatically invoke the constructor for the base class `PFArrayD`, which would delete the member array `a`. So, with the base class destructor marked as virtual, all the memory is returned to the freestore. To prepare for eventualities such as these, it is best to always mark destructors as virtual. ■

Downcasting and Upcasting

You might think some sort of type casting would allow you to easily get around the slicing problem. However, things are not that simple. The following is illegal:

```
Pet vpet;
Dog vdog; //Dog is a derived class with base class Pet.
  . . .
vdog = static_cast<Dog>(vpet); //ILLEGAL!
```

However, casting in the other direction is perfectly legal and does not even need a casting operator:

```
vpet = vdog; //Legal (but does produce the slicing problem.)
```

upcasting

Casting from a descendant type to an ancestor type is known as **upcasting**, since you are moving up the class hierarchy. Upcasting is safe because you are simply disregarding some information (disregarding member variables and functions). So, the following is perfectly safe:

```
vpet = vdog;
```

downcasting

Casting from an ancestor type to a descended type is called **downcasting** and is very dangerous, since you are assuming that information is being added (added member variables and functions). The dynamic_cast that we discussed briefly in Chapter 1 is used for downcasting. It is of some possible use in defeating the slicing problem but is dangerously unreliable and fraught with pitfalls. A dynamic_cast may allow you to downcast, but it works only for pointer types, as in the following:

```
Pet *ppet;
ppet = new Dog;
Dog *pdog = dynamic_cast<Dog*>(ppet); //Dangerous!
```

We have had downcasting fail even in situations as simple as this, and so we do not recommend it.

The dynamic_cast is supposed to inform you if it fails. If the cast fails, the dynamic_cast should return NULL (which is really the integer 0).[2]

If you want to try downcasting, keep the following points in mind:

1. You need to keep track of things so that you know the information to be added is indeed present.

2. Your member functions must be virtual, since dynamic_cast uses the virtual function information to perform the cast.

How C++ Implements Virtual Functions

You need not know how a compiler works in order to use it. That is the principle of information hiding, which is basic to all good program design philosophies. In particular, you need not know how virtual functions are implemented in order to use virtual functions. However, many people find that a concrete model of the implementation helps their understanding; when reading about virtual functions in other books you are likely to encounter references to the implementation of virtual functions. So, we will give a brief outline of how they are implemented. All compilers for all languages (including C++) that have virtual functions typically implement them in basically the same way.

---

[2]The standard says "The value of a failed cast to pointer type is the null pointer of the required result type. A failed cast to a reference type throws a bad_cast."

Display 15.8   Review of the Classes `PFArrayD` and `PFArrayDBak`

```
class PFArrayD
{
public:
    PFArrayD( );
        . . .
    ~PFArrayD( );
protected:
    double *a; //for an array of doubles.
    int capacity; //for the size of the array.
    int used; //for the number of array positions currently in use.
};
```

```
PFArrayD::PFArrayD( ) : capacity(50), used(0)
{
    a = new double[capacity];
}
```

Some details about the base class `PFArrayD`.
A more complete definition of `PFArrayD` is given in Displays 14.8 and 14.9, but this display has all the details you need for this.

```
PFArrayD::~PFArrayD( )
{
    delete [] a;
}
```

The destructors should be virtual, but we had not yet covered virtual functions when we wrote these classes.

```
class PFArrayDBak : public PFArrayD
{
public:
    PFArrayDBak( );
        . . .
    ~PFArrayDBak( )
private:
    double *b; //for a backup of main array.
    int usedB; //backup for inherited member variable used.
};
```

Some details about the derived class `PFArrayDBak`.
A complete definition of `PFArrayDBak` is given in Displays 14.10 and 14.11, but this display has all the details you need for this chapter.

```
PFArrayDBak::PFArrayDBak( ) : PFArrayD( ), usedB(0)
{
    b = new double[capacity];
}
```

```
PFArrayDBak::~PFArrayDBak( )
{
    delete [] b;
}
```

virtual function table

If a class has one or more member functions that are virtual, the compiler creates what is called a **virtual function table** for that class. This table has a pointer (memory address) for each virtual member function. The pointer points to the location of the correct code for that member function. If one virtual function was inherited and not changed, then its table entry points to the definition for that function that was given in the parent class (or other ancestor class if need be). If another virtual function had a new definition in the class, then the pointer in the table for that member function points to that definition. (Remember that the property of being a virtual function is inherited, so once a class has a virtual function table, then all its descendant classes have a virtual function table.)

Whenever an object of a class with one or more virtual functions is created, another pointer is added to the description of the object that is stored in memory. This pointer points to the class's virtual function table. When you make a call to a member function using a pointer (yep, another one) to the object, the run-time system uses the virtual function table to decide which definition of a member function to use; it does not use the type of the pointer.

Of course, this all happens automatically, so you need not worry about it. A compiler writer is even free to implement virtual functions in some other way as long as it works correctly (although it never actually is implemented in a different way).

Self-Test Exercise

8. Why is the following illegal?

```
Pet vpet;
Dog vdog; //Dog is a derived class with base class Pet.
...
vdog = static_cast(vpet); //ILLEGAL!
```

MyProgrammingLab™

Chapter Summary

- *Late binding* means that the decision of which version of a member function is appropriate is decided at run time. In C++, member functions that use late binding are called *virtual* functions. *Polymorphism* is another word for late binding.

- A *pure virtual function* is a member function that has no definition. It is indicated by the word virtual and the notation = 0 in the member function declaration. A class with one or more pure virtual functions is called an *abstract class*.

- An abstract class is a type and can be used as a base class to derive other classes. However, you cannot create an object of an abstract class type (unless it is an object of some derived class).

- You can assign an object of a derived class to a variable of its base class (or any ancestor class), but the member variables that are not in the base class are lost. This is known as the *slicing problem*.

- If the domain type of the pointer `pAncestor` is a base class for the domain type of the pointer `pDescendant`, then the following assignment of pointers is allowed:

  `pAncestor = pDescendant;`

  Moreover, none of the data members or member functions of the dynamic variable being pointed to by `pDescendant` will be lost. Although all the extra fields of the dynamic variable are there, you will need virtual member functions to access them.

- It is a good programming practice to make destructors virtual.

Answers to Self-Test Exercises

1. In essence there is no difference among the three terms. They all refer to the same topic. There is only a slight difference in their usage. (*Virtual function* is a kind of member function; *late binding* refers to the mechanism used to decide which function definition to use when a function is virtual; and *polymorphism* is another name for late binding.)

2. The output would change to the following:

   `Discounted item is not cheaper.`

3. Yes, it is legal to have an abstract class in which all member functions are pure virtual functions.

4. a. Illegal, because `Employee` is an abstract class.
   b. Legal.
   c. Legal, because an abstract class is a type.

5. There would be no members to assign to the derived class's added members.

6. Although it is legal to assign a derived class object to a base class variable, this discards the parts of the derived class object that are not members of the base class. This situation is known as *the slicing problem*.

7. If the base class function carries the `virtual` modifier, then the derived class member function is called. If the base class member function does not have the `virtual` modifier, then the base class member function is called.

8. Since `Dog` can have more member variables than `Pet`, the object `vpet` may not have enough data for all the member variables of type `Dog`.

Programming Projects

Visit www.myprogramminglab.com to complete select exercises online and get instant feedback.

1. Consider a graphics system that has classes for various figures—say, rectangles, squares, triangles, circles, and so on. For example, a rectangle might have data members height, width, and center point, while a square and circle might have only a center point and an edge length or radius, respectively. In a well-designed system, these would be derived from a common class, `Figure`. You are to implement such a system.

The class `Figure` is the base class. You should add only `Rectangle` and `Triangle` classes derived from `Figure`. Each class has stubs for member functions erase and draw. Each of these member functions outputs a message telling what function has been called and what the class of the calling object is. Since these are just stubs, they do nothing more than output this message. The member function center calls erase and draw to erase and redraw the figure at the center. Because you have only stubs for erase and draw, center will not do any "centering" but will call the member functions erase and draw. Also, add an output message in the member function center that announces that center is being called. The member functions should take no arguments. There are three parts to this project:

a. Do the class definitions using no virtual functions. Compile and test.

b. Make the base class member functions virtual. Compile and test.

c. Explain the difference in results.

For a real example, you would have to replace the definition of each of these member functions with code to do the actual drawing. You will be asked to do this in Programming Project 15.2.

Use the following main function for all testing:

```
//This program tests Programming Problem 15.1.

#include <iostream>
#include "figure.h"
#include "rectangle.h"
#include "triangle.h"
using std::cout;
int main( )
{
    Triangle tri;
    tri.draw( );
    cout <<
        "\nDerived class Triangle object calling center( ).\n";
    tri.center( ); //Calls draw and center

    Rectangle rect;
    rect.draw( );
    cout <<
        "\nDerived class Rectangle object calling center( ).\n";
    rect.center( ); //Calls draw and center
    return 0;
}
```

2. Flesh out Programming Problem 15.1. Give new definitions for the various constructors and member functions `Figure::center`, `Figure::draw`, `Figure::erase`, `Triangle::draw`, `Triangle::erase`, `Rectangle::draw`, and

Rectangle::erase so that the draw functions actually draw figures on the screen by placing the character '*' at suitable locations on the screen. For the erase functions, you can simply clear the screen (by outputting blank lines or by doing something more sophisticated). There are a lot of details in this and you will have to decide on some of them on your own.

3. The goal for this programming project is to create a simple 2D predator-prey simulation. In this simulation, the prey are ants and the predators are doodlebugs. These critters live in a 20×20 grid of cells. Only one critter may occupy a cell at a time. The grid is enclosed, so a critter is not allowed to move off the edges of the world. Time is simulated in steps. Each critter performs some action every time step.

The ants behave according to the following model:

- *Move.* For every time step, the ants randomly try to move up, down, left, or right. If the neighboring cell in the selected direction is occupied or would move the ant off the grid, then the ant stays in the current cell.

- *Breed.* If an ant survives for three time steps, at the end of the time step (i.e., after moving) the ant will breed. This is simulated by creating a new ant in an adjacent (up, down, left, or right) cell that is empty. If there is no empty cell available, no breeding occurs. Once an offspring is produced, an ant cannot produce an offspring again until it has survived three more time steps.

The doodlebugs behave according to the following model:

- *Move.* For every time step, the doodlebug will move to an adjacent cell containing an ant and eat the ant. If there are no ants in adjoining cells, the doodlebug moves according to the same rules as the ant. Note that a doodlebug cannot eat other doodlebugs.

- *Breed.* If a doodlebug survives for eight time steps, at the end of the time step it will spawn off a new doodlebug in the same manner as the ant.

- *Starve.* If a doodlebug has not eaten an ant within three time steps, at the end of the third time step it will starve and die. The doodlebug should then be removed from the grid of cells.

During one turn, all the doodlebugs should move before the ants.

Write a program to implement this simulation and draw the world using ASCII characters of "O" for an ant and "X" for a doodlebug. Create a class named Organism that encapsulates basic data common to ants and doodlebugs. This class should have a virtual function named move that is defined in the derived classes of Ant and Doodlebug. You may need additional data structures to keep track of which critters have moved.

Initialize the world with 5 doodlebugs and 100 ants. After each time step, prompt the user to press Enter to move to the next time step. You should see a cyclical pattern between the population of predators and prey, although random perturbations may lead to the elimination of one or both species.

4. This Programming Project requires that you first complete Programming Project 14.9 from Chapter 14.

```
class Creature
{
    private:
        int type; // 0 human, 1 cyberdemon, 2 balrog, 3 elf
        int strength; // How much damage we can inflict
        int hitpoints; // How much damage we can sustain
        string getSpecies(); // Returns type of species
    public:
        Creature();
        // Initialize to human, 10 strength, 10 hit points

        Creature(int newType, int newStrength, int newHit);
        // Initialize creature to new type, strength, hit points

        // Also add appropriate accessor and mutator functions
        // for type, strength, and hit points

        int getDamage();
        // Returns amount of damage this creature
        // inflicts in one round of combat

};
```

Here is an implementation of the getSpecies( ) function:

```
string Creature::getSpecies()
{
    switch (type)
    {
        case 0: return "Human";
        case 1: return "Cyberdemon";
        case 2: return "Balrog";
        case 3: return "Elf";
    }
    return "Unknown";
}
```

The getDamage( ) function outputs and returns the damage this creature can inflict in one round of combat. The rules for calculating the damage are as follows:

- *Every creature inflicts damage that is a random number r, where $0 < r <=$ strength.*
- Demons have a 5% chance of inflicting a demonic attack, which is an additional 50 damage points. Balrogs and Cyberdemons are demons.
- Elves have a 10% chance to inflict a magical attack that doubles the normal amount of damage.
- Balrogs are very fast, so they get to attack twice.

An implementation of getDamage( ) is given here:

```
int Creature::getDamage( )
{
    int damage;

    // All creatures inflict damage, which is a
    // random number up to their strength
    damage = (rand( ) % strength) + 1;
    cout << getSpecies( ) << " attacks for " <<
        damage << "points!" << endl;

    // Demons can inflict damage of 50 with a 5% chance
    if ((type = 2) || (type == 1))
    if ((rand( ) % 100) < 5)
    {

        damage = damage + 50;
        cout << "Demonic attack inflicts 50 "
            << "additional damage points!" << endl;

    }

    // Elves inflict double magical damage with a 10% chance
    if (type == 3)
    {

        if ((rand( ) % 10)==0)
        {
            cout << "Magical attack inflicts " << damage<<
                "additional damage points!" << endl;
            damage = damage * 2;

        }

    }

    // Balrogs are so fast they get to attack twice
    if (type == 2)
    {

        int damage2 = (rand() % strength) + 1;
        cout << "Balrog speed attack inflicts " << damage2 <<
            "additional damage points!" << endl;
        damage = damage + damage2;

    }

    return damage;
}
```

One problem with this implementation is that it is unwieldy to add new creatures. Rewrite the class to use inheritance, which will eliminate the need for the variable type. The Creature class should be the base class. The classes Demon, Elf, and Human should be derived from Creature. The classes Cyberdemon and Balrog should be derived from Demon. You will need to rewrite the getSpecies( ) and getDamage( ) functions so they are appropriate for each class.

For example, the getDamage( ) function in each class should only compute the damage appropriate for that object. The total damage is then calculated by combining the results of getDamage( ) at each level of the inheritance hierarchy. As an example, invoking getDamage( ) for a Balrog object should invoke getDamage( ) for the Demon object, which should invoke getDamage( ) for the Creature object. This will compute the basic damage that all creatures inflict, followed by the random 5% damage that demons inflict, followed by the double damage that balrogs inflict.

Also include mutator and accessor functions for the private variables. Write a main function that contains a driver to test your classes. It should create an object for each type of creature and repeatedly outputs the results of getDamage( ). First, make the getDamage( ) function virtual. Then, make a function in your main program, battleArena(Creature &creature1, Creature &creature2), that takes two Creature objects as input. The function should calculate the damage done by creature1, subtract that amount from creature2's hit points, and vice versa. If both creatures end up with zero or less hit points, then the battle is a tie. Otherwise, at the end of a round, if one creature has positive hit points but the other does not, then the battle is over. The function should loop until the battle is either a tie or over. Since the getDamage( ) function is virtual, it should invoke the getDamage( ) function defined for the specific creature. Test your program with several battles involving different creatures.

5. The following shows code to play a guessing game in which two players attempt to guess a number. Your task is to extend the program with objects that represent either a human player or a computer player.

```
bool checkForWin(int guess, int answer)
{
    if (answer == guess)
    {
        cout << "You're right! You win!" << endl;
        return true;
    }
    else if (answer < guess)
        cout << "Your guess is too high." << endl;
    else
        cout << "Your guess is too low." << endl;
    return false;
}

void play(Player &player1, Player &player2)
{
    int answer = 0, guess = 0;
    answer = rand( ) % 100;
    bool win = false;
```

VideoNote
Solution to Programming Project 15.5

```
    while (!win)
    {
        cout << "Player 1's turn to guess." << endl;
        guess = player1.getGuess();
        win = checkForWin(guess, answer);
        if (win) return;

        cout << "Player 2's turn to guess." << endl;
        guess = player2.getGuess();
        win = checkForWin(guess, answer);
    }
}
```

The play function takes as input two Player objects. Define the Player class with a virtual function named getGuess(). The implementation of Player::getGuess() can simply return 0. Next, define a class named HumanPlayer derived from Player. The implementation of HumanPlayer::getGuess() should prompt the user to enter a number and return the value entered from the keyboard. Next, define a class named ComputerPlayer derived from Player. The implementation of ComputerPlayer::getGuess() should randomly select a number from 0 to 100. Finally, construct a main function that invokes play(Player &player1, Player &player2) with two instances of a HumanPlayer and ComputerPlayer (human versus human), an instance of a HumanPlayer and ComputerPlayer (human versus computer), and two instances of ComputerPlayer (computer versus computer).

6. The computer player in Programming Project 15.5 does not play the number guessing game very well, since it makes only random guesses. Modify the program so that the computer plays a more informed game. The specific strategy is up to you, but you must add function(s) to the Player and ComputerPlayer classes so that the play(Player &player1, Player &player2) function can send the results of a guess back to the computer player. In other words, the computer must be told if its last guess was too high or too low, and it also must be told if its opponent's last guess was too high or too low. The computer can then use this information to revise its next guess.

VideoNote
Solution to
Programming
Project 15.7

7. The following lists a Dice class that simulates rolling a die with a different number of sides. The default is a standard die with six sides. The rollTwoDice function simulates rolling two dice objects and returns the sum of their values. The srand function requires including cstdlib.

```
class Dice
{
public:
    Dice();
    Dice(int numSides);
    virtual int rollDice() const;
protected:
    int numSides;
};
```

```
Dice::Dice()
{
    numSides = 6;
    srand(time(NULL)); // Seeds random number generator
}

Dice::Dice(int numSides)
{
    this->numSides = numSides;
    srand(time(NULL)); // Seeds random number generator
}

int Dice::rollDice() const
{
    return (rand() % numSides) + 1;
}

    // Take two dice objects, roll them, and return the sum
    int rollTwoDice(const Dice& die1, const Dice& die2)
    {
        return die1.rollDice() + die2.rollDice();
    }
```

Write a main function that creates two Dice objects with a number of sides of your choosing. Invoke the rollTwoDice function in a loop that iterates ten times and verify that the functions are working as expected.

Next create your own class, LoadedDice, that is derived from Dice. Add a default constructor and a constructor that takes the number of sides as input. Override the rollDice function in LoadedDice so that with a 50% chance the function returns the largest number possible (i.e., numSides), otherwise it returns what Dice's rollDice function returns.

Test your class by replacing the Dice objects in main with LoadedDice objects. You should not need to change anything else. There should be many more dice rolls with the highest possible value. Polymorphism results in LoadedDice's rollDice function to be invoked instead of Dice's rollDice function inside rollTwoDice.

Templates 16

16 Templates

All men are mortal.

Aristotle is a man.

Therefore, Aristotle is mortal.

All X's are Y.

Z is an X.

Therefore, Z is Y.

All cats are mischievous.

Garfield is a cat.

Therefore, Garfield is mischievous.

A Short Lesson on Syllogisms

Introduction

This chapter discusses C++ templates, which allow you to define functions and classes that have parameters for type names. This enables you to design functions that can be used with arguments of different types and to define classes that are much more general than those you have seen before this chapter.

Section 16.1 requires only material from Chapters 1 through 5. Section 16.2 uses material from Section 16.1 as well as Chapters 1 through 11 but does not require the material from Chapters 12 through 15. Section 16.3 requires the previous sections as well as Chapter 14 on inheritance and all the chapters needed for Section 16.2. Section 16.3 does mark some member functions as `virtual`. Virtual functions are covered in Chapter 15. However, this use of virtual functions is not essential to the material presented. It is possible to read Section 16.3 ignoring (or even omitting) all occurrences of the keyword `virtual`.

16.1 Function Templates

Many of our previously discussed C++ function definitions have an underlying algorithm that is much more general than the algorithm we gave in the function definition. For example, consider the function `swapValues`, which we first discussed in Chapter 4. For reference, we now repeat the function definition:

```
void swapValues(int& variable1, int& variable2)
{
    int temp;
    temp = variable1;
    variable1 = variable2;
    variable2 = temp;
}
```

Notice that the function swapValues applies only to variables of type int. Yet the algorithm given in the function body could just as well be used to swap the values in two variables of type char. If we want to also use the function swapValues with variables of type char, we can overload the function name swapValues by adding the following definition:

```
void swapValues(char& variable1,  char& variable2)
{
    char temp;

    temp = variable1;
    variable1 = variable2;
    variable2 = temp;
}
```

But there is something inefficient and unsatisfying about these two definitions of the swapValues function: They are almost identical. The only difference is that one definition uses the type int in three places and the other uses the type char in the same three places. Proceeding in this way, if we wanted to have the function swapValues apply to pairs of variables of type double, we would have to write a third, almost identical function definition. If we wanted to apply swapValues to still more types, the number of almost identical function definitions would be even larger. This would require a good deal of typing and would clutter up our code with lots of definitions that look identical. We should be able to say that the following function definition applies to variables of any type:

```
void swapValues(Type_Of_The_Variables& variable1,
                Type_Of_The_Variables& variable2)
{
    Type_Of_The_Variables temp;

    temp = variable1;
    variable1 = variable2;
    variable2 = temp;
}
```

As we will see, something like this is possible. We can define one function that applies to all types of variables, although the syntax is a bit more complicated than what we have just shown. The proper syntax is described in the next subsection.

Syntax for Function Templates

Display 16.1 shows a C++ template for the function swapValues. This function template allows you to swap the values of any two variables, of any type, as long as the two variables have the same type. The definition and the function declaration begin with the line

```
template<class T>
```

template prefix

type parameter

This is often called the **template prefix**. It tells the compiler that the definition or function declaration that follows is a **template** and that T is a **type parameter**. In this context, the word class actually means *type*.[1] As we will see, the type parameter T can be replaced by any type, whether the type is a class or not. Within the body of the function definition, the type parameter T is used just like any other type.

A template overloads the function name

The function template definition is, in effect, a large collection of function definitions. For the function template for swapValues shown in Display 16.1, there is, in effect, one function definition for each possible type name. Each of these definitions is obtained by replacing the type parameter T with a type name. For example, the function definition shown next is obtained by replacing T with the type name double:

```
void swapValues(double& variable1, double& variable2)
{
    double temp;

    temp = variable1;
    variable1 = variable2;
    variable2 = temp;
}
```

Another definition for swapValues is obtained by replacing the type parameter T in the function template with the type name int. Yet another definition is obtained by replacing the type parameter T with char. The one function template shown in Display 16.1 overloads the function name swapValues so that there is a slightly different function definition for every possible type.

The compiler will not literally produce definitions for every possible type for the function name swapValues, but it will behave exactly as if it had produced all those function definitions. A separate definition will be produced for each different type for which you use the template, but not for any types you do not use. Only one definition is generated for a single type regardless of the number of times you use the template for that type. Notice that the function swapValues is called twice in Display 16.1: One time the arguments are of type int, and the other time the arguments are of type char. Consider the following function call from Display 16.1:

```
swapValues(integer1, integer2);
```

---

[1] In fact, the ANSI/ISO standard provides that the keyword typename may be used instead of class in the template prefix. It would make more sense to use the keyword typename rather than class, but everybody uses class, so we will do the same. (It is often true that consistency in coding is more important than optimality.)

Display 16.1 A Function Template

```
1   //Program to demonstrate a function template.
2   #include <iostream>
3   using std::cout;
4   using std::endl;

5   //Interchanges the values of variable1 and variable2.
6   //The assignment operator must work for the type T.
7   template<class T>
8   void swapValues(T& variable1, T& variable2)
9   {
10      T temp;

11      temp = variable1;
12      variable1 = variable2;
13      variable2 = temp;
14  }

15  int main( )
16  {
17      int integer1 = 1, integer2 = 2;
18      cout << "Original integer values are "
19           << integer1 << " " << integer2 << endl;
20      swapValues(integer1, integer2);
21      cout << "Swapped integer values are "
22           << integer1 << " " << integer2 << endl;

23      char symbol1 = 'A', symbol2 = 'B';
24      cout << "Original character values are: "
25           << symbol1 << " " << symbol2 << endl;
26      swapValues(symbol1, symbol2);
27      cout << "Swapped character values are: "
28           << symbol1 << " " << symbol2 << endl;
29      return 0;
30  }
```

Many compilers still have problems with templates. To be certain that your templates work on the widest selection of compilers, place the template definition in the same file in which it is used and have the template definition precede all uses of the template.

Sample Dialogue

```
Original integer values are: 1 2
Swapped integer values are: 2 1
Original character values are: A B
Swapped character values are: B A
```

When the C++ compiler gets to this function call, it notices the types of the arguments—in this case, int—and then it uses the template to produce a function definition with the type parameter T replaced with the type name int. Similarly, when the compiler sees the function call

```
swapValues(symbol1, symbol2);
```

calling a function template

it notices the types of the arguments—in this case, char—and then it uses the template to produce a function definition with the type parameter T replaced with the type name char.

Notice that you need not do anything special when you call a function that is defined with a function template; call it just as you would any other function. The compiler does all the work of producing the function definition from the function template.

A function template may have a function declaration and a definition, just like an ordinary function. You may be able to place the function declaration and definition for a function template in the same locations that you place function declarations and definitions for ordinary functions. However, separate compilation of template definitions and template function declarations is not yet implemented on most compilers, so it is safest to place your template function definition in the file where you invoke the template function, as we did in Display 16.1. In fact, most compilers require that the template function definition appear before the first invocation of the template. You may simply #include the file containing your template function definitions prior to calling the template function. Your particular compiler may behave differently; you should ask a local expert about the details.

In the function template in Display 16.1, we used the letter T as the parameter for the type. This is traditional but is not required by the C++ language. The type parameter can be any identifier (other than a keyword). T is a good name for the type parameter, but other names can be used.

more than one type parameter

It is possible to have function templates that have more than one type parameter. For example, a function template with two type parameters named T1 and T2 would begin as follows:

```
template<class T1, class T2>
```

However, most function templates require only one type parameter. You cannot have unused template parameters; that is, each template parameter must be used in your template function.

PITFALL: Compiler Complications

Many compilers do not allow separate compilation of templates, so you may need to include your template definition within your code that uses it. As usual, at least the function declaration must precede any use of the function template.

Some C++ compilers have additional special requirements for using templates. If you have trouble compiling your templates, check your manuals or check with a local expert. You may need to set special options or rearrange the way you order the template definitions and the other items in your files.

PITFALL: (continued)

The template program layout that seems to work with the widest selection of compilers is the following: Place the template definition in the same file in which it is used and have the template definition precede all uses (all invocations) of the template. If you want to place your function template definition in a file separate from your application program, you can #include the file with the function template definition in the application file. ∎

Self-Test Exercises

1. Write a function template named maximum. The function takes two values of the same type as its arguments and returns the larger of the two arguments (or either value if they are equal). Give both the function declaration and the function definition for the template. You will use the operator < in your definition. Therefore, this function template will apply only to types for which < is defined. Write a comment for the function declaration that explains this restriction.

2. We have used three kinds of absolute value functions: abs, labs, and fabs. These functions differ only in the type of their argument. It might be better to have a function template for the absolute value function. Give a function template for an absolute value function called absolute. The template will apply only to types for which < is defined, for which the unary negation operator is defined, and for which the constant 0 can be used in a comparison with a value of that type. Thus, the function absolute can be called with any of the number types, such as int, long, and double. Give both the function declaration and the function definition for the template.

3. Define or characterize the template facility for C++.

4. In the template prefix

   template <class T>

   what kind of variable is the parameter T? Choose from the answers listed here.

   a. T must be a class.
   b. T must *not* be a class.
   c. T can be only a type built into the C++ language.
   d. T can be any type, whether built into C++ or defined by the programmer.
   e. T can be any kind of type, whether built into C++ or defined by the programmer, but T does have some requirements that must be met. (What are they?)

Algorithm Abstraction

As we saw in our discussion of the swapValues function, there is a very general algorithm for interchanging the value of two variables that applies to variables of any type. Using a function template, we were able to express this more general algorithm in C++. This is a very simple example of algorithm abstraction. When we say we are using **algorithm abstraction**, we mean that we are expressing our algorithms in a very general way so that we can ignore incidental detail and concentrate on the substantive part of the algorithm. Function templates are one feature of C++ that supports algorithm abstraction.

TIP: How to Define Templates

When we defined the function templates in Display 16.1, we started with a function that sorts an array of elements of type int. We then created a template by replacing the base type of the array with the type parameter T. This is a good general strategy for writing templates. If you want to write a function template, first write a version that is not a template at all but is just an ordinary function. Then completely debug the ordinary function, and finally convert the ordinary function to a template by replacing some type names with a type parameter. There are two advantages to this method. First, when you are defining the ordinary function, you are dealing with a much more concrete case, which makes the problem easier to visualize. Second, you have fewer details to check at each stage; when worrying about the algorithm itself, you need not concern yourself with template syntax rules. ∎

Function Template

The function definition and the function declaration for a function template are each prefaced with the following:

```
template<class Type_Parameter>
```

The function declaration (if used) and definition are then the same as any ordinary function declaration and definition, except that the Type_Parameter can be used in place of a type.

For example, the following is a function declaration for a function template:

```
template<class T>
void showStuff(int stuff1, T stuff2, T stuff3);
```

The definition for this function template might be as follows:

```
template<class T>
void showStuff(int stuff1, T stuff2, T stuff3)
{
    cout << stuff1 << endl
         << stuff2 << endl
         << stuff3 << endl;
}
```

The function template given in this example is equivalent to having one function declaration and one function definition for each possible type name. The type name is substituted for the type parameter (which is T in the preceding example). For instance, consider the following function call:

```
showStuff(2, 3.3, 4.4);
```

When this function call is executed, the compiler uses the function definition obtained by replacing T with the type name double. A separate definition will be produced for each different type for which you use the template, but not for any types you do not use. Only one definition is generated for a specific type regardless of the number of times you use the template.

EXAMPLE: A Generic Sorting Function

Chapter 5 gave the selection sorting algorithm for sorting an array of values of type int. The algorithm was realized in C++ code as the function sort, given in Display 5.8. In the following, we repeat the definitions of this function sort:

```
void sort(int a[], int numberUsed)
{
    int indexOfNextSmallest;
    for (int index = 0; index < numberUsed - 1; index++)
    {//Place the correct value in a[index]:
        indexOfNextSmallest =
            indexOfSmallest(a, index, numberUsed);
        swapValues(a[index], a[indexOfNextSmallest]);
        //a[0] <= a[1] <=...<= a[index] are the smallest of the
        // original array elements. The rest of the elements
        //are in the remaining positions.
    }
}
```

If you study the preceding definition of the function sort, you will see that the base type of the array is never used in any significant way. If we replaced the base type of the array in the function header with the type double, we would obtain a sorting function that applies to arrays of values of type double. Of course, we also must adjust the helping functions so that they apply to arrays of elements of type double. Let's consider the helping functions that are called inside the body of the function sort. The two helping functions are swapValues and indexOfSmallest.

We already saw that swapValues can apply to variables of any type for which the assignment operator works, provided we define it as a function template (as in Display 16.1). Let's see if indexOfSmallest depends in any significant way on the

(continued)

EXAMPLE: (continued)

base type of the array being sorted. The definition of `indexOfSmallest` is repeated next so you can study its details.

```
int indexOfSmallest(const int a[], int startIndex, int numberUsed)
{
    int min = a[startIndex],
        indexOfMin = startIndex;
    for (int index = startIndex + 1; index < numberUsed; index++)
        if (a[index] < min)
        {
            min = a[index];
            indexOfMin = index;
            //min is the smallest of a[startIndex] through
            //a[index]
        }

    return indexOfMin;
}
```

The function `indexOfSmallest` also does not depend in any significant way on the base type of the array. If we replace the two highlighted instances of the type `int` with the type `double`, then we will have changed the function `indexOfSmallest` so that it applies to arrays whose base type is `double`.

To change the function `sort` so that it can be used to sort arrays with the base type `double`, we need only to replace a few instances of the type name `int` with the type name `double`. Moreover, there is nothing special about the type `double`. We can do a similar replacement for many other types. The only thing we need to know about the type is that the assignment operator and the operator, `<`, are defined for that type. This is the perfect situation for function templates. If we replace a few instances of the type name `int` (in the functions `sort` and `indexOfSmallest`) with a type parameter, then the function `sort` can sort an array of values of any type, provided that the values of that type can be assigned with the assignment operator and compared using the `<` operator. In Display 16.2, we have written just such a function template.

Notice that the function template `sort` shown in Display 16.2 can be used with arrays of values that are not numbers. In the demonstration program, the function template `sort` is called to sort an array of characters. Characters can be compared using the `<` operator, which compares characters according to the order of their ASCII numbers (see Appendix 3). Thus, when applied to two uppercase letters, the operator, `<`, tests to see if the first character comes before the second in alphabetic order. Also, when applied to two lowercase letters, the operator, `<`, tests to see if the first character comes before the second in alphabetic order. When you mix upper- and lowercase letters, the situation is not so well behaved, but the program shown in Display 16.2 deals only with uppercase letters. In that program, an array of uppercase letters is sorted into alphabetical order with a call to the function template `sort`. (The function template `sort` will even sort an array of objects of a class that you define, provided you overload the `<` operator to apply to objects of the class.)

EXAMPLE: (continued)

Our generic sorting function has separated the implementation from the declaration of the sorting function by placing the definition of the sorting function in the file sort.cpp (Display 16.3). However, most compilers do not allow for separate compilation of templates in the usual sense. So, we have separated the implementation from the programmer's point of view, but from the compiler's point of view it looks like everything is in one file. The file sort.cpp is #included in our main file, so it is as if everything were in one file. Note that the include directive for sort.cpp is placed before any invocation of the functions defined by templates. For most compilers, this is the only way you can get templates to work.

Display 16.2   A Generic Sorting Function (part 1 of 2)

```
1    //Demonstrates a template function that implements
2    //a generic version of the selection sort algorithm.
3    #include <iostream>
4    using std::cout;
5    using std::endl;

6    template<class T>
7    void sort(T a[], int numberUsed);
8    //Precondition: numberUsed <= declared size of the array a.
9    //The array elements a[0] through a[numberUsed - 1] have values.
10   //The assignment and < operator work for values of type T.
11   //Postcondition: The values of a[0] through a[numberUsed - 1] have
12   //been rearranged so that a[0] <= a[1] <=... <= a[numberUsed - 1].

13   template<class T>
14   void swapValues(T& variable1, T& variable2);
15   //Interchanges the values of variable1 and variable2.
16   //The assignment operator must work correctly for the type T.

17   template<class T>
18   int indexOfSmallest(const T a[], int startIndex, int numberUsed);
19   //Precondition: 0 <= startIndex < numberUsed. Array elements have
     //values.
20   //The assignment and < operator work for values of type T.
21   //Returns the index i such that a[i] is the smallest of the values
22   //a[startIndex], a[startIndex + 1],..., a[numberUsed - 1].

23   #include "sort.cpp"          This is equivalent to placing the function
                                  template definitions in this file at this
                                  location.
24   int main( )
25   {
26       int i;
27       int a[10] = {9, 8, 7, 6, 5, 1, 2, 3, 0, 4};
28       cout << "Unsorted integers:\n";
```

(continued)

Display 16.2   A Generic Sorting Function (part 2 of 2)

```
29      for (i = 0; i < 10; i++)
30          cout << a[i] << " ";
31      cout << endl;
32      sort(a, 10);
33      cout << "In sorted order the integers are:\n";
34      for (i = 0; i < 10; i++)
35          cout << a[i] << " ";
36      cout << endl;
37      double b[5] = {5.5, 4.4, 1.1, 3.3, 2.2};
38      cout << "Unsorted doubles:\n";
39      for (i = 0; i < 5; i++)
40          cout << b[i] << " ";
41      cout << endl;
42      sort(b, 5);
43      cout << "In sorted order the doubles are:\n";
44      for (i = 0; i < 5; i++)
45          cout << b[i] << " ";
46      cout << endl;

47      char c[7] = {'G', 'E', 'N', 'E', 'R', 'I', 'C'};
48      cout << "Unsorted characters:\n";
49      for (i = 0; i < 7; i++)
50          cout << c[i] << " ";
51      cout << endl;
52      sort(c, 7);
53      cout << "In sorted order the characters are:\n";
54      for (i = 0; i < 7; i++)
55          cout << c[i] << " ";
56      cout << endl;

57      return 0;
58  }
```

Sample Dialogue

```
Unsorted integers:
9 8 7 6 5 1 2 3 0 4
In sorted order the integers are:
0 1 2 3 4 5 6 7 8 9
Unsorted doubles:
5.5 4.4 1.1 3.3 2.2
In sorted order the doubles are:
1.1 2.2 3.3 4.4 5.5
Unsorted characters:
G E N E R I C
In sorted order the characters are:
C E E G I N R
```

Display 16.3   Implementation of the Generic Sorting Function

```
1   // This is the file sort.cpp.

2   template<class T>
3   void sort(T a[],int numberUsed)
4   {
5       int indexOfNextSmallest;
6       for (int index = 0; index < numberUsed - 1; index++)
7       {//Place the correct value in a[index]:
8           indexOfNextSmallest =
9               indexOfSmallest(a, index, numberUsed);
10          swapValues(a[index], a[indexOfNextSmallest]);
11          //a[0] <= a[1] <=...<= a[index] are the smallest of the original
12          //array elements. The rest of the elements are in the remaining
13          //positions.
14      }
15  }

15  template<class T>
16  void swapValues(T& variable1, T& variable2)
            <The rest of the definition of swapValues is given in Display 16.1.>

17  template<class T>
18  int indexOfSmallest(const T a[ ], int startIndex, int numberUsed)
19  {
20      T min = a[startIndex];          Note that the type parameter may be used
21      int indexOfMin = startIndex;        in the body of the function definition.

22      for (int index = startIndex + 1; index < numberUsed; index++)
23          if (a[index] < min)
24          {
25              min = a[index];
26              indexOfMin = index;
27              //min is the smallest of a[startIndex] through a[index].
28          }

29      return indexOfMin;
30  }
```

PITFALL: Using a Template with an Inappropriate Type

You can use a template function with any type for which the code in the function definition makes sense. However, all the code in the template function must be clear and must behave in an appropriate way. For example, you cannot use the swapValues template (Display 16.1) with the type parameter replaced

(continued)

PITFALL: (continued)

by a type for which the assignment operator does not work at all, or does not work "correctly."

As a more concrete example, suppose that your program defines the template function `swapValues` as in Display 16.1. You cannot add the following to your program:

```
int  a[10], b[10];
<some code to fill arrays>
swapValues(a, b);
```

This code will not work, because assignment does not work with array types. ∎

MyProgrammingLab™

Self-Test Exercises

5. Display 5.6 shows a function called `search`, which sequentially searches an array for a specified integer. Give a function template version of `search` that can be used to search an array of elements of any type. Give both the function declaration and the function definition for the template. (*Hint:* It is almost identical to the function given in Display 5.6.)

6. Compare and contrast overloading of a function name with the definition of a function template for the function name.

7. (This exercise is only for those who have already read at least Chapter 6 on structures and classes and preferably also read Chapter 8 on overloading operators.) Can you use the `sort` template function (Display 16.3) to sort an array with base type `DayOfYear` defined in Display 6.4?

8. (This exercise is only for those who have already read Chapter 10 on pointers and dynamic arrays.)

   Although the assignment operator does not work with ordinary array variables, it does work with pointer variables that are used to name dynamic arrays. Suppose that your program defines the template function `swapValues` (as in Display 16.1) and contains the following code. What is the output produced by this code?

```
typedef int* ArrayPointer;
ArrayPointer a, b, c;
a = new int[3];
b = new int[3];

int i;
for (i = 0; i < 3; i++)
{
    a[i] = i;
    b[i] = i * 100;
}
c = a;
```

Self-Test Exercises (continued)

```
        cout << "a contains: ";
        for (i = 0; i < 3; i++)
            cout << a[i] << " ";
        cout << endl;
        cout << "b contains: ";
        for (i = 0; i < 3; i++)
            cout << b[i] << " ";
        cout << endl;
        cout << "c contains: ";
        for (i = 0; i < 3; i++)
            cout << c[i] << " ";
        cout << endl;

        swapValues(a, b);
        b[0] = 42;

        cout << "After swapping a and b, \n"
             << "and changing b:\n";
        cout << "a contains: ";
        for (i = 0; i < 3; i++)
            cout << a[i] << " ";
        cout << endl;
        cout << "b contains: ";
        for (i = 0; i < 3; i++)
            cout << b[i] << " ";
        cout << endl;
        cout << "c contains: ";
        for (i = 0; i < 3; i++)
            cout << c[i] << " ";
        cout << endl;
```

16.2 Class Templates

Equal wealth and equal opportunities of culture ... have simply made us all members of one class.

EDWARD BELLAMY, *Looking Backward 2000–1887*

As you saw in the previous section, function definitions can be made more general by using templates. In this section, you will see that templates can also make class definitions more general.

Syntax for Class Templates

The syntax details for class templates are basically the same as those for function templates. The following is placed before the template definition:

```
template<class T>
```

type parameter

The type parameter T is used in the class definition just like any other type. As with function templates, the type parameter T represents a type that can be any type at all; the type parameter does not have to be replaced with a class type. As with function templates, you may use any (nonkeyword) identifier instead of T, although it is traditional to use T.

Display 16.4 shows an example of a class template. An object of this class contains a pair of values of type T: If T is int, the object values are pairs of integers; if T is char, the object values are pairs of characters, and so on.[2]

declaring objects

Once the class template is defined, you can declare objects of this class. The declaration must specify what type is to be filled in for T. For example, the following declares the object score so it can record a pair of integers, and it declares the object seats so it can record a pair of characters:

```
Pair<int> score;
Pair<char> seats;
```

The objects are then used just like any other objects. For example, the following sets score to be 3 for the first team and 0 for the second team:

```
score.setFirst(3);
score.setSecond(0);
```

Display 16.4   Class Template Definition (part 1 of 2)

```
1    //Class for a pair of values of type T:
2    template<class T>
3    class Pair
4    {
5    public:
6        Pair( );
7        Pair(T firstValue, T secondValue);
8        void setFirst(T newValue);
9        void setSecond(T newValue);
10       T getFirst( ) const;
11       T getSecond( ) const;
12    private:
13       T first;
14       T second;
15    };
```

---

[2] Pair is a template version of the class intPair given in Display 8.6. However, since they would not be appropriate for all types T, we have omitted the increment and decrement operators.

Display 16.4   Class Template Definition (part 2 of 2)

```
16   template<class T>
17   Pair<T>::Pair(T firstValue, T secondValue)
18   {
19       first = firstValue;
20       second = secondValue;
21   }

22   template<class T>
23   void Pair<T>::setFirst(T newValue)
24   {
25       first = newValue;
26   }

27   template<class T>
28   T Pair<T>::getFirst( ) const
29   {
30       return first;
31   }
```

*Not all the member functions
are shown here.*

**defining
member
functions**

The member functions for a class template are defined the same way as member functions for ordinary classes. The only difference is that the member function definitions are themselves templates. For example, Display 16.4 shows appropriate definitions for the member functions setFirst and getFirst, and for the constructor with two arguments for the template class Pair. Notice that the class name before the scope resolution operator is Pair<T>, and not simply Pair. However, the constructor name after the scope resolution operator is the simple name Pair without any <T>.

**class templates
as parameters**

The name of a class template may be used as the type for a function parameter. For example, the following is a possible function declaration for a function with a parameter for a pair of integers:

```
int addUp(const Pair<int>& thePair);
//Returns the sum of the two integers in thePair.
```

Note that we specified the type—in this case, int—that is to be filled in for the type parameter T.

You can even use a class template within a function template. For example, rather than defining the specialized function addUp given in the preceding code, you could instead define a function template as follows so that the function applies to all kinds of numbers:

```
template<class T>
T addUp(const Pair<T>& thePair);
//Precondition: The operator + is defined for values of type T.
//Returns the sum of the two values in thePair.
```

restrictions on the type parameter

Almost all template class definitions have some restrictions on what types can reasonably be substituted for the type parameter (or parameters). Even a straightforward template class such as Pair does not work well with absolutely all types T. The type Pair<T> will not be well behaved unless the assignment operator and copy constructor are well behaved for the type T, since the assignment operator is used in member function definitions and since there are member functions with call-by-value parameters of type T. If T involves pointers and dynamic variables, then T should also have a suitable destructor. However, these are requirements you might expect a well-behaved class type T to have. So, these requirements are minimal. With other template classes, the requirements on the types that can be substituted for a type parameter may be more restrictive.

Class Template Syntax

A class template definition and the definitions of its member functions are prefaced with the following:

```
template<class Type_Parameter>
```

The class and member function definitions are then the same as for any ordinary class, except that the Type_Parameter can be used in place of a type.

For example, the following is the beginning of a class template definition:

```
template<class T>
class Pair
{
public:
    Pair( );
    Pair(T firstValue, T secondValue);
    ...
```

Member functions and overloaded operators are then defined as function templates. For example, the definition of the two-argument constructor for the preceding sample class template would begin as follows:

```
template<class T>
Pair<T>::Pair(T firstValue, T secondValue)
{
    ...
```

You can specialize a class template by giving a type argument to the class name, as in the following example:

```
Pair<int>
```

The specialized class name, like Pair<int>, can then be used just like any class name. It can be used to declare objects or to specify the type of a formal parameter.

Type Definitions

You can define a new class type name that has the same meaning as a specialized class template name, such as Pair<int>. The syntax for such a defined class type name is as follows:

typedef Class_Name<Type_Argument> New_Type_Name;

For example,

typedef Pair<int> PairOfInt;

The type name PairOfInt can then be used to declare objects of type Pair<int>, as in the following example:

PairOfInt pair1, pair2;

The type name PairOfInt can also be used to specify the type of a formal parameter or used anyplace else a type name is allowed.

Self-Test Exercises

9. Give the definition for the default (zero-argument) constructor for the class template Pair in Display 16.4.

10. Give the complete definition for the following function, which was discussed in the previous subsection:

```
int addUp(const Pair<int>& thePair);
//Returns the sum of the two integers in thePair.
```

11. Give the complete definition for the following template function, which was discussed in the previous subsection:

```
template<class T>
T addUp(const Pair<T>& thePair);
//Precondition: The operator + is defined for values of type T.
//Returns the sum of the two values in thePair
```

EXAMPLE: An Array Template Class

In Chapter 10, we defined a class for a partially filled array of doubles (Displays 10.10 and 10.11). In this example, we convert that definition to a template class for a partially filled array of values of any type. The template class PFArray has a type parameter T for the base type of the array.

The conversion is routine. We just replace double (when it occurs as the base type of the array) with the type parameter T and convert both the class definition and the member function definitions to template form. The template class definition is given in Display 16.5. The member function template definitions are given in Display 16.6. Note that we have placed the template definitions in a namespace. Namespaces are used with templates in the same way as they are used with simple, nontemplate definitions.

A sample application program is given in Display 16.7. Note that we have separated the class template interface, implementation, and application program into three files. Unfortunately, these files cannot be used for the traditional method of separate compilation. Most compilers do not yet accommodate such separate compilation. So, we do the best we can by #include-ing the interface and implementation files in the application file. To the compiler, that makes it look like everything is in one file.

Display 16.5 Interface for the PFArray Template Class (part 1 of 2)

```
1   //This is the header file pfarray.h. This is the interface for the class
2   //PFArray. Objects of this type are partially filled arrays with base
3   //type T.
4   #define PFARRAY_H
3   #ifndef PFARRAY_H
5   namespace PFArraySavitch
6   {
7       template<class T>
8       class PFArray
9       {
10      public:
11          PFArray( ); //Initializes with a capacity of 50.
12          PFArray(int capacityValue);
13          PFArray(const PFArray<T>& pfaObject);
14          void addElement(const T& element);
15          //Precondition: The array is not full.
16          //Postcondition: The element has been added.
```

Display 16.5 Interface for the **PFArray** Template Class (part 2 of 2)

```
17      bool full( ) const; //Returns true if the array is full;
                            //false, otherwise.

18      int getCapacity( ) const;

19      int getNumberUsed( ) const;

20      void emptyArray( );
21      //Resets the number used to zero, effectively emptying the
        //array.

22      T& operator[](int index);
23      //Read and change access to elements 0 through numberUsed - 1.

24      PFArray<T>& operator =(const PFArray<T>& rightSide);

25      virtual ~PFArray( );
26  private:
27      T *a; //for an array of T.
28      int capacity; //for the size of the array.
29      int used; //for the number of array positions currently in use.
30      };
31  }// PFArraySavitch
32  #endif //PFARRAY_H
```

Display 16.6 Implementation for **PFArray** Template Class (part 1 of 3)

```
1  //This is the implementation file pfarray.cpp.
2  //This is the implementation of the template class PFArray.
3  //The interface for the template class PFArray is in the file pfarray.h.

4  #include "pfarray.h"
5  #include <iostream>
6  using std::cout;

7  namespace PFArraySavitch
8  {
9      template <class T>
10     PFArray<T>::PFArray( )  :capacity(50), used(0)
11     {
12         a = new T[capacity];
13     }
```

Note that the T is used before the scope resolution operator, but no T is used for the constructor name.

(continued)

Display 16.6 Implementation for `PFArray` Template Class (part 2 of 3)

```
14  template<class T>
15  PFArray<T>::PFArray(int size) :capacity(size), used(0)
16  {
17      a = new T[capacity];
18  }
19
20  template<class T>
21  PFArray<T>::PFArray(const PFArray<T>& pfaObject)
            :capacity(pfaObject.getCapacity( )),
            used(pfaObject.getNumberUsed( ))
22  {
23      a = new T[capacity];
24      for (int i = 0; i < used; i++)
25          a[i] = pfaObject.a[i];
26  }
27
28  template<class T>
29  void PFArray<T>::addElement(const T& element)
30  {
31      if (used >= capacity)
32      {
33          cout << "Attempt to exceed capacity in PFArray.\n";
34          exit(0);
35      }
36      a[used] = element;
37      used++;
38  }
39
40  template<class T>
41  bool PFArray<T>::full( ) const
42  {
43      return (capacity == used);
44  }
45
46  template<class T>
47  int PFArray<T>::getCapacity( ) const
48  {
49      return capacity;
50  }
51
52  template<class T>
53  int PFArray<T>::getNumberUsed( ) const
54  {
55      return used;
56  }
```

Display 16.6   Implementation for **PFArray** Template Class (part 3 of 3)

```
54    template<class T>
55    void PFArray<T>::emptyArray( )
56    {
57        used = 0;
58    }

59    template<class T>
61    T& PFArray<T>::operator[] (int index)
62    {
63        if (index >= used)
64        {
65            cout << "Illegal index in PFArray.\n";
66            exit(0);
67        }
68        return a[index];
69    }

70    template<class T>
71    PFArray<T>& PFArray<T>::operator =(const PFArray<T>& rightSide)
72    {
73        if (capacity != rightSide.capacity)
74        {
75            delete [] a;
76            a = new T[rightSide.capacity];
77        }

78        capacity = rightSide.capacity;
79        used = rightSide.used;
80        for (int i = 0; i < used; i++)
81            a[i] = rightSide.a[i];

82        return *this;
83    }

84    template<class T>
85    PFArray<T>::~PFArray( )
86    {
87        delete [] a;
88    }
89    }// PFArraySavitch
```

Display 16.7   Demonstration Program for Template Class PFArray (part 1 of 2)

```
1   //Program to demonstrate the template class PFArray.
2   #include <iostream>
3   #include <string>
4   using std::cin;
5   using std::cout;
6   using std::endl;
7   using std::string;

8   #include "pfarray.h"
9   #include "pfarray.cpp"
10  using PFArraySavitch::PFArray;

11  int main( )
12  {
13      PFArray<int> a(10);

14      cout << "Enter up to 10 nonnegative integers.\n";
15      cout << "Place a negative number at the end.\n";
16      int next;
17      cin >> next;
18      while ((next >= 0) && (!a.full( )))
19      {
20          a.addElement(next);
21          cin >> next;
22      }
23      if (next >= 0)
24      {
25          cout << "Could not read all numbers.\n";
26          //Clear the unread input:
27          while (next >= 0)
28              cin >> next;
29      }

30      cout << "You entered the following:\n ";
31      int index;
32      int count = a.getNumberUsed( );
33      for (index = 0; index < count; index++)
34          cout << a[index] << " ";
35      cout << endl;
36      PFArray<string> b(3);
37      cout << "Enter three words:\n";
38      string nextWord;
```

Display 16.7   Demonstration Program for Template Class `PFArray` (part 2 of 2)

```
39    for (index = 0; index < 3; index++)
40    {
41        cin >> nextWord;
42        b.addElement(nextWord);
43    }

44    cout << "You wrote the following:\n";
45    count = b.getNumberUsed( );
46    for (index = 0; index < count; index++)
47        cout << b[index] << " ";
48    cout << endl;
49    cout << "I hope you really mean it.\n";

50        return 0;
51 }
```

Sample Dialogue

```
Enter up to 10 nonnegative integers.
Place a negative number at the end.
1 2 3 4 5 -1
You entered the following:
1 2 3 4 5
Enter three words:
I love you
You wrote the following:
I love you
I hope you really mean it
```

Friend Functions

Friend functions are used with template classes in the same way that they are used with ordinary classes. The only difference is that you must include a type parameter where appropriate.

Self-Test Exercise

12. What do you have to do to make the following function a friend of the template class `PFArray` in Display 16.5?

```
void showData(PFArray<T> theObject);
//Displays the data in theObject to the screen.
//Assumes that << is defined for values of type T.
```

The `vector` and `basic_string` Templates

If you have not yet done so, this would be a good time to read Section 7.3 of Chapter 7, which covers the template class `vector`.

Another predefined template class is the `basic_string` template class. This class can deal with strings of elements of any type. The class `basic_string<char>` is the class for strings of characters. The class `basic_string<double>` is the class for strings of numbers of type `double`. The class `basic_string<YourClass>` is the class for strings of objects of the class `YourClass` (whatever that may be).

You have already been using a special case of the `basic_string` template class. The unadorned name `string`, which we have been using, is an alternate name for the class `basic_string<char>`. All the member functions you learned for the class `string` apply and behave similarly for the template class `basic_string<T>`.

The template class `basic_string` is defined in the library with header file `<string>`, and the definition is placed in the `std` namespace. When using the class `basic_string`, you therefore need the following or something similar near the beginning of your file:

```
#include <string>
using namespace std;
```

or

```
#include <string>
using std::basic_string;
using std::string; //Only if you use the name string by itself
```

16.3   Templates and Inheritance

The ruling ideas of each age have ever been the ideas of its ruling class.

KARL MARX and FRIEDRICH ENGELS, *The Communist Manifesto*

There is very little new to learn about templates and inheritance. To define a derived template class, start with a template class (or sometimes a nontemplate class) and derive another template class from it. Do this in the same way that you derive an ordinary class from an ordinary base class. An example should clarify any questions you might have about syntax details.

EXAMPLE: Template Class For a Partially Filled Array with Backup

Chapter 14 (Displays 14.10 and 14.11) defined the class PFArrayDBak for partially filled arrays of double with backup. We defined it as a derived class of PFArrayD (Displays 14.8 and 14.9). The class PFArrayD was a class for a partially filled array, but it only worked for the base type double. Displays 16.5 and 16.6 converted the class PFArrayD to the template class PFArray so that it would work for any type as the array base type. In this program, we will define a template class PFArrayBak for a partially filled array with backup that will work for any type as the array base type. We will define the template class PFArrayBak as a derived class of the template PFArray. We can do this almost automatically by starting with the regular derived class PFArarryDBak and replacing all occurrences of the array base type double with a type parameter T, replacing the class PFArrayD with the template class PFArray, and cleaning up the syntax so it fully conforms to template syntax.

The interface to the template class PFArrayBak is given in Display 16.8. Note that the base class is PFArray<T> with the array parameter, not simply PFArray. If you think about it, you will realize that you need the <T>. A partially filled array of T with backup is a derived class of a partially filled array of T. The T, and how it is used, is important. The implementation for the template class PFArrayBak is given in Display 16.9. In what follows, we reproduce the first constructor definition in the implementation:

```
template<class T>
PFArrayBak<T>::PFArrayBak( )  :  PFArray<T>( ), usedB(0)
{
    b = new T[getCapacity( )];
}
```

Note that, as with any definition of a template class function, it starts with

```
template<class T>
```

Also notice that the base type of the array (given after the new) is the type parameter T. Other details may not be quite as obvious, but do make sense.

Next consider the following line:

```
PFArrayBak<T>::PFArrayBak( )  :  PFArray<T>( ), usedB(0)
```

As with any definition of a template class function, the definition has PFArray<T> with the type parameter before the scope resolution operator, but the constructor name is just plain, old PFArrayBak without any type parameter. Also notice that the base class constructor includes the type parameter T in the initialization PFArray<T>( ). This is so that the constructor will match the base type PFArray<T> as given in the following line of the interface:

```
class PFArrayBak : public PFArray<T>
```

A sample program using the template class PFArrayBak is given in Display 16.10.

Display 16.8   Interface for the Template Class PFArrayBak

```
1   //This is the header file pfarraybak.h. This is the interface for the
2   //template class PFArrayBak. Objects of this type are partially filled
3   //arrays of any type T. This version allows the programmer to make a
4   //backup copy and restore to the last saved copy of the partially filled
    //array.
5   #ifndef PFARRAYBAK_H
6   #define PFARRAYBAK_H
7   #include "pfarray.h"

8   namespace PFArraySavitch
9   {
10      template<class T>
11      class PFArrayBak : public PFArray<T>
12      {
13      public:
14          PFArrayBak( );
15          //Initializes with a capacity of 50.

16          PFArrayBak(int capacityValue);

17          PFArrayBak(const PFArrayBak<T>& Object);

18          void backup( );
19          //Makes a backup copy of the partially filled array.

20          void restore( );
21          //Restores the partially filled array to the last saved version.
22          //If backup has never been invoked, this empties the partially
23          //filled array.

24          PFArrayBak<T>& operator =(const PFArrayBak<T>& rightSide);
25          virtual ~PFArrayBak( );
26      private:
27          T *b; //for a backup of main array.
28          int usedB; //backup for inherited member variable used.
29      };

30   }// PFArraySavitch
31   #endif //PFARRAY_H
```

Display 16.9   Implementation for the Template Class PFArrayBak (part 1 of 3)

```
1   //This is the file pfarraybak.cpp.
2   //This is the implementation for the template class PFArrayBak. The
3   //interface for the template class PFArrayBak is in the file
    //pfarraybak.h.
4   #include "pfarraybak.h"
5   #include <iostream>
```

Display 16.9   Implementation for the Template Class **PFArrayBak** (part 2 of 3)

```
6   using std::cout;

7   namespace PFArraySavitch
8   {

9       template<class T>
10      PFArrayBak<T>::PFArrayBak( ) : PFArray<T>( ),usedB(0)
11      {
12          b = new T[getCapacity( )];
13      }

14      template<class T>
15      PFArrayBak<T>::PFArrayBak(int capacityValue)
16                      : PFArray<T>(capacityValue),usedB(0)
17      {
18          b = new T[getCapacity( )];
19      }

20      template<class T>
21      PFArrayBak<T>::PFArrayBak(const PFArrayBak<T>& oldObject)
22                      : PFArray<T>(oldObject),usedB(0)
23      {
24          b = new T[getCapacity( )];
25          usedB = oldObject.getNumberUsed( );
26          for (int i = 0; i < usedB; i++)
27              b[i] = oldObject.b[i];
28      }

29      template<class T>
30      void PFArrayBak<T>::backup( )
31      {
32          usedB = getNumberUsed( );
33          for (int i = 0; i < usedB; i++)
34              b[i] = operator[](i);
35      }

36      template<class T>
37      void PFArrayBak<T>::restore( )
38      {
39          emptyArray( );

40          for (int i = 0; i < usedB; i++)
41              addElement(b[i]);
42      }

43      template<class T>
44      PFArrayBak<T>& PFArrayBak<T>::operator =
                        (const PFArrayBak<T>& rightSide)
```

(continued)

Display 16.9 Implementation for the Template Class `PFArrayBak` (part 3 of 3)

```
45    {
46        PFArray<T>::operator =(rightSide);

47        if (getCapacity( ) != rightSide.getCapacity( ))
48        {
49            delete [] b;
50            b = new T[rightSide.getCapacity( )];
51        }
52        usedB = rightSide.usedB;
53        for (int i = 0; i < usedB; i++)
54            b[i] = rightSide.b[i];

55        return *this;
56    }

57    template<class T>
58    PFArrayBak<T>::~PFArrayBak( )
59    {
60        delete [] b;
61    }
62    }// PFArraySavitch
```

Display 16.10 Demonstration Program for Template Class `PFArrayBak` (part 1 of 2)

```
1    //Program to demonstrate the template class PFArrayBak.
2    #include <iostream>
3    #include <string>
4    using std::cin;
5    using std::cout;
6    using std::endl;
7    using std::string;

8    #include "pfarraybak.h"
9    #include "pfarray.cpp"
10   #include "pfarraybak.cpp"
11   using PFArraySavitch::PFArrayBak;

12   int main( )
13   {
14       int cap;
15       cout << "Enter capacity of this super array: ";
16       cin >> cap;
17       PFArrayBak<string> a(cap);

18       cout << "Enter " << cap << " strings\n";
19       cout << "separated by blanks.\n";

20       string next;
```

Do not forget to include the implementation of the base class template.

Display 16.10   Demonstration Program for Template Class **PFArrayBak** (part 2 of 2)

```
21      for (int i = 0; i < cap; i++)
22      {
23          cin >> next;
24          a.addElement(next);
25      }
26      int count = a.getNumberUsed( );
27      cout << "The following " << count
28           << " strings read and stored:\n";
29      int index;
30      for (index = 0; index < count; index++)
31          cout << a[index] << " ";
32      cout << endl;

33      cout << "Backing up array.\n";
34      a.backup( );
35      cout << "Emptying array.\n";
36      a.emptyArray( );
37      cout << a.getNumberUsed( )
38           << " strings are now stored in the array.\n";
39      cout << "Restoring array.\n";
40      a.restore( );
41      count = a.getNumberUsed( );
42      cout << "The following " << count
43           << " strings are now stored:\n";
44      for (index = 0; index < count; index++)
45          cout << a[index] << " ";
46      cout << endl;

47      cout << "End of demonstration.\n";
48      return 0;
49  }
```

Sample Dialogue

```
Enter capacity of this super array: 3
Enter 3 strings
separated by blanks.
I love you
The following 3 strings read and stored:
I love you
Backing up array.
Emptying array.
0 strings are now stored in the array.
Restoring array.
The following 3 strings are now stored:
I love you
End of demonstration.
```

Self-Test Exercises

13. Is it legal for a derived template class to start as shown in the following code? The template class `TwoDimPFArrayBak` is designed to be a two-dimensional partially filled array with backup.

```
template<class T>
class TwoDimPFArrayBak : public PFArray< PFArray<T> >
{
public:
    TwoDimPFArrayBak( );
```

Note that the space in `< PFArray<T> >` is important, or at least the last space is. If the space between the next-to-last `>` and the last `>` is omitted, then the compiler may interpret `>>` to be the extraction operator used for input in expressions such as `cin >> n;` rather than interpreting it as a nested `<` `>`.

14. Give the heading for the default (zero-argument) constructor for the class `TwoDimPFArrayBak` given in Self-Test Exercise 13. (Assume all instance variables are initialized in the body of the constructor definition, so you are not being asked to do that.)

Chapter Summary

- Using function templates, you can define functions that have a parameter for a type.

- Using class templates, you can define a class with a type parameter for subparts of the class.

- The predefined `vector` and `basic_string` classes are actually template classes.

- You can define a template class that is a derived class of a template base class.

Answers to Self-Test Exercises

1. Function declaration:

```
template<class T>
T maximum(T first, T second);
//Precondition: The operator < is defined for the type T.
//Returns the maximum of first and second.
```

Definition:

```
template<class T>
T maximum(T first, T second)
{
    if (first < second)
        return second;
    else
        return first;
}
```

2. Function declaration:

```
template<class T>
T absolute(T value);
//Precondition: The expressions x < 0 and -x are defined
//whenever x is of type T.
//Returns the absolute value of its argument.
```

Definition:

```
template<class T>
T absolute(T value)
{
    if (value < 0)
        return -value;
    else
        return value;
}
```

3. Templates provide a facility to allow the definition of functions and classes that have parameters for type names.

4. e. Any type, whether a primitive type (provided by C++) or a type defined by the user (a class or struct type, an enum type, or a type defined array, or int, float, double, etc.), but T must be a type for which the code in the template makes sense. For example, for the swapValues template function (Display 16.1), the type T must have a correctly working assignment operator.

5. The function declaration and function definition are given in the following code. They are basically identical to those for the versions given in Display 5.6 except that two instances of int are changed to T in the parameter list.

Function declaration:

```
template<class T>
int search(const T a[], int numberUsed, T target);
//Precondition: numberUsed is <= the declared size of a.
//Also, a[0] through a[numberUsed -1] have values.
//Returns the first index such that a[index] == target,
//provided there is such an index, otherwise returns -1.
```

Definition:

```
template<class T>
int search(const T a[], int numberUsed, T target)
{
    int index = 0;
    bool found = false;
    while ((!found) && (index < numberUsed))
        if (target == a[index])
            found = true;
        else
            index++;

    if (found)
        return index;
    else
        return -1;
}
```

6. Function overloading works only for types for which an overloading is provided. (Overloading may work for types that automatically convert to some type for which an overloading is provided, but it may not do what you expect.) The template solution will work for any type that is defined at the time of invocation, provided that the template function body makes sense for that type.

7. No, you cannot use an array with base type DayOfYear with the template function sort because the < operator is not defined on values of type DayOfYear. (If you overload <, as we discussed in Chapter 8, to give a suitable ordering on values of type DayOfYear, then you can use an array with base type DayOfYear with the template function sort. For example, you might overload < so it means one date comes before the other on the calendar and then sort an array of dates by calendar ordering.)

8. a contains: 0 1 2
b contains: 0 100 200
c contains: 0 1 2
After swapping a and b,
and changing b:
a contains: 0 100 200
b contains: 42 1 2
c contains: 42 1 2

Note that before swapValues(a, b); c is an alias (another name) for the array a. After swapValues(a, b); c is an alias for b. Although the values of a and b are in some sense swapped, things are not as simple as you might have hoped. With pointer variables, there can be side effects of using swapValues.

The point illustrated here is that the assignment operator is not as well behaved as you might want on array pointers and so the template swapValues does not work as you might want with variables that are pointers to arrays. The assignment operator does not do element-by-element swapping but merely swaps two pointers. So, the swapValues function used with pointers to arrays simply swaps two pointers. It might be best to not use swapValues with pointers to arrays (or any other pointers), unless you are very aware of how it behaves on the pointers. The swapValues template function used with a type T is only as good, or as bad, as the assignment operator is on type T.

9. Since the type can be any type at all, there are no natural candidates for the default initialization values. So this constructor does nothing, but it does allow you to declare (uninitialized) objects without giving any constructor arguments.

```
template<class T>
Pair<T>::Pair( )
{
    //Do nothing.
}
```

10. `int addUp(const Pair<int>& thePair)`

```
{
    return (thePair.getFirst( ) + thePair.getSecond( ));
}
```

11. `template<class T>`

```
T addUp(const Pair<T>& thePair)
{
    return (thePair.getFirst( ) + thePair.getSecond( ));
}
```

12. Add the following to the public section of the template class definition of PFArray:

```
friend void showData(PFArray<T> theObject);
//Displays the data in theObject to the screen.
//Assumes that << is defined for values of type T.
```

You also need to add a function template definition of showData. One possible definition is as follows:

```
namespace PFArraySavitch
{
    template<class T>
    void showData(PFArray< T > theObject)
    {
        for (int i = 0; i < theObject.used; i++)
            cout << theObject[i] << endl;
    }
}//PFArraySavitch
```

13. Yes, it is perfectly legal. There are other, possibly preferable, ways to accomplish the same thing, but this is legal and not even crazy.

14. `template<class T>`

```
TwoDimPFArrayBak<T>::TwoDimPFArrayBak( )
                        : PFArray< PFArray<T> >( )
```

MyProgrammingLab™   **Programming Projects**

Visit www.myprogramminglab.com to complete select exercises online and get instant feedback.

1. Write a template version of the iterative binary search algorithm from Display 13.8 which only searches an array of integers for an integer key. Specify requirements on the template parameter type.

2. Write a template version of the recursive binary search function from Display 13.6. Specify requirements on the template parameter type. Discuss the requirements on the template parameter type.

3. The template sort routine in Display 16.3 is based on an algorithm called the *selection sort*. Another related sorting algorithm is called **insertion sort**. The insertion sort algorithm is the sort method often used to sort a Bridge hand. Consider each element in turn, inserting it into its proper place among the elements at the start of the array that are already sorted. The element being considered is inserted by moving the larger elements "to the right" to make space and inserting the vacated place. For example, the following shows the steps in a selection sort of an array of ints a. The values of a[0] through a[4] are given on each line. The asterisk marks the boundary between the sorted and unsorted portions of the array.

```
2 * 5 3 4
2 5 * 3 4
2 3 5 * 4
2 3 4 5 *
```

First, write an insertion sort function that works for ints. Next, write the template version of this sort function. Finally, test thoroughly using several primitive types, using a type you create with the minimal machinery necessary to use the sort routine.

4. Write a template-based function that calculates and returns the absolute value of two numeric values passed in. The function should operate with any numeric data types (e.g., float, int, double, char).

5. Write a template-based class that implements a set of items. The class should allow the user to

   a. Add a new item to the set.
   b. Get the number of items in the set.
   c. Get a pointer to a dynamically created array containing each item in the set. The caller of this function is responsible for deallocating the memory.

   Test your class by creating sets of different data types (e.g., integers, strings).

6. Do Programming Project 10.6 for the wrapper class around a dynamic array of strings that allowed for the deletion and addition of string entries. Except this time, use a template-based class so the implementation is not limited to strings. Test the class with dynamic arrays of integers in addition to strings.

7. In this chapter, we used only a single template class type parameter. C++ allows you to specify multiple type parameters. For example, the following code specifies that the class accepts two type parameters:

```
template
<class T, class V>
class Example
{
    ...
}
```

When creating an instance of the class, we must now specify two data types, such as

```
Example<int, char> demo;
```

Modify the Pair class given in Display 16.4 so that the pair of items can be different data types. Write a main function that tests the class with pairs of different data types.

17 Linked Data Structures

17 Linked Data Structures

If somebody there chanced to be
Who loved me in a manner true
My heart would point him out to me
And I would point him out to you.

GILBERT AND SULLIVAN, *Ruddigore*

Introduction

A *linked list* is a list constructed using pointers. A linked list is not fixed in size but can grow and shrink while your program is running. A *tree* is another kind of data structure constructed using pointers. This chapter introduces the use of pointers for building such data structures. The Standard Template Library (STL) has predefined versions of these and other similar data structures. The STL is covered in Chapter 19. It often makes more sense to use the predefined data structures in the STL rather than defining your own. However, there are cases where you need to define your own data structures using pointers. (Somebody had to define the STL.) Also, this material will give you some insight into how the STL might have been defined and will introduce you to some basic widely used material.

Linked data structures produce their structures using dynamic variables, which are created with the `new` operator. The linked data structures use pointers to connect these variables. This gives you complete control over how you build and manage your data structures, including how you manage memory. This allows you to sometimes do things more efficiently. For example, it is easier and faster to insert a value into a sorted linked list than into a sorted array.

There are basically three ways to handle data structures of the kind discussed in this chapter:

1. The C-style approach of using global functions and `struct`s with everything public
2. Using classes with all member variables private and using accessor and mutator functions
3. Using friend classes (or something similar, such as private or protected inheritance or locally defined classes)

We give examples of all three methods. We introduce linked lists using method 1. We then present more details about basic linked lists and introduce both the stack and queue data structures using method 2. We give an alternate definition of our queue template class using friend classes (method 3), and also use friend classes (method 3) to present a tree template class. This way you can see the virtues and shortcomings of each approach. Our personal preference is to use friend classes, but each method has its own advocates.

Sections 17.1 through 17.3 do not use the material in Chapters 13 through 15 (recursion, inheritance, and polymorphism), with one small exception: We have marked our class destructors with the modifier virtual following the advice given in Chapter 15. If you have not yet read about virtual functions (Chapter 15), you can pretend that "virtual" does not appear in the code. For in the purposes of this chapter, it makes no difference whether "virtual" is present or not. Section 17.4 uses recursion (Chapter 13) but does not use Chapters 14 and 15.

17.1   Nodes and Linked Lists

A linked list, such as the one diagrammed in Display 17.1, is a simple example of a dynamic data structure. It is called a **dynamic data structure** because each of the boxes in Display 17.1 is a variable of a struct or class type that has been dynamically created with the new operator. In a dynamic data structure, these boxes, known as **nodes**, contain pointers, diagrammed as arrows, that point to other nodes. This section introduces the basic techniques for building and maintaining linked lists.

Nodes

A structure like the one shown in Display 17.1 consists of items that we have drawn as boxes connected by arrows. The boxes are called *nodes*, and the arrows represent pointers. Each of the nodes in Display 17.1 contains a string value, an integer, and a pointer that can point to other nodes of the same type. Note that pointers point to the entire node, not to the individual items (such as 10 or "rolls") that are inside the node.

Nodes are implemented in C++ as structs or classes. For example, the struct type definitions for a node of the type shown in Display 17.1, along with the type definition for a pointer to such nodes, can be as follows:

```
struct ListNode
{
    string item;
    int count;
    ListNode *link;
}

Typedef ListNode* ListNodePtr;
```

The order of the type definitions is important. The definition of ListNode must come first, since it is used in the definition of ListNodePtr.

The box labeled head in Display 17.1 is not a node but a pointer variable that can point to a node. The pointer variable head is declared as follows:

```
ListNodePtr head;
```

dynamic data structure

node structures

node type definition

Even though we have ordered the type definitions to avoid some illegal forms of circularity, the preceding definition of the type `ListNode` is still circular. The definition of the type `ListNode` uses the type name `ListNode` to define the member variable `link`. There is nothing wrong with this particular circularity, which is allowed in C++. One indication that this definition is not logically inconsistent is the fact that you can draw pictures, such as Display 17.1, that represent such structures.

We now have pointers inside `struct`s and have these pointers pointing to `struct`s that contain pointers, and so forth. In such situations the syntax can sometimes get involved, but in all cases the syntax follows those few rules we have described for pointers and `struct`s. As an illustration, suppose the declarations are as just shown, the situation is as diagrammed in Display 17.1, and you want to change the number in the first node from `10` to `12`. One way to accomplish this is with the following statement:

changing node data

```
(*head).count = 12;
```

The expression on the left side of the assignment operator may require a bit of explanation. The variable `head` is a pointer variable. The expression `*head` is thus the thing it points to, namely the node (dynamic variable) containing `"rolls"` and the integer `10`. This node, referred to by `*head`, is a `struct`, and the member variable of this `struct`, which contains a value of type `int`, is called `count`; therefore, `(*head).count` is the name of the `int` variable in the first node. The parentheses around `*head` are not optional. You want the dereferencing operation, `*`, to be performed before the dot operation. However, the dot operator has higher precedence than the dereferencing

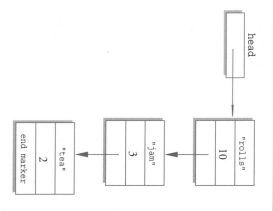

head

"rolls"
10

"jam"
3

"tea"
2
end marker

Display 17.1   Nodes and Pointers

operator, `*`, and so without the parentheses, the dot operation would be performed first (which would produce an error). The next paragraph describes a shortcut notation that can avoid this worry about parentheses.

C++ has an operator that can be used with a pointer to simplify the notation for specifying the members of a `struct` or a class. Chapter 10 introduced the arrow operator, `->`, but we have not used it extensively before now. So, a review is in order. The arrow operator combines the actions of a dereferencing operator, `*`, and a dot operator to specify a member of a dynamic `struct` or class object that is pointed to by a given pointer. For example, the previous assignment statement for changing the number in the first node can be written more simply as

```
head->count = 12;
```

This assignment statement and the previous one mean the same thing, but this one is the form normally used.

The string in the first node can be changed from `"rolls"` to `"bagels"` with the following statement:

```
head->item = "bagels";
```

The result of these changes to the first node in the list is diagrammed in Display 17.2.

the -> operator

Display 17.2   Accessing Node Data

```
head->count = 12;
head->item = "bagels";
```

Before

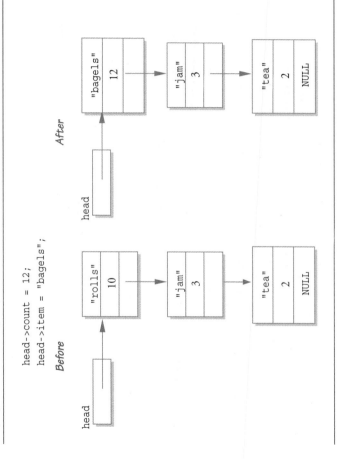

After

The Arrow Operator, ->

The arrow operator, `->`, specifies a member of a struct or a member of a class object that is pointed to by a pointer variable. The syntax is

```
Pointer_Variable->Member_Name
```

This refers to a member of the struct or class object pointed to by the Pointer_Variable. Which member it refers to is given by the Member_Name. For example, suppose you have the following definition:

```
struct Record
{
    int number;
    char grade;
};
```

The following creates a dynamic variable of type Record and sets the member variables of the dynamic struct variable to 2001 and 'A':

```
Record *p;
p = new Record;
p->number = 2001;
p->grade = 'A';
```

Look at the pointer member in the last node in the list shown in Display 17.2. This last node has the word NULL written where there should be a pointer. In Display 17.1, we filled this position with the phrase "end marker," but "end marker" is not a C++ expression. In C++ programs we use the constant NULL as a marker to signal the end of a linked list (or the end of any other kind of linked data structure).

NULL is typically used for two different (but often coinciding) purposes. First, NULL is used to give a value to a pointer variable that otherwise would not have any value. This prevents an inadvertent reference to memory, since NULL is not the address of any memory location. The second category of use is that of an end marker. A program can step through the list of nodes as shown in Display 17.2 and know that it has come to the end of the list when the program reaches the node that contains NULL.

NULL

As noted in Chapter 10, the constant NULL is actually the number 0, but we prefer to think of it and spell it as NULL to make it clear that it means this special-purpose value that you can assign to pointer variables. The definition of the identifier NULL is in a number of the standard libraries, such as `<iostream>` and `<cstddef>`, so you should use an include directive with either `<iostream>`, `<cstddef>`, or some other suitable library when you use NULL. The definition of NULL is handled by the C++ preprocessor, which replaces NULL with 0. Thus, the compiler never actually sees "NULL", so there are no namespace issues; therefore, no using directive is needed for NULL.

NULL is 0

A pointer can be set to NULL using the assignment operator, as in the following, which declares a pointer variable called there and initializes it to NULL:

```
double *there = NULL;
```

The constant NULL can be assigned to a pointer variable of any pointer type.

NULL

NULL is a special constant value that is used to give a value to a pointer variable that would not otherwise have a value. NULL can be assigned to a pointer variable of any type. The identifier NULL is defined in a number of libraries including the library with header file <cstddef> and the library with header file <iostream>. The constant NULL is actually the number 0, but we prefer to think of it and spell it as NULL.

Linked Lists as Arguments

You should always keep one pointer variable pointing to the head of a linked list. This pointer variable is a way to name the linked list. When you write a function that takes a linked list as an argument, this pointer (which points to the head of the linked list) can be used as the linked list argument.

Self-Test Exercises

1. Suppose your program contains the following type definitions:

```
struct Box
{
    string name;
    int number;
    Box *next;
};

typedef Box* BoxPtr;
```

What is the output produced by the following code?

```
BoxPtr head;
head = new Box;
head->name = "Sally";
head->number = 18;
cout << (*head).name << endl;
cout << head->name << endl;
cout << (*head).number << endl;
cout << head->number << endl;
```

(continued)

Self-Test Exercises (continued)

2. Suppose that your program contains the type definitions and code given in Self-Test Exercise 1. That code creates a node that contains the string "Sally" and the number 18. What code would you add to set the value of the member variable next of this node equal to NULL?

3. Consider the following structure definition:

```
struct ListNode
{
    string item;
    int count;
    ListNode *link;
};
ListNode *head = new ListNode;
```

Give code to assign the string "Wilbur's brother Orville" to the member variable item of the variable to which head points.

Linked Lists

Lists such as those shown in Display 17.1 are called *linked lists*. A **linked list** is a list of nodes in which each node has a member variable that is a pointer that points to the next node in the list. The first node in a linked list is called the **head**, which is why the pointer variable that points to the first node is named head. Note that the pointer named head is not itself the head of the list but only points to it. The last node has no special name, but it does have a special property: It has NULL as the value of its member pointer variable. To test whether a node is the last node, you need only test whether the pointer variable in the node is equal to NULL.

Our goal in this section is to write some basic functions for manipulating linked lists. For variety, and to simplify the notation, we will use a simpler type of data for the nodes than that used in Display 17.2. These nodes will contain only an integer and a pointer. However, we will make our nodes more complicated in one sense. We will make them objects of a class, rather than just a simple struct. The node and pointer type definitions that we will use are as follows:

```
class IntNode
{
public:
    IntNode( ) {}
    IntNode(int theData, IntNode* theLink)
        : data(theData), link(theLink) {}
    IntNode* getLink( ) const { return link; }
    int getData( ) const { return data; }
```

linked list

head

node type definition

```
     void setData(int theData)  { data = theData; }
     void setLink(IntNode* pointer) { link = pointer; }
private:
     int data;
     IntNode *link;
};
typedef IntNode* IntNodePtr;
```

Note that all the member functions in the class IntNode are simple enough to have inline definitions.

Notice the two-parameter constructor for the class IntNode. It will allow us to create nodes with a specified integer as data and with a specified link member. For example, if p1 points to a node n1, then the following creates a new node pointed to by p2 such that this new node has data 42 and has its link member pointing to n1:

```
IntNodePtr p2 = new IntNode(42, p1);
```

After we derive some basic functions for creating and manipulating linked lists with this node type, we will convert the node type and the functions to template versions so they will work to store any type of data in the nodes.

As a warm-up exercise, let us see how we might construct the start of a linked list with nodes of this type. We first declare a pointer variable, called head, that will point to the head of our linked list:

```
IntNodePtr head;
```

To create our first node, we use the operator new to create a new dynamic variable that will become the first node in our linked list:

```
head = new IntNode;
```

We then give values to the member variables of this new node:

```
head->setData(3);
head->setLink(NULL);
```

Notice that the pointer member of this node is set equal to NULL because this node is the last node in the list (as well as the first node in the list). At this stage our linked list looks like this:

That was more work than we needed to do. By using the IntNode constructor with two parameters, we can create our one-node linked list much easier. The following is an easier way to obtain the one-node linked list just pictured:

```
head = new IntNode(3, NULL);
```

a one-node linked list

As it turns out, we will always create new nodes using this two-argument constructor for `IntNode`. Many programs would even omit the zero-argument constructor from the definition of `IntNode` so that it would be impossible to create a node without specifying values for each member variable.

Our one-node list was built in an ad hoc way. To have a larger linked list, your program must be able to add nodes in a systematic way. We next describe one simple way to insert nodes in a linked list.

Inserting a Node at the Head of a List

In this subsection we assume that our linked list already contains one or more nodes, and we develop a function to add another node. The first parameter for the insertion function will be a call-by-reference parameter for a pointer variable that points to the head of the linked list—that is, a pointer variable that points to the first node in the linked list. The other parameter will give the number to be stored in the new node. The function declaration for our insertion function is as follows:

```
void headInsert(IntNodePtr& head, int theData);
```

To insert a new node into the linked list, our function will use the `new` operator and our two-argument constructor for `IntNode`. The new node will have `theData` as its data and will have its link member pointing to the first node in the linked list (before insertion). The dynamic variable is created as follows:

```
new IntNode(theData, head)
```

We want the pointer `head` to point to this new node, so the function body can simply be

```
{
    head = new IntNode(theData, head);
}
```

Display 17.3 contains a diagram of the action

```
head = new IntNode(theData, head);
```

when `theData` is 12. The complete function definition is given in Display 17.4.

You will want to allow for the possibility that a list contains nothing. For example, a shopping list might have nothing in it because there is nothing to buy this week. A list with nothing in it is called an **empty list**. A linked list is named by naming a pointer that points to the head of the list, but an empty list has no head node. To specify an empty list, use the value `NULL`. If the pointer variable `head` is supposed to point to the head node of a linked list and you want to indicate that the list is empty, then set the value of `head` as follows:

```
head = NULL;
```

Whenever you design a function for manipulating a linked list, you should always check to see if it works on the empty list. If it does not, you may be able to add a special case for the empty list. If you cannot design the function to apply to the empty

Display 17.3   Adding a Node to the Head of a Linked List

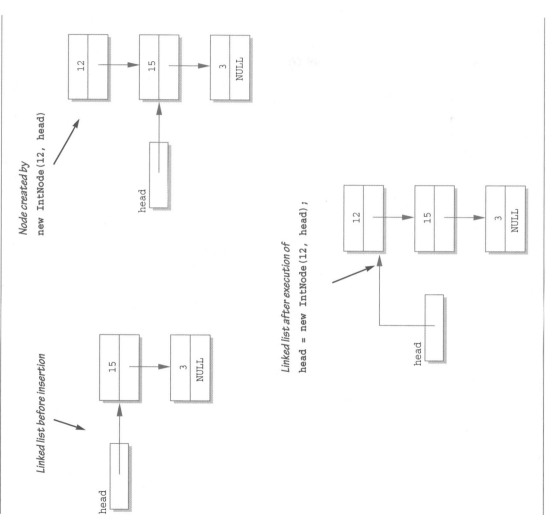

Linked list before insertion

head

| 15 | → | 3 | NULL |

Node created by
new IntNode(12, head)

head

| 12 | → | 15 | → | 3 | NULL |

Linked list after execution of
head = new IntNode(12, head) ;

head

| 12 | → | 15 | → | 3 | NULL |

list, then your program must be designed to handle empty lists some other way or to avoid them completely. Fortunately, the empty list can often be treated just like any other list. For example, the function headInsert in Display 17.4 was designed with nonempty lists as the model, but a check will show that it works for the empty list as well.

Display 17.4   Functions for Adding a Node to a Linked List

NODE AND POINTER TYPE DEFINITIONS

```
class IntNode
{
public:
    IntNode( ) {}
    IntNode(int theData, IntNode* theLink)
        : data(theData), link(theLink) {}
    IntNode* getLink( ) const { return link; }
    int getData( ) const { return data; }
    void setData(int theData) { data = theData; }
    void setLink(IntNode* pointer) { link = pointer; }
private:
    int data;
    IntNode *link;
};

typedef IntNode* IntNodePtr;
```

FUNCTION TO ADD A NODE AT THE HEAD OF A LINKED LIST
FUNCTION DECLARATION

```
void headInsert(IntNodePtr& head, int theData);
//Precondition: The pointer variable head points to
//the head of a linked list.
//Postcondition: A new node containing theData
//has been added at the head of the linked list.
```

FUNCTION DEFINITION

```
void headInsert(IntNodePtr& head, int theData)
{
    head = new IntNode(theData, head);
}
```

FUNCTION TO ADD A NODE IN THE MIDDLE OF A LINKED LIST
FUNCTION DECLARATION

```
void insert(IntNodePtr afterMe, int theData);
//Precondition: afterMe points to a node in a linked list.
//Postcondition: A new node containing theData
//has been added after the node pointed to by afterMe.
```

FUNCTION DEFINITION

```
void insert(IntNodePtr afterMe, int theData)
{
    afterMe->setLink(new IntNode(theData, afterMe->getLink( )));
}
```

PITFALL: Losing Nodes

You might be tempted to write the function definition for `headInsert` (Display 17.4) using the zero-argument constructor to set the member variables of the new node. If you were to try, you might start the function as follows:

```
head = new IntNode;
head->setData(theData);
```

At this point, the new node is constructed, contains the correct data, and is pointed to by the pointer `head`—all as it is supposed to be. All that is left to do is attach the rest of the list to this node by setting the pointer member in this new node so that it points to what was formerly the first node of the list. You could do it with the following, if only you could figure out what pointer to put in place of the question mark:

```
head->setLink(?);
```

Display 17.5 shows the situation when the new data value is 12 and illustrates the problem. If you were to proceed in this way, there would be nothing pointing to the node containing 15. Since there is no named pointer pointing to it (or to a chain of pointers extending to that node), there is no way the program can reference this node. The node and all nodes below this node are lost. A program cannot make a pointer point to any of these nodes, nor can it access the data in these nodes or do anything else to them. It simply has no way to refer to the nodes. Such a situation ties up memory for the duration of the program. A program that loses nodes is sometimes said to have a **memory leak**. A significant memory leak can result in the program running out of memory and terminating abnormally. Worse, a memory leak (lost nodes) in an ordinary users program can, in rare situations, cause the operating system to crash. To avoid such lost nodes, the program must always keep some pointer pointing to the head of the list, usually the pointer in a pointer variable like `head`. ∎

memory leak

Inserting and Removing Nodes Inside a List

We next design a function to insert a node at a specified place in a linked list. If you want the nodes in some particular order, such as numerical or alphabetical, you cannot simply insert the node at the beginning or end of the list. We will therefore design a function to insert a node after a specified node in the linked list.

We assume that some other function or program part has correctly placed a pointer called `afterMe` pointing to some node in the linked list. We want the new node to be placed after the node pointed to by `afterMe`, as illustrated in Display 17.6. The same technique works for nodes with any kind of data, but to be concrete, we are using

inserting in the middle of a list

Display 17.5   Lost Nodes

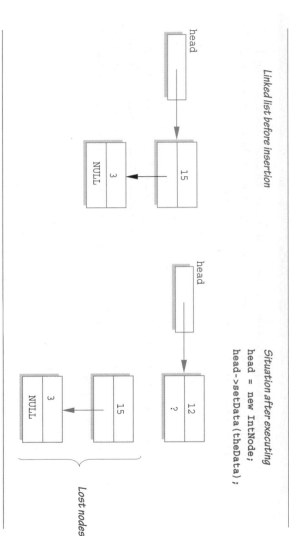

Linked list before insertion

head

| 15 | → | 3 | NULL |

Situation after executing

```
head = new IntNode;
head->setData(theData);
```

head

| 12 | ? | → | 15 | → | 3 | NULL |

Lost nodes

the same type of nodes as in previous subsections. The type definitions are given in Display 17.4. The function declaration for the function we want to define is given in the following:

```
void insert(IntNodePtr afterMe, int theData);
//Precondition: afterMe points to a node in a linked list.
//Postcondition: A new node containing theData
//has been added after the node pointed to by afterMe.
```

The new node is inserted inside the list in basically the same way a node is added to the head (start) of a list, which we have already discussed. The only difference is that we use the pointer afterMe->link instead of the pointer head. The insertion is done as follows:

```
afterMe->setLink(new IntNode(theData, afterMe->getLink( )));
```

The details with theData equal to 5 are pictured in Display 17.6, and the final function definition is given in Display 17.4.

insertion at the ends

If you go through the code for the function insert, you will see that it works correctly even if the node pointed to by afterMe is the last node in the list. However, insert will not work for inserting a node at the beginning of a linked list. The function headInsert given in Display 17.4 can be used to insert a node at the beginning of a list.

comparison to arrays

By using the function insert, you can maintain a linked list in numerical or alphabetical order or in some other ordering. You can squeeze a new node into the correct position by simply adjusting two pointers. This is true no matter how long the linked list is or where in the list you want the new data to go. If you instead use an array, much—and in extreme cases, all—of the array would have to be copied in order

Display 17.6   Inserting in the Middle of a Linked List

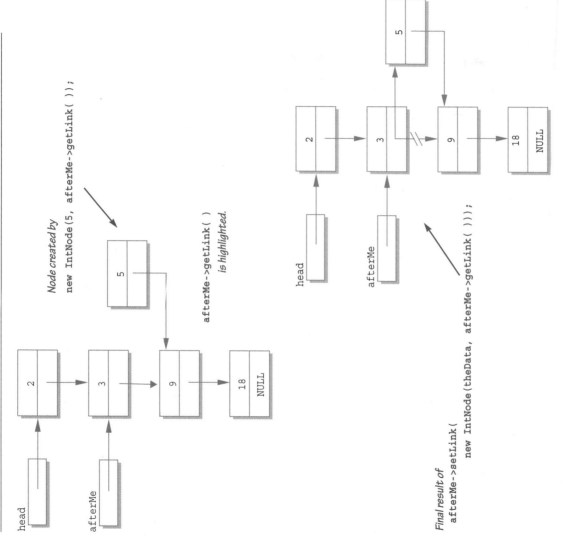

Node created by
`new IntNode(5, afterMe->getLink( ));`

`afterMe->getLink( )`
is highlighted.

Final result of
`afterMe->setLink(`
    `new IntNode(theData, afterMe->getLink( ));`

to make room for a new value in the correct spot. Despite the overhead involved in positioning the pointer `afterMe`, inserting into a linked list is frequently more efficient than inserting into an array.

Removing a node from a linked list is also quite easy. Display 17.7 illustrates the method. Once the pointers `before` and `discard` have been positioned, all that is required to remove the node is the following statement:

`before->setLink(discard->getLink( ));`

removing a node

Display 17.7   Removing a Node

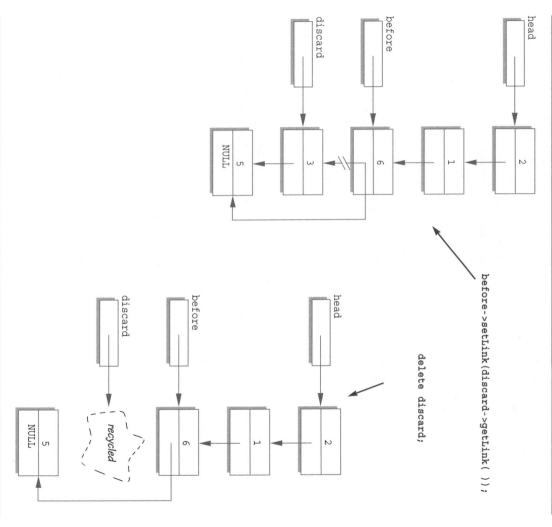

This is sufficient to remove the node from the linked list. However, if you are not using this node for something else, you should destroy the node and return the memory it uses for recycling; you can do this with a call to delete as follows:

```
delete discard;
```

As we noted in Chapter 10, the memory for dynamic variables is kept in an area of memory known as the *freestore*. Because the freestore is not unlimited, when a dynamic variable (node) is no longer needed by your program, you should return this memory for recycling using the delete operator. We include a review of the delete operator in the accompanying box.

The delete Operator

The delete operator eliminates a dynamic variable and returns the memory that the dynamic variable occupied to the freestore. The memory can then be reused to create new dynamic variables. For example, the following eliminates the dynamic variable pointed to by the pointer variable p:

```
delete p;
```

After a call to delete, the value of the pointer variable, like p just shown, is undefined.

PITFALL: Using the Assignment Operator with Dynamic Data Structures

If head1 and head2 are pointer variables and head1 points to the head node of a linked list, the following will make head2 point to the same head node and hence the same linked list:

```
head2 = head1;
```

However, you must remember that there is only one linked list, not two. If you change the linked list pointed to by head1, then you will also change the linked list pointed to by head2, because they are the same linked lists.

If head1 points to a linked list and you want head2 to point to a second, identical *copy* of this linked list, the preceding assignment statement will not work. Instead, you must copy the entire linked list node by node. ■

Searching a Linked List

Next we will design a function to search a linked list in order to locate a particular node. We will use the same node type, called IntNode, that we used in the previous subsections. (The definitions of the node and pointer types are given in Display 17.4.) The function we design will have two arguments: the linked list and the integer we want to locate. The function will return a pointer that points to the first node that contains that integer. If no node contains the integer, the function will return NULL.

This way our program can test whether the `int` is in the list by checking to see if the function returns a pointer value that is not equal to `NULL`. The function declaration and header comment for our function are as follows:

search

```
IntNodePtr search(IntNodePtr head, int target);
//Precondition: The pointer head points to the head of a
//linked list. The pointer variable in the last node is NULL.
//If the list is empty, then head is NULL.
//Returns a pointer that points to the first node that contains the
//target. If no node contains the target, the function returns NULL.
```

We will use a local pointer variable, called `here`, to move through the list looking for the target. The only way to move around a linked list, or any other data structure made up of nodes and pointers, is to follow the pointers. Thus, we will start with `here` pointing to the first node and move the pointer from node to node, following the pointer out of each node. This technique is diagrammed in Display 17.8.

Since empty lists present some minor problems that would clutter our discussion, we will at first assume that the linked list contains at least one node. Later we will come back and make sure the algorithm works for the empty list as well. This search technique yields the following algorithm:

Pseudocode for search Function

Make the pointer variable here point to the head node (that is, first node) of the linked list.

algorithm

```
while (here is not pointing to a node containing target
                and here is not pointing to the last node)
{
        Make here point to the next node in the list.
}
if (the node pointed to by here contains target)
        return here;
else
        return NULL;
```

To move the pointer `here` to the next node, we must think in terms of the named pointers we have available. The next node is the one pointed to by the pointer member of the node currently pointed to by `here`. The pointer member of the node currently pointed to by `here` is given by the expression

```
here->getLink( )
```

To move `here` to the next node, we want to change `here` so that it points to the node that is pointed to by the above-named pointer. Hence, the following will move the pointer `here` to the next node in the list:

```
here = here->getLink( );
```

Display 17.8   Searching a Linked List

target *is* 6

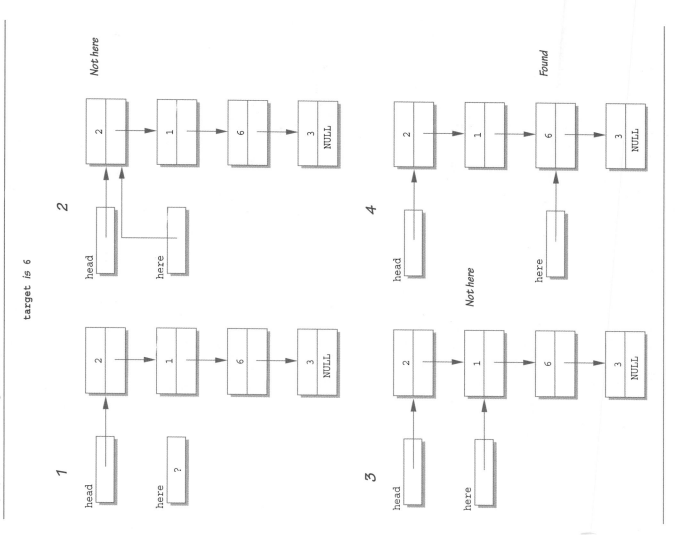

Putting these pieces together yields the following refinement of the algorithm pseudocode for the search function:

```
here = head;

while (here->getData( ) != target && here->getLink( ) != NULL)
    here = here->getLink( );

if (here->getData( ) == target)
    return here;
else
    return NULL;
```

Notice the Boolean expression in the `while` statement. We test to see if `here` is pointing to the last node by testing to see if the member variable `here->getLink( )` is equal to `NULL`.

empty list

We still must go back and take care of the empty list. If we check the previous code, we find that there is a problem with the empty list. If the list is empty, then `here` is equal to `NULL` and hence the following expressions are undefined:

```
here->getData( )
here->getLink( )
```

When `here` is `NULL`, it is not pointing to any node, so there is no data member or link member. Hence, we make a special case of the empty list. The complete function definition is given in Display 17.9.

Doubly Linked Lists

doubly linked list

An ordinary linked list allows you to move down the list in only one direction (following the links). A **doubly linked list** has one link that is a pointer to the next node and an additional link that is a pointer to the previous node. In some cases the link to the previous node can simplify our code. For example, if removing a node from the list, we will no longer need to have a `before` variable to remember the node that links to the node we wish to discard. Diagrammatically, a doubly linked list looks like the sample list in Display 17.10.

Display 17.9   Function to Locate a Node in a Linked List (part 1 of 2)

FUNCTION DECLARATION

```
IntNodePtr search(IntNodePtr head, int target);
//Precondition: The pointer head points to the head of a
//linked list. The pointer variable in the last node is NULL.
//If the list is empty, then head is NULL.
//Returns a pointer that points to the first node that contains the
//target. If no node contains the target, the function returns NULL.
```

FUNCTION DEFINITION

```
//Uses cstddef:
```

Display 17.9   Function to Locate a Node in a Linked List (part 2 of 2)

```
IntNodePtr search(IntNodePtr head, int target)
{
    IntNodePtr here = head;                    The definitions of IntNode
                                               and IntNodePtr are given in
    if (here == NULL) //if empty list          Display 17.4.
    {
        return NULL;
    }
    else
    {
        while (here->getData( ) != target && here->getLink( ) != NULL)
            here = here->getLink( );

        if (here->getData( ) == target)
            return here;
        else
            return NULL;
    }
}
```

Display 17.10   A Doubly Linked List

head

The node class for a doubly linked list of integers can be defined as follows:

```
class DoublyLinkedIntNode
{
public:
    DoublyLinkedIntNode ( ) {}
    DoublyLinkedIntNode (int theData, DoublyLinkedIntNode* previous,
                         DoublyLinkedIntNode* next)
        : data(theData), nextLink(next), previousLink(previous) {}
    DoublyLinkedIntNode* getNextLink( ) const { return nextLink; }
    DoublyLinkedIntNode* getPreviousLink( ) const
        { return previousLink; }
    int getData( ) const { return data; }
    void setData(int theData) { data = theData; }
    void setNextLink(DoublyLinkedIntNode* pointer)
                         { nextLink = pointer; }
```

```
        void setPreviousLink(DoublyLinkedIntNode* pointer)
        { previousLink = pointer; }
    private:
        int data;
        DoublyLinkedIntNode *nextLink;
        DoublyLinkedIntNode *previousLink;
};
typedef DoublyLinkedIntNode* DoublyLinkedIntNodePtr;
```

The code is almost identical to the version for the singly linked list except that we have added a private member variable, `previousLink`, to store a link to the previous node in the list. The functions `setPreviousLink` and `getPreviousLink` have been added to get and set the link, along with an additional parameter to the constructor to initialize `previousLink`. What used to be called `link` has also been renamed `nextLink` to differentiate between linking to the previous node or to the next node.

Adding a Node to a Doubly Linked List

To add a new `DoublyLinkedIntNode` to the front of the list, we must set links on two nodes instead of one. The general process is shown in Display 17.11. The declaration for the insertion function is basically the same as in the singly linked case:

```
    void headInsert(DoublyLinkedIntNodePtr& head, int theData);
```

First, we create a new node whose `nextLink` points to the old head and whose `previousLink` is `NULL`, because it will become the new head:

```
    DoublyLinkedIntNode* newHead = new DoublyLinkedIntNode
        (theData, NULL, head);
```

The old head has to link its previous pointer to the new head:

```
    head->setPreviousLink(newHead);
```

Finally, we set head to the new head:

```
    head = newHead;
```

The complete function definition is given in Display 17.13.

Deleting a Node from a Doubly Linked List

To remove a node from the doubly linked list also requires updating the references on both sides of the node we wish to delete. Thanks to the backward link we do not need a separate variable to keep track of the previous node in the list as we did for the singly linked list. The general process of deleting a node referenced by `position` is shown in Display 17.12. Note that some special cases must be handled separately, such as deleting a node from the beginning or the end of the list.

adding a node to a doubly linked list

deleting a node from a doubly linked list

Display 17.11   Adding a Node to the Front of a Doubly Linked List

Existing list before adding new node

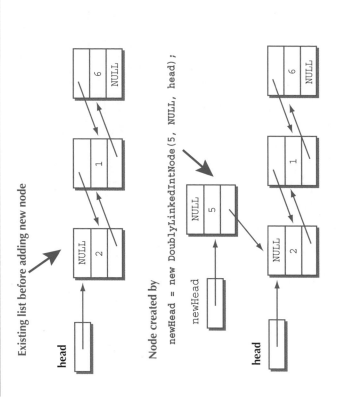

Node created by

```
newHead = new DoublyLinkedIntNode(5, NULL, head);
```

Set the previous link of the original head node

```
head->setPreviousNode(newHead);
```

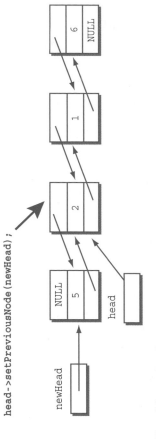

Set head to newHead

```
head = newHead;
```

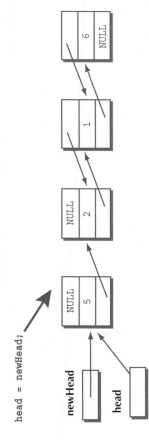

Display 17.12　Deleting a Node from a Doubly Linked List

Existing list before deleting `discard`

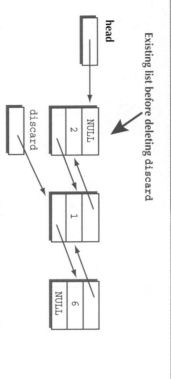

Set pointers to the previous and next nodes

```
DoublyLinkedIntNodePtr prev = discard->getPreviousLink ( ) ;
DoublyLinkedIntNodePtr next = discard->getNextLink ( ) ;
```

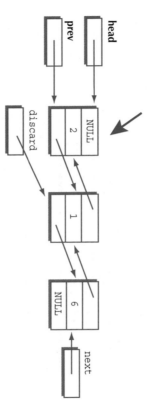

Bypass `discard`

```
prev->setNextLink(next) ;
next->setPreviousLink(prev) ;
```

Delete `discard`

```
delete discard;
```

The function declaration for our delete function is now

```
void delete(DoublyLinkedIntNodePtr& head,
            DoublyLinkedIntNodePtr discard);
```

The parameter discard is a pointer to the node we wish to remove. We must also input the head of the list to handle the case where discard is the same as head:

```
if (head == discard)
{
    head = head->getNextLink();
    head->setPreviousLink(NULL);
}
```

In this case we have to advance head to the next node in the list. We then set the previous link to NULL because there is no prior node. In the more general case, the variable discard points to any other node that is not the head. We handle this case by redirecting the links to bypass discard, as shown in Display 17.12:

```
else
{
    DoublyLinkedIntNodePtr prev = discard->getPreviousLink();
    DoublyLinkedIntNodePtr next = discard->getNextLink();
    prev->setNextLink(next);
    if (next != NULL)
    {
        next->setPreviousLink(prev);
    }
}
```

The previous node now links to discard's next node, and the next node now links to discard's previous node. Since discard might be the last node in the list, we have to check and make sure that next != NULL so we do not try to dereference a NULL pointer in the function setPreviousLink.

The complete function definition is given in Display 17.13.

Display 17.13   Functions to Add and Remove a Node from a Doubly Linked List (part 1 of 3)

NODE AND POINTER TYPE DEFINITIONS

```
class DoublyLinkedIntNode
{
public:
    DoublyLinkedIntNode( ) {}
    DoublyLinkedIntNode (int theData, DoublyLinkedIntNode* previous,
                         DoublyLinkedIntNode* next)
        : data(theData), nextLink(next), previousLink(previous) {}
    DoublyLinkedIntNode* getNextLink( ) const
        { return nextLink; }
```

(continued)

Display 17.13   Functions to Add and Remove a Node from a Doubly Linked List (part 2 of 3)

```
    DoublyLinkedIntNode* getPreviousLink( ) const
    { return previousLink; }
int getData( ) const
    { return data; }
void setData(int theData)
    { data = theData; }
void setNextLink(DoublyLinkedIntNode* pointer)
    { nextLink = pointer; }
void setPreviousLink(DoublyLinkedIntNode* pointer)
    { previousLink = pointer; }
private:
    int data;
    DoublyLinkedIntNode *nextLink;
    DoublyLinkedIntNode *previousLink;
}
typedef DoublyLinkedIntNode* DoublyLinkedIntNodePtr;
```

FUNCTION TO ADD A NODE AT THE HEAD OF A LINKED LIST

FUNCTION DECLARATION

```
void headInsert(DoublyLinkedIntNode& head, int theData);
//Precondition: The pointer variable head points to
//the head of a linked list.
//Postcondition: A new node containing theData
//has been added at the head of the linked list.
```

FUNCTION DEFINITION

```
void headInsert(DoublyLinkedIntNodePtr& head, int theData)
{
    DoublyLinkedIntNode* newHead = new DoublyLinkedIntNode
                                       (theData, NULL, head);

    head->setPreviousLink(newHead);
    head = newHead;
}
```

FUNCTION TO REMOVE A NODE

FUNCTION DECLARATION

```
void deleteNode(DoublyLinkedIntNodePtr& head,
                DoublyLinkedIntNodePtr discard);
//Precondition: The pointer variable head points to
//the head of a linked list and discard points to the node to remove.
//Postcondition: The node pointed to by discard is removed from the list.
```

Display 17.13   Functions to Add and Remove a Node from a Doubly Linked List (part 3 of 3)

FUNCTION DEFINITION

```
void deleteNode(DoublyLinkedIntNodePtr& head,
                DoublyLinkedIntNodePtr discard) ;
{
    if (head == discard)
    {
        head = head->getNextLink( ) ;
        head->setPreviousLink(NULL) ;
    }
    else
    {
        DoublyLinkedIntNodePtr prev = discard->getPreviousLink( ) ;
        DoublyLinkedIntNodePtr next = discard->getNextLink( ) ;
        prev->setNextLink(next) ;
        if (next != NULL)
        {
            next->setPreviousLink(prev) ;
        }
    }
    delete discard;
}
```

Self-Test Exercises

4. Write type definitions for the nodes and pointers in a linked list. Call the node type NodeType and call the pointer type PointerType. The linked lists will be lists of letters.

5. A linked list is normally referred to via a pointer that points to the first node in the list, but an empty list has no first node. What pointer value is normally used to represent an empty list?

6. Suppose your program contains the following type definitions and pointer variable declarations:

```
struct Node
{
    double data;
    Node *next;
}

typedef Node* Pointer;
Pointer p1, p2;
```

(continued)

Self-Test Exercises (continued)

Suppose p1 points to a node of the above type that is in a linked list. Write code that will make p1 point to the next node in this linked list. (The pointer p2 is for the next exercise and has nothing to do with this exercise.)

7. Suppose your program contains type definitions and pointer variable declarations as in Self-Test Exercise 6. Suppose further that p2 points to a node of the above type that is in a linked list and that is not the last node on the list. Write code that will delete the node *after* the node pointed to by p2. After this code is executed, the linked list should be the same, except that there will be one less node in the linked list. (*Hint:* You may want to declare another pointer variable to use.)

8. Suppose your program contains the following type definitions and pointer variable declarations:

```
class Node
{
public:

    Node(double theData, Node* theLink)
        : data(theData), next(theLink) {}

    Node* getLink( ) const { return next; }
    double getData( ) const { return data; }
    void setData(double theData) { data = theData; }
    void setLink(Node* pointer) { next = pointer; }

private:

    double data;
    Node *next;

}

typedef Node* Pointer;
Pointer p1, p2;
```

9. Suppose p1 points to a node of the above type that is in a linked list. Write code that will make p1 point to the next node in this linked list. (The pointer p2 is for the next exercise and has nothing to do with this exercise.)

Suppose your program contains type definitions and pointer variable declarations as in Self-Test Exercise 8. Suppose further that p2 points to a node of the above type that is in a linked list and that is not the last node on the list. Write code that will delete the node *after* the node pointed to by p2. After this code is executed, the linked list should be the same, except that there will be one less node in the linked list. (*Hint:* You may want to declare another pointer variable to use.)

Self-Test Exercises (continued)

10. Choose an ending to the following statement, and explain:

    For a large array and a large list holding the same type objects, inserting a new object at a known location into the middle of a linked list compared to insertion in an array is

    a. more efficient.

    b. less efficient.

    c. about the same.

11. Complete the body of the following function:

    ```
    void insert(DoublyLinkedIntNodePtr afterMe, int theData);
    ```

    The function should insert a new node with the value in theData after the node afterMe in a doubly linked list.

12. What operations are easier to implement with a doubly linked list than with a singly linked list? What operations are more difficult?

EXAMPLE: A Generic Sorting Template Version of Linked List Tools

It is a routine matter to convert our type definitions and function definitions to templates so that they will work for linked lists with data of any type T in the nodes. However, there are some details to worry about. The heart of what you need to do is replace the data type of the data in a node (the type int in Display 17.4) by a type parameter T and insert the following at the appropriate locations:

```
template<class T>
```

However, you should also do a few more things to account for the fact that the type T might be a class type. Since the type T might be a class type, a value parameter of type T should be changed to a constant reference parameter and a returned type of type T should have a const added so that it is returned by constant value. (The reason for returning by const value is explained in Chapter 8.)

The final templates with the changes we described are shown in Displays 17.14 and 17.15. It was necessary to do one more change from the simple case of a linked list of integers. Since template typedefs are not implemented in most compilers, we have not been able to use them. This means that on occasion we needed to use the following hard-to-read parameter type specification:

```
Node<T>*&
```

(continued)

```
template<class T>
void headInsert(Node<T>*& head, const T& theData);
```

EXAMPLE: (continued)

This is a call-by-reference parameter for a pointer to a node of type Node<T>. Next, we have reproduced a function declaration from Display 17.15 so you can see this parameter type specification in context:

Display 17.14   Interface File for a Linked List Library (part 1 of 2)

```
1   //This is the header file listtools.h. This contains type definitions
2   //and function declarations for manipulating a linked list to store
3   //data of any type T. The linked list is given as a pointer of type
4   //Node<T>* that points to the head (first) node of the list. The
5   //implementation of the functions is given in the file listtools.cpp
6   #ifndef LISTTOOLS_H
7   #define LISTTOOLS_H
8   namespace LinkedListSavitch
9   {
10      template<class T>
11      class Node
12      {
13      public:
14          Node(const T& theData, Node<T>* theLink) : data(theData),
                                                       link(theLink){}
15          Node<T>* getLink( ) const { return link; }
16          const T getData( ) const { return data; }
17          void setData(const T& theData) { data = theData; }
18          void setLink(Node<T>* pointer) { link = pointer; }
19      private:
20          T data;
21          Node<T> *link;
22      };
23      template<class T>
24      void headInsert(Node<T>*& head, const T& theData);
25      //Precondition: The pointer variable head points to
26      //the head of a linked list.
27      //Postcondition: A new node containing theData
28      //has been added at the head of the linked list.
29      template<class T>
30      void insert(Node<T>* afterMe, const T& theData);
31      //Precondition: afterMe points to a node in a linked list.
32      //Postcondition: A new node containing theData
33      //has been added after the node pointed to by afterMe.
```

It would be acceptable to use T as a parameter type where we have used const T&. We used a constant reference parameter because we anticipate that T will frequently be a class type.

Display 17.14   Interface File for a Linked List Library (part 2 of 2)

```
34    template<class T>
35    void deleteNode(Node<T>* before);
36    //Precondition: The pointer before points to a node that has
37    //at least one node after it in the linked list.
38    //Postcondition: The node after the node pointed to by before
39    //has been removed from the linked list and its storage
40    //returned to the freestore.

41    template<class T>
42    void deleteFirstNode(Node<T>*& head);
43    //Precondition: The pointer head points to the first
44    //node in a linked list with at least one node.
45    //Postcondition: The node pointed to by head has been removed
46    //from the linked list and its storage returned to the freestore.

47    template<class T>
48    Node<T>* search(Node<T>* head, const T& target);
49    //Precondition: The pointer head points to the head of a linked list.
50    //The pointer variable in the last node is NULL.
51    //== is defined for type T.
52    //(== is used as the criterion for being equal.)
53    //If the list is empty, then head is NULL.
54    //Returns a pointer that points to the first node that
55    //is equal to the target. If no node equals the target,
56    //then the function returns NULL.
57    }//LinkedListSavitch

58    #endif //LISTTOOLS_H
```

Display 17.15   Implementation File for a Linked List Library (part 1 of 2)

```
1     //This is the implementation file listtools.cpp. This file contains
2     //function definitions for the functions declared in listtools.h.
3     #include <cstddef>
4     #include "listtools.h"

5     namespace LinkedListSavitch
6     {
7         template<class T>
8         void headInsert(Node<T>*& head, const T& theData)
9         {
10            head = new Node<T>(theData, head);
11        }
```

(continued)

Display 17.15   Implementation File for a Linked List Library (part 2 of 2)

```
12    template<class T>
13    void insert(Node<T>* afterMe, const T& theData)
14    {
15        afterMe->setLink(new Node<T>(theData, afterMe->getLink( )));
16    }
17    template<class T>
18    void deleteNode(Node<T>* before)
19    {
20        Node<T> *discard;
21        discard = before->getLink( );
22        before->setLink(discard->getLink( ));
23        delete discard;
24    }
25    template<class T>
26    void deleteFirstNode(Node<T>*& head)
27    {
28        Node<T> *discard;
29        discard = head;
30        head = head->getLink( );
31        delete discard;
32    }
33    //Uses cstddef:
34    template<class T>
35    Node<T>* search(Node<T>* head, const T& target)
36    {
37        Node<T>* here = head;
38        if (here == NULL) //if empty list
39        {
40            return NULL;
41        }
42        else
43        {
44            while (here->getData( ) != target && here->getLink( ) != NULL)
45                here = here->getLink( );
46            if (here->getData( ) == target)
47                return here;
48            else
49                return NULL;
50        }
51    }
52    }//LinkedListSavitch
```

17.2   Linked List Applications

But many who are first now will be last, and many who are last now will be first.

Matthew 19:30

First come first served

A common (and more secular) saying

Linked lists have many applications. This section presents only a few small examples of their use—namely, common data structures that all use a linked list as the heart of their implementation.

EXAMPLE: A Stack Template Class

A **stack** is a data structure that retrieves data in the reverse of the order in which the data is stored. Suppose you place the letters 'A', 'B', and then 'C' in a stack. When you take these letters out of the stack, they will be removed in the order 'C', then 'B', and then 'A'. This use of a stack is diagrammed in Display 17.16. As shown there, you can think of a stack as a hole in the ground. In order to get something out of the stack, you must first remove the items on top of the one you want. For this reason a stack is often called a *last-in/first-out* data structure.

(continued)

Display 17.16   A Stack

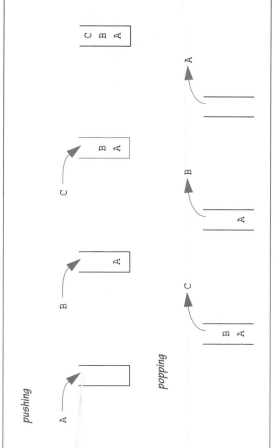

EXAMPLE: (continued)

Stacks are used for many language processing tasks. Chapter 13 discussed how the computer system uses a stack to keep track of C++ function calls. However, here we will only be concerned with one very simple application. Our goal in this example is to show how you can use the linked list techniques to implement specific data structures, such as a stack.

The interface for our `stack` class is given in Display 17.17. This is a template class with a type parameter `T` for the type of data stored in the stack. One item stored in the stack is a value of type `T`. In the example we present, `T` is replaced by the type `char`. However, in most applications, an item stored in the stack is likely to be a `struct` or class object. Each record (item of type `T`) that is stored in the stack is called a **stack frame**, which will explain why we occasionally use stackFrame as an identifier name in the definition of the stack template class. There are two basic operations you can perform on a stack: adding an item to the stack and removing an item from the stack. Adding an item is called **pushing** the item onto the stack, and so we called the member function that does this push. Removing an item from a stack is called **popping** the item off the stack, and so we called the member function that does this pop.

The names push and pop derive from a particular way of visualizing a stack. A stack is analogous to a mechanism that is sometimes used to hold plates in a cafeteria. The mechanism stores plates in a hole in the countertop. There is a spring underneath the plates with its tension adjusted so that only the top plate protrudes above the countertop. If this sort of mechanism were used as a stack data structure, the data would be written on plates (which might violate some health laws, but still makes a good analogy). To add a plate to the stack, put it on top of the other plates, and the weight of this new plate pushes down the spring. When you remove a plate, the plate below it pops into view.

Display 17.18 shows a simple program that illustrates how the `stack` class is used. This program reads a line of text one character at a time and places the characters in a stack. The program then removes the characters one by one and writes them to the screen. Because data is removed from a stack in the reverse of the order in which it enters the stack, the output shows the line written backward. We have `#included` the implementation of the `Stack` class in our application program, as we normally do with template classes. That means we cannot run or even compile our application program until we do the implementation of our `Stack` class template.

The definitions of the member functions for the template class `Stack` are given in the implementation file shown in Display 17.19. Our stack class is implemented as a linked list in which the head of the list serves as the `top` of the stack. The member

(continued on page 769)

push

pop

Display 17.17   Interface File for a Stack Template Class

```
1   //This is the header file stack.h. This is the interface for the class
2   //Stack, which is a template class for a stack of items of type T.
3   #ifndef STACK_H
4   #define STACK_H
                                            You might prefer to replace the
                                            parameter type T with const T&.
5   namespace StackSavitch
6   {
7       template<class T>
8       class Node
9       {
10      public:
11          Node(T theData, Node<T>* theLink) : data(theData), link(theLink) {}
12          Node<T>* getLink( ) const { return link; }
13          const T getData( ) const { return data; }
14          void setData(const T& theData) { data = theData; }
15          void setLink(Node<T>* pointer) { link = pointer; }
16      private:
17          T data;
18          Node<T> *link;
19      };
20      template<class T>
21      class Stack
22      {
23      public:
24          Stack( );
25          //Initializes the object to an empty stack.    Copy Constructor.
26          Stack(const Stack<T>& aStack);
27          Stack<T>& operator =(const Stack<T>& rightSide);
                                            The destructor destroys the stack
                                            and returns all the memory to the
28          virtual ~Stack( );              freestore.
29          void push(T stackFrame);
30          //Postcondition: stackFrame has been added to the stack.
31          T pop( );
32          //Precondition: The stack is not empty.
33          //Returns the top stack frame and removes that top
34          //stack frame from the stack.
35          bool isEmpty( ) const;
36          //Returns true if the stack is empty. Returns false otherwise.
37      private:
38          Node<T> *top;
39      };
40  } //StackSavitch
41  #endif //STACK_H
```

Display 17.18   Program Using the stack Template Class (part 1 of 2)

```
1    //Program to demonstrate use of the Stack template class.
2    #include <iostream>
3    #include "stack.h"
4    #include "stack.cpp"
5    using std::cin;
6    using std::cout;
7    using std::endl;
8    using StackSavitch::Stack;
9    int main( )
10   {
11       char next, ans;

12       do
13       {
14           Stack<char> s;
15           cout << "Enter a line of text:\n";
16           cin.get(next);
17           while (next != '\n')
18           {
19               s.push(next);
20               cin.get(next);
21           }

22           cout << "Written backward that is:\n";
23           while ( ! s.isEmpty( ) )
24               cout << s.pop( );
25           cout << endl;

26           cout << "Again?(y/n): ";
27           cin >> ans;
28           cin.ignore(10000, '\n');
29       }while (ans != 'n' && ans != 'N');

30       return 0;
31   }
```

Sample Dialogue

```
Enter a line of text:
straw
Written backward that is:
warts
Again?(y/n): y
```

The ignore member of cin is discussed in Chapter 9. It discards input remaining on the line.

Display 17.18   Program Using the stack Template Class (part 2 of 2)

```
Enter a line of text:
I love C++
Written backward that is:
++C evol I
Again?(y/n): n
```

Display 17.19   Implementation of the stack Template Class (part 1 of 2)

```
1   //This is the implementation file stack.cpp.
2   //This is the implementation of the template class Stack.
3   //The interface for the template class Stack is in the header file
    //stack.h.

4   #include <iostream>
5   #include <cstdlib>
6   #include <cstddef>
7   #include "stack.h"
8   using std::cout;

9   namespace StackSavitch
10  {

11      //Uses cstddef:
12      template<class T>
13      Stack<T>::Stack( ) : top(NULL)
14      {
15          //Intentionally empty
16      }

17      template<class T>
18      Stack<T>::Stack(const Stack<T>& aStack)
19      <The definition of the copy constructor is Self-Test Exercise 14.>

20      template<class T>
21      Stack<T>& Stack<T>::operator =(const Stack<T>& rightSide)
22      <The definition of the overloaded assignment operator is Self-Test Exercise 15.>

23      template<class T>
24      Stack<T>::~Stack( )
25      {
26          T next;
```

(continued)

Display 17.19   Implementation of the stack Template Class (part 2 of 2)

```
27        while (! isEmpty( ))
28            next = pop( );//pop calls delete.
29        }
30    }
31
32    //Uses cstddef:
33    template<class T>
34    bool Stack<T>::isEmpty( ) const
35    {
36        return (top == NULL);
37    }
38
39    template<class T>
40    void Stack<T>::push(T stackFrame)
41    <The rest of the definition is Self-Test Exercise 13.>
42
43    //Uses cstdlib and iostream:
44    template<class T>
45    T Stack<T>::pop( )
46    {
47        if (isEmpty( ))
48        {
49            cout << "Error: popping an empty stack.\n";
50            exit(1);
51        }
52
53        T result = top->getData( );
54
55        Node<T> *discard;
56        discard = top;
57        top = top->getLink( );
58
59        delete discard;
60        return result;
61    }
62    //StackSavitch
```

EXAMPLE: (continued)

variable top is a pointer that points to the head of the linked list. The pointer top serves the same purpose as the pointer head did in our previous discussions of linked lists.

Self-Test Exercise 13 is to write the definition of the member function push. However, we have already given the algorithm for this task. The code for the push member function is essentially the same as the function headInsert shown in Display 17.15, except that in the member function push we use a pointer named top in place of a pointer named head.

An empty stack is just an empty linked list, so an empty stack is implemented by setting the pointer top equal to NULL. Once you realize that NULL represents the empty stack, the implementations of the default constructor and of the member function empty are obvious.

The definition of the copy constructor is a bit more complicated but does not use any techniques we have not already discussed. The details are left to Self-Test Exercise 14.

The pop member function first checks to see if the stack is empty. If it is not empty, it proceeds to remove the top character in the stack. It sets the local variable result equal to the top symbol on the stack as follows:

```
T result = top->getData( );
```

After the data in the top node is saved in the variable result, the pointer top is moved to the next node in the linked list, effectively removing the top node from the list. The pointer top is moved with the statement

```
top = top->getLink( );
```

However, before the pointer top is moved, a temporary pointer, called discard, is positioned so that it points to the node that is about to be removed from the list. The storage for the removed node can then be recycled with the following call to delete:

```
delete discard;
```

Each node that is removed from the linked list by the member function pop has its memory recycled with a call to delete, so all that the destructor needs to do is remove each item from the stack with a call to pop. Each node will then have its memory returned to the freestore for recycling.

Stacks

A *stack* is a last-in/first-out data structure; that is, data items are retrieved in the opposite order to which they were placed in the stack.

Push and Pop

Adding a data item to a stack data structure is referred to as *pushing* the data item onto the stack. Removing a data item from a stack is referred to as *popping* the item off the stack.

Self-Test Exercises

13. Give the definition of the member function push of the template class Stack described in Displays 17.17 and 17.19.

14. Give the definition of the copy constructor for the template class Stack described in Displays 17.17 and 17.19.

15. Give the definition of the overloaded assignment operator for the template class Stack described in Displays 17.17 and 17.19.

EXAMPLE: A Queue Template Class

A stack is a last-in/first-out data structure. Another common data structure is a **queue**, which handles data in a *first-in/first-out* fashion. A queue can be implemented with a linked list in a manner similar to our implementation of the stack template class. However, a queue needs a pointer at both the head of the list and at the end of the linked list, since action takes place in both locations. It is easier to remove a node from the head of a linked list than from the other end of the linked list. Therefore, our implementation will remove nodes from the head of the list (which we will now call the **front** of the list) and will add nodes to the other end of the list, which we will now call the **back** of the list (or the back of the queue).

The definition of the Queue template class is given in Display 17.20. A sample application that uses the class Queue is shown in Display 17.21. The definitions of the member functions are left as Self-Test Exercises (but remember that the answers are given at the end of the chapter should you have any problems filling in the details).

Display 17.20   Interface File for a Queue Template Class (part 1 of 2)

```
1    //This is the header file queue.h.  This is the interface for the class
2    //Queue, which is a template class for a queue of items of type T.
3    #ifndef QUEUE_H
4    #define QUEUE_H
5
6    namespace QueueSavitch
7    {
8        template<class T>
9        class Node
10       {
11       public:
12           Node(T theData, Node<T>* theLink)  : data(theData),
13                link(theLink){}
14           Node<T>* getLink( ) const { return link; }
15           const T getData( ) const { return data; }
16           void setData(const T& theData)  { data = theData; }
17           void setLink(Node<T>* pointer)  { link = pointer; }
18       private:
19           T data;
20           Node<T> *link;
21       };
22
23       template<class T>
24       class Queue
25       {
26       public:
27           Queue( );
28           //Initializes the object to an empty queue.
29
30           Queue(const Queue<T>& aQueue);
31
32           Queue<T>& operator =(const Queue<T>& rightSide);
33
34           virtual ~Queue( );
35
36           void add(T item);
37           //Postcondition: item has been added to the back of the queue.
38
39           T remove( );
40           //Precondition: The queue is not empty.
41           //Returns the item at the front of the queue
42           //and removes that item from the queue.
```

This is the same definition of the template class Node that we gave for the stack interface in Display 17.17. See the "Tip: A Comment on Namespaces" for a discussion of this duplication.

Copy constructor.

You might prefer to replace the parameter type T with const T&.

The destructor destroys the queue and returns all the memory to the freestore.

(continued)

Display 17.20   Interface File for a Queue Template Class (part 2 of 2)

```
37        bool isEmpty( ) const;
38        //Returns true if the queue is empty. Returns false otherwise.
39     private:
40        Node<T> *front; //Points to the head of a linked list.
41                        //Items are removed at the head
42        Node<T> *back;  //Points to the node at the other end of the
43                        //linked list.
44                        //Items are added at this end.
45     };
46     } //QueueSavitch

47     #endif //QUEUE_H
```

Display 17.21   Program Using the Queue Template Class (part 1 of 2)

Contrast this with the similar program using a stack instead of a queue that we gave in Display 17.18.

```
1   //Program to demonstrate use of the Queue template class.
2   #include <iostream>
3   #include "queue.h"
4   #include "queue.cpp"
5   using std::cin;
6   using std::cout;
7   using std::endl;
8   using QueueSavitch::Queue;

9   int main( )
10  {
11     char next, ans;

12     do
13     {
14         Queue<char> q;
15         cout << "Enter a line of text:\n";
16         cin.get(next);
17         while (next != '\n')
18         {
19             q.add(next);
20             cin.get(next);
21         }

22         cout << "You entered:\n";
23         while ( ! q.isEmpty( ) )
24             cout << q.remove( );
25         cout << endl;
```

Display 17.21   Program Using the Queue Template Class (part 2 of 2)

```
26        cout << "Again?(y/n): ";
27        cin >> ans;
28        cin.ignore(10000, '\n');
29    } while (ans != 'n' && ans != 'N');

30    return 0;
31    }
```

Sample Dialogue

```
Enter a line of text:
straw
You entered:
straw
Again?(y/n): y
Enter a line of text:
I love C++
You entered:
I love C++
Again?(y/n): n
```

Queue

A *queue* is a *first-in/first-out* data structure; that is, the data items are removed from the queue in the same order that they were added to the queue.

TIP: A Comment on Namespaces

Notice that both of the namespaces StackSavitch (Display 17.17) and QueueSavitch (Display 17.20) define a template class called Node. As it turns out, the two definitions of Node are the same, but the point discussed here is the same whether the two definitions are the same or different. C++ does not allow you to define the same identifier twice, even if the two definitions are the same, unless the two names are somehow distinguished. In this case, the two definitions are allowed because they are in two different namespaces. It is even legal to use both the Stack template class and the Queue template class in the same program. However, you should use

```
using StackSavitch::Stack;
using QueueSavitch::Queue;
```

(continued)

CHAPTER 17

TIP: (continued)

rather than

```
using namespace StackSavitch;
using namespace QueueSavitch;
```

Most compilers will allow either set of using directives if you do not use the identifier Node, but the second set of using directives provides two definitions of the identifier Node and therefore should be avoided.

It would be fine to use either, but not both, of the following:

```
using StackSavitch::Node;
```

or

```
using QueueSavitch::Node; ■
```

MyProgrammingLab

Self-Test Exercises

16. Give the definitions for the default (zero-argument) constructor and the member functions Queue<T>::isEmpty for the template class Queue (Display 17.20).

17. Give the definitions for the member functions Queue<T>::add and Queue<T>::remove for the template class Queue (Display 17.20).

18. Give the definition for the destructor for the template class Queue (Display 17.20).

19. Give the definition for the copy constructor for the template class Queue (Display 17.20).

20. Give the definition for the overloaded assignment operator for the template class Queue (Display 17.20).

Friend Classes and Similar Alternatives

You may have found it a nuisance to use the accessor and mutator functions getLink and setLink in the template class Node (see Display 17.17 or Display 17.20). You might be tempted to avoid the invocations of getLink and setLink by simply making the member variable link of the class Node public instead of private. Before you abandon the principle of making all member variables private, note two things. First, using getLink and setLink is not really any harder for you, the programmer, than directly accessing the links in the nodes. (However, getLink and setLink do introduce some overhead and so may slightly reduce efficiency.) Second, there is a way to avoid using getLink and setLink and instead directly access the links of nodes without making the link member variable public. Let us explore this second possibility.

Chapter 8 discussed friend functions. As you will recall, if f is a friend function of a class C, then f is not a member function of C; however, when you write the definition

friend class

of the function `f`, you can access private members of `c` just as you can in the definitions of member functions of `c`. A class can be a **friend** of another class in the same way that a function can be a friend of a class. If the class `F` is a friend of the class `C`, then every member function of the class `F` is a friend of the class `C`. Thus, if, for example, the `Queue` template class were a friend of the `Node` template class, then the private link member variables would be directly available in the definitions of the member functions of `Queue`. The details are outlined in Display 17.22.

Display 17.22 A Queue Template Class as a Friend of the `Node` Class (part 1 of 2)

```
1    //This is the header file queue.h. This is the interface for the class
2    //Queue, which is a template class for a queue of items of type T.
3    #ifndef QUEUE_H
4    #define QUEUE_H
5    namespace QueueSavitch
6    {
7        template<class T>                                    A forward declaration. Do not forget
8        class Queue;                                         the semicolon.

9        template<class T>                                    This is an alternate approach to that given in
10       class Node                                           Display 17.20. In this version, the Queue template
11       {                                                    class is a friend of the Node template class.
12       public:
13           Node(T theData, Node<T>* theLink) :  data(theData),
                      link(theLink) {}
14           friend class Queue<T>;                           If Node<T> is only used in the definition
15       private:                                             of the friend class Queue<T>, there is no
16           T data;                                          need for mutator or accessor functions.
17           Node<T> *link;
18       };

19       template<class T>
20       class Queue
21       {
22          <The definition of the template class Queue is identical to the one given in Display 17.20.
            However, the definitions of the member functions will be different from the ones we gave
            (in the Self-Test Exercises) for the nonfriend version of Queue.>
23          }
24       }   //QueueSavitch
25   }   //QueueSavitch

26   #endif //QUEUE_H                                         The implementation file would contain these
27   #include <iostream>                                      definitions and the definitions of the other member
28   #include <cstdlib>                                       functions similarly modified to allow access by name
29   #include <cstddef>                                       to the link and data member variables of the nodes.
30   #include "queue.h"
31   using std::cout;
32   namespace QueueSavitch
```

(continued)

Display 17.22　A Queue Template Class as a Friend of the Node Class (part 2 of 2)

```
33    {
34        template<class T>    //Uses cstddef:
35        void Queue<T>::add(T item)
36        {
37            if (isEmpty( ))
38                front = back = new Node<T>(item, NULL);
39            else
40            {
41                back->link = new Node<T>(item, NULL);
42                back = back->link;
43            }
44        }
45
46        template<class T>    //Uses cstdlib and iostream:
47        T Queue<T>::remove( )
48        {
49            if (isEmpty( ))
50            {
51                cout << "Error: Removing an item from an empty queue.\n";
52                exit(1);
53            }
54            T result = front->data;

55            Node<T> *discard;
56            discard = front;
57            front = front->link;
58            if (front == NULL) //if you removed the last node
59                back = NULL;

60            delete discard;
61            return result;
62        }
63    } //QueueSavitch
```

If efficiency is a major issue, you might want to use
(front == NULL) instead of (isEmpty( )).

Contrast these implementations with the ones given
as the answer to Self-Test Exercise 17.

forward
declaration

When one class is a friend of another class, it is typical for the classes to reference each other in their class definitions. This requires that you include a **forward declaration** to the class or class template defined second, as illustrated in Display 17.22. Note that the forward declaration is just the heading of the class or class template definition followed by a semicolon. A complete example using a friend class is given in Section 17.4 (see the programming example "A Tree Template Class").

Two approaches that serve pretty much the same purpose as friend classes and that can be used in pretty much the same way with classes and template classes such as Node and Queue are (1) using protected or private inheritance to derive Queue from Node, and (2) giving the definition of Node within the definition of Queue, so that Node is a local class (template) definition. (Protected inheritance is discussed in Chapter 14, and classes defined locally within a class are discussed in Chapter 7.)

EXAMPLE: Hash Tables with Chaining

hash table
hash map

A **hash table** or **hash map** is a data structure that efficiently stores and retrieves data from memory. There are many ways to construct a hash table; in this section we will use an array in combination with singly linked lists. In Section 17.1, we searched a linked list by iterating through every node in the list looking for a target. This process might require the examination of every node in the list, a potentially time-consuming process if the list is very long. In contrast, a hash table has the potential to find the target very quickly, although in a worst-case (but highly unlikely) scenario our implementation would run as slowly as using a singly linked list.

An object is stored in a hash table by associating it with a *key*. Given the key, we can retrieve the object. Ideally, the key is unique to each object. If the object has no intrinsically unique key, then we can use a **hash function** to compute one. In most cases the hash function computes a number.

hash function

For example, let us use a hash table to store a dictionary of words. Such a hash table might be useful to make a spell-checker—words missing from the hash table might not be spelled correctly. We will construct the hash table with a fixed array, where each array element references a linked list. The key computed by the hash function will map to the index of the array. The actual data will be stored in a linked list at the hash value's index. Display 17.23 illustrates the idea with a fixed array of ten entries. Initially each entry of the array hasharray contains a reference to an empty singly linked list. First, we add the word "cat," which has been assigned the key or hash value of 2 (we will show how this was computed shortly). Next, we add "dog" and "bird," which are assigned hash values of 4 and 7, respectively. Each of these strings is inserted as the head of the linked list using the hash value as the index in the array. Finally, we add "turtle," which also has a hash of 2. Since "cat" is already stored at index 2, we now have a **collision**. Both "turtle" and "cat" map to the same index in the array. When this occurs in a hash table with **chaining**, we simply insert the new node onto the existing linked list. In our example, there are now two nodes at index 2: "turtle" and "cat."

collision
chaining

To retrieve a value from the hash table, we first compute the hash value of the target. Next we sequentially search the linked list that is stored at hasharray[hashvalue] for the target. If the target is not found in this linked list, then the target is not stored in the hash table. If the size of the linked list is small, then the retrieval process will be quick.

(continued)

EXAMPLE: (continued)

A HASH FUNCTION FOR STRINGS

A simple way to compute a numeric hash value for a string is to sum the ASCII value of every character in the string and then compute the modulus of the sum using the size of the fixed array. A subset of ASCII codes is given in Appendix 3. Code to compute the hash value is shown in the function computeHash.

```
int computeHash(string s)
{
    int hash = 0;
    for (int i = 0; i < s.length( ); i++)
    {
        hash = hash + s[i];
    }
    return hash % SIZE;    //SIZE = 10 in example
}
```

For example, the ASCII codes for the string "dog" are

```
d    ->    100
o    ->    111
g    ->    103
```

The hash function is computed as

```
Sum       = 100 + 111 + 103 = 314
Hash = Sum % 10 = 314 % 10   = 4
```

In this example, we first compute an unbounded value, the sum of the ASCII values in the string. However, the array was defined to hold a finite number of elements. To scale the sum to the size of the array, we compute the modulus of the sum with respect to the size of the array, which is 10 in the example. In practice, the size of the array is generally a prime number larger than the number of items that will be put into the hash table[1]. The computed hash value of 4 serves as a fingerprint for the string "dog." However, other strings may also map to the same value. For example, we can verify that "cat" maps to $(99 + 97 + 116)$ % 10 = 2 and "turtle" maps to $(116 + 117 + 114 + 116 + 108 + 101)$ % 10 = 2.

A complete code listing for a hash table class is given in Displays 17.24 and 17.25. A demo is shown in Display 17.26. The hash table definition uses an array where each element is a Node class defined in Display 17.14. The linked list is implemented using the generic linked list library defined in Displays 17.14 and 17.15.

---

[1]A prime number avoids common divisors after modulus that can lead to collisions.

Display 17.23   Constructing a Hash Table

Existing hash table with 10 empty linked lists

```
Node<string> *hashArray[10];
for (int i=0; i<10; i++) hashArray[i] = NULL;
```

hashArray	0	1	2	3	4	5	6	7	8	9
	NULL	NULL	NULL	NULL	NULL	NULL	NULL	NULL	NULL	NULL

After adding "cat" with a hash of 2

hashArray	0	1	2	3	4	5	6	7	8	9
	NULL	NULL	→ cat	NULL	NULL	NULL	NULL	NULL	NULL	NULL

After adding "dog" with a hash of 4 and "bird" with a hash of 7

hashArray	0	1	2	3	4	5	6	7	8	9
	NULL	NULL	→ cat	NULL	→ dog	NULL	NULL	→ bird	NULL	NULL

After adding "turtle" with a hash of 2 - collision and chained to linked list with "cat"

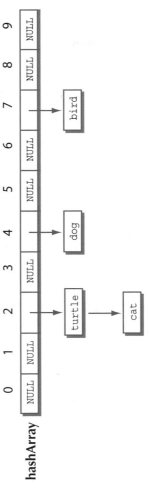

hashArray	0	1	2	3	4	5	6	7	8	9
	NULL	NULL	→ turtle → cat	NULL	→ dog	NULL	NULL	→ bird	NULL	NULL

Display 17.24 Interface File for a HashTable Class

```
1   //This is the header file hashtable.h. This is the interface
2   //for the class HashTable, which is a class for a hash table
3   //of strings.
4   #ifndef HASHTABLE_H
5   #define HASHTABLE_H

6   #include <string>
7   #include "listtools.h"                    The library "listtools.h" is the linked list
                                              library interface from Display 17.14.
8   using LinkedListSavitch::Node;
9   using std::string;

10  namespace HashTableSavitch
11  {
12      const int SIZE = 10;   //Maximum size of the hash table array

13      class HashTable
14      {
15      public:
16          HashTable( );    //Initialize empty hash table.

17          //Normally a copy constructor and overloaded assignment
18          //operator would be included. They have been omitted
19          //to save space.

20          virtual ~HashTable( );    //Destructor destroys hash table.

21          bool containsString(string target) const;
22          //Returns true if target is in the hash table,
23          //false otherwise.

24          void put(string s);
25          //Adds a new string to the hash table.

26      private:
27          Node<string> *hashArray[SIZE];         //The actual hash table
28          static int computeHash(string s);      //Compute a hash value
29      }; //HashTable
30  }; //HashTableSavitch
31  #endif  //HASHTABLE_H
```

Display 17.25 Implementation of the HashTable Class (part 1 of 2)

```cpp
1  //This is the implementation file hashtable.cpp.
2  //This is the implementation of the class HashTable.

3  #include <string>
4  #include "listtools.h"
5  #include "hashtable.h"

6  using LinkedListSavitch::Node;
7  using LinkedListSavitch::search;
8  using LinkedListSavitch::headInsert;
9  using std::string;

10 namespace HashTableSavitch
11 {
12     HashTable::HashTable( )
13     {
14         for (int i = 0; i < SIZE; i++)
15         {
16             hashArray[i] = NULL;
17         }
18     }

19     HashTable::~HashTable( )
20     {
21         for (int i=0; i<SIZE; i++)
22         {
23             Node<string> *next = hashArray[i];
24             while (next != NULL)
25             {
26                 Node<string> *discard = next;
27                 next = next->getLink( );
28                 delete discard;
29             }
30         }
31     }

32     int HashTable::computeHash(string s)
33     {
34         int hash = 0;
35         for (int i = 0; i < s.length( ); i++)
36         {
37             hash = hash + s[i];
38         }
39         return hash % SIZE;
40     }
```

(continued)

Display 17.25   Implementation of the HashTable Class (part 2 of 2)

```
41      void HashTable::put(string s)
42      {
43          int hash = computeHash(s);
44          if (search(hashArray[hash], s)==NULL)
45          {
46              //Only add the target if it's not in the list
47              headInsert(hashArray[hash], s);
48          }
49      }
50  //HashTableSavitch
```

Display 17.26   Hash Table Demonstration (part 1 of 2)

```
1   //Program to demonstrate use of the HashTable class
2   #include <string>
3   #include <iostream>
4   #include "hashtable.h"
5   #include "listtools.cpp"
6   #include "hashtable.cpp"
7   using std::string;
8   using std::cout;
9   using std::endl;
10  using HashTableSavitch::HashTable;

11  int main( )
12  {
13      HashTable h;

14      cout << "Adding dog, cat, turtle, bird" << endl;
15      h.put("dog");
16      h.put("cat");
17      h.put("turtle");
18      h.put("bird");
19      cout << "Contains dog? " << h.containsString("dog") << endl;
20      cout << "Contains cat? " << h.containsString("cat") << endl;
21      cout << "Contains turtle? " << h.containsString("turtle") << endl;
22      cout << "Contains bird? " << h.containsString("bird") << endl;
23      cout << "Contains fish? " << h.containsString("fish") << endl;
24      cout << "Contains cow? " << h.containsString("cow") << endl;
25      return 0;
26  }
```

Display 17.26   Hash Table Demonstration (part 2 of 2)

Sample Dialogue

```
Adding dog, cat, turtle, bird
  Contains dog? 1
  Contains cat? 1
  Contains turtle? 1
  Contains bird? 1
  Contains fish? 0
  Contains cow? 0
```

Hash Table

A *hash table* is a data structure that associates a data item with a key. The key is computed by a hash function.

Efficiency of Hash Tables

The efficiency of our hash table depends on several factors. First, let us examine some extreme cases. The worst-case run-time performance occurs if every item inserted into the table has the same hash key. Everything will then be stored in a single linked list, and the `find` operation may require searching through each item in the list. Fortunately, if the items that we insert are somewhat random, the possibility that all of them hash to the same key is highly unlikely. In contrast, the best-case run-time performance occurs if every item inserted into the table has a different hash key. This means that there will be no collisions, so the `find` operation will only need to search through a one-item list because the target will always be the first node in the linked list.

We can decrease the chance of collisions by using a better hash function. For example, the simple hash function that sums each letter of a string ignores the ordering of the letters. The words "rat" and "tar" would hash to the same value. A better hash function for a string `s` is to multiply each letter by an increasing weight depending on the position in the word:

```
int hash = 0;
for (int i = 0; i < s.length( ); i++)
{
    hash = 31 * hash + s[i];
}
```

Another way to decrease the chance of collisions is by making the hash table bigger. For example, if the hash table array had a 10,000-entry capacity but we were only inserting 1000 items, then the probability of a collision would be much smaller than if the hash table array could store only 1000 entries. However, inserting only 1000 items in a 10,000-entry hash table would mean 9000 memory locations will go unused, which is a waste of memory. This illustrates the **time-space tradeoff**. It is usually possible to increase run-time performance at the expense of memory space, and vice versa.

MyProgrammingLab™

Self-Test Exercises

21. Suppose that every student in your university is assigned a unique nine-digit ID number. You would like to create a hash table that indexes ID numbers to an object representing a student. The hash table has a size of N where N has fewer than nine digits. Describe a simple hash function that you can use to map from ID number to a hash index.

22. Write an `outputHashTable( )` function for the `HashTable` class that ouputs every item stored in the hash table.

EXAMPLE: A Set Template Class

A *set* is a collection of elements in which no element occurs more than once. Many problems in computer science can be solved with the aid of a set data structure. A variation on linked lists is a straightforward way to implement a set. In this implementation, the items in each set are stored using a singly linked list. The data variable for each node simply contains an item in the set.

Display 17.27 illustrates two sample sets stored using this data structure. The set round contains "peas," "ball," and "pie" while the set green contains "peas" and "grass." The string "peas" is in both sets because it is both round and green. Note that if the data type used to fill the Node template is a pointer to an object, then multiple lists might reference a common object instead of creating multiple copies of the same object in each list.

FUNDAMENTAL SET OPERATIONS

Some fundamental operations that our set class should support are

add element. Add a new item into a set.

contains. Determine if a target item is a member of the set.

union. Return a set that is the union of two sets.

intersection. Return a set that is the intersection of two sets.

We should also include a way to iterate through each element in the set. Other useful set operations include functions to retrieve the cardinality of the set and to remove items from the set. The implementation of these operations is given as an exercise in Programming Project 17.7.

EXAMPLE: (continued)

The code for implementing a generic set of elements appears in Displays 17.28 and 17.29. The Set class uses the linked list tools from Display 17.14. The add function simply adds a node to the front of the linked list, but only if the item is not already in the set. The contains function uses the search function from the linked list library. We simply loop through every item in the list looking for the target.

The union function combines the elements in the calling objects set with the elements from the set of the input argument, otherSet. To union these sets we first create a new empty Set object. Next, we iterate through both the calling object's set and otherSet's set. All elements are added to the new set. The add function enforces uniqueness so we do not have to check for duplicate elements in the union function.

The intersection function is similar to the union function in that it also creates a new, empty Set object. In this case, we populate the set with items that are common to both the calling object's set and otherSet's set. This is accomplished by iterating through every item in the calling object's set. For each item, we invoke the contains function for otherSet. If contains returns true, then the item is in both sets and can be added to the new set.

A short demonstration program is in Display 17.30.

Display 17.27   Set Implementation Using Linked Lists

Set

A set is an unordered collection of data elements.

Display 17.28 Interface File for a Set Template Class

```
1    //This is the header file set.h. This is the interface
2    //for the class Set, which is a class for a generic set.
3    #ifndef SET_H
4    #define SET_H
5    #include "listtools.h"
6    using LinkedListSavitch::Node;
7    namespace SetSavitch
8    {
9        template<class T>
10       class Set
11       {
12       public:
13           Set( ) { head = NULL; } //Initialize empty set.
14           //Normally a copy constructor and overloaded assignment
15           //operator would be included. They have been omitted
16           //to save space.
17           virtual ~Set( ); //Destructor destroys set.
18           bool contains(T target) const;
19           //Returns true if target is in the set, false otherwise.
20           void add(T item);
21           //Adds a new element to the set.
22           void output( );
23           //Outputs the set to the console.
24           Set<T>* setUnion(const Set<T>& otherSet);
25           //Union calling object's set with otherSet
26           //and return a pointer to the new set.
27           Set<T>* setIntersection(const Set<T>& otherSet);
28           //Intersect calling object's set with otherSet
29           //and return a pointer to the new set.
30       private:
31           Node<T> *head;
32       }; //Set
33    } //SetSavitch
34    #endif //SET_H
```

The library "listtools.h" is the linked list
library interface from Display 17.14.

Display 17.29   Implementation File for a Set Template Class (part 1 of 2)

```
1    //This is the implementation file set.cpp.
2    //This is the implementation of the class Set.

3    #include <iostream>
4    #include "listtools.h"
5    #include "set.h"
6    using std::cout;
7    using std::endl;
8    using LinkedListSavitch::Node;
9    using LinkedListSavitch::search;
10   using LinkedListSavitch::headInsert;

11   namespace SetSavitch
12   {
13       template<class T>
14       Set<T>::~Set( )
15       {
16           Node<T> *toDelete = head;
17           while (head != NULL)
18           {
19               head = head->getLink( );
20               delete toDelete;
21               toDelete = head;
22           }
23       }

24       template<class T>
25       bool Set<T>::contains(T target) const
26       {
27           Node<T>* result = search(head, target);
28           if (result == NULL)
29               return false;
30           else
31               return true;
32       }

33       void Set<T>::output( )
34       {
35           Node<T> *iterator = head;
36           while (iterator != NULL)
37           {
38               cout << iterator->getData( ) << " ";
39               iterator = iterator->getLink( );
40           }
```

(continued)

Display 17.29   Implementation File for a Set Template Class (part 2 of 2)

```cpp
41        cout << endl;
42    }

43    template<class T>
44    void Set<T>::add(T item)
45    {
46        if (search(head, item)==NULL)
47        {
48            //Only add the target if it's not in the list
49            headInsert(head, item);
50        }
51    }

52    template<class T>
53    Set<T>* Set<T>::setUnion(const Set<T>& otherSet)
54    {
55        Set<T> *unionSet = new Set<T>( );
56        Node<T>* iterator = head;
57        while (iterator != NULL)
58        {
59            unionSet->add(iterator->getData( ));
60            iterator = iterator->getLink( );
61        }
62        iterator = otherSet.head;
63        while (iterator != NULL)
64        {
65            unionSet->add(iterator->getData( ));
66            iterator = iterator->getLink( );
67        }
68        return unionSet;
69    }

70    template<class T>
71    Set<T>* Set<T>::setIntersection(const Set<T>& otherSet)
72    {
73        Set<T> *interSet = new Set<T>( );
74        Node<T>* iterator = head;
75        while (iterator != NULL)
76        {
77            if (otherSet.contains(iterator->getData( )))
78            {
79                interSet->add(iterator->getData( ));
80            }
81            iterator = iterator->getLink( );
82        }
83        return interSet;
84    }
85    } //SetSavitch
```

Display 17.30   Program Using the Set Template Class (part 1 of 2)

```
1   //Program to demonstrate use of the Set class

2   #include <iostream>
3   #include <string>
4   #include "set.h"
5   #include "listtools.cpp"
6   #include "set.cpp"
7   using std::cout;
8   using std::endl;
9   using std::string;
10  using namespace SetSavitch;

11  int main( )
12  {
13      Set<string> round; //Round things
14      Set<string> green; //Green things

15      round.add("peas");  //Sample data for both sets
16      round.add("ball");
17      round.add("pie");
18      round.add("grapes");
19      green.add("peas");
20      green.add("grapes");
21      green.add("garden hose");
22      green.add("grass");

23      cout << "Contents of set round: ";
24      round.output( );
25      cout << "Contents of set green: ";
26      green.output( );

27      cout << "ball in set round? " <<
28          round.contains("ball") << endl;
29      cout << "ball in set green? " <<
30          green.contains("ball") << endl;

31      cout << "ball and peas in same set? ";
32      if ((round.contains("ball") && round.contains("peas")) ||
33          (green.contains("ball") && green.contains("peas")))
34          cout << " true" << endl;
35      else
36          cout << " false" << endl;

37      cout << "pie and grass in same set? ";
38      if ((round.contains("pie") && round.contains("grass")) ||
39          (green.contains("pie") && green.contains("grass")))
40          cout << " true" << endl;
```

(continued)

Display 17.30   Program Using the Set Template Class (part 2 of 2)

```
41    else
42        cout << " false" << endl;

43    cout << "Union of green and round: " << endl;
44    Set<string> *unionset = round.setUnion(green);
45    unionset->output( );
46    delete unionset;

47    cout << "Intersection of green and round: " << endl;
48    Set<string> *interset = round.setIntersection(green);
49    interset->output( );
50    delete interset;

51    return 0;
52 }
```

Sample Dialogue

```
Contents of set round: grapes pie ball peas
Contents of set green: grass garden hose grapes peas
ball in set round? 1
ball in set green? 0
ball and peas in same set? true
pie and grass in same set? false
Union of green and round:
garden hose grass peas ball pie grapes
Intersection of green and round:
peas grapes
```

Some compilers may output true and false instead of 1 and 0.

Efficiency of Sets Using Linked Lists

set

We can analyze the run-time efficiency of our set data structure in terms of the fundamental set operations. Adding an item to the set always inserts a new node on the front of the list. This requires setting only one link on the linked list. The contains function iterates through the entire set looking for the target, which may require examining every node in the list. When we invoke the setUnion function for sets A and B, it iterates through both sets and adds each item into a new set. If there are n items in set A and m items in set B, then this requires examining n + m items. However, there is a hidden cost because the add function searches through its entire list for any duplicates before a new item is added. This cost becomes significant as the number of items added to the new set increases. Finally, the setIntersection function applied to sets A and B invokes the contains function of set B for each item in set A. Since the contains function requires examining up to m nodes for each item in set A, then setIntersection requires examining at most m × n nodes. These are inefficient functions in our implementation of sets. A different approach to represent the set—for example, one that used hash tables instead of a linked list—could result in a setIntersection function that examines at most $n + m$ nodes. Nevertheless, our linked list implementation would probably be fine for an application that uses small sets or for an application that does not frequently invoke the setIntersection function, and we have the benefit of relatively simple code that is easy to understand.

If we really needed the efficiency, we could maintain the same interface to the Set<T> class but replace our linked list implementation with something else. If we used the hash table implementation from Display 17.25, the contains function would run much more quickly. However, switching to a hash table makes it more difficult to iterate through the set of items. Instead of traversing a single linked list to retrieve every item in the set, the hash table version must now iterate through the hash table array and then, for each index in the array, iterate through the linked list at that index. Examination of each entry in the hash table array takes extra time that was not necessary in the singly linked list implementation of a set. So while we have decreased the number of steps it takes to look up an item, we have increased the number of steps it takes to iterate over every item. If this were troublesome, you could overcome this problem with an implementation of Set<T> that used both a linked list (to facilitate iteration) and a hash table (for fast lookup). However, the complexity of the code is significantly increased using such an approach. You are asked to explore the hash table implementation in Programming Project 17.10.

Self-Test Exercise

23. Write a function named difference for the Set class that returns the difference between two sets. The function should return a pointer to a new set that has items from the first set that are not in the second set.
    For example, if setA contains {1, 2, 3, 4} and setB contains {2, 4, 5}, then setA.difference(setB) should return the set {1, 3}.

17.3   Iterators

The white rabbit put on his spectacles. "Where shall I begin, please your Majesty?" he asked.
"Begin at the beginning," the King said, very gravely, "And go on till you come to the end: then stop."

LEWIS CARROLL, *Alice in Wonderland*

iterator   An important notion in data structures is that of an iterator. An **iterator** is a construct (typically an object of some iterator class) that allows you to cycle through the data items stored in a data structure so that you can perform whatever action you want on each data item.

An *iterator* is a construct (typically an object of some iterator class) that allows you to cycle through the data items stored in a data structure so that you can perform whatever action you want on each data item in the data structure.

Iterator

Pointers as Iterators

The basic idea, and in fact the prototypical model, for iterators can easily be seen in the context of linked lists. A linked list is one of the prototypical data structures, and a pointer is a prototypical example of an iterator. You can use a pointer as an iterator by moving through the linked list one node at a time starting at the head of the list and cycling through all the nodes in the list. The general outline is as follows:

```
Node_Type *iterator;
for (iterator = Head; iterator != NULL;
     iterator = iterator->Link)
    Do whatever you want with the node pointed to by iterator;
```

where *Head* is a pointer to the head node of the linked list and *Link* is the name of the member variable of a node that points to the next node in the list.

For example, to output the data in all the nodes in a linked list of the kind we discussed in Section 17.1, you could use the following:

```
IntNode *iterator;
for(iterator = head; iterator != NULL;
    iterator = iterator->getLink( ))
    cout << (iterator->getData( ));
```

The definition of IntNode is given in Display 17.4.

Note that you test to see if two pointers are pointing to the same node by comparing them with the equal operator, ==. A pointer is a memory address. If two pointer variables contain the same memory address, then they compare as equal and point to the same node. Similarly, you can use != to compare two pointers to see if they do not point to the same node.

Iterator Classes

An **iterator class** is a more versatile and more general notion than a pointer. It very often does have a pointer member variable as the heart of its data, as in the next programming example, but that is not required. For example, the heart of the iterator might be an array index. An iterator class has functions and overloaded operators that allow you to use pointer syntax with objects of the iterator class no matter what you use for the underlying data structure, node type, or basic location marker (pointer or array index or whatever). Moreover, it provides a general framework that can be used across a wide range of data structures.

**iterator
class**

An iterator class typically has the following overloaded operators:

++ Overloaded increment operator, which advances the iterator to the next item.

-- Overloaded decrement operator, which moves the iterator to the previous item.

== Overloaded equality operator to compare two iterators and return true if they both point to the same item.

!= Overloaded not-equal operator to compare two iterators and return true if they do not point to the same item.

* Overloaded dereferencing operator that gives access to one item. (Often it returns a reference to allow both read and write access.)

When thinking of this list of operators, you can use a linked list as a concrete example. In that case, remember that the items in the list are the data in the list, not the entire nodes and not the pointer members of the nodes. Everything but the data items is implementation detail that is meant to be hidden from the programmer who uses the iterator and data structure classes.

An iterator is used in conjunction with some particular structure class that stores data items of some type. The data structure class normally has the following member functions that provide iterators for objects of that class:

begin( ): A member function that takes no argument and returns an iterator that is located at ("points to") the first item in the data structure.

end( ): A member function that takes no argument and returns an iterator that can be used to test for having cycled through all items in the data structure. If i is an iterator and it has been advanced *beyond* the last item in the data structure, then i should equal end( ).

Using an iterator, you can cycle through the items in a data structure ds as follows:

```
for (i = ds.begin( ); i != ds.end( ); i++)
    process *i //*i is the current data item.
```

Iterator Class

An iterator class typically has the following overloaded operators: ++, move to next item; --, move to previous item; ==, overloaded equality; !=, overloaded not-equal operator; and *, overloaded dereferencing operator that gives access to one data item.

The data structure corresponding to an iterator class typically has the following two member functions: begin( ), which returns an iterator that is located at ("points to") the first item in the data structure; and end( ), which returns an iterator that can be used to test for having cycled through all items in the data structure. If i is an iterator and it has been advanced *beyond* the last item in the data structure, then i should equal end( ).

Using an iterator, you can cycle through the items in a data structure ds as follows:

```
for (i = ds.begin( ); i != ds.end( ); i++)
    process *i //*i is the current data item.
```

where i is an iterator. Chapter 19 discusses iterators with a few more items and refinements than these, but these will do for an introduction.

This abstract discussion will not come alive until we give an example. So, let us walk through one.

EXAMPLE: An Iterator Class

Display 17.31 contains the definition of an iterator class that can be used for data structures (such as a stack or queue) that are based on a linked list. We have placed the node class and the iterator class into a namespace of their own. This makes sense, since the iterator is intimately related to the node class and since any class that uses this node class can also use the iterator class. This iterator class does not have a decrement operator, because a definition of a decrement operator depends on the details of the linked list and does not depend solely on the type `Node<T>`. (There is nothing wrong with having the definition of the iterator depend on the underlying linked list. We have just decided to avoid this complication.)

As you can see, the template class `ListIterator` is essentially a pointer wrapped in a class so that it can have the needed member operators. The definitions of the overload operators are straightforward and in fact so short that we have defined all of them as inline functions. Note that the dereferencing operator, `*`, produces the data member variable of the node pointed to. Only the data member variable is data. The pointer member variable in a node is part of the implementation detail that the user programmer should not need to be concerned with.

You can use the `ListIterator` class as an iterator for any class based on a linked list that uses the template class `Node`. As an example, we have rewritten the template class `Queue` so that it has iterator facilities. The interface for the template class `Queue` is given in Display 17.32. This definition of the `Queue` template is the same as our previous version (Display 17.20) except that we have added a type definition as well as the following two member functions:

```
Iterator begin( ) const { return Iterator(front); }
Iterator end( ) const { return Iterator( ); }
//The end iterator has end( ).current == NULL.
```

Let us discuss the member functions first.

The member function `begin( )` returns an iterator located at ("pointing to") the front node of the queue, which is the head node of the underlying linked list. Each application of the increment operator, `++`, moves the iterator to the next node. Thus, you can move through the nodes, and hence the data, in a queue named q as follows:

```
for (i = q.begin( ); stopping_Condition; i++)
    process *i     //*i is the current data item.
```

where i is a variable of the iterator type.

(continued)

Display 17.31   An Iterator Class for Linked Lists (part 1 of 2)

```
1   //This is the header file iterator.h. This is the interface for the
2   //class ListIterator, which is a template class for an iterator to use
3   //with linked lists of items of type T. This file also contains the
4   //node type for a linked list
5   #ifndef ITERATOR_H
6   #define ITERATOR_H

7   namespace ListNodeSavitch
8   {
9       template<class T>
10      class Node
11      {
12      public:
13          Node(T theData, Node<T>* theLink) : data(theData),
                                                link(theLink){}
14          Node<T>* getLink( ) const  { return link; }
15          const T& getData( ) const  { return data; }
16          void setData(const T& theData)  { data = theData; }
17          void setLink(Node<T>* pointer)  { link = pointer; }
18      private:
19          T data;
20          Node<T> *link;
21      };

22      template<class T>
23      class ListIterator
24      {
25      public:
26          ListIterator( ) : current(NULL)  {}

27          ListIterator(Node<T>* initial) : current(initial)  {}
28          const T& operator *( ) const  { return current->getData( ); }
29          //Precondition: Not equal to the default constructor object;
30          //that is, current != NULL.
31          ListIterator& operator ++( )  //Prefix form
32          {
33              current = current->getLink( );
34              return *this;
35          }
36          ListIterator operator ++(int)  //Postfix form
37          {
38              ListIterator startVersion(current);
39              current = current->getLink( );
40              return startVersion;
```

Note that the dereferencing operator * produces the data member of the node, not the entire node. This version does not allow you to change the data in the node.

(continued)

Display 17.31   An Iterator Class for Linked Lists (part 2 of 2)

```
41      }
42      bool operator ==(const ListIterator& rightSide) const
43      { return (current == rightSide.current); }

44      bool operator !=(const ListIterator& rightSide) const
45      { return (current != rightSide.current); }

46      //The default assignment operator and copy constructor
47      //should work correctly for ListIterator.

48      private:
49          Node<T> *current;
50      };

51  } //ListNodeSavitch

52  #endif //ITERATOR_H
```

EXAMPLE: (continued)

The member function end( ) returns an iterator whose current member variable is NULL. Thus, when the iterator i has passed the last node, the Boolean expression

```
i != q.end( )
```

changes from true to false. This is the desired *Stopping_Condition*. This queue class and iterator class allow you to cycle through the data in the queue in the way we outlined for an iterator:

```
for (i = q.begin( ); i != q.end( ); i++)
    process *i //*i is the current data item.
```

Note that i is not equal to q.end( ) when i is at the last node. The iterator i is not equal to q.end( ) until i has been advanced one position past the last node. To remember this detail, think of q.end( ) as being an end marker like NULL; in this case, it is essentially a version of NULL. A sample program that uses such a for loop is shown in Display 17.33.

Notice the type definition in our new queue template class:

```
typedef ListIterator<T> Iterator;
```

(continued on page 799)

Display 17.32   Interface File for a Queue with Iterators Template Class

```
1   //This is the header file queue.h.  This is the interface for the class
2   //Queue, which is a template class for a queue of items of type T,
3   //including iterators.            The definitions of Node<T> and
4   #ifndef QUEUE_H                   ListIterator<T> are in the namespace
5   #define QUEUE_H                   ListNodeSavitch in the file iterator.h.
6   #include "iterator.h"
7   using namespace ListNodeSavitch;

8   namespace QueueSavitch
9   {
10      template<class T>
11      class Queue
12      {
13      public:
14          typedef ListIterator<T> Iterator;

15          Queue( );
16          Queue(const Queue<T>& aQueue);
17          Queue<T>& operator =(const Queue<T>& rightSide);
18          virtual ~Queue( );
19          void add(T item);
20          T remove( );
21          bool isEmpty( ) const;

22          Iterator begin( ) const { return Iterator(front);}
23          Iterator end( ) const { return Iterator( ); }
24          //The end iterator has end( ).current == NULL.
25          //Note that you cannot dereference the end iterator.
26      private:
27          Node<T> *front;//Points to the head of a linked list.
28                         //Items are removed at the head.
29          Node<T> *back; //Points to the node at the other end of
30                         //the linked list.
31                         //Items are added at this end.
32      };
33   }  //QueueSavitch

34   #endif //QUEUE_H
```

Display 17.33   Program Using the Queue Template Class with Iterators

```
1   //Program to demonstrate use of the Queue template class with iterators.
2   #include <iostream>
3   #include "queue.h"  //not needed
4   #include "queue.cpp"
5   #include "iterator.h"  //not needed
6   using std::cin;
7   using std::cout;
8   using std::endl;
9   using namespace QueueSavitch;
10  int main( )
11  {
12      char next, ans;
13      do
14      {
15          Queue<char> q;
16          cout << "Enter a line of text:\n";
17          cin.get(next);
18          while (next != '\n')
19          {
20              q.add(next);
21              cin.get(next);
22          }
23          cout << "You entered:\n";
24          Queue<char>::Iterator i;
25          for (i = q.begin( ); i != q.end( ); i++)
26              cout << *i;
27          cout << endl;
28          cout << "Again?(y/n): ";
29          cin >> ans;
30          cin.ignore(10000, '\n');
31      }while (ans != 'n' && ans != 'N');
32      return 0;
33  }
```

Even though they are not needed, many programmers prefer to include these include directives for the sake of documentation.

If your compiler is unhappy with `Queue<char>::Iterator i;` *try using namespace* `ListNodeSavitch;` `ListIterator<char> i;`

Sample Dialogue

```
Enter a line of text:
Where shall I begin?
You entered:
Where shall I begin?
Again?(y/n): y
Enter a line of text:
Begin at the beginning
You entered:
Begin at the beginning
Again?(y/n): n
```

EXAMPLE: (continued)

This `typedef` is not absolutely necessary. You can always use `ListIterator<T>` instead of the type name `Iterator`. However, this type definition does make for cleaner code. With this type definition, an iterator for the class `Queue<char>` is written

```
Queue<char>::Iterator i;
```

This makes it clear with which class the iterator is meant to be used.

The implementation of our new template class `Queue` is given in Display 17.34. Since the only member functions we added to this new `Queue` class are defined inline, the implementation file contains nothing really new, but we include the implementation file to show how it is laid out and to show which directives it would include.

Display 17.34   Implementation File for a Queue with Iterators Template Class (part 1 of 2)

```
1   //This is the file queue.cpp. This is the implementation of the
2   //template class Queue. The interface for the template class Queue is
3   //in the header file queue.h.
4   #include <iostream>
5   #include <cstdlib>
6   #include <cstddef>           The member function definitions are the same as in
7   #include "queue.h"           the previous version of the Queue template. This is
8   using std::cout;             given to show the file layout and use of namespaces.

9   using namespace ListNodeSavitch;
10  namespace QueueSavitch
11  {
12      template<class T>
13      Queue<T>::Queue( ) : front(NULL), back(NULL)
14      <The rest of the definition is given in the answer to Self-Test Exercise 16.>

15      template<class T>
16      Queue<T>::Queue(const Queue<T>& aQueue)
17      <The rest of the definition is given in the answer to Self-Test Exercise 19.>

18      template<class T>
19      Queue<T>& Queue<T>::operator =(const Queue<T>& rightSide)
20      <The rest of the definition is given in the answer to Self-Test Exercise 20.>

21      template<class T>
22      Queue<T>::~Queue( )
```

(continued)

Display 17.34 Implementation File for a Queue with Iterators Template Class (part 2 of 2)

23 *The rest of the definition is given in the answer to Self-Test Exercise 18.*

24 template<class T>

25 bool Queue<T>::isEmpty( ) const

26 *The rest of the definition is given in the answer to Self-Test Exercise 16.*

27 template<class T>

28 void Queue<T>::add(T item)

29 *The rest of the definition is given in the answer to Self-Test Exercise 17.*

30 template<class T>

31 T Queue<T>::remove( )

32 *The rest of the definition is given in the answer to Self-Test Exercise 17.*

33 }//QueueSavitch

34 #endif //QUEUE_H

Self-Test Exercise

24. Write the definition of the template function inQ shown here. Use iterators. Use the definition of Queue given in Display 17.32.

```
template<class T>
bool inQ(Queue<T> q, T target);
//Returns true if target is in the queue q;
//otherwise, returns false.
```

17.4 Trees

I think that I shall never see a data structure as useful as a tree.

Anonymous

A detailed treatment of trees is beyond the scope of this chapter. The goal of this chapter is to teach you the basic techniques for constructing and manipulating data structures based on nodes and pointers. The linked list served as a good example for our discussion. However, there is one detail about the nodes in a singly linked list that is quite restricted: They have only one pointer member variable to point to another node. A tree node has two (and in some applications more than two) member variables for pointers to other nodes. Moreover, trees are a very important and widely used data structure. So, we will briefly outline the general techniques used to construct and manipulate trees.

This section uses recursion, which is covered in Chapter 13.

Tree Properties

A tree is a data structure that is structured as shown in Display 17.35. Note that a tree must have the sort of structure illustrated in Display 17.35. In particular, in a tree you can reach any node from the top (root) node by some path that follows the links (pointers). Note that there are no cycles in a tree. If you follow the pointers, you eventually get to an end. A definition for a node class for this sort of tree of ints is also shown in Display 17.35. Note that each node has two links (two pointers) coming from it. This sort of tree is called a binary tree because it has exactly two link member

Display 17.35   A Binary Tree

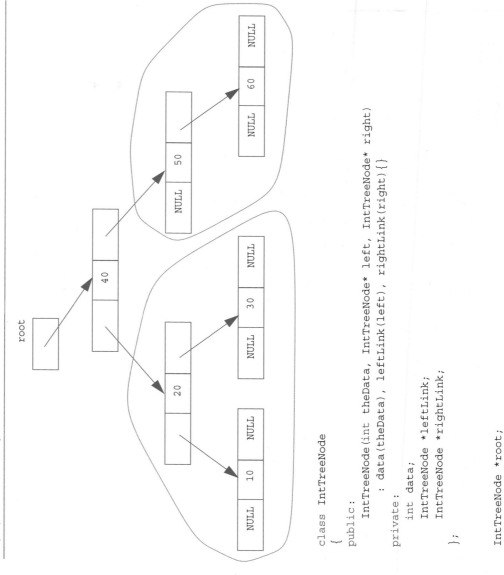

```
class IntTreeNode
{
public:
    IntTreeNode(int theData, IntTreeNode* left, IntTreeNode* right)
        : data(theData), leftLink(left), rightLink(right) {}
private:
    int data;
    IntTreeNode *leftLink;
    IntTreeNode *rightLink;
};

IntTreeNode *root;
```

binary tree

root node

empty tree

leaf node

preorder

in order

postorder

binary
search tree

variables. There are other kinds of trees with different numbers of link member variables, but the **binary tree** is the most common case.

The pointer named root serves a purpose similar to that of the pointer head in a linked list (Display 17.1). The node pointed to by the root pointer is called the **root node**. Note that the pointer root is not itself the root node, but rather points to the root node. Any node in the tree can be reached from the root node by following the links.

The term *tree* may seem like a misnomer. The root is at the top of the tree and the branching structure looks more like a root branching structure than a true tree branching structure. The secret to the terminology is to turn the picture (Display 17.35) upside down. The picture then does resemble the branching structure of a tree and the root node is where the trees root would begin. The nodes at the ends of the branches with both link member variables set to NULL are known as **leaf nodes**, a terminology that may now make some sense.

By analogy to an empty linked list, an empty tree is denoted by setting the pointer variable root equal to NULL.

Note that a tree has a recursive structure. Each tree has two subtrees whose root nodes are the nodes pointed to by the leftLink and rightLink of the root node. These two subtrees are circled in Display 17.35. This natural recursive structure make trees particularly amenable to recursive algorithms. For example, consider the task of searching the tree in such a way that you visit each node and do something with the data in the node (such as writing it to the screen). The general plan of attack is as follows:

Preorder Processing

1. Process the data in the root node.
2. Process the left subtree.
3. Process the right subtree.

You can obtain a number of variants on this search process by varying the order of these three steps. Two more versions are given next.

In-order Processing

1. Process the left subtree.
2. Process the data in the root node.
3. Process the right subtree.

Postorder Processing

1. Process the left subtree.
2. Process the right subtree.
3. Process the data in the root node.

The tree in Display 17.35 has stored each number in the tree in a special way known as the **Binary Search Tree Storage Rule**. The rule is given in the accompanying box. A tree that satisfies the Binary Search Tree Storage Rule is referred to as a **binary search tree**.

Binary Search Tree Storage Rule

1. All the values in the left subtree are less than the value in the root node.
2. All the values in the right subtree are greater than or equal to the value in the root node.
3. This rule applies recursively to each of the two subtrees.

(The base case for the recursion is an empty tree, which is always considered to satisfy the rule.)

Note that if a tree satisfies the Binary Search Tree Storage Rule and you output the values using the in-order processing method, the numbers will be output in order from smallest to largest.

For trees that follow the Binary Search Tree Storage Rule that are short and fat rather than long and thin, values can be very quickly retrieved from the tree using a binary search algorithm that is similar in spirit to the binary search algorithm presented in Display 13.5. The topic of searching and maintaining a binary storage tree to realize this efficiency is a large topic that goes beyond what we have room for here.

EXAMPLE: A Tree Template Class

Display 17.36 contains the definition of a template class for a binary search tree. In this example, we have made the SearchTree class a friend class of the TreeNode class. This allows us to access the node member variables by name in the definitions of the tree class member variables. The implementation of this SearchTree class is given in Display 17.37, and a demonstration program is given in Display 17.38.

This template class is designed to give you the flavor of tree processing, but it is not really a complete example. A real class would have more member functions. In particular, a real tree class would have a copy constructor and an overloaded assignment operator. We have omitted these to conserve space.

There are some things to observe about the function definitions in the class SearchTree. The functions insert and inTree are overloaded. The single-argument versions are the ones we need. However, the clearest algorithms are recursive, and the recursive algorithms require one additional parameter for the root of a subtree. Therefore, we defined private helping functions with two arguments for each of these functions and implemented the recursive algorithms in the two-parameter function. The single-parameter function then simply makes a call to the two-parameter version with the subtree root parameter set equal to the root of the entire tree. A similar situation holds for the overloaded member function name inorderShow. The function deleteSubtree serves a similar purpose for the destructor function.

(continued on page 808)

Display 17.36 Interface File for a Tree Template Class

```
1   //Header file tree.h. The only way to insert data in a tree is with the
2   //insert function. So, the tree satisfies the Binary Search Tree Storage
3   //Rule. The function inTree depends on this. < must be defined and
4   //give a well-behaved ordering to the type T.
5   #ifndef TREE_H
6   #define TREE_H
7   namespace TreeSavitch
8   {
9      template<class T>
10     class SearchTree;//forward declaration

11     template<class T>
12     class TreeNode
13     {
14     public:
15         TreeNode( ) : root(NULL) {}
16         TreeNode(T theData, TreeNode<T>* left, TreeNode<T>* right)
17             : data(theData), leftLink(left), rightLink(right) {}
18         friend class SearchTree<T>;
19     private:
20         T data;
21         TreeNode<T> *leftLink;
22         TreeNode<T> *rightLink;
23     };

24     template<class T>
25     class SearchTree
26     {
27     public:
28         SearchTree( ) : root(NULL) {}
29         virtual ~SearchTree( );
30         void insert(T item);//Adds item to the tree.
31         bool inTree(T item) const;
32         void inorderShow( ) const;
33     private:
34         void insert(T item, TreeNode<T>*& subTreeRoot);
35         bool inTree(T item, TreeNode<T>* subTreeRoot) const;
36         void deleteSubtree(TreeNode<T>*& subTreeRoot);
37         void inorderShow(TreeNode<T>* subTreeRoot) const;
38         TreeNode<T> *root;
39     };
40   }//TreeSavitch
41   #endif
```

The SearchTree template class should have a copy constructor, an overloading of the assignment operator, and other member functions. However, we have omitted these functions to keep this example short. A real template class would contain more member functions and overloaded operators.

Display 17.37   Implementation File for a Tree Template Class (part 1 of 2)

```cpp
1    //This is the implementation file tree.cpp. This is the implementation
2    //for the template class SearchTree. The interface is in the file tree.h.
3    namespace TreeSavitch
4    {
5        template<class T>
6        void SearchTree<T>::insert(T item, TreeNode<T>*& subTreeRoot)
7        {
8            if (subTreeRoot == NULL)
9                subTreeRoot = new TreeNode<T>(item, NULL, NULL);       If all data is entered using the
10           else if (item < subTreeRoot->data)                         function insert, the tree will
11               insert(item, subTreeRoot->leftLink);                   satisfy the Binary Search Tree
12           else//item >= subTreeRoot->data                            Storage Rule.
13               insert(item, subTreeRoot->rightLink);
14       }
15       template<class T>
16       void SearchTree<T>::insert(T item)
17       {
18           insert(item, root);
19       }
20       template<class T>
21       bool SearchTree<T>::inTree(T item, TreeNode<T>* subTreeRoot) const      The function inTree
22       {                                                                       uses a binary search
23           if (subTreeRoot == NULL)                                            algorithm that is a
24               return false;                                                   variant of the one given
25           else if (subTreeRoot->data == item)                                 in Display 13.5.
26               return true;
27           else if (item < subTreeRoot->data)
28               return inTree(item, subTreeRoot->leftLink);
29           else//item >= link->data
30               return inTree(item, subTreeRoot->rightLink);
31       }
32       template<class T>
33       bool SearchTree<T>::inTree(T item) const
34       {
35           return inTree(item, root);
```

(continued)

Display 17.37   Implementation File for a Tree Template Class (part 2 of 2)

```
36      }
37      template<class T>//uses iostream:
38      void SearchTree<T>::inorderShow(TreeNode<T>* subTreeRoot) const
39      {
40          if (subTreeRoot != NULL)
41          {
42              inorderShow(subTreeRoot->leftLink);                    Uses in-order traversal
43              cout << subTreeRoot->data << " ";                      of the tree.
44              inorderShow(subTreeRoot->rightLink);
45          }
46      }
47      template<class T>//uses iostream:
48      void SearchTree<T>::inorderShow( ) const
49      {
50          inorderShow(root);
51      }
52      template<class T>
53      void SearchTree<T>::deleteSubtree(TreeNode<T>*& subTreeRoot)
54      {
55          if (subTreeRoot != NULL)
56          {
57              deleteSubtree(subTreeRoot->leftLink);                  Uses postorder
58              deleteSubtree(subTreeRoot->rightLink);                 traversal of the tree.
59              //subTreeRoot now points to a one node tree.
60              delete subTreeRoot;
61              subTreeRoot = NULL;
62          }
63      }
64      template<class T>
65      SearchTree<T>::~SearchTree( )
66      {
67          deleteSubtree(root);
68      }
69      }//TreeSavitch
```

Display 17.38   Demonstration Program for the Tree Template Class

```
1   //Demonstration program for the Tree template class.
2   #include <iostream>
3   #include "tree.h"
4   #include "tree.cpp"
5   using std::cout;
6   using std::cin;
7   using std::endl;
8   using TreeSavitch::SearchTree;

9   int main( )
10  {
11      SearchTree<int> t;

12      cout << "Enter a list of nonnegative integers.\n"
13           << "Place a negative integer at the end.\n";

14      int next;
15      cin >> next;
16      while (next >= 0)
17      {
18          t.insert(next);
19          cin >> next;
20      }

21      cout << "In sorted order: \n";
22      t.inorderShow( );
23      cout << endl;

24      return 0;
25  }
```

Sample Dialogue

```
Enter a list of nonnegative integers.
Place a negative integer at the end.
40 30 20 10  11  22  33  44  -1
In sorted order:
10  11  20  22  30  33  40  44
```

EXAMPLE: (continued)

Finally, it is important to note that the `insert` function builds a tree that satisfies the Binary Search Tree Storage Rule. Since `insert` is the only function available to build trees for this template class, objects of this tree template class will always satisfy the Binary Search Tree Storage Rule. The function `inTree` uses the fact that the tree satisfies the Binary Search Tree Storage Rule in its algorithms. This makes searching the tree very efficient. Of course this means that the < operator must be defined for the type `T` of data stored in the tree. To make things work correctly, the operation < should satisfy the following rules when applied to values of type `T`:

- *Transitivity:* $a < b$ and $b < c$ implies $a < c$.
- *Antisymmetry:* If a and b are not equal, then either $a < b$ or $b < a$, but not both.
- *Irreflexive:* You never have $a < a$.

Most natural orders satisfy these rules.[2]

Self-Test Exercise

25. Define the following member functions, which could be added to the class `SearchTree` in Display 17.36. These functions display the data encountered in a pre- and postorder traversal of the tree, respectively. Define a private helping function for each function, as we did for `SearchTree<T>::inorderShow`.

```
void SearchTree<T>::preorderShow( ) const
void SearchTree<T>::postorderShow( ) const
```

Chapter Summary

- A *node* is a `struct` or class object that has one or more member variables that are pointer variables. These nodes can be connected by their member pointer variables to produce data structures that can grow and shrink in size while your program is running.

- A *linked list* is a list of nodes in which each node contains a pointer to the next node in the list.

- The end of a linked list (or other linked data structure) is indicated by setting the pointer member variable equal to `NULL`.

[2]Note that you normally have both a "less-than-or-equal" relation and a "less-than" relation. These rules apply only to the "less-than" relation. You can actually make do with an even weaker notion of ordering known as a *strict weak ordering*, which is defined in Chapter 19, but that is more detail than you need for normally encountered orderings.

- Nodes in a *doubly linked list* have two links—one to the previous node in the list and one to the next node. This makes operations such as insertion and deletion slightly easier.

- A *stack* is a first-in/last-out data structure. A *queue* is a first-in/first-out data structure. Both can be implemented using a linked list.

- A *hash table* is a data structure that is used to store objects and retrieve them efficiently. A *hash function* is used to map an object to a value that can then be used to index the object.

- Linked lists can be used to implement sets, including common operations such as union, intersection, and set membership.

- An *iterator* is a construct (typically an object of some iterator class) that allows you to cycle through data items stored in a data structure.

- A *tree* is a data structure whose nodes have two (or more) member variables for pointers to other nodes. If a tree satisfies the *Binary Search Tree Storage Rule*, then a function can be designed to rapidly find data in the tree.

Answers to Self-Test Exercises

1. sally
   sally
   18
   18

   Note that (*head).name and head->name mean the same thing. Similarly, (*head).number and head->number mean the same thing.

2. The best answer is

   head->next = NULL;

   However, the following is also correct:

   (*head).next = NULL;

3. head->item = "Wilbur's brother Orville";

4. class NodeType
   {
   public:
       NodeType( ){}
       NodeType(char theData, NodeType* theLink)
                : data(theData), link(theLink){}
       NodeType* getLink( ) const { return link; }

```
        char getData( ) const { return data; }
        void setData(char theData) { data = theData; }
        void setLink(NodeType* pointer) { link = pointer; }
    private:
        char data;
        NodeType *link;
};

typedef NodeType* PointerType;
```

5. The value NULL is used to indicate an empty list.

6. `p1 = p1-> next;`

7. Pointer discard;
```
discard = p2->next;//discard points to the node to be deleted.
p2->next = discard->next;
```
This is sufficient to delete the node from the linked list. However, if you are not using this node for something else, you should destroy the node with a call to delete as follows:
```
delete discard;
```

8. `p1 = p1->getLink( );`

9. Pointer discard;
```
discard = p2->getLink( );//points to node to be deleted.
p2->setLink(discard->getLink( ));
```
This is sufficient to delete the node from the linked list. However, if you are not using this node for something else, you should destroy the node with a call to delete as follows:
```
delete discard;
```

10. a. Inserting a new item at a known location into a large linked list is more efficient than inserting into a large array. If you are inserting into a list, you have about five operations, most of which are pointer assignments, regardless of the list size. If you insert into an array, on the average you have to move about half the array entries to insert a data item.

    For small lists, the answer is c, about the same.

11. ```
    void insert(DoublyLinkedIntNodePtr afterMe, int theData)
    {
        DoublyLinkedIntNode* newNode = new
            DoublyLinkedIntNode(theData, afterMe,
            afterMe->getNextLink( ));
        afterMe->setNextLink(newNode);
        if (newNode->getNextLink( ) != NULL)
    ```
    ```

```
            {
                newNode->getNextLink( )->setPreviousLink(newNode);
            }
    }
```

12. Insertion and deletion are slightly easier with the doubly linked list because we no longer need a separate variable to keep track of the previous node. Instead, we can access this node through the previous link. However, all operations require updating more links (e.g., both the next and previous instead of just the previous).

13. Note that this function is essentially the same as headInsert in Display 17.15.

```
template<class T>
void Stack<T>::push(T stackFrame)
{
    top = new Node<T>(stackFrame, top);
}
```

14. //Uses cstddef:

```
template<class T>
Stack<T>::Stack(const Stack<T>& aStack)
{
    if (aStack.isEmpty( ))
        top = NULL;
    else
    {
        Node<T> *temp = aStack.top;//temp moves through
                      //the nodes from top to bottom of aStack.
        Node<T> *end;//Points to end of the new stack.
        end = new Node<T>(temp->getData( ), NULL);
        top = end;
        //First node created and filled with data.
        //New nodes are now added AFTER this first node.
        temp = temp->getLink( );//move temp to second node
                      //or NULL if there is no second node.
        while (temp != NULL)
        {
            end->setLink(
                new Node<T>(temp->getData( ), NULL));
            temp = temp->getLink( );
            end = end->getLink( );
        }
        //end->link == NULL;
    }
}
```

15. ```
template<class T>
Stack<T>& Stack<T>::operator =(const Stack<T>& rightSide)
{
    if (top == rightSide.top)//if two stacks are the same
        return *this;
    else   //send left side back to freestore
    {
        T next;
        while (! isEmpty( ))
            next = pop( );//remove calls delete.
    }
    if (rightSide.isEmpty( ))
    {
        top = NULL;
        return *this;
    }
    else
    {
        Node<T> *temp = rightSide.top;//temp moves through
                     //the nodes from front top to bottom of rightside.
        Node<T> *end;//Points to end of the left-side stack.
        end = new Node<T>(temp->getData( ), NULL);
        top = end;;
        //First node created and filled with data.
        //New nodes are now added AFTER this first node.
        temp = temp->getLink( );//Move temp to second node
                 //or set to NULL if there is no second node.
        while (temp != NULL)
        {
            end->setLink(
                    new Node<T>(temp->getData( ),NULL));
            temp = temp->getLink( );
            end = end->getLink( );
        }
        //end->link == NULL;
        return *this;
    }
}
```

16. The following should be placed in the namespace QueueSavitch:
```
//Uses cstddef:
template<class T>
Queue<T>::Queue( ) : front(NULL), back(NULL)
```
```

```
    {
        //Intentionally empty.
    }

    //Uses cstddef:
    template<class T>
    bool Queue<T>::isEmpty( ) const
    {
        return (back == NULL);//front == NULL would also work
    }
```

17. The following should be placed in the namespace QueueSavitch:

```
    //Uses cstddef:
    template<class T>
    void Queue<T>::add(T item)
    {
        if (isEmpty( ))
            front = back = new Node<T>(item, NULL);//Sets both
                            //front and back to point to the only node

        else
        {
            back->setLink(new Node<T>(item, NULL));
            back = back->getLink( );
        }
    }

    //Uses cstdlib and iostream:
    template<class T>
    T Queue<T>::remove( )
    {
        if (isEmpty( ))
        {
            cout << "Error: Removing an item from an empty queue.\n";
            exit(1);
        }

        T result = front->getData( );
        Node<T> *discard;
        discard = front;
        front = front->getLink( );
        if (front == NULL)//if you removed the last node
            back = NULL;

        delete discard;
        return result;
    }
```

18. The following should be placed in the namespace QueueSavitch:

```
template<class T>
Queue<T>::~Queue( )
{
    T next;
    while (! isEmpty( ))
        next = remove( );//remove calls delete.
}
```

19. The following should be placed in the namespace QueueSavitch:

```
//Uses cstddef:
template<class T>
Queue<T>::Queue(const Queue<T>& aQueue)
{
    if (aQueue.isEmpty( ))
        front = back = NULL;
    else
    {
        Node<T> *temp = aQueue.front;//temp moves
        //through the nodes from front to back of aQueue.
        back = new Node<T>(temp->getData( ), NULL);
        front = back;
        //First node created and filled with data.
        //New nodes are now added AFTER this first node.
        temp = temp->getLink( );//temp now points to second
            //node or NULL if there is no second node.
        while (temp != NULL)
        {
            back->setLink(new Node<T>(temp->getData( ), NULL));
            back = back->getLink( );
            temp = temp->getLink( );
        }
        //back->link == NULL
    }
}
```

20. The following should be placed in the namespace QueueSavitch:

```
//Uses cstddef:
template<class T>
Queue<T>& Queue<T>::operator =(const Queue<T>& rightSide)
```

```
    {
        if (front == rightSide.front)//if the queues are the same
            return *this;
        else//send left side back to freestore
        {
            T next;
            while (! isEmpty( ))
                next = remove( );//remove calls delete.
        }

        if (rightSide.isEmpty( ))
        {
            front = back = NULL;
            return *this;
        }
        else
        {
            Node<T> *temp = rightSide.front;//temp moves
                //through the nodes from front to back of rightSide.
            back = new Node<T>(temp->getData( ), NULL);
            front = back;
            //First node created and filled with data.
            //New nodes are now added AFTER this first node.
            temp = temp->getLink( );//temp now points to second
                                    //node or NULL if there is no second node.

            while (temp != NULL)
            {
                back->setLink(
                    new Node<T>(temp->getData( ), NULL));

                back = back->getLink( );
                temp = temp->getLink( );
            }

            //back->link == NULL;
            return *this;
        }
    }
```

21. The simplest hash function is to map the ID number to the range of the hash table using the modulus operator:

```
hash = ID % N; //N is the hash table size.
```

22.
```
void HashTable::outputHashTable()
{
    for (int i=0; i<SIZE; i++)
    {
        Node<string> *next = hashArray[i];
        cout << "In slot " << i << endl;
        cout << " ";
        while (next != NULL)
        {
            cout << next->getData() << " ";
            next = next->getLink();
        }
    }
    cout << endl;
}
```

23. This code is similar to intersection, but adds elements if they are not in otherSet:
```
template<class T>
Set<T>* Set<T>::setDifference(const Set<T>& otherSet)
{
    Set<T> *diffSet = new Set<T>();
    Node<T>* iterator = head;
    while (iterator != NULL)
    {
        if (!otherSet.contains(iterator->getData()))
        {
            diffSet->add(iterator->getData());
        }
        iterator = iterator->getLink();
    }
    return diffSet;
}
```

24.
```
using namespace ListNodeSavitch;
using namespace QueueSavitch;
template<class T>
bool inQ(Queue<T> q, T target)
{
    Queue<T>::Iterator i;
    i = q.begin();
    while ((i != q.end()) && (*i != target))
    {
        i++;
    }
    return (i != q.end());
}
```

Note that the following return statement does not work, since it can cause a dereferencing of NULL, which is illegal. The error would be a run-time error, not a compiler error.

```
return (*i == target);
```

25. The template class SearchTree needs function declarations added. These are just the definitions.

```
template<class T>//uses iostream:
void SearchTree<T>::preorderShow( ) const
{
    preorderShow(root);
}

template<class T>//uses iostream:
void SearchTree<T>::preorderShow(
                   TreeNode<T>* subTreeRoot) const
{
    if (subTreeRoot != NULL)
    {
        cout << subTreeRoot->data << " ";
        preorderShow(subTreeRoot->leftLink);
        preorderShow(subTreeRoot->rightLink);
    }
}

template<class T>//uses iostream:
void SearchTree<T>::postorderShow( ) const
{
    postorderShow(root);
}

template<class T>//uses iostream:
void SearchTree<T>::postorderShow(
                   TreeNode<T>* subTreeRoot) const
{
    if (subTreeRoot != NULL)
    {
        postorderShow(subTreeRoot->leftLink);
        postorderShow(subTreeRoot->rightLink);
        cout << subTreeRoot->data << " ";
    }
}
```

MyProgrammingLab™

Programming Projects

Visit www.myprogramminglab.com to complete select exercises online and get instant feedback.

1. Write a void function that takes a linked list of integers and reverses the order of its nodes. The function will have one call-by-reference parameter that is a pointer to the head of the list. After the function is called, this pointer will point to the head of a linked list that has the same nodes as the original list but in the reverse of the order they had in the original list. Note that your function will neither create nor destroy any nodes. It will simply rearrange nodes. Place your function in a suitable test program.

2. Write a function called mergeLists that takes two call-by-reference arguments that are pointer variables that point to the heads of linked lists of values of type int. The two linked lists are assumed to be sorted so that the number at the head is the smallest number, the number in the next node is the next smallest, and so forth. The function returns a pointer to the head of a new linked list that contains all the nodes in the original two lists. The nodes in this longer list are also sorted from smallest to largest values. Note that your function will neither create nor destroy any nodes. When the function call ends, the two pointer variable arguments should have the value NULL.

3. Design and implement a class that is a class for polynomials. The polynomial

$$a_n x^n + a_{n-1} x^{n-1} + \ldots + a_0$$

will be implemented as a linked list. Each node will contain an int value for the power of x and an int value for the corresponding coefficient. The class operations should include addition, subtraction, multiplication, and evaluation of a polynomial. Overload the operators +, -, and * for addition, subtraction, and multiplication. Evaluation of a polynomial is implemented as a member function with one argument of type int. The evaluation member function returns the value obtained by plugging in its argument for x and performing the indicated operations. Include four constructors: a default constructor, a copy constructor, a constructor with a single argument of type int that produces the polynomial that has only one constant term that is equal to the constructor argument, and a constructor with two arguments of type int that produces the one-term polynomial whose coefficient and exponent are given by the two arguments. (In the previous notation, the polynomial produced by the two-argument constructor is of the simple form consisting of only a_0. The polynomial produced by the two-argument constructor is of the slightly more complicated form $a_n x^n$.) Include a suitable destructor. Include member functions to input and output polynomials.

When the user inputs a polynomial, the user types in the following:

$$a_n x^n + a_{n-1} x^n-1 + \ldots + a_0$$

However, if a coefficient a_i is 0, the user may omit the term $a_ix^{} i$. For example, the polynomial

$$3x^4 + 7x^2 + 5$$

can be input as

```
3x^4 + 7x^2 + 5
```

It could also be input as

```
3x^4 + 0x^3 + 7x^2 + 0x^1 + 5
```

If a coefficient is negative, a minus sign is used in place of a plus sign, as in the following examples:

```
3x^5 - 7x^3 + 2x^1 - 8
```

```
-7x^4 + 5x^2 + 9
```

A minus sign at the front of the polynomial, as in the second of the previous two examples, applies only to the first coefficient; it does not negate the entire polynomial. Polynomials are output in the same format. In the case of output, the terms with 0 coefficients are not output. To simplify input, you can assume that polynomials are always entered one per line and that there will always be a constant term a_0. If there is no constant term, the user enters 0 for the constant term, as in the following:

```
12x^8 + 3x^2 + 0
```

4. a. The annotation in Display 17.36 says that a real SearchTree template class should have a copy constructor, an overloaded assignment operator, other overloaded operators, and other member functions. Obtain the code for Display 17.36 and add declarations for the following functions and overloaded operators: the default constructor, copy constructor, delete, overloaded operator, =, makeEmpty, height, size, preOrderTraversal, inOrderTraversal, and postOrderTraversal. The functions preOrderTraversal, inOrder-Traversal, and postOrderTraversal each call a global function process to process the nodes as they are encountered. The function process is a friend of the SearchTree class. For this exercise, it is only a stub.

Supply preconditions and postconditions for these functions describing what each function should do.

The function height has no parameters and returns the height of the tree. The height of the tree is the maximum of the heights of all the nodes. The height of a node is the number of links between it and the root node.

The function size has no parameters and returns the number of nodes in the tree.

The function makeEmpty removes all the nodes from the tree and returns the memory used by the nodes for reuse. The makeEmpty function leaves the root pointer with the value NULL.

b. Implement the member and friend functions and overloaded operators. Note that some of the functions listed here are already implemented in the text. You should make full use of the text's code. You should test your package thoroughly.

c. Design and implement an iterator class for the tree class. You will need to decide what a begin and end element means for your searchTree, and what will be the next element the ++ operator will point to.

   Hint 1: You might maintain a private size variable that is increased by insertion and decreased by deletion, and whose value is returned by the size function. An alternative (use this if you know calls to size will be quite infrequent) is to calculate the size when you need it by traversing the tree. Similar techniques, though with more sophisticated details, can be used to implement the height function.

   Hint 2: Do these a few members at a time. Compile and test after doing each group of a few members. You will be glad you did it this way.

   Hint 3: Before you write the operator, =, and copy constructor, note that their jobs have a common task—duplicating another tree. Write a copyTree function that abstracts out the common task of the copy constructor and operator, =. Then write these two important functions using the common code.

   Hint 4: The function makeEmpty and the destructor have a common tree destruction task.

VideoNote
Solution to
Programming
Project 17.5

5. In an ancient land, the beautiful princess Eve had many suitors. She decided on the following procedure to determine which suitor she would marry. First, all of the suitors would be lined up one after the other and assigned numbers. The first suitor would be number 1, the second number 2, and so on up to the last suitor, number *n*. Starting at the first suitor, she would then count three suitors down the line (because of the three letters in her name) and the third suitor would be eliminated from winning her hand and removed from the line. Eve would then continue, counting three more suitors, and eliminating every third suitor. When she reached the end of the line, she would continue counting from the beginning. For example, if there were six suitors, then the elimination process would proceed as follows:

123456	Initial list of suitors, start counting from 1
12456	Suitor 3 eliminated, continue counting from 4
1245	Suitor 6 eliminated, continue counting from 1
125	Suitor 4 eliminated, continue counting from 5
15	Suitor 2 eliminated, continue counting from 5
1	Suitor 5 eliminated, 1 is the lucky winner

Write a program that creates a circular linked list of nodes to determine which position you should stand in to marry the princess if there are *n* suitors. Your program should simulate the elimination process by deleting the node that corresponds to the suitor that is eliminated for each step in the process. Be careful that you do not leave any memory leaks.

6. Modify the `Queue Template` class given in Section 17.2 so that it implements a **priority queue**. A priority queue is similar to a regular queue except that each item added to the queue also has an associated priority. For this problem, make the priority an integer where 0 is the highest priority and larger values are increasingly lower in priority.

The `remove` function should return and remove the item that has the highest priority. For example,

```
q.add('X', 10);
q.add('Y', 1);
q.add('Z', 3);

cout << q.remove();  //Returns Y
cout << q.remove();  //Returns Z
cout << q.remove();  //Returns X
```

Test your queue on data with priorities in various orders (e.g., ascending, descending, mixed). You can implement the priority queue by performing a linear search in the `remove()` function. In future courses, you may study a data structure called a *heap* that affords a more efficient way to implement a priority queue.

7. Add a `remove` function, a `cardinality` function, and an iterator for the `Set` class given in Displays 17.28 and 17.29. Write a suitable test program.

8. The hash table from Displays 17.24 and 17.25 hashed a string to an integer and stored the same string in the hash table. Modify the program so that instead of storing strings it stores `Employee` objects. Define the `Employee` class so that it contains private string member variables for the combined first and last name, job title, and phone number. Include functions to get and set these member variables. Use the employee name as the input to the hash function. The modification will require changes to the linked list, since the `LinkedList2` class created only linked lists of strings. For the most generality, modify the hash table so that it uses generic types. You will also need to add a `get` function to the `HashTable` class that returns the `Employee` object stored in the hash table that corresponds to the input name. The `Employee` class may require defining the `==` and `!=` operators. Test your program by adding and retrieving several names, including names that hash to the same slot in the hash table.

9. Displays 17.24 through 17.26 provide the beginnings of a spell-checker. Refine the program to make it more useful. The modified program should read in a text file, parse each word, and determine whether each word is in the hash table and if not

output the line number and word of the potentially misspelled word. Discard any punctuation in the original text file. Use the `words.txt` file, which can be found on the website accompanying the textbook and on the book's Web site, as the basis for the hash table dictionary. The file contains 45,407 common words and names in the English language. Note that some words are capitalized. Test your spell-checker on a short text document.

10. Change the `Set<T>` class of Displays 17.28 and 17.29 so that internally it uses a hash table to store its data instead of a linked list. The headers of the public functions should remain the same so that a program such as the demonstration in Display 17.30 will work without any changes. Add a constructor that allows the user of the new `Set<T>` class to specify the size of the hash table array.

The class for type `T` must override the `<<` operator. To convert the return value of `<<` to a string, do the following:

```
# include <sstream>
...
stringstream temp;
temp << instance of Class;
string s = temp.str();
```

For an additional challenge, implement the set using both a hash table and a linked list. Items added to the set should be stored using both data structures. Any operation requiring lookup of an item should use the hash table, and any operation requiring iteration through the items should use the linked list.

11. The following figure is called a graph. The circles are called nodes and the lines are called edges. An edge connects two nodes. You can interpret the graph as a maze of rooms and passages. The nodes can be thought of as rooms and an edge connects one room to another. Note that each node has at most four edges in the following graph.

Write a program that implements the previous maze using references to instances of a Node class. Each node in the graph will correspond to an instance of Node. The edges correspond to links that connect one node to another and can be represented in Node as instance variables that reference another Node class. Start the user in node A. The user's goal is to reach the finish in node L. The program should output possible moves in the north, south, east, or west direction. Sample execution is shown next.

```
You are in room A of a maze of twisty little passages, all alike.
You can go east or south.
E

You are in room B of a maze of twisty little passages, all alike.
You can go west or south.
S

You are in room F of a maze of twisty little passages, all alike.
You can go north or east.
E
```

12. First, complete Programming Project 17.11. Then, write a recursive algorithm that finds a path from node A to node L. Your algorithm should work with any pair of start and finish nodes, not just nodes A and L. Your algorithm should also work if there are loops such as a connection between nodes E and F.

Exception Handling 18

It's the exception that proves the rule.

Common maxim

Introduction

One way to write a program is to first assume that nothing unusual or incorrect will happen. For example, if the program takes an entry off a list, you might assume that the list is not empty. Once you have the program working for the core situation where things always go as planned, you can then add code to take care of the exceptional cases. C++ has a way to reflect this approach in your code. Basically, you write your code as if nothing very unusual happens. After that, you use the C++ exception handling facilities to add code for those unusual cases.

Exception handling is commonly used to handle error situations, but perhaps a better way to view exceptions is as a way to handle exceptional situations. After all, if your code correctly handles an "error," then it no longer is an error.

Perhaps the most important use of exceptions is to deal with functions that have some special case that is handled differently depending on how the function is used. Perhaps the function will be used in many programs, some of which will handle the special case in one way, while others will handle it in some other way. For example, if there is a division by zero in the function, then it may turn out that for some invocations of the function the program should end, but for other invocations something else should happen. You will see that such a function can be defined to throw an exception if the special case occurs; that exception will allow the special case to be handled outside the function. Thus, the special case can be handled differently for different invocations of the function.

In C++, exception handling proceeds as follows: Either some library software, or your code, provides a mechanism that signals when something unusual happens. This is called *throwing an exception*. You place the code that deals with the exceptional case at another place in your program. This is called *handling the exception*. This method of programming makes for cleaner code. Of course, we still need to explain the details of how you do this in C++.

Most of this chapter uses only material from Chapters 1 through 9. However, the sections "Exception Specification in Derived Classes" and "Exception Class Hierarchies" use material from Chapter 14. The section "Testing for Available Memory" uses material from Chapter 17. Any or all of these listed sections may be omitted without hurting the continuity of the chapter. The section "Exception Specification" has one paragraph that refers to derived classes (Chapter 14), but that paragraph may be omitted.

18.1 Exception Handling Basics

Well, the program works for most cases. I didn't know it had to work for that case.

Computer Science Student, *Appealing a grade*

Exception handling is meant to be used sparingly and in situations that are more involved than what is reasonable to include in a simple introductory example. So, we will teach you the exception handling details of C++ by means of simple examples that would not normally use exception handling. This makes a lot of sense for learning about the exception handling details of C++, but do not forget that these first examples are toy examples; in practice, you would not use exception handling for anything that simple.

A Toy Example of Exception Handling

For this example, suppose that milk is such an important food in our culture that people almost never run out of it, but still we would like our programs to accommodate the very unlikely situation of this happening. The basic code, which assumes we do not run out of milk, might be as follows:

```
cout << "Enter number of donuts:\n";
cin >> donuts;
cout << "Enter number of glasses of milk:\n";
cin >> milk;
dpg = donuts / static_cast<double>(milk);
cout << donuts << " donuts.\n"
     << milk << " glasses of milk.\n"
     << "You have " << dpg
     << " donuts for each glass of milk.\n";
```

If there is no milk, then this code will include a division by zero, which is an error. To take care of this special situation where we run out of milk, we can add a test. The complete program with this added test for the special situation is shown in Display 18.1. The program in Display 18.1 does not use exception handling. Now, let us see how this program can be rewritten using the C++ exception handling facilities.

In Display 18.2, we have rewritten the program from Display 18.1 using an exception. This is only a toy example, and you would probably not use an exception in this case. However, it does give us a simple example to work with. Although the program as a whole is not simpler, at least the part between the words try and catch is cleaner, which hints at the advantage of using exceptions. Look at the code between the words try and catch. It is basically the same as the code in Display 18.1, except that

Display 18.1 Handling a Special Case without Exception Handling

```
1   #include <iostream>
2   using std::cin;
3   using std::cout;

4   int main( )
5   {
6       int donuts, milk;
7       double dpg;
8       cout << "Enter number of donuts:\n";
9       cin >> donuts;
10      cout << "Enter number of glasses of milk:\n";
11      cin >> milk;

12      if (milk <= 0)
13      {
14          cout << donuts << " donuts, and No Milk!\n"
15               << "Go buy some milk.\n";
16      }
17      else
18      {
19          dpg = donuts / static_cast<double>(milk);
20          cout << donuts << " donuts.\n"
21               << milk << " glasses of milk.\n"
22               << "You have " << dpg
23               << " donuts for each glass of milk.\n";
24      }

25      cout << "End of program.\n";
26      return 0;
27  }
```

Sample Dialogue

```
Enter number of donuts:
12
Enter number of glasses of milk:
0
12 donuts, and No Milk!
Go buy some milk.
End of program.
```

Display 18.2 Same Thing Using Exception Handling (part 1 of 2)

```
1    #include <iostream>
2    using std::cin;
3    using std::cout;
4
5    int main( )
6    {
7        int donuts, milk;
8        double dpg;
9
10       try
11       {
12           cout << "Enter number of donuts:\n";
13           cin >> donuts;
14           cout << "Enter number of glasses of milk:\n";
15           cin >> milk;
16
17           if (milk <= 0)
18               throw donuts;
19
20           dpg = donuts / static_cast<double>(milk);
21           cout << donuts << " donuts.\n"
22                << milk << " glasses of milk.\n"
23                << "You have " << dpg
24                << " donuts for each glass of milk.\n";
25       }
26       catch(int e)
27       {
28           cout << e << " donuts, and No Milk!\n"
29                << "Go buy some milk.\n";
30       }
31
32       cout << "End of program.\n";
33       return 0;
34   }
```

This is just a toy example to learn C++ syntax. Do not take it as an example of good typical use of exception handling.

(continued)

Display 18.2   Same Thing Using Exception Handling (part 2 of 2)

Sample Dialogue 1

```
Enter number of donuts:
12
Enter number of glasses of milk:
6
12 donuts.
6 glasses of milk.
You have 2 donuts for each glass of milk.
End of program.
```

Sample Dialogue 2

```
Enter number of donuts:
12
Enter number of glasses of milk:
0
12 donuts, and No Milk!
Go buy some milk.
End of program.
```

---

rather than the big if-else statement (highlighted in Display 18.1), this new program has the following smaller if statement (plus some simple nonbranching statements):

```
if (milk <= 0)
    throw donuts;
```

This if statement says that if there is no milk, then do something exceptional. That something exceptional is given after the word catch. The idea is that the normal situation is handled by the code following the word try, and that exceptional situations are handled by the code following the word catch. Thus, we have separated the normal case from the exceptional case. In this toy example, that does not really buy us too much, but in other situations it will prove to be very helpful. Let us look at the details.

The basic way of handling exceptions in C++ consists of the try-throw-catch threesome. A **try block** has the following syntax:

try block

```
try
{
    Some_Code
}
```

This try block contains the code for the basic algorithm that tells what to do when everything goes smoothly. It is called a try block because you are not 100% sure that all will go without a hitch, but you want to "give it a try."

If something unusual does happen, the way to indicate this is to throw an exception. So the basic outline, when we add a throw, is as follows:

```
try
{
    Code_To_Try
    Possibly_Throw_An_Exception
    More_Code
}
```

The following is an example of a try block with a throw statement included (copied from Display 18.2):

```
try
{
    cout << "Enter number of donuts:\n";
    cin >> donuts;
    cout << "Enter number of glasses of milk:\n";
    cin >> milk;

    if (milk <= 0)
        throw donuts;

    dpg = donuts / static_cast<double>(milk) ;
    cout << donuts << " donuts.\n"
         << milk << " glasses of milk.\n"
         << "You have " << dpg
         << " donuts for each glass of milk.\n";
}
```

The following statement **throws** the int value donuts:

```
throw donuts;
```

The value thrown (in this case, donuts) is sometimes called an **exception**; the execution of a throw statement is called **throwing an exception**. You can throw a value of any type. In this case, an int value is thrown.

- throw
- **statement**
- **exception**
- **throwing an exception**

---

throw Statement

SYNTAX

```
throw Expression_for_Value_to_Be_Thrown;
```

When the throw statement is executed, the execution of the enclosing try block is stopped. If the try block is followed by a suitable catch block, then flow of control is transferred to the catch block. A throw statement is almost always embedded in a branching statement, such as an if statement. The value thrown can be of any type.

EXAMPLE

```
if (milk <= 0)
    throw donuts;
```

When something is "thrown," something goes from one place to another place. In C++, what goes from one place to another is the flow of control (as well as the value thrown). When an exception is thrown, the code in the surrounding try block stops executing and another portion of code, known as a **catch block**, begins execution. Executing the catch block is called **catching the exception** or **handling the exception.** When an exception is thrown, it should ultimately be handled by (caught by) some catch block. In Display 18.2, the appropriate catch block immediately follows the try block. We repeat the catch block in what follows:

```
catch (int e)
{
    cout << e << " donuts, and No Milk!\n"
         << "Go buy some milk.\n";
}
```

This catch block looks very much like a function definition that has a parameter of type int. It is not a function definition, but in some ways a catch block is like a function. It is a separate piece of code that is executed when your program encounters (and executes) the following (within the preceding try block):

```
throw Some_int;
```

So, this throw statement is similar to a function call, but instead of calling a function, it calls the catch block and says to execute the code in the catch block. A catch block is often referred to as an **exception handler,** which is a term that suggests that a catch block has a function-like nature.

What is that identifier e in the following line from a catch block?

```
catch(int e)
```

That identifier e looks like a parameter and acts very much like a parameter. In fact, the identifier, such as e, in the catch-block heading is called the **catch-block parameter.** Each catch block can have at most one catch-block parameter. The catch-block parameter does two things:

1. The catch-block parameter is preceded by a type name that specifies what kind of thrown value the catch block can catch.

2. The catch-block parameter gives you a name for the thrown value that is caught, so you can write code in the catch block that does things with that value.

We will discuss these two functions of the catch-block parameter in reverse order. This subsection discusses using the catch-block parameter as a name for the value that was thrown and is caught. The subsection entitled "Multiple Throws and Catches," later in this chapter, discusses which catch block (which exception handler) will process a value that is thrown. Our current example has only one catch block. A common name for a catch-block parameter is e, but you can use any legal identifier in place of e.

Let us see how the catch block in Display 18.2 works. When a value is thrown, execution of the code in the try block ends and control passes to the catch block (or

catch block
handling the
exception
exception
handler
catch-block
parameter

blocks) that is placed right after the try block. The catch block from Display 18.2 is reproduced here:

```
catch(int e)
{
    cout << e << " donuts, and No Milk!\n"
         << "Go buy some milk.\n";
}
```

When a value is thrown, the thrown value must be of type int in order for this particular catch block to apply. In Display 18.2, the value thrown is given by the variable donuts; because donuts is of type int, this catch block can catch the value thrown.

Suppose the value of donuts is 12 and the value of milk is 0, as in the second sample dialogue in Display 18.2. Since the value of milk is not positive, the throw statement within the if statement is executed. In that case, the value of the variable donuts is thrown. When the catch block in Display 18.2 catches the value of donuts, the value of donuts is plugged in for the catch-block parameter e and the code in the catch block is executed, producing the following output:

```
12 donuts, and No Milk!
Go buy some milk.
```

If the value of donuts is positive, the throw statement is not executed. In this case, the entire try block is executed. After the last statement in the try block is executed, the statement after the catch block is executed. Note that if no exception is thrown, the catch block is ignored.

This discussion makes it sound like a try-throw-catch setup is equivalent to an if-else statement. It almost is equivalent, except for the value thrown. A try-throw-catch setup is like an if-else statement *with the added ability to send a message to one of the branches*. This does not sound much different from an if-else statement, but it turns out to be a big difference in practice.

To summarize in a more formal tone, a try block contains some code that we are assuming includes a throw statement. The throw statement is normally executed only in exceptional circumstances, but when it is executed, it throws a value of some type. When an exception (a value such as donuts in Display 18.2) is thrown, the try block ends. All the rest of the code in the try block is ignored and control passes to a suitable catch block. A catch block applies only to an immediately preceding try block. If the exception is thrown, then that exception object is plugged in for the catch-block parameter, and the statements in the catch block are executed. For example, if you look at the dialogues in Display 18.2, you will see that as soon as the user enters a nonpositive number, the try block stops and the catch block is executed. For now, we will assume that every try block is followed by an appropriate catch block. We will later discuss what happens when there is no appropriate catch block.

catch-Block Parameter

The catch-block parameter is an identifier in the heading of a catch block that serves as a placeholder for an exception (a value) that might be thrown. When a suitable value is thrown in the preceding try block, that value is plugged in for the catch-block parameter. (In order for the catch block to be executed, the value thrown must be of the type given for its catch-block parameter.) You can use any legal (nonreserved word) identifier for a catch-block parameter.

EXAMPLE

```
{
    catch(int e)

        cout << e << " donuts, and No Milk!\n"
             << "Go buy some milk.\n";
}
```

e is the catch-block parameter.

If no exception (no value) is thrown in the try block, then after the try block is completed, program execution continues with the code after the catch block. In other words, if no exception is thrown, the catch block is ignored. Most of the time when the program is executed, the throw statement will not be executed, and so in most cases the code in the try block will run to completion and the code in the catch block will be ignored completely.

try-throw-catch

The basic mechanism for throwing and catching exceptions is a try-throw-catch sequence. The throw statement throws the exception (a value). The catch block catches the exception (the value). When an exception is thrown, the try block ends and then the code in the catch block is executed. After the catch block is completed, the code after the catch block or blocks is executed (provided the catch block has not ended the program or performed some other special action).

(The type of the thrown exception must match the type listed for the catch-block parameter or else the exception will not be caught by that catch block. This point is discussed further in the subsection "Multiple Throws and Catches.")

If no exception is thrown in the try block, then after the try block is completed, program execution continues with the code after the catch block or blocks. (In other words, if no exception is thrown, the catch block or blocks are ignored.)

SYNTAX

```
try
{
    Some_Statements
    <Either some code with a throw statement or
        a function invocation that might throw an exception>
    Some_More_Statements
}
catch(Type e)
{
    <Code to be performed if a value of the
        catch-block parameter type is thrown in the try block>
}
```

EXAMPLE

See Display 18.2 for an example.

Self-Test Exercises

1. What output is produced by the following code?

```
int waitTime = 46;

try
{
    cout << "Try block entered.\n";
    if (waitTime > 30)
        throw waitTime;
    cout << "Leaving try block.\n";
}
catch(int thrownValue)
{
    cout << "Exception thrown with\n"
         << "waitTime equal to " << thrownValue << endl;
}
cout << "After catch block" << endl;
```

2. What would be the output produced by the code in Self-Test Exercise 1 if we made the following change? Change the line

```
int waitTime = 46;
```

to

```
int waitTime = 12;
```

(continued)

Self-Test Exercises (continued)

3. In the code given in Self-Test Exercise 1, what is the throw statement?

4. What happens when a throw statement is executed? (Tell what happens in general, not simply what happens in the code in Self-Test Exercise 1 or some other sample code.)

5. In the code given in Self-Test Exercise 1, what is the try block?

6. In the code given in Self-Test Exercise 1, what is the catch block?

7. In the code given in Self-Test Exercise 1, what is the catch-block parameter?

Defining Your Own Exception Classes

A throw statement can throw a value of any type. It is common to define a class whose objects can carry the precise kinds of information you want thrown to the catch block. An even more important reason for defining a specialized exception class is so that you can have a different type to identify each possible kind of exceptional situation.

An exception class is just a class. What makes it an exception class is how it is used. Still, it pays to take some care in choosing an exception class's name and other details. Display 18.3 contains an example of a program with a programmer-defined exception class. This is just a toy program to illustrate some C++ details about exception handling. It uses much too much machinery for such a simple task, but it is an otherwise uncluttered example of some C++ details.

Notice the throw statement, reproduced in what follows:

```
throw NoMilk(donuts);
```

The part NoMilk(donuts) is an invocation of a constructor for the class NoMilk. The constructor takes one int argument (in this case, donuts) and creates an object of the class NoMilk. That object is then thrown.

Multiple Throws and Catches

A try block can potentially throw any number of exception values, which can be of differing types. In any one execution of the try block, at most one exception will be thrown (since a throw statement ends the execution of the try block), but different types of exception values can be thrown on different occasions when the try block is executed. Each catch block can only catch values of one type, but you can catch exception values of differing types by placing more than one catch block after a try block. For example, the program in Display 18.4 has two catch blocks after its try block.

Display 18.3   Defining Your Own Exception Class

```
1   #include <iostream>
2   using std::cin;
3   using std::cout;
```

*This is just a toy example to learn
C++ syntax. Do not take it as an
example of good typical use of
exception handling.*

```
4   class NoMilk
5   {
6   public:
7       NoMilk( ) {}
8       NoMilk(int howMany) : count(howMany)  {}
9       int getCount( ) const { return count; }
10  private:
11      int count;
12  };
```

```
13  int main( )
14  {
15      int donuts, milk;
16      double dpg;
17      try
18      {
19          cout << "Enter number of donuts:\n";
20          cin >> donuts;
21          cout << "Enter number of glasses of milk:\n";
22          cin >> milk;
```

*The sample dialogues are
the same as in Display 18.2.*

```
23          if (milk <= 0)
24              throw NoMilk(donuts);
```

```
25          dpg = donuts / static_cast<double>(milk);
26          cout << donuts << " donuts.\n"
27               << milk << " glasses of milk.\n"
28               << "You have " << dpg
29               << " donuts for each glass of milk.\n";
30      }
31      catch (NoMilk e)
32      {
33          cout << e.getCount( ) << " donuts, and No Milk!\n"
34               << "Go buy some milk.\n";
35      }
36      cout << "End of program.\n";
37      return 0;
38  }
```

Display 18.4 Catching Multiple Exceptions (part 1 of 2)

Exception classes can have their own interface and implementation files and can be put in a namespace. This is another toy example.

```
1   #include <iostream>
2   #include <string>
3   using std::cin;
4   using std::cout;
5   using std::endl;
6   using std::string;

7   class NegativeNumber
8   {
9   public:
10      NegativeNumber( ){}
11      NegativeNumber(string theMessage) : message(theMessage) {}
12      string getMessage( ) const { return message; }
13  private:
14      string message;
15  };

16  class DivideByZero
17  {};

18  int main( )
19  {
20      int pencils, erasers;
21      double ppe; //pencils per eraser

22      try
23      {
24          cout << "How many pencils do you have?\n";
25          cin >> pencils;
26          if (pencils < 0)
27              throw NegativeNumber("pencils");
28          cout << "How many erasers do you have?\n";
29          cin >> erasers;
30          if (erasers < 0)
31              throw NegativeNumber("erasers");

32          if (erasers != 0)
33              ppe = pencils / static_cast<double>(erasers);
34          else
35              throw DivideByZero( );
36          cout << "Each eraser must last through "
37              << ppe << " pencils.\n";
38      }
```

Display 18.4   Catching Multiple Exceptions (part 2 of 2)

```
39    catch(NegativeNumber e)
40    {
41        cout << "Cannot have a negative number of "
42             << e.getMessage( ) << endl;
43    }
44    catch(DivideByZero)                          If the catch-block
45    {                                            parameter is not used,
46        cout << "Do not make any mistakes.\n";   you need not give it in the
47    }                                            heading.

48    cout << "End of program.\n";
49    return 0;
50    }
```

Sample Dialogue 1

```
How many pencils do you have?
5
How many erasers do you have?
2
Each eraser must last through 2.5 pencils
End of program.
```

Sample Dialogue 2

```
How many pencils do you have?
-2
Cannot have a negative number of pencils
End of program.
```

Sample Dialogue 3

```
How many pencils do you have?
5
How many erasers do you have?
0
Do not make any mistakes.
End of program.
```

Note that there is no parameter in the catch block for DivideByZero. If you do not need a parameter, you can simply list the type with no parameter. This is discussed a bit more in the Programming Tip section entitled "Exception Classes Can Be Trivial."

PITFALL: Catch the More Specific Exception First

When catching multiple exceptions, the order of the catch blocks can be important. When an exception value is thrown in a try block, the catch blocks that follow it are tried in order, and the first one that matches the type of the exception thrown is the one that is executed.

For example, the following is a special kind of catch block that will catch a thrown value of any type:

```
catch (...)
{
    <Place whatever you want in here.>
}
```

The three dots do not stand for something omitted. You actually type in those three dots in your program. This makes a good default catch block to place after all other catch blocks. For example, we could add it to the catch blocks in Display 18.4 as follows:

```
catch(NegativeNumber e)
{
    cout << "Cannot have a negative number of "
         << e.getMessage( ) << endl;
}
catch(DivideByZero)
{
    cout << "Do not make any mistakes.\n";
}
catch (...)
{
    cout << "Unexplained exception.\n";
}
```

However, it only makes sense to place this default catch block at the end of a list of catch blocks. For example, suppose we instead used

```
catch(NegativeNumber e)
{
    cout << "Cannot have a negative number of "
         << e.getMessage( ) << endl;
}
catch (...)
{
    cout << "Unexplained exception.\n";
}
catch(DivideByZero)
{
    cout << "Do not make any mistakes.\n";
}
```

PITFALL: (continued)

With this second ordering, an exception (a thrown value) of type NegativeNumber will be caught by the NegativeNumber catch block as it should be. However, if a value of type DivideByZero were thrown, it would be caught by the block that starts catch(...). So, the DivideByZero catch block could never be reached. Fortunately, most compilers will tell you if you make this sort of mistake. ∎

TIP: Exception Classes Can Be Trivial

In the following, we have reproduced the definition of the exception class DivideByZero from Display 18.4:

```
class DivideByZero
{};
```

This exception class has no member variables and no member functions (other than the default constructor). It has nothing but its name, but that is useful enough. Throwing an object of the class DivideByZero can activate the appropriate catch block, as it does in Display 18.4.

When using a trivial exception class, you normally do not have anything you can do with the exception (the thrown value) once control gets to the catch block. The exception is just being used to get you to the catch block. Thus, you can omit the catch-block parameter. In fact, you can omit the catch-block parameter any time you do not need it, whether the exception type is trivial or not. ∎

Throwing an Exception in a Function

Sometimes it makes sense to delay handling an exception. For example, you might have a function with code that throws an exception if there is an attempt to divide by zero, but you may or may not want to catch the exception in that function. Perhaps some programs that use that function should simply end if the exception is thrown, and other programs that use the function should do something else. Thus, you would not know what to do with the exception if you caught it inside the function. In these cases, it makes sense to not catch the exception in the function definition, but instead to have any program (or other code) that uses the function to place the function invocation in a try block and catch the exception in a catch block that follows that try block.

Look at the program in Display 18.5. It has a try block, but there is no throw statement visible in the try block. The statement that does the throwing in that program is

```
if (bottom == 0)
    Throw DivideByZero( );
```

Display 18.5   Throwing an Exception Inside a Function (part 1 of 2)

```
1   #include <iostream>
2   #include <cstdlib>
3   using std::cin;
4   using std::cout;
5   using std::endl;

6   class DivideByZero
7   {};

8   double safeDivide(int top, int bottom) throw (DivideByZero);

9   int main( )
10  {
11      int numerator;
12      int denominator;
13      double quotient;
14      cout << "Enter numerator:\n";
15      cin >> numerator;
16      cout << "Enter denominator:\n";
17      cin >> denominator;

18      try
19      {
20          quotient =  safeDivide(numerator, denominator) ;
21      }
22      catch (DivideByZero)
23      {
24          cout << "Error: Division by zero!\n"
25               << "Program aborting.\n";
26          exit(0);
27      }

28      cout << numerator << "/" << denominator
29           << " = " << quotient << endl;

30      cout << "End of program.\n";
31      return 0;
32  }

33  double safeDivide(int top, int bottom) throw (DivideByZero)
34  {
35      if (bottom == 0)
36          throw DivideByZero( ) ;
37
38      return top / static_cast<double>(bottom) ;
39  }
```

Display 18.5   Throwing an Exception Inside a Function (part 2 of 2)

Sample Dialogue 1

```
Enter numerator:
5
Enter denominator:
10
5/10 = 0.5
End of Program.
```

Sample Dialogue 2

```
Enter numerator:
5
Enter denominator:
0
Error: Division by zero!
Program aborting.
```

This statement is not visible in the `try` block. However, it is in the `try` block in terms of program execution, because it is in the definition of the function `safeDivide` and there is an invocation of `safeDivide` in the `try` block.

The meaning of `throw (DivideByZero)` in the declaration of `safeDivide` is discussed in the next subsection.

Exception Specification

exception specification

If a function does not catch an exception, it should at least warn programmers that any invocation of the function might possibly throw an exception. If there are exceptions that might be thrown but not caught in the function definition, those exception types should be listed in an **exception specification**, which is illustrated by the following function declaration from Display 18.5:

```
double safeDivide(int top, int bottom) throw (DivideByZero);
```

As illustrated in Display 18.5, the exception specification should appear in both the function declaration and the function definition. If a function has more than one function declaration, then all the function declarations must have identical exception specifications. The exception specification for a function is also sometimes called the **throw list**.

throw list

If more than one possible exception can be thrown in the function definition, the exception types are listed separated by commas, as illustrated in what follows:

```
void someFunction( ) throw (DivideByZero, SomeOtherException);
```

All exception types listed in the exception specification are treated normally. When we say the exception is treated normally, we mean it is treated as we have described before this subsection. In particular, you can place the function invocation in a `try` block followed by a `catch` block to catch that type of exception, and if the function throws the exception (and does not catch it inside the function), then the `catch` block following the `try` block will catch the exception.

If there is no exception specification (no throw list) at all (not even an empty one), then the code behaves the same as if all possible exception types were listed in the exception specification; that is, any exception that is thrown is treated normally.

What happens when an exception is thrown in a function but is not listed in the exception specification (and not caught inside the function)? This is neither a compile-time error nor a run-time error. In such cases, the function `unexpected( )` is called. You can change the behavior of the function `unexpected( )`, which ends the program. In particular, notice that if an exception is thrown in a function but is not listed in the exception specification (and not caught inside the function), then it will not be caught by any `catch` block in your program but will instead result in an invocation of `unexpected( )` whose default behavior is to end your program.

Keep in mind that the exception specification is for exceptions that "get outside" the function. If they do not get outside the function, they do not belong in the exception specification. If they get outside the function, they belong in the exception specification no matter where they originate. If an exception is thrown in a `try` block that is inside a function definition and is caught in a `catch` block inside the function definition, then its type need not be listed in the exception specification. If a function definition includes an invocation of another function and that other function can throw an exception that is not caught, then the type of the exception should be placed in the exception specification.

You might think that the possibility of throwing an exception that is not caught and is not on the throw list should be checked by the compiler and produce a compiler error. However, because of the details of exceptions in C++, it is not possible for the compiler to perform the check. The check must be done at run time.[1]

To say that a function should not throw any exceptions that are not caught inside the function, use an empty exception specification like so:

By way of summary,

```
void someFunction( )  throw ( ) ;
```

```
void someFunction( )  throw (DivideByZero,  SomeOtherException) ;
//Exceptions of type DivideByZero or SomeOtherException are
//treated normally.  All other exceptions invoke unexpected( ).
```

---

[1] This is not true in all programming languages. It depends on the details of how the exception specification details are defined for the language.

```
void someFunction( ) throw ( );
//Empty exception list, so all exceptions invoke unexpected( ).

void someFunction( );
//All exceptions of all types are treated normally.
```

The default action of unexpected( ) is to end the program. You need not use any special include or using directives to gain the default behavior of unexpected( ). You normally have no need to redefine the behavior of unexpected( ); however, the behavior of unexpected( ) can be changed with the function set_unexpected. If you need to use set_unexpected, you should consult a more advanced book for the details.

Keep in mind that an object of a derived class is also an object of its base class. So, if D is a derived class of class B and B is in the exception specification, then a thrown object of class D will be treated normally, since it is an object of class B. However, no automatic type conversions are done. If double is in the exception specification, this does not account for throwing an int value. You would need to include both int and double in the exception specification.

Warning!

One final warning: Not all compilers treat the exception specification as they are supposed to. Some compilers essentially treat the exception specification as a comment; with those compilers, the exception specification has no effect on your code. This is another reason to place all exceptions that might be thrown by your functions in the throw specification. This way all compilers will treat your exceptions in the same manner. Of course, you could get the same compiler consistency by not having any throw specification at all, but then your program would not be as well documented and you would not get the extra error checking provided by compilers that do use the throw specification. With a compiler that does process the throw specification, your program will terminate as soon as it throws an exception that you did not anticipate. (Note that this is a run-time behavior—but which run-time behavior you get depends on your compiler.)

PITFALL: Exception Specification in Derived Classes

When you redefine or override a function definition in a derived class, it should have the same exception specification as it had in the base class, or it should have an exception specification whose exceptions are a subset of those in the base class exception specification. Put another way, when you redefine or override a function definition, you cannot add any exceptions to the exception specification (but you can delete some exceptions if you want). This makes sense, since an object of the derived class can be used anyplace an object of the base class can be used, and so a redefined or overwritten function must fit any code written for an object of the base class. ■

Self-Test Exercises

8. What is the output produced by the following program?

```cpp
#include <iostream>
using std::cout;

void sampleFunction(double test) throw (int);

int main( )
{
    try
    {
        cout << "Trying.\n";
        sampleFunction(98.6);
        cout << "Trying after call.\n";
    }
    catch(int)
    {
        cout << "Catching.\n";
    }

    cout << "End program.\n";
    return 0;
}

void sampleFunction(double test) throw (int)
{
    cout << "Starting sampleFunction.\n";
    if (test < 100)
        throw 42;
}
```

9. What is the output produced by the program in Self-Test Exercise 8 when the following change is made to the program? Change

```
sampleFunction(98.6);
```

in the try block to

```
sampleFunction(212);
```

18.2 Programming Techniques for Exception Handling

Only use this in exceptional circumstances.

WARREN PEACE, *The Lieutenant's Tool*

So far we have shown lots of code that explains how exception handling works in C++, but we have not shown an example of a program that makes good and realistic use of exception handling. However, now that you know the mechanics of exception handling, this section can go on to explain exception handling techniques.

When to Throw an Exception

We have given some very simple code to illustrate the basic concepts of exception handling. However, our examples were unrealistically simple. A more complicated but better guideline is to separate throwing an exception and catching the exception into separate functions. In most cases, you should include any `throw` statement within a function definition, list the exception in an exception specification for that function, and place the `catch` clause in a different function. Thus, the preferred use of the `try-throw-catch` triad is as illustrated here:

```
void functionA( ) throw (MyException)
{
    .
    .
    .
    throw MyException (<Maybe an argument>) ;
    .
    .
    .
}
```

Then, in some other function (perhaps even some other function in some other file), you have the following:

```
void functionB( )
{
    .
    .
    .
    try
    {
        .
        .
        .
        functionA( ) ;
        .
        .
        .
    }
    catch(MyException e)
    {
        <Handle exception>
    }
    .
    .
    .
}
```

Even this kind of use of a throw statement should be reserved for cases where it is unavoidable. If you can easily handle a problem in some other way, do not throw an exception. Reserve throw statements for situations in which the way the exceptional condition is handled depends on how and where the function is used. If the way that the exceptional condition is handled depends on how and where the function is invoked, then the best thing to do is let the programmer who invokes the function handle the exception. In all other situations, it is preferable to avoid throwing exceptions. Let us outline a sample scenario of this kind of situation.

Suppose you are writing a library of functions to deal with patient monitoring systems for hospitals. One function might compute the patient's average daily temperature by accessing the patient's record in some file and dividing the sum of the temperatures by the number of times the temperature was taken. Now suppose these functions are used for creating different systems to be used in different situations. What should happen if the patient's temperature was never taken and so the averaging would involve a division by zero? In an intensive care unit, this would indicate something is very wrong, such as the patient is lost. (It has been known to happen.) So for that system, when this potential division by zero would occur, an emergency message should be sent out. However, for a system to be used in a less urgent setting, such as outpatient care or even in some noncritical wards, it might have no significance and so a simple note in the patient's records would suffice. In this scenario, the function for doing the averaging of the temperatures should throw an exception when this division by zero occurs, list the exception in the exception specifications, and let each system handle the exception case in the way that is appropriate to that system.

When to Throw an Exception

For the most part, throw statements should be used within functions and listed in an exception specification for the function. Moreover, they should be reserved for situations in which the way the exceptional condition is handled depends on how and where the function is used. If the way that the exceptional condition is handled depends on how and where the function is invoked, then the best thing to do is let the programmer who invokes the function handle the exception. In other situations, it is almost always preferable to avoid throwing an exception.

PITFALL: Uncaught Exceptions

Every exception that is thrown by your code should be caught someplace in your code. If an exception is thrown but not caught anywhere, the program will end.

Technically speaking, if an exception is thrown but not caught, then the function terminate( ) is called. The default meaning for terminate( ) is to end your program. You can change the meaning from the default, but that is seldom needed and we will not go into the details here.

terminate( )

unexpected( )

PITFALL: (continued)

An exception that is thrown in a function but is not caught either inside or outside the function has two possible cases. If the exception is not listed in the exception specification, then the function unexpected( ) is called. If the exception is not listed in the exception specification, the function terminate( ) is called. But unless you change the default behavior of unexpected( ), unexpected( ) calls terminate( ). So, the result is the same in both cases. If an exception is thrown in a function but not caught either inside or outside the function, then your program ends. ■

PITFALL: Nested try-catch Blocks

You can place a try block and following catch blocks inside a larger try block or inside a larger catch block. In rare cases, this may be useful, but if you are tempted to do this, you should suspect that there is a nicer way to organize your program. It is almost always better to place the inner try-catch blocks inside a function definition and place an invocation of the function in the outer try or catch block (or maybe just eliminate one or more try blocks completely).

If you place a try block and following catch blocks inside a larger try block, and an exception is thrown in the inner try block but not caught in any of the inner catch blocks, then the exception is thrown to the outer try block for processing and might be caught by a catch block following the outer try block. ■

PITFALL: Overuse of Exceptions

Exceptions allow you to write programs whose flow of control is so involved that it is almost impossible to understand the program. Moreover, this is not hard to do. Throwing an exception allows you to transfer flow of control from anyplace in your program to almost anyplace else in your program. In the early days of programming, this sort of unrestricted flow of control was allowed via a construct known as a *goto*. Programming experts now agree that such unrestricted flow of control is very poor programming style. Exceptions allow you to revert to these bad old days of unrestricted flow of control. Exceptions should be used sparingly and in certain ways only. A good rule is the following: If you are tempted to include a throw statement, then think about how you might write your program or class definition without this throw statement. If you can think of an alternative that produces reasonable code, then you probably do not want to include the throw statement. ■

Exception Class Hierarchies

It can be very useful to define a hierarchy of exception classes. For example, you might have an ArithmeticError exception class and then define an exception class DivideByZeroError that is a derived class of ArithmeticError. Since a DivideByZeroError is an ArithmeticError, every catch block for an ArithmeticError will catch a DivideByZeroError. If you list ArithmeticError in the exception specification, then you have, in effect, also added DivideByZeroError to the exception specification, whether or not you list DivideByZeroError by name in the exception specification.

Testing for Available Memory

In Chapter 17 we created new dynamic variables with code similar to the following:

```
struct Node
{
    int data;
    Node *link;
};
typedef Node* NodePtr;
    ...
NodePtr pointer = new Node;
```

This works fine as long as there is sufficient memory available to create the new node. But what happens if there is not? If there is insufficient memory to create the node, then a **bad_alloc** exception is thrown.

Since new will throw a bad_alloc exception when there is not enough memory to create the node, you can check for running out of memory as follows:

```
try
{
    NodePtr pointer = new Node;
}
catch (bad_alloc)
{
    cout << "Ran out of memory!";
}
```

Of course, you can do other things besides simply giving a warning message, but the details of what you do will depend on your particular programming task.

The definition of bad_alloc is in the library with the header file <new> and is placed in the std namespace. So, when using bad_alloc, your program should contain the following (or something similar):

```
#include <new>
using std::bad_alloc;
```

Rethrowing an Exception

It is legal to throw an exception within a catch block. In rare cases, you may want to catch an exception and then, depending on the details, decide to throw the same or a different exception for handling farther up the chain of exception handling blocks.

Self-Test Exercises

10. What happens when an exception is never caught?

11. Can you nest a try block inside another try block?

Chapter Summary

- Exception handling allows you to design and code the normal case for your program separately from the code that handles exceptional situations.

- An *exception* can be thrown in a try *block*. Alternatively, an exception can be thrown in a function definition that does not include a try block (or does not include a catch block to catch that type of exception). In this case, an invocation of the function can be placed in a try block.

- An exception is caught in a catch *block*.

- A try block may be followed by more than one catch block. In this case, always list the catch block for a more specific exception class before the catch block for a more general exception class.

- The best use of exceptions is to throw an exception in a function (but not catch it in the function) whenever the way the exception is handled will vary from one invocation of the function to another. There is seldom any other situation that can profitably benefit from throwing an exception.

- If an exception is thrown in a function but not caught in that function, then the exception type should be listed in an exception specification for that function.

- If an exception is thrown but never caught, then the default behavior is to end your program.

- Do not overuse exceptions.

Answers to Self-Test Exercises

1. Try block entered.
   Exception thrown with
   waitTime equal to 46
   After catch block.

2. Try block entered.
   Leaving try block.
   After catch block.

3. throw waitTime;

   Note that the following is an if statement, not a throw statement, even though it
   contains a throw statement:

   ```
   if (waitTime > 30)
       throw waitTime;
   ```

4. When a throw statement is executed, that is the end of the enclosing try block. No
   other statements in the try block are executed, and control passes to the following
   catch block or blocks. When we say control passes to the following catch block,
   we mean that the value thrown is plugged in for the catch-block parameter (if any)
   and the code in the catch block is executed.

5. ```
   try
   {
       cout << "Try block entered.";
       if (waitTime > 30)
           throw waitTime;
       cout << "Leaving try block.";
   }
   ```

6. ```
   catch(int thrownValue)
   {
       cout << "Exception thrown with\n"
            << "waitTime equal to" << thrownValue << endl;
   }
   ```

7. thrownValue is the catch-block parameter.

8. Trying.
   Starting sampleFunction.
   Catching.
   End of program.

9. Trying.
   Starting sampleFunction.
   Trying after call.
   End of program.

10. If an exception is not caught anywhere, then your program ends. Technically
    speaking, if an exception is thrown but not caught, then the function terminate ( )
    is called. The default meaning for terminate ( ) is to end your program.

11. Yes, you can have a try block and corresponding catch blocks inside another larger
    try block. However, it would probably be better to place the inner try and catch
    blocks in a function definition and place an invocation of the function in the larger
    try block.

Programming Projects

Visit www.myprogramminglab.com to complete select exercises online and get instant feedback.

1. Obtain the source code for the `PFArray` class from Chapter 10 shown in Display 10.11. Modify the definition of the overloaded operator, `[]`, so it throws an `OutOfRange` exception if an index is out of range is used or if an attempt is made to add an element beyond the capacity of the implementation. `OutOfRange` is an exception class that you define. The exception class should have a private `int` member and a private `string` member, and a public constructor that has `int` and `string` arguments. The offending index value along with a message should be stored in the exception object. You choose the message to describe the situation. Write a suitable test program to test the modified class `PFArray`.

2. (Based on a problem in Stroustrup, *The C++ Programming Language*, 3rd edition) Write a program consisting of functions calling one another to a calling depth of 10. Give each function an argument that specifies the level at which it is to throw an exception. The `main` function prompts for and receives input that specifies the calling depth (level) at which an exception will be thrown. The `main` function then calls the first function. The `main` function catches the exception and displays the level at which the exception was thrown. Do not forget the case in which the depth is 0, where `main` must both throw and catch the exception.

   Hints: You could use ten different functions or ten copies of the same function that call one another, but do not do this. Rather, for compact code, use a `main` function that calls another function that calls itself recursively. Suppose you do this; is the restriction on the calling depth necessary? This can be done without giving the function any additional arguments, but if you cannot do it that way, try adding an additional argument to the function.

3. Modify the source code for the `Stack` class from Chapter 17, shown in Displays 17.17 through 17.19. Currently, if the user of the class attempts to pop from an empty stack the program prints out an error message and exits. Modify the program so that it instead throws an exception named `PopEmptyStackException`.

   Write a `main` function that tests the new `Stack` class, attempts to pop from an empty stack, and catches the `PopEmptyStackException` exception.

4. The following code uses two arrays, one to store products and another to store product IDs (a better organization would be to use a single array of a class or struct, but that is not the subject of this Programming Project). The function `getProductID` takes as input the two arrays, the length of the arrays, and a target product to search for. It then loops through the product name array; if a match is found, it returns the corresponding product ID:

```
int getProductID(int ids[], string names[],
                 int numProducts, string target)
{
    for (int i=0; i < numProducts; i++)
```

```cpp
    {
        if (names[i] == target)
            return ids[i];
    }
    return -1; // Not found
}

int main() // Sample code to test the getProductID function
{
    int productIds[] = {4, 5, 8, 10, 13};
    string products[] = {"computer", "flash drive",
                         "mouse", "printer", "camera"};

    cout << getProductID(productIds, products, 5, "mouse") << endl;
    cout << getProductID(productIds, products, 5, "camera")
         << endl;
    cout << getProductID(productIds, products, 5, "laptop")
         << endl;

    return 0;
}
```

One problem with the implementation of the getProductID function is that it returns the special error code of −1 if the target name is not found. The caller might ignore the −1, or later we might actually want to have −1 as a valid product ID number. Rewrite the program so that it throws an appropriate exception when a product is not found instead of returning −1.

5. A function that returns a special error code is usually better accomplished throwing an exception instead. The following class maintains an account balance.

```cpp
class Account
{
private:
    double balance;
public:
    Account()
    {
        balance = 0;
    }
    Account(double initialDeposit)
    {
        balance = initialDeposit;
    }
    double getBalance()
    {
        return balance;
    }
    // returns new balance or -1 if error
    double deposit(double amount)
    {
        if (amount > 0)
            balance += amount;
```

```
        else
            return -1;        // Code indicating error
        return balance;
    }
    // returns new balance or -1 if invalid amount
    double withdraw(double amount)
    {
        if ((amount > balance) || (amount < 0))
            return -1;
        else
            balance -= amount;
        return balance;
    }
};
```

Rewrite the class so that it throws appropriate exceptions instead of returning −1 as an error code. Write test code that attempts to withdraw and deposit invalid amounts and catches the exceptions that are thrown.

Standard Template Library 19

Libraries are not made; they grow.

AUGUSTINE BIRRELL

STL

Introduction

In Chapter 17 we constructed our own versions of the stack and queue data structures. A large collection of standard structures for holding data exists. Because they are so standard, it makes sense to have standard portable implementations of these data structures. The **Standard Template Library (STL)** includes libraries for such data structures. Included in the STL are implementations of the stack, queue, and many other standard data structures. When discussed in the context of the STL, these data structures are usually called *container classes* because they are used to hold collections of data. Chapter 7 presented a preview of the STL by describing the `vector` template class, which is one of the container classes in the STL. This chapter presents an overview of some of the basic classes included in the STL. Because the STL is very large, we will not be able to give a comprehensive treatment of it here, but we will present enough to get you started using some basic STL container classes as well as some of the other items in the STL.

The STL was developed by Alexander Stepanov and Meng Lee at Hewlett-Packard and was based on research by Stepanov, Lee, and David Musser. It is a collection of libraries written in the C++ language. Although the STL is not part of the core C++ language, it is part of the C++ standard, and so any implementation of C++ that conforms to the standard includes the STL. As a practical matter, you can consider the STL to be part of the C++ language.

As its name suggests, the classes in the STL are template classes. A typical container class in the STL has a type parameter for the type of data to be stored in the container class.

The STL container classes make extensive use of iterators, which are objects that facilitate cycling through the data in a container. An introduction to the general concept of an iterator was given in Section 17.3 of Chapter 17. Although this chapter does not presuppose that you have read that section, most readers will find it helpful to read that section before reading this chapter. As defined in the STL, iterators are very general and can be used for more than just cycling through the few container classes we will cover. Our discussion of iterators will be specialized to simple uses with the container classes discussed in this chapter. This should make the concept come alive in a concrete setting and should give you enough understanding to feel comfortable reading more advanced texts on the STL (there are numerous books dedicated to the STL).

The STL also includes implementations of many important generic algorithms, such as searching and sorting. The algorithms are implemented as template functions. After discussing the container classes, we will describe some of these algorithm implementations.

The STL differs from other C++ libraries—such as `<iostream>`, for example—in that the classes and algorithms are *generic*, which is another way of saying that they are template classes and template functions.

If you have not already done so, you should read Section 7.3 of Chapter 7, which covers the `vector` template class of the STL. Although the current chapter does not use any of the material in Chapter 17, most readers will find that reading Chapter 17 before reading this one will aid his or her comprehension of this chapter by giving sample concrete implementations of some of the abstract ideas intrinsic to the STL. This chapter does not use any of the material in Chapters 12 to 15.

19.1 Iterators

To iterate is human, and programmers are human.

ANONYMOUS

If you have not yet done so, you should read Chapter 10 on pointers and arrays and also read Section 7.3 of Chapter 7, which covers vectors. Vectors are one of the container template classes in the STL. Iterators are a generalization of pointers. This section shows how to use iterators with vectors. Other container template classes that we introduce in Section 19.2 use iterators in the same way. So, all that you learn about iterators in this section will apply across a wide range of containers rather than applying solely to vectors. This reflects one of the basic tenets of the STL philosophy: The semantics, naming, and syntax for iterator usage should be (and is) uniform across different container types.

Iterator Basics

iterator An **iterator** is a generalization of a pointer, and in fact is typically even implemented using a pointer, but the abstraction of an iterator is designed to spare you the details of the implementation and give you a uniform interface to iterators that is the same across different container classes. Each container class has its own iterator types, just like each data type has its own pointer type. But just as all pointer types behave essentially the same for dynamic variables of their particular data type, so too does each iterator type behave the same, but each iterator is used only with its own container type.

An iterator is not a pointer, but you will not go far wrong if you think of it and use it as if it were. Like a pointer variable, an iterator variable is located at (meaning, it points to) one data entry in the container. You manipulate iterators using the following overloaded operators that apply to iterator objects:

- Prefix and postfix increment operators (++) for advancing the iterator to the next data item.
- Prefix and postfix decrement operators (--) for moving the iterator to the previous data item.
- Equal and unequal operators (== and !=) to test whether two iterators point to the same data location.

- A dereferencing operator (*) so that if p is an iterator variable, then *p gives access to the data located at (pointed to by) p. This access may be read only or write only, or it may allow both reading and changing of the data, depending on the particular container class.

Not all iterators have all of these operators. However, the vector template class is an example of a container whose iterators have all these operators and more.

A container class has member functions that get the iterator process started. After all, a new iterator variable is not located at (pointing to) any data in the container. Many container classes, including the vector template class, have the following member functions that return iterator objects (iterator values) that point to special data elements in the data structure:

- c.begin( ) returns an iterator for the container c that points to the "first" data item in the container c.

- c.end( ) returns something that can be used to test when an iterator has passed beyond the last data item in a container c. The iterator c.end( ) is completely analogous to NULL when used to test whether a pointer has passed the last node in a linked list of the kind discussed in Chapter 17. The iterator c.end( ) is thus an iterator that is not located at a data item but that is a kind of end marker or sentinel.

For many container classes, these tools allow you to write for loops that cycle through all the elements in a container object c, as follows:

```
//p is an iterator variable of the type for the container object c.
for (p = c.begin( ); p != c.end( ); p++)
    process *p //*p is the current data item.
```

That is the big picture. Now let us look at the details in the concrete setting of the vector template container class.

Display 19.1 illustrates the use of iterators with the vector template class. Keep in mind that each container type in the STL has its own iterator types, although they are all used in the same basic ways. The iterators we want for a vector of ints are of type

```
std::vector<int>::iterator
```

Another container class is the list template class. Iterators for lists of ints are of type

```
std::list<int>::iterator
```

In the program in Display 19.1, we specialize the type name iterator so it applies to iterators for vectors of ints. The type name iterator that we want in Display 19.1 is defined in the template class vector. Thus, if we specialize the template class vector to ints and want the iterator type for vector<int>, we want the type

```
vector<int>::iterator;
```

Display 19.1   Iterators Used with a Vector

```
1    //Program to demonstrate STL iterators.
2    #include <iostream>
3    #include <vector>
4    using std::cout;
5    using std::endl;
6    using std::vector;

7    int main( )
8    {
9        vector<int> container;

10       for (int i = 1; i <= 4; i++)
11           container.push_back(i);

12       cout << "Here is what is in the container:\n";
13       vector<int>::iterator p;
14       for (p = container.begin( ); p != container.end( ); p++)
15           cout << *p << " ";
16       cout << endl;

17       cout << "Setting entries to 0:\n";
18       for (p = container.begin( ); p != container.end( ); p++)
19           *p = 0;

20       cout << "Container now contains:\n";
21       for (p = container.begin( ); p != container.end( ); p++)
22           cout << *p << " ";
23       cout << endl;

24       return 0;
25   }
```

Sample Dialogue

```
Here is what is in the container:
1 2 3 4
Setting entries to 0:
Container now contains:
0 0 0 0
```

The basic use of iterators with `vector` (or any container class) is illustrated by the following lines from Display 19.1:

```
vector<int>::iterator p;
for (p = container.begin( ) ; p != container.end( ) ; p++)
    cout << *p << " ";
```

Recall that container is of type `vector<int>`, and that the type `iterator` really means `std::vector<int>::iterator`.

A vector v can be thought of as a linear arrangement of its data elements. There is a first data element v[0], a second data element v[1], and so forth. An iterator p is an object that can be located at one of these elements (or points to one of these elements). An iterator can move its location from one element to another element. If p is located at, say, v[7], then p++ moves p so it is located at v[8]. This allows an iterator to move through the vector from the first element to the last element, but it needs to find the first element and needs to know when it has seen the last element.

You can tell if an iterator is at the same location as another iterator by using the operator, ==. Thus, if you have an iterator pointing to the first, last, or other element, you could test another iterator to see if it is located at the first, last, or other element.

If p1 and p2 are two iterators, then the comparison

```
p1 == p2
```

is true when and only when p1 and p2 are located at the same element. (This is analogous to pointers. If p1 and p2 were pointers, this comparison would be true if they pointed to the same thing.) As usual, != is just the negation of ==, and so

```
p1 != p2
```

is true when p1 and p2 are not located at the same element.

The member function `begin( )` is used to position an iterator at the first element in a container. For vectors, and many other container classes, the member function `begin( )` returns an iterator located at the first element. (For a vector v the first element is v[0].) Thus,

begin( )

```
vector<int>::iterator p = v.begin( );
```

initializes the iterator variable p to an iterator located at the first element. The basic `for` loop for visiting all elements of the vector v is therefore

```
vector<int>::iterator p;
for (p = v.begin( ); Boolean_Expression; p++)
    Action_At_Location p;
```

The desired stopping condition is

```
p = v.end( )
```

end( )

The member function end( ) returns a sentinel value that can be checked to see if an iterator has passed the last element. If p is located at the last element, then after p++, the test p = v.end( ) changes from false to true. So the correct Boolean_Expression is the negation of this stopping condition:

```
vector<int>::iterator p;
for (p = v.begin( ); p != v.end( ); p++)
    Action_At_Location p;
```

Note that p != v.end( ) does not change from true to false until after p's location has advanced past the last element. So, v.end( ) is not located at any element. The value v.end( ) is a special value that serves as a sentinel. It is not an iterator, but you can compare v.end( ) to an iterator using == and !=. The value v.end( ) is analogous to the value NULL that is used to mark the end of a linked list of the kind discussed in Chapter 17.

The following for loop from Display 19.1 uses this same technique with the vector named container:

```
vector<int>::iterator p;
for (p = container.begin( ); p != container.end( ); p++)
    cout << *p << " ";
```

The action taken at the location of the iterator p is

```
cout << *p << " ";
```

The dereferencing operator, *, is overloaded for STL container iterators so that *p produces the element at location p. In particular, for a vector container, *p produces the element located at the iterator p. The preceding cout statement thus outputs the element located at the iterator p, and so the entire for loop outputs all the elements in the vector container.

The dereferencing operator *p always produces the element located at the iterator p. In some situations *p produces read-only access, which does not allow you to change the element. In other situations it gives you access to the element and will let you change it. For vectors, *p will allow you to change the element located at p, as illustrated by the following for loop from Display 19.1:

```
for (p = container.begin( ); p != container.end( ); p++)
    *p = 0;
```

This for loop cycles through all the elements in the vector container and changes all the elements to 0.

PITFALL: Compiler Problems

Some compilers have problems with iterator declarations. You can declare an iterator in different ways. For example, we have been using the following:

```
using std::vector;
. . .
vector<char>::iterator p;
```

Alternatively, you could use the following:

```
using std::vector<char>::iterator;
. . .
iterator p;
```

You could also use the following, which is not quite as nice:

```
using namespace std;
. . .
vector<char>::iterator p;
```

There are other, similar variations.

Your compiler should accept any of these alternatives. However, we have found that some compilers will accept only certain of these alternatives. If one form does not work with your compiler, try another. ■

Iterator

An *iterator* is an object that can be used with a container to gain access to elements in the container. An iterator is a generalization of the notion of a pointer. The operators ==, !=, ++, and -- behave the same for iterators as they do for pointers. The basic outline of how an iterator can cycle through all the elements in a container is as follows:

```
STL_container<datatype>::iterator p;
for (p = container.begin( ); p != container.end( ); p++)
    Process_Element_At_Location p;
```

STL_container is the name of the container class (e.g., vector) and datatype is the data type of items to be stored in the container. The member function begin( ) returns an iterator located at the first element. The member function end( ) returns a value that serves as a sentinel value one location past the last element in the container.

Dereferencing

The dereferencing operator, *p, when applied to an iterator p, produces the element located at the iterator p. In some situations *p produces read-only access, which does not allow you to change the element. In other situations it gives you access to the element and will let you change the element.

Self-Test Exercises

1. If v is a vector, what does v.begin( ) return? What does v.end( ) return?

2. If p is an iterator for a vector object v, what is *p?

3. Suppose v is a vector of ints. Write a for loop that will output all the elements of p except for the first element.

Kinds of Iterators

Different containers have different kinds of iterators. Iterators are classified according to the kinds of operations that work on them. Vector iterators are of the most general form; that is, all the operations work with vector iterators. Thus, we will again use the vector container to illustrate iterators. In this case we use a vector to illustrate the iterator operations of *decrement* and *random access*. Display 19.2 shows another program using a vector object named container and an iterator p.

The decrement operator is used on line 29 of Display 19.2. As you would expect, p-- moves the iterator p to the previous location. The decrement operator, --, is similar to the increment operator, ++, but it moves the iterator in the opposite direction.

The increment and decrement operators can be used in either prefix (++p) or postfix (p++) notation. In addition to changing p, they also return a value. The details of the value returned are completely analogous to what happens with the increment and decrement operators on int variables. In prefix notation, first the variable is changed and then the changed value is returned. In postfix notation, the value is returned before the variable is changed. We prefer not to use the increment and decrement operators as expressions that return a value; we use them only to change the variable value.

The following lines from Display 19.2 illustrate the fact that with vector iterators you have random access to the elements of a vector, such as container:

```
vector<char>::iterator p = container.begin( );
cout << "The third entry is " << container[2] << endl;
cout << "The third entry is " << p[2] << endl;
cout << "The third entry is " << *(p + 2) << endl;
```

random access **Random access** means that you can go directly to any particular element in one step. We have already used container[2] as a form of random access to a vector. This is simply the square bracket operator that is standard with arrays and vectors. What is new is that you can use this same square bracket notation with an iterator. The expression p[2] is a way to obtain access to the element indexed by 2.

The expressions p[2] and *(p + 2) are completely equivalent. By analogy to pointer arithmetic (see Chapter 10), (p + 2) names the location two places beyond p. Since p is at the first (index 0) location in the previous code, (p + 2) is at the third (index 2) location. The expression (p + 2) returns an iterator. The expression *(p + 2) dereferences that iterator. Of course, you can replace 2 with a different nonnegative integer to obtain a pointer to a different element.

Display 19.2 Bidirectional and Random-Access Iterator Use (part 1 of 2)

```
1   //Program to demonstrate bidirectional and random-access iterators.
2   #include <iostream>
3   #include <vector>
4   using std::cout;
5   using std::endl;
6   using std::vector;
7
8   int main()
9   {
10      vector<char> container;
11      container.push_back('A');
12      container.push_back('B');
13      container.push_back('C');
14      container.push_back('D');
15
16      for (int i = 0; i < 4; i++)
17          cout << "container[" << i << "] == "
18               << container[i] << endl;
19
20      vector<char>::iterator p = container.begin();
21      cout << "The third entry is " << container.begin() << endl;
22      cout << "The third entry is " << p[2] << endl;
23      cout << "The third entry is " << *(p + 2) << endl;
24
25      cout << "Back to container[0].\n";
26      p = container.begin();
27      cout << "which has value " << *p << endl;
28
29      cout << "Two steps forward and one step back:\n";
30      p++;
31      cout << *p << endl;
32      p++;
33      cout << *p << endl;
34
35      p--;
36      cout << *p << endl;
37
38      return 0;
39  }
```

Three different notations for the same thing.

This notation is specialized to vectors and arrays.

These two work for any random-access iterator.

This works for any bidirectional iterator.

Display 19.2   Bidirectional and Random-Access Iterator Use (part 2 of 2)

Sample Dialogue

```
container[0] == A
container[1] == B
container[2] == C
container[3] == D
The third entry is C
The third entry is C
The third entry is C
Back to container[0].
which has value A
Two steps forward and one step back:
B
C
B
```

Be sure to note that neither p[2] nor (p + 2) changes the value of the iterator in the iterator variable p. The expression (p + 2) returns another iterator at another location, but it leaves p where it was. Something similar happens with p[2] behind the scenes. Also note that the meaning of p[2] and (p + 2) depends on the location of the iterator in p. For example, (p + 2) means two locations beyond the location of p, wherever that may be.

For example, suppose the previously discussed code from Display 19.2 were replaced with the following (note the added p++):

```
vector<char>::iterator p = container.begin( );
p++;
cout << "The third entry is " << container[2] << endl;
cout << "The third entry is " << p[2] << endl;
cout << "The third entry is " << *(p + 2) << endl;
```

The output of these three couts would no longer be

```
The third entry is C
The third entry is C
The third entry is C
```

but would instead be

```
The third entry is C
The third entry is D
The third entry is D
```

The p++ moves p from location 0 to location 1, and so (p+2) is now an iterator at location 3, not location 2. So, *(p+2) and p[2] are equivalent to container[3], not container[2].

We now know enough about how to operate on iterators to make sense of how iterators are classified. The main kinds of iterators are as follows.

Forward iterators: ++ works on the iterator.

Bidirectional iterators: Both ++ and --- work on the iterator.

Random-access iterators: ++, ---, and random access all work with the iterator.

Note that these are increasingly strong categories: Every random-access iterator is also a bidirectional iterator, and every bidirectional iterator is also a forward iterator.

As we will see, different template container classes have different kinds of iterators. The iterators for the vector template class are random-access iterators.

Note that the names *forward iterator*, *bidirectional iterator*, and *random-access iterator* refer to kinds of iterators, not type names. An actual type name would be something like std::vector<int>::iterator, which in this case happens to be a random-access iterator.

Kinds of Iterators

Different containers have different kinds of iterators. The following are the main kinds of iterators.

Forward iterators: ++ works on the iterator.

Bidirectional iterators: Both ++ and --- work on the iterator.

Random-access iterators: ++, ---, and random access all work with the iterator.

Self-Test Exercise

4. Suppose the vector v contains the letters 'A', 'B', 'C', and 'D' in that order. What is the output of the following code?

```
vector<char>::iterator i = v.begin( ) ;
i++;
cout << *(i + 2) << " ";
i--;
cout << i[2] << " ";
cout << *(i + 2) << " ";
```

Constant and Mutable Iterators

The categories of forward iterator, bidirectional iterator, and random-access iterator each subdivide into two categories—*constant* and *mutable*—depending on how the dereferencing operator behaves with the iterator. With a **constant iterator** the dereferencing operator produces a read-only version of the element. With a constant iterator p, you can use *p to assign it to a variable or output it to the screen, for example, but you cannot change the element in the container by, for example, assigning

mutable iterator

to `*p`. With a **mutable iterator** `p`, `*p` can be assigned a value, which will change the corresponding element in the container. Phrased another way, with a mutable iterator `p`, `*p` returns an lvalue. The vector iterators are mutable, as shown by the following lines from Display 19.1:

```
cout << "Setting entries to 0:\n";
for (p = container.begin( ); p != container.end( ); p++)
    *p = 0;
```

If a container has only constant iterators, you cannot obtain a mutable iterator for the container. However, if a container has mutable iterators and you want a constant iterator for the container, you can have it. You might want a constant iterator as a kind of error-checking device if you intend that your code should not change the elements in the container. For example, the following will produce a constant iterator for a vector container named `container`:

```
std::vector<char>::const_iterator p = container.begin( );
```

or equivalently

```
using std::vector<char>::const_iterator;
const_iterator p = container.begin( );
```

With `p` declared in this way, the following would produce an error message:

```
*p = 'Z';
```

For example, Display 19.2 would behave exactly the same if you replaced

```
vector<char>::iterator p;
```

with

```
vector<char>::const_iterator p;
```

However, a similar change would not work in Display 19.1 because of the following line from the program in Display 19.1:

```
*p = 0;
```

Note that `const_iterator` is a type name, whereas *constant iterator* is the name of a kind of iterator. However, every iterator of a type named `const_iterator` will be a constant iterator.

Constant Iterator

A *constant iterator* is an iterator that does not allow you to change the element at its location.

Reverse Iterators

Sometimes you want to cycle through the elements in a container in reverse order. If you have a container with bidirectional iterators, you might be tempted to try the following:

```
vector<int>::iterator p;
for (p = container.end( ); p != container.begin( ); p--)
    cout << *p << " ";
```

This code will compile, and you may be able to get something like this to work on some systems, but there is something fundamentally wrong with it: container.end( ) is not a regular iterator but only a sentinel, and container.begin( ) is not a sentinel.

Fortunately, there is an easy way to do what you want. For a container with bidirectional iterators, there is a way to reverse everything using a kind of iterator known as a **reverse iterator**. The following will work fine:

reverse
iterator

```
vector<int>::reverse_iterator rp;
for (rp = container.rbegin( ); rp != container.rend( ); rp++)
    cout << *rp << " ";
```

rbegin( )
rend( )

The member function rbegin( ) returns an iterator located at the last element. The member function rend( ) returns a sentinel that marks the "end" of the elements in the reverse order. Note that for an iterator of type reverse_iterator, the increment operator, ++, moves backward through the elements. In other words, the meanings of -- and ++ are interchanged. The program in Display 19.3 demonstrates a reverse iterator. reverse_iterator type also has a constant version, which is named const_reverse_iterator.

Reverse Iterators

A *reverse iterator* can be used to cycle through all elements of a container with bidirectional iterators. The elements are visited in reverse order. The general scheme is as follows:

```
STL_container<datatype>::reverse_iterator rp;
for (rp = c.rbegin( ); rp != c.rend( ); rp++)
    Process_At_Location p;
```

The object c is a container class with bidirectional iterators.

When using reverse_iterator, you need to have some sort of using declaration or something equivalent. For example, if c is a vector<int>, the following will suffice:

```
vector<int>::reverse_iterator rp;
```

Display 19.3   Reverse Iterator

```cpp
1   //Program to demonstrate a reverse iterator.
2   #include <iostream>
3   #include <vector>
4   using std::cout;
5   using std::endl;
6   using std::vector;

7   int main( )
8   {
9       vector<char> container;

10      container.push_back('A');
11      container.push_back('B');
12      container.push_back('C');

13      cout << "Forward:\n";
14      vector<char>::iterator p;
15      for (p = container.begin( ); p != container.end( ); p++)
16          cout << *p << " ";
17      cout << endl;

18      cout << "Reverse:\n";
19      vector<char>::reverse_iterator rp;
20      for (rp = container.rbegin( ); rp != container.rend( ); rp++)
21          cout << *rp << " ";
22      cout << endl;

23      return 0;
24  }
```

Sample Dialogue

```
Forward:
A B C
Reverse:
C B A
```

Other Kinds of Iterators

input iterator

output iterator

There are other kinds of iterators, which we will not cover in this book. We will briefly mention two kinds of iterators whose names you may encounter. An **input iterator** is essentially a forward iterator that can be used with input streams. An **output iterator** is essentially a forward iterator that can be used with output streams. For more details you will need to consult a more advanced reference.

Self-Test Exercises

5. Suppose the vector v contains the letters 'A', 'B', 'C', and 'D' in that order. What is the output of the following code?

```
vector<char>::reverse_iterator i = v.rbegin();
i++;
i++;
cout << *i << " ";
i--;
cout << *i << " ";
```

6. Suppose you want to run the following code, where v is a vector of ints:

```
for (p = v.begin(); p != v.end(); p++)
    cout << *p << " ";
```

Which of the following are possible ways to declare p?

```
std::vector<int>::iterator p;
std::vector<int>::const_iterator p;
```

19.2   Containers

You can put all your eggs in one basket, but be sure it's a good basket.

WALTER SAVITCH, *Absolute C++*

container class

The **container classes** of the STL are different kinds of structures for holding data, such as lists, queues, and stacks. Each is a template class with a parameter for the particular type of data to be stored. So, for example, you can specify a list to be a list of ints or doubles or strings, or any class or struct type you wish. Each container template class may have its own specialized accessor and mutator functions for adding data and removing data from the container. Different container classes may have different kinds of iterators. For example, one container class may have bidirectional iterators, whereas another container class may have only forward iterators. However, whenever they are defined, the iterator operators and the member functions begin() and end() have the same meaning for all STL container classes.

Sequential Containers

singly linked list

A sequential container arranges its data items into a list such that there is a first element, a next element, and so forth, up to a last element. The linked lists we discussed in Chapter 17 are examples of a kind of sequential container; these kinds of lists are sometimes called **singly linked lists** because there is only one link from one location to another. The STL has no container corresponding to such a singly linked list, although some implementations do offer an implementation of a singly linked list, typically under

**doubly
linked list**

the name `slist`.[1] The simplest list that is part of the STL is the **doubly linked list**, which is the template class named `list`. The difference between these two kinds of lists is illustrated in Display 19.4 and is described in more detail in Section 17.1.

The lists in Display 19.4 contain the three integer values `1`, `2`, and `3` in that order.

**`slist` and
`list`**

The types for the two lists are `slist<int>` and `list<int>`. The display also indicates the location of the iterators `begin( )` and `end( )`. We have not yet told you how you can enter the integers into the lists.

In Display 19.4 we have drawn our singly and doubly linked lists as nodes and pointers of the form discussed in Chapter 17. The STL class `list` and the nonstandard class `slist` might (or might not) be implemented in this way. However, when using the STL template classes, you are shielded from these implementation details. So, you simply think in terms of locations for the data (which may or may not be nodes) and of iterators (not pointers). You can think of the arrows in Display 19.4 as indicating the directions for `++` (which is down) and `– –` (which is up).

We presented the template class `slist` to help give a context for the sequential containers. It corresponds to what we discussed in Chapter 17 and is the first thing

Display 19.4 Two Kinds of Lists

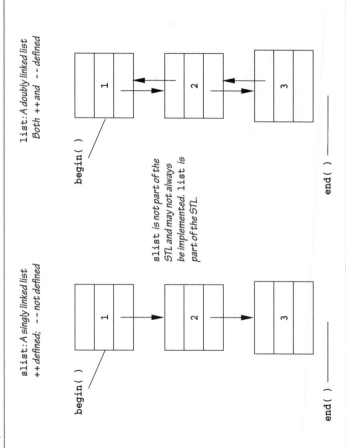

`slist`: A singly linked list
`++` defined; `– –` not defined

`list`: A doubly linked list
Both `++` and `– –` defined

begin( )

begin( )

`slist` is not part of the STL and may not always be implemented. `list` is part of the STL.

end( )

end( )

[1] The Silicon Graphics version of the STL includes `slist` and is distributed with the g++ compiler. SGI provides a very useful reference document for its STL version that is applicable to almost everyone's STL.

that comes to the mind of most programmers when you mention *linked lists*. However, since the template class `slist` is not standard, we will not discuss it further. If your implementation offers the template class `slist` and you want to use it, the details are similar to those we will describe for `list`, except that the decrement operators -- (prefix and postfix) are not defined for `slist`.

A simple program using the STL template class `list` is given in Display 19.5. The function `push_back` adds an element to the end of the list. Notice that for the `list` template class, the dereferencing operator gives you access for reading and for changing the data. Also notice that with the `list` template class and all the template classes and iterators of the STL, all definitions are placed in the `std` namespace.

push_back

Note that Display 19.5 would compile and run exactly the same if we replaced `list` and `list<int>` with `vector` and `vector<int>`, respectively. This uniformity of usage is a key part of the STL syntax.

There are, however, differences between a vector and a list container. One of the main differences is that a vector container has random-access iterators, whereas a list has only bidirectional iterators. For example, if you start with Display 19.2, which uses random access, and replace all occurrences of `vector` and `vector<char>` with `list` and `list<char>`, respectively, and then compile the program, you will get a compiler error. (You will get an error message even if you delete the statements containing `container[i]` or `container[2]`.)

memory management

The basic sequential container template classes of the STL are listed in Display 19.6. Other containers, such as stacks and queues, can be obtained from these using techniques discussed in the subsection entitled "The Container Adapters `stack` and `queue`." A sample of some member functions of the sequential container classes is given in Display 19.7. All these sequence template classes have a destructor that returns storage for recycling.

deque

Deque is pronounced "d-queue" or "deck" and stands for "doubly ended queue." A deque is a kind of super queue. With a queue, you add data at one end of the data sequence and remove data from the other end. With a deque, you can add data at either end and remove data from either end. The template class `deque` is a template class for a deque with a parameter for the type of data stored.

Sequential Containers

A **sequential container** arranges its data items into a list so that there is a first element, a next element, and so forth, up to a last element. The sequential container template classes that we have discussed are `slist`, `list`, `vector`, and `deque`.

Display 19.5   Using the list Template Class

```
1   //Program to demonstrate the STL template class list.
2   #include <iostream>
3   #include <list>
4   using std::cout;
5   using std::endl;
6   using std::list;

7   int main( )
8   {
9       list<int> listObject;

10      for (int i = 1; i <= 3; i++)
11          listObject.push_back(i);

12      cout << "List contains:\n"
13      list<int>::iterator iter;
14      for (iter = listObject.begin( ); iter != listObject.end( );
                                        iter++)
15          cout << *iter << " ";
16      cout << endl;

17      cout << "Setting all entries to 0:\n"
18      for (iter = listObject.begin( ); iter != listObject.end( );
                                        iter++)
19          *iter = 0;

20      cout << "List now contains:\n"
21      for (iter = listObject.begin( ); iter != listObject.end( );
                                        iter++)
22          cout << *iter << " ";
23      cout << endl;

24      return 0;
25  }
```

Sample Dialogue

```
List contains:
1 2 3
Setting all entries to 0:
List now contains:
0 0 0
```

Display 19.6 STL Basic Sequential Containers

TEMPLATE CLASS NAME	ITERATOR TYPE NAMES	KIND OF ITERATORS	LIBRARY HEADER FILE
slist (Warning: slist is not part of the STL.)	slist<T>::iterator slist<T>::const_iterator	Mutable forward Constant forward	<slist> Depends on implemen-tation and may not be available.)
list	list<T>::iterator list<T>::const_iterator list<T>::reverse_iterator list<T>::const_reverse_ iterator	Mutable bidirectional Constant bidirectional Mutable bidirectional Constant bidirectional	<list>
vector	vector<T>::iterator vector<T>::const_iterator vector<T>::reverse_ iterator vector<T>::const_reverse_ iterator	Mutable random access Constant random access Mutable random access Constant random access	<vector>
deque	deque<T>::iterator deque<T>::const_iterator deque<T>::reverse_ iterator deque<T>::const_reverse_ iterator	Mutable random access Constant random access Mutable random access Constant random access	<deque>

Display 19.7 Some Sequential Container Member Functions (part 1 of 2)

MEMBER FUNCTION (c IS A CONTAINER OBJECT)	MEANING
c.size( )	Returns the number of elements in the container.
c.begin( )	Returns an iterator located at the first element in the container.
c.end( )	Returns an iterator located one beyond the last element in the container.
c.rbegin( )	Returns an iterator located at the last element in the container. Used with reverse_iterator. Not a member of slist.

Display 19.7   Some Sequential Container Member Functions (part 2 of 2)

c.rend( )	Returns an iterator located one beyond the first element in the container. Used with reverse_iterator. Not a member of slist.
c.push_back(Element)	Inserts the Element at the end of the sequence. Not a member of slist.
c.push_front(Element)	Inserts the Element at the front of the sequence. Not a member of vector.
c.insert(Iterator, Element)	Inserts a copy of Element before the location of Iterator.
c.erase(Iterator)	Removes the element at location Iterator. Returns an iterator at the location immediately following. Returns c.end( ) if the last element is removed.
c.clear( )	A void function that removes all the elements in the container.
c.front( )	Returns a reference to the element in the front of the sequence. Equivalent to *(c.begin( )).
c1 == c2	True if c1.size( ) == c2.size( ) and each element of c1 is equal to the corresponding element of c2.
c1 != c2	!(c1 == c2)

All the sequence containers discussed in this section also have a default constructor, a copy constructor, and various other constructors for initializing the container to default or specified elements. Each also has a destructor that returns all storage for recycling, and a well-behaved assignment operator.

PITFALL: Iterators and Removing Elements

Adding or removing an element to or from a container can affect other iterators. In general, there is no guarantee that the iterators will be located at the same element after an addition or deletion. Some containers do, however, guarantee that the iterators will not be moved by additions or deletions, except of course if the iterator is located at an element that is removed.

Of the template classes we have seen so far, list and slist guarantee that their iterators will not be moved by additions or deletions, except of course if the iterator is located at an element that is removed. The template classes vector and deque make no such guarantee. ■

TIP: Type Definitions in Containers

The STL container classes contain type definitions that can be handy when programming with these classes. We have already seen that STL container classes may contain the type names `iterator`, `const_iterator`, `reverse_iterator`, and `const_reverse_iterator` (and hence must contain their type definitions behind the scene). There are typically other type definitions as well.

The type `value_type` is the type of the elements stored in the container, and `size_type` is an unsigned integer type that is the return type for the member function `size`. For example, `list<int>::value_type` is another name for `int`. All the template classes we have discussed so far have the defined types `value_type` and `size_type`. ∎

MyProgrammingLab™

Self-Test Exercises

7. What is a major difference between `vector` and `list`?

8. Which of the template classes `slist`, `list`, `vector`, and `deque` have the member function `push_back`?

9. Which of the template classes `slist`, `list`, `vector`, and `deque` have random-access iterators?

10. Which of the template classes `slist`, `list`, `vector`, and `deque` can have mutable iterators?

The Container Adapters `stack` and `queue`

Container adapters are template classes that are implemented on top of other classes. For example, the `stack` template class is by default implemented on top of the `deque` template class, which means that buried in the implementation of the stack is a `deque` where all the data resides. However, you are shielded from this implementation detail and see a stack as a simple last-in/first-out data structure.

Other container adapter classes are the `queue` and `priority_queue` template classes. Stacks and queues were discussed in Chapter 17. A **priority queue** is a queue with the additional property that each entry is given a priority when it is added to the queue. If all entries have the same priority, then entries are removed from a priority queue in the same manner as they are removed from a queue. If items have different priorities, the higher-priority items are removed before lower-priority items. We will not discuss priority queues in any detail, but mention it for those who may be familiar with the concept.

priority queue

Although an adapter template class has a default container class on top of which it is built, you may choose to specify a different underlying container, for efficiency or other reasons, depending on your application. For example, any sequence container may serve as the underlying container for the `stack` template class, and any sequence container other than `vector` may serve as the underlying container for the `queue` template class. The default underlying data structure is the `deque` for both the `stack` and the `queue`. For a `priority_queue`, the default underlying container is a `vector`. If you are happy with the default underlying container type, then a container adapter looks like any other template container class to you. For example, the type name for the `stack` template class using the default underlying container is `stack<int>` for a stack of `int`s. If you wish to specify that the underlying container is instead the `vector` template class, you would use `stack<int, vector<int>>` as the type name. Make sure to always insert a space between the two `>` symbols. We will always use the default underlying container.

The member functions and other details about the `stack` template class are given in Display 19.8. The details for the `queue` template class are given in Display 19.9. A simple example of using the `stack` template class is given in Display 19.10.

Warning!

PITFALL: Underlying Containers

If you specify an underlying container, be warned that you should not place two `>` symbols in the type expression without a space in between them, or the compiler can be confused. Use `stack<int, vector<int> >`, with a space between the last two `>`s. Do not use `stack<int, vector<int>>`. ∎

Self-Test Exercises

11. What kind of iterators (forward, bidirectional, or random access) does the stack template adapter class have?

12. What kind of iterators (forward, bidirectional, or random access) does the queue template adapter class have?

13. If `s` is a `stack<char>`, what is the type of the returned value of `s.pop()`?

Display 19.8   The **stack** Template Class

stack ADAPTER TEMPLATE CLASS DETAILS

Type name: stack<T> or stack<T, Sequence_Type> for a stack of elements of type T.

Library header: <stack>, which places the definition in the std namespace.

Defined types: value_type, size_type.

There are no iterators.

SAMPLE MEMBER FUNCTIONS

MEMBER FUNCTION (s IS A STACK OBJECT)	MEANING
s.size( )	Returns the number of elements in the stack.
s.empty( )	Returns true if the stack is empty; otherwise, returns false.
s.top( )	Returns a mutable reference to the top member of the stack.
s.push(Element)	Inserts a copy of *Element* at the top of the stack.
s.pop( )	Removes the top element of the stack. Note that pop is a void function. It does not return the element removed.
s1 == s2	True if s1.size( ) == s2.size( ) and each element of s1 is equal to the corresponding element of s2; otherwise, returns false.

The stack template class also has a default constructor, a copy constructor, and a constructor that takes an object of any sequence class and initializes the stack to the elements in the sequence. It also has a destructor that returns all storage for recycling, and a well-behaved assignment operator.

Display 19.9   The **queue** Template Class (part 1 of 2)

queue ADAPTER TEMPLATE CLASS DETAILS

Type name: queue<T> or queue<Sequence_Type, T> for a queue of elements of type T. For efficiency reasons, the Sequence_Type cannot be a vector type.

Library header: <queue>, which places the definition in the std namespace.

Defined types: value_type, size_type.

There are no iterators.

Display 19.9 The queue Template Class (part 2 of 2)

SAMPLE MEMBER FUNCTIONS

MEMBER FUNCTION (q IS A QUEUE OBJECT)	MEANING
q.size( )	Returns the number of elements in the queue.
q.empty( )	Returns true if the queue is empty; otherwise, returns false.
q.front( )	Returns a mutable reference to the front member of the queue.
q.back( )	Returns a mutable reference to the last member of the queue.
q.push(Element)	Adds Element to the back of the queue.
q.pop( )	Removes the front element of the queue. Note that pop is a void function. It does not return the element removed.
q1 == q2	True if q1.size( ) == q2.size( ) and each element of q1 is equal to the corresponding element of q2; otherwise, returns false.

The queue template class also has a default constructor, a copy constructor, and a constructor that takes an object of any sequence class and initializes the stack to the elements in the sequence. It also has a destructor that returns all storage for recycling, and a well-behaved assignment operator.

Display 19.10 Program Using the stack Template Class (part 1 of 2)

```
1   //Program to demonstrate use of the stack template class from the STL.
2   #include <iostream>
3   #include <stack>
4   using std::cin;
5   using std::cout;
6   using std::endl;
7   using std::stack;

8   int main( )
9   {
10      stack<char> s;
11      cout << "Enter a line of text:\n";
12      char next;
13      cin.get(next);
```

(continued)

Display 19.10   Program Using the stack Template Class (part 2 of 2)

```
14    while (next != '\n')
15    {
16        s.push(next);
17        cin.get(next);
18    }
19    cout << "Written backward that is:\n";
20    while ( ! s.empty() )
21    {
22        cout << s.top();
23        s.pop();
24    }
25    cout << endl;
26    return 0;
27    }
```

The member function pop removes one element, but does not return that element. pop is a void function. Therefore, we needed to use top to read the element we removed.

Sample Dialogue

```
Enter a line of text:
straw
Written backward that is:
warts
```

The Associative Containers set and map

Associative containers are basically very simple databases. They store data, such as structs or any other type of data. Each data item has an associated value known as its **key**. For example, if the data is a struct with an employee's record, the key might be the employee's Social Security number. Items are retrieved on the basis of the key. The key type and the type for data to be stored need not have any relationship to one another, although they often are related. A very simple case is when each data item is its own key. For example, in a set, every element is its own key.

The set template class is, in some sense, the simplest container you can imagine. It stores elements without repetition. The first insertion places an element in the set. Additional insertions after the first have no effect, so that no element appears more than once. Each element is its own key. Basically, you just add or delete elements and ask if an element is in the set or not. Like all STL classes, the set template class was written with efficiency as a goal. To work efficiently, a set object stores its values in sorted order. You can specify the order used for storing elements as follows:

```
set<T, Ordering> s;
```

map

ordering should be a well-behaved ordering relation that takes two arguments of type T and returns a bool value.[2] T is the type of elements stored. If no ordering is specified, then the ordering is assumed to use the < relational operator. Some basic details about the set template class are given in Display 19.11. A simple example that shows how to use some of the member functions of the template class set is given in Display 19.12.

A **map** is essentially a function given as a set of ordered pairs. For each value first that appears in a pair, there is at most one value second such that the pair (first, second) is in the map. The template class map implements map objects in the STL. For example, if you want to assign a unique number to each string name, you could declare a map object as follows:

    map<string, int> numberMap;

For string values known as *keys*, the numberMap object can associate a unique int value.

associative array

An alternate way to think of a map is as an **associative array**. A traditional array maps from a numerical index to a value. For example, a[10]=5 would store the number 5 at index 10. An associative array allows you to define your own indices using the data type of your choice. For example, numberMap["c++"]=5 would associate the integer 5 with the string "c++". For convenience, the [] square bracket operator is defined to allow you to use an array-like notation to access a map, although you can also use the insert or find methods if you want.

Like a set object, a map object stores its elements sorted by its key values. You can specify the ordering on keys as a third entry in the angular brackets, < >. If you do not specify an ordering, a default ordering is used. The restrictions on orderings you can use are the same as those on the orderings allowed for the set template class. Note that the ordering is on key values only. The second type can be any type and need not have anything to do with any ordering. As with the set object, the sorting of the stored entries in a map object is done for reasons of efficiency.

The easiest way to add and retrieve data from a map is to use the [] operator. Given a map object m, the expression m[key] will return a reference to the data element associated with key. If no entry exists in the map for key then a new entry will be created with the default value for the data element. This can be used to add a new item to the map or to replace an existing entry. For example, the statement m[key] = newData; will create a new association between key and newData. Note that care must be taken to ensure that map entries are not created by mistake. For example, if you execute the statement val = m[key]; with the intention of retrieving the value associated with key but mistakenly enter a value for key that is not already in the map, then a new entry will be made for key with the default value and assigned into val.

---

[2]The ordering must be a *strict weak ordering*. Most typical ordering used to implement the < operator is strict weak ordering. For those who want the details, a strict weak ordering must be one of the following: (irreflexive) Ordering(x, x) is always false; (antisymmetric) Ordering(x, y) implies !Ordering(y, x); (transitive) Ordering(x, y) and Ordering(y, z) implies Ordering(x, z); and (transitivity of equivalence) if x is equivalent to y and y is equivalent to z, then x is equivalent to z. Two elements x and y are equivalent if Ordering(x, y) and Ordering(y, x) are both false.

Display 19.11   The set Template Class

set TEMPLATE CLASS DETAILS

Type name: set<T> or set<T, Ordering> for a set of elements of type T. The *Ordering* is used to sort elements for storage. If no *Ordering* is given, the ordering used is the binary operator, <.
Library header: <set>, which places the definition in the std namespace.
Defined types include value_type, size_type.
Iterators: iterator, const_iterator, reverse_iterator, and const_reverse_iterator. All iterators are bidirectional and those not including const_ are mutable. begin(), end(), rbegin(), and rend() have the expected behavior. Adding or deleting elements does not affect iterators, except for an iterator located at the element removed.

SAMPLE MEMBER FUNCTIONS

MEMBER FUNCTION (s IS A SET OBJECT)	MEANING
s.insert(Element)	Inserts a copy of *Element* in the set. If *Element* is already in the set, this has no effect.
s.erase(Element)	Removes *Element* from the set. If *Element* is not in the set, this has no effect.
s.find(Element)	Returns an iterator located at the copy of *Element* in the set. If *Element* is not in the set, s.end() is returned. Whether the iterator is mutable or not is implementation dependent.
s.erase(Iterator)	Erases the element at the location of the *Iterator*.
s.size()	Returns the number of elements in the set.
s.empty()	Returns true if the set is empty; otherwise, returns false.
s1 == s2	Returns true if the sets contain the same elements; otherwise, returns false.

The set template class also has a default constructor, a copy constructor, and other specialized constructors not mentioned here. It has a destructor as well that returns all storage for recycling, and a well-behaved assignment operator.

Display 19.12   Program Using the set Template Class (part 1 of 2)

```
1  //Program to demonstrate use of the set template class.
2  #include <iostream>
3  #include <set>
4  using std::cout;
5  using std::endl;
6  using std::set;
```

Display 19.12 Program Using the set Template Class (part 2 of 2)

```
7   int main( )
8   {
9       set<char> s;

10      s.insert('A');
11      s.insert('D');
12      s.insert('D');
13      s.insert('C');
14      s.insert('C');
15      s.insert('B');

16      cout << "The set contains:\n";
17      set<char>::const_iterator p;
18      for (p = s.begin( ); p != s.end( ); p++)
19          cout << *p << " ";
20      cout << endl;

21      cout << "Set contains 'C': ";
22      if (s.find('C')==s.end( ))
23          cout << " no " << endl;
24      else
25          cout << " yes " << endl;

26      cout << "Removing C.\n";
27      s.erase('C');
28      for (p = s.begin( ); p != s.end( ); p++)
29          cout << *p << " ";
30      cout << endl;

31      cout << "Set contains 'C': ";
32      if (s.find('C')==s.end( ))
33          cout << " no " << endl;
34      else
35          cout << " yes " << endl;

36      return 0;
37  }
```

No matter how many times you add an element to a set, the set contains only one copy of that element.

Sample Dialogue

```
The set contains:
A B C D
Set contains 'C': yes
Removing C.
A B D
Set contains 'C': no
```

Some basic details about the map template class are given in Display 19.13. In order to understand these details, you need to first know something about the pair template class.

Display 19.13   The map Template Class

map TEMPLATE CLASS DETAILS

Type name: map<KeyType, T> or map<KeyType, T, Ordering> for a map that associates ("maps") elements of type KeyType to elements of type T. The *Ordering* is used to sort elements by key value for efficient storage. If no *Ordering* is given, the ordering used is the binary operator, <.

Library header: <map>, which places the definition in the std namespace.

Defined types: include key_type for the type of the key values, mapped_type for the type of the values mapped to, and size_type. (So, the defined type key_type is simply what we called *KeyType* above.)

Iterators: iterator, const_iterator, reverse_iterator, and const_reverse_iterator. All iterators are bidirectional. Those iterators not including const_ are neither constant nor mutable but something in between. For example, if p is of type iterator, then you can change the key value but not the value of type T. Perhaps it is best, at least at first, to treat all iterators as if they were constant. begin( ), end( ), rbegin( ), and rend( ) have the expected behavior. Adding or deleting elements does not affect iterators, except for an iterator located at the element removed.

SAMPLE MEMBER FUNCTIONS

MEMBER FUNCTION (m IS A MAP OBJECT)	MEANING
m.insert(*Element*)	Inserts *Element* in the map. *Element* is of type pair<KeyType, T>. Returns a value of type pair<iterator, bool>. If the insertion is successful, the second part of the returned pair is true and the iterator is located at the inserted element.
m[*Target_Key*]	Returns a reference to the object associated with the *Target_Key*. If the map does not already contain such an object, then a default object of type T is inserted.
m.find(*Target_Key*)	Returns an iterator located at the element with key value *Target_Key*. Returns m.end( ) if there is no such element.
m.erase(*Target_Key*)	Removes the element with the key *Target_Key*.
m.size( )	Returns the number of pairs in the map.
m.empty( )	Returns true if the map is empty; otherwise, returns false.
m1 == m2	Returns true if the maps contain the same pairs; otherwise, returns false.

The map template class also has a default constructor, a copy constructor, and other specialized constructors not mentioned here. It has a destructor as well that returns all storage for recycling, and a well-behaved assignment operator.

The STL template class pair<T1, T2> has objects that are pairs of values such that the first element is of type T1 and the second is of type T2. If aPair is an object of type pair<T1, T2>, then aPair.first is the first element, which is of type T1, and aPair.second is the second element, which is of type T2. The member variables first and second are public member variables, so no accessor or mutator functions are needed.

The header file for the pair template is <utility>. So, to use the pair template class, you need the following (or something like it) in your file:

```
#include <utility>
using std::pair;
```

The map template class uses the pair template class to store the association between the key and a data item. For example, given the definition

```
map<string, int> numberMap;
```

if we add to the map

```
numberMap["c++"] = 10;
```

then when we access this pair using an iterator, iterator->first will refer to the key "c++" while iterator->second will refer to the data value 10.

A simple example that shows how to use some of the member functions of the template class map is given in Display 19.14.

We will mention four other associative containers, although we will not give any details about them. The template classes multiset and multimap are essentially the same as set and map, respectively, except that multiset allows repetition of elements and multimap allows multiple values to be associated with each key value. Some implementations of STL also include the hash_set and hash_map classes. These template classes are essentially the same as set and map, except they are implemented using a hash table. Hash tables are described in Chapter 17. Instead of hash tables, most implementations of the set and map classes use balanced binary trees. In a balanced binary tree, the number of nodes to the left of the root is approximately equal to the number of nodes to the right of the root. Binary search trees are also described in Chapter 17, although we do not discuss details of balancing them.

Efficiency

The STL implementations strive to be optimally efficient. For example, the set and map elements are stored in sorted order so that algorithms that search for the elements can be more efficient.

Each of the member functions for each of the template classes has a guaranteed maximum running time. These maximum running times are expressed using what is called *big-O notation*, which we discuss in Section 19.3. (Section 19.3 also gives some guaranteed running times for some of the container member functions we have already discussed. These are given in the subsection entitled "Container Access Running Times.") You will be told the guaranteed maximum running times for certain functions described in the rest of this chapter.

Display 19.14   Program Using the map Template Class (part 1 of 2)

```
1   //Program to demonstrate use of the map template class.
2   #include <iostream>
3   #include <map>
4   #include <string>
5   using std::cout;
6   using std::endl;
7   using std::map;
8   using std::string;

9   int main( )
10  {
11      map<string, string> planets;

12      planets["Mercury"] = "Hot planet";
13      planets["Venus"] = "Atmosphere of sulfuric acid";
14      planets["Earth"] = "Home";
15      planets["Mars"] = "The Red Planet";
16      planets["Jupiter"] = "Largest planet in our solar system";
17      planets["Saturn"] = "Has rings";
18      planets["Uranus"] = "Tilts on its side";
19      planets["Neptune"] = "1500 mile-per-hour winds";
20      planets["Pluto"] = "Dwarf planet";

21      cout << "Entry for Mercury - " << planets["Mercury"]
22           << endl << endl;

23      if (planets.find("Mercury") != planets.end( ))
24          cout << "Mercury is in the map." << endl;
25      if (planets.find("Ceres") == planets.end( ))
26          cout << "Ceres is not in the map." << endl << endl;

27      cout << "Iterating through all planets: " << endl;
28      map<string, string>::const_iterator iter;
29      for (iter = planets.begin( ); iter != planets.end( ); iter++)
30      {
31          cout << iter->first << " - " << iter->second << endl;
32      }
33      return 0;
34  }
```

The iterator will output the map in order sorted by the key. In this case, the output will be listed alphabetically by planet.

Sample Dialogue

```
Entry for Mercury - Hot planet

Mercury is in the map.
Ceres is not in the map.
```

Display 19.14   Program Using the map Template Class (part 2 of 2)

```
Iterating through all planets:
Earth - Home
Jupiter - Largest planet in our solar system
Mars - The Red Planet
Mercury - Hot planet
Neptune - 1500 mile-per-hour winds
Pluto - Dwarf planet
Saturn - Has rings
Uranus - Tilts on its side
Venus - Atmosphere of sulfuric acid
```

Self-Test Exercises

14. Why are the elements in the set template class stored in sorted order?

15. Can a set have elements of a class type?

16. Suppose s is of the type set<char>. What value is returned by s.find('A') if 'A' is in s? What value is returned if 'A' is not in s?

17. How many elements will be in the map mymap after the following code executes?

```
map<int, string> mymap;
mymap[5] = "c++";
cout << mymap[4] << endl;
```

19.3   Generic Algorithms

"And if you take one from three hundred and sixty-five, what remains?"

"Three hundred and sixty-four, of course."

Humpty Dumpty looked doubtful. *"I'd rather see that done on paper,"* he said.

LEWIS CARROLL, *Through the Looking-Glass*

This section covers some basic function templates in the STL. We cannot give you a comprehensive description of them all here, but we will present a large enough sample to give you a good feel for what is contained in the STL and to give you sufficient detail to start using these template functions.

These template functions are sometimes called **generic algorithms**. The term **generic algorithm** *algorithm* is used for a reason. Recall that an algorithm is just a set of instructions for performing a task. An algorithm can be presented in any language, including a programming language like C++. But, when using the word *algorithm*, programmers typically have in mind a less formal presentation given in English or pseudocode. As such, it is often thought of as an abstraction of the code defining a function. It gives the important details but not the fine details of the coding. The STL specifies certain details about the algorithms underlying the STL template functions, which is why they are sometimes called *generic algorithms*. These STL function templates do more than just deliver a value in any way that the implementers wish. The function templates in the STL come with minimum requirements that must be satisfied by their implementations if they are to satisfy the standard. In most cases, they must be implemented with a guaranteed running time. This adds an entirely new dimension to the idea of a function interface. In the STL, the interface not only tells a programmer what the function does and how to use the functions, but also how rapidly the task will be done. In some cases, the standard even specifies the particular algorithm that is used, although not the exact details of the coding. Moreover, when it does specify the particular algorithm, it does so because of the known efficiency of the algorithm. The key new point is the specification of an efficiency guarantee for the code. In this chapter, we will use the terms *generic algorithm, generic function, and STL function template* to all mean the same thing.

In order to have some terminology to discuss the efficiency of these template functions or generic algorithms, we first present some background on how the efficiency of algorithms is usually measured.

Running Times and Big-O Notation

If you ask a programmer how fast his or her program is, you might expect an answer like "two seconds." However, the speed of a program cannot be given by a single number. A program will typically take a longer amount of time on larger inputs than it will on smaller inputs. You would expect that a program for sorting numbers would take less time to sort 10 numbers than it would to sort 1000 numbers. Perhaps it takes 2 seconds to sort 10 numbers, but 10 seconds to sort 1000 numbers. How then should the programmer answer the question "How fast is your program?" The programmer would have to give a table of values showing how long the program takes for different sizes of input. For example, the table might be as shown in Display 19.15. This table does not give a single time, but instead gives different times for a variety of different input sizes.

The table is a description of what is called a **function** in mathematics. Just as a (non-void) C++ function takes an argument and returns a value, so too does this function take an argument, which is an input size, and returns a number, which is the time the program takes on an input of that size. If we call this function T, then $T(10)$ is 2 seconds, $T(100)$ is 2.1 seconds, $T(1000)$ is 10 seconds, and $T(10,000)$ is 2.5 minutes. The table is just a sample of some of the values of this function T. The program will take some amount of time on inputs of every size. So although they are not shown in the table, there are also values for $T(1)$, $T(2)$, . . ., $T(101)$, $T(102)$, and so forth. For any positive integer N, $T(N)$ is the amount of time it takes for the program to sort N numbers. The function T is called the **running time** of the program.

So far we have been assuming that this sorting program will take the same amount of time on any list of N numbers. That need not be true. Perhaps it takes much less time if the list is already sorted or almost sorted. In that case, $T(N)$ is defined to be the time taken by the "hardest" list—that is, the time taken on that list of N numbers that

margin terms:
mathematical function

running time

worst-case running time

makes the program run the longest. This is called the **worst-case running time**. In this chapter, we will always mean worst-case running time when we give a running time for an algorithm or for some code.

The time taken by a program or algorithm is often given by a formula, such as $4N + 3$, $5N + 4$, or N^2. If the running time $T(N)$ is $5N + 5$, then on inputs of size N the program will run for $5N + 5$ time units.

The following is some code to search an array a with N elements to determine whether a particular value target is in the array:

```
int i = 0;
bool found = false;
while ( ( i < N) && !(found) )
    if (a[i] == target)
        found = true;
    else
        i++;
```

Display 19.15   Some Values of a Running Time Function

INPUT SIZE	RUNNING TIME
10 numbers	2 seconds
100 numbers	2.1 seconds
1000 numbers	10 seconds
10,000 numbers	2.5 minutes

We want to compute some estimate of how long it will take a computer to execute this code. We would like an estimate that does not depend on which computer we use, either because we do not know which computer we will use or because we might use several different computers to run the program at different times.

One possibility is to count the number of "steps," but it is not easy to decide what a step is. In this situation the normal thing to do is count the number of **operations**. The term *operations* is almost as vague as the term *step*, but there is at least some agreement in practice about what qualifies as an operation. Let us say that, for this C++ code, each application of any of the following will count as an operation: =, <, &&, !, [], ==, and ++. The computer must do other things besides carry out these operations, but these seem to be the main things that it is doing, and we will assume that they account for the bulk of the time needed to run this code. In fact, our analysis of time will assume that everything else takes no time at all and that the total time for our program to run is equal to the time needed to perform these operations. Although this is an idealization that clearly is not completely true, it turns out that this simplifying assumption works well in practice, and so it is often made when analyzing a program or algorithm.

Even with our simplifying assumption, we still must consider two cases: Either the value target is in the array or it is not. Let us first consider the case when target is not in the array. The number of operations performed will depend on the number of array elements searched. The operation = is performed two times before the loop is

operations

executed. Since we are assuming that target is not in the array, the loop will be executed N times, one for each element of the array. Each time the loop is executed, the following operations are performed: <, &&, !, [], ==, and ++. This adds five operations for each of N loop iterations. Finally, after N iterations, the Boolean expression is again checked and found to be false. This adds a final three operations (<, &&, !).[3] If we tally all these operations, we get a total of 6N + 5 operations when the target is not in the array. We will leave it as an exercise for the reader to confirm that if the target is in the array, then the number of operations will be 6N + 5 or fewer. Thus, the worst-case running time is T(N) = 6N + 5 operations for any array of N elements and any value of target.

We just determined that the worst-case running time for our search code is 6N + 5 operations. But an operation is not a traditional unit of time, like a nanosecond, second, or minute. If we want to know how long the algorithm will take on some particular computer, we must know how long it takes that computer to perform one operation. If an operation can be performed in one nanosecond, then the time will be 6N + 5 nanoseconds. If an operation can be performed in one second, the time will be 6N + 5 seconds. If we use a slow computer that takes ten seconds to perform an operation, the time will be 60N + 50 seconds. In general, if it takes the computer c nanoseconds to perform one operation, then the actual running time will be approximately c(6N + 5) nanoseconds. (We said *approximately* because we are making some simplifying assumptions, and therefore the result may not be the absolutely exact running time.) This means that our running time of 6N + 5 is a very crude estimate. To get the running time expressed in nanoseconds, you must multiply by some constant that depends on the particular computer you are using. Our estimate of 6N + 5 is only accurate to within a constant multiple.

Estimates on running time, such as the one we just went through, are normally expressed in something called **big-O notation.** (The O is the letter "Oh," not the digit zero.) Suppose we estimate the running time to be, say, 6N + 5 operations, and suppose we know that no matter what the exact running time of each different operation may turn out to be, there will always be some constant factor c such that the real running time is less than or equal to

$$c\,(6N + 5)$$

big-O notation

Under these circumstances, we say that the code (or program or algorithm) runs in time O(6N + 5). This is usually read as "big-O of 6N + 5." We need not know what the constant c will be. In fact, it will undoubtedly be different for different computers, but we must know that there is one such c for any reasonable computer system. If the computer is very fast, the c might be less than 1—say, 0.001. If the computer is very slow, the c might be very large—say, 1000. Moreover, since changing the units (say from nanosecond to second) involves only a constant multiple, there is no need to give any units of time.

Be sure to notice that a big-O estimate is an upper-bound estimate. We always approximate by taking numbers on the high side rather than the low side of the true

---

[3]Because of short-circuit evaluation, !(found) is not evaluated, so we actually get two, not three, operations. However, the important thing is to obtain a good upper bound. If we add in one extra operation, that is not significant.

count. Also notice that when performing a big-O estimate, we need not determine an exact count of the number of operations performed. We need only an estimate that is correct up to a constant multiple. If our estimate is twice as large as the true number, that is good enough.

size of task

An order-of-magnitude estimate, such as the previous $6N + 5$, contains a parameter for the size of the task solved by the algorithm (or program or piece of code). In our sample case, this parameter N was the number of array elements to be searched. Not surprisingly, it takes longer to search a larger number of array elements than it does to search a smaller number of array elements. Big-O running-time estimates are always expressed as a function of the size of the problem. In this chapter, all our algorithms will involve a range of values in some container. In all cases, N will be the number of elements in that range.

The following is an alternative, pragmatic way to think about big-O estimates:

Look only at the term with the highest exponent and do not pay attention to constant multiples.

For example, all of the following are $O(N^2)$:

$$N^2 + 2N + 1, \; 3N^2 + 7, \; 100N^2 + N$$

All of the following are $O(N^3)$:

$$N^3 + 5N^2 + N + 1, \; 8N^3 + 7, \; 100N^3 + 4N + 1$$

These big-O running-time estimates are admittedly crude, but they do contain some information. They will not distinguish between a running time of $5N + 5$ and a running time of $100N$, but they do let us distinguish between some running times and so determine that some algorithms are faster than others. Look at the graphs in Display 19.16 and notice that all the graphs for functions that are $O(N)$ eventually fall below the graph for the function $0.5N^2$. The result is inevitable: An $O(N)$ algorithm will always run faster than any $O(N^2)$ algorithm, provided we use large enough values of N. Although an $O(N^2)$ algorithm could be faster than an $O(N)$ algorithm for the problem size you are handling, programmers have found that, in practice, $O(N)$ algorithms perform better than $O(N^2)$ algorithms for most practical applications that are intuitively "large." Similar remarks apply to any other two different big-O running times.

linear running time

quadratic running time

Some terminology will help with our descriptions of generic algorithm running times. **Linear running time** means a running time of $T(N) = aN + b$. A linear running time is always an $O(N)$ running time. **Quadratic running time** means a running time with a highest term of N^2. A quadratic running time is always an $O(N^2)$ running time. We will also occasionally have logarithms in running-time formulas. Those normally are given without any base, since changing the base is just a constant multiple. If you see log N, think log base 2 of N, but it would not be wrong to think log base 10 of N. Logarithms are very slow-growing functions. So, an $O(\log N)$ running time is very fast.

In many cases, our running-time estimates will be better than big-O estimates. In particular, when we specify a linear running time, that is a tight upper bound; you can think of the running time as being exactly $T(N) = cN$, although the c is still not specified.

Container Access Running Times

Now that we know about big-O notation, we can express the efficiency of some of the accessing functions for container classes that we discussed in Section 19.2. Insertions at the back of a vector (push_back), the front or back of a deque (push_back and push_front), and anywhere in a list (insert) are all $O(1)$ (that is, a constant upper bound on the running time that is independent of the size of the container). Insertion or deletion of an arbitrary element for a vector or deque is $O(N)$ where N is the number of elements in the container. For a set or map finding, (find) is $O(\log N)$ where N is the number of elements in the container.

Self-Test Exercises

18. Show that a running time $T(N) = aN + b$ is an $O(N)$ running time. (*Hint:* The only issue is the plus b. Assume N is always at least 1.)

19. Show that for any two bases a and b for logarithms, if a and b are both greater than 1, then there is a constant c such that $\log_a N \le c (\log_b N)$. Thus, there is no need to specify a base in $O(\log N)$. That is, $O(\log_a N)$ and $O(\log_b N)$ mean the same thing.

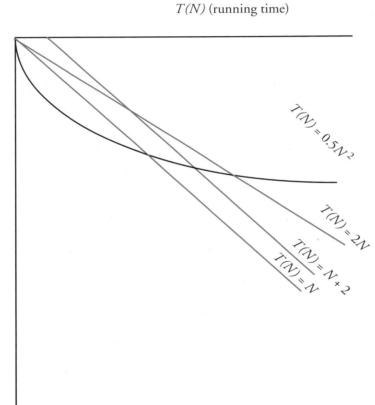

Display 19.16   Comparison of Running Times

Nonmodifying Sequence Algorithms

This section describes template functions that operate on containers but do not modify the contents of the container in any way. A good simple and typical example is the generic find function.

The generic find function is similar to the find member function of the set template class but is a different find function. The generic find function can be used with any of the STL sequence container classes. Display 19.17 shows a sample use of the generic find function used with the class vector<char>. The function in Display 19.17 would behave exactly the same if we replaced vector<char> by list<char> throughout, or if we replaced vector<char> by any other sequence container class. That is one of the reasons why the functions are called *generic*. One definition of the find function works for a wide selection of containers.

Display 19.17 The Generic find Function (part 1 of 2)

```
1   //Program to demonstrate use of the generic find function.
2   #include <iostream>
3   #include <vector>
4   #include <algorithm>
5   using std::cin;
6   using std::cout;
7   using std::endl;
8   using std::vector;
9   using std::find;

10  int main( )
11  {
12      vector<char> line;

13      cout << "Enter a line of text:\n";
14      char next;
15      cin.get(next);
16      while (next != '\n';
17                                          If find does not find what it is looking
18          line.push_back(next);           for, it returns its second argument.
19          cin.get(next);
20      }

21      vector<char>::const_iterator where;
22      where = find(line.begin( ), line.end( ), 'e');
23      //where is located at the first occurrence of 'e' in v.

24      vector<char>::const_iterator p;
25      cout << "You entered the following before you"
                << "entered your first line:\n";
26      for (p = line.begin( ); p != where; p++)
27          cout << *p;
28      cout << endl;
```

(continued)

Display 19.17   The Generic `find` Function (part 2 of 2)

```
29      cout << "You entered the following after that:\n";
30      for (p = where; p != line.end( ); p++)
31          cout << *p;
32      cout << endl;

33      cout << "End of demonstration.\n";
34      return 0;
35  }
```

Sample Dialogue 1

```
Enter a line of text
A line of text.
You entered the following before you entered your first e:
A lin
You entered the following after that:
e of text.
End of demonstration.
```

Sample Dialogue 2

```
Enter a line of text
I will not!
You entered the following before you entered your first e:
I will not!
You entered the following after that:
```
←

*If `find` does not find what it
is looking for, it returns
`line.end( )`.*

```
End of demonstration.
```

If the `find` function does not find the element it is looking for, it returns its second iterator argument, which need not be equal to some `end( )` as it is in Display 19.17. Sample Dialogue 2 in that display shows the situation when `find` does not find what it is looking for.

Does `find` work with absolutely any container? No, not quite. To start with, it takes iterators as arguments, and some containers, such as `stack`, do not have iterators. To use the `find` function, the container must have iterators, the elements must be stored in a linear sequence so that the `++` operator moves iterators through the container, and the elements must be comparable using `==`. In other words, the container must have forward iterators (or some stronger kind of iterators, such as bidirectional iterators).

When presenting generic function templates, we will describe the iterator type parameter by using the name of the required kind of iterator as the type parameter name. So, `ForwardIterator` should be replaced by a type that is a type for some kind of forward iterator, such as the `iterator` type in a `list`, `vector`, or other container template class. Remember, a bidirectional iterator is also a forward iterator, and a random-access iterator is also a bidirectional iterator. Thus, the type name `ForwardIterator` can be used with any iterator type that is a bidirectional or random-access iterator type as well as a plain-old forward iterator type. In some cases, when we specify ForwardIterator, you can use an even simpler iterator kind—namely, an input iterator or output iterator. Because we have not discussed input and output iterators, however, we do not mention them in our function template declarations.

Remember that the names *forward iterator, bidirectional iterator,* and *random-access iterator* refer to kinds of iterators, not type names. The actual type names will be something like std::vector<int>::iterator, which in this case happens to be a random-access iterator.

Display 19.18 gives a sample of some nonmodifying generic functions in the STL. Display 19.18 uses a notation that is common when discussing container iterators. The iterator locations encountered in moving from an iterator first to—but not including—an iterator last are called the **range**. For example, the following for loop outputs all the elements in the range [first,last):

```
for (iterator p = first; p != last; p++)
    cout << *p << endl;
```

range
[first,
last)

Note that when two ranges are given, they need not be in the same container or even the same type of container. For example, for the search function, the ranges [first1,last1) and [first2,last2) may be in the same or different containers.

Notice that there are three search functions in Display 19.18: find, search, and binary_search. The function search searches for a subsequence, while the find and binary_search functions search for a single value. How do you decide whether to use find or binary_search when searching for a single element? One function returns an iterator whereas the other returns just a Boolean value, but that is not the biggest difference. The binary_search function requires that the range being searched be sorted (into ascending order using <) and run in time $O(\log N)$, whereas the find function does not require that the range be sorted, but guarantees only linear time. If you have or can have the elements in sorted order, you can search for them much more quickly by using binary_search.

Range [first, last)

The movement from some iterator first, often container.begin( ), up to but not including some location last, often container.end( ), is so common it has come to have a special name, *range [first, last)*. For example, the following code outputs all elements in the range [c.begin( ), c.end( )), where c is some container object, such as a vector:

```
for (iterator p = c.begin( ); p != c.end( ); p++)
    cout << *p << endl;
```

Note that with the binary_search function, you are guaranteed that the implementation will use the binary search algorithm, which was discussed in Chapter 13. The importance of using the binary search algorithm is that it guarantees a very fast running time, $O(\log N)$. If you have not read Chapter 13 and have not otherwise heard of a binary search, just think of it as a very efficient search algorithm that requires that the elements be sorted. Those are the only two points about binary searches that are relevant to the material in this chapter.

Display 19.18 Some Nonmodifying Generic Functions

These functions all work for forward iterators, which means they also work for bidirectional and random-access iterators. (In some cases, they even work for other kinds of iterators that we have not covered in any detail.)

```
template <class ForwardIterator, class T>
ForwardIterator find(ForwardIterator first, ForwardIterator last,
                     const T& target);
//Traverses the range [first, last) and returns an iterator located at
//the first occurrence of target. Returns second if target is not found.
//Time complexity: linear in the size of the range [first, last).

template <class ForwardIterator, class T>
int[4] count(ForwardIterator first, ForwardIterator last, const T& target);
//Traverse the range [first, last) and returns the number
//of elements equal to target.
//Time complexity: linear in the size of the range [first, last).

template <class ForwardIterator1, class ForwardIterator2>
bool equal(ForwardIterator1 first1, ForwardIterator1 last1,
           ForwardIterator2 first2);
//Returns true if [first1, last1) contains the same elements in the same
//order as the first last1-first1 elements starting at first2.
//Otherwise, returns false.
//Time complexity: linear in the size of the range [first, last).

template <class ForwardIterator1, class ForwardIterator2>
ForwardIterator1 search(ForwardIterator1 first1, ForwardIterator1 last1,
                        ForwardIterator2 first2, ForwardIterator2 last2);
//Checks to see if [first2, last2) is a subrange of [first1, last1).
//If so, it returns an iterator located in [first1, last1) at the start
//of the first match. Returns last1 if a match is not found.
//Time complexity: quadratic in the size of the range [first1, last1).

template <class ForwardIterator, class T>
bool binary_search(ForwardIterator first, ForwardIterator last,
                   const T& target);
//Precondition: The range [first, last) is sorted into ascending order
//using <.
//Uses the binary search algorithm to determine if target is in the
//range [first, last).
//Time complexity: For random-access iterators O(log N). For nonrandom-
//access iterators linear in N, where N is the size of the range [first,
//last).
```

---

[4] The actual return type is an integer type that we have not discussed, but the returned value should be assignable to a variable of type int.

Self-Test Exercises

20. Replace all occurrences of the identifier vector with the identifier list in Display 19.17. Compile and run the program.

21. Suppose v is an object of the class vector<int>. Use the search generic function (Display 19.18) to write some code to determine whether or not v contains the number 42 immediately followed by 43. You need not give a complete program, but do give all necessary include and using directives. (*Hint:* It may help to use a second vector.)

Modifying Sequence Algorithms

Display 19.19 contains descriptions of some of the generic functions in the STL that change the contents of a container in some way.

Remember that adding or removing an element to or from a container can affect any of the other iterators. There is no guarantee that the iterators will be located at the same element after an addition or deletion unless the container template class makes such a guarantee. Of the template classes we have seen, list and slist guarantee that their iterators will not be moved by additions or deletions, except of course if the iterator is located at an element that is removed. The template classes vector and deque make no such guarantee. Some of the function templates in Display 19.19 guarantee the values of some specific iterators; you can, of course, count on those guarantees no matter what the container is.

Display 19.19   Some Modifying Generic Functions (part 1 of 2)

The name of the iterator type parameter tells the kind of iterator for which the function works. Remember that these are minimum iterator requirements. For example, ForwardIterator works for forward iterators, bidirectional iterators, and random-access iterators.

```
template <class T>
void swap(T& variable1, T& variable2);
//Interchanges the values of variable1 and variable2.

template <class ForwardIterator1, class ForwardIterator2>
ForwardIterator2 copy(ForwardIterator1 first1, ForwardIterator1 last1,
                      ForwardIterator2 first2);
//last2 is such that the ranges [first1, last1) and [first2, last2) are
//the same size.
//Action: Copies the elements at locations [first1, last1) to
//locations [first2, last2). Returns last2.
//Time complexity: linear in the size of the range [first1, last1).
template <class ForwardIterator, class T>
ForwardIterator remove(ForwardIterator first, ForwardIterator last,
                          const T& target);
```

(continued)

Display 19.19   Some Modifying Generic Functions (part 2 of 2)

```
//Removes those elements equal to target from the range [first, last).
//The size of the container is not changed. The removed values equal to
//target are moved to the end of the range [first, last). There is then
//an iterator i in this range such that all the values not equal to
//target are in [first, i). This i is returned. Time complexity: linear
//in the size of the range [first, last).

template <class BidirectionalIterator>
void reverse(BidirectionalIterator first, BidirectionalIterator last);
//Reverses the order of the elements in the range [first, last).
//Time complexity: linear in the size of the range [first, last).

template <class RandomAccessIterator>
void random_shuffle(RandomAccessIterator first,
                    RandomAccessIterator last);
//Uses a pseudorandom number generator to randomly reorder the elements
//in the range [first, last).
//Time complexity: linear in the size of the range [first, last).
```

Self-Test Exercises

22. Can you use the random_shuffle template function with a list container?

23. Can you use the copy template function with vector containers, even though copy requires forward iterators and vector has random-access iterators?

Set Algorithms

Display 19.20 shows a sample of the generic set operation functions defined in the STL. Note that generic algorithms assume that the containers store their elements in sorted order. The containers set, map, multiset, and multimap do store their elements in sorted order; therefore, all the functions in Display 19.20 apply to these four template class containers. Other containers, such as vector, do not store their elements in sorted order; these functions should not be used with such containers. The reason for requiring that the elements be sorted is so that the algorithms can be more efficient.

Display 19.20 Set Operations

These functions work for sets, maps, multisets, and multimaps (and other containers)
but do not work for all containers. For example, they do not work for vectors, lists,
or deques unless their contents are sorted. For these to work, the elements in the container
must be stored in sorted order. These all work for forward iterators, which means
they also work for bidirectional and random-access iterators. (In some cases, they
even work for other kinds of iterators that we have not covered in any detail.)

```
template <class ForwardIterator1, class ForwardIterator2>
bool includes(ForwardIterator1 first1, ForwardIterator1 last1,
              ForwardIterator2 first2, ForwardIterator2 last2);
```

```
//Returns true if every element in the range [first2, last2) also occurs
//in the range [first1, last1). Otherwise, returns false.
//Time complexity: linear in the size of [first1, last1) plus [first2,
//last2).
```

```
template <class ForwardIterator1, class ForwardIterator2,
          class ForwardIterator3>
void⁵ set_union(ForwardIterator1 first1, ForwardIterator1 last1,
                ForwardIterator2 first2, ForwardIterator2 last2,
                                    ForwardIterator3 result);
```

```
//Creates a sorted union of the two ranges [first1, last1) and [first2,
//last2). The union is stored starting at result.
//Time complexity: linear in the size of [first1, last1) plus [first2,
//last2).
```

```
template <class ForwardIterator1, class ForwardIterator2,
          class ForwardIterator3>
void⁵ set_intersection(ForwardIterator1 first1, ForwardIterator1 last1,
                ForwardIterator2 first2, ForwardIterator2 last2,
                                    ForwardIterator3 result);
```

```
//Creates a sorted intersection of the two ranges [first1, last1) and
//[first2, last2). The intersection is stored starting at result.
//Time complexity: linear in the size of [first1, last1) plus [first2,
//last2).
```

```
template <class ForwardIterator1, class ForwardIterator2,
          class ForwardIterator3>
void⁵ set_difference(ForwardIterator1 first1, ForwardIterator1 last1,
                ForwardIterator2 first2, ForwardIterator2 last2,
                                    ForwardIterator3 result);
```

```
//Creates a sorted set difference of the two ranges [first1, last1) and
//[first2, last2). The difference consists of the elements in the first
//range that are not in the second. The result is stored starting at
//result. Time complexity: linear in the size of [first1, last1) plus
//[first2, last2).
```

---

[5]Returns an iterator of type ForwardIterator3 but can be used as a void function.

Self-Test Exercise

24. The mathematics course version of a set does not keep its elements in sorted order, and it has a union operator. Why does the set_union template function require that the containers keep their elements in sorted order?

Sorting Algorithms

Display 19.21 gives the declarations and documentation for two template functions: one to sort a range of elements and one to merge two sorted ranges of elements. Note that the sorting function sort guarantees a running time of $O(N \log N)$. Although it is beyond the scope of this book, it can be shown that you cannot write a sorting algorithm that is faster than $O(N \log N)$. So, this function guarantees that the sorting algorithm is as fast as possible, up to a constant multiple.

Display 19.21   Some Generic Sorting Algorithms

```
template <class RandomAccessIterator>
void sort(RandomAccessIterator first, RandomAccessIterator last);
//Sorts the elements in the range [first, last) into ascending order.
//Time complexity: O(N log N), where N is the size of the range [first,
//last).

template <class ForwardIterator1, class ForwardIterator2,
          class ForwardIterator3>
void merge(ForwardIterator1 first1, ForwardIterator1 last1,
           ForwardIterator2 first2, ForwardIterator2 last2,
           ForwardIterator3 result);
//Precondition: The ranges [first1, last1) and [first2, last2) are
//sorted.
//Action: Merges the two ranges into a sorted range [result, last3)
//where last3 = result + (last1 - first1) + (last2 - first2).
//Time complexity: linear in the size of the range [first1, last1)
//plus the size of [first2, last2).

Sorting uses the < operator, and so the < operator must be defined.
There are other versions, not given here, that allow you to provide the ordering relation.
"Sorted" means sorted into ascending order.
```

Chapter Summary

- An *iterator* is a generalization of a pointer. Iterators are used to move through the elements in some range of a container. The operations ++, --, and dereferencing * are usually defined for an iterator.

- *Container classes* with iterators have member functions `end()` and `begin()` that return iterator values such that you can process all the data in the container as follows:

```
for (p = c.begin( ); p != c.end( ); p++)
    process *p //*p is the current data item.
```

- The main kinds of iterators are as follows.
  Forward iterators: `++` works on the iterator.
  Bidirectional iterators: Both `++` and `--` work on the iterator.
  Random-access iterators: `++`, `--`, and random access all work with the iterator.

- With a *constant iterator* p, the dereferencing operator `*p` produces a read-only version of the element. With a *mutable iterator* p, `*p` can be assigned a value.

- A bidirectional container has reverse iterators that allow your code to cycle through the elements in the container in reverse order.

- The main container template classes in the STL are `list`, which has mutable bidirectional iterators; and the template classes `vector` and `deque`, both of which have mutable random-access iterators.

- `stack` and `queue` are container adapter classes, which means they are built on top of other container classes. A `stack` is a last-in/first-out container. A `queue` is a first-in/first-out container.

- The `set`, `map`, `multiset`, and `multimap` container template classes store their elements in sorted order for efficiency of search algorithms. A `set` is a simple collection of elements. A `map` allows storing and retrieving by key values. The `multiset` class allows repetitions of entries. The `multimap` class allows a single key to be associated with multiple data items.

- The *STL* includes template functions to implement generic algorithms with guarantees on their maximum running time.

Answers to Self-Test Exercises

1. `v.begin( )` returns an iterator located at the first element of `v`. `v.end( )` returns a value that serves as a sentinel value at the end of all the elements of `v`.

2. `*p` is the dereferencing operator applied to p. `*p` is a reference to the element at location p.

3. `using std::vector<int>::iterator;`

   ```
   iterator p;
   for (p = v.begin( ), p++; p != v.end( ); p++)
       cout << *p << " ";
   ```

4. D C C

5. B C

6. Either would work.

7. A major difference is that a vector container has random-access iterators, whereas list has only bidirectional iterators.

8. All except slist.

9. vector and deque.

10. They all can have mutable iterators.

11. The stack template adapter class has no iterators.

12. The queue template adapter class has no iterators.

13. No value is returned; pop is a void function.

14. To facilitate an efficient search for elements.

15. Yes, they can be of any type, although there is only one type for each object. The type parameter in the template class is the type of element stored.

16. If 'A' is in s, then s.find('A') returns an iterator located at the element 'A'. If 'A' is not in s, then s.find('A') returns s.end().

17. mymap will contain two entries. One is a map from 5 to "c++" and the other is a map from 4 to the default string, which is blank.

18. Just note that $aN + b \leq (a + b)N$ as long as $1 \leq N$.

19. This is mathematics, not C++. So, = will mean *equals*, not *assignment*.

First note that $\log_a N = (\log_a b)(\log_b N)$.

To see this first identity, just note that if you raise a to the power $\log_a N$, you get N and if you raise a to the power $(\log_a b)(\log_b N)$, you also get N.

If you set $c = (\log_a b)$ you get $\log_a N = c (\log_b N)$.

20. The programs should run exactly the same.

21.
```
#include <iostream>
#include <vector>
#include <algorithm>
using std::cout;
using std::vector;
using std::search;

    ...

vector<int> target;
target.push_back(42);
target.push_back(43);
vector<int>::const_iterator result = search(v.begin( ), v.end( ),
                                            target.begin( ), target.end( ));
if (result != v.end( ))
    cout << "Found 42, 43.\n";
else
    cout << "42, 43 not there.\n";
```

22. No, you must have random-access iterators, and the list template class only has bidirectional iterators.

23. Yes, a random-access iterator is also a forward iterator.

24. The set_union template function requires that the containers keep their elements in sorted order to allow the function template to be implemented in a more efficient way.

Programming Projects

Visit www.myprogramminglab.com to complete select exercises online and get instant feedback.

1. The point of this exercise is to demonstrate that an object that *behaves* like an iterator *is* an iterator. More precisely, if an object accesses some container and behaves like an iterator of a particular strength, then that object can be used as an iterator to manipulate the container with any of the generic functions that require an iterator having that strength. However, while the generic algorithms can be used with this container, the *member* functions, such as begin and end, will (of course) not be present (for example, in an array) unless they have been explicitly coded for that container. We will restrict this exercise to arrays of double, but the same message would hold true for any base type.

   a. Argue from the properties of random-access iterators that a pointer that points to an element of an array behaves exactly as a random-access iterator.

   b. Argue further that

      i) the name of the array is a pointer to double that points to the first element and so the array name can serve as a "begin" iterator and

      ii) (the array's name) + (the size of the array) can serve as an "end" pointer. (Of course, this points *one past* the end, as it should.)

   c. Write a short program in which you declare an array of double of size 10, and populate this array with 10 doubles. Then call the sort generic algorithm with these pointer values as arguments and display the results.

2. This problem intends to illustrate removal of several instances of a particular item from a container with the remove generic function. A side effect is to examine the behavior of the generic function remove that comes with your compiler. (We have observed some variation in the behavior of remove from one compiler to another.) Before you start, look up the behavior of the remove generic algorithm as described by your favorite STL document or Web site. (For example, point your browser at http://www.sgi.com/tech/stl/remove.html. This worked as of the publication date.)

   a. Modify the array declaration in Programming Project 19.1 to include several elements with the same value (say, 4.0, but you can use any value for this exercise). Make sure that some of these are not all together. Use the modifying generic function remove (see Display 19.19) to remove all elements 4.0 (that is, the value you duplicated in building the array). Test.

   b. Use the array of double from part a to build a list and a vector that have the same contents as the array. Do this using the container constructor that takes two iterators as arguments. The vector and list classes each have a constructor that takes two iterators as arguments and initializes the vector or list to the items in the iterator interval. The iterators can be located in any container, including in an array. Build the `vector` and `list` using the array name for the begin iterator and the name + array length as the end iterator for the two constructor arguments. Use the modifying algorithm `remove` (Display 19.19) to remove from the `list` and from the `vector` all elements equal to 4.0 (or the value you duplicated in building the array). Display the contents of the `vector` and `list` and explain the results.

c. Modify the code from part b to assign to an iterator variable of appropriate type the iterator value returned by the call to the `remove` generic function. Review the documentation for `remove` to be certain you know what these iterator values mean. Output the contents of the array, the `vector` and the `list`, `begin( )` to `end( )`, using the "begin" and "end" we described previously for the array. Output the contents of the two containers starting at the iterator returned from `remove` to the `end( )` of each container. Explain your results.

3. A **prime** number is an integer greater than 1 and divisible only by itself and 1. An integer `x` is **divisible** by an integer `y` if there is another integer `z` such `x = y*z`. The Greek mathematician Eratosthenes (pronounced Er-ah-tos-thin-eeze) gave an algorithm for finding all prime numbers less than some integer N. This algorithm is called the *Sieve of Eratosthenes*. It works like this: Begin with a list of integers 2 through N. The number 2 is the first prime. (It is instructive to consider why this is true.) The *multiples of 2*—that is, 4, 6, 8, etc.—are *not prime*. We cross these off through N. The first number after 2 that was not crossed off, which is 3, is the next prime. The *multiples of 3 are not primes*. Cross these off the list. Note that 6 is already gone, cross off 9, 12 is already gone, cross off 15, etc. The first number not crossed off is the next prime. The algorithm continues on this fashion until we reach N. All the numbers not crossed off the list are primes.

a. Write a program using this algorithm to find all primes less than a user-supplied number N. Use a vector container for the integers. Use an array of `bool` initially set to all `true` to keep track of crossed off integers. Change the entry to `false` for integers that are crossed off the list.

b. Test for $N = 10, 30, 100,$ and 300.

Improvements:

c. Actually, we do not need to go all the way to N. You can stop at $N/2$. Try this and test your program. $N/2$ works and is better, but is not the smallest number we could use. Argue that to get all the primes between 1 and N the minimum limit is the square root of N.

d. Modify your code from part a to use the square root of N as an upper limit.

4. Suppose you have a collection of student records. The records are structures of the following type:

```
struct StudentInfo
{
    string name;
    int grade;
};
```

The records are maintained in a vector<StudentInfo>. Write a program that prompts for and fetches data and builds a vector of student records, then sorts the vector by name, calculates the maximum and minimum grades, and the class average, then prints this summarizing data along with a class roll with grades. (We are not interested in who had the maximum and minimum grade, though, just the maximum, minimum, and average statistics.) Test your program.

5. Continuing Programming Project 19.4, write a function that separates the students in the vector of StudentInfo records into two vectors, one containing records of passing students and one containing records of failing students. (Use a grade of 60 or better for passing.)

You are asked to do this in two ways, and to give some run-time estimates.

a. Consider continuing to use a vector. You could generate a second vector of passing students and a third vector of failing students. This keeps duplicate records for at least some of the time, so do not do it that way. You could create a vector of failing students and a test-for-failing function. Then you push_back failing student records, then erase (which is a member function) the failing student records from the original vector. Write the program this way.

b. Consider the efficiency of this solution. You are potentially erasing $O(N)$ members from the middle of a vector. You have to move a lot of members in this case. Erase from the middle of a vector is an $O(N)$ operation. Give a big-O estimate of the running time for this program.

c. If you used a list<StudentInfo>, what is the run time for the erase and insert functions? Consider how the time efficiency of erase for a list affects the runtime for the program. Rewrite this program using a list instead of a vector. Remember that a list provides neither indexing nor random access, and its iterators are only bidirectional, not random access.

6. a. Here is pseudocode for a program that inputs a value n from the user and then inserts n random numbers, ensuring that there are no duplicates:

```
Input n from user
Create vector v of type int
Loop i = 1 to n
    r = random integer between 0 and n-1
    Linearly search through v for value r
    if r is not in vector v then add r to the end of v
End Loop
Print out number of elements added to v
```

Implement this program with your own linear search routine and add wrapper code that will time how long it takes to run. Test the program for different values of n. Depending on the speed of your system, you may need to input large values for n so that the program takes at least one second to run. Here is a sample that indicates how to calculate the difference in time: (time.h is a library that should be available on your version of C++).

```
#include <time.h>

time_t start,end;
double dif;

time (&start);                              // Record start time
// Rest of program goes here.
time (&end);                                // Record end time
dif = difftime(end,start);
cout << "It took " << dif << " seconds to execute. " << endl;
```

b. Next, create a second program that has the same behavior except that it uses an STL set to store the numbers instead of a vector:

```
Input n from user
Create set s of type int
Loop i = 1 to n
    r = random integer between 0 to n-1
    Use s.find(r) to search if r is already in the set
    if r is not in set s then add r to s
End Loop
Print out number of elements added to s
```

Time your new program with the same values of n that you used in the vector version. What do the results tell you about the Big-O run time of the find( ) function for the set compared with linear search through the vector? Note that the find( ) function is really redundant because insert has no effect if the element is already in the set. However, use the find( ) function anyway to create a program comparable to the vector algorithm.

7. Modify your program from part a of Programming Project 19.6 so that the generic find function is used to search the vector for an existing value in place of your own code. You may wish to test your program with sample data to make sure that it is working correctly.

8. The field of information retrieval is concerned with finding relevant electronic documents based on a query. For example, given a group of keywords, a search engine retrieves Web pages (documents) and displays them in order, with the most relevant documents listed first. This technology requires a way to compare a document with the query to see which is most relevant to the query.

A simple way to make this comparison is to compute the binary cosine coefficient. The coefficient is a value between 0 and 1, where 1 indicates that the query is very similar to the document and 0 indicates that the query has no keywords in common with the document. This approach treats each document as a set of words. For example, consider the following sample document:

"Cows are big. Cows go moo. I love cows."

This document would be parsed into keywords where case is ignored and punctuation discarded and turned into the set containing the words "{cows, are, big, go, moo, i, love}". An identical process is performed on the query.

Once we have a query Q represented as a set of words and a document D represented as a set of words, the similarity between the query and document is computed by

$$Sim = \frac{|Q \cap D|}{\sqrt{|Q|}\sqrt{|D|}}$$

For example, if $D = \{cows, are, big, go, moo, i, love\}$ and $Q = \{love, holstein, cows\}$ then

$$Sim = \frac{|\{love, cows\}|}{\sqrt{|Q|}\sqrt{|D|}} = \frac{2}{\sqrt{3}\sqrt{7}} = 0.436$$

Write a program that allows the user to input a set of strings that represents a document and a set of strings that represents a query. (If you are more ambitious, you could write a program that parses an actual text file and computes the set of unique strings.) Represent the document and query as an STL set of strings. Then compute and print out the similarity between the query and document using the binary cosine coefficient. The `sqrt` function is in `cmath`. Use the generic `set_intersection` function to compute the intersection of Q and D.

Here is an example of `set_intersection` to intersect set A with B and store the result in C, where all sets are sets of strings:

```
#include <iterator>
#include <algorithm>
#include <set>
#include <string>
...
using std::insert_iterator;

set<string> A,B,C;
// Code below assumes strings have been inserted into A and B
// Note space between > > in line below
insert_iterator<set<string> > cIterator(C, C.begin());
set_intersection(A.begin(), A.end(),
                 B.begin(),B.end(),
                 cIterator);

// set C now contains the intersection of A and B
```

9. Re-do or do for the first time Programming Project 5.8 in Chapter 5. This project asks you to approximate through simulation the probability that two or more people in the same room have the same birthday, for two to fifty people in the room.

VideoNote
Solution to Programming Project 19.9

However, instead of creating a solution that uses arrays, write a solution that uses a map. Over many trials (say, 5000), randomly assign birthdays (i.e., the numbers 1 through 365, assuming each number has an equal probability) to everyone in the room. Use a `map<int, int>` to map from the birthday (1–365) to a count of how many times that birthday occurs. Initially, each birthday should map to a count of 0. As the birthdays are randomly generated, increment the corresponding counter in the map. If a duplicate birthday is detected, then increment a counter for that trial. Over all trials this counter should indicate how many of those trials had a duplicate birthday. Divide the counter by the number of trials to get an estimated probability that two or more people share the same birthday for a given room size. Your output should look the same as the output for Programming Project 5.8 in Chapter 5.

10. You have collected a file of movie ratings where each movie is rated from 1 (bad) to 5 (excellent). The first line of the file is a number that identifies how many ratings are in the file. Each rating then consists of two lines: the name of the movie followed by the numeric rating from 1 to 5. Here is a sample rating file with four unique movies and seven ratings:

```
7
Happy Feet
4
Happy Feet
5
Pirates of the Caribbean
3
Happy Feet
4
Pirates of the Caribbean
4
Flags of Our Fathers
5
Gigli
1
```

Write a program that reads in a file in this format, calculates the average rating for each movie, and outputs the average along with the number of reviews. Here is the desired output for the sample data:

```
Happy Feet: 3 reviews, average of 4.3 / 5
Pirates of the Caribbean: 2 reviews, average of 3.5 / 5
Flags of Our Father: 1 review, average of 5 / 5
Gigli: 1 review, average of 1 / 5
```

Use a map or multiple maps to generate the output. Your map should index from a string representing each movie's name to integers that store the number of reviews for the movie and the sum of the ratings for the movie.

11. Write a program that outputs a histogram of grades for an assignment given to a class of students. The program should input each student's grade as an integer and store the grade in a vector. Grades should be entered until the user enters −1 for a grade. Use a map from an int to an int to compute the histogram. The first integer in the map represents the grade, and the second integer represents the number of times that grade occurred. Output the histogram to the console. See Programming Project 5.7 for information on how to compute a histogram. There should be no restrictions on the minimum and maximum grade for this programming project.

12. Consider a text file of names, with one name per line, that has been compiled from several different sources. A sample is shown in the following:

```
Brooke Trout
Dinah Soars
Jed Dye
Brooke Trout
Jed Dye
Paige Turner
```

There are duplicate names in the file. We would like to generate an invitation list but do not want to send multiple invitations to the same person. Write a program that eliminates the duplicate names by using the set template class. Read each name from the file, add it to the set, and then output all names in the set to generate the invitation list without duplicates.

13. Reverse Polish Notation (RPN) or postfix notation is a format to specify mathematical expressions. In RPN the operator comes after the operands instead of the more common format in which the operator is between the operands (this is called infix notation). Starting with an empty stack, a RPN calculator can be implemented with the following rules:

- If a number is input, push it on the stack.
- If + is input, then pop the last two operands off the stack, add them, and push the result on the stack.
- If - is input, then pop value1, pop value2, then push value2 - value1 on the stack.
- If * is input, then pop the last two operands off the stack, multiply them, and push the result on the stack.
- If / is input, then pop value1, pop value2, then push value2 / value1 on the stack.
- If q is input, then stop inputting values, print out the top of the stack, and exit the program.

VideoNote
**Solution to
Programming
Project 19.12**

Use the stack template class to implement a RPN calculator. Output an appropriate error message if there are not two operands on the stack when given an operator. Here is sample input and output that is equivalent to $((10 - (2 + 3))*2)/5$:

```
10
2
3
+
-
2
*
5
/
q
```

The top of the stack is: 2

Patterns and UML

This chapter is available on the book's website.

The following keywords should not be used for anything other than their predefined purposes in the C++ language. In particular, do not use them for variable names or names for programmer-defined functions. In addition to the keywords in the following list, identifiers containing a double underscore (__) are reserved for use by C++ implementations and standard libraries and should not be used in your code.

asm	do	inline	short	typeid
auto	double	int	signed	typename
bool	dynamic_cast	long	sizeof	union
break	else	mutable	static	unsigned
case	enum	namespace	static_cast	using
catch	explicit	new	struct	virtual
char	extern	operator	switch	void
class	false	private	template	volatile
const	float	protected	this	wchar_t
const_cast	for	public	throw	while
continue	friend	register	true	
default	goto	reinterpret_cast	try	
delete	if	return	typedef	

These alternative representations for operators and punctuation are reserved and also should not be used otherwise.

and &&	and_eq &=	bitand &
not_eq !=	or ||	or_eq |=
bitor |	compl ^	not ~
xor ^	xor_eq ^=	

All the operators in a given box have the same precedence. Operators in higher boxes have higher precedence than operators in lower boxes. Unary operators and the assignment operator are done right to left when operators have the same precedence. For example, $x = y = z$ means $x = (y = z)$. Other operators that have the same precedences are done left to right. For example, $x + y + z$ means $(x + y) + z$.

Highest precedence (done first)

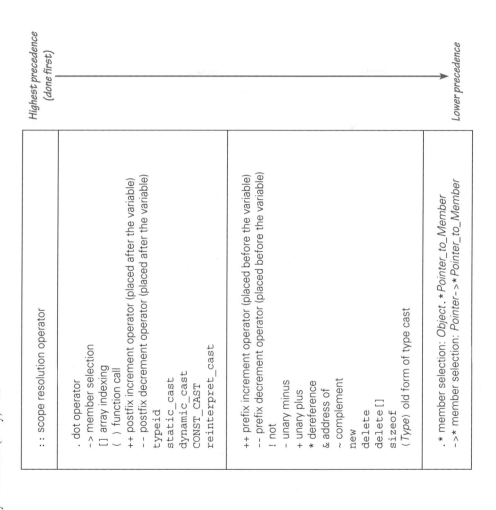

```
:: scope resolution operator
```

```
.  dot operator
-> member selection
[] array indexing
( ) function call
++ postfix increment operator (placed after the variable)
-- postfix decrement operator (placed after the variable)
typeid
static_cast
dynamic_cast
CONST_CAST
reinterpret_cast
```

```
++ prefix increment operator (placed before the variable)
-- prefix decrement operator (placed before the variable)
!  not
-  unary minus
+  unary plus
*  dereference
&  address of
~  complement
new
delete
delete []
sizeof
(Type) old form of type cast
```

```
.* member selection: Object.*Pointer_to_Member
->* member selection: Pointer->*Pointer_to_Member
```

Lower precedence

Higher precedence

Operators	
* multiply / divide % remainder (modulo)	
+ addition - subtraction	
<< insertion operator (output), bitwise left shift >> extraction operator (input), bitwise right shift	
< less than <= less than or equal > greater than >= greater than or equal	
== equal != not equal	
& bitwise and	
^ bitwise exclusive or	
| bitwise or	
&& and	
|| or	
= assignment += add and assign -= subtract and assign *= multiply and assign %= modulo and assign <<= << and assign >>= >> and assign &= & and assign ^= ^ and assign |= | and assign /= division and assign	
?: conditional operator	
throw throw exception	
, comma	

Lowest precedence
(done last)

Only the printable characters are shown. Character number 32 is the blank.

#	Char	#	Char	#	Char	#	Char
32		56	8	80	P	104	h
33	!	57	9	81	Q	105	i
34	"	58	:	82	R	106	j
35	#	59	;	83	S	107	k
36	$	60	<	84	T	108	l
37	%	61	=	85	U	109	m
38	&	62	>	86	V	110	n
39	'	63	?	87	W	111	o
40	(	64	@	88	X	112	p
41	)	65	A	89	Y	113	q
42	*	66	B	90	Z	114	r
43	+	67	C	91	[	115	s
44	,	68	D	92	\	116	t
45	-	69	E	93	]	117	u
46	.	70	F	94	^	118	v
47	/	71	G	95	_	119	w
48	0	72	H	96	`	120	x
49	1	73	I	97	a	121	y
50	2	74	J	98	b	122	z
51	3	75	K	99	c	123	{
52	4	76	L	100	d	124		
53	5	77	M	101	e	125	}
54	6	78	N	102	f	126	~
55	7	79	O	103	g		

The following lists are organized according to what the function is used for, rather than what library it is in.

Arithmetic Functions

FUNCTION DECLARATION	DESCRIPTION	HEADER FILE
`int abs(int);`	Absolute value	`cstdlib`
`long labs(long);`	Absolute value	`cstdlib`
`double fabs(double);`	Absolute value	`cmath`
`double sqrt(double);`	Square root	`cmath`
`double pow(double, double);`	Returns the first argument raised to the power of the second argument	`cmath`
`double exp(double);`	Returns e (base of the natural logarithm) to the power of its argument	`cmath`
`double log(double);`	Natural logarithm (*ln*)	`cmath`
`double log10(double);`	Base 10 logarithm	`cmath`
`double ceil(double);`	Returns the smallest integer that is greater than or equal to its argument	`cmath`
`double floor(double);`	Returns the largest integer that is less than or equal to its argument	`cmath`

Input and Output Member Functions

FORM OF A FUNCTION CALL	DESCRIPTION	HEADER FILE
Stream_Var.open(*External_File_Name*);	Connects the file with the *External_File_Name* to the stream named by the *Stream_Var*. The *External_File_Name* is a C-string value.	`fstream`
Stream_Var.fail( );	Returns true if the previous operation (such as open) on the stream *Stream_Var* has failed.	`fstream` or `iostream`

FORM OF A FUNCTION CALL	DESCRIPTION	HEADER FILE
Stream_Var.close ( );	Disconnects the stream *Stream_Var* from the file it is connected to.	fstream
Stream_Var.bad ( );	Returns true if the stream *Stream_Var* is corrupted.	fstream or iostream
Stream_Var.eof ( );	Returns true if the program has attempted to read beyond the last character in the file connected to the input stream *Stream_Var*. Otherwise, it returns false.	fstream or iostream
Stream_Var.get(*Char_Variable*);	Reads one character from the input stream *Stream_Var* and sets the *Char_Variable* equal to this character. Does *not* skip over whitespace.	fstream or iostream
Stream_Var.getline(*String_Var*, *Max_Characters* +1);	One line of input from the stream *Stream_Var* is read and the resulting string is placed in *String_Var*. If the line is more than *Max_Characters* long, only the first *Max_Characters* are read. The declared size of the *String_Var* should be *Max_Characters* +1 or larger.	fstream or iostream
Stream_Var.peek ( );	Reads one character from the input stream *Stream_Var* and returns that character. The character read is *not* removed from the input stream; the next read will read the same character.	fstream or iostream
Stream_Var.put (*Char_Exp*);	Writes the value of the *Char_Exp* to the output stream *Stream_Var*.	fstream or iostream
Stream_Var.putback (*Char_Exp*);	Places the value of *Char_Exp* in the input stream *Stream_Var* so that that value is the next input value read from the stream. The file connected to the stream is not changed.	fstream or iostream
Stream_Var.precision (*Int_Exp*);	Specifies the number of digits output after the decimal point for floating-point values sent to the output stream *Stream_Var*.	fstream or iostream
Stream_Var.width (*Int_Exp*);	Sets the field width for the next value output to the stream *Stream_Var*.	fstream or iostream

FORM OF A FUNCTION CALL	DESCRIPTION	HEADER FILE
Stream_Var.setf(*Flag*);	Sets flags for formatting output to the stream *Stream_Var*. See Display 12.5 for the list of possible flags.	fstream or iostream
Stream_Var.unsetf(*Flag*);	Unsets flags for formatting output to the stream *Stream_Var*. See Display 12.5 for the list of possible flags.	fstream or iostream

Character Functions

For all of these, the actual type of the argument is int, but for most purposes you can think of the argument type as char. For tolower and toupper, the type returned is truly an int. To use the value returned as a value of type char, you must perform an explicit or implicit typecast.

FUNCTION DECLARATION	DESCRIPTION	HEADER FILE
bool isalnum(char);	Returns true if its argument satisfies either isalpha or isdigit. Otherwise returns false.	cctype
bool isalpha(char);	Returns true if its argument is an upper- or lowercase letter. It may also return true for other arguments. The details are implementation dependent. Otherwise returns false.	cctype
bool isdigit(char);	Returns true if its argument is a digit. Otherwise returns false.	cctype
bool ispunct(char);	Returns true if its argument is a printable character that does not satisfy isalnum and that is not whitespace. (These characters are considered punctuation characters.) Otherwise returns false.	cctype
bool isspace(char);	Returns true if its argument is a whitespace character (e.g., blank, tab, newline). Otherwise returns false.	cctype
bool iscntrl(char);	Returns true if its argument is a control character. Otherwise returns false.	cctype

FUNCTION DECLARATION	DESCRIPTION	HEADER FILE
bool islower(char);	Returns true if its argument is a lowercase letter. Otherwise returns false.	cctype
bool isupper(char);	Returns true if its argument is an uppercase letter. Otherwise returns false.	cctype
int tolower(char);	Returns the lowercase version of its argument. If there are no lowercase versions, returns its argument unchanged.	cctype
int toupper(char);	Returns the uppercase version of its argument. If there are no uppercase versions, returns its argument unchanged.	cctype[a]

C-String Functions

FUNCTION DECLARATION	DESCRIPTION	HEADER FILE
int atoi(const char a[]);	Converts a C-string of characters to an integer.	cstdlib
long atol(const char a[]);	Converts a C-string of characters to a long integer.	cstdlib
double atof(const char a[]);	Converts a C-string of characters to a double.	cstdlib[a]
strcat(C-String_Variable, C-String_Expression);	Appends the value of the C-String_Expression to the end of the string in the C-String_Variable.	cstring
strcmp(C-String_Exp1, C-String_Exp2);	Returns true if the values of the two string expressions are different; otherwise, returns false.[b]	cstring
strcpy(C-String_Variable, C-String_Expression);	Changes the value of the C-String_Variable to the value of the C-String_Expression.	cstring
strlen(C-String_Expression)	Returns the length of the C-String_Expression.	cstring

[a]Some implementations place it in cmath.
[b]Returns an integer that is less than zero, zero, or greater than zero accordingly as C-String_Exp1 is less than, equal to, or greater than C-String_Exp2, respectively. The ordering is lexicographic ordering.

FUNCTION DECLARATION	DESCRIPTION	HEADER FILE
strncat (*C-String_Variable, C-String_Expression, Limit*);	Same as strcat except that at most *Limit* characters are appended.	cstring
strncmp (*C-String_Exp1, C-String_Exp2, Limit*)	Same as strcmp except that at most *Limit* characters are compared.	cstring
strncpy (*C-String_Variable, C-String_Expression, Limit*);	Same as strcat except that at most *Limit* characters are copied.	cstring
strstr (*C-String_Expression, Pattern*)	Returns a pointer to the first occurrence of the string *Pattern* in *C-String_Expression*. Returns NULL if the *Pattern* is not found.	cstring
strchr (*C-String_Expression, Character*)	Returns a pointer to the first occurrence of the *Character* in *C-String_Expression*. Returns NULL if *Character* is not found.	cstring
strrchr (*C-String_Expression, Character*)	Returns a pointer to the last occurrence of the *Character* in c-String_Expression. Returns NULL if *Character* is not found.	cstring

string Class Functions

In all cases the header file is string.

CONSTRUCTORS	
string *Variable_Name*;	Default constructor constructs an empty string.
string *Variable_Name* (*string_Object*);	Copy constructor.
string *Variable_Name* (*C-String*);	C-string to string constructor.

ELEMENT ACCESS	
string_Object[i]	Read/write access to character at index i.
string_Object.at (i)	Read/write access to character at index i.
string_Object.substr (*Position, Length*)	Returns the substring of the calling object starting at *Position* and having *Length* character.

	ASSIGNMENT/MODIFIERS
string_Object1 = string_Object2;	Allocates space and initializes it to *string_Object2*'s data, releases memory allocated for *string_Object1*, sets *string_Object1*'s size to that of *string_Object2*.
string_Object1 += string_Object2;	Character data of *string_Object2* is concatenated to the end of *string_Object1*; the size is set appropriately.
string_Object.empty( )	Returns true if *string_Object* is an empty string; otherwise, returns false.
string_Object1 + string_Object2	Returns a string that has *string_Object2*'s data concatenated onto the end of *string_Object1*'s data. The size is set appropriately.
string_Object1.insert (Position, string_Object2) ;	Inserts *string_Object2* into *string_Object1* beginning at Position.
string_Object.remove (Position, Length) ;	Removes substring of size Length starting at Position.

	COMPARISONS
string_Object1 == string_Object2 *string_Object1 != string_Object2*	Compare for equality or inequality; returns a Boolean value.
string_Object1 < string_Object2 *string_Object1 > string_Object2* *string_Object1 <= string_Object2* *string_Object1 >= string_Object2*	Lexicographical comparisons.

	FINDS
string_Object1.find (string_Object2)	Returns index of the first occurrence of *string_Object2* in *string_Object1*.
string_Object1.find (string_Object2, Position)	Returns index of the first occurrence of *string_Object2* in *string_Object1*; the search starts at Position.
string_Object1.find_first (string_Object2, Position)	Returns the index of the first instance in *string_Object1* of any character in *string_Object2*, starting the search at Position.
string_Object1.find_first_not_of (string_Object2, Position)	Returns the index of the first instance in *string_Object1* of any character not in *string_Object2*, starting the search at Position.

[a]Some implementations place it in cmath.

Random Number Generator

FUNCTION DECLARATION	DESCRIPTION	HEADER FILE
`int random(int);`	The call `random(n)` returns a pseudorandom integer greater than or equal to 0 and less than or equal to n - 1. (Not available in all implementations. If not available, then you must use `rand`.)	`cstdlib`
`int rand( );`	The call `rand( )` returns a pseudorandom integer greater than or equal to 0 and less than or equal to `RAND_MAX`. `RAND_MAX` is a predefined integer constant that is defined in `cstdlib`. The value of `RAND_MAX` is implementation dependent but will be at least 32767.	`cstdlib`
`void srand(unsigned int);` (The type `unsigned int` is an integer type that allows only nonnegative values. You can think of the argument type as `int` with the restriction that it must be nonnegative.)	Reinitializes the random number generator. The argument is the seed. Calling `srand` multiple times with the same argument will cause `rand` or `random` (whichever you use) to produce the same sequence of pseudorandom numbers. If `rand` or `random` is called without any previous call to `srand`, the sequence of numbers produced is the same as if there had been a call to `srand` with an argument of 1.	`cstdlib`

Trigonometric Functions

These functions use radians, not degrees.

FUNCTION DECLARATION	DESCRIPTION	HEADER FILE
`double acos(double);`	Arc cosine	`cmath`
`double asin(double);`	Arc sine	`cmath`
`double atan(double);`	Arc tangent	`cmath`
`double cos(double);`	Cosine	`cmath`
`double cosh(double);`	Hyperbolic cosine	`cmath`
`double sin(double);`	Sine	`cmath`
`double sinh(double);`	Hyperbolic sine	`cmath`
`double tan(double);`	Tangent	`cmath`
`double tanh(double);`	Hyperbolic tangent	`cmath`

In this book, we have used the header files for standard libraries that are part of the new ANSI/ISO C++ standard. If you have an older compiler, you may need to use the older header files. In the following, we list the new header file names that we have used in this book along with their corresponding older header file names. If the new header files do not work for you, then try the older header file names instead.

If your compiler requires the older header file names, then it also may not accommodate namespaces. In that case, you may have to eliminate all references to namespaces. If you have a compiler that requires the older header file names and/or does not support namespaces, you should consider obtaining a new compiler that comes closer to meeting the new standard.

NEW HEADER FILE	CORRESPONDING OLDER HEADER FILE
cassert	assert.h
ctype	ctype.h
cstddef	stddef.h
cstdlib	stdlib.h
cmath	math.h
cstring	string.h
fstream	fstream.h
iomanip	iomanip.h
iostream	iostream.h
string	string or no corresponding library